Lecture Notes in Computer Science 8627

Commenced Publication in 1973
Founding and Former Series Editors:
Gerhard Goos, Juris Hartmanis, and Jan van Leeuwen

Paris Avgeriou   Uwe Zdun (Eds.)

Software
Architecture

8th European Conference, ECSA 2014
Vienna, Austria, August 25-29, 2014
Proceedings

 Springer

Volume Editors

Paris Avgeriou
University of Groningen
Johann Bernoulli Institute for Mathematics and Computer Science
Groningen, The Netherlands
E-mail: paris@cs.rug.nl

Uwe Zdun
University of Vienna
Research Group Software Architecture
Vienna, Austria
E-mail: uwe.zdun@univie.ac.at

ISSN 0302-9743   e-ISSN 1611-3349
ISBN 978-3-319-09969-9   e-ISBN 978-3-319-09970-5
DOI 10.1007/978-3-319-09970-5
Springer Cham Heidelberg New York Dordrecht London

Library of Congress Control Number: 2014945553

LNCS Sublibrary: SL 2 – Programming and Software Engineering

Typesetting: Camera-ready by author, data conversion by Scientific Publishing Services, Chennai, India

Printed on acid-free paper

Springer is part of Springer Science+Business Media (www.springer.com)

Preface

These are the proceedings of the European Conference on Software Architecture (ECSA), which is the premier European conference dedicated to the field of software architecture. ECSA provides researchers and practitioners with a platform to present and discuss the most recent, innovative, and significant findings and experiences in the field of software architecture research and practice. The eighth edition of ECSA was built upon a history of a successful series of European workshops on software architecture held from 2004 through 2006 and a series of European software architecture conferences from 2007 through 2013. ECSA was merged with the Working IEEE/IFIP Conference on Software Architecture (WICSA) in 2009 and 2012.

Apart from the traditional technical program consisting of keynote talks, a main research track, discussion panels, and a tool demonstration track, the scope of ECSA 2014 was broadened to incorporate a rich industry day aiming to bring closer together the academic and industrial communities. The industry day featured additional keynote talks, presentations, and a discussion panel, with contributions by prominent software architects and other practitioners. In addition, we also offered several workshops and tutorials on diverse topics related to software architecture, as well as "MiniPLoP", a Pattern Languages of Programs mini-conference.

We received 91 submissions in the four main categories: full research papers and experience reports, as well as "emerging" (short) research papers and experience reports. The conference attracted papers (co-)authored by researchers, practitioners, and academics from 30 countries (Algeria, Australia, Austria, Belgium, Brazil, Canada, China, Czech Republic, Denmark, Finland, France, Germany, India, Iran, Ireland, Israel, Italy, Japan, The Netherlands, New Zealand, Norway, Pakistan, Poland, Spain, Sweden, Switzerland, Tunisia, Turkey, UK and USA). Each paper, independently of the category, was peer-reviewed by at least three reviewers, and discussed by the Program Committee.

Based on the recommendations of the Program Committee, we accepted only 16 full papers out of 75 full papers submitted. The acceptance rate for the full papers was 21.33% for ECSA 2014. In the "Emerging" research papers and experience reports category, we accepted only three out of 16 papers submitted. Based on the reviews and quality of the submissions, 15 full papers were invited to be converted into "Emerging" research papers and experience reports.

It was a great pleasure to have four eminent keynote speakers at ECSA 2014. The industry day was opened by a keynote from Uwe Dumslaff, Vice President and Chief Technology Officer at Capgemini, Germany. The second keynote in the industry day was presented by Markus Völter, an independent consultant, on "Language Shapes (Architectural) Thought." The third keynote was delivered by Hans van Vliet, professor at the VU University Amsterdam,

The Netherlands. Hans argued that "Architecting = Decision Making." The fourth and final keynote was given by Gregor Hohpe, who is Chief IT Architect at Allianz, Germany, and spoke about "The Age of Architecture."

We are grateful to the members of the Program Committee for helping us to seek submissions and provide valuable and timely reviews. Their efforts enabled us to put together a high-quality technical program for ECSA 2014. We are also indebted to the members of the Organizing Committee of ECSA 2014 for playing an enormously important role in successfully organizing the event with several tracks and collocated events, especially the industry day. We also thank the workshop organizers and tutorials presenters, who also made significant contributions to the success of an extended version of ECSA. The ECSA 2014 submission and review process was extensively supported by the EasyChair Conference Management System. We acknowledge the prompt and professional support from Springer, who published these proceedings in printed and electronic volumes as part of the *Lecture Notes in Computer Science* series. Finally, we are grateful to the team of the of University of Vienna, for providing its facilities and professionally trained staff for the organization of ECSA 2014.

June 2014   Paris Avgeriou
                                                                   Uwe Zdun

Organization

General Chair

Uwe Zdun   University of Vienna, Austria

Program Chair

Paris Avgeriou   University of Groningen, The Netherlands

Organizing Committee

Tutorial Chairs

Philippe Kruchten   University of British Columbia, Canada
Tomi Männistö   University of Helsinki, Finland

Panel Chair

Eoin Woods   UBS, UK

Industry Chairs

Olaf Zimmermann   Hochschule fur Technik Rapperswill
                              (HSR FHO), Switzerland
Uwe van Heesch   Capgemini, Germany

Doctoral Symposium Chairs

Rick Kazman   University of Hawaii, USA
Ivica Crnkovic   Mälardalen University, Sweden

Publicity Chair

Henry Muccini   University of L'Aquila, Italy

Workshop Chair

Danny Weyns   Linnaeus University, Sweden

Tool Demo Chairs

Ipek Ozkaya   Software Engineering Institute, Carnegie
                              Mellon University, USA
Rich Hilliard   Independent Architect, USA

Steering Committee

Paris Avgeriou	University of Groningen, The Netherlands
Muhammad Ali Babar	University of Adelaide, Australia
Ivica Crnkovic	Mälardalen University, Sweden
Carlos E. Cuesta	Rey Juan Carlos University, Spain
Khalil Drira	LAAS-CNRS, University of Toulouse, France
Ian Gorton	SEI, Software Engineering Institute, USA
Volker Gruhn	University of Duisburg-Essen, Germany
Tomi Männistö	University of Helsinki, Finland
Flavio Oquendo	IRISA, University of Brittany, France
Uwe Zdun	University of Vienna, Austria

Program Committee

Eduardo Almeida	Federal University of Bahia and Fraunhofer Project Center for Software and Systems Engineering
Jesper Andersson	Linnaeus University, Sweden
Muhammad Ali Babar	University of Adelaide, Australia
Rami Bahsoon	University of Birmingham, UK
Thais Batista	Federal University of Rio Grande do Norte, Brazil
Jan Bosch	Chalmers University of Technology, Sweden
Janet Burge	Miami University, USA
Rafael Capilla	Universidad Rey Juan Carlos, Spain
Ivica Crnkovic	Mälardalen University, Sweden
Carlos E. Cuesta	Rey Juan Carlos University, Spain
Khalil Drira	LAAS-CNRS, France
Laurence Duchien	Inria, University of Lille, France
Cristina Gacek	City University London, UK
Matthias Galster	University of Canterbury, New Zealand
David Garlan	Carnegie Mellon University, USA
Ian Gorton	Software Engineering Institute, Carnegie Mellon, USA
Volker Gruhn	Universität Duisburg-Essen, Germany
John Grundy	Swinburne University of Technology, Australia
Wilhelm Hasselbring	Kiel University, Germany
Rich Hilliard	Independent architect, USA
Paola Inverardi	University of L'Aquila, Italy
Anton Jansen	ABB Corporate Research, Sweden
Rick Kazman	Software Engineering Institute, Carnegie Mellon, and University of Hawaii, USA
Gerald Kotonya	Lancaster University

Table of Contents

Architecture Description Languages

Enterprise Architecture, SOA and Cloud Computing

Components and Connectors

Quality Attributes

Architecture Analysis and Verification

A Fresh Look at Codification Approaches for SAKM: A Systematic Literature Review

Rainer Weinreich and Iris Groher

Johannes Kepler University Linz, Austria
{rainer.weinreich,iris.groher}@jku.at

Abstract. The last 10 years have seen a rise of approaches for Software Architecture Knowledge Management (SAKM), with a focus on codification of architecture knowledge. Still there is no common meta-model for describing architectural knowledge nor is there a common terminology for the main concepts of such a model. While this might lead to the question whether such a common meta-model is even possible, it is certainly desirable. We decided to tackle this question based on the results of 10 years of research in this area. As part of a systematic literature survey we analyzed and compared model-based approaches for SAKM. Specifically we analyzed the models of SAKM approaches with the highest-rated evidence for different knowledge management activities like capturing, maintaining, reuse, sharing, and using. As a result we identified important aims and elements of proven SAKM approaches, which could be used as a driver for the next generation of AK codification approaches.

Keywords: Architecture Knowledge Management (AKM), AKM Codification Approaches, AKM Models, AKM Activities.

1 Introduction

The last 10 years have seen a rise of software architecture knowledge management (SAKM) as a major research topic within software architecture research. Numerous approaches for SAKM have been developed, most of them following the basic notion of design decisions as first-class entities as proposed by Bosch in 2004 [1]. To preserve the otherwise tacit knowledge, the majority of the approaches developed within the last 10 years supports the codification (i.e., capturing, storing, and retrieving) of architectural knowledge. An early template for representing architectural knowledge has been presented by Tyree et al. [2]. It identifies central elements like decisions, their rationale, and relationships between decisions. This template has been the basis for many of the approaches that have been developed subsequently, yet a common meta-model for representing architectural knowledge is still missing.

As part of our current work we are transforming the architecture management infrastructure we have developed the past years (cf. [3]) into a service-based offering. This has led us to rethink the SAKM support of our approach. Specifically, we assume that we can learn from existing approaches on SAKM, especially

P. Avgeriou and U. Zdun (Eds.): ECSA 2014, LNCS 8627, pp. 1–16, 2014.

from those that have shown some evidence of their usefulness through empirical studies or application in practice.

The work presented in this paper is part of a systematic literature review we performed on SAKM papers published in the last 10 years. The literature review is even broader than what can be presented in this paper, so we concentrate on two research questions that are related to the objective outlined above: (1) What are the main aims of approaches for SAKM within the last 10 years showing the highest evidence for different knowledge management activities and (2) What are the important elements of the SAKM models of these approaches.

The contribution of this paper is a list of requirements on a versatile approach for SAKM that has been derived from published approaches within the last 10 years that have shown some evidence of their usefulness, and important elements of an SAKM model that are the result of these requirements. A distinctive characteristic of our study is that we are not only looking at specific papers but that we are aggregating related papers and studies to approaches. A further distinctive characteristic is that we are not only looking at particular approaches for SAKM but specifically at their support for a particular SAKM activity. The provided evidence is specifically rated with regard to the supported activity.

Expected benefits of the presented work are a better basis for creating a new and versatile approach for SAKM as part of our architecture management infrastructure. Apart from this, the presented work could be a basis for next generation SAKM approaches and a further step towards a commonly agreed on model for SAKM. Such a unified model and terminology is still desirable, since it might lead to a higher adoption rate of SAKM in practice.

2   Research Method

The systematic literature review has been performed following the guidelines of Kitchenham [4]. The main goal of our study was to identify the focus of research in terms of the different SAKM activities, how the activities are supported by tools and techniques, the evidence provided for the different activities, and what gaps exist in supporting the different activities. The study has been conducted from June 2013 to February 2014 and thus only includes papers published before June 2013.

2.1   SAKM Activities

Since we analyze how various approaches support SAKM activities, we briefly define the activities investigated in this study. We derive the main activities from two general definitions of knowledge management [5][6], which identify knowledge creation, capturing, and application (using) as main activities. We add additional activities like maintenance and reuse not contained in the original definitions, and define the investigated activities as follows: AK Capturing makes AK explicit by documenting knowledge about design decisions in a dedicated form; AK Maintaining refers to the activity of keeping the documented knowledge up-to-date; AK Sharing aims at distributing the documented knowledge among different stakeholders and in different contexts; AK Using refers to using the knowledge in different architecture-related activities such as architecture analysis and architecture review; AK Reusing refers to using AK from one project in another project.

2.2   Research Questions

Even though the primary goal of our systematic literature survey was the analysis of support for the different SAKM activities, our search strategy (cf. Section 2.3) allows us to answer additional research questions since the primary studies include existing codification approaches for SAKM published in the last 10 years. In this study we analyze them to answer the following two research questions:

- **RQ1**: What are the main aims of approaches for SAKM within the last 10 years showing the highest evidence for different knowledge management activities?
- **RQ2**: What are the main elements of the SAKM models of these approaches?

In RQ1 we analyze the selected approaches with respect to their goals. In RQ2 we identify the main elements of the SAKM models of the selected approaches and discuss how they relate to the goals identified in RQ1.

2.3   Search Strategy

We used an automated search in four different scientific databases: IEEE, ACM, Springer, and Elsevier. To identify a suitable search string we conducted a pilot study on five venues (WICSA, ECSA, MODELS, QoSA) to verify and refine our initial key words. In particular, we manually examined the venues for relevant papers published in the last five years (since 1.1.2008). Table 1 shows the final search string that resulted from this analysis. The automatic search process in the four scientific databases yielded 440 publications.

2.4   Study Selection

First, we defined a number of inclusion and exclusion criteria for pre-selecting papers for the final review: We only include papers available in electronic form (I1), written in English (I2), written since 2003 (I3), and only take into account peer-reviewed publications appearing in journals, conferences, and workshops (I4). We exclude introductions to special issues, workshops, tutorials, conferences, and conference tracks, as well as editorials (E1), and presentations and short/extended abstracts (E2).

286 publications (about 65 % of the initial set of papers obtained by the automatic search) were left after the exclusion of papers on the basis of the formal criteria. All publications meeting all inclusion criteria and not meeting any of the exclusion criteria were subjected to a voting stage. The voting stage

Table 1. Search string for automatic search in scientific databases

		OR		OR
software architecture	AND	architectural knowledge, architecture knowledge, architecture decision, architectural decision, architecture decisions, architectural decisions, design issue, design issues, design decision, design decisions, design rationale, decision structure, design reasoning, architecture information, architectural information, knowledge management, decision management	AND	model, models, modeling, documentation, documenting, decision making, decision-making, decision process, ontology, ontologies, framework, metamodel, meta-model, metamodeling, modelling (Br.E), decision structure, capture, representation, reuse, sharing, recovery, reasoning, evaluation, analysis, understanding

involved four researchers (2 senior researchers and 2 PhD students). Based on the title and abstract of each publication the reviewers rated whether the publication can contribute to answering the research questions or not. After the rating, publications in which the researchers strongly disagreed were discussed by at least two researchers with opposing opinions.

To determine the overall inter-rater agreement between the four reviewers we calculated the Fleiss Kappa coefficient [7]. The final value was 0.78 and according to Landis and Koch [8] this means substantial agreement. After the voting stage 62 papers (about 22 % of papers included after the application of the inclusion and exclusion criteria) were selected to be potentially relevant for answering our research questions. To ensure that no relevant publications had been forgotten, we conducted a snowball sampling process [9]. We went through all references of the 62 selected primary studies and searched for potentially relevant publications. In total we found 1728 referenced publications. After removing multiple entries 984 referenced publications remained.

From the 984 references we excluded all publications that did not meet the formal criteria or that were not within the scope of AKM. After applying the formal criteria 72 potential publications were left of which 27 publications were already in the list of selected primary studies. The voting (as described above) for the remaining 42 publications resulted in 28 newly selected publications.

In total, 90 primary studies were selected through the search and selection process described above. The data extraction was performed for this final set of studies.

2.5   Data Extraction and Synthesis

Each publication from the final set of publications was read in detail to extract information about both the quality of the publication and specific information about the approaches or concepts, like model-, process- and tool-support for different SAKM activities and the evidence provided. We also extracted information about the main elements of a potential SAKM meta-model and/or ontology.

Each of the four reviewers extracted the data from about one fourth of the overall papers. The extracted data of each paper was additionally cross-checked by another reviewer. The papers were assigned randomly to the four reviewers. Own publications were not self-extracted or checked. To get the same level of knowledge with respect to the data to be extracted, we performed a first round of extraction. Each reviewer extracted the data of one publication and all four reviewers discussed the data of these four publications. Afterwards the data extraction forms were adjusted according to the results of the discussions.

During the extraction process, we further excluded 14 publications, as they either did not meet the formal criteria or because they could not contribute to answering our research questions. This left us with a set of 76 papers we included in our analysis.

Each publication in the final set was assessed for its quality. The quality criteria are based on the protocol for a published systematic literature review [10] and a systematic mapping study [11].

The quality assessment and the data extraction process were conducted in parallel. In addition to general information about the selected study (such as authors, title, year of publication, publication venue, research context, relevance of approach) we focused on support for the different SAKM activities. We analyzed whether and how capturing, maintaining, sharing, using, and reusing of decisions are supported either by a model, a process, or a tool.

Regarding SAKM codification we asked about the representation of AK (formal, informal, or semi-formal). If the approach was based on a decision model we extracted the main elements and their purpose from the studies. We furthermore extracted the goals and motivation of each study.

After extracting the data from all selected primary studies we grouped the papers by approaches. Typically more than one paper is published for an approach, each having a different goal or focus. To be able to draw meaningful conclusions from our study regarding existing SAKM approaches and their codification support we aggregated the results from the individual papers for each approach. In total we identified 47 different SAKM approaches.

We then analyzed each approach with respect to the supported SAKM activities (capturing, sharing, using, maintaining, reusing) and the evidence provided in the supported activities. The evidence levels are rated from 0.0 (no evidence) to 1.0 (evidence obtained from industrial practice). Additional evidence levels are 0.2 (evidence obtained from demonstration or working out toy examples), 0.4 (evidence obtained from expert opinions; evidence obtained from observations and application examples in an industrial setting), 0.6 (evidence obtained from academic studies, case studies, or experiments), and 0.8 (evidence obtained from industrial studies). We first assessed the evidence level for each supported activity separately for each paper and then aggregated the evidence levels per approach and activity.

In total we identified 47 different SAKM approaches containing 32 approaches with support for capturing (27 with evidence), 11 with support for maintaining (0 with evidence), 7 with support for sharing (3 with evidence), 21 with support for using (15 with evidence), and 6 with support for reuse (4 with evidence).

3   Results Analysis

As described in the previous section, each approach has an associated overall evidence level for each SAKM activity it supports. To get an equal distribution of analyzed approaches over the different SAKM activities, we selected for each activity the 3 approaches with the highest evidence level. If two approaches had the same overall level of evidence for a specific activity, both were included. We excluded approaches with an evidence level of less than 0.4 because this means that only examples are presented in the respective papers. Table 2 lists the 7 approaches selected for comparison with their evidence levels in the different SAKM activities[1]. In the table we only present approaches with evidence levels greater than 0.2. Overall, the approaches offer the highest level of evidence for capturing and using, while there is only little evidence both in number of approaches with evidence and in the provided evidence level for the other SAKM activities.

Table 2. Selected approaches based on evidence levels of SAKM activities

	Approach		Evidence Capturing	Evidence Maintaining	Evidence Using	Evidence Sharing	Evidence Reusing
A1	PAKME	[12][13]	0.8		**0.8**	**0.8**	
A4	ADF	[14][15][16]	**0.8**	**0.6**	**0.6**		**0.8**	0.6
A5	ABC/DD	[17][18]	0.8	0.8	**0.8**	0.8	
A8	Knowledge Architect	[19][20]			0.8	**0.8**	
A13	LISA	[3][21]	**0.6**	**0.8**	0.8		
A14	RADM	[22]	0.4				**0.4**
A15	NDR	[23][24]	0.6	0.4	0.6		**0.4**

3.1   RQ1: What Are the Main Aims of Approaches for SAKM within the Last 10 Years Showing the Highest Evidence for Different Knowledge Management Activities?

PAKME [12][13] is a web-based approach for SAKM, which provides a central repository for managing AK through a web interface. The knowledge repository

---

[1] A list of all approaches and associated papers we identified in the systematic literature review can be found at http://www.se.jku.at/akm_slr.zip

supports two types of knowledge: (1) generic knowledge like general scenarios, patterns, quality attributes, and design options and (2) project specific knowledge including concrete scenarios, contextualized patterns, quality factors, and architecture decisions. The approach also supports distilling architecture knowledge from patterns. A main characteristic of the approach is support for architecture evaluation, where it has also been validated in an industrial setting.

Heesch et al. [14][15][16] propose a view-based architectural documentation framework (ADF) for documenting architecture decisions in the sense of ISO / IEC / IEEE 42010-2011. Available viewpoints are a *Decision Detail* (*Decision Rationale*) viewpoint, a *Decision Relationship* viewpoint, a *Decision Chronological* viewpoint, a *Decision Stakeholder Involvement* viewpoint, and a *Decision Forces* viewpoint. The main driver for these views is stakeholder-related concerns like "What decisions have been made?" or "Which stakeholders are affected by a decision?". A more comprehensive list of these concerns and a mapping of concerns to stakeholders can be found in [14]. The approach has been validated with regard to capturing support, support for understanding and review, and support for reuse.

ABC/DD [17][18] is a decision-centric architecture design approach. The main aim is to provide support for the design process. Issues (architecturally significant requirements) lead to issue solutions. Issue solutions can be automatically synthesized to candidate architecture solutions using rules for issue solution compatibility. By deciding on a candidate architecture solution it becomes an architecture decision and the involved issue solutions are automatically captured as issue decisions. Also the pros and cons of the involved issue solutions become the rationale of the issue decisions and collectively make up the rationale of the architecture decision. Finally, the rationale of the architecture decision can be manually extended by additional rationale provided by the people making the decision.

The Knowledge Architect / Astron approach [19][20] supports the enrichment of traditional architecture documentation with formal architectural knowledge to facilitate automatic processing [19]. Main challenges to be addressed by the approach include understandability, change impact analysis, design maturity assessment, locating relevant AK, traceability, and trust. These challenges are supported by activities for identifying documentation issues, defining a domain-specific AK model, capturing AK, using AK, integrating AK, and evolving AK. The approach only provides a validation for the first four activities and leaves out the last two. Validation is limited to one challenge (understandability) and one use case: incremental architecture review. The approach also provides support for the description and the integration of different quantitative analysis models [20] for analyzing complex software systems. Validation has been performed on the context of sharing a cost model for a large telescope (www.skatelescope.org), however with mixed results [20].

The LISA approach [3][21] aims at integrating architecture knowledge management into architecture design and implementation to facilitate agile and iterative development processes. As an architecture model is extracted from and synchronized with an implementation, requirements and design decisions can be added continuously during design and implementation. The approach supports traceability between requirements, design decisions, design structures, and implementation elements, and the automatic capturing of such traces during design and implementation. The LISA toolkit provides multiple views for impact analysis on the basis of the captured traces. The AKM features of the approach have been validated in an industrial project (using Scrum), though with mixed results.

The goal of RADM [22] is to support proactive capturing of reusable background information about recurring design issues. A dedicated decision-making process supports decision identification, decision making, and decision enforcement. The process is supported by a meta-model for capturing and reusing architectural decisions. The meta-model separates reusable information on decisions (issues and proven solutions) from the outcome (project-specific information about the decision made) to facilitate reuse. It is implemented in the Architectural Decision Knowledge Wiki tool, a collaboration system and decision modeling tool. RADM has been practically applied to enterprise application development and SOA.

NDR/TREx [23][24] supports the recovery of rationale from text documents. The goal is to make use of design information that is hidden in casual and semi-structured records such as emails, notes, or documents. Textual documents are parsed and the extracted rationale is described in the NDR ontology using Softgoal Interdependency Graphs (SIGs). After a manual validation the rationale is stored in a knowledge base. Reuse of rationale is tool-supported by comparing and reviewing different SIGs to explore alternative rationale. The approach has been validated with regard to the extraction of rationale from text documents and the comparison of the rationale of two projects.

Discussion of Results RQ1: In analyzing the aims and application scenarios of the approaches with the highest evidence for the different knowledge management activities it becomes evident that a broad application of AKM is still missing. Most of the approaches have been developed in the context of one industrial project or application scenario and have been driven by this scenario. On the other hand, the application to different scenarios with some evidence of their usefulness in practice uncovers important requirements for codification approaches for AKM in general.

For example, the ADF highlights the importance of different views for different stakeholder concerns and provides evidence of the usefulness for the captured AK for use and review. PAKME highlights the need for supporting architecture evaluation using AKM. Evaluation and review support is also one of the main application scenarios of the ADF and of the Knowledge Architect. Extracting architecture knowledge from existing documentation are central aims of the Knowledge Architect approach and of NDR. RADM, NDR, and also PAKME aim at supporting reuse; NDR through comparing the rationale of different projects; RADM and PAKME through splitting generic knowledge from project-specific knowledge. An example for AK-generic knowledge is patterns, which are supported by PAKME but also by other approaches not listed here (e.g., [25]). ABC/DD and RADM specifically support the decision making process. LISA explores capturing decisions and decision traces in an agile context. The main aims and areas of interest of the discussed approaches are summarized in Table 3.

Table 3. Summary of the main goals of the analyzed approaches

Goals	Approaches
Different stakeholder views	ADF
Architecture evaluation	PAKME, Knowledge Architect
Knowledge extraction	Knowledge Architect, NDR
Reuse	RADM, NDR, PAKME
Decision-making process	ABC/DD, RADM
Capturing in agile processes	LISA

3.2 RQ2: What Are Important Elements of SAKM Models of the Selected Approaches?

Tyree and Ackermann [2] present a template for capturing decisions. They define concepts like issue (to be addressed), decision (the outcome of the decision), group, assumptions, constraints, positions (alternatives), argument (rationale), implications, as well as related decisions, requirements, artifacts, and principles as part of a decision documentation [2]. We use the concepts of the Tyree and Ackermann template as a baseline for describing the concepts provided by the other approaches.

The PAKME meta-model supports the documentation of architecture decisions as part of the design history. PAKME provides templates for capturing patterns and scenarios as AK. Scenarios are either user-defined or originate from a pattern. Patterns consist of a name, a description, context, problem, solution, and forces. The repository contains design options that are composed of patterns and each of them is composed of tactics. Rationale for design options can also be captured. An architectural decision is a selected design option. The concepts are similar to what is provided in the Tyree template, except that PAKME also supports the capturing of general design options. The repository is thus divided into generic knowledge (general scenarios, patterns, quality attributes, design options) and project specific knowledge (concrete scenarios, contextualized patterns, quality factors, architecture decisions). Using of AK is supported by searching the repository.

The AKM model of the ADF provides concepts like problem/issue, decision, decision groups, arguments, alternatives, and related decisions, which can be mapped directly to the concepts of the Tyree template. Additional elements are related concerns, decision states, decision relationships, and decision history. Related concerns include requirements, constraints, business goals, assumptions, risks, and design rules. Most of these concepts again map to the elements in the Tyree template. Decision states and decision relation types are taken from the Kruchten

Ontology [26]. The history contains decision state changes and is required for providing the *Decision Chronology* Viewpoint. All in all, the model is rather general, resembling its intended use cases as outlined in the previous section.

The ABC/DD meta-model provides requirement, issue, solution, decision, and rationale as the main elements. Notable is the separation of issue and architecture solution, issue and architecture decision, and issue and architecture rationale. This is due to the fact that issue solutions are combined to form candidate architecture solutions, which, when selected by the architect, become architecture decisions. Pros and cons of an issue solution form its rationale. If an issue solution becomes an issue decision because it is part of an architecture decision, its rationale contributes to the rationale of the architecture decision and vice versa. Since the model has mainly been created for supporting the decision process, it lacks concepts like related decisions or concern though all issue decisions within an architecture decision can be viewed as related.

The Knowledge Architect /Astron approach uses a basic AK (core) model, which can be used for constructing a more (domain-) specific domain model. The basic model only consists of related knowledge entities, which are created by authors and which are described by artifact fragment, which are part of artifacts. The authors have presented two domain models, one for AK in documentation and one for quantitative analysis models. The elements of the AK meta-model very much resemble the elements of the Tyree template: concerns (requirement, risks) raise decision topics, which are addressed by potentially multiple alternatives. The chosen alternative (with its rationale) is represented by the decision. A quick decision resembles a decision with only one alternative. Since some of the authors of the approach are also involved in the ADF described above, the AK model also contains information about the status of a decision and decision relationships as defined in the Kruchten ontology. The AK meta-model for quantitative analysis models supports the evaluation of different design options, or alternatives. Each alternative is a design concept, which is specialized in one or more scenarios, which in turn are analyzed using one or more analysis models. The model also contains concepts for describing analysis functions in more detail. For integrating different analysis models, a mapping can be defined between them. Finally, additional concepts like review and rating are provided to support the review and evaluation process itself.

The LISA meta-model provides concepts like concern, requirement, and design decisions. Rationale is captured as part of design decisions. Requirements and design decisions are first-class elements of the architecture model and specializations of the concept of an issue. Grouping of requirements and design decisions and alternatives are supported through relations among issues. Relation types are modeled according to the Kruchten ontology. The model also supports traces from requirements and design decisions to architectural solution structures and implementation artifacts. During automatic capturing of traces, existing traces are used for proposing relations between design decisions (and requirements).

The RADM meta-model provides concepts like issue, alternative, and outcome to capture AK. Issues represent single architectural design problems and alternatives are possible solutions to this problem. Outcome is an actual decision made to solve the design problem including its rationale. The separation between alternatives and outcome fosters reuse of proactively captured design issues and their proven solutions. RADM also provides topic groups to bundle related issues and levels to represent different refinement levels. The concepts provided in RADM can be mapped to the Tyree template. Issues and groups are used in both approaches. Assumptions, arguments, and implications in the Tyree template are modeled as attributes of decisions in RADM. Also, both support linking decisions to design artifacts. The main difference is the separation of alternatives and outcomes in RADM that is driven by the reuse attempt.

The NDR ontology describes AK using Softgoal Interdependency Graphs (SIGs). SIGs describe non-functional requirements as softgoals that can be decomposed into more specific softgoals until they can be *satisfied* (satisfied sufficiently) by one or more solutions (operationalizing softgoal in SIG). SIGs further support the capturing of interdependencies among softgoals, argumentation rationale, and evaluation of adopted and discarded design decisions. Architectural alternative, pattern, and technology are subclasses of operationalizing softgoal. Driver, requirement, and issue are subclasses of softgoal. In NDR reuse is facilitated through comparison of different SIGs. The comparison algorithm checks softgoals, claims, interdependencies, and argumentations for equality. NDR concepts can be compared to the Tyree template as both provide concepts for describing issues and their solutions. The main difference is that NDR mainly targets nonfunctional requirements to be modeled as softgoals whereas issues in the Tyree template represent any kind of architectural design issue.

Discussion of Results RQ2: In analyzing the elements of the different SAKM models with the highest evidence for the different knowledge management activities we found that the models are not that different, as they might seem at first glance. Overall, the models typically contain a set of core elements to represent issues, decisions, and rationale that map to the concepts provided in the Tyree template. Nearly all models we analyzed support this set of concepts. Some models additionally provide support for capturing relationships between decisions. The ADF and LISA use relationship types that map to the Kruchten Ontology. Decision states are also captured in some models (e.g. ADF and Knowledge Architect) but not all. A notable commonality between most approaches is the support for capturing traces between decisions and design artifacts. LISA and NDR, for example, provide concepts for documenting how decisions are addressed in the architecture. The common concepts of the analyzed SAKM models are listed in Table 4. Some approaches are distinguishing with respect to reuse of decisions. These approaches (e.g. RADM and PAKME) separate general knowledge from project specific knowledge. This is typically achieved by supporting the capturing of reusable knowledge in the form of patterns or recurring design options. During decision making, a concrete option is selected and its rationale is captured. Finally, PAKME is very much focused on architecture analysis and thus support concepts like quality attribute, quality factor, scenario, and risk.

In our analysis we did not include any approaches that focus on the maintaining activity because none of these approaches did provide sufficient evidence. Even though it is worth mentioning that some approaches exist that support evolution and maintenance of architectural knowledge like ADDSS [27] and TVM [25].

Table 4. Summary of the common concepts supported by the analyzed approaches

Model Concepts	Approaches
Issue	Tyree, ADF, ABC/DD, Knowledge Architect, LISA, RADM, NDR
Requirement	PAKME (ASRs), ADF, Knowledge Architect, LISA, NDR
Design Decision	all
Decision Status	Tyree, ADF, Knowledge Architect, LISA, RADM
Group	Tyree, ADF, LISA, RADM
Assumptions	Tyree, ADF, RADM
Alternatives	all
Constraints	Tyree
Rationale	all
Implications	Tyree, RADM
Related decisions	Tyree, ADF, Knowledge Architect, LISA, NDR
Related artifacts (Tracing)	Tyree, Knowledge Architect, LISA, RADM, NDR
Patterns	PAKME, NDR
Scenario	PAKME, Knowledge Architect, LISA
Quality attributes	PAKME, LISA
Decision history	ADF, PAKME

4   Threats to Validity

There are several factors that may influence the results of this study. These are in particular factors that influence the search we conducted, the study selection we performed, and the extraction of the data from the selected studies.

Reliability refers to the question whether the study is reproducible by other researchers [28]. To ensure reliability we present the search terms, the sources of our automatic search and the inclusion and exclusion criteria used. The voting leaves room for variation between researchers, since researchers are likely to have different opinions on whether a publication can contribute to answering the research questions. To reduce this bias, four researchers performed the voting in parallel and discussed publications where they strongly disagreed. The data extraction and especially the quality assessment of the study strongly affect the classification and thus the selection of approaches in this paper. To reduce the personal bias in study assessment, the extracted data was checked by at least two reviewers. Also, own publications were not self-extracted or checked and a pilot extraction was performed. Furthermore, we looked at related studies (such as [11]) and analyzed how papers that were contained in both our study and the related study were rated. We found a strong agreement between the quality assessment results in most cases.

Construct validity refers to the question whether the constructs are measured and interpreted correctly [28]. To ensure a common understanding of the relevant concepts and terms we checked the relevant literature and analyzed the definitions. To ensure that our search terms were accurate, we conducted a pilot study to verify and refine the initial key words. To ensure a common understanding of the data to be extracted from the studies we performed a pilot extraction. Each reviewer extracted the data of one publication and four reviewers discussed the data of these four publications. The data extraction forms were adjusted according to the results of the discussions.

Internal validity refers to the question whether the study results really follow from the data [28]. This does not really apply in our case, as we did not use any statistical analysis in our study.

External validity refers to the question whether claims for the generality of the results are justified [28]. The goal of this study is to identify the aims of SAKM approaches with some evidence and the most important elements of the SAKM models of these approaches. The approaches included in this study were identified by a systematic literature review following the guidelines of Kitchenham [4]. From the set of identified approaches from the systematic review we selected for each SAKM activity the 3 approaches with the highest evidence level to ensure an equal distribution of studies among the different activities and to obtain a representative set of studies.

5   Related Work

Li et al. [11] conducted a systematic mapping study to assess the state of the art in how knowledge-based approaches are applied in software architecture. They used similar inclusion and exclusion criteria and they also assessed the quality of publications in a similar way. In contrast to our work, they did not combine related publications. They state that knowledge capturing and representation is most frequently used, which supports our results. Also architecture evaluation has been identified as a very frequent application scenario. This result also supports our findings, as knowledge using is the activity with the second most approaches that provide evidence in our study.

Tang et al. [29] present a comparative study of five architecture knowledge management tools. Also, concepts of the different AK tools have been compared with the result that all tools support the concepts rationale and concern from IEEE 1471-2000. Our study does not focus on tools but rather on AKM approaches and analyzes them regarding their goals and model elements. The results of our study also show that the analyzed models have many concepts in common and largely match the concepts proposed in the Tyree template.

Tofan et al. [30] present a systematic mapping study to assess the state of research on architectural decisions. They look at various aspects like support for quality attributes and group decision making, which has not been a focus in our study. In terms of documenting decisions they find that numerous approaches for documenting decisions exist and conclude "so practitioners can incorporate documentation approaches in their activities." As we found that there is still no sufficient evidence for basic requirements like maintenance of decisions in existing approaches, we cannot support this specific claim. Also, the authors did not combine papers to approaches nor did they compare the underlying decision models. While they state that only half of the papers in their study provide empirical evidence, they did not analyze the evidence with regard to the supported knowledge management activities like we did in our work.

Shahin et al. [31] compared 9 models for capturing architectural design decisions and related tools. Similar to our study they tried to map the important elements of the surveyed models to the Tyree template. In contrast to our study, Shahin et al. did not take the evidence of the approaches into account nor did they systematically identify the models under comparison. Furthermore, they did not take the different AKM activities into account.

6 Conclusion

Analyzing AKM codification approaches published in the last 10 years with the highest rated evidence for a specific AKM activity shows that approaches for capturing and using dominate. Capturing approaches with evidence aim to support manual capturing, extraction from existing artifacts, and automatic capturing of traces during design and development. The dominant use cases of the analyzed approaches in terms of using are understanding and architecture evaluation. Also approaches aiming to support reuse, decision making, and different stakeholder views provide some evidence. A main finding is that there is still no evidence for core knowledge management activities like AK maintenance and only weak evidence for AK sharing and reusing. This is a prerequisite to address adoption of AKM approaches in practice.

If we look at the supported concepts and model elements, the Tyree template has been amazingly resilient over the last 10 years. The essential concepts of the analyzed approaches still largely resemble the original concepts introduced in the Tyree template. There is some difference in how these concepts are implemented, but these differences are not significant. There is, however, no agreement on the used terminology and this is something we as a research community need to address in the future. A commonly agreed on terminology is a significant part to foster broader adoption of the topic. Some approaches have introduced additional concepts required to support specific use cases like scenarios in the case of architecture evaluation and patterns as a means for easily capturing and reusing decisions. But this only shows that these concepts are closely related to design decisions and discussing this relationship in more detail could be another step in better aligning the different terminology used in some approaches.

References

1. Bosch, J.: Software architecture: The next step. In: Oquendo, F., Warboys, B.C., Morrison, R. (eds.) EWSA 2004. LNCS, vol. 3047, pp. 194–199. Springer, Heidelberg (2004)

2. Tyree, J., Akerman, A.: Architecture decisions: Demystifying architecture. IEEE Software 22(2), 19–27 (2005)
3. Weinreich, R., Buchgeher, G.: Towards supporting the software architecture life cycle. Journal of Systems and Software 85(3), 546–561 (2012)
4. Kitchenham, B.A., Charters, S.: Guidelines for performing systematic literature reviews in software engineering. Technical report, Software Engineering Group, School of Computer Science and Mathematics, Keele University, UK, and Department of Computer Science, University of Durham, Durham, UK (July 2007)
5. Davenport, T.H., Prusak, L.: Working knowledge: How organizations manage what they know. Harvard Business School Press, Boston (1998)
6. Alavi, M., Leidner, D.E.: Review: Knowledge management and knowledge management systems: Conceptual foundations and research issues. MIS Quarterly, 107–136 (2001)
7. Fleiss, J.L.: Measuring nominal scale agreement among many raters. Psychological Bulletin 76(5), 378 (1971)
8. Landis, J.R., Koch, G.G.: The measurement of observer agreement for categorical data. Biometrics 33(1), 159–174 (1977)
9. Goodman, L.A.: Snowball sampling. The Annals of Mathematical Statistics, 148–170 (1961)
10. Weyns, D., Ahmad, T.: Claims and evidence for architecture-based self-adaptation: A systematic literature review. In: Drira, K. (ed.) ECSA 2013. LNCS, vol. 7957, pp. 249–265. Springer, Heidelberg (2013)
11. Li, Z., Liang, P., Avgeriou, P.: Application of knowledge-based approaches in software architecture: A systematic mapping study. Information and Software Technology (2012)
12. Babar, M.A., Northway, A., Gorton, I., Heuer, P., Nguyen, T.: Introducing tool support for managing architectural knowledge: An experience report. In: 15th Conference on the Engineering of Computer Based Systems, pp. 105–113. IEEE (2008)
13. Babar, M.A., Capilla, R.: Capturing and using quality attributes knowledge in software architecture evaluation process. In: First International Workshop on Managing Requirements Knowledge, MARK 2008, pp. 53–62. IEEE (2008)
14. van Heesch, U., Avgeriou, P., Hilliard, R.: A documentation framework for architecture decisions. Journal of Systems and Software 85(4), 795–820 (2012)
15. van Heesch, U., Avgeriou, P., Tang, A.: Does decision documentation help junior designers rationalize their decisions?-a comparative multiple-case study. Journal of Systems and Software (2013)
16. van Heesch, U., Avgeriou, P., Hilliard, R.: Forces on architecture decisions-a viewpoint. In: 2012 Joint Working IEEE/IFIP Conference on Software Architecture (WICSA) and European Conference on Software Architecture (ECSA), pp. 101–110. IEEE (2012)
17. Cui, X., Sun, Y., Xiao, S., Mei, H.: Architecture design for the large-scale software-intensive systems: A decision-oriented approach and the experience. In: 2009 14th IEEE International Conference on Engineering of Complex Computer Systems, pp. 30–39. IEEE (2009)
18. Cui, X., Sun, Y., Mei, H.: Towards automated solution synthesis and rationale capture in decision-centric architecture design. In: Seventh Working IEEE/IFIP Conference on Software Architecture, pp. 221–230. IEEE (2008)
19. Jansen, A., Avgeriou, P., van der Ven, J.S.: Enriching software architecture documentation. Journal of Systems and Software 82(8), 1232–1248 (2009)

20. Jansen, A., de Vries, T., Avgeriou, P., van Veelen, M.: Sharing the architectural knowledge of quantitative analysis. In: Becker, S., Plasil, F., Reussner, R. (eds.) QoSA 2008. LNCS, vol. 5281, pp. 220–234. Springer, Heidelberg (2008)

21. Weinreich, R., Buchgeher, G.: Integrating requirements and design decisions in architecture representation. In: Babar, M.A., Gorton, I. (eds.) ECSA 2010. LNCS, vol. 6285, pp. 86–101. Springer, Heidelberg (2010)

22. Zimmermann, O., Gschwind, T., Küster, J., Leymann, F., Schuster, N.: Reusable architectural decision models for enterprise application development. In: Overhage, S., Ren, X.-M., Reussner, R., Stafford, J.A. (eds.) QoSA 2007. LNCS, vol. 4880, pp. 15–32. Springer, Heidelberg (2008)

23. López, C., Codocedo, V., Astudillo, H., Cysneiros, L.M.: Bridging the gap between software architecture rationale formalisms and actual architecture documents: An ontology-driven approach. Science of Computer Programming 77(1), 66–80 (2012)

24. López, C., Inostroza, P., Cysneiros, L.M., Astudillo, H.: Visualization and comparison of architecture rationale with semantic web technologies. Journal of Systems and Software 82(8), 1198–1210 (2009)

25. Che, M., Perry, D.E.: Scenario-based architectural design decisions documentation and evolution. In: 2011 18th IEEE International Conference and Workshops on Engineering of Computer Based Systems, ECBS 2011, pp. 216–225. IEEE (2011)

26. Kruchten, P.: An ontology of architectural design decisions in software intensive systems. In: 2nd Groningen Workshop on Software Variability, pp. 54–61 (2004)

27. Capilla, R., Nava, F., Dueas, J.C.: Modeling and documenting the evolution of architectural design decisions. In: Second Workshop on Sharing and Reusing Architectural Knowledge- Architecture, Rationale, and Design Intent, SHARK/ADI 2007: ICSE Workshops 2007, p. 9. IEEE (2007)

28. Easterbrook, S., Singer, J., Storey, M.A.A., Damian, D.: Selecting empirical methods for software engineering research. In: Guide to advanced empirical software engineering, pp. 285–311. Springer (2008)

29. Tang, A., Avgeriou, P., Jansen, A., Capilla, R., Babar, M.A.: A comparative study of architecture knowledge management tools. Journal of Systems and Software 83(3), 352–370 (2010)

30. Tofan, D., Galster, M., Avgeriou, P., Schuitema, W.: Past and future of software architectural decisions–a systematic mapping study. Information and Software Technology (2014)

31. Shahin, M., Liang, P., Khayyambashi, M.R.R.: Architectural design decision: Existing models and tools. In: Joint Working IEEE/IFIP Conference on Software Architecture, 2009 & European Conference on Software Architecture, WICSA/ECSA 2009, pp. 293–296. IEEE (2009)

Suitability of Software Architecture Decision Making Methods for Group Decisions

Smrithi Rekha V.[1,2] and Henry Muccini[3]

[1] Amrita School of Business, Amrita Vishwa Vidyapeetham, India
[2] Center for Research in Advanced Technologies for Education (CREATE),
Amrita Vishwa Vidyapeetham, India
[3] Department of Engineering, Computer Science, and Mathematics,
University of L'Aquila, Italy
smrithirekha@gmail.com, henry.muccini@univaq.it

Abstract. Software architecture design decisions are central to the architecting process. Hence, the software architecture community has been constantly striving towards making the decision-making process robust and reliable to create high-quality architectures. Surveys of practitioners has demonstrated that most decisions made by them are group decisions. Hence, for any tool or method to be useful to them, it must include provision for making group decisions.

In this paper we analyse *if* and *how* current software architecture decision-making techniques support Group Decision Making (GDM). We use an evaluation framework with eight criteria, identified by the GDM community, to evaluate selected SA decision-making techniques in order to check their adequacy and suitability to support group decisions. As per our analysis, most of the selected methods in their current form are not yet fully suitable for group decision making and may need to integrate more aspects like provision for stakeholders to explicitly indicate their preferences, conflict resolution mechanisms, and group decision rules meant to specify how stakeholders' preferences are taken into account.

1 Introduction

Software architects find themselves making numerous decisions while architecting software systems. These decisions could be related to the architecture style of the system, technological or even economical decisions. The decision-making process is highly complex since it has to satisfy multiple-criteria and the concerns of multiple-stakeholders. As testified by related work [1,2,3], the software architecture (SA) decision-making process involves several decision makers, that with their different skills and concerns, participate in a (typically) distributed decision process. Looking at SA decision-making as a group process helps in including perspectives and opinions of multiple stakeholders thereby making the process more holistic in nature leading to a high quality system.

In this paper, we analyse the suitability of current SA decision-making methods to support group decision making. We essentially want to provide an answer to two main research questions, namely: *RQ1) how to evaluate the architecture design decision methods' suitability for group decision making?*, and *RQ2) how adequate existing architecture design decision methods are for group decision making?*

P. Avgeriou and U. Zdun (Eds.): ECSA 2014, LNCS 8627, pp. 17–32, 2014.

For those purposes, we define an evaluation framework with eight criteria extracted by a list identified by the group decision making (GDM) community. Then, we apply such criteria to state of the art architecture design decision methods. Such an analysis, we believe, will have the following benefits:

• pave the way for explicitly including multiple stakeholders into SA decision-making methods and tools;
• help to accommodate the preferences of these stakeholders;
• facilitate a more democratic and robust method of SA decision-making where preferences, priorities, objectives etc., are included to make optimal decisions.

The current tools and methods for capturing Architectural Design Decisions (ADDs), which are typically modeled around the ISO/IEC/IEEE 42010 standard for architectural description [4], do not explicitly cover all aspects of GDM. Given that most decisions in practice are group decisions, it may be necessary to integrate GDM into these methods and tools.

Our paper is organized as follows. In Section 2 we present background information on various GDM techniques, the details of a comparative study as discussed by Saaty and Vargas in their book titled *Decision making with the analytic network process* [5], and a generic *Group Problem Solving Model* presented by Aldag in [6]. In Section 3 we highlight the need for integrating GDM into mainstream SA decision-making. Details of our evaluation framework and its application to various SA decision-making techniques are presented in Section 4 and 5. Results are discussed in Section 6. Related work are presented in Section 7, while conclusions and future work are discussed in Section 8.

2   Background

It is a common practice in organizations to involve groups for making decisions. While making important decisions, groups are preferred to individuals as groups bring in a) diverse perspectives, b) greater information exchange, and c) better sense of involvement and accountability [7]. Given these benefits, management researchers have evolved several GDM methods for effective decision-making. Some popular *GDM methods* are:

• Brainstorming: it involves group discussion moderated by a facilitator. An alternative is brainwriting.
• Voting: participants vote on a predetermined set of alternatives and the solutions with majority votes are selected.
• Nominal Group Technique (NGT): NGT encourages all members to participate freely and prevents dominant ones from hijacking the discussions. This results in a prioritized set of alternatives and recommendations.
• Delphi Technique: it involves several rounds of structured communication among participants.
• Analytic Hierarchy Processing (AHP): considered to be one of the most effective techniques, AHP involves pairwise comparison and ranking of alternatives, and mathematically computing the best solution.

Other GDM methods include matrix evaluation, goal programming, conjoint analysis, outranking and bayesian analysis.

Each of these methods has their own pros and cons. These plethora of GDM methods have helped decision-makers enhance the quality of decisions. In addition to this, various other factors are said to influence the quality of decisions made by groups some of which include group size, group cohesiveness, task significance, group norms and group composition [8]. Each of these factors have been studied in great detail by several researchers in the field of GDM.

The following Section 2.1 and 2.2 will introduce state-of-the-art GDM evaluation criteria and a generic GDM model, respectively. Those will be used as the baseline to answer RQ1 (*how to evaluate the architecture design decision methods' suitability for group decision making?*).

2.1 Criteria for Evaluating Group Decision Making Methods

A detailed comparison of the various techniques has been performed by Thomas L. Saaty and Luis G. Vargas in [5]. These authors have identified and used 16 criteria for evaluating various GDM methods. These criteria are reported and briefly illustrated in Table 1.

Table 1. Criteria for evaluating GDM methods

Criteria	Description
1. Leadership Effectiveness	Importance given to Leader and provides other collaborative tools and the necessary control mechanisms to guide the facilitator's leadership actions in pursuing the group's achievement
2. Learning	Facilitates group learning and enables one to produce the necessary materials to facilitate learning beyond the membership of the group
3. Scope	Involves problem analysis that serves as feedback to broaden problem abstraction
4. Development of Alternatives	Alternatives evolve with group discussion and helps to satisfy certain properties to ensure the validity of the outcome
5. Breadth	Problem is modeled such that there are many distinct elements (criteria) that are assumed to be independent of each other
6. Depth	Problem is modeled such that each element is broken down into sub-elements, each sub-element into sub-sub elements and so on down to the most detailed elements
7. Breadth and Depth of Analysis	Facilitates careful thinking and review
8. Cardinal Separation of Alternatives	Uses an interval scale, a ratio scale, or an absolute scale to rate the alternatives
9. Faithfulness of Judgment	The method is elicited in the most elementary way (pairwise comparison with respect to a property), expressed in a way that fits the decision maker best (numerically, verbally, or graphically), or, if it is by design an objective method
10. Prioritizing Group Members	Provides a method to determine the weights for the members as the group wishes.
11. Consideration of other Actors and Stakeholders	Involves External Stakeholders and addresses the issue both explicitly and quantitatively
12. Scientific and Mathematical Generality	Theorems are axiomatized and generalizable in a natural and less taxing way by not requiring many new assumptions
13. Applicability to Intangibles	Measurement is applicable to intangibles and gives an assessment of their relative importance, either absolutely or relatively, as the user wishes
14. Psychophysical Applicability	Applicable psychophysically and addresses issues of stimulusresponse
15. Applicability to Conflict Resolution	Facilitates finding the best solution for a group conflict that is understandable, acceptable, practical, flexible, and has been demonstrated to work well in practice
16. Validity of the Outcome (prediction)	The method uses cardinal measurement, but its mathematical validity sets limits on the structural representation of a problem

2.2 Generic Model of Group Decision Making

In order to understand whether the current SA decision-making methods are suitable for GDM i.e to answer our RQ2, we use a generic model as a basis.

Our review of literature and the review presented in [6] reveals that though GDM has been researched from many perspectives, most of the works look at specific aspects and there are very few works that give a *generic model of GDM*. We use the General Group Problem-Solving (GGPS) model proposed in [6] which is actually an expansion of the groupthink model proposed by Janis [9]. The GGPS model has four components, namely: (a) *antecedents conditions*, (b) *the group characteristics*, (c) *the decision process characteristics*, and (d) *the decision process outcomes*. The model is comprehensive in that it covers several aspects of GDM with neutral connotation (as opposed to the groupthink model of Janis). The antecedent conditions examine various aspects preceding the GDM process like group structure, decision characteristics and the decision making context. Once the group is formed, certain characteristics of the group emerge that impact the decision-making process and its outcome.

The decision-making process has three important stages namely *problem identification*, *alternative generation* and *evaluation and choice*. The outcome of the decision-making process are the final decisions and their implementation. The model is shown in Figure 1.

Both the evaluation criteria outlined in Section 2.1 and the GGPS model summarized in this section are going to be used to shape our evaluation framework presented in Section 4.

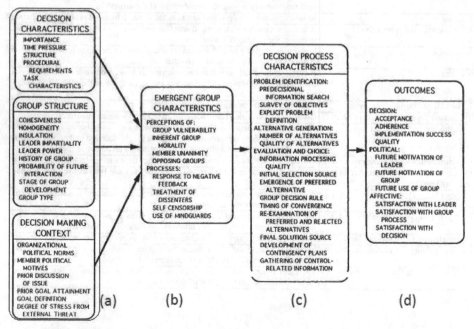

Fig. 1. Generic Group Problem Solving Model proposed by Aldag and Fuller [6]

3 The Rationale for GDM in SA

With more than 85% of the decisions made by software architects being group decisions [1], [3], the SA community is yet to harness this vast body of literature available on GDM. In this section we briefly discuss why we need to explicitly model GDM in the SA decision-making process. The needs are as follows:

1. As discussed earlier, what is seen in practice is that most SA decisions are not made in isolation but through a process of discussion and deliberation by a group of experts who have different preferences. Group decision rules may be required to process these preferences to arrive at optimal decisions.
2. A review of literature done by Falessi et al. in [10] points out that the various methods so far used in SA decision-making are focused more on identifying quality attributes and alternatives, scoring them using pairwise comparison or other ranking techniques and making a decision based on the scores. These methods involve multi-criteria/multi-attribute decision-making. While a few of these include multiple stakeholders, many of them do not account for group processes like brainstorming alternatives, preference ranking, prioritizing stakeholders or using a group decision support system. Hence these methods in literature may have to be extended to suit the practical setting.
3. If at all the decision-making methods in literature involve several decision-makers, they have predetermined set of alternatives from to choose from, i.e., the function as a group only in certain stages of decision-making. This seems to be a limited way of involving stakeholders. What may be required is a way of involving stakeholders right from the problem identification, to generation of alternatives to arriving at a consensus.
4. The results of our study of SA decision-making practices in the industry [1] shows that GDM isn't just about indicating preferences but a detailed process of: a) preparing documentation b) face-to-face and virtual discussions c) group members listing alternatives and indicating preferences d) making trade-offs e) deciding to take risks f) facing and resolving challenges and conflicts g) arriving at a consensus and make a decision with or without arbitration.
5. Decision-making involves uncertainty i.e decision-makers may not have knowledge about all the consequences of their decisions. This may be caused due to incomplete information, inadequate understanding and undifferentiated alternatives [11]. Such a situation may be better handled by a group of decision-makers who share different perspectives and information thereby reducing the level of uncertainty.

Hence, a more holistic decision-making method is required for SA which accounts for multiple stakeholder perspective and uses a combination of formal and non-formal approaches to GDM.

4 Evaluation Framework

In this section we present details of the criteria that we use for checking the adequacy of current SA decision-making methods to support GDM. The evaluation framework is primarily based on the GGPS model presented in Section 2.2. We draw these criteria from the *Decision Process Characteristics* (see Figure 1.c) which focuses on various steps in GDM, namely problem identification, survey of objectives, generation of alternatives, evaluation, and selection based on decision rules. We also draw insights from the criteria discussed by Saaty and Vargas in [5] (summarised in Section 2.1). We have not used the evaluation criteria as-is but adapted them to suit SA decision-making. While adapting we have combined a few criteria and process discussed in the two references mentioned above as well from the steps involved in generic SA decision-making. For instance the "Problem Identification" criteria is combination of "Problem Abstraction" from [5] and "Problem Identification" from [6]. "Preference Indication" is adapted from "Cardinal Separation of Alternatives" from [5] and "Evaluation and Choice" step from [6].

The evaluation criteria are as follows:

1. **Problem Identification:** We use this criteria to see if groups are involved right from the problem identification stage where the problem is identified and defined, broken down into sub-problems or issues and mapped to specific requirements.

2. **Development of Alternatives:** Instead of a pre-determined set of alternatives, the process of identification of alternatives is integrated in the GDM process, where the entire group discusses and identifies/filters the alternatives. There may be a specific technique to identify alternatives and the GDM process shall also allow the evolution of preferred alternatives during the process.

3. **Preference Indication:** The heart of any GDM process is the indication of preferences by the stakeholders. Hence there should be provision for multiple stakeholders to indicate preferences either through a process of ranking or scoring through comparisons or simple ratings. The preferences could be based on the criteria to be satisfied by the system or any other organizational criteria.

4. **Prioritizing Group Members:** Not all group members are equally important. The voice of senior experts could be more important than junior architects. Hence hierarchy and expertise play an important role in GDM. The method could include ways of prioritizing decision-makers.

5. **Provision for Conflict Resolution:** There should be explicit mechanisms of avoiding conflicts or resolving conflicts if they occur. Conflict resolution is key to the quality of decisions made. Conflicts could occur due to conflicting objectives, presence of a few dominant members in the group, political issues and task related issues. So a formal conflict resolution strategy may be required or the process could be fair enough that conflicts are as minimal as possible.

6. **Group Decision Rules:** Group decision rules help specifying how the preferences of various stakeholders are taken into account. It could be the aggregation of various preferences in case of methods like AHP. Unanimity, plurality and minority rules are used during voting. Complex mathematical calculations can be involved to arrive at a decision. Decision rules can ensure that decisions are made in a timely manner and that all stakeholder preferences are factored in.

7. **Information Exchange and Recall:** A very important factor in any GDM process is the exchange of shared and unshared information [12], [13]. Shared information is the one known by all, while unshared is that known only by one member in the

group. The success of a GDM lies in bringing out the unshared information during the process of discussion so that optimal decisions are made. Balanced information exchange can help to avoid issues like Groupthink [6]. Also, information recall is a key factor impacting the effectiveness of decisions. The more information the group is able to recall, the better the decisions would be [14]. Hence any GDM process, specially if it is tool based, should facilitate appropriate representation of information for quick and effective recall.

8. **Revisiting Information:** Individuals often come with certain preferential biases before the GDM process [15] and during the discussion as more and more information is exchanged, the members tend to revisit their preferences. Hence any GDM process must be able to accommodate the revisiting of alternatives, preferences and decisions made. It would also be appropriate if there was a way of members to indicate their individual pre-group preferences to avoid discussion biases.

5 Evaluation of the Various SA Decision-Making Techniques

In this section we present our evaluation of various SA decision-making techniques using the framework discussed in Section 4. We choose a subset from the several SA decision-making methods discussed in [10] and [16] and apply our framework to them. We have chosen reference works that do not have tool support but only discuss a decision-making process/method.

The reference works we have chosen are represented in Table 2. The rationale for choosing these works is as follows:

- SA decision-making involves several aspects that include right from understanding the requirements to the generation of high-level architecture of the system. We needed SA decision-making methods in literature that represented these wide range activities. The selected references include COTS selection, architectural candidate selection, architectural design decisions, components selection and evaluation of scenarios thereby covering broad aspects of SA decision-making.
- There is no one single SA decision-making method. A variety of scientific methods of decision-making methods are available in literature. The subset of reference works adopts many of these methods including Utility Function based methods, Weighted Score methods, Trade-offs, Analytic Hierarchy Processing and Cost Benefit Analysis Method (CBAM)[1].
- Most of the reference works chosen involve conflicting multiple objectives. Hence it may be useful to check their suitability to accommodate multiple stakeholder perspectives as well.

1. Problem Identification: The methods discussed in [19], ATAM and CBAM 2 discussed in [25] and [21] involves several stakeholders who at the beginning elicit and discuss a set of scenarios relevant to the problem. [27], [28] explicitly models the presence of multiple-stakeholders by branching out on different nodes of a decision-tree depending on the stakeholder concerns but does not discuss problem identification.

---

[1] Hereafter we do focus on CBAM and not to the ATAM, since the former builds on the latter

Table 2. Methods Selected for Applying Evaluation Framework

Methods and Authors	Reference and Title
ArchDesigner: Al-Naeem et al	[17]: A Quality-Driven Systematic Approach for Architecting Distributed Software Applications
Andrews et al	[18]: A Framework for Design Tradeoffs
Comparative Evolution Process (CEP):Phillips and Polen	[19]: Add Decision Analysis to Your COTS Selection Process
BAREMO:Lozano et al	[20]: BAREMO: How to Choose the Appropriate Software Component Using the Analytic Hierarchy Process
CBAM 2: Moore et al	[21]: Quantifying the Value of Architecture Design Decisions: Lessons from the field
Svahnberg et al	[22]: A Quality-Driven Decision-Support Method for Identifying Software Architecture Candidates
Vijayalakshmi et al	[23]: Multicriteria Decision Analysis Method for Evaluation of Software Architectures
RGT: Tofan et al	[24]: Capturing tacit architectural knowledge using the repertory grid technique
Wallin et al	[25]: Making decisions in integration of automotive software and electronics: A method based on ATAM and AHP
Stoll et al	[26]:Guiding architectural decisions with the influencing factors method
Fabian Gilson and Vincent Englebert	[27]:Rationale, Decisions and Alternatives Traceability for Architecture Design
Orlic et al	[28]:Concepts and diagram elements for architectural knowledge management
Weihang Wu and Tim Kelly	[29]:Managing Architectural Design Decisions for Safety Critical Software Systems
AQUA: Heeseok Choi et al	[30]:An Integrated Approach to Quality Achievement with Architectural Design Decisions
Hoh In	[31]:From Requirements Negotiation to Software Architectural Decisions
Lars Grunske	[32]:Identifying "Good" Architectural Design Alternatives with Multi-Objective Optimization Strategies
Qing Gu et al	[33]:A template for SOA design decision making in an educational setting
Carmen Zannier and Frank Maurer	[34]:A Qualitative Empirical Evaluation of Design Decisions
Olaf Zimmermann et al	[35]:Reusable Architectural Decision Models for Enterprise Application Development
Riebisch, Matthias and Wohlfarth, Sven	[36]:Introducing impact analysis for architectural decisions
Bingfeng Xu et al	[37]:Making Architectural Decisions Based on Requirements: Analysis and Combination of Risk-Based and Quality Attribute-Based Methods
CEADA: Nakakawa et al	[38]: Requirements for Collaborative Decision Making in Enterprise Architecture

[26] gathers the opinion of several stakeholders in formulating the decision factors. [38] provides detailed set of steps for collaborative decision-making. The steps discussed in [38] not only focus on problem definition but on collaboratively defining organizational goals. References [18], [22], [26], [30] and [32] start with the identification of alternatives or decision, decision factors, directly. They do not mention any specific *problem identification* stage that involves a group. Though both [17] and [20] are based on AHP, only [20] discusses problem identification and building of a hierarchy tree for the problem. [24], [29], [36], [37] and [31] start with the identification of topic, negative scenarios, objectives and requirements respectively, all of which resembles problem identification. However, none of the above works discuss the involvement of a group in problem identification, definition and decomposition. Reference [23] does not start with a problem identification stage.

2. Development of Alternatives: We expect that the alternatives will emerge and evolve during the process of group discussion and a good GDM process should facilitate the same. In [21] the group discusses alternative responses (best, worst, desired etc.) for a given scenario. Scenarios are generated in an iterative process as more and more information is available. This is also the case with [31]. [25] and [38] discuss a collaborative evolution of alternatives. References [19] and [22] both discuss the search for suitable alternatives. References [17], [29], [32], [24] and [36] discuss steps where alternatives/negative scenarios and criteria are identified. In [20] identification of alternatives is integrated into the step where a hierarchy tree for the problem is created. A similar approach is used by [28] where there are alternate lines of reasoning. [23] and [27] involve the identification of alternative architectures/solutions for a given set of requirements. Each of these works, though talk of identification of alternatives, do not seem to involve a group in discussing and deliberating upon suitable alternatives and hence does not involve the *development of alternatives*. Reference [30], [18] and [26] do not specifically talk of alternative solutions.

3. Preference Indication: Stakeholders participating in GDM shall be enabled to indicate preferences. In [21] the alternative scenarios are scored and the stakeholders vote the alternatives. The voting method has been chosen to enable the groups to arrive at consensus in a timely manner. We find an explicit mention of several stakeholders involved in indicating the preferences by a process of pairwise comparison of alternatives and criteria satisfaction in [17]. Though not explicitly, [26] indicates the involvement of a voting procedure to choose influencing factors and a binary approach to indicate preferences. References [20], [22] and [25] are AHP-based, hence involve pairwise comparison of alternatives and scoring. Reference [19] evaluates the alternatives against criteria and then ranks the alternatives. Reference [18] determines the value level of each factor by using utility functions. A numerical approach that involves rating, ranking or scoring is used by [23], [24], [32], [31], [29], [36] and [37]. [28], [27], [30] and [38] vaguely discuss how alternatives are evaluated. However all these methods do not seem to explicitly involve a group of people in ranking the alternatives.

4. Prioritizing of Group Members: Each group member brings in their unique expertise and hold different positions in the hierarchy, hence need to be treated differently. References [17] and [21] acknowledge that different stakeholders have different preferences but the stakeholders themselves are not ranked as per hierarchy or expertise i.e all stakeholders are given equal weightage. Reference [38] involves multiple stakeholders right from the start. The initial set of requirements and scope are defined in consultation with senior members. None of the other works acknowledge the active involvement of stakeholders hence do not talk of treating the stakeholders differently. This could be due to several reasons: a) group members expect fairness and hence the method adopted gives equal weightage to all stakeholders, b) current tools and methods may not be capable of factoring in differences in hierarchy, and c) hierarchy could be implicit in cases where the final decision lies in the hands of the senior most executive in the organization.

5. Provision for Conflict Resolution: References [17] acknowledges that different stakeholder groups have divergent views and preferences. But there is no mention of inter or intra group conflict and hence conflict resolution mechanisms have not been discussed. References [18] [28], [32] and [30] mention conflict but in a different connotation i.e conflicts occurring among decisions or between decisions and requirements or criteria. The remaining works do not mention about conflicts of any type.

6. Group Decision Rules: Reference [17] accounts for multiple stakeholder preferences by computing the geometric mean to arrive at the ranks. Reference [21] uses the votes as weights along with the utility scores to make decisions. Group scoring is summed up in [31]. [25] uses a combination of ATAM and AHP to combine multiple stakeholder preferences. Though [38] discusses the presence of multiple stakeholders, a specific decision rule is not mentioned. Other works involve value score computation using aggregation but do not involve multiple stakeholder preferences hence no group decision rule is discussed.

7. Information Exchange and Recall: For effective information exchange, an active group discussion is required. [38] proposes CEADA method for Enterprise Architect which includes visualizations. In their future work, Al-Naeem et al. [17] plan to develop a visual representation of their approach. This would probably facilitate better information exchange and recall. Only [17] [21], [31] and [25] involve active groups. There is no mention of visual representation of information like alternatives, criteria, scores etc in each of the selected references. Reference [21] acknowledges elicitation of information has been done keeping in mind the attention span and time availability of members.

8. Revisiting Information: This is an important criteria as it facilitates group learning and evolution of preferences and decisions during the lifetime of the GDM process. With the exception of [21] and [25], the other works do not specifically refer to a feedback mechanism where revisiting of alternatives or solutions can happen. [21] does it in the second iteration where factors that were not given importance in the first iteration due to time constraints are taken up and included in the decision-making process. Such a step will help uncover more hidden information for better decision-making.

6   Discussion

Table 3 presents a summary of our evaluation of the six SA decision-making methods. The reference works that involve a group while meeting a particular criteria are included in the table. The "*" indicates that the reference work satisfies the criteria only partially or implicitly.

To summarise our findings and offer some suggestions in the light of each criteria:

Table 3. Reference Works that Address a Criteria

Criteria	References
1. Problem Identification	[21], [25],[26], [38]
2. Development of Alternatives	[21], [31], [25], [38]
3. Preference Indication	[21], [17], [26]*
4. Prioritizing of Group Members	[38]*
5. Provision for Conflict Resolution	None
6. Group Decision Rules	[21], [31], [25], [38]
7. Information Exchange and Recall	[17]*,[38]
8. Revisiting Information	[21],[25]

1. Problem Identification: Except very few methods, all others do not have a specific problem identification step that involves a group. Some of these analyzed methods directly begin from identification of alternatives, which may be a limited way of decision-making. It may be useful for methods to involve a group of stakeholders in discussing the problem, breaking it down into sub-problems or specific issues. This ensures that the problem space is presented in a more granular form indicating a high quality GDM practice as defined by [5].

2. Development of Alternatives: We see that very few of these methods allow for a group to discuss and evolve alternatives. Multi-criteria decision-making methods (MCDM) must allow for the generation and filtering of alternatives through a process of discussion and deliberation which ensures more participation of group members [5]. When experts from various fields discuss, several alternative solutions emerge which may be important for architecting the system. Hence it is best that a group is involved even at this stage.

3. Preference Indication: Though the selected methods allow for preference indication in someway, it is mostly individuals who rank the alternatives. They do not seem to allow multiple stakeholders to indicate preferences. When the entire group is involved in ranking/rating the alternatives, the decisions are of high quality because they have factored in the perspective and expertise of all the stakeholders involved.

4. Prioritizing of Group Members: It is surprising to note that none of the methods account for hierarchy or expertise differences among stakeholders. As criteria and alternatives are prioritized, it would be useful to prioritize stakeholders based on some criteria like seniority or expertise to make the process more robust [5]. However this need not be the general case. Some organizations have flat structures where all stake-holders enjoy equal priority and have equal access to information.

5. Provision for Conflict Resolution: Again we see that no method accounts for conflict management strategies. Conflicts are inherent to GDM. The sources of conflict, levels of conflict and appropriate conflict resolution styles could be applied to the SA decision-making method. Our interviews with practitioner demonstrates that collabora-tive style of conflict resolution seems to be the most popular [1].

6. Group Decision Rules: Very few of the selected references allow for multiple-stakeholder preference and hence they alone discuss decision-rules. The more rigorous and scientific the decision-rule is, the better the quality of decisions made [5], [14].

7. Information Exchange and Recall: Two of the chosen methods seem to indicate the presence of visual representation of information. Information recall has been found to be key in making the knowledge pool more rich. It could be facilitated through the use of charts, pictures or tool based representation of decision knowledge [13].

8. Revisiting Information: Only one method is iterative in nature. The more number of times the group is able to exchange information, uncover unshared information and revisit the alternatives, the higher the quality of decisions. Hence feedback should be an inherent part of the GDM process [6].

Reflection: Most of the selected method, in their current form, do not seem to indi-cate the involvement of groups in the decision-making process and hence may not be directly suitable. This is indeed an unexpected result, considering that the playing the role of a Software Architect brings him in contact with a number of diverse stakehold-ers. The lack of support in current architecture design decisions methods might have been brought by different factors, such as the need to first carefully understand how the architecture design decision process works for individuals before moving to a group decision making task, or the fact that current methods may inherit and expand over state-of-the art work (e.g., the Questions Option Criteria) that where mostly focusing on capturing concerns, alternatives, and criteria.

What may be required is an expansion of the current methods, based on our criteria, to incorporate the views of multiple-stakeholders, their preferences, addressing of con-flicts thereby enabling better flow information among all stakeholders. It may be more useful for the various techniques to assume at a fundamental level that SA decision-making is inherently a group process and hence must facilitate the participation of all concerned.

7 Related Work

In this section we present details of few selected related works and why these works are important for our analysis. The authors of [10] have done a detailed comparison of var-ious decision-making methods for SA design. The main objective is to help architects choose the best method as per their needs. They have formulated a characterization schema, used to compare eight SA decision-making techniques in literature. We use this paper for gaining knowledge of various decision-making techniques used in SA literature. Tofan et al, in [16], have done an extensive and systematic study of state of research in SA decisions. They have covered a total of 144 published papers and classified them based on their six research questions. This work has been very useful for us in identifying those works that discuss SA decision process with or without tool support. We apply our evaluation framework to a subset of the works discussed in this paper.

A detailed comparison of various Architectural Knowledge (AK) management tools has been been presented in [39]. They compare five tools by using an evaluation framework consisting of 10 criteria. The comparison is based on the various AK management activities that take place during the SA life-cycle. They observe that architectural evolution and design patterns are well supported by these tools which are not part of the IEEE 42010 standard. They have observed that the current version of the tools lack knowledge sharing facility which is key for collaborative activities. This has been an important references for us to see if SA KM tools support GDM.

In our previous work [1], we have presented the findings of our study on GDM in Software Architecture. We had interviewed 29 practitioners and researchers working on SA to understand how practitioners make group decisions in architecting software systems, how practiced group decision-making techniques relate to state-of-the-art techniques, and challenges companies face when making architecture-related group decisions. Our main findings is that architectural decisions are made in reasonably sized groups that interact both face-face and online. Though there is a lot of emphasis on documentation, there seems to be no specific tool for facilitating GDM. SA groups often face a lot of issues and challenges that are found in management literature and making time-bound decisions seem to be a top priority. They adopt a collaborative strategy to manage conflicts. The analysis of survey responses and the findings from this previous work motivates our current work as we see that the industry faces a lot of challenges in decision-making and a more comprehensive SA decision-making method may be required for creating good quality architectures.

Miesbauer and Weinreich conducted a survey with software architects, software team leads, and senior developers from six different companies in Austria. They have presented their findings in [2]. They mainly look at how decisions are made in practice, what kind of decisions are made and what factors influence these decisions. They have classified the decisions types into 22 categories. They have noted that all architectural decisions are made in groups with the final decision taken by a competent authority. Among the several factors that impact decisions, Expertise, Requirements and Constraints have more impact.

Tofan et al have presented the results of their survey of 43 architects in [3]. They identified the characteristics of ADDs, the factors that make decision-making difficult, the differences between senior and junior architects and differences between good and bad decisions.They have identified that only 14% of the decisions are individual decisions the rest are all group decisions.

8   Conclusion and Future Work

The architecture design decision (ADD) process is a group decision making (GDM) activity, as analyzed in a number of work [1,2,39,3]. Therefore, ADD methods shall incorporate practices and methods coming from the group decision making community. The main research question we wanted to investigate through this research work is how much of the group *Decision Process Characteristics* discussed in [6,5] have been taken into consideration in existing ADD methods.

More specifically, we designed two research questions: *RQ1) how to evaluate the architecture design decision methods' suitability for group decision making?*, and *RQ2) how adequate existing architecture design decision methods are for group decision making?* As far as concern RQ1, we rely on and build upon the GDM evaluation criteria proposed by Saaty and Vargas in [5] and on the General Group Problem-Solving model proposed in [6]. We therefore extract eight criteria. Related to RQ2, we select a subset of state of the art SA decision-making methods and apply our framework to them.

The results show that there is ample space for improvements. Some of the analyzed ADD methods though implicitly acknowledge the presence of groups, need to bring GDM to the fore where the entire process assumes and acknowledges the presence of a group hence tailored to include collaborative decision-making.

We hope that this work can drive new research on this topic, and bring together the ADD and GDM communities. Still, a lot needs to be done, and we plan to further contribute on this direction by: i) including in our future work an analysis on how ADD *tools* support GDM, and what shall be improved on existing tools, ii) running a survey with practitioners to evaluate how much the proposed methods and tools improvements are considered to be useful by them, iii) running a case study to evaluate how enhanced ADD may improve the group decision making process with respect to the traditional ADD methods. More specifically, we plan to select one (or more) tool supported ADD methods, and enhance it based on the findings of this study and of our previous research [1]. Then, the traditional and enhanced version of the approach/tool will be used by different groups through a controlled experiment, so to record how much they like them and the output itself.

References

1. Rekha, V.S., Muccini, H.: A study on group decision-making in software architecture. In: Proc. WICSA 2014 the 11th Working IEEE/IFIP Conference on Software Architecture (2014)
2. Miesbauer, C., Weinreich, R.: Classification of design decisions an expert survey in practice. In: Drira, K. (ed.) ECSA 2013. LNCS, vol. 7957, pp. 130–145. Springer, Heidelberg (2013)
3. Tofan, D., Galster, M., Avgeriou, P.: Difficulty of architectural decisions a survey with professional architects. In: Drira, K. (ed.) ECSA 2013. LNCS, vol. 7957, pp. 192–199. Springer, Heidelberg (2013)
4. ISO: ISO/IEC/IEEE 42010, Systems and software engineering — Architecture description (2011)
5. Saaty, T.L., Vargas, L.G.: Decision making with the analytic network process. Springer (2006)
6. Aldag, R.J., Fuller, S.R.: Beyond fiasco: A reappraisal of the groupthink phenomenon and a new model of group decision processes. Psychological Bulletin 113(3), 533 (1993)
7. Ambrus, A., Greiner, B., Pathak, P.: Group versus individual decision-making: Is there a shift? Economics Working Papers from Institute for Advanced Study (91) (2009)

8. Kerr, N.L., Tindale, R.S.: Group performance and decision making. Annu. Rev. Psychol. 55, 623–655 (2004)
9. Janis, I.L.: Groupthink. Houghton Mifflin, Boston (1983)
10. Falessi, D., Cantone, G., Kazman, R., Kruchten, P.: Decision-making techniques for software architecture design: A comparative survey. ACM Computing Surveys (CSUR) 43(4), 33 (2011)
11. Lipshitz, R., Strauss, O.: Coping with uncertainty: A naturalistic decision-making analysis. Organizational Behavior and Human Decision Processes 69(2), 149–163 (1997)
12. Dennis, A.R.: Information processing in group decision making: You can lead a group to information, but you can't make it think. Proceedings of the Academy of Management, 283–287 (1993)
13. Brodbeck, F.C., Kerschreiter, R., Mojzisch, A., Schulz-Hardt, S.: Group decision making under conditions of distributed knowledge: The information asymmetries model. Academy of Management Review 32(2), 459–479 (2007)
14. Hinsz, V.B., Tindale, R.S., Vollrath, D.A.: The emerging conceptualization of groups as information processors. Psychological Bulletin 121(1), 43 (1997)
15. Stasser, G., Titus, W.: Pooling of unshared information in group decision making: Biased information sampling during discussion. Journal of Personality and Social Psychology 48(6), 1467 (1985)
16. Tofan, D., Galster, M., Avgeriou, P., Schuitema, W.: Past and future of software architectural decisions a systematic mapping study. Information and Software Technology 56(8), 850–872 (2014)
17. Al-Naeem, T., Gorton, I., Babar, M.A., Rabhi, F., Benatallah, B.: A quality-driven systematic approach for architecting distributed software applications. In: Proceedings of the 27th International Conference on Software Engineering, pp. 244–253. ACM (2005)
18. Andrews, A., Mancebo, E., Runeson, P., France, R.: A framework for design tradeoffs. Software Quality Journal 13(4), 377–405 (2005)
19. Phillips, B.C., Polen, S.M.: Add decision analysis to your cots selection process. Software Technology Support Center Crosstalk (2002)
20. Lozano-Tello, A., Gómez-Pérez, A.: Baremo: how to choose the appropriate software component using the analytic hierarchy process. In: Proceedings of the 14th International Conference on Software Engineering and Knowledge Engineering, pp. 781–788. ACM (2002)
21. Moore, M., Kazman, R., Klein, M., Asundi, J.: Quantifying the value of architecture design decisions: lessons from the field. In: Proceedings of the 25th International Conference on Software Engineering, pp. 557–562. IEEE Computer Society (2003)
22. Svahnberg, M., Wohlin, C., Lundberg, L., Mattsson, M.: A quality-driven decision-support method for identifying software architecture candidates. International Journal of Software Engineering and Knowledge Engineering 13(05), 547–573 (2003)
23. Vijayalakshmi, S., Zayaraz, G., Vijayalakshmi, V.: Multicriteria decision analysis method for evaluation of software architectures. International Journal of Computer Applications 1(25), 22–27 (2010)
24. Tofan, D., Galster, M., Avgeriou, P.: Capturing tacit architectural knowledge using the repertory grid technique (nier track). In: Proceedings of the 33rd International Conference on Software Engineering, pp. 916–919. ACM (2011)
25. Wallin, P., Froberg, J., Axelsson, J.: Making decisions in integration of automotive software and electronics: A method based on atam and ahp. In: Proceedings of the 4th International Workshop on Software Engineering for Automotive Systems, p. 5. IEEE Computer Society (2007)
26. Stoll, P., Wall, A., Norstrom, C.: Guiding architectural decisions with the influencing factors method. In: Seventh Working IEEE/IFIP Conference on Software Architecture, WICSA 2008, pp. 179–188. IEEE (2008)

27. Gilson, F., Englebert, V.: Rationale, decisions and alternatives traceability for architecture design. In: Proceedings of the 5th European Conference on Software Architecture, Companion Volume, p. 4. ACM (2011)
28. Orlic, B., Mak, R., David, I., Lukkien, J.: Concepts and diagram elements for architectural knowledge management. In: Proceedings of the 5th European Conference on Software Architecture, Companion Volume, p. 3. ACM (2011)
29. Wu, W., Kelly, T.: Managing architectural design decisions for safety-critical software systems. In: Hofmeister, C., Crnković, I., Reussner, R. (eds.) QoSA 2006. LNCS, vol. 4214, pp. 59–77. Springer, Heidelberg (2006)
30. Choi, H., Choi, Y., Yeom, K.: An integrated approach to quality achievement with architectural design decisions. JSW 1(3), 40–49 (2006)
31. In, H., Kazman, R., Olson, D.: From requirements negotiation to software architectural decisions. In: Proc. From Software Requ. to Architectures Workshop STRAW (2001)
32. Grunske, L.: Identifying good architectural design alternatives with multi-objective optimization strategies. In: Proceedings of the 28th International Conference on Software Engineering, pp. 849–852. ACM (2006)
33. Gu, Q., Lago, P., van Vliet, H.: A template for soa design decision making in an educational setting. In: 2010 36th EUROMICRO Conference on Software Engineering and Advanced Applications (SEAA), pp. 175–182. IEEE (2010)
34. Zannier, C., Maurer, F.: A qualitative empirical evaluation of design decisions. ACM SIGSOFT Software Engineering Notes 30(4), 1–7 (2005)
35. Zimmermann, O., Gschwind, T., Küster, J., Leymann, F., Schuster, N.: Reusable architectural decision models for enterprise application development. In: Overhage, S., Szyperski, C.A., Reussner, R., Stafford, J.A. (eds.) QoSA 2007. LNCS, vol. 4880, pp. 15–32. Springer, Heidelberg (2008)
36. Riebisch, M., Wohlfarth, S.: Introducing impact analysis for architectural decisions. In: 14th Annual IEEE International Conference and Workshops on the Engineering of Computer-Based Systems, ECBS 2007, pp. 381–392. IEEE (2007)
37. Xu, B., Huang, Z., Wei, O.: Making architectural decisions based on requirements: Analysis and combination of risk-based and quality attribute-based methods. In: 2010 7th International Conference on Ubiquitous Intelligence Computing and 7th International Conference on Autonomic Trusted Computing (UIC/ATC), pp. 392–397 (2010)
38. Nakakawa, A., Bommel, P.: Requirements for collaborative decision making in enterprise architecture. In: Proceedings of the 4th SIKS/BENAIS Conference on Enterprise Information Systems, The Netherlands, Nijmegen (2009)
39. Tang, A., Avgeriou, P., Jansen, A., Capilla, R., Ali Babar, M.: A comparative study of architecture knowledge management tools. Journal of Systems and Software 83(3), 352–370 (2010)

Modeling the Interactions between Decisions within Software Architecture Knowledge

Mohamed Soliman and Matthias Riebisch

Universität Hamburg
Vogt-Kölln-Str. 30, 22527 Hamburg, Germany
{soliman,riebisch}@informatik.uni-hamburg.de

Abstract. Software architecture is developed as a result of a selection process for software architectural solutions. The complexity, diversity and evolution nature of architectural solutions' interactions forces the architect to make critical design decisions based only on his own experience. Even though, the same design problem has already been addressed by another architect in a similar situation. In this paper, we are presenting a model for reusable software architectural knowledge to support the architect within the design process in understanding the relationship between the different architectural solutions, and how they impact the architectural design reasoning. In addition, the model acts as a base for organizational software architectural knowledge sharing. Our contribution in this paper is classifying and modeling the solutions and decisions' interactions, as well as how the design decision can be used as a reusable element for sharing the architectural experience.

Keywords: Software architecture, design decision, architecture knowledge, design reasoning.

1   Introduction

The software architect is responsible on taking the most important design decisions within the software design process. These architectural decisions [1] must be identified early in the project lifecycle due to their long-term impact on the system quality, and their tenacious behavior, which makes them quite expensive to change [2]. Even with their well-known impact, the architect is forced to take design decisions based solely on his personal experience, due to the enormous amount of possibilities for interacting architectural solutions[1], that must be selected in a limited project budget and schedule. Morever, the current state of the art approaches for architectural knowledge and solutions lack the required support for analyzing the interactions between solutions. Within this situation, the architect is restricted in discovering the right series of architectural solutions, and analyzing their impact on the system quality. This leads to sub-optimal decisions, which can significantly influence the system quality.

---

[1] In this paper, we use the term 'architectural solution' to refer to the different solutions that the architects use, such as patterns, tactics, technologies and products.

P. Avgeriou and U. Zdun (Eds.): ECSA 2014, LNCS 8627, pp. 33–40, 2014.

One of the main reasons that promotes this problem is the heterogeneous nature of architectural solutions, such that it is hard to set a common handling during design between the different solutions. In the past two decades, several classes of architectural solutions were captured separately in the current state of the art (e.g. architectural styles [3], patterns [3,4], tactics [2], unit operations and different technologies and products). Each class is concerned with solving different types of design problems using different notions. In addition, each class is described originally in a different way, such that its arduous to combine two members from different classes together. Nevertheless, a combination of various members is required to develop the system software architecture. Such a diversity nature of software architectural solutions represents a challenge within the design process, because each solution has its unique impact on the subsequent design decisions as well as on the behavior of other solutions.

In addition to the above-mentioned problems, the interaction between the architectural solutions and decisions are constantly evolving, through new design ideas that emerge everyday from the mind of the designers. Thus, maintaining an evolvable reusable architectural knowledge[2] would support the organisation to share the design experience and solutions between the different software architects. This objective is derived by the notion of characterizing the architecture design process as a knowledge intensive process [5], such that losing this knowledge, recollecting and transferring it again is an expensive process. This idea of maintaining an architectural knowledge would improve the quality and productivity of the software architecture design process within the organization through learning, verification and improvement of existing solutions.

In this paper, we are proposing a model for a reusable software architectural knowledge to support the architect and the organisations in reasoning about software architecture design, as well as maintaining and sharing architectural knowledge. We concentrated our work on trying to understand and model the impact of selecting an architectural solution on the subsequent architectural decisions and the reasoning process, as well as providing the fundamental elements for sharing the architectural design decisions among different projects. This paper is organized as follows. First, related work to architectural knowledge and solutions are presented and discussed. Then, our research steps are explained, follwed by our result model which is explained with several examples. The paper ends with a discussion, future work, and some concluding words.

2   Related Work

In the patterns community, pattern languages are proposed (e.g. [6]). However, the relationships between patterns are modeled in a high level, without specifying clearly how the patterns interact with each other. Harrison et al. [7] modeled the relationships between architectural patterns and tactics. Their approach

---

[2] we use the term 'architectural knowledge' to refer to the reusable information that supports the architect within the design process.

is based on relating the solutions through their impact on the system components. Such modeling supports the architect to describe the solutions within
the software architecture. However, with less guidance on how to take the design decisions. Since the paradigm shift of modeling the software architecture as
a set of design decisions [1], several models and tools [8] have been proposed.
The main target for the former suggested approaches is to document and share
the design decisions of a specific software system for the sake of preventing the
software architecture erosion phenomena. The recent work by Zimmerman et.
al. [9] and its extension [10] distinguish between project specific design decision
outcomes and its reusable part of design issues and solutions. Zimmermann et
al. formally described the relationships between the design issues and the architectural solutions, as a way to support the architect in the decision making
process. Nevertheless, the distinct behaviors of the different types of solutions are
not explicitly described. To the best of our knowledge, there are no more recent
work which address the mentioned problem. Therefore, our approach in this paper is an extension to the model proposed by Zimmerman et al. to address the
aforementioned points.

3   Research Method and Steps

To achieve our goal, we followed an inductive qualitative content analysis process
[11]. First, we analyzed the influence of selecting an architectural solution on the
design reasoning independent from other solutions. Then, we experimented with
the relationships between the different solutions. In order to implement these
steps, we selected samples from the architectural solutions. Two main criteria
were considered in the selection process: A) Diversity: The chosen solutions
belong to different classes, B) Popularity and success in the industry. The chosen
architectural solutions were the Layer architectural style, the MVC architectural
pattern, the architectural tactics by Bass et al. [2], basic unit operations and the
GoF design patterns. We performed our analysis through the design realization
steps, descriptions and examples provided in the solutions' sources, as well as
case studies, which used the mentioned architectural solutions.

4   Reusable Software Architectural Knowledge Modeling

Fig. 1 shows our view for a high level contextual diagram for the reusable architectural knowledge. The diagram shows how an architectural knowledge is
used within an organisation. First, the architect - influenced by the stakeholders' concerns and constrains - utilize the data and the reasoning logic within
the architectural knowledge in order to support him taking the design decisions
of the system. This process is followed by or intervened with capturing and
documenting the system design decisions, which would act later as a source for
enriching the architectural knowledge with new design solutions or logic in a separate harvesting process. Our main goal in this paper is to model the reusable
architectural knowledge in relation to other contextual entities.

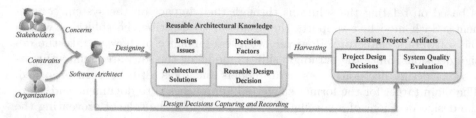

Fig. 1. Reusable Architectural Knowledge Context Diagram

We describe our model into two sections. The first section concentrates on the interaction between the architectural solutions and their influence on the design reasoning process, while the second section shows how the design decisions can act as a reusable component, in connection with existing software systems.

4.1 Solutions' Interactions within a Reusable Architectural Knowledge

Fig. 2 shows the proposed model. In the core of this model is the *Design Issue* concept, which represents the architectural design problems [3] that the architects need to solve, and associated to each design issue, there is a set of *alternative architectural solutions* which address this design problem [9]. Each architectural solution has a different impact on the quality attribute of the system, as well as a different impact on the resulting structure of the system components. Based on our described analysis process, we classified the architectural solutions into two main types:

1. **Triggering Architectural Solutions**: They are the type of solutions that have the ability to trigger new architectural design issues, such that in order to complete the architectural design of these solutions, new architectural design issues must be addressed. In this group belong architectural styles and architectural patterns.
2. **Elementary Architectural Solutions**: These are architectural solutions that do not trigger new architectural design issues. They are either as architectural unit operations (e.g. Component Decomposition) or solutions recommendations for a subsequent detailed design (e.g. Design Patterns [4]).

Architectural tactics [2] have a different nature as other solutions, such that it is hard to classify them all in a single group. Therefore, we divided the tactics among the two groups, into elementary and triggering tactics. Elementary tactics are tactics that do not triger new architectural design issues. For example, to improve the performance of a well-known process (e.g. Products sorting), selecting or changing the algorithm usually would not produce new architectural

---

[3] We diffrentiate between an architectural design issue and other detailed design or implementation issues, based on the software architecture definition of Bass [2].

Reusable Architectural Design Decisions

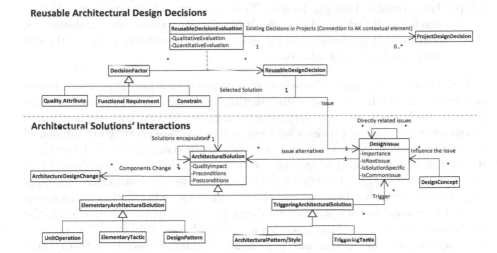

Fig. 2. Reusable Architectural Knowledge Domain Model

design issues, however, it can produce algorithmic or implementation issues. On the other hand, triggering tactics require more architectural design issues to be addressed in order to realize the design of the tactic. For example, improving the performance through caching, this would require to answer other design questions such as: which and where to cach the data? and how to synchronize the cached data?

Architectural design issues vary in their importance, types, scope and position within the reasoning process. Zimmerman et. al classified design issues based on their abstraction level. In order to support the architect in understanding when design issues occur within the reasoning process. We propose a classification for design issues, based on their occurance within the design reasoning process and their relationship to the architectural solutions.

1. **Root Design Issues**: They are design issues which are stimulated independently from previously selected architectural solutions. Enterprise or principal high level design issues (e.g. deciding the high level architectural style of the system or the main implementation technology) are popular examples that belong to this group.
2. **Solutions-Triggered Design Issues**: They are design issues that must be triggered based on a stimulation from a previously selected architectural solution. We further classified these issues based on their relationship to the architectural solutions into the following groups:
   (a) **Solution-Specific Design Issues**: They can only be triggered as a result of selecting a specific solution. They can't be triggered by any other solutions.
   (b) **Joined Design Issues**: A common design issue which can be triggered by different solutions.

(c) **Integration Design Issues**: This is a type of design issue which is conditionally triggered as a result of selecting two or more architectural solutions. It represents the integration design problem between the different architectural solutions.

Fig. 3 shows an example of a subset of issues and solutions that are triggered as a result of selecting the Layer architectural style and the MVC architectural pattern. Both solutions were triggered as a result of two root design issues, independently from any previous solution selected. However, they are influenced by several decision factors (e.g. requirements, team structure, ...). In order to realize the design of both triggering solutions, several design issues have to be addressed. For example, to define the Layer structure, an abstraction paradigm (e.g. distance from hardware or complexity) must be defined, this decision can depend on several factors (e.g. system domain). Similarly, in order to design the relationship between the Model and Views/Controllers within the MVC pattern, a 'change propagation mechanism' (e.g. using a Publish-Subscribe pattern) must be selected. Both of these issues are examples of solution specific design issues. On the other hand, designing the domain components of the system is required to be addressed for both solutions, however, for two different purposes. Firstly, to define how objects are communicated between layers, and secondly to provide a separation of concerns between the Model and View components. Finally, the introduction of both the Layer and MVC solutions together triggers an issue, whose purpose is the integration of both solutions components.

4.2   Reusable Architectural Design Decisions

In contradiction to other models, which consider an architectural design decision only as a project-specific entity, we argue that design decisions taken within different projects constitute a part of a reusable software architecture knowledge, such that a design decision consists of three main elements; A) The design issue addressed by this decision, B) The selected architectural solution, and C) The decison factors which influence the selection of this architectural solution to the design issue. The combination of the three elements acts as a reusable tuple which can be used among other projects.

The quality and success of design decisions varies from one project to another, such that a design decision concerned with a certain design issue and influenced by the same factors may be supported by different architectural solutions with different qualities. Therefore, a quality measurement factor should be associated with each of the reusable architectural design decisions. This quality measurement factor is originally obtained from the actual system quality or an evaluation for the architecture of the harvested projects. Fig. 2 shows the connection of the three tuples that constitutes a reusable architectural decision within the proposed model, as well as how the quality evaluation values are associated to the decisions and related to it's original sources in referenced projects.

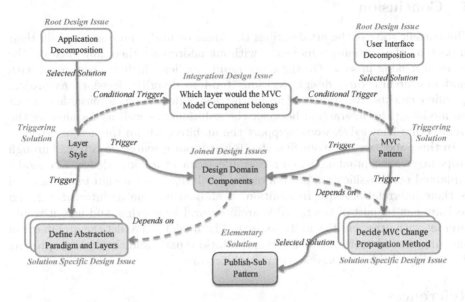

Fig. 3. An example showing the interaction of objects based on the proposed architectural knowledge domain model

5   Discussion and Future Work

In our analysis work, we selected solutions, which are well known and more used within the software development industry, specifically within the information systems domain. In addition, we considered various architectural solutions from different groups, in order to discover the different relationships and their impact on the design process. However, based just on this research, our results are not yet generalized to all types of architectural solutions in different domains. Throughout our analysis of solutions, we assumed that the design issues mentioned in their sources represent the expected solutions decisions. Nevertheless, it is possible that other design issues can be generated in different other contexts, providing more relations.

The proposed model is a first step in our research plan, which seeks promoting ideas and solutions for the purpose of architectural knowledge sharing within organizations and architectural communities. Our plan involves several research steps: A) Developing a process to support the architect in utilizing the model, and how it relates with the existing design processes. B) Propose an approach for the harvesting process, to show how the project specific decisions can contribute to the architecture knowledge. C) Providing a tool support for the architect in using the model within the design process. We are working to verify our model in an industrial environment, through experimenting the model to support software architects in driving architectural designs.

6   Conclusion

The current state of the art describes the architectural solutions based on their impact on the system components, without addressing their influence on the decision making process. On the other hand, studies which are concerned with modeling architectural design decisions tend to describe decisions as project specific elements. We argue that using the design decision as a reusable element for modeling the interaction between the solutions, as well as for sharing the architecture knowledge, would support the architect within the design process.

In this paper, we made our first step towards our research objective. Through proposing a conceptual model for a reusable architectural knowledge. The model explained our classification of architectural solutions and design issues, as well as their interrelationships. In addition, it showed how an architectural design decision can be part of the reusable architectural knowledge, and how it would interact with other entities in its context. The model can assist the architects in selecting the right software architectural solutions path, and therefore, improving the quality of the produced software architecture.

References

1. Jansen, A., Bosch, J.: Software architecture as a set of architectural design decisions. In: 5th Working Conf. on Software Architecture, pp. 109–120 (2005)
2. Bass, L., Clements, P., Kazman, R.: Software Architecture in Practice, 2nd edn. Addison-Wesley Longman Publishing Co., Inc., Boston (2003)
3. Buschmann, F., Meunier, R., Rohnert, H., Sommerlad, P., Stal, M.: Pattern-Oriented Software Architecture: A System of Patterns, 1st edn. John Wiley & Sons (July 1996)
4. Gamma, E., Helm, R., Johnson, R., Vlissides, J.M.: Design Patterns: Elements of Reusable Object-Oriented Softwaresystemen. Addison-Wesley Professional (1994)
5. Lago, P., Avgeriou, P., Capilla, R., Kruchten, P.: Wishes and boundaries for a software architecture knowledge community. In: WICSA. IEEE Computer Society, 271–274 (2008)
6. Avgeriou, P., Zdun, U.: Architectural patterns revisited - a pattern language. In: Longshaw, A., Zdun, U., eds.: EuroPLoP, UVK - Universitaetsverlag Konstanz, pp. 431–470 (2005)
7. Harrison, N.B., Avgeriou, P.: How do architecture patterns and tactics interact? a model and annotation. Journal of Systems and Software 83(10), 1735–1758 (2010)
8. Shahin, M., Liang, P., Khayyambashi, M.R.: Architectural design decision: Existing models and tools. In: WICSA/ECSA. IEEE, pp. 293–296 (2009)
9. Zimmermann, O., Koehler, J., Leymann, F., Polley, R., Schuster, N.: Managing architectural decision models with dependency relations, integrity constraints, and production rules. Journal of Systems and Software 82(8), 1249–1267 (2009)
10. Capilla, R., Zimmermann, O., Zdun, U., Avgeriou, P., Küster, J.M.: An enhanced architectural knowledge metamodel linking architectural design decisions to other artifacts in the software engineering lifecycle. In: Crnkovic, I., Gruhn, V., Book, M. (eds.) ECSA 2011. LNCS, vol. 6903, pp. 303–318. Springer, Heidelberg (2011)
11. Elo, S., Kyngas, H.: The qualitative content analysis process. Journal of Advanced Nursing 62(1)(2), 107–115 (2007)

Semi-automated Design Guidance Enhancer (SADGE): A Framework for Architectural Guidance Development

Mohsen Anvaari[1] and Olaf Zimmermann[2]

[1] Norwegian University of Science and Technology, Trondheim, Norway
mohsena@idi.ntnu.no
[2] University of Applied Sciences of Eastern Switzerland, Rapperswil, Switzerland
ozimmerm@hsr.ch

Abstract. Architectural decision making is a non-trivial task for architects in the software development projects. Researchers have developed several concepts, methods and tools to assist practitioners in their decision making and decision capturing activities. One of these approaches is a decision identification technique that creates architectural guidance models from decisions made in previous projects and from knowledge about a domain found in the literature. To apply this technique, significant manual knowledge engineering effort has to be invested initially. In this paper, we introduce a framework that automatically extracts architectural knowledge entities from architectural related documents by applying natural language processing. A knowledge engineer then manually post processes and fine-tunes the extracted knowledge entities. We applied evaluation techniques from the information retrieval community to measure the sensitivity and accuracy of the framework. Our results show that the automatic approach has the highest recall and shortest processing time while the semi-automatic approach has the highest precision.

Keywords: Architectural decision making, design guidance, information extraction, natural language processing, automatic annotation.

1 Introduction

Architectural decision making is a non-trivial task for architects in software development projects. Since 2000, researchers have developed several concepts, methods, frameworks and tools to assist practitioners in their decision making and decision capturing procedures [2][6][11]. However, a recent study shows practitioners still have difficulties to make and manage decisions [13].

One of the difficulties the practitioners have in making decisions is recognizing and highlighting architectural issues in a specific project to make decisions about them (we call these issues *architectural issues* or *decisions required*). Our previous study shows that architects mostly rely on their intuitions to recognize architectural issues [1]. One of the promising approaches to help practitioners in their decision making is a decision identification technique that enhances architectural guidance (decisions required) from decisions made in previous projects and from knowledge

P. Avgeriou and U. Zdun (Eds.): ECSA 2014, LNCS 8627, pp. 41–49, 2014.

about a domain that can be found in the literature. Through decision identification rules, this approach tasks a knowledge engineer to study pattern languages, genre- and style-specific extensions to software engineering methods, technical papers, industrial standards and project documentation to identify architectural issues [15]. To do so, the technique advises knowledge engineers to read the natural language texts of the documents and to annotate the texts manually. The intention is to extract architectural knowledge entities (i.e., issues, alternatives, outcomes[1]) from documents and to develop an architectural guidance model from the extracted information. Such architectural guidance model is a reusable asset containing knowledge about architectural decisions recurring in a particular domain [16]. Several case studies have shown that the developed architectural guidance is promising in assisting the practitioners in their decision making, e.g. in SOA design and cloud computing [15]. However, this decision identification approach is manual; significant knowledge engineering effort that has to be invested initially before benefits can be realized.

In this paper, we introduce a framework called Semi Automated Design Guidance Enhancer (SADGE) that automatically extracts architectural issues (decisions required) from architecture documents by applying natural language processing (NLP) first (we refer to this automated step as automatic approach). In a second step, a knowledge engineer manually post processes and fine-tunes the extracted knowledge entities to increase the accuracy of the framework (we refer to the first automated and the second manual step together as semi-automatic approach). We validated and evaluated the SADGE framework in an experiment with students. The intention of this evaluation was to compare the effort, sensitivity and accuracy of architectural entities extraction process between manual, automatic and semi-automatic approaches. More specifically, by conducting the experiment we were going to find out:

- Research Question (RQ) 1: Which approach does have the shortest processing time for extracting the architectural entities?
- RQ 2: Which approach does have the highest sensitivity in extracting the architectural entities?
- RQ 3: Which approach does have the highest accuracy in extracting the architectural entities?

The contribution of this paper is twofold: 1) It applies NLP-based knowledge extraction to the architectural knowledge area and proposes a novel framework architecture and process model for doing so. 2) It demonstrates the efficiency, sensitivity and accuracy of this framework in enhancing architectural guidance from architectural related documents.

The rest of the paper is organized as follows. In the Section 2 we introduce the framework by describing how we have developed the framework and how users should operate and maintain the framework. Section 3 presents the design of the experiment and analyses and discusses the result of the experiment. Section 4 describes the related work in the software architecture domain. Finally, Section 5 concludes the paper and outlines future work.

---

[1] *Architectural issue* represents any design concern or problem that a decision should be made about; *alternative* presents a solution to the problem and *outcome* is the chosen solution among different alternatives [14].

2   SADGE – Framework for Semi-Automatic Architectural Knowledge Extraction

In this section, we explain how we developed the framework and how the framework operates.

2.1   SADGE Framework Development

SADGE has to be set up first (by a researcher) before practitioners in the projects can use it. As we mentioned earlier, the framework applies natural language processing (NLP) to extract architectural knowledge entities from a document. There are two main approaches in NLP to do so, machine learning approach and rule-based approach [5]. We tried both approaches, but due to the lack of enough training data, the machine learning approach did not work well; therefore in the current version of the framework we only use the rule-based approach. The stages of framework development will be described in the following subsections.

D1. Initializing the annotation rule. For developing the annotation rules we started with the simplest rule that an expert in the software architecture intuitively applies to manually annotate a sentence: *If a sentence contains at least one of the terms from catalog of terms* (a list of predefined keywords) *annotate it as an architectural issue.* For example, an architect would annotate the sentence "determine your validation strategy" in a document as an architectural issue (decision required) because of keywords "determine" and "strategy". Therefore, to apply the rule, the keywords (i.e., the catalog of terms) should be developed as well.

D2. Initializing the catalog of terms. To develop the catalog, we first interviewed an expert in the software architecture domain and identified terms that the expert considers as indicator to annotate a sentence as an architectural issue. When the first versions of the rule and the catalog of terms became ready, we applied them on some sample texts. We started by automatically annotating one document. To evaluate the result, we compared the automatic annotated entities against the entities that had been annotated manually by the expert. The evaluator presents the precision, recall, f-measure[2] and also shows those entities that have positively or negatively annotated.

D3. Evolving the annotation rule. When we applied the first version of the rule, the average recall of automatic annotation was high but the precision was very low. Hence, we decided to change the rule to reduce the amount of negatively annotated sentences and increase the precision. We divided the catalog of terms into two catalogs: high priority terms and low priority terms. Then the new rule is presented in Fig. 1.

This rule resulted in a higher f-measure, so we replaced the first rule with the newer version. To decide whether a term is a low priority term or high priority term, we put the term in either category to see which one results to a higher f-measure.

D4. Evolving the catalog of terms. By looking at the sentences that should be annotated (according to the manually annotated text) but had not been annotated by the automated annotator, we found new terms to add to the catalog of terms. This resulted

---

[2] *Precision, Recall and F-measure* are the measures used in the information retrieval domain to measure how well an information retrieval system retrieves the relevant entities requested by a user. See [12] for definitions.

> *if*
>   (a sentence contains at least one of the terms
>   from the catalog of high priority terms)   →   annotate it as an architectural issue
> *or*
>   (contains at least two terms
>   from the catalog of low priority terms)

Fig. 1. The rule for annotating "architectural issues"

to higher f-measure. We added other sample texts one by one and did the same procedure for each text to develop the catalog of terms further. We finished the iterative procedure when the improvement of f-measure was not significant anymore. In total, we annotated seven documents that contained architecture related text. We selected the sample texts from various types of documents to make them representative in the software architecture domain. The texts were two industrial standards for software integration, three software design guidelines and two academic papers.

D5. Refining the catalog of terms. There is a possibility that some of the terms have positive impact on annotating one document whereas have negative effect on annotating some other documents. So in this stage of the framework development we decided to measure the impact of each of the terms on the average f-measure of all of sample documents. To do so, we removed each term from the catalog of terms and calculate the f-measure and then put the term back to check how the presence of a term affects the average f-measure. Those terms that their presence had negative effect on the average of f-measure were removed from the catalog of terms permanently. We call this stage of the development *sensitivity test*. The final version of catalog of terms after conducting the sensitivity test is presented in Fig. 2. We should mention that we use *stemming* for applying the annotation rule. Stemming is the process of reducing a word to its root. Therefore the terms in Fig. 2 are the roots of the terms and in the case another form of the word appears in a sentence the automated annotator considers it as an instance of the term.

> **High Priority Terms**
> agree on, choose
> **Low Priority Terms**
> approach, articulate, class, component, construct, concern, define, design, determine, different
> employ, establish, evaluate, exchange, facilitate, framework, investigate, limitation, make
> philosophy, principle, profile, provide, protocol, recommend, refactor, require, schema
> select, service, several, strategy, support, topology, transaction management, type, various

Fig. 2. Catalog of terms for annotating "architectural issues"

When both annotation rules and catalog of terms are developed, the framework is ready to be used.

2.2 SADGE Framework Operation and Maintenance

The steps of framework operation and maintenance are described as follows. Note that in sections 1 and 3 by automatic approach we mean step O2 of the framework while O2 and O3 together make the semi-automatic part of the framework.

O1. Preparing documents for annotation. The input of the framework comprises text files that can be either project documents or domain literature. The knowledge engineer edits the text files in a way that the file doesn't include non-text objects (for example images) or non-relevant texts (cover page, table of contents, etc.). Then (s)he converts the text files to the types that automated annotator accepts.

O2. Automatically annotate the documents. The knowledge engineer loads the annotation rules, the catalog of terms, and the batch of text files to the automated annotator. The automated annotator applies the rules and annotate the architectural issues in the text files. The output of this step is a list of sentences that automated annotator suggests as architectural issues. Besides, the knowledge engineer also receives a list of sentences that automated annotator doesn't consider as architectural issues.

O3. Manually fine-tune the results. The knowledge engineer in this stage looks through the list of tool suggestions and reject the sentences that (s)he doesn't consider as architectural entities.

O4. Generate the design guide out of annotated text. Now that the annotated sentences from all of the text files are finalized, guidance generator merges them and produce design guide for a specific project. It includes all of the potential issues (decisions required) in the project. The knowledge engineer can shorten the sentences, classify issues into sub-projects and add alternatives (including pros and cons for each alternative) to each issue. (S)he can also remove the redundant issues.

M1. Suggest new terms for catalog of terms. In step O3, the knowledge engineer may find some terms that would be an indicator for annotating architectural issues. In that case (s)he can suggest them to catalog enhancer.

M2. Add new terms to the catalog of terms: The catalog enhancer conducts the sensitivity test for the suggested term and if the average f-measure is positive, the term will be added to the catalog of terms. So the framework evolves during projects.

3   Framework Evaluation

The main purpose of developing SADGE is to reduce the efforts that manual approach of decision identification technique demands. However, the accuracy and sensitivity of the framework should not be too lower than manual approach; otherwise the framework will not be effective. Therefore these three quality attributes of the framework should be evaluated: processing time (effort), sensitivity and accuracy. The metrics we use for evaluating the effort is time and for evaluating the other two attributes we use the classical metrics in information retrieval domain, recall and precision. In the current stage of the research, we preliminary evaluate the framework by conducting an experiment with students. In the following sections, we first describe the design of the experiment, then we present the results of the experiment and in the discussion section we interpret and discuss the results and describe the potential threats to validity.

3.1   Evaluation Design (Setup)

Participants: We asked students of a bachelor's program in information technology to participate the experiment. They are familiar with the software architecture. However, they were not familiar with the concept of architectural knowledge (including architectural issues). 19 students (randomly selected) participated in the experiment. We divided them into two groups of ten and nine students. Before the experiment, an introduction about the task and the concept of architectural issue were presented to the students.

Stages: In the first stage, students were supposed to read a text carefully and annotate the sentences they think are architectural issues. In the second stage, the list of automatically annotated sentences from the text given to group 1 in the first stage was given to the students of group 2 and vice versa to avoid the testing effects. They were asked to reject the sentences they disagreed with automated annotator to fine-tune the results.

Material: In the first stage of the experiment each group received two pages of a text from a book chapter on web application design guidance. The texts of two groups are not identical. The book chapter is one of the documents we had used to evaluate the automated annotator (automatic part of the framework). The reason we chose this document among all of the tested documents was that this document had the smallest deviation from the mean of precision and recall of annotating all of the documents and therefore can be considered as a representative of the tested documents.

3.2   Evaluation Results

Table 1 summarizes the results of the experiment. In the manual approach, the students spent nine minutes on average to annotate the architectural issues. The automated annotator ran the annotation procedure in two sec. In the semi-automated approach the students spent 3 minutes on average to reject those sentences they didn't agree is an architectural issue (we neglect the two second that automated annotator ran the procedure). To calculate the recall and precision we needed reference texts. Two experts in the software architecture domain annotated the two texts and the annotated texts were used as the reference text. The recall and precision for all three approaches are presented in Table 1. In the next section, we analyse the results and discuss about their validity.

Table 1. Results of experiment

Approach	Time (min)	Recall (%)	Precision (%)
Manual	9	38	25
Automatic	**0.03**	**86**	57
Semi-automatic	3	55	**62**

3.3   Discussion

As Table 1 shows, automated annotator has the highest effort reduction (lowest annotation time) and the highest recall while semi-automatic approach has the highest precision. The effort reduction results are in correspondence to our expectation. Regarding the precision and recall, in the real projects we expect that when those practitioners who are experts in the software architecture domain annotate a text manually, both precision and recall should be near to 100 percent, because the practitioners' knowledge are almost the same as our reference experts' knowledge. Whereas here the results show that the recall and precision of student annotations are very low (38 and 25 respectively). The results for automated annotator are relatively high (86 and 57) and these show that if the people in charge of enhancing architectural guidance are not expert enough, automated approach will perform more accurate and more sensitive by spending much less time. We expected that the semi-automatic approach has the highest precision rate that is in line with the experiment results; but we expected higher precision rate.

The other result that doesn't meet our expectation is the recall rate of semi-automatic approach. Although it cannot be higher than the automatic approach (because some of the positive results have been already neglected by the automated annotator) we expected that the recall would not be lower than the automatic approach. But the results show that some of the positive results are rejected by the participants. This might be caused by the expertise level of the participants. Our expectation is that if the participants were expert enough in the domain, the semi-automatic approach would have almost the same recall rate as the automatic approach and much higher precision rate than the automatic approach. However, this hypothesis needs to be investigated with subject matter experts.

Threats to validity: The potential threat to the internal validity of the evaluation is the testing effect [4]. To avoid the issue, as we explained we divided the participants into two groups and swapped the two documents between the groups. As a result the group 1 in the second stage examined the sentences that group 2 had in the first stage and vice versa.

The potential threat to the external validity of the research is the selection of the material for the experiment because one document cannot be enough for generalizing the evaluation of the framework. We were aware of this issue but to evaluate the framework by applying it on diverse documents we would need to ask students to stay much longer for the experiment that was not feasible. Also as we explained before this document has the smallest deviation from the mean of accuracy and sensitivity of annotating several documents that we tested the automated annotator on.

4   Related Work

Using NLP for knowledge extraction is not novel in software engineering. For instance several researchers have developed tools and methods for generating object oriented models from natural language texts by applying NLP [3][9][10]. However, most of these methods and tools are applied on specific software documents such as design documents and requirements specifications while more general or informal texts such as meeting minutes, wikis and industrial standards are not considered. Besides, the majority of work has been done to extract the object oriented data from the documents whereas extraction of architectural knowledge (specifically architectural decisions) is not mainly in focus. Even though, there is still few work focusing on architectural knowledge extraction. Figueiredo et al. have developed a rule-based NLP approach to search architectural knowledge entities in documents [7]. TREx is another approach that annotates architectural related documents by applying NLP to retrieve architectural knowledge entities (including issues, drivers, rationale) [8]. Although the development and operation stages of both approaches are very similar to

SADGE, the catalog of terms and annotation rules are not presented in the papers nor publicly accessible. Therefore, it is not possible to replicate the approaches and as a result the comparison is not feasible. So the catalog of terms and annotation rules presented in this paper are the contribution of our research to extracting architectural issues from documents and generating architectural guidance.

5   Conclusion and Future Work

In this paper we introduced Semi-Automated Design Guidance Enhancer (SADGE), a framework for obtaining design guidance from architectural knowledge in project documents and domain literature. SADGE applies Natural Language Processing (NLP) to the architectural knowledge domain to reduce the efforts of manually creating architectural guidance from architecture documentation. More specifically, SADGE automatically annotates (highlight) the architectural issues to reduce the knowledge engineering effort that has to be invested initially to identify architectural knowledge from the documents.

We presented the five development stages of SADGE, D1 initializing the annotation rule, D2 initializing the catalog of terms, D3 evolving the annotation rule, D4 evolving the catalog of terms, and D5 refining the catalog of terms. This makes the design of the framework replicable for researchers.

The four operation steps of the SADGE are preparing documents for annotation (O1), automatically annotate the documents (O2), manually fine-tune the results (O3), generate the design guide out of annotated text (O4). The two maintenance steps of the framework are (M1) suggest new terms for catalog of terms and (M2) add new terms to the catalog of terms. This makes the application of the framework understandable for practitioners.

The results of the framework evaluation are: the automatic approach has the shortest processing time (research question RQ1) and the highest sensitivity (RQ2) while the semi-automatic approach has the highest accuracy (RQ3). In summary, using NLP in the architectural knowledge domain reduces the amount of manual decision identification work and has the potential to improve existing decision identification techniques.

Practitioners can use SADGE in the first stages of their architectural decision making process to rapidly identify architectural issues (decisions required) that are relevant to their project. This helps them accelerate the orientation in the problem-solution space and, consequently, to make architectural decisions in a more confident way.

In the next stage of our research, we plan to improve the sensitivity and accuracy of the automated annotator by applying machine learning algorithms (so far, we were missing adequate training data, but we expect to receive more architectural related documents from real projects in the industry). Furthermore, we plan to evaluate the framework by conducting case studies that involve expert architects and also include more real-world project documents.

References

1. Anvaari, M., Conradi, R., Jaccheri, L.: Architectural Decision-Making in Enterprises: Preliminary Findings from an Exploratory Study in Norwegian Electricity Industry. In: Drira, K. (ed.) ECSA 2013. LNCS, vol. 7957, pp. 162–175. Springer, Heidelberg (2013)

2. Babar, M.A., Dingsøyr, T., Lago, P., van Vliet, H.: Software Architecture Knowledge Management. Springer (2009)
3. Bajwa, I.S., Samad, A., Mumtaz, S.: Object Oriented Software Modeling Using NLP Based Knowledge Extraction. European Journal of Scientific Research 35(01), 22–33 (2009)
4. Campbell, D.T., Stanley, J.C.: Experimental and Quasi-experimental Designs for Research. Houghton Mifflin, Boston (1963)
5. Crowston, K., Liu, X., Allen, E.E.: Machine Learning and Rule-based Automated Coding of Qualitative Data. Proceedings of the American Society for Information Science and Technology 47(1), 1–2 (2010)
6. Falessi, D., Cantone, C., Kazman, R., Kruchten, P.: Decision-Making Techniques for Software Architecture Design: A Comparative Survey. ACM Computing Surveys 43(4) (2011)
7. Figueiredo, A.M., dos Reis, J.C., Rodrigues, M.: Improving Access to Software Architecture Knowledge: An Ontology-based Search Approach. International Journal Multimedia and Image Processing (IJMIP) 2(1/2) (2012)
8. López, C., Codocedo, V., Astudillo, H., Cysneiros, L.M.: Bridging the Gap between Software Architecture Rationale Formalisms and Actual Architecture Documents: An Ontology-Driven Approach. Science of Computer Programming 77(1), 66–80 (2012)
9. Perez-Gonzalez, H.G.: Automatically Generating Object Models from Natural Language Analysis. In: 17th Annual ACM SIGPLAN Conference on Object-Oriented Programming, Systems, Languages, and Applications, pp. 86–87. ACM, New York (2002)
10. Soeken, M., Wille, R., Drechsler, R.: Assisted Behavior Driven Development Using Natural Language Processing. In: Furia, C.A., Nanz, S. (eds.) TOOLS 2012. LNCS, vol. 7304, pp. 269–287. Springer, Heidelberg (2012)
11. Tang, A., Avgeriou, P., Jansen, A., Capilla, R., Babar, M.A.: A Comparative Study of Architecture Knowledge Management Tools. Journal of Systems and Software 83(3), 352–370 (2010)
12. Ting, K.M.: Precision and Recall, Encyclopedia of Machine Learning. Springer, US (2010)
13. Tofan, D., Galster, M., Avgeriou, P.: Difficulty of Architectural Decisions–A Survey with Professional Architects. In: Drira, K. (ed.) ECSA 2013. LNCS, vol. 7957, pp. 192–199. Springer, Heidelberg (2013)
14. Zimmermann, O., Koehler, J., Leymann, F., Polley, R., Schuster, N.: Managing Architectural Decision Models with Dependency Relations, Integrity Constraints, and Production Rules. Journal of Systems and Software 82(8), 1249–1267 (2009)
15. Zimmermann, O.: An Architectural Decision Modeling Framework for Service-Oriented Architecture Design. PhD Dissertation, University of Stuttgart (2009)
16. Zimmermann, O.: Architectural Decisions as Reusable Design Assets. IEEE Software 28(1), 64–69 (2011)

Combining Architectural Design Decisions and Legacy System Evolution

Sebastian Gerdes[1], Steffen Lehnert[2], and Matthias Riebisch[1]

[1] Universität Hamburg
Vogt-Kölln-Str. 30, 22527 Hamburg, Germany
{gerdes,riebisch}@informatik.uni-hamburg.de
[2] Technische Universität Ilmenau
Ehrenbergstraße 29, 98693 Ilmenau, Germany
steffen.lehnert@tu-ilmenau.de

Abstract. Software development is characterized by ongoing design decisions that must take into account numerous requirements, goals, and constraints. When changing long-living and legacy systems, former decisions have to be considered. In order to minimize the risk of taking wrong or misleading decisions an explicit representation of the relevant aspects is crucial. Architectural decision modeling has proven to be an effective means to represent these aspects, the required knowledge, and properties of a potential solution. However, existing approaches do not sufficiently cover the ongoing evolution of decisions and artifacts. They fail in particular to represent relations to existing systems on a fine-grained level to allow for impact analysis and a later comprehension of decisions. Furthermore, the effort for capturing and modeling of design decisions has to be reduced. In our paper we integrate existing approaches for software architectural design decision making. We extend them by fine-grained traceability to elements of existing systems and explicit means for modeling the evolution of decisions. We show how relevant decisions can easily be identified and developers are supported in decision making.

Keywords: Software architecture, design decision, traceability, evolution, reengineering, legacy software.

1 Introduction

The majority of today's software engineering efforts are spent on continuous and evolutionary development of existing systems [1]. Hence, development faces the ongoing integration, maintenance, and reengineering of existing (legacy) systems. An increasing amount of software is also composed of pre-existing building blocks, such as COTS-components, which therefore represent another type of existing items that have to be considered during design decision making [2].

As software architectures cover many important design decisions, evolutionary development of software systems demands for traceability between decisions and the resulting artifacts to comprehend *who* made *which* decision *when* and *why* [3].

P. Avgeriou and U. Zdun (Eds.): ECSA 2014, LNCS 8627, pp. 50–57, 2014.

Additional traceability between (legacy) decisions is required to enable comprehensive change impact analysis in response to changes. However, this support is not yet sufficiently provided by current research on the documentation and utilization of design decisions. Therefore, our goals are to:

1. Support the evolution of design decisions.
2. Document the origins and potential impacts of design decisions.
3. Establish fine-grained couplings between design decisions, requirements, constraints, and elements of existing systems.
4. Reduce the effort for the modeling of dependencies.

To accomplish these goals, we consolidate the decision models as proposed by Zimmermann [4] and Capilla *et al.* [5]. We augment the resulting decision model with means for fine-grained traceability towards software artifacts which are either impacted by the design decisions or contribute towards them, to help developers understand the implications of their changes. As our main contribution we illustrate how the evolution of every aspect of the decision model is addressed by our approach to allow for a seamless documentation of design decisions. We emphasize how developers are enabled to identify (legacy) decisions relevant to their current tasks and how our approach helps developers to answer the questions arising during software maintenance.

The remainder of this paper is organized as follows. In Section 2 we describe requirements to design decisions, which will be derived from developer's needs represented by use cases. We introduce our revised decision model in Section 3 and explain how our model assists with decision making in Section 4. Related work is discussed based on our requirements in Section 6 and finally Section 7 outlines future research and concludes the paper.

2 Requirements to Architectural Design Decisions

Before analyzing existing works on documenting architectural design decisions we have to define valid criteria for the analysis of the proposed models. These criteria are derived from studies that elicited questions frequently asked by developers during software maintenance and evolution [6,7,8]. These studies revealed general information needs and special demands on software evolution, for which they conducted interviews with developers working in different domains.

2.1 Derived Use Cases and Requirements

In a next step we distilled three use cases from these questions and illustrate how they benefit from explicit design decisions and support developers.

Identifying Relevant Legacy Decisions: If legacy decisions shall support developers with their current tasks, means going beyond simple text searches are required for identifying relevant decisions by querying the set of legacy decisions in a more structured way. The derived use case comprises the efficient access to decisions by limiting the search space, focusing on relevant information, and revealing links to elements of existing systems to support evolution.

Decision Support Based on Legacy Decisions: Once relevant legacy decisions are identified, they must be aligned with the current task to select potentially suitable solutions. Afterwards and in combination with fine-grained traceability towards software artifacts and requirements they enable change impact analysis as one of the key requirements of developers [6]. Legacy decisions and related requirements and constraints reveal why code was implemented in a particular way, which is crucial when trying to understand the rationale behind existing solutions and the evolution of code [6,8]. Historical decisions also expose information about previous issues in terms of constraints, requirements, etc.

Documenting Design Decisions: Developers must be able to populate the decision repository with recent decisions and related information to enable further reuse. This task must be accomplished with as little overhead as possible.

Based on the needs and use cases, we distilled requirements for a metamodel to capture design decisions, which can be summarized as follows.

1. **Explicit support for evolution of decisions and related artifacts:** Considering the evolutionary characteristics of decisions will expose potential pitfalls developers already experienced in the past.
2. **Explicit traceability to related software artifacts:** Fine-grained traceability will show which legacy decision leads to certain artifacts, such as code or models, which will make developers aware of potential impacts of changes.
3. **Explicit traceability to constraints and requirements:** This will reveal the drivers of a decision and the reasons of the developer why code and design are the way they are. They need to be represented as first-class entities.

3   Consolidated Metamodel for Design Decisions

Based on our requirements we propose a consolidated decision model which is displayed by Figure 1 to better capture the evolution of decisions and their relations to other software artifacts, requirements, and constraints.

3.1   Consolidating the Decision Model

The consolidation of the existing decision models is comprised of two steps aimed to increase the applicability of the resulting model. Firstly, we remove several elements from the models which are not necessary for documenting architectural issues and decisions in a real-world context, but complicate the application of the model for developers. Secondly, we revise the attributes of remaining elements and purge those that do not contribute towards the comprehension of decisions.

The first element to be removed is the *ADLevel* as introduced in [4]. There are two reasons, on the one hand its limited benefit when exploring legacy decisions to assist developers to accomplish their task. On the other hand, the boundaries between the different *ADLevels* are quite fluid and most classifications are rather ambiguous, thus misleading developers when documenting issues and decisions.

Furthermore, we identified cases of redundancy in the existing models which should be resolved to streamline the decision model. The first candidates are

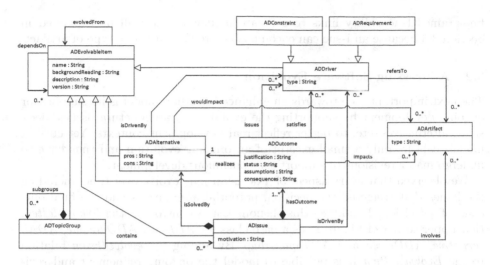

Fig. 1. Our revised decision model represented by a class diagram

ADRequirement, ADRequirementType, and *ADRequirementsArtifact* introduced
in [5]. We integrated the *ADRequirementType* as an attribute into *ADRequirement*, thereby diminishing the need for a separate class (upper right corner of
Figure 1). Likewise, there is little conceptual difference between *ADDesignArtifact* and *ADRequirementsArtifact* as both represent real software artifacts,
regardless of whether it is a free text, a use case, etc. By renaming *ADDesignArtifact* into *ADArtifact* and by adding both an attribute *type* to it and a reference
from *ADRequirement* towards it we can omit the additional classes.

A similar level of redundancy can be observed in the instances of *ADDesignArtifact, ADDesignElementType, ADDesignElement, ADRuntimeElement,* and
ADRuntimeArtifact. In this case we also propose to merge the classes into the
ADArtifact class (right side of Figure 1) for the following reasons: First of all,
for the traceability of decisions and issues with design elements the additional
layer as introduced by the *ADDesignArtifact* is not required if the granularity
of the traceability concept is refined. This will be discussed in detail in Section
3.3. Additionally, the *ADDesignElementType* is dispensable as this information
is already encoded in the metamodels of the actual design artifacts.

Finally, we have to reorganize and purge several attributes of the remaining
model constituents. To begin with, there is a redundancy in *ADOutcome* class
of [4], namely the *candidateAlternatives* attribute which is already encoded by
the *isSolvedBy* references of the containing *ADIssue*. This is likely to introduce
inconsistencies as architects and developers are forced to link the same entities
twice in two different places. There are also various attributes of the *ADIssue*
class which turned out to hamper the capturing of issues in practice or were
never used, but in turn complicated the representation of recorded information. Therefore, the attributes *phase, role,* and *shortName* are removed from our
model. Moreover, the attribute *scope* is omitted and instead replaced by more

fine-grained traceability links to software artifacts. This will be explained in Section 3.3 because an issue can encompass more than just one type of artifact.

3.2   Addressing Software Evolution

The next important step towards an enhanced decision model is its support for ongoing development by supporting the evolution of architectural issues, decisions, alternatives, etc. to better reflect real development contexts. Yet current models capture only a small excerpt of an ongoing evolution and thus have to undergo major revisions to support the continuous development.

We observed that every aspect of a decision may evolve over time, including the issues that triggered the decision, potential alternatives and the final outcome of a decision. To address this phenomenon, we introduce the *EvolvableItem* (left upper corner of Figure 1) as a base-class for *ADIssue*, *ADOutcome*, *ADAlternative*, *ADDriver*, and *ADTopicGroup*. By adding the *evolvedFrom* relation to the *EvolvableItem* it is possible to model the ongoing refinement and revision of entities, for example when new constraints were introduced or existing requirements changed. This enables architects and developers to explore and inspect the various influences leading to the current state of the issue, decision, alternatives, and so forth. Moreover, by providing the link back to the previous version of a certain entity developers are able to trace and understand the effects of changes. The mere presence of evolutionary links helps to inform developers about changes of issues etc. which would be lost if all entities would simply be overwritten or replaced. This is especially important for developers joining development at a later stage to focus their attention on recent changes.

3.3   Interweaving Traceability Support and Decision Modeling

Finally, we incorporate an enhanced traceability scheme into our decision model to allow for fine-grained traceability between its constituents. While we keep the relations of Zimmermann and Capilla *et al.*, we add further relations towards software artifacts and provide means for linking dependent entities.

We first introduce *impact*-relations between *ADOutcome* entities and software artifacts represented by the *ADArtifact* entity. Using these relations developers can clearly highlight those artifacts that are impacted by a certain decision, thus assisting with software maintenance. Likewise, potential impacts between *ADAlternatives* and *ADArtifacts* can be expressed as *wouldImpact*-traceability links to signify the consequences of implementing a certain alternative.

Secondly, developers must be able to link architectural issues with the involved software artifacts, as the origin of an issue might result from their interplay. We therefore add the *involves*-relation between *ADIssues* and *ADArtifacts*, which acts as the inverse relation to the aforementioned *impact*-relation.

Moreover, the outcome of a decision (*ADOutcome*) might entail new architectural drivers, like for example when the decision to utilize a SQL-database would impose a new constraint on the storage layer of the software. Hence, the *ADOutcome* is also related through an *issues*-link with the *ADDriver*.

We further extend the scope the *dependsOn*-relation by moving it from the *ADIssue* to the *EvolvableItem*, since our model should support traceability links between different decision entities. As for example, an *ADAlternative* may depends on a previously decided *ADOutcome*, which is not expressible with the current models. Another advantage of this relation is that it provides information about temporal dependencies. It indicates whether a decision has been made before or after another one and would justify it from today's perspective.

4 Supporting Decision Making and Comprehension

The following illustrates how our revised decision model assists developers dealing with the use cases outlined in Section 2.1.

Identifying Relevant Legacy Decisions: As previously stated, simple text searches are not the most feasible way to identify an entry point to documented (legacy) decisions which are related to the current task. Instead, a more structured search approach should be used, both limiting the search space and reducing irrelevant information at the same time. This can be accomplished by exploring the topics in which architectural issues are grouped, allowing a stepwise navigation through the available (legacy) data. We support this by using hierarchic *ADTopicGroup* entities where the lowest level of topic groups finally links towards architectural issues (*ADIssue*). By classifying and refining a current problem, developers can navigate the topic hierarchy to find the topic group(s) containing the most similar issues.

Decision Support Based on Legacy Decisions: Once an initial set of relevant issues and decisions has been identified, the developer must be enabled to decide which of those are most relevant to him. For this purpose three novel aspects of our decision model come into play. Firstly, with the help of our traceability concept the developer can inspect the software artifacts that were impacted by the decisions or which the decisions are based on. Hence, by correlating the impacted artifacts to his current situation he can estimate potential impacts and identify problems. This is further strengthened by the traceability of alternatives and software artifacts to reveal artifacts which would have been impacted. Previous experiences allow to track and understand possible issues and support in balancing current decisions. Secondly, due to our support for linking constraints and requirements with issues, decisions and alternatives, a developer can judge whether similar constraints hold for a project. If so, those (legacy) decisions and alternatives, which do not meet the constraints, can be excluded. This is especially important since similar issues appear in many projects, whereas the outcome is project-specific due to project-specific constraints. Finally, analyzing the "historical" development of a design decision might reveal issues a developer is not yet aware of. By comparing the evolution of a decision, issues which occurred at a certain point in time and might have altered the course of a decision are revealed, thus enabling him to judge the impacts of similar scenarios on the current case. Moreover, it allows to study the refinement of decisions over time which might support in taking the right decision earlier.

5   Evaluation Plans - The CoCoME Case Study

Our evaluation plan is built on the *Common Component Modeling Example* (CoCoME)[1] which was developed to evaluate and compare component-based modeling approaches in a real world context based on the implementation of a trading system for handling supermarket sales and enterprise management. We identified two works that performed various refactorings on CoCoME using different modeling methodologies and also documented their decisions, yet in an unstructured and semi-formal manner [9,10]. Our goal is to apply our model for the documentation of their decisions and to establish the linkage between software artifacts, requirements, and constraints to support software evolution.

6   Related Work

Tang *et al.* [11] proposed AREL as a rationale-based architecture model to document architectural design by means of a UML profile. However, the model lacks dependencies to design elements from design alternatives, which would expose potential impacts. Furthermore, it does not distinguish between constraints and requirements and lacks direct linkage of interdependent decisions. Van Heesch *et al.* [12] proposed a documentation framework consisting of four viewpoints for architectural decisions, which satisfy several stakeholders' concerns but neglect fine-grained traceability to related software artifacts and requirements. Capilla *et al.* [13] developed a web-based approach to capture and manage design decisions, yet it still lacks support for ongoing evolution which is only supplied in a partial manner [14] and fine-grained linking of decisions and software artifacts. Furthermore, Capilla *et al.* [5] extended the metamodel of Zimmermann *et al.* for decision modeling and reuse [4]. Due to their focus on capturing and reusing decisions, the model has various shortcomings in regard to decision evolution and traceability, which were not addressed in a comprehensive manner. They neglect traceability links required for maintenance, i.e. traceability links from issues or alternatives to fine-grained artifacts. Malavolta *et al.* [15] proposed an approach for systematically defining traceability links between decisions to enable "decision impact analysis". However, their linking concept does not provide means to link decisions with artifacts impacted by them. Likewise, linking the artifacts a decision is based on with the actual decision is also not possible either. Che and Perry [16] introduced the Triple View Model (TVM) to manage the documentation and evolution of decisions. The core of TVM is almost identical to Capilla's model, hence both share the same disadvantages. Its major derivation is its support for best practices that are interweaved with the decisions.

7   Conclusion and Future Work

Architectural design decisions provide urgently needed support for evolutionary development, yet current approaches are not fully capable of capturing the evolution of decisions and their fine-grained traceability. Thus we propose a revised

---

[1] http://cocome.org/index.htm

version of an architectural decision model for which we consolidated existing decision models and extended them with comprehensive means for expressing the evolution of their constituents to enable developers to trace the historical development of decisions, their drivers, and their outcomes. We enhanced the obtained decision model with means for fine-grained traceability to enable impact analysis and to further strengthen the integration of decisions when changing long-living software systems during software evolution. Currently, we evaluate our approach in a controlled lab experiment and plan an industrial case study. Further works will focus on the recovery of design decisions and the rationale behind them, as well as on constraints induced by legacy systems to differentiate their impact on design decisions and to underpin their necessity.

References

1. Vliet, H.: Software Engineering: Principles and Practice, 2nd edn. Wiley (2007)
2. Perry, D., Grisham, P.: Architecture and Design Intent in Component & COTS Based Systems. In: ICCBSS 2005, pp. 155–164 (2006)
3. Jansen, A., Bosch, J.: Software Architecture as a Set of Architectural Design Decisions. In: 5th Working Conf. on Software Architecture, pp. 109–120 (2005)
4. Zimmermann, O., Koehler, J., Leymann, F., Polley, R., Schuster, N.: Managing architectural decision models with dependency relations, integrity constraints, and production rules. Journal of Systems and Software 82(8), 1249–1267 (2009)
5. Capilla, R., Zimmermann, O., Zdun, U., Küster, J.M.: An enhanced architectural knowledge metamodel linking architectural design decisions to other artifacts in the software engineering lifecycle. In: Software Architecture, pp. 303–318 (2011)
6. Ko, A.J., DeLine, R., Venolia, G.: Information Needs in Collocated Software Development Teams. In: 29th Intl. Conf. on Software Engineering, pp. 344–353 (2007)
7. Sillito, J., Murphy, G.C., De Volder, K.: Questions programmers ask during software evolution tasks. In: SIGSOFT 2006/FSE-14, pp. 23–33 (2006)
8. Fritz, T., Murphy, G.C.: Using information fragments to answer the questions developers ask. In: 32nd Intl. Conf. on Software Engineering, pp. 175–184 (2010)
9. Knapp, A., Janisch, S., Hennicker, R., Clark, A., Gilmore, S., Hacklinger, F., Baumeister, H., Wirsing, M.: Modelling the CoCoME with the Java/A Component Model. In: Rausch, A., Reussner, R., Mirandola, R., Plášil, F. (eds.) Common Component Modeling Example. LNCS, vol. 5153, pp. 207–237. Springer, Heidelberg (2008)
10. Küster, M., Trifu, M.: A case study on co-evolution of software artifacts using integrated views. In: WICSA/ECSA 2012, pp. 124–131 (2012)
11. Tang, A., Jin, Y., Han, J.: A rationale-based architecture model for design traceability and reasoning. Journal of Systems and Software 80(6), 918–934 (2007)
12. van Heesch, U., Avgeriou, P., Hilliard, R.: A documentation framework for architecture decisions. Journal of Systems and Software 85(4), 795–820 (2012)
13. Capilla, R., Nava, F., Pérez, S., Dueñas, J.: A web-based tool for managing architectural design decisions. SIGSOFT Softw. Eng. Notes 31(5) (2006)
14. Capilla, R., Nava, F., Dueñas, J.C.: Modeling and Documenting the Evolution of Architectural Design Decisions. In: SHARK/ADI 2007, pp. 9–15 (2007)
15. Malavolta, I., Muccini, H., Smrithi Rekha, V.: Supporting architectural design decisions evolution through model driven engineering. In: Troubitsyna, E.A. (ed.) SERENE 2011. LNCS, vol. 6968, pp. 63–77. Springer, Heidelberg (2011)
16. Che, M., Perry, D.E.: Managing architectural design decisions documentation and evolution. International Journal of Computers 6(2), 137–148 (2012)

Specification and Detection of SOA Antipatterns in Web Services

Francis Palma[1,2], Naouel Moha[2], Guy Tremblay[2], and Yann-Gaël Guéhéneuc[1]

[1] Ptidej Team, DGIGL, École Polytechnique de Montréal, Canada
{francis.palma,yann-gael.gueheneuc}@polymtl.ca
[2] Département d'informatique, Université du Québec à Montréal, Canada
{moha.naouel,tremblay.guy}@uqam.ca

Abstract. Service Based Systems, composed of Web Services (WSs), offer promising solutions to software development problems for companies. Like other software artefacts, WSs evolve due to the changed user requirements and execution contexts, which may introduce poor solutions—*Antipatterns*—may cause (1) degradation of design and quality of service (QoS) and (2) difficult maintenance and evolution. Thus, the automatic detection of antipatterns in WSs, which aims at evaluating their design and QoS requires attention. We propose SODA-W (Service Oriented Detection for Antipatterns in Web services), an approach supported by a framework for specifying and detecting antipatterns in WSs. Using SODA-W, we specify ten antipatterns, including *God Object Web Service* and *Fine Grained Web Service*, and perform their detection in two different corpora: (1) 13 weather-related and (2) 109 financial-related WSs. SODA-W can specify and detect antipatterns in WSs with an average precision of more than 75% and a recall of 100%.

Keywords: Antipatterns, Web Services, Specification, Detection.

1 Introduction

Service Oriented Architecture (SOA) has already become the prevailing architectural style used in the industry [6]. SOA helps developing low-cost, reusable, and distributed business solutions by combining *services*, which are independent, portable, and interoperable program units that can be discovered and invoked through the Internet. In practice, SOA can be realised using various technologies and architectural styles including SCA (Service Component Architecture) [5], REST (REpresentational State Transfer), and Web services.

Web services is the leading SOA technology used nowadays to develop *Service-based systems* (SBSs) [15]. Amazon, Google, eBay, FedEx, PayPal, and many more companies, all leverage Web services. In the distributed systems literature, the term *Web service* is commonly used to refer to both SOAP-based and RESTful Web services. Nevertheless, in this paper, we focus on SOAP-based Web services because currently they are more widely adopted than those based on REST [15].

SBSs evolve to meet new requirements or to adapt to the changed execution contexts, *e.g.*, changes in transport protocols or in service contracts. Such changes

P. Avgeriou and U. Zdun (Eds.): ECSA 2014, LNCS 8627, pp. 58–73, 2014.

may deteriorate the design and implementation, and worsen the QoS of Web services, and may cause the introduction of poor solutions, known as *Antipatterns*—in opposition to *design patterns* that are good solutions to recurring problems. In general, it has been shown that antipatterns negatively impact the evolution and maintenance of software systems [12].

God Object Web Service and *Fine Grained Web Service* are the two most common antipatterns in Web services [4]. The *God Object Web Service* describes a Web service that contains a large number of very low cohesive operations in its interface, related to different business abstractions. Being overloaded with a multitude of operations, a *God Object Web Service* may also have high response time and low availability. In contrast, *Fine Grained Web Service*, with few low cohesive operations, implements only a part of an abstraction. Such Web services often require several other coupled Web services to complete an abstraction, resulting in higher architectural complexity.

Despite the importance and extensive usage of Web services, no specification and automated approach for the detection of such antipatterns in Web services has been proposed. Such an approach to analyse the design and QoS of Web services and automatically identify antipatterns would help the maintenance and evolution of Web services. In fact, a few contributions have been made in the literature for the detection of SOA antipatterns in Web services including those in [14, 17, 18]. Yet, none of them provide the specification and all of them focus on the static analysis of Web service description files (*e.g.*, [17, 18]) or on antipatterns in other SOA technologies (*e.g.*, SCA [14]).

With the goal of assessing the design and QoS of Web services and filling the gap in the literature, we propose the SODA-W approach (Service Oriented Detection for Antipatterns in Web services) inspired from SODA [14]. SODA, supported by an underlying framework SOFA (Service Oriented Framework for Antipatterns), was the first approach dedicated to the specification and detection of antipatterns in SCA systems; it is, however, restricted to SCA. Instead, SODA-W is supported by an extended version of SOFA and is dedicated to the specification of SOA antipatterns and their automatic detection in Web services. The extended SOFA provides the means to analyse Web services statically, dynamically, or combining them. Static analyses refer to measuring the structural properties of Web services, whereas dynamic analyses invoke the real Web services and measure different properties, such as response time.

Therefore, the main contributions of this paper that leverage SODA-W are: (1) we add ten new metrics to our previous language proposed in [14] and adapt five other existing metrics in SOFA, (2) we specify ten Web service-specific antipatterns and perform the structural and semantic analysis of service interfaces, and finally (3) we perform detection for those ten antipatterns to validate SODA-W with more than 120 Web services in two different experiments. For the validation, we implement detection algorithms for the ten SOA antipatterns from their specifications, which we then apply on Web services. We perform the manual validation of the detection results in terms of precision, recall, and specificity.

Our results show that SODA-W allows to specify and detect SOA antipatterns with an average precision of more than 75% and a recall of 100%.

The remainder of this paper is organised as follows. Section 2 surveys related work on the detection of antipatterns, and in SBSs in particular. Section 3 lays out the approach, SODA-W, along with the language and the underlying framework, SOFA. Section 4 presents the experiments performed on Web services for validating SODA-W. Finally, Section 5 concludes and sketches future work.

2 Related Work

SOA antipatterns, Web service-specific antipatterns in particular, and their specification and detection are still in their infancy. A few books and articles address SOA antipatterns and most of the references are online [4, 13, 19]. Dudney *et al.* [4] first suggested a list of 52 antipatterns that are common in service-based architectures, and particularly in Web services. Antipatterns from that book are described informally. Rotem-Gal-Oz *et al.* [19] in their book listed some other SOA antipatterns also informally. In their paper, Král *et al.* [11] introduced seven SOA antipatterns that appear due to the improper use of SOA principles and standards. All the above works contributed to the existing catalogue of SOA antipatterns, but did not discuss their specification or detection.

A number of detection approaches [10, 16, 21] exist for object-oriented (OO) antipatterns. However, OO approaches are not applicable to the detection of SOA antipatterns because: (1) SOA is concerned with *services* as building blocks, whereas OO is concerned with *classes*, *i.e.*, services are coarser than classes in terms of granularity and (2) the highly dynamic nature of SOA compared to OO systems. Just a few works studied the detection of SOA antipatterns in Web services. Rodriguez *et al.* [18] performed detection for a set of Web service-specific antipatterns related to WSDL proposed by Heß *et al.* [9]. However, the primary focus of the work was not analysing or improving the design of Web services, rather on the WSDL writing conventions to improve their discoverability.

Moha *et al.* [14] proposed the SODA approach for specifying and detecting antipatterns in SCA systems (Service Component Architecture), relying on a rule-based language to specify antipatterns at a higher-level of abstraction than detection algorithms. In SODA, the detection algorithms are generated automatically and applied on SCA systems with a high accuracy. However, the proposed approach can only deal with local SCA components developed with plain JAVA and cannot handle remote Web services.

In another study, Rodriguez *et al.* [17] described *EasySOC* and provided a set of guidelines for service providers to avoid bad practices while writing WSDLs. Based on some heuristics, the authors detected eight bad practices in the writing of WSDL for Web services. The heuristics are simple rules based on pattern matching. The authors did not consider the design and QoS of the Web services and analysed the WSDL files statically. In this paper, instead, we analyse the Web services both statically and dynamically.

More recently, Coscia *et al.* [3] performed a statistical correlation analysis between a set of traditional code-level OO metrics and WSDL-level service metrics, and found a statistically significant correlation between them. Still, the main focus was not on identifying bad practices or poor design decisions in the service interfaces. Also, Sindhgatta *et al.* [22] performed a thorough literature survey on service cohesion, coupling, and reusability metrics, and proposed five new cohesion and coupling metrics, which they described as new quality criteria for service design. These metrics are even at the WSDL code-level; in contrast, we assess the design and QoS of Web services.

Given the above limitations in the literature, we try to come up with a viable solution for specifying and detecting SOA antipatterns in Web services.

3 Approach

We now describe the SODA-W (Service Oriented Detection for Antipatterns in Web services) approach dedicated to Web services (WSs). SODA-W involves three steps from the specification of Web service-specific antipatterns to their detection.

Step 1. Specification of SOA Antipatterns: We identify the relevant properties of Web service-specific antipatterns that we use to extend our previous domain-specific language (DSL) [14]. We then use this DSL to specify antipatterns.

Step 2. Generation of Detection Algorithms: This step involves the generation of detection algorithms from the specifications in the former step. In this paper, we performed this step manually by implementing concretely the algorithms in conformance with the rules specified in Step 1. We plan to automate this step.

Step 3. Detection of SOA Antipatterns: We apply the detection algorithms on a set of real WSs to detect antipatterns.

The following sections detail the first two steps. The last step is discussed in Section 4, where we perform the validation of SODA-W.

3.1 Specification of SOA Antipatterns

To specify SOA antipatterns, we performed a thorough domain analysis of antipatterns for WSs. We investigated their definitions and descriptions in the literature [4, 9, 11, 13, 18] because these mostly discussed WS-specific antipatterns. We identified a set of properties related to each antipattern, including static properties related to service design, *e.g.*, cohesion and coupling; and dynamic properties, *e.g.*, response time and availability. In general, static properties are recoverable from service interfaces. In contrast, dynamic properties are obtained by concretely invoking the WSs. We used these relevant properties to extend our DSL from [14]. Using this DSL, engineers can specify SOA antipatterns in the form of a rule-based language, using their own judgment and experience. A DSL allows engineers to focus on *what* to detect without being concerned about *how* to detect [2]. In fact, our DSL is implementation-independent, *i.e.*, it can be used regardless of the underlying technology of the system under analysis. However, the DSL needs to be extended for each new technology.

The syntax of our DSL is shown in Figure 1 using a Backus-Naur Form (BNF) grammar. We apply a rule-based technique for specifying antipatterns, *i.e.*, each

```
1  rule_card    ::= RULE_CARD: rule_cardName { (rule)+ };
2  rule         ::= RULE: ruleName { content_rule };

3  content_rule ::= metric | relationship | operator ruleType (ruleType)+
4                 | RULE_CARD: rule_cardName

5  ruleType     ::= ruleName | rule_cardName

6  operator     ::= INTER | UNION | DIFF | INCL | NEG

7  metric       ::= id_metric ordi_value
8                 | id_metric comparator num_value
9  id_metric    ::= ALS | ANIO | ANP | ANPT | ANAO | ARIP | ARIO | ARIM | CPL | COH | NCO
10                | NOD | NOPT | NPT | NVMS | NVOS | RGTS
11                | A | RT
12 ordi_value   ::= VERY_HIGH | HIGH | MEDIUM | LOW | VERY_LOW
13 comparator   ::= < | ≤ | = | ≥ | >

14 rule_cardName, ruleName, ruleClass ∈ string
15 num_value ∈ double
```

Fig. 1. BNF grammar of rule cards for SODA-W

rule card combines a set of rules. The different constituents of our DSL are as follows: a *rule_card* is characterised by a name and a set of related rules (Figure 1, line 1). A *rule* (lines 3 and 4) is associated with a metric or it may combine other rules using different set operators (line 6) including intersection (INTER) or union (UNION). A rule can be a singleton rule or it can refer to another rule card (line 4). A metric may involve an ordinary value or it can have a comparator with a numeric value (lines 7 and 8). Ordinal values range from VERY_LOW to VERY_HIGH (line 12), and are used to define values compared to other candidate WSs under analysis. We use the box-plot statistical technique [1] to associate ordinal values with numeric values, to automatically set thresholds. Finally, the comparators include common mathematical operators (line 13).

Our metric suite (lines 9 to 11) includes both static (lines 9 and 10) and dynamic metrics (line 11). In [14], we had a set of 13 metrics defined for SCA domain. In this paper, we extend the DSL by adding ten new metrics specific to the domain of WSs as shown in Table 1. We also adapt some previously existing metrics (see Table 1). This adaptation is essential due to the non-trivial differences between SCA and WSs. For instance, SCA applications are built with *components*, while WSs use *services* as their first class entities. The other metrics remain the same as in [14] as noted in Table 1.

The ARIP, ARIO, and ARIM metrics combine both the structural and semantic similarity computation. Structural similarity uses the well-known Levenshtein Distance algorithm, whereas semantic similarity uses WordNet[1(a)] and CoreNLP[3(b)]. WordNet is a widely used lexical database that groups nouns, verbs, adjectives, etc. into the sets of synsets, *i.e.*, cognitive synonyms, each representing a distinct concept. We use WordNet to find the cognitive similarity between two (sets of) operations, messages, or port-types. We use Stanford's

---

[1] (a) wordnet.princeton.edu (b) nlp.stanford.edu/software/corenlp.shtml

Table 1. The list of 19 metrics in SODA-W approach

Metrics	Full Names	Versions
ALS	Average Length of Signatures	new
ARIP	Average Ratio of Identical Port-Types	new
ARIO	Average Ratio of Identical Operations	new
ARIM	Average Ratio of Identical Messages	new
NCO	Number of Crud Operations	new
NOPT	Number of Operations in Port-Types	new
NPT	Number of Port-Types	new
NVMS	Number of Verbs in Message Signatures	new
NVOS	Number of Verbs in Operation Signatures	new
RGTS	Ratio of General Terms in Signatures	new
ANP	Average Number of Parameters in Operations	adapted
ANPT	Average Number of Primitive Type Parameters	adapted
NOD	Number of Operations Declared	adapted
ANIO	Average Number of Identical Operations	adapted
ANAO	Average Number of Accessor Operations	adapted
CPL	Coupling	same
COH	Cohesion	same
A	Availability	same
RT	Response Time	same

```
1 RULE_CARD: GodObjectWebService {
2 RULE: GodObjectWebService {INTER
      LowCohesion MultiOperation
      HighRT LowA};
3 RULE: LowCohesion {COH VERY_LOW};
4 RULE: MultiOperation {NOD HIGH};
5 RULE: HighRT {RT VERY_HIGH};
6 RULE: LowA {A LOW};
7 };
```
(a) God Object Web Service

```
1 RULE_CARD: FineGrainedWebService {
2 RULE: FineGrainedWebService {INTER
      FewOperation HighCoupling
      LowCohesion};
3 RULE: FewOperation {NOD LOW};
4 RULE: HighCoupling {CPL VERY_HIGH};
5 RULE: LowCohesion {COH LOW};
6 };
```
(b) Fine Grained Web Service

Fig. 2. Rule cards for *God Object Web Service* and *Fine Grained Web Service*

CoreNLP: (1) to find the base forms of a set of signatures of operations, messages, or port-types and (2) to annotate them with the part-of-speech (POS) tagger after we split the signatures based on the CamelCase.

Figure 2 shows the rule cards of the *God Object Web Service* [4] and *Fine Grained Web Service* [4] antipatterns as discussed in Section 1. A *God Object Web Service* (Figure 2(a)) is characterised by a high number of low cohesive operations and results in very high response time with low availability. A *Fine Grained Web Service* (Figure 2(b)) contains a fewer number of low cohesive operations with a high coupling resulting in higher development complexity. We also specify eight other WS-specific SOA antipatterns, whose rule cards are available in Section 4.

3.2 Generation of Detection Algorithms

The second step involves the implementation of the detection algorithms from the rule cards specified for each SOA antipattern. For each antipattern, we implement all the related metrics following its specification and write the detection algorithm in JAVA, which can directly be applied on any WSs. In the future, we will automate this algorithm generation process following a similar technique presented in [14].

3.3   Underlying Framework

We further develop the SOFA framework (Service Oriented Framework for Antipatterns) [14] to support the detection of SOA antipatterns in WSs. SOFA itself is developed as an SBS based on the SCA (Service Component Architecture) standards [5] and is composed of several SCA components. Figure 3 depicts the SOFA's key components: (1) *Rule Specification*—specifies rules relying on several other components, such as *Rule, Metric, Operator*, and *Boxplot*. The *Box-Plot* determines the ordinal values based on the numerical values computed for all the services under analysis; (2) *Algorithm Generation*—generates detection algorithms based on specified rules; and (3) *Detection*—applies detection algorithms generated in *Algorithm Generation* component on WSs.

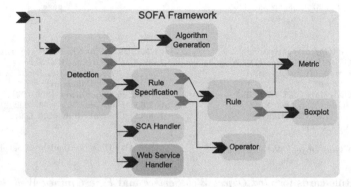

Fig. 3. The SOFA framework

We added a new *Web Service Handler* component to the SOFA to allow the detection of Web service-specific antipatterns. The different functionalities performed by the *Web Service Handler* component include: (1) given *keywords*, it returns a list of WSs from a search engine, (2) it then filters broken service descriptions or unavailable services, and finally (3) for all WSs, it generates a list of SCA components. Concretely, these SCA components wrap WSs as our SOFA framework can only introspect SCA components.

We extended the SOFA framework by: (1) adding ten new Web service-specific metrics and (2) adapting five existing SCA-specific metrics. Combining those new and adapted metrics, we specify ten Web service-specific antipatterns as described in Figure 4 and perform their detection using SOFA. The addition of an antipattern requires the implementation of each metric following its specification. A metric can be reused for other antipatterns if they share the same metric in their specifications.

We use FraSCAti [20] as SOFA's runtime support. FraSCAti, itself developed as an SCA 1.1 application [5], provides a runtime environment for SCA applications.

Being based on SCA, FraSCAti can provide component-based systems on top of diverse SOA technologies including Web services. In SOFA, we wrap each technology-specific services within an SCA component, thus providing a technology-agnostic platform to detect SOA antipatterns.

4   Validation

We want to show the completeness and the extensibility of our DSL, the preciseness of the detection algorithms, and the specificity of our rule cards. Therefore, we perform experiments with two sets of Web services (WSs) collected using a search engine: (1) 13 weather-related and (2) 109 finance-related WSs.

4.1   Hypotheses

We state three hypotheses that we want to examine in our experiments.

H1. Generality: *Our DSL allows the specification of various SOA antipatterns, from simple to more complex ones.* This hypothesis claims the applicability of our SODA-W approach that relies on metric-based (*i.e.*, 17 static and 2 dynamic metrics) rule cards for specifying ten Web service-specific SOA antipatterns.

H2. Accuracy: *The detection algorithms have an average precision of more than 75% and a recall of 100%, i.e., more than three-quarters of detected antipatterns are true positive and we do not miss any existing antipatterns.* Having a trade-off between precision and recall, we presume that 75% precision is acceptable while our objective is to detect all existing antipatterns, *i.e.*, 100% recall. We also show the specificity of the rule cards. This hypothesis claims the accuracy of the specified rule cards and the detection algorithms.

H3. Extensibility: *Our DSL and SOFA framework are extensible for adding new metrics and new SOA antipatterns.* In this hypothesis, we claim that the new metrics can be added and combined to specify new SOA antipatterns and that the SOFA framework can handle new antipatterns, including some specific to WSs, and detect them automatically.

4.2   Subjects

We specify ten different SOA antipatterns that are commonly found in WSs by applying our SODA-W approach. Figure 4 lists those Web service-specific SOA antipatterns. Among those ten antipatterns, eight are collected from the literature [4, 9, 11, 13, 18]. We also define two new antipatterns, namely *Duplicated Web Service* and *Data Web Service* inspired from OO antipatterns: *Silo Approach* and *Data Class*. Figure 4 emphasises the relevant properties of each antipattern in **bold-italics**. Figure 5 shows the specifications of those antipatterns. We give concrete examples of those antipatterns and show how they manifest in practice on our site[2].

---

[2] http://sofa.uqam.ca/soda-w/

Ambiguous Name [18] is an antipattern where the developers use the names of *interface elements* (*e.g., port-types, operations*, and *messages*) that are *very short* or *long*, include too *general terms*, or even show the improper *use of verbs*, etc. *Ambiguous names* are not *semantically* and *syntactically* sound and impact the *discoverability* and the *reusability* of a Web service.

Chatty Web Service [4] is an antipattern where a *high* number of *operations* are required to complete one abstraction where the *operations* are typically attribute-level *setters* or *getters*. A chatty Web service may have many *fine grained operations* for which: (1) *maintenance* becomes harder since inferring the *order of invocation* is difficult and (2) *many interactions* are required, which *degrades* the overall *performance* with *higher response time*.

CRUDy Interface [7] is an antipattern where the design encourages services the *RPC-like behavior* by creating *CRUD-type operations*, *e.g., create_X(), read_Y()*, etc. Interfaces designed in that way might be *chatty* because multiple operations need to be invoked to achieve one goal. In general, *CRUD operations* should *not be exposed* via *interfaces*.

Data Web Service typically contains *accessor operations*, *i.e., getters* and *setters*. In a distributed environment, some Web services that may only perform some simple *information retrieval* or *data access* operations. A *Data Web Service* usually deals with *very small messages* of *primitive types* and may have *high data cohesion*.

Duplicated Web Service, corresponds to a set of *highly similar* Web services. Because Web services are implemented multiple times as a result of the silo approach, there might exist *common* or *identical operations* with the *same names and–or message parameters*.

Fine Grained Web Service [4] is a small Web service with *few operations* implementing only a part of an abstraction. Such a Web service often requires *several coupled* Web services to complete an abstraction, resulting in higher development complexity, *reduced usability*. Moreover, since the *related operations* for an abstraction spread across services, individual services are *less cohesive*.

God Object Web Service [4] corresponds to a Web service that contains a *large number of operations* related to different business abstractions. Often the client *interactions break* due to frequent changes in the Web service definition, hence cause *low availability*. This antipattern affects the reusability because the operations are *very low cohesive*. Moreover, being overloaded with a multitude of operations, this antipattern may also result in *high response time*.

Low Cohesive Operations in the Same PortType [18] is an antipattern where developers place *low cohesive operations* in a *single prototype*. From the Web services perspective, if the operations belonging to the same *prototype* do not provide a set of *semantically related* operations, the *prototype* becomes *less cohesive*.

Maybe It's Not RPC [4] is an antipattern where the Web service mainly provides *CRUD operations* with a *large number of parameters*. This antipattern causes *poor system performance* because the clients *often wait* for the synchronous *responses*.

Redundant PortTypes [9] is an antipattern where *multiple port-types* are *duplicated* with the *similar set* of *operations*. Very often, such *port-types* deal with the *same messages*. The *Redundant PortType* antipattern may *negatively impact* the *ranking* of the Web Services.

Fig. 4. List of the ten SOA antipatterns in Web services

4.3   Objects

Unlike open-source systems in OO, freely available real WSs are difficult to find for validating detection algorithms. There are some Web service search engines, like eil.cs.txstate.edu/ServiceXplorer, programmableweb.com, myexperiment. org, and taverna.org.uk, however, the number of such search engines is limited and often may not provide healthy service interface.

We perform experiments on two different sets of WSs collected from a Web service search engine, programmableweb.com. The first set includes 13 weather-related WSs (keyword *'Weather'*); and the second set includes 109 finance-related WSs (keyword *'Finance'*). The complete list of all service interfaces that we experimented with is available online on our site[2].

```
1 RULE_CARD: AmbiguousName {
2   RULE: AmbiguousName {INTER GeneralTerm
3   ShortORLongSignature VerbedMessage
4   MultiVerbedOperation};
5   RULE: ShortORLongSignature {UNION
6   ShortSignature LongSignature};
7   RULE: LongSignature {ALS VERY_HIGH};
8   RULE: ShortSignature {ALS VERY_LOW};
9   RULE: GeneralTerm {RGTS HIGH};
10  RULE: VerbedMessage {NVMS > 0};
11  RULE: MultiVerbedOperation {NVOS > 1};
12 };
```
(a) Ambiguous Name

```
1 RULE_CARD: ChattyWebService {
2   RULE: ChattyWebService {INTER LowCohesion
3   HighDataAccessor MultiOperation
4   LowPerformance};
5   RULE: LowCohesion {COH LOW};
6   RULE: HighDataAccessor {ANAO VERY_HIGH};
7   RULE: MultiOperation {NOD HIGH};
8   RULE: LowPerformance {INTER HighRT LowA};
9   RULE: HighRT {RT HIGH};
10  RULE: LowA {A LOW};
11 };
```
(b) Chatty Web Service

```
1 RULE_CARD: CRUDyInterface {
2   RULE: CRUDyInterface {INTER ChattyInterface
3   HighCRUDOperation};
4   RULE: ChattyInterface {RULE_CARD:
5   ChattyWebService};
6   RULE: HighCRUDOperation {NCO > 1};
7 };
```
(c) CRUDy Interface

```
1 RULE_CARD: DataWebService {
2   RULE: DataWebService {INTER HighCohesion
3   PrimitiveParameter HighAccessor
4   LowParameter};
5   RULE: HighCohesion {COH HIGH};
6   RULE: PrimitiveParameter {ANPT HIGH};
7   RULE: HighAccessor {ANAO HIGH};
8   RULE: LowParameter {ANP LOW};
9 };
```
(d) Data Web Service

```
1 RULE_CARD: DuplicatedWebService {
2   RULE: DuplicatedWebService {INTER
3   IdenticalPortType IdenticalOperation};
4   RULE: IdenticalPortType {ARIP HIGH};
5   RULE: IdenticalOperation {ARIO HIGH};
6 };
```
(e) Duplicated Web Service

```
1 RULE_CARD: LowCohesiveOperations {
2   RULE: LowCohesiveOperations {INTER
3   MultiOperation LowCohesivePT};
4   RULE: MultiOperation {NOD HIGH};
5   RULE: LowCohesivePT {ARIO LOW};
6 };
```
(f) Low Cohesive Operations

```
1 RULE_CARD: MaybeItsNotRPC {
2   RULE: MaybeItsNotRPC {INTER HighRT
3   HighCRUDOperation HighParameter};
4   RULE: HighRT {RT HIGH};
5   RULE: HighCRUDOperation {NCO VERY_HIGH};
6   RULE: HighParameter {ANP HIGH};
7 };
```
(g) Maybe It's Not RPC

```
1 RULE_CARD: RedundantPortType {
2   RULE: RedundantPortType {INTER
3   MultiPortType MultiOps HighCohesivePT};
4   RULE: MultiPortType {NPT > 1};
5   RULE: MultiOps {NOPT > 1};
6   RULE: HighCohesivePT {ARIP VERY_HIGH};
7 };
```
(h) Redundant PortTypes

Fig. 5. Rule cards for different SOA antipatterns in Web services

4.4   Process

We specified the rule cards for ten Web service-specific antipatterns and implemented their detection algorithms using our SOFA framework. Then, we applied those algorithms on the WSs and reported any existing antipatterns. We manually validated the detection results to: (1) identify the true positives and (2) to find false negatives. The validation was performed by two students; we provided them with the descriptions of antipatterns and the service description file for each Web service along with its average response time. To measure the response time regardless of the network latency and physical location of a Web service, using the SAAJ[3(a)] standard implementation and SoapUI[3(b)], we arbitrarily invoked at least

---

[3] (a) saaj.java.net (b) www.soapui.org/

three operations from each real Web service, measured their response times, and
took the average. We used precision and recall [8] to measure our detection accuracy. Precision concerns the ratio between the true detected antipatterns and all
detected antipatterns, and recall is the ratio between the true detected antipatterns and all existing true antipatterns. Finally, we also calculate the specificity
of our rule cards, *i.e.*, the ratio between all WSs identified as non-antipattern and
total existing true negatives.

4.5 Results

Tables 2 and 3 present the detailed detection results for the ten SOA antipatterns.
Each table reports the antipatterns in the first column followed by the involved
WSs in the second. The third column shows the metric values for each Web
service once it is identified as an antipattern. The fourth and fifth columns
report the box-plot threshold values for each metric and the detection time for
each antipattern, respectively. The last two columns show the precision (P) and
recall (R) of our detection algorithms.

4.6 Details of the Results on 13 Weather Web Services

We briefly explain the detection results obtained from the first experiment as presented in Table 2. We identified five WSs involved in four antipatterns, namely,
Ambiguous Name, Fine Grained Web Service, Low Cohesive Operations, and
Redundant PortTypes. For instance, the AIP3_PV_ImpactCallback in Table 2 is
identified as an *Ambiguous Name* antipattern because this Web service offers operations with the signatures that (1) are very long (ALS=0.675), (2) use too many
general terms (RGTS=0.85), (3) deal with many messages having verbs in their
signatures (NVMS=26), and (4) have multiple verbs or action names (NVOS=7).
In comparison to the median values, those values are high, *i.e.*, greater than
the median but less or equal to the max. Therefore, we appropriately detected
AIP3_PV_ImpactCallback as *Ambiguous Name* and had a precision and recall of
100% as confirmed by the manual validation.

We also detected SrtmWs-PortType, ShadowWs-PortType, and Hydro1KWs-
PortType as *Fine Grained Web Service* antipatterns because they have very low
values for NOD (*i.e.*, 2) and COH (*i.e.*, 0.0). As calculated by the *Box-Plot* component, the NOD values are low in comparison with the median of 5.5. Similarly, with
only two operations defined, the cohesion values are not significant compared to
other WSs, whose COH values are between 0.216 and 0.443. The manual validation
revealed the correct identification of this antipattern for ShadowWs-PortType
and Hydro1KWs-PortType. However, for the SrtmWs-PortType, the manual validation suggested that the operations defined in its service interface could fulfill
an abstraction, and did not consider SrtmWs-PortType as an antipattern. Thus,
we have precision of 66.67% with 100% recall for this detection.

For this first experiment, our detection algorithms did not detect six other
antipatterns (see Table 2).

Table 2. Details on detection results for 13 Weather-related Web services

Antipatterns	Involved Web Services	Metrics	Boxplot Values Min|Median|Max	Detect Time	P	R
Ambiguous Name	AIP3_PV_Impact-Callback	ALS 0.675 RGTS 0.85 NVMS 26 NVOS 7	0.027|0.463|0.675 0.0|0.0|0.85 4|6|54 1|3|20	0.69s	[1/1] 100%	[1/1] 100%
Chatty Web Service	*none detected*	*n/a*	*n/a*	300.23s	–	–
CRUDy Interface	*none detected*	*n/a*	*n/a*	244.48s	–	–
Data Web Service	*none detected*	*n/a*	*n/a*	1.03s	–	–
Duplicated Web Service	*none detected*	*n/a*	*n/a*	1.21s	–	–
Fine Grained Web Service	SrtmWsPortType	NOD 2 COH 0.0	2|5.5|27 0.0|0.216|0.443	1.04s	[2/3] 66.67%	[2/2] 100%
	Hydro1KWsPortType	NOD 2 COH 0.0	*same as above*			
	ShadowWsPortType	NOD 2 COH 0.0	*same as above*			
God Object Web Service	*none detected*	*n/a*	*n/a*	235.47s	–	–
Low Cohesive Operations	ndfdXMLPortType	NOD 12 ARIO 0.221	2|3|27 0.221|0.473|0.998	1.13s	[1/1] 100%	[1/1] 100%
May be It's Not RPC	*none detected*	*n/a*	*n/a*	235.47s	–	–
Redundant PortTypes	AIP3_PV_Impact	NOPT 3 ARIP 0.378	2|3|27 0.378|0.378|0.378	1.11s	[2/2] 100%	[2/2] 100%
	AIP3_PV_Impact-Callback	NOPT 9 ARIP 0.378	*same as above*			
Average				102.19s	[6/7] 85.71%	[6/6] 100%

4.7 Details of the Results on 109 Finance Web services

Table 3 shows the detail on each antipattern detected in the second experiment with 109 Finance-related WSs. We briefly describe here some antipatterns: ForeignExchangeRates and TaarifCustoms are both identified as the *Chatty Web Service* and *CRUDy Interface* antipatterns because of their low cohesion (COH≈0.015), high average number of accessor operations (ANAO between 50 and 72.22), high number of operations (NOD between 9 and 24), and high response time (RT more than 3s), compared to other WSs. The box-plot values are shown in the corresponding rows for each metric. However, the manual analysis did not confirm ForeignExchangeRates as a *Chatty Web Service* because the order of invocation of the operations could easily be inferred from the service interface. The *CRUDy Interface* includes the rule card of *Chatty Web Service* in its specification. Therefore, the detection of ForeignExchangeRates as a *CRUDy Interface* was also not confirmed by the manual validation. Hence, we had the precision of 50% and recall of 100% for these two antipatterns.

We also identified wsIndicadoresEconomicosHttpPost, wsIndicadores-EconomicosSoap, and wsIndicadoresEconomicosHttpGet as *Redundant Port-Types* antipattern with multiple identical port-types (*i.e.*, NPT>1 and NOPT>1) defined in their service interfaces, thus have ARIP=1.0, *i.e.*, a very high value compared to the median of 0.465. If a Web service has redundant *port-types*, it is a good practice to merge them, while making sure that this merge does not introduce a *God Object Web Service* antipattern. Seven other WSs were identified

Table 3. Details on detection results for 109 Finance-related Web services

Antipatterns	Involved Web Services	Metrics	Boxplot Values Min|Median|Max	Detect Time	P	R
Ambiguous Name	BLiquidity	ALS 0.576 RGTS 0.682 NVMS 42 NVOS 7	0.013|0.226|0.81 0.0|0.613|0.75 1|64|482 0|6.5|48	1.02s	[8/8] 100%	[8/8] 100%
	CurrencyServerWebService	ALS 0.136 RGTS 0.682 NVMS 42 NVOS 5	same as above			
	ProhibitedInvestors-Service	ALS 0.158 RGTS 0.684 NVMS 12 NVOS 4	same as above			
Chatty Web Service	ForeignExchangeRates	COH 0.155 ANAO 50 NOD 24 RT 3286	0.0|0.25|0.667 0.0|0.961|100 1|12|70 172|1985|8592	1.89s	[1/2] 50%	[1/1] 100%
	TaarifCustoms	COH 0.116 ANAO 72.222 NOD 18 RT 4105	same as above			
CRUDy Interface	ForeignExchangeRates	COH 0.155 ANAO 66.667 NOD 9 RT 3113 NCO 9	0.0|0.25|0.667 0|0.96|100 1|11.5|70 172|1985|8592 0|9.5|62	1.81s	[1/2] 50%	[1/1] 100%
	TaarifCustoms	COH 0.103 ANAO 72.222 NOD 18 RT 4105 NCO 18	same as above			
Data Web Service	none detected	n/a	n/a	0.91s	–	–
Duplicated Web Service	none detected	n/a	n/a	1343.97s	–	–
Fine Grained Web Service	XigniteTranscripts	NOD 4 COH 0.125	1|12|70 0.0|0.25|0.667	0.85s	[2/2] 100%	[2/2] 100%
	BGCantorUSTreasuries	NOD 3 COH 0.083	same as above			
God Object Web Service	none detected	n/a	n/a	1.16s	–	–
Low Cohesive Operations	ServiceSoap	NOD 24 ARIO 0.253	1|12|70 0.0|0.435|1.0	242.49s	[7/7] 100%	[7/7] 100%
	XigniteSecuritySoap	NOD 25 ARIO 0.177	same as above			
	... ...	... ...	... ...			
	XigniteSecurityHttpPost	NOD 25 ARIO 0.177	same as above			
	XigniteCorporate-ActionsSoap	NOD 37 ARIO 0.268	same as above			
May be It's Not RPC	none detected	n/a	n/a	0.91s	–	–
Redundant PortTypes	wsIndicadores-EconomicosHttpPost	NOPT 2 ARIP 1.0	2|14|70 0.127|0.465|0.557	334.12s	[3/3] 100%	[3/3] 100%
	wsIndicadores-EconomicosSoap	NOPT 2 ARIP 1.0	same as above			
	wsIndicadores-EconomicosHttpGet	NOPT 2 ARIP 1.0	same as above			
Average				192.91s	[22/24] 91.67%	[22/22] 100%

as *Low Cohesive Operations* antipatterns (see Table 3), and two other WSs, *i.e.*, XigniteTranscripts and BGCantorUSTreasuries as *Fine Grained Web Service*. Both those WSs have a very small number of operations defined (NOD is 3 and 4) and have a low cohesion (COH between 0.083 and 0.125), compared to the maximum values (*i.e.*, 70 for NOD, and 0.667 for COH) from other WSs. Manual analysis also confirmed their detection, hence, we have precision and recall of 100% for *Redundant PortTypes* and *Fine Grained Web Service* antipatterns.

Again, for this experiment, we also did not identify four antipatterns on the set of 109 Finance-related WSs. As in Section 4.6 (see Table 2), we do not consider them to calculate the precision and recall. However, it is worth pointing out, the manual validation for 109 WSs is indeed a labor intensive task, and for each Web service it may take from 20 minutes to few hours based on the size of its interface.

4.8   Discussion on the Hypotheses

Following the results, we examine here three hypotheses stated in Section 4.1.

H1. Generality: In this paper, we specified ten WS-specific SOA antipatterns from the literature as shown in Figure 5 and described in Figure 4. We specified simpler antipatterns with fewer rules, such as *Low Cohesive Operations in the Same PortType* but also more complex antipatterns with composite rules, such as *CRUDy Interface* that is composed of another rule card, *i.e.*, *Chatty Web Service*. We also specified antipatterns combining six different rules, *Ambiguous Name* antipattern, for instance. Hence, this confirms our first hypothesis regarding the generality of our DSL. In fact, engineers can only use this DSL after analysing and integrating antipatterns properties to specify them.

H2. Accuracy: As shown in Tables 2 and 3, we obtained an average recall of 100% and an average precision of 88.69%. In the first experiment, with 13 WSs, we have a precision of 85.71%, whereas for the second experiment with 109 WSs, we have a precision and recall of 91.67% and 100%, respectively. Besides, we have the specificity of 98% for 13 WSs and 99% for 109 WSs. Thus, on average, we hold a precision of 88.69%, a recall of 100%, and a specificity 98.5%, which positively support our second hypothesis on the accuracy of our detection algorithms.

H3. Extensibility: We claim that our DSL and the SOFA framework are extensible for new antipatterns. In [14], we specified and detected ten antipatterns in SCA systems using our framework. In this paper, we specified and detected ten more Web service-specific antipatterns, and added them in the DSL and SOFA framework. More specifically, we added ten new metrics, such as NVMS, NOPT, RGTS, and NCO, etc. In addition, we added some variants of already existing metrics in the SOFA, *i.e.*, NOD, ANIO, ANAO, etc. Furthermore, we added new Web service-specific SOA antipatterns, such as *Low Cohesive Operations in the Same PortType, Maybe Its Not RPC*, and so forth. The designed language is flexible enough for integrating new metrics in the DSL. Our framework also supports the addition of new antipatterns through the implementation of new metrics and adaptation of existing ones to the new technology. This extensibility feature of our DSL and framework thus supports our third hypothesis.

4.9   Threats to Validity

As future work, we plan to generalise our findings to other large set of WSs. However, we tried to minimise the threat to the *external validity* of our results by performing two experiments with more than 120 WSs in two different domains. The detection results may vary based on the specification of the rule cards, and the way the components are implemented in the SOFA framework. *Internal validity* refers to the effectiveness of our approach and the framework. We made sure that the SOFA itself does not introduce antipatterns, to minimise the threat to the internal validity. Engineers may have different views and different levels of expertise on antipatterns, which may affect the specification of rule cards. We attempted to lessen the threat to *construct validity* by performing the specification of rule cards after a thorough literature review.

5   Conclusion

Web services are key artefacts for building Service-based systems. Like other systems, SBSs evolve due to new user requirements, which may lead to the introduction of antipatterns. The presence of SOA antipatterns may hinder software maintenance and evolution. This paper presented the SODA-W approach (Service Oriented Detection for Antipatterns in Web services) to specify and detect SOA antipatterns in Web services. Detection of antipatterns in Web services requires an in-depth analysis of their design, implementation, and QoS.

We applied SODA-W to specify ten common SOA antipatterns in Web services domain. Using an extended SOFA framework (Service Oriented Framework for Antipatterns), in an extensive validation with ten SOA antipatterns, we showed that SODA-W can specify and detect different Web services-specific antipatterns. We analysed more than 120 Web services and showed the accuracy of SODA-W with an average precision of more than 75% and recall of 100%.

In future work, we plan to enhance our approach to support other SOA styles, in particular REST services that follow different principles and standards for service design and consumption. Furthermore, we plan to conduct additional experiments with more Web services and antipatterns.

Acknowledgment. The authors are thankful to Ons Mlouki for initiating the study. This study is supported by NSERC and FRQNT research grants.

References

1. Chambers, J., Cleveland, W., Tukey, P., Kleiner, B.: Graphical Methods for Data Analysis. Wadsworth International (1983)
2. Consel, C., Marlet, R.: Architecturing Software Using A Methodology for Language Development. In: Palamidessi, C., Meinke, K., Glaser, H. (eds.) ALP 1998 and PLILP 1998. LNCS, vol. 1490, pp. 170–194. Springer, Heidelberg (1998)
3. Coscia, J.A.L.O., Crasso, M., Mateos, C., Zunino, A.: Estimating Web Service Interface Quality Through Conventional Object-oriented Metrics. CLEI Electronic Journal 16 (April 2013)
4. Dudney, B., Asbury, S., Krozak, J.K., Wittkopf, K.: J2EE AntiPatterns. John Wiley & Sons Inc. (August 2003)
5. Edwards, M.: Service Component Architecture (SCA), OASIS, USA (April 2011), http://oasis-opencsa.org/sca

6. Erl, T.: Service-Oriented Architecture: Concepts, Technology, and Design. Prentice Hall PTR (August 2005)

7. Evdemon, J.: Principles of Service Design: Service Patterns and Anti-Patterns (August 2005), msdn.microsoft.com/en-us/library/ms954638.aspx

8. Frakes, W.B., Baeza-Yates, R.A.: Information Retrieval: Data Structures & Algorithms. Prentice-Hall (1992)

9. Heß, A., Johnston, E., Kushmerick, N.: ASSAM: A Tool for Semi-Automatically Annotating Semantic Web Services. In: McIlraith, S.A., Plexousakis, D., van Harmelen, F. (eds.) ISWC 2004. LNCS, vol. 3298, pp. 320–334. Springer, Heidelberg (2004)

10. Kessentini, M., Kessentini, W., Sahraoui, H., Boukadoum, M., Ouni, A.: Design Defects Detection and Correction by Example. In: IEEE 19th International Conference on Program Comprehension (ICPC), pp. 81–90 (June 2011)

11. Král, J., Žemlička, M.: Crucial Service-Oriented Antipatterns, vol. 2, pp. 160–171. International Academy, Research and Industry Association, IARIA (2008)

12. Mäntylä, M.V., Lassenius, C.: Subjective Evaluation of Software Evolvability Using Code Smells: An Empirical Study. Empirical Software Engineering 11(3), 395–431 (2006)

13. Modi, T.: SOA Management: SOA Antipatterns (August 2006), http://www.ebizq.net/topics/soa_management/features/7238.html

14. Moha, N., Palma, F., Nayrolles, M., Conseil, B.J., Guéhéneuc, Y.-G., Baudry, B., Jézéquel, J.-M.: Specification and Detection of SOA Antipatterns. In: Liu, C., Ludwig, H., Toumani, F., Yu, Q. (eds.) Service Oriented Computing. LNCS, vol. 7636, pp. 1–16. Springer, Heidelberg (2012)

15. zur Muehlen, M., Nickerson, J.V., Swenson, K.D.: Developing Web Services Choreography Standards the Case of REST vs. SOAP. Decision Support Systems 40(1), 9–29 (2005)

16. Munro, M.J.: Product Metrics for Automatic Identification of "Bad Smell" Design Problems in Java Source-Code. In: Proceedings of the 11th International Software Metrics Symposium. IEEE Computer Society Press (September 2005)

17. Rodriguez, J.M., Crasso, M., Mateos, C., Zunino, A.: Best Practices for Describing, Consuming, and Discovering Web Services: A Comprehensive Toolset. Software: Practice and Experience 43(6), 613–639 (2013)

18. Rodriguez, J.M., Crasso, M., Zunino, A., Campo, M.: Automatically Detecting Opportunities for Web Service Descriptions Improvement. In: Cellary, W., Estevez, E. (eds.) Software Services for e-World. IFIP AICT, vol. 341, pp. 139–150. Springer, Heidelberg (2010)

19. Rotem-Gal-Oz, A., Bruno, E., Dahan, U.: SOA Patterns. Manning Publications Co. (2012)

20. Seinturier, L., Merle, P., Rouvoy, R., Romero, D., Schiavoni, V., Stefani, J.B.: A Component-Based Middleware Platform for Reconfigurable Service-Oriented Architectures. Software: Practice and Experience 42(5), 559–583 (2012)

21. Settas, D.L., Meditskos, G., Stamelos, I.G., Bassiliades, N.: SPARSE: A Symptom-based Antipattern Retrieval Knowledge-based System using Semantic Web Technologies. Expert Systems with Applications 38(6), 7633–7646 (2011)

22. Sindhgatta, R., Sengupta, B., Ponnalagu, K.: Measuring the Quality of Service Oriented Design. In: Baresi, L., Chi, C.-H., Suzuki, J. (eds.) ICSOC-ServiceWave 2009. LNCS, vol. 5900, pp. 485–499. Springer, Heidelberg (2009)

Co-evolving Pattern Synthesis and Class Responsibility Assignment in Architectural Synthesis[*]

Yongrui Xu and Peng Liang[**]

State Key Lab of Software Engineering
School of Computer, Wuhan University, Wuhan, China
{xuyongrui,liangp}@whu.edu.cn

Abstract. Architectural synthesis (AS) activity plays a key role in architecture design as it essentially links the problem to the solution space. To reuse successful design experience, architects may use architectural patterns in AS to generate candidate solutions. In a pattern-based AS, there are two challenges: one is class responsibility assignment (CRA) when using specific patterns and the other is pattern synthesis which attempts to avoid the pattern constraint violations. In this paper, we propose a cooperative coevolution approach to assign class responsibility and synthesize pattern automatically in a pattern-based AS. We formally translate the problem of the automated pattern-based AS into a multi-objective optimization problem, and describe the approach in detail.

Keywords: Automated architectural synthesis, class responsibility assignment, architectural patterns, cooperative coevolution.

1 Introduction

During the architecting process, architects perform various activities for different purposes towards the construction of the architecture of a software-intensive system. Hofmeister *et al.* defined a general model of architecture design including three activities, i.e., *architectural analysis*, *architectural synthesis*, and *architectural evaluation* [1]. Architectural synthesis (AS) activity proposes a collection of candidate architecture solutions, which are composed of a set of architectural elements (e.g., classes, components, and connectors) to address architecturally significant requirements (ASRs) identified during architectural analysis. AS is the core activity of architecture design as it essentially links the problem to the solution space of architecture design. However, how to propose architecture solutions to a set of ASRs largely depends on the experience of architects in traditional AS.

To reduce the complexity and reuse successful design experience when designing software architectures, architects rely on a set of idiomatic architectural patterns, which are packages of architectural design decisions and are identified and used repeatedly in practice [2], such as MVC, pipe and filter, and layer patterns. Using architectural patterns for architectural synthesis gets lots of benefits, and the architecture of

---

[*] This work is partially sponsored by the NSFC under Grant No. 61170025.
[**] Corresponding author.

P. Avgeriou and U. Zdun (Eds.): ECSA 2014, LNCS 8627, pp. 74–81, 2014.
© Springer International Publishing Switzerland 2014

large and complex systems is increasingly designed by composing architectural patterns [2]. However, existing research has observed that the resulting architecture of a system does not always conform to the initial patterns employed which guide the design at the beginning [3]. It is mainly due to the reasons that (1) existing work mostly focuses on pattern recommendation and selection, but pays less attention to the conceptual gap between the abstract elements and the implementation units in the employed patterns; (2) each pattern has a set of design constraints when using it, and architects may use the pattern being unaware of the constraints or misinterpreting the constraints due to lack of experience (especially for novice architects). If the pattern constraints are not satisfied, architects may have to redesign the architecture in order to avoid negative impact to the quality of the system. In summary, most existing work focuses on "architectural patterns recommendation and selection" instead of "architectural patterns implementation" which is part of architectural synthesis [1], and they did not address how to arrange structural elements (e.g., components and connectors) elegantly in a pattern to avoid the violations to the pattern constraints.

On the other hand, assigning responsibilities to classes is another vital task in object-oriented architectural synthesis [4], in which responsibilities are represented in terms of methods and attributes. Class responsibility assignment (CRA) has a great impact on the overall design of the application [4], and many methods were developed to help recognize the responsibilities of a system and assign them to classes [4] [5]. But one of deficiencies of these works is that they addressed the CRA problem in isolation. In practical software design, architects should not only consider CRA issues, but also think about the quality impact of architecture (e.g., which patterns can be used to satisfy given quality attributes). In most situations, the system quality attributes have great influences on CRA (e.g., some responsibilities may be replicated in both client- and server-side when using Client-Server pattern in order to improve the performance or reliability of a system), and CRA should be considered together with the quality aspects of the system.

To this end, we propose a cooperative coevolution approach that aims at synthesizing pattern-based architecture solutions automatically. It is composed of two processes: *responsibility synthesis* (RS) and *pattern synthesis* (PS). RS process addresses the CRA problem while PS process focuses on pattern implementation at architectural level. This approach tries to avoid the violations to the pattern constraints while considering the responsibility assignment to architecture elements (e.g., classes) in the resulting architecture solutions. In our approach, we use meta-heuristic search techniques (e.g., NSGA-II) to explore (i.e., to visit entirely new regions of a search space) and exploit (i.e., to visit those regions that are explored within the neighborhood of previous visited points) [6] pattern-based architecture design space automatically when the populations of RS and PS cooperatively coevolve. On one hand, we use pattern metrics that were proposed in our previous work [7] to evaluate the pattern constraint violations; on the other hand, we use CK object-oriented metrics to evaluate the quality of CRA [8]. We demonstrate how the proposed approach can help architects arrange architectural elements with minimum constraint violations to implement architectural patterns in specific design context. The contributions of this work are: (1) the first attempt to consider responsibility synthesis (i.e., CRA) and pattern synthesis simultaneously in pattern-based architectural synthesis; (2) translating the pattern-based architectural synthesis to a cooperative coevolution problem, which can be automated.

2   Background

For pattern synthesis (PS) process, our work is rooted in the concept of pattern metrics [7], which is based on pattern constraints. For responsibility synthesis (RS) process, we employ the responsibility collecting techniques. We describe these concepts and techniques as well as their relationships to our proposed approach below.

Architectural Pattern Metrics are used to measure the pattern constraint violations of candidate architecture solutions generated in automated architectural synthesis in PS. We introduce the pattern metrics definition process and describe MVC pattern metrics as an example in [7], which helps architects to translate the pattern constraints of an architectural pattern to its pattern metrics.

Responsibility Collecting Techniques help to collect responsibilities of a system and the dependencies between the responsibilities. Some of these techniques directly identify classes from requirements specifications that can be used to further collect responsibilities of a system, such as common class pattern, and class responsibility collaboration (CRC) card [5]. In this paper, we focus on the part of automated RS, and we assume that the responsibilities of a system and their dependencies have been collected and made available using abovementioned techniques.

Fig. 1 shows the relationship between our proposed cooperative coevolution approach for architectural synthesis (inside the rectangle) and the concepts and techniques mentioned above. On one hand, architects use a definition process [7] to define pattern metrics from constraints of the patterns they plan to use; on the other hand, using certain responsibility collecting technique, architects acquire responsibilities from requirement specifications. Pattern metrics and responsibilities are used as inputs for pattern synthesis and responsibility synthesis respectively in our approach to finally generate architecture solutions. We will present the formal definition of the automated pattern-based AS problem in the next section, which is further translated into a cooperative coevolution problem detailed in Section 4.

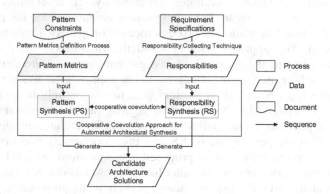

Fig. 1. The relationship between our cooperative coevolution approach and related techniques

3   The Problem

A pattern provides a generic solution for a recurring problem: a solution that can be implemented in many ways without necessarily being "twice the same", and there is no configurable generic implementations for patterns that cover their whole design space [9]. However, every pattern has its invariable roles, such as *model, view,* and *controller* in MVC pattern, and we define these invariable roles as the set of pattern roles for each pattern, e.g., {*model, view, controller*} for MVC pattern.

Let R represent a set of responsibilities which are derived from requirement specifications by responsibility collecting techniques, and every element in R represents which class one specific responsibility belongs to. Hence the number of elements in R equals the number of responsibilities, and let the number as n. In addition, let P represent the pattern role that each responsibility plays for the chosen pattern plus the connector type of all the relations among the responsibilities during pattern synthesis. Let the number of relations between responsibilities as m, hence the number of elements in P equals to the number of responsibilities in R (i.e., n) plus the number of relations (i.e., m). The first n elements in P represent the pattern role that each responsibility plays in a specific pattern, while the last m elements indicate the connector type (e.g., procedure call, event, and data access) [10] for each relation.

Fig. 2 depicts an example of R and P set that has two classes (Class 1 and Class 2) with five responsibilities: three operations and two attributes, and there is a relation between Operation 2 (O2) and Operation 3 (O3) that O3 *depends on* O2. This example uses Layer pattern and the two classes are located in different layers. The number of elements in R (i.e., number of responsibilities) is five, and each element indicates which class the responsibility belongs to. For instance, O1 belongs to Class 1, while Attribute 2 (A2) belongs to Class 2. Hence the value of R set is {C1, C1, C2, C1, C2}. In Layer pattern, layers constitute the set of pattern roles. The first five elements in P represent the layers that corresponding responsibilities belongs to, for example O1 belongs to Layer 0 (L0), while O3 belongs to Layer 1 (L1). In addition, as there is one dependency between responsibilities O2 and O3, P set has one extra element which describes the connector type of this relation, remote procedure call (RPC).

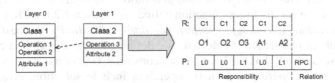

Fig. 2. An example of R and P set in Layer pattern

Formally speaking, the automated pattern-based AS problem consists in establishing an automated search for two optimal sets R and P following the definitions below:

- *The individuals from the responsibility population (IndR)*: IndR is an individual (chromosome) from responsibility population expressed as R set, and the value of each element v_i in R set represents one specific class. If two elements have the same value, it means the responsibilities these two elements represent belong to the same class. Therefore, v_i represents one feasible design decision of responsibility R_i, which assigns this responsibility to one class, in the whole design space.
- *The individual from pattern population (IndP)*: IndP is an individual (chromosome) from pattern population expressed as P set. P has two parts: responsibility and relation parts. The value of each element v_i in responsibility part represents the type of

pattern role for the corresponding responsibility. If two elements in the responsibility part have the same value, it means these two responsibilities play the same pattern role for a given pattern (e.g., they are in the same layer in Layer pattern). For relation part, the value of each element v_i represents the connector type (e.g., RPC, event) of this relation. Therefore, the value v_i of each element in P also represents one feasible design decision of pattern synthesis in the whole design space.

An optimal set R means this individual gets the highest score for evaluation metrics of CRA in responsibility population, while an optimal set P means this individual has the least pattern constraint violations in pattern population. For automated pattern-based AS problem, our objective is to acquire the solutions which not only achieve a high cohesion, low coupling and complexity design for CRA, but also have minimal pattern constraint violations. Therefore, the problem can be featured as a multi-objective optimization problem, and the responsibility and pattern population have a cooperative coevolution relationship for acquiring the final optimal architecture solutions.

4   Cooperative Coevolution Approach

The proposed approach coevolves two populations: responsibility and pattern populations. Fig. 3 illustrates the cooperative coevolution procedure with following steps:

1. *Population initialization*: The two populations are randomly generated, taking into account the set of responsibilities, pattern roles of these responsibilities, and all the relations among these responsibilities. Each population has a fixed size to form individuals (i.e., a series of IndR and IndP), which is described in Section 3.
2. *Calculating the fitness of population*:
   (a) *Best individual selection for responsibility population (BestIndR)*: in the first generation, an individual from responsibility population is randomly selected as the best individual. From the second generation, BestIndR is the individual with the best score for the fitness function defined in Section 4.2 for CRA problem.
   (b) *Best individual selection for pattern population (BestIndP)*: the best individual from pattern population is selected. We define a fitness function in Section 4.2 to ensure BestIndP has the least pattern constraint violations.
3. *Applying genetic operators*. Genetic operators include selection, crossover, and mutation operators [11]. In this step, for each population, a selection operator is used to select parents from all individuals for the crossover operation which generates sons using a crossover operator. Then mutation is performed using a mutation operator for each individual to produce the next generation for the two populations.
4. *Stopping condition satisfied*. If the limit of generations established by the input parameters of the meta-heuristic algorithm is reached, the execution of the cooperative coevolution procedure is stopped. As there are two objectives to be optimized (i.e., maximized cohesion metrics, minimized coupling and complexity metrics for CRA; and minimized pattern constraint violations for pattern implementation at architectural level), our approach returns a Pareto front (i.e., a set of solutions represent the best possible trade-offs among the two objectives) constructed by BestIndR and BestIndP when the stopping condition is satisfied.

It is expected that using this cooperative coevolution approach architects can acquire optimized solutions with better CRA and minimized pattern constraint violations.

In the following sub-sections, we describe representation of individuals for each population, and the fitness functions in detail.

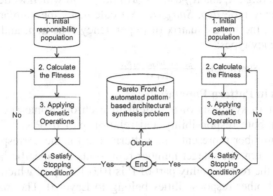

Fig. 3. Cooperative coevolution procedure of our approach

4.1 Representation of Individual

As illustrated in Fig. 2, there are two kinds of individuals, one is R set from responsibility population, and the other is P set from pattern population. We describe them in the next two sub-sections.

a)   Individuals in Responsibility Population

To encode the class responsibility assignment of a system in a chromosome (i.e., R set), we define the concept *centroid responsibility* (CR) similar to the concept *centroid use case* in [12]. In our approach, for each class, a CR is considered as a representative of other responsibilities belonging to that class, and R set is represented as a binary string of length n, where n is the total number of responsibilities. If the value of an element is "1", its corresponding responsibility is a CR; and otherwise when the value of the element is "0", then its corresponding responsibility is a non-CR. Therefore, the number of "1" in the binary string of R set shows the number of classes. For instance, one possible binary string in Fig. 2 is [10100], in which O1, O3 are CRs of Class 1 and Class 2. For those responsibilities that are not CRs, they are assigned to the most similar class. Here, the similarity between a non-CR and a class is equivalent to the similarity between the non-CR and the CR of that class. For example, in Fig. 2, if O2 is more similar to O1 compared with O3, then O2 is assigned to Class 1.

The core part of the encoding scheme for responsibility population is to define the similarity function to calculate the similarity between any two responsibilities. When using responsibility collecting techniques to collect the responsibilities of a system and the dependencies between responsibilities, we can acquire many types of dependencies between two responsibilities, such as Direct Method-Method dependency (DMM), Direct Method-Attribute dependency (DMA), and Direct Responsibility-Responsibility Semantic dependency (DRRS) [5]. For each type of dependency, we use a binary matrix to show the presence or absence of dependencies between responsibilities, and we use Jaccard binary similarity measurement [5] to calculate the similarity between two vectors in binary matrix.

As many types of dependencies (e.g., DMM) exist between two responsibilities, we assign each dependency type a specific weight to calculate the similarity between two responsibilities (e.g., R_i and R_j) using Formula (1), in which w_k denotes the weight of certain dependency type dep, $Sim_{dep}(R_i, R_j)$ calculates the similarity between two responsibilities with the binary matrix of dependency type dep, and n represents the number of dependency types:

$$Sim(R_i, R_j) = \frac{\sum_{k=1}^{n} w_k Sim_{dep}(R_i, R_j)}{\sum_{k=1}^{n} w_k} \tag{1}$$

b)   Individuals in Pattern Population

To encode the pattern synthesis of a system in a chromosome (i.e., P set), we use integer number for both responsibility and relation part of P set. For responsibility part, each integer number represents the pattern role for the corresponding responsibility. For Layer pattern, the integer number represents the specific layer directly. For instance, in Fig. 2, the responsibility part of P is [0,0,1,0,1], in which only O3 and A2 are in Layer 1, and other responsibilities belong to Layer 0. The maximum value of the integer number equals the total number of responsibilities, which means in an extreme condition, every responsibility belongs to a separate layer. For other patterns (e.g., MVC), the specific value of the integer number represents a specific role in that pattern (e.g., in MVC, 0 for model, 1 for view, and 2 for controller). For relation part, each integer number represents the connector type for corresponding relation. For example, we can use 0 to 6 to represent the 7 different connector types in [10].

4.2   Fitness Function

Many approaches have been proposed to address the CRA problem, and most of them use object-oriented metrics which are based on the CK metrics to define their fitness function. We also use these metrics. Formula (2) shows the fitness function for CRA problem, which is used to maximize the overall cohesion and minimize the overall coupling and complexity of software. The details about the cohesion, coupling, and complexity metrics are introduced respectively in [5].

$$\text{Fitness Score}_{RS} = \text{SoftwareCohesion} - \text{SoftwareCoupling} - \text{SoftwareComplexity} \tag{2}$$

For pattern synthesis, our objective is to minimize the violations of pattern constraints. In our recent work [7], we proposed a definition process for pattern metrics, which is composed of three steps (identify the roles of a pattern, the relations within a pattern, and the domain related metrics). The definition process takes pattern constraints as input, and output a series of pattern metrics. Each metric measures the number of violations for a specific type of pattern constraint. It is worth noting that every pattern has its own metrics, and different metrics have different weights [7]. Hence we can quantify the pattern constraint violations for a specific pattern using Formula (3), in which w_k represents the weight of a specific metric $metric_k$ of the chosen pattern, and n is the number of pattern metrics for that pattern.

$$\text{Fitness Score}_{PS} = \frac{\sum_{k=1}^{n} w_k metric_k}{\sum_{k=1}^{n} w_k} \tag{3}$$

Architects can acquire architecture solutions which consider both CRA and pattern synthesis. In each generation, the Pareto front can be established and updated with these solutions automatically. When the cooperative coevolution procedure terminates, any solution of the Pareto front may be considered as optimal, since it means that no further improvement can be made for an objective without degrading another.

5   Conclusions

Architectural synthesis essentially links the problem to the solution space and plays a key role in architecting process from requirements to initial architecture design. However, due to its complexity, this architecting activity heavily depends on the experience of architects. In this paper, we propose a cooperative coevolution approach to assign class responsibility and synthesize pattern automatically in the pattern-based AS. We formally translate the problem of the automated pattern-based AS into a multi-objective optimization problem. One objective is to maximize the cohesion and minimize the coupling and complexity of solutions for class responsibility assignment, and the other objective is to minimize the pattern constraint violations for the chosen pattern. We then describe the cooperative coevolution approach, including the representation of the problem, and the fitness function to evaluate the solutions. In the next step, we plan to conduct controlled experiments that compare the quality of architecture design between the generated pattern-based AS solutions using our approach and the solutions by human architects based on the same design problems.

References

1. Hofmeister, C., Kruchten, P., Nord, R.L., Obbink, H., Ran, A., America, P.: A general model of software architecture design derived from five industrial approaches. J. Syst. Softw. 80(1), 106–126 (2007)
2. Bass, L., Clements, P., Kazman, R.: Software Architecture in Practice, 3rd edn. Addison-Wesley Professional (2012)
3. Belle, A., El Boussaidi, G., Desrosiers, C., Mili, H.: The layered architecture revisited: Is it an optimization problem? In: SEKE, pp. 344–349 (2013)
4. Bowman, M., Briand, L.C., Labiche, Y.: Solving the class responsibility assignment problem in object-oriented analysis with multi-objective genetic algorithms. IEEE Trans. Softw. Eng. 36(6), 817–837 (2010)
5. Masoud, H., Jalili, S.: A clustering-based model for class responsibility assignment problem in object-oriented analysis. J. Syst. Softw. (2014)
6. Črepinšek, M., Liu, S., Mernik, M.: Exploration and exploitation in evolutionary algorithms: A survey. ACM Comput. Surv. 45(3), 1–33 (2013)
7. Xu, Y., Liang, P.: Automated software architectural synthesis using patterns: A cooperative coevolution approach. In: SEKE, pp. 174–180 (2014)
8. Chidamber, S.R., Kemerer, C.F.: A metrics suite for object oriented design. IEEE Trans. Softw. Eng. 20(6), 476–493 (1994)
9. Buschmann, F., Henney, K., Schmidt, D.C.: Pattern-Oriented Software Architecture: On Patterns and Pattern Languages, 1st edn. Wiley (2007)
10. Mehta, N.R., Medvidovic, N., Phadke, S.: Towards a taxonomy of software connectors. In: ICSE, pp. 178–187 (2000)
11. Harman, M., McMinn, P., de Souza, J.T., Yoo, S.: Search based Software Engineering: Techniques, Taxonomy, Tutorial. In: Meyer, B., Nordio, M. (eds.) Empirical Software Engineering and Verification. LNCS, vol. 7007, pp. 1–59. Springer, Heidelberg (2012)
12. Hasheminejad, S.M.H., Jalili, S.: SCI-GA: Software component identification using genetic algorithm. J. Object Technol. 12(2), 1–34 (2013)

Ontology-Driven Pattern Selection and Matching in Software Design

Tommaso Di Noia, Marina Mongiello, and Eugenio Di Sciascio

Dipartimento di Ingegneria Elettrica e Dell'informazione – Politecnico di Bari
Via E. Orabona, 4 – 70125 BARI, Italy
{firstname.lastname}@poliba.it

Abstract. Design patterns are a meaningful technology for supporting the construction and modeling of software systems. Besides their use is related to the non-functional requirements fulfillment that is also an open challenge in the field of software design. In this work we propose a theoretical approach for modeling relationships and sequences of patterns and for modeling the taxonomy that relates patterns with ensured non-functional requirements for given application contexts. The approach is based on the use of Description Logics for modeling the domain of patterns and for reasoning tasks on the modeled domain. We developed a framework for supporting the architectural modeling phase and used it to verify the effectiveness of both the patterns conceptualization and the use of non-standard reasoning tasks for querying the pattern ontology.

1 Introduction and Motivation

The past two decades have witnessed the explosive growth and diffusion of distributed systems that moved beyond traditional application areas, namely industrial automation, defense and telecommunication to several domains, such as e-commerce, financial services, health care, and so on. Anyway, though the quick and wide diffusion and the increasing ubiquity of distributed systems, their design yet faces a number of challenges. Best practices in developing and refactoring distributed systems mainly refer to the use and implementation of reusable solutions conveyed through design models and patterns that provide verified and tested solutions to given situations in distributed computing. Patterns derive from the experience gathered by designers over the last three or four decades and are based on the idea of finding solutions to given problems by recalling a similar problem that has already been tackled and solved and by adopting that abstract solution to solve the problem at hand [5], [3],[2]. Design patterns are somewhat related to Non-functional requirements [7], that play an important role in the design of a software system. Even though several quality models are available to classify and characterize software quality [9], there is not a formal definition and taxonomy of non-functional requirements, neither an explicit definition of their treatment in software modelling and development.

To this purpose we propose a modeling solution for design patterns and non functional requirements by using an ontology, that is a common terminology supported by semantics and algorithms linked to the reasoning services that allow

P. Avgeriou and U. Zdun (Eds.): ECSA 2014, LNCS 8627, pp. 82–89, 2014.
© Springer International Publishing Switzerland 2014

one to query and retrieve in the given domain also on specific sub-problems. We also implemented a framework to manage the ontology and run reasoning services on it. The framework retrieves a set of patterns compliant with the set that the experience would have proposed and selects the most appropriate solution for the set of specified requirements. The remaining of this paper is organized as follows. Section 2 recalls basics of ontologies and Description Logics. Section 3 describes the approach we use to model the ontology and defines a theoretical algorithm. Section 4 draws the component based model of our framework and presents a case study to explain the proposed idea. Section 5 presents a brief state of the art. Conclusions and future works are drawn in the last section.

2 Ontologies and Languages for Reasoning Tasks

Description Logics (DLs) are a family of formalisms well-established in the field of knowledge representation. In the following we only recap elements we use in the presented approach and refer the interested reader to [1]. DLs are usually endowed with a model-theoretic formal semantics. A semantic *interpretation* is a pair $\mathcal{I} = (\Delta, \cdot^{\mathcal{I}})$, where Δ represents the *domain* and $\cdot^{\mathcal{I}}$ is the *interpretation function*. Basic elements of DLs are *concept names*, *role names* and *individuals*. The interpretation function $\cdot^{\mathcal{I}}$ maps every concept to a subset of Δ, every property to a subset of $\Delta \times \Delta$ and every individual to a single element of Δ. Then, given a concept name CN, a role name R and an individual name a we have: $CN^{\mathcal{I}} \subseteq \Delta^{\mathcal{I}}$, $R^{\mathcal{I}} \subseteq \Delta^{\mathcal{I}} \times \Delta^{\mathcal{I}}$ and $a^{\mathcal{I}} \in \Delta^{\mathcal{I}}$. The symbols $\top$ and $\bot$ are used, respectively, to represent the most generic concept and the most specific concept. Hence their formal semantics correspond to $\top^{\mathcal{I}} = \Delta^{\mathcal{I}}$ and $\bot^{\mathcal{I}} = \emptyset$. Concept names, role names and individual names can be combined to form concept expressions. The ones allowed in our DL are built according to the following syntax represented in the left-hand column of Table 1 where we use CN, R and a to denote a concept name, a role name and an individual name respectively. In the right-hand column of Table 1 the formal semantics of DL formulas is shown. We call TBox (terminological box) a set of axioms of the form $C \sqsubseteq D$ (inclusion) and $C \equiv D$ (definition) with C and D being concept expressions. We say C is subsumed by D w.r.t. $\mathcal{T}$ when $\mathcal{T} \models C \sqsubseteq D$; C is not satisfiable w.r.t. the ontology $\mathcal{T}$ when it is subsumed by the most specific concept $\mathcal{T} \models C \sqsubseteq \bot$. Besides axioms encoding *intensional* information about a knowledge domain, we can also have statements related to *extensional* information, i.e., about individuals and their mutual relationships. In particular we have two possible expressions: $C(a)$ and $R(a, b)$. The former stating that a is an instance of C, the latter saying that b is related to a via R. The set of extensional statements are called ABox (assertional box). A knowledge base is composed by a set a TBox and an ABox.

3 Problem Statement and Approach

Requirements for modeling Software and Architecture Design are made up of Functional Requirements (FRs) and Non-functional Requirements (NRFs). While FRs

Table 1. Syntax and formal semantics of the DL used in our approach

Syntax	Semantics
Concept expressions	
CN	$CN^{\mathcal{I}} \subseteq \Delta^{\mathcal{I}}$
$\top$	$\top^{\mathcal{I}} = \Delta^{\mathcal{I}}$
$\bot$	$\bot^{\mathcal{I}} = \emptyset$
$C \sqcap D$	$(C \sqcap D)^{\mathcal{I}} = C^{\mathcal{I}} \cap D^{\mathcal{I}}$
$C \sqcup D$	$(C \sqcup D)^{\mathcal{I}} = C^{\mathcal{I}} \cup D^{\mathcal{I}}$
$\exists R$	$(\exists R)^{\mathcal{I}} = \{x \in \Delta^{\mathcal{I}} \mid \exists y : (x,y) \in R^{\mathcal{I}}\}$
$\exists R.\{a\}$	$(\exists R.\{a\})^{\mathcal{I}} = \{x \in \Delta^{\mathcal{I}} \mid (x,a) \in R^{\mathcal{I}}, a^{\mathcal{I}} \in \Delta^{\mathcal{I}}\}$
$\forall R.C$	$(\forall R.C)^{\mathcal{I}} = \{x \in \Delta^{\mathcal{I}} \mid \forall y : (x,y) \in R^{\mathcal{I}} \to b \in C^{\mathcal{I}}\}$
$\neg C$	$(\neg C)^{\mathcal{I}} = \Delta^{\mathcal{I}} \setminus C^{\mathcal{I}}$

Syntax	Semantics
TBox	
$C \sqsubseteq D$	$(C \sqsubseteq D)^{\mathcal{I}} = C^{\mathcal{I}} \subseteq D^{\mathcal{I}}$
$C \equiv D$	$(C \sqsubseteq D)^{\mathcal{I}} = C^{\mathcal{I}} = D^{\mathcal{I}}$
ABox	
$C(a)$	$(C(a))^{\mathcal{I}} = a^{\mathcal{I}} \in C^{\mathcal{I}}$
$R(a,b)$	$(R(a,b))^{\mathcal{I}} = (a,b)^{\mathcal{I}} \in R^{\mathcal{I}}$

modeling and definition is strongly supported in software process development a formal and rigorous method to model, implement and validate NFRs is still missing. Anyway, compliance of NFRs should be comprised and validated in the system design and implementation since it would impact on the long-term value of the system. In the set of NFRs a wide subset is made of **quality attributes** that take part in the software quality evaluation and prediction. Nevertheless prediction, evaluation and use of quality attributes is still an open challenge when building software systems. NFRs are related to design patterns that are interrelated in sets of families grouped for problem areas [2]. Each problem area addresses a specific topic related to building distributed systems and intrinsically addresses some specific non-functional requirements or quality attributes that are not explicitly deducible.

Let us now consider the following typical problem of software design: "'*Given a set of requirements define the software design that (better) models the given requirements*"'. Generally its solution is based on empirical solutions depending on the designer's know-how and experience. Hence, the designer is looking for the best design solution given a set of non-functional requirements given some problem areas and/or pattern families related to the system. Providing an answer to the previous question is not trivial as, for example, NFRs may be disjoint with each other and cannot be satisfied at the same time; some families may not contain patterns satisfying some of the non-functional requirements. Moreover, the designer may not be aware of all the patterns available given a NFR or given a pattern family. We propose to model the knowledge related to the patterns domain via a set of Description Logics statements in order to have a high level model of the domain we are dealing with and to represent relations among non-functional properties. Moreover, we can exploit DL reasoning, in particular *instance retrieval* to retrieve patterns satisfying a set of requirements. Patterns are interrelated in sets of families grouped for problem areas [2]. Each problem area addresses a specific topic related to building distributed systems Besides each problem area intrinsically addresses some specific non-functional requirements or quality attributes that are not explicitly elicitable. So when we state

Table 2. Families of patterns

Family	Description	NFRs
Distribution Infrastructure	Patterns regarding middleware	Stability Performance Scalability
Object Interaction	Patterns that manage interaction between objects in standalone programs	Scalability
Application Control	Patterns used to separate interface from applications core functionality	Functionality Maintainability Security
Adaptation and Extension	Patterns to ensure the adaptability of applications and components to specific environments	Adaptability Extensibility Evolution
Resource Management	Patterns used to manage the lifecycle and availability of resource to clients	Quality of service Performance Scalability Flexibility Availability Reliability Portability Security

that a pattern belongs to a *family* we assume that the pattern could inherit non-functional requirements of that family, and then we state that a design pattern has a given set of non-functional requirements. In Table 2 we summarize the scope of some families and a number of nonfunctional requirements that each of them ensures: a set of non-functional requirements can be intrinsically considered inside each problem area. The set of non-functional requirements that we consider belongs to two international quality models of software product: FURPS [6] and ISO-IEC9126 [8]. The latter is a standard that defines a quality model based on six main features: *functionality, reliability, usability, efficiency, maintainability, portability* while FURPS, developed by Robert Grady at Hewlett Packard, is an acronym for: *F*unctionality, *U*sability, *U*sability, *P*erformance, *S*upportability. In order to encode all the information related to non-functional requirements, patterns and corresponding families we need a formalization of the domain knowledge. The ontology we use to cope with this task can be seen as composed by two main modules: the one describing at a very high level the connections between patterns and families, the other modeling connections between patterns and NFRs. The model is depicted in Figure 1 and its formal definition is encoded in DL as:

- $\exists isInFamily \sqsubseteq Software\_design\_pattern$
- $\top \sqsubseteq \forall isInFamily.Families$
- $\exists nFR \sqsubseteq Software\_design\_pattern$
- $\top \sqsubseteq \forall nFR.Non\text{-}functional\_requirement$

Please note that the structure of the high level ontology we model makes it possible to easily extend it to deal also with other elements, e.g, functional requirements. Given the ontology we can state explicit facts about the description of a pattern in terms of pattern family it belongs to and non-functional requirements it guarantees.

Fig. 1. A graphical representation of our high-level ontology

Software_design_pattern(adapter_pattern), *Families(adaptation_extension)*,
Non-functional_requirement(adaptability), *Non-functional_requirement*
(portability),
Non-functional_requirement(stability), *nFR(adapter_pattern, portability)*,
isInFamily(adapter_pattern, adaptation_extension)
Besides the modelling of the relations represented in Figure 1, we use DL language also to explicitly model relations between NFRs in the TBox. Consider the non-functional requirements *portability, adaptability, stability* as previously defined. With respect to our ontology they are defined as instances (individuals) of the class *Non-functional_requirement*. Now we need to formally represent relations between these individuals to model, for instance, interactions between non-functional requirements. An example of mutual relation between NFRs is the one between *portability* and *adaptability*. Indeed the former implies the latter. The above statement can be encoded with the Description Logics axiom
$\exists nFR.\{portability\} \sqsubseteq \exists nFR.\{adaptability\}$
We also know that a system cannot be *adaptable* and *stable* at the same time. Hence, if a pattern guarantees *adaptability* it cannot guarantees also *stability*. We encode such disjoint relations with the following DL statement
$\exists nFR.\{stability\} \sqsubseteq \neg\exists nFR.\{adaptability\}$
Given the above formulation, if we are looking for the patterns that guarantee *adaptability* and that belong to the *adaptation and extension* family we retrieve all the individual instantiating the formula:
$SoftwareDesignPattern \sqcap \exists nFR.\{adaptability\} \sqcap \exists isInFamily.\{adaptation\_$
extension}
Based on all the statements previously introduced we will get *adapter_pattern*. Indeed, by using automated reasoning we see that this pattern also guarantees *adaptability*. Summing up, the ABox of the knowledge base we built is composed by a set statements of the form:

- *Software_design_pattern(p)*
- *Families(f)*
- *Non-functional_requirement(nfr)*
- *isInFamily(p, f)*
- *nFR(p, nfr)*

where *p*, *f* and *nfr* are individuals representing a pattern, a family of patterns and a non-functional requirement respectively. On the other side, the TBox contains statements of the following two types:

- $\exists nFR.\{a\} \sqsubseteq \exists nFR.\{b\}$
- $\exists nFR.\{c\} \sqsubseteq \neg\exists nFR.\{d\}$

where *a, b, c, d* are instances of the class *Non-functional_requirement*.

Based on this modelling of the ABox and of the TBox, we may retrieve instances of concept expressions in the form:
$SoftwareDesignPattern \sqcap (\exists nFR.\{a\} \sqcup \exists nFR.\{b\} \sqcup \ldots \sqcup \exists nFR.\{c\} \sqcup \exists nFR.\{d\})$
$\sqcap (\exists isInFamily.\{x\} \sqcup \exists isInFamily.\{y\} \sqcup \ldots \sqcup \exists isInFamily.\{z\} \sqcup \exists isInFamily.$
$\{t\})$ with x, y, z, t being instances of the class $Families$. The previous general formula allows to look for patterns that satisfy one or more NFRs and belong to one or more family patterns. Besides instance retrieval tasks, we can use automated reasoning also to check the *consistency* of the information encoded in the knowledge base and, in case of inconsistency provide a possible explanation [4] useful for knowledge revision. With respect to the statements encoded so far, we see that a pattern that satisfies both *portability* and *stability* is not consistent. Hence, while populating the knowledge base, it would be nice to have a service that catches the inconsistency and provides ad explanation for it. A procedure for consistency checking and explanation generation is provided in Algorithm 1. It computes the transitive closure $\mathcal{TR}$ of a pattern description p only with respect to the information related to non-functional requirements ($nFR : s_i$). Then, by looking at the elements available $\mathcal{TR}$ it checks if two or more NFRs are conflicting with each others and adds them to the set $\mathcal{EXP}$ (for explanation). Algorithm 1 uses the recursive function described in Algorithm 2 to compute the transitive closure of a pattern description.

Data: A pattern description p and a TBox $\mathcal{T}$
Result: The set of inconsistent sub-parts of p with the inconsistency explanation: $\mathcal{EXP}$
1 $\mathcal{TC} = \emptyset$;
2 $\mathcal{EXP} = \emptyset$;
3 **foreach** $nFR : s_i \in p$ **do**
4      $\mathcal{TC} = \mathcal{TC} \cup \texttt{transitiveClosure}(\exists nFR.\{s_i\}, \exists nFR.\{s_i\}, \mathcal{T})$;
5 **end**
6 **foreach** $(\langle \exists nFR.\{x\}, \exists nFR.\{s_k\}\rangle, \langle \neg(\exists nFR.\{x\}), \exists nFR.\{s_j\}\rangle) \in \mathcal{TC} \times \mathcal{TC}$, with $k \neq j$ **do**
7      $\mathcal{EXP} = (\langle \exists nFR.\{x\}, \exists nFR.\{s_k\}\rangle, \langle \neg(\exists nFR.\{x\}), \exists nFR.\{s_j\}\rangle)$;
8 **end**
9 **foreach** $(\langle \neg(\exists nFR.\{x\}), \exists nFR.\{s_k\}\rangle, \langle \exists nFR.\{x\}, \exists nFR.\{s_j\}\rangle) \in \mathcal{TC} \times \mathcal{TC}$, with $k \neq j$ **do**
10     $\mathcal{EXP} = (\langle \neg(\exists nFR.\{x\}), \exists nFR.\{s_k\}\rangle, \langle \exists nFR.\{x\}, \exists nFR.\{s_j\}\rangle)$;
11 **end**

Algorithm 1. Inconsistency detection and explanation in a pattern description.

4   Framework Overview and System Evaluation

In this section we briefly expose the main functionalities of our framework. Currently the framework supports two main functionalities: *insertion* of a new pattern or of a new non functional requirement and *search* of patterns or of non functional requirements. The web based framework includes the Pellet[1] reasoner that uses standard services and a microreasoner that implements the algorithm of inconsistency explanation.

As an example scenario let us consider in a Security Information and Event Monitoring System (SIEM), the problem of designing a subsystem able to provide security services, like authentication and access control, and able to adapt to the rapidly changing contexts of the spaces. The system evaluates events and

---

[1] http://http://clarkparsia.com/pellet/

```
 1  Function transitiveClosure(gen, seed, T)is
        Data: A piece of a pattern description of the form ∃R.{s} (seed) and an expression of
              the form ∃R.{x} or ¬∃R.{x} (gen) generated starting from seed via the set of
              axioms composing the TBox T.
        Result: The transitive closure of seed.
 2      switch gen do
 3          case ∃R.{x}
 4              if ∃R.{x} ⊑ ∃R.{y} ∈ T then
 5                  |  return {⟨∃R.{x}, ∃R.{s}⟩}∪ transitiveClosure(∃R.{y}, ∃R.{s}, T);
 6              end
 7              if ∃R.{x} ⊑ ¬(∃R.{y}) ∈ T or ∃R.{y} ⊑ ¬(∃R.{x}) ∈ T then
 8                  |  return {⟨∃R.{x}, ∃R.{s}⟩}∪ transitiveClosure(¬(∃R.{y}), ∃R.{s}, T);
 9              end
10              return {⟨∃R.{x}, ∃R.{s}⟩};
11          end
12          case ¬(∃R.{x})
13              if ∃R.{y} ⊑ ∃R.{x} ∈ T then
14                  |  return {⟨¬(∃R.{x}), ∃R.{s}⟩}∪ transitiveClosure(¬(∃R.{y}), ∃R.{s},
                       |  T);
15              end
16              return {⟨¬(∃R.{x}), ∃R.{s}⟩};
17          end
18      endsw
19  end
```

Algorithm 2. Computation of the transitive closure of a pattern description

security policies based on the context. We refer to an *adaptive authentication* subsystem that when the user logs in, takes into account a number of context parameters (IP and place, time and date, etc..) and decide whether or not to authenticate the user and the mechanism by which to authenticate (more or less secure mechanism). A non functional requirement here should be clearly adaptability. The most appropriate architectural styles for realizing adaptability are in the family of "Adaptation and Extension"', as the Adapter pattern. Besides, patterns belonging to others families achieve other functionalities required by the system and fulfill other non functional requirements. Other properties that the system should provide are stability, availability and reliability – hence dependability – and portability. The decision problem is that of selecting the strategy that properly considers the right balance between attributes. In fact dynamic adaptation can hamper both dependability, and stability hence the modeled architecture must be the result of the best balancing between those parameters. So the method should select the pattern or the combination of patterns that provides the right balancing of the trade-off between stability and adaptability, and between adaptability and dependability. Portability is instead implied by adaptability.

To manage the interprocesses communication, let us consider patterns of the "Distribution infrastructure" family: styles that require direct dependencies among the components such as virtual machines or distributed objects can hamper adaptability, so we choose patterns that support event-based interaction such as publish-subscribe and implicit invocation.

Patterns useful for implementing *publish-subscribe* or *implicit invocation* can be respectively Broker and Observer. Now, when implementing a Broker for a component based system, we try to decouple a component from the technical details of its environment. In the described scenario we further need to integrate components into diverse application deployment scenarios and execute them on various system platforms without explicit programmer intervention. Also having different ways of accessing to system resources and having different security policies we need to initialize and provide a run-time context for the component. This is a typical environment for the application of Container pattern. Container defines operations that enable component objects to access the common middleware services such as persistence, event notification, security. Container belongs to "Resource Management" family that has reliability, availability and security as NFRs, so ensures dependability. Observer inherits security as NFR from the "Application Control" family.

5   Conclusion and Future Work

In this paper we introduce a formal model to relate non-functional requirements and design patterns in a DL ontology. The scope of the ontology is to provide a formal representation of the relations among design areas, non-functional requirements and design patterns and to reason with such a representation to help the designer during the selection of the right set of patterns that best match the initial requirements. We are currently performing extensive experiments on a structured benchmark to test the framework functionalities and performance on simple and on composable schemes also in more advanced architectural environments.

References

1. Baader, F., Calvanese, D., McGuinness, D.L., Nardi, D., Patel-Schneider, P.F. (eds.): The Description Logic Handbook: Theory, Implementation, and Applications. Cambridge University Press (2003)
2. Buschmann, F., Henney, K., Schmidt, D.C.: Pattern-oriented software architecture: A pattern language for distributed computing, vol. 4 (2007)
3. Buschmann, F., Meunier, R., Rohnert, H., Sommerlad, P., Stal, M.: Pattern-oriented software architecture: A system of patterns. John Wiley & Sons, Inc., New York (1996)
4. Di Noia, T., Di Sciascio, E., Donini, F.M.: Semantic Matchmaking as Non-Monotonic Reasoning: A Description Logic Approach. Journal of Artificial Intelligence Research 16, 209–257 (2006)
5. Gamma, E., Helm, R., Johnson, R., Vlissides, J.: Design patterns: Elements of reusable object-oriented software. Pearson Education (1994)
6. Grady, R.B.: Successfully applying software metrics. Computer 27(9), 18–25 (1994)
7. Gross, D., Yu, E.: From non-functional requirements to design through patterns. Requirements Engineering 6(1), 18–36 (2001)
8. ISO/IEC. Software product evaluation: Quality characteristics and guidelines for their use (1991)
9. Naragani, D.P., Uniyal, P.: Comparative analysis of software quality models. International Journal of Computer Science and Management Research 2(3) (2013)

Towards an Improved Stakeholder Management
for Software Reference Architectures

Samuil Angelov[1] and Rich Hilliard[2]

[1] Software Engineering, Fontys University of Applied Sciences, The Netherlands
s.angelov@fontys.nl
[2] Consulting software systems architect, USA
r.hilliard@computer.org

Abstract. A recent survey on software reference architectures (RA) indicates their widespread usage. Among the leading problems when designing and using RA, practitioners point to various aspects of stakeholder management (e.g., stakeholder identification, involvement). In this paper, we identify and analyze issues that lie at the basis of the problems reported in stakeholder management, with a goal to improve the state of the practice.

Keywords: Reference architecture, stakeholder management and identification.

1 Introduction

Software reference architectures have emerged as reusable resources for creating software architectures within a domain of application [1]. Definitions for the term software reference architecture (RA) and software architectures of individual systems (SA) are discussed in [1], [2]. RA are used to lower costs, improve software quality, improve communications, etc. While RA have an indisputable role in the software community, practitioners indicate facing a substantial number of problems when designing and using RA [3]. Among the leading problems reported during design are the identification and involvement of stakeholders and the dissemination of the RA to the stakeholders for usage. Problems reported during usage of RA are poor quality and lack of clear benefits for the stakeholders [3], which indicate that stakeholder management was not properly performed during the RA design. We conclude that stakeholder management in RA is a problem that needs to be investigated.

Literature does not address particular methods for stakeholder management for RA and knowledge from the design of system architectures must be applied to cases of RA. In this paper, we show that RA exhibit a number of specifics that existing work on stakeholder management in system architectures does not address. In Sections 2 and 3, we review the literature on stakeholders and stakeholder management and analyze the results from our literature overview, and build a model that we use for structuring and positioning our research. In Section 4, we analyze RA and identify their specifics compared to SA from the perspective of stakeholder management. In Section 5, we validate our findings and draw final conclusions.

P. Avgeriou and U. Zdun (Eds.): ECSA 2014, LNCS 8627, pp. 90–97, 2014.

2   Literature Review

We start our literature review with an overview of the domain of organizational science, as it sets the fundaments of the stakeholder notion. Next, we discuss the software engineering and software architecting domains.

2.1   Stakeholders in Organization Management

Definitions of "Stakeholder". Freeman [4] defines a stakeholder in an organization as "any group or individual who can affect or is affected by the achievement of the organization's objectives". Mitchell *et al.* summarize definitions found in the organizational literature until 1997 [5] and categorize them as either broad [4] or narrow (based on various "relevance properties" an entity may have for an organization). They point out that the notion of a "stake" is the leading one in defining who can be a stakeholder. Project management methods (e.g., PRINCE2, PMI) naturally focus on the relationship between entities and a project [6]. An overview of the historical development of the stakeholder concept is provided in [7].

Stakeholder Categories and Methods. In [5], a method for stakeholder identification is proposed. The method is based on three attributes: power, legitimacy and urgency. Possession of one or more of these attributes indicates a stakeholder. Classes of stakeholders are defined on the basis of combinations of the three attributes. The method is applied in a number of case studies (e.g., in [8]). Two approaches for stakeholder identification are discussed in [9]. In the first approach, named the *relationship approach*, stakeholders are identified on the basis of their relations with the organization. The types of relations which serve as a basis for the identification of stakeholders are defined to be voluntarism, mutual benefit, and community membership. In the second approach, named the *assignment approach*, the relations are based on moral considerations. The classification scheme in [10] identifies two classes of stakeholders, *actively involved* and *passively involved*. A stakeholders management process model is proposed in [7]. Stakeholder identification, defined as the first step in this process model, is based on the stakeholder categorization scheme proposed in [11], where primary (critical for the organization's survival), secondary (not critical), and public (infrastructure and legislation framework providers) types of stakeholders are defined. Vos and Achterkamp [10] argue that in addition to the stakeholder classification, stakeholder identification should be augmented with procedural guidelines that define how a stakeholder classification scheme should be applied to identify actual stakeholders and that classification schemes should be *context specific*, shifting the focus from the organization at-large to specific types of projects. In [7], [10] references to other stakeholder classification schemes are provided.

2.2   Stakeholders in Software Engineering

Definitions of "Stakeholder". Within software engineering, the focus on stakeholders pertains to requirements definition: "Requirements are the basis for every project, defining what the stakeholders (...) in a potential new system need from it" [12].

The authors of [13] provide references to stakeholder definitions. According to [14], a *project* stakeholder is "someone who gains or loses (…) as a result of that project".

In software architecting, a *software system* stakeholder is an "individual, team, or organization (or classes thereof) with interests in, or concerns relative to, a system" [15][1]. Stakeholders and their concerns drive architecture-related decisions, in particular architecture representation [16]. Rozanski and Woods [17], following IEEE Std 1471:2000 [15], define a stakeholder in a *software architecture* as "a person, group, or entity with an interest in or concern about the realization of the architecture".

Stakeholder Categories and Methods. Stakeholder categorization has been seen as the core of stakeholder identification and management in software engineering. Efforts to categorize stakeholders are reported for example in [18], [19], [17], [20]. McManus notes that "stakeholder involvement is generally context-specific; what works in one situation may not be appropriate in another" [21]. He classifies stakeholders into *primary*, *secondary*, *external*, and *extended*. Preis *et al.* propose a stakeholder classification framework based on system science techniques [22]. The stakeholders are divided into two classes: *goal oriented* and *means oriented*. A conceptual summary of classifications schemes in the literature is provided in [23].

A number of efforts defining methods for stakeholder identification exist. Sharp *et al.* [13] propose an approach for identification of stakeholders of a software system based on categorizing the interactions in a project between the stakeholders. The stakeholders are typed as *baseline*, *satellite*, *client* and *supplier* stakeholders. Baseline stakeholders (users, developers, legislators and decision-makers) are the starting point from which stakeholders of the other types are identified. In [14], an approach for the stakeholder identification and managing their involvement is proposed. The stakeholder classification scheme is based on the "onion model", where stakeholders may take different positions depending on how closely they are related to the system (at the center of the onion). MacManus also pays attention to the stakeholders' involvement [21]. He notes that stakeholder involvement is based on the central goal and project objectives. The work in [23] focuses on stakeholder identification in the development projects for inter-organizational systems.

2.3   Stakeholders in Reference Architectures

In [1], the stakeholders are classified based on the number of RA receiving organizations, their role in the RA design process, and the type of organization they represent. In a case study made of five Dutch municipalities [24], Galster *et al.* discuss two stakeholder categories: the customers and software vendors who are applying RA. Martínez-Fernández *et al.* [25] consider RA in a specific context: a software consultancy company defining for their clients RA and define two types of stakeholders: the RA team (software architects and architecture developers) and "concrete software architecture teams" (the application builders). Cloutier *et al.* [26] mention stakeholders of RA to be ranging from engineers to business managers and customers. Notably, one of their conclusions is that further research on the stakeholders of RA is needed.

---

[1] The stakeholder concept is treated in a broader sense in [8] and [9].

3   An Approach for RA Stakeholder Analysis

From the literature overview, it can be observed that the term "stakes" presents several ambiguities and that authors search for substitute terminology (e.g., "affect", "interest"). We use the definition from [15]: "A *stakeholder* of a *P* is an individual, team, organization, or classes thereof, with an *interest* in *P*". With respect to the issues at stake, in organizational sciences the broad notion of "organization" (or "projects" within it) is seen as the basic issue. In software engineering the issues at stakes lie in the software system [16], [27], or in the project for its creation [14], [18]. The precise issue at stake, however, is often weakly defined. In architecting, the focus lies on identifying *all stakeholders* whose concerns will influence the architecture [16]. Most efforts focus on providing one or a combination of categorization schemes that facilitate stakeholder identification. Specifically for RA, the stakeholder categories are defined only for specific contexts [24], [28] or in an informal manner [1].

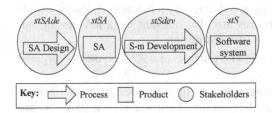

Fig. 1. Areas of stakes in software system design and development

Fig. 2. Relationship between the stakeholder sets [Venn diagram]

Based on our observations from the literature review, we define a model in which we ascribe to each major sub-process and product of the notional software development cycle an "area" with its stakeholders (see Fig. 1). The "stakeholder areas" cover all the entities with an interest in the specific process or product. The "system stakeholders" (*stS*) include stakeholders with developmental, technological, business, etc. influences (as defined in [16]). The "development process stakeholders" (*stSdev*) are the stakeholders of the development process. The "SA design stakeholders" (*stSAde*) are those with concerns about the design process (architects, project leaders, project managers, etc.). Obviously, an entity may be a stakeholder in several of the stakeholder areas (see Fig. 2). The model in Fig. 1 is inspired by the approach of [5] and our observation that the issues at stake need to be well-defined – we focus on the elements of a project, i.e., main processes and products.

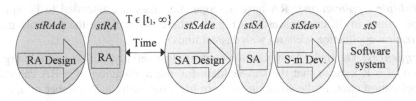

Fig. 3. Areas of stakes in the case of RA, usage decoupled (S_2)

The process of elaborating a reference architecture is conceptually comparable to the process of SA elaboration. Therefore, we extend the initial model with the corresponding RA sub-process and product (see Fig. 3, time gap is explained in Section 4). The stakeholders of the RA design process (*stRAde*) and the RA (*stRA*) are the new elements in the scenario and are the focus of our research. We also investigate if stakeholder management in the other elements changes when a RA is used.

4   Specifics of RA in Stakeholder Management

In this section, we identify the specifics (S_i) of stakeholder management for RA contrasted with SA. The set of specifics was defined by studying and analyzing publications on RA (e.g., [2], [3], [25], [26], [28], [29]).

Looking at the types of purposes and goals of a RA design discussed in [3], [26], [28], (e.g., "decrease development costs", "speed up projects", "standardization"), we observe that they are predominantly stemming from *stSAde* and *stSdev*. In the case of SA, the purposes and goals of architecting are defined by a balance of design, development, and system drivers. These concerns are also relevant for a RA design, but they are not defining the purpose and goals of a RA design.

S_1 *(New concerns, New dominant drivers):* The purpose of a RA is typically targeted towards *stSAde* and *stSdev*.

Consequences: The incentives for getting involved in a RA design project for requirements elicitation and architecture evaluation may be lower for the *stSA* who are neither *stSAde* nor *stSdev*. At the same time, the *stSAde* and SA-interested part of the *stSdev* become the main beneficiaries of the effort. For the *stSAde*, this implies changes in their roles, as they become *consumers* of the effort, while previously their role was in *producing* a SA. Furthermore, the new purposes require the involvement of new (not typical for SA) *stRA*. For example, standardization purposes can lead to the introduction of *standardization organizations* [29]. Cost reduction and project efficiency concerns may arise from the interests of higher management levels (e.g., *program managers, governance bodies*) and *enterprise architects*.

S_2 *(Usage Decoupled):* The RA design and its usage may be separated with a substantial period of time, often unknown at design-time (see Fig. 3). In certain scenarios, a RA may be defined without any specific planned usages.

Consequences: The decoupling of usage from design means that concerns that need to be reflected in the RA will come from stakeholders not seeing directly the results of their inputs. This allows us to distinguish *actual* (where RA usage is planned) and *potential stRA* (where the RA usage is not planned). Involvement and retention of the *potential stRA* may be difficult due to insufficient motivation.

S_3 *(Multiple Applications):* RA have a scope, i.e., they are intended to be applied multiple times in different cases (see Fig. 4, where we indicate the possible multi-organization application scenario with dashed lines).

Consequences: The multiple application contexts (potentially, across multiple organizations) of a RA mean that the stakeholders for the application of a RA can differ per application case. In the situations of very high (or unlimited) number of application contexts, across multiple organizations, not all stakeholders can be involved

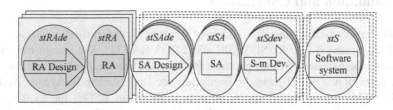

Fig. 4. Multiple applications of RA (S₃) and design organizations (S₄)

and choices need to be made. To indicate the multiple application contexts, we refer to the stakeholders of an eventual system *i* targeted by a RA as *stS_i, stSdev_i, stSA_i, stSAde_i*.

S_4 (Cross-organizational design): The design of RA can be of cross-organizational nature, i.e., a RA may be designed by several, independent organizations (see Fig. 4).

Consequences: A cross-organizational effort puts the organizations involved in a RA design in a complex communication and management situation. Different organizations may have different policies, rules, and strategies, leading potentially to conflicts with the concerns of other stakeholders and the selection of the design organizations is challenging. To tackle these problems a *coordination (management) body* of some type may be introduced.

S_5 (Long-life): A RA is an investment. It is intended to be applied over a period of time in which the initial investment will pay out. A RA has a life beyond the life of individual systems.

Consequences: The longer life of RA means that the *stRAde* need to remain active after the initial design and ensure RA evolution for the time the RA is intended to be maintained (leading to a more complicated management of the *stRAde* involvement).

S_6 (Abstract): Because RA are to be applied in multiple contexts, they are typically defined at a higher level of abstraction, where specific choices are deferred.

Consequences: RA may be harder to understand, use, and communicate due to this increased abstractness. This may lead to an inability to (properly) apply a RA by its users, frustration, criticism, etc. This may be the cause for stakeholders abandoning or not (fully) engaging in RA application projects.

The specifics identified by us have not been addressed in the software engineering and architecting literature on stakeholder management reviewed in Sections 2.2 and 2.3. Based on the consequences of the specifics, we have made a number of observations on the *stRA* and *stRAde*, which we summarize in Table 1.

Table 1. Observations on the stakeholders of RA

Stakeholders of RA	Source
A *stRAde* is a *stRA*.	definition
The *stSA_i* and *stSAde_i* of an eventual system *i* targeted by the RA are *potential stRA*.	S₁, S₂, S₃
For RA with efficiency goals, higher management roles (program managers, enterprise architects) are *stRA*. For RA with standardization goals, standardization bodies are *stRA*.	S₁
For *stRAde* from multiple organizations, a coordination body may be a *stRAde*.	S₄
stRAde may be *stSAde_i* in order to obtain feedback on the RA and evolve it.	S₅

5   Validation and Conclusions

As initial steps in establishing the validity of the specifics identified, we have studied two well-documented RA: RASDS [30] and ESDS RA [31]. We sought evidence to demonstrate the existence of the specifics. Both the Reference Architecture for Space Data Systems (RASDS) [30] and the Earth Science Data System Reference Architecture ESDS [31] exemplify all specifics, except for S_4 in ESDS due to the single-organization application scope of the RA. Next, we validated the specifics for completeness. Our approach is to study "framework papers" that define the fundaments of RA and which were not used in our initial analysis. We have considered [26] and [32] for this purpose, where [26] focuses on the RA purposes, contexts, and processes and [32] on the RA elements making them complimentary in covering the RA landscape. As a result from this step, we have identified the omission of the "evolution" of RA, which has led to the addition of S_5 to our list of specifics.

Therefore we conclude that the six specifics of RA identified do exist. Their critical role for stakeholder management can be traced back in their relation to the problems reported in [3]. Existing literature on stakeholder management in system architecting does not provide direct solutions for these specifics. We conclude that a dedicated method for stakeholder management for RA is desired. The results presented in this paper are a first step towards such a method.

References

1. Angelov, S., Grefen, P., Greefhorst, D.: A Framework for Analysis and Design of Software Reference Architectures. Inf. and Soft. Technology 54(4), 417–431 (2012)
2. Angelov, S., Trienekens, J.J.M., Grefen, P.: Towards a Method for the Evaluation of Reference Architectures: Experiences from a Case. In: Morrison, R., Balasubramaniam, D., Falkner, K. (eds.) ECSA 2008. LNCS, vol. 5292, pp. 225–240. Springer, Heidelberg (2008)
3. Angelov, S., Trienekens, J., Kusters, R.: Software Reference Architectures - Exploring Their Usage and Design in Practice. In: Drira, K. (ed.) ECSA 2013. LNCS, vol. 7957, pp. 17–24. Springer, Heidelberg (2013)
4. Freeman, R.E.: Strategic Management: A Stakeholder Approach. Pitman, Boston (1984)
5. Mitchell, R., Agle, B., Wood, D.: Toward a Theory of Stakeholder Identification and Salience: Defining the Principle of Who and What Really Counts. Academy of Management Review 22(4), 853–886 (1997)
6. Project Management Institute, A Guide to the Project Management Body of Knowledge (PMBOK Guide), 4th ed. Project Management Institute Inc., Pennsylvania (2008)
7. Preble, J.: Toward a Comprehensive Model of Stakeholder Management. Business and Society Review 10(4), 407–431 (2005)
8. Parent, M., Deephouse, D.: A Case Study of Stakeholder Identification and Prioritization by Managers. Journal of Business Ethics 75, 1–23 (2007)
9. Cappelen, A.: Two Approaches to Stakeholder Identification. Ethics and Economics 2(2), 1–9 (2004)
10. Vos, J., Achterkamp, M.: Stakeholder Identification in Innovation Projects - Going Beyond Classification. European J. of Innovation Management 9(2), 161–177 (2006)

11. Clarkson, M.: A Stakeholder Framework for Analyzing and Evaluating Corporate Social Performance. Academy of Management Review 20, 65–91 (1995)
12. Hull, E., Jackson, K., Dick, J.: Requirements Engineering, 3rd edn. Springer (2011)
13. Sharp, H., Finkelstein, A., Galal, G.: Stakeholder Identification in the Requirements Engineering Process. In: Proceedings of the Tenth International Workshop on Database and Expert Systems Applications. IEEE Computer Society (1999)
14. Alexander, I., Robertson, S.: Understanding Project Sociology by Modeling Stakeholders. IEEE Software 21(1), 23–27 (2004)
15. IEEE: Recommended Practice for Architectural Description of Software-Intensive Systems.Std 1471-2000. IEEE (2000)
16. ISO/IEC/IEEE: Systems and software engineering —Architecture description. 42010, ISO/IEC/IEEE (2011)
17. Rozanski, N., Woods, E.: Software Systems Architecture: Working With Stakeholders Using Viewpoints and Perspectives. Addison-Wesley Professional (2005)
18. Cotterell, M., Hughes, B.: Software Project Management. Int. Thomson Publishing (1995)
19. Newman, W., Lamming, M.: Interactive System Design. Addison-Wesley (1995)
20. Clements, P., Kazman, R., Klein, M.: Evaluating Software Architectures: Methods and Case Studies. Addison-Wesley (2002)
21. McManus, J.: A Stakeholder Perspective within Software Engineering Projects. In: Proceedings of the 2004 IEEE International I Engineering Management Conference, vol. 2, pp. 880–884. IEEE (2004)
22. Preiss, O., Wegmann, A.: Stakeholder Discovery and Classification Based on Systems Science Principles. In: Proceedings of the Second Asia-Pacific Conference on Quality Software, pp. 194–198. IEEE (2001)
23. Ballejos, L., Montagna, J.: Method for Stakeholder Identification in Interorganizational Environments. Requirements Eng. 13, 281–297 (2008)
24. Galster, M., Avgeriou, P., Tofan, D.: Constraints for the Design of Variability-Intensive Service-Oriented Reference Architectures – An Industrial Case Study. Information and Software Technology 55(2), 428–441 (2013)
25. Martínez-Fernández, S., Ameller, D., Ayala, C., Franch, X., Terradellas, X.: Conducting Empirical Studies on Reference Architectures in IT Consulting Firms. UPC (2012)
26. Cloutier, R., et al.: The Concept of Reference Architectures. Systems Engineering 13(1), 14–27 (2010)
27. Conger, S.: The New Software Engineering. International Thomson Publishing (1994)
28. Muller, G.: A Reference Architecture Primer (2008)
29. Angelov, S., Grefen, P., Greefhorst, D.: A Classification of Software Reference Architectures: Analyzing their Success and Effectiveness. In: Joint Working IEEE/IFIP Conference on Software Architecture, 2009 & European Conference on Software Architecture, WICSA/ECSA 2009, September 14-17, pp. 141–150. IEEE, Cambridge (2009)
30. CCSDS: CCSDS Recommended Practice - Reference Architecture for Space Data Systems. CCSDS, NASA (2008)
31. ESDS Reference Architecture Working Group: ESDS Reference Architecture for the Decadal Survey Era. NASA ESDS Reference Architecture v1.0, NASA (2011)
32. Nakagawa, E., Oquendo, F., Becker, M.: RAModel: A Reference Model for Reference Architectures. In: SPLC 2011 Proceedings of the 15th International Software Product Line Conference, vol. 2(28). IEEE Computer Society (2012)

RA-Ubi: A Reference Architecture for Ubiquitous Computing

Carlos Alberto Machado[1,2], Eduardo Silva[2], Thais Batista[2], Jair Leite[2],
and Elisa Nakagawa[3]

[1] Federal University of Paraíba, João Pessoa, PB, Brazil
[2] Federal University of Rio Grande do Norte, Natal, RN, Brazil
[3] University of São Paulo, São Carlos, SP, Brazil
carlos@ccen.ufpb.br, eduardoafs@ppgsc.ufrn.br,
{thais,jair}@ufrn.br, elisa@icmc.usp.br

Abstract. Successful ubiquitous systems need to integrate several underlying technologies including different operating systems, advanced middleware, several Internet protocols, sensors, actuators, I/O drivers and many others elements. This scenario means that ubiquitous systems software should cope with different kinds of software/hardware components, programming languages, and interaction protocols. In order to easy software development in this heterogeneous context, software architecture elements provide high abstractions that hide the details of specific platforms. However, a clear and common understanding of the elements that compose a ubiquitous system architecture and their relationship is still missing. Reference Architectures have been used to provide a common ground and to give directions for the construction of software architectures for different classes of systems. In this paper, we propose RA-Ubi, a reference architecture for ubiquitous systems that was build based on PROSA-SA, a process for the establishment of new reference architectures. Following PROSA-SA's steps, RA-Ubi defines the architectural requirements of ubiquitous systems by following the literature about this subject, applying literature systematic review technique. As main results, we present RA-Ubi reference architecture detailing the role of each element and their relationships.

Keywords: Software architecture, reference architecture, ubiquitous computing.

1   Introduction

Ubiquitous Computing (UC) encompasses sensor-instrumented environments often endowed with wireless network interfaces, in which devices, software agents, and services are integrated in a seamless, transparent way and cooperate to meet high-level goals for satisfying human users. This computational power distribution provides new functionality through support of personalized services and omnipresent applications. Advances in technology have made ubiquitous computing permeate our daily lives, even if we are not always aware of it. There are many challenges in ubiquitous computing [4]: (i) to handle the various types of events, such as application

P. Avgeriou and U. Zdun (Eds.): ECSA 2014, LNCS 8627, pp. 98–105, 2014.

events, change of environment, data exchange events, and domain-specific events, (ii) to adapt the system at runtime to support service discovering and location sensing, (iii) to integrate various types of computational elements, such as smartphones, sensors, actuators, and (iv) to manage their communications, including mobility and security issues. Solutions to those problems are not trivial and may involve various cooperating elements to support the system operation.

This heterogeneous, multi-faced nature hampers the design and implementation of ubiquitous systems, and has increased the cost of building them. In order to systematically organize the main building blocks of a ubiquitous system, their responsibilities, and their interactions, providing a clear and common understanding of the architecture of this domain, a reference architecture (RA) [2] can be quite useful. As ubiquitous systems are becoming commonplace in our daily life, it is essential to provide a reference architecture to capture the essence of this important class of system and to ensure standardization and interoperability between them. We envision that the future of software architecture involves the definition of reference architectures to several domains, mainly for those that encompass long-lasting and heterogeneous systems. Considering the ubiquitous system domain, their critical aspects regarding complexity and interoperability, demands a reference architecture for both architectural definition and evolution of ubiquitous systems. Interoperability, one of the most essential requirements of ubiquitous systems, can be achieved by a systematic and disciplined architecture-centric development approach.

In this paper we present RA-Ubi, a reference architecture for ubiquitous systems. It was built in a systematic manner, following the ProSA-SA [3] process for the establishment of new reference architectures. This process defines four basic steps that involve literature reviews, requirements elicitation, development of the RA, and evaluation. Regarding to the evaluation process, we evaluated RA-Ubi by comparing its elements with the elements of existing concrete ubiquitous systems. As main results, we have observed that RA-Ubi can be considered an important contribution to the UC area, by intending to support Ubiquitous Systems development.

This paper is structured as follows. Section 2 discusses the background on ubiquitous computing, reference architecture, and the related work. Section 3 presents RA-Ubi. Section 4 contains the final remarks.

2   Background and Related Work

2.1   Ubiquitous Computing

According to Weiser [1], UC is a form of invisible computing, whereas the computation devices are spread among the environments and interact to themselves in order to provide services. UC aims to provide access to relevant information in a senseless way, wherever users need at any time. Since computational systems are becoming even more part of our daily lives, UC emerges as a solution that eases user's life, by hiding the devices interfaces and automatically handling mobility and communication issues. In summary, mobility and context-awareness are the most notorious characteristic of ubiquitous systems, followed by the implicit interaction. It means that as the user moves on, ubiquitous systems should be able to retrieve and use context information, to implicitly interact with the user using devices that are embedded in the environments, and to adapt to multiple environments. The context information must be updated very often at run time, since the system must be able to interpret and make decisions according to these data.

2.2 Reference Architecture

Software architecture defines a high-level structure of a software system as a set of components and their relationship and properties. The software architectural design is one of the most critical activities in system development, especially in large and complex systems. In this context, reference architectures provide common understanding and directions for the construction of concrete software architectures for a class of systems. It contains architectural elements, domain experiences, design rules, architectural styles and other several elements that may be useful for specifying a concrete architecture of a specific system, which is an instance of the reference architecture. For the establishment of RA-Ubi in a systemic way, we adopted the PROSA-RA process that defines the following four steps for the establishment of reference architectures: (i) *Information Source Investigation*, with the domain-related information as the main output; (ii) *Architectural Requirement Establishment*, which produces the architectural requirements and concepts; (iii) *Reference Architecture Design*, which produces the architectural description of the reference architecture; and finally (iv) *Reference Architecture Evaluation*, which produces an evaluated reference architecture. .

2.3 Related Work

There are various reference architectures for different domains, such as service-oriented systems [5], embedded systems [6], and robotic systems [7]. However, for ubiquitous computing, there are very few proposals, and they target specific applications, such as smart environments [9]. In this subsection, we discuss three main related works: *Pervasive Computing Architecture (PCA) [10], Pervasive Service Composition – Reference Model (PSC-RM) [11] and Smart Environment Software Reference Architecture [9].* PCA [10] proposes an architecture that divides the pervasive computing in two parts: Network-oriented pervasive computing and Personality-oriented pervasive computing. The first one is focused on intelligent distributed computing, mobile computing, etc. The second part deals with applications focused on the user, as smart homes, smart cars, intelligent navigation. This second part encompasses four layers: application, middleware and security mechanism, computing, and embedded system and hardware. PCA does not handle adaptation and mobility issues. Thus, the reference architecture does not cover the whole purpose of ubiquitous systems. PSC-RM [11] proposes a reference model for pervasive computing focused on web services. It proposes a tree-layer structure, whereas the first one is responsible for describing the services, human-computer interfaces, mobility issues, P2P collaboration, etc. PSC-RM is a very complex reference model focused on service composition. The reference model does not handle service discovery nor event management, which are some of the main challenges of ubiquitous systems. Thus, it is not enough for describing ubiquitous systems. The Smart Environment Software Reference Architecture [9] proposes a reference model for smart environments.

It organizes smart environments in tasks implemented by one or more architectural components: *Perception*, *Reasoning*, and *Acting*. Although this work is proposed as a reference architecture, it is not a real reference architecture since it does not define architectural elements (components and interfaces) to be further used to derive concrete architecture for this domain. All the above-mentioned studies do not encompass the architectural elements identified by a previous work [12]; thus, a new reference architecture is needed.

3   RA-Ubi

This session presents RA-Ubi, a reference architecture for ubiquitous systems. RA-Ubi was defined based on ProSA-RA. This process encompasses four steps: (i) identification of information sources; (ii) requirements elicitation; (iii) reference architecture design; and (iv) reference architecture evaluation. The evaluation is available in the project website (http://consiste.dimap.ufrn.br/projects/ra-ubi).

Identification of Information Sources. In this work, several sources of information were used to get knowledge about ubiquitous systems. In particular, RA-Ubi inherits from our previous work [12] that reports a systematic review to identify in the existing literature the essential architectural elements for ubiquitous systems. Furthermore, this work is also based on [8], which presents a systematic review that classified existing ubiquitous projects based on their characteristics.

Table 1. Ubiquitous Systems' Features, provided by [8]

Feature	Description
Service Omnipresence	The system must enable users to move around with the feeling of carrying the computer services with them.
Invisibility	The system must have the ability of integrating devices to such degree that the user is no longer aware of them.
Context Sensitivity	The system must be able to retrieve information from the environment in which it is being used.
Adaptable Behavior	The system must be able of dynamically adapting itself to the provided services according to the current environment.
Experience Capture	The system must be able to capture and register experiences for later use.
Service Discovery	The system must be able to discover new services according to the environment that it is being used
Function Composition	The system must be able to create new services by composing existing services.
Spontaneous Interoperability	The system must be able to change its partners (i.e. sensors, actuators and collaborating parts) during operation.
Heterogeneity of Devices	The system must be able to migrate among devices, adjusting itself to each of them.
Fault Tolerance	The system must be able to recover from error states

Elicited Requirements. The requirements of RA-Ubi are basically based on two previous works. The first one [8] elicited a set of features of ubiquitous systems on 31 existing projects. We use these features as the basis for the requirements of our reference architecture. Table 1 summarizes the first set of requirements, which are based on the features of ubiquitous systems.

The second work is our systematic review [12]. It has identified the most common architectural elements of ubiquitous systems, based on the application-specific (smart living) reference architecture and also on existing middleware for ubiquitous computing.

Reference Architecture Design. In order to define the reference architecture, the elements identified as common were established as components of RAUbi. Although simplistic, this approach gave a starting point to the reference architecture that may be refined in a later process. After defined these components, it was necessary to specify the communications among them, aiming to encompass all the features mentioned in Table 1. This task was performed by using the knowledge acquired on previous studies and previous specifications of ubiquitous systems. Additionally, some experts' suggestions were applied in order to create a more realistic reference architecture. The experts are renowned researchers on ubiquitous computing domain, and their suggestions aimed mainly to establish and fix some issues on the communication among the components.

RA-Ubi was designed to encompass the essential elements of ubiquitous systems based on the architectural requirements. In order to represent our architecture, three architectural views are used: (i) the *component view* that is responsible for defining the components of the architecture, their interfaces and how they communicate with each other; (ii) the *deployment view* relies on the   UML deployment diagram to show how the components of RA-Ubi are organized in the system operating context. This is a very important view for ubiquitous systems, since these systems use heterogeneous devices; (iii) the *process view*, described using a set of activity diagrams, gives a better understanding of the components communications, and the component behavior while running a given task. An additional view, not detailed in this paper, is the *implementation view*, which organizes components into packages, displaying their dependency relationships.

Fig.1 depicts the component view of RA-Ubi, which is divided into four layers: *Infrastructure, Services, Context-Aware Computing,* and *Application*. The first layer, the *Infrastructure layer*, encompasses two elements: Sensor and Actuator. These elements are physical elements that the system needs to interact with the environment. Sensors are responsible for collecting context information and Actuators are responsible for controlling some devices and for providing feedback to the user. The second layer, named *Services,* contains the components responsible for providing the software interface to access the physical elements of the first layer: *Context Service*, for sensors data; and *Actuation Service*, for controlling actuators. A single context service may involve several sensors, as a single actuation service may control several actuators. They also need to handle the context data, using statistical methods to correct missing values [9]. This layer provides the context information and actuator access through the services; thus, the hardware elements of the first layer can only be accessed by those services. The third layer, named *Context-Aware Computing,* contains the core elements of a ubiquitous system. It encompasses six components:

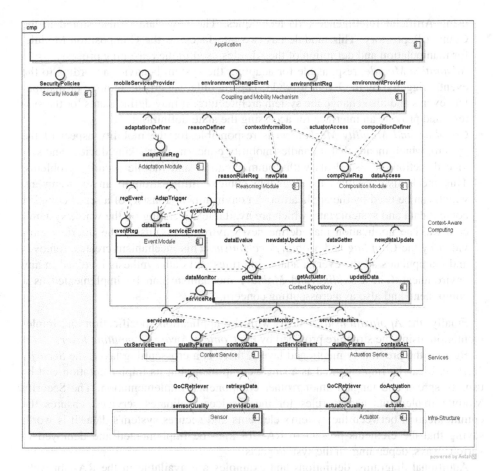

Fig. 1. Component Diagram of RA-Ubi

- *Context Repository*, responsible for storing and providing an interface to access context data and actuator services. This component requests the context data from the context service, in the second layer, and maintains a set of assessable actuation services, being also responsible for updating the repository with new data;
- *Event Module*, responsible for service and context data monitoring. This module provides an interface for defining events and monitoring their triggers, which can be defined through QoS (Quality of Service) and QoC (Quality of Context) parameters provided by the services, or through the context data itself. The Event Module is similar to an Observer (design pattern), since it monitors the services and the context data;
- *Composition Module*, responsible for composing context data. It retrieves data and stores the composed data in the Context Repository. It provides an interface for the definition of composed data and an interface for accessing these data;
- The *Reasoning Module* has a behavior similar to the Composition Module. However, it retrieves data from the Context Repository and creates new context data,

using Artificial Intelligence (AI) techniques. The new data is also stored in the Context Repository. This module has two interfaces, as the Composition Module, for manipulation and definition of the AI rules used in the reasoning process;

- *Adaptation Module*, responsible for adapting the system behavior according to the events triggered by the Event Module. This module can create, remove or manipulate events and also change the system architecture. It may define states for the system, and provide an interface for accessing the state definition;
- *Coupling and Mobility Mechanism* is responsible for the mobility aspect of the system, which means that it handles mobility concerns as tracking devices and service detection. It also deals with communication and mobile security problems. This mechanism couples the available context information in an environment, which can be used by the application. An environment consists of a set of complex context data and system state, which are available depending on the whole system's context. The application may define new environments, using the interface provided by the *Coupling* and *MobilityMechanism*. This mechanism creates, removes and manipulates all the events, adaptation rules and data synthesis involved in any environment. The *Coupling* and *Mobility* mechanism can be implemented as a component, and also as a crosscutting concern.

Finally, the *Application layer* deals with the application specification and implementation, using the structure provided by the *Context-Aware Computing layer*.

Besides the previously mentioned layers, there is a crosscutting layer, the *Security Module*. It can be implemented as a single component, but its implementation will be usually spread and tangled among other components' implementation. The Security Module implements access rules for the services, validates services, ensures the communication between the system's elements and secures system's data. It is worth saying that the elements present in RA-Ubi may be implemented and deployed in various ways, depending on the system goals.

Additional diagrams, definitions and examples are available in the RA-Ubi webpage: http://consiste.dimap.ufrn.br/projects/raubi/

4   Final Remarks

This paper presented RA-Ubi, a reference architecture for ubiquitous computing that was built based on ProSA-RA, a process for the establishment of reference architectures. RA-Ubi relies on UML diagrams to depict the different architectural views that describe the architecture. It was developed based on existing systems and applications for the domain of ubiquitous systems. The diagrams used in this paper and others are available at the project webpage (http://consiste.dimap.ufrn.br/projects/ra-ubi). In addition, the project webpage also contains an simple evaluation using a comparison-based technique and focusing on a specific quality attribute of the architecture, reusability, in order to verify if it can be a basis for deriving concrete architecture, i.e., if the elements of RA-Ubi cover the spectrum of existing systems and applications.

The main findings in our evaluation of RA-Ubi are: (i) some fundamental characteristics of ubiquitous computing are missing in some of the first work in this domain, such as the Service Omnipresence, Service Discovery, and Spontaneous Interoperability; (ii) recent works have a strong focus on reasoning and service composition; and (iii) actuation services are often neglected on the existing projects, although the importance of these components for providing feedback to the user.

As future work, RA-Ubi is being evaluated through other evaluation techniques, such as scenario-based evaluation and architectural-prototype evaluation, adopting other qualities attributes. Further evaluations are under development involving a checklist and interview with specialists.

References

1. Weiser, M.: The computer for 21st century. In: SIGMOOBILE Mob. Comput. Commun. Rev., pp. 3–11. ACM (1999)
2. Nakagawa, E.Y., Oliveira Antonino, P., Becker, M.: Reference architecture and product line architecture: A subtle but critical difference. In: Crnkovic, I., Gruhn, V., Book, M. (eds.) ECSA 2011. LNCS, vol. 6903, pp. 207–211. Springer, Heidelberg (2011)
3. Nakagawa, E.Y., et al.: Consolidating a Process for the Design, Representation, and Evaluation of Reference Architectures. In: Proc. Working IEEE/IFIP Conf. of Software Architecture (WICSA 2014), Sydney, Australia (2014)
4. Kumar, S.: Challenges for Ubiquitous Computing. In: Proceedings of the Fifth International Conference on Network and Services (ICNS 2009), pp. 526–535 (2009)
5. Arsanjani, A.: A service-oriented reference architecture. In: IEEE IT Professional (2007)
6. Eklund, U., et al.: Experience of introducing reference architectures in the development of automotive electronics systems. ACM Sigsoft Software Engineering Notes (2005)
7. Blackand, B., Knapp, C.: Reference architecture for mobile robotics. Technical Report, National Instruments (2010)
8. Spínola, R., Travassos, G.: Towards a framework to characterize ubiquitous software projects. Information and Software Technology 54, 759–785 (2012)
9. Fernandez-Montes, A., et al.: Smart Environment Software Reference Architecture. In: Proc. of the Fifth Int. Joint Conference on INC, IMS and IDC (NCM 2009), pp. 397–403 (2009)
10. Liu, Y., Li, F.: PCA: A Reference Architecture for Pervasive Computing. In: Proc. of the 1st International Symposium on Pervasive Computing and Applications, pp. 99–103 (2006)
11. Zhou, J., et al.: PSC-RM: Reference Model for Pervasive Service Composition. In: Proc. Fourth Int. Conf. on Frontier of Computer Science and Technology, pp. 705–709 (2009)
12. Machado, C., et al.: Architectural Elements of Ubiquitous Systems: A Systematic Review. In: Proc. of The Eighth Int. Conf. on Software Engineering Advances (ICSEA 2013), Venice, Italy, pp. 208–213 (2013)

Towards a Coordination-Centric Architecture Metamodel for Social Web Applications

Juergen Musil, Angelika Musil, and Stefan Biffl

CDL-Flex, Institute of Software Technology and Interactive Systems,
Vienna University of Technology,
Favoritenstrasse 9/188, 1040 Vienna, Austria
{jmusil,angelika}@computer.org
stefan.biffl@tuwien.ac.at

Abstract. Social web applications like wikis, social networks, and crowdsourcing markets have provided people with new dynamic forms of communication and collaboration. Although communities have widely adopted these systems, the methodological support for their architecting is still at the beginning. Since social web applications are mediation environments for human interaction, environment-based coordination models like stigmergy have increased in relevance. Therefore, we propose the concept of a Stigmergic Information System (SIS) architecture metamodel, which embeds a stigmergy-like coordination model. The metamodel defines key system elements and organizes a system into four layers: agent, artifact data, analysis & control and workflow. The metamodel should support the systematic investigation of common architecture elements, their relations and interdependencies, and future approaches for the description and modeling of social web applications. In this work we introduce the SIS architecture metamodel and evaluate the metamodel's validity with preliminary results from a pilot survey on groupware systems.

Keywords: Architecture Metamodel, Collective Intelligence, Coordination, Social Web Application, Stigmergic Information System, Stigmergy.

1 Introduction

Over the last decade, new forms of online collaboration platforms like wikis, social networks and crowdsourcing markets have enabled individuals to communicate and work together on problems effectively. While social web applications have been widely adopted in a variety of domains, the understanding and methodological support for architecting and "programming" them on a higher, more abstract, system level is still at an early stage [4], [8]. Social web applications mediate the interaction among their users by realizing a certain coordination model. Thus modifications of the coordination model highly affect a social web application's main regulatory capabilities. Therefore, research which investigates the models and mechanisms for computational support of mediated social interaction and human cognitive processes is highly relevant as well

P. Avgeriou and U. Zdun (Eds.): ECSA 2014, LNCS 8627, pp. 106–113, 2014.

as approaches, which enable the systematic design and analysis of these socio-technical systems [13], [16].

In this paper we explore the concept of a Stigmergic Information System (SIS) architecture metamodel, which realizes stigmergy-like coordination and self-organization and which also covers common key features of popular social web applications. Stigmergy (from Greek *stigma*: sign, and *ergon*: work) is a nature-inspired coordination mechanism to describe the environment-mediated task coordination of social insects [2]. Stigmergy promotes *awareness* among agents about the activities of other agents, which in turn reinforces their own activities [16]. In computer science, stigmergy is well-known as an effective coordination model, which provides computational systems with bottom-up, environment-mediated coordination capabilities [1], [12], [16]. The SIS metamodel represents a first step towards a common system model on which basis architectures for social web applications can be designed. Furthermore, the metamodel should also assist in the identification of design patterns, thus support architecture decision making and tradeoff considerations.

The remainder of this paper summarizes related work in section 2 and the research question and approach in 3. The architecture metamodel concept is detailed in section 4 and section 5 discusses preliminary results from the pilot survey. Finally, section 6 concludes and outlines future work.

2   Related Work

This section presents an overview on architecting coordination in social web applications and the stigmergy model for self-organizational, environment-mediated coordination.

The challenge of architecting social web applications is well known: In 2001, Tiwana and Bush [17] presented with the KNOWeb architecture one of the first approaches, which uses positive feedback mechanisms to deliberately reinforce the social/knowledge exchange in distributed virtual communities. Girgensohn and Lee [7] described their experiences from designing two "social interaction web sites" for two social groups. Similar to Tiwana and Bush, they concluded that in order to retain user engagement (1) the role of the social software system as a merely supportive infrastructure is not sufficient, and (2) mechanisms to maintain a continuous influx of new user contributions are needed. In recent time, Dorn and Taylor [4] presented a human Architecture Description Language hADL to describe collaboration structures and patterns in social web applications. Minder and Bernstein [8] focused on human computation and propose with CrowdLang a programming framework for interaction mechanisms and the design of human computation systems.

Software architectures are known, besides coordination languages, to be the primary means to embed coordination models [3]. When using a computational system to coordinate a multi-agent system (MAS) through stigmergy, the concepts of environment and artifact are essential [14], [16]. Weyns et al. [19] noted on the environment that it *"mediates both the interaction among agents and the access to resources"*. The *artifact* is used as a coordination medium, as an environment abstraction, through which the agents communicate. Advantages of environment-based coordination approaches are that processes can be decoupled in space and time as well as that producer and consumer can be anonymous [15]. For social web applications, stigmergy is of particular relevance, since the interaction between the human agents is predominantly mediated/regulated by the software infrastructure [13]. Parunak [18] surveyed stigmergic computational systems, which are used to coordinate human interactions. So far, some types of social web applications (social networking services, wikis) have been identified as stigmergic systems [13], [16], [18].

3   Research Question and Approach

The research question of this work is to **explore the possibility of a hypothetical metamodel with a built-in coordination mechanism, which is capable to cover common key features of dominant social web application types**.

We follow best-practice processes from software architecture discovery and reconstruction (SAR) to derive and validate a conceptual architecture metamodel. The metamodel should support the research for a future architecture viewpoint in order to assist software architects in the description and modeling of social web applications. We have chosen a hybrid bottom-up and top-down process as described by Ducasse and Pollet [5], which follows a metamodel focus like the CacOphoNy approach introduced by Favre [6]. Favre's approach has been deemed promising by Ducsasse and Pollet as it focusses on different abstraction levels horizontally and vertically.

We proceed in three phases: (1) design of a hypothetical architecture metamodel based on literature and experience from industry, (2) derivation of a catalogue of key features using the metamodel and formal concept analysis method, and (3) top-down exploration of the architecture hypothesis' validity in an initial pilot survey by mapping model constructs to features from systems from the field. Insights from the pilot should support the design of a following large-scale system survey.

4   The Stigmergic Information System (SIS) Architecture Metamodel

This section presents the Stigmergic Information System (SIS) architecture metamodel. An initial description of the SIS approach has been presented in [9], where the overall system concept and its key areas have been outlined. Further a simplified subset of metamodel elements has been described in [10]. This work extends previous research by contributing (a) a coherent, hypothetical architecture metamodel, and (b) a set of key features, with which systems can be tested for compliance with the proposed metamodel. A detailed description of the metamodel and its elements can be found online in a technical report [11].

The SIS metamodel is organized in four layers: I. agent layer, II. artifact data layer, III. analysis & control layer and IV. workflow layer (see Fig. 1). Human agents in layer I provide a continuous stream of information, whereby layer II and III form the computational coordination infrastructure, which maintains and enforces the workflows from layer IV.

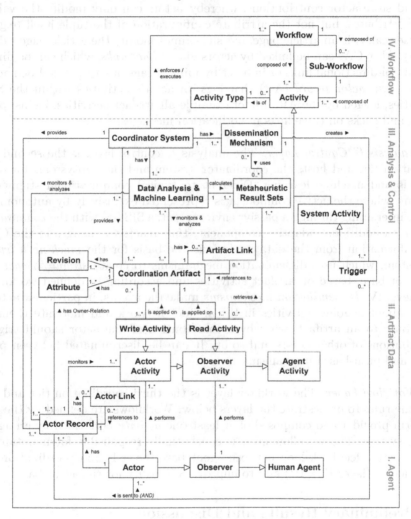

Fig. 1. UML class diagram of the hypothetical architecture metamodel for Stigmergic Information Systems

I. Agent Layer: The agent layer encompasses types of *human agents*, who interact with the system and are an active component in a SIS. Human agents are divided into *observers*, who have read-only access to the artifact content, and *actors*, who can also create artifacts and modify their content. Typically the actor role requires an agent to sign in with some sort of user account in the system.

II. Artifact Data Layer: The artifact data layer is the first coordination tier and consists of the coordination artifacts and the actor records. A *coordination artifact* (CA) is a characteristic tuple of *attributes*, which is the same for all CAs within a SIS. The coordination artifacts are the passive components in a SIS and store actor contributions, whereby actors can only modify the values of the attributes, but not the attribute configuration of the tuple itself (e.g., a wiki user can edit an article page, but she cannot modify the article page's data model). Also, CAs can be linked by actors via *artifact links*, which can be direct via uni-/bi-directional links or indirect by joins of tags or categories. Each actor has her own *actor record* (AR) that logs an actor's activities within the SIS. Activities, logged by the AR, are for example all artifact activities, logins, page views, and clicks on trace links in notification messages.

III. Analysis & Control Layer: The analysis & control layer is the second coordination tier and hosts the coordinator system and the subsystems for data analysis and machine learning. Different to typical computational stigmergic systems, where the active component is represented exclusively by autonomous agents interacting through a passive environment, a SIS has with the *coordinator system* an additional adaptive component, that reacts to changes in the CAs. The information from the data analysis is the basis for the *machine learning* subsystem, which uses dissemination mechanisms to create *stimuli/trigger* for the actor base, based on artifact activities and according to defined workflows from level IV. *Dissemination mechanisms* make the agents, in particular actors, *aware* about ongoing activities in the artifact network and motivate them to contribute to an artifact, whereby a contribution of one actor should trigger contributions of other actors and so on. It can be discriminated between pull-based and push-based mechanisms.

IV. Workflow Layer: The workflow layer is the third coordination tier and defines the rules to orchestrate the layers below. Workflows are defined by the SIS platform provider and composed of at least one *activity* performed by an agent or the system. The workflow layer is conceptually responsible for maintaining the perpetual feedback loop between agent base (layer I) and coordination infrastructure (layer II + III) and to improve SIS utility for the agent base.

5   Preliminary Results and Discussion

To evaluate the SIS metamodel's validity and scope, we conducted a pilot survey of 14 space/time-asynchronous groupware systems. Where possible, dominant systems with high Alexa[1] web-traffic rankings have been chosen. We examine

---

[1] www.alexa.com (last visited at 06/18/2014)

6 characteristic features, which we derived from the metamodel and a concept lattice using formal concept analysis method. Features 1-4 focus on capabilities of the individual coordination artifact and features 5-6 address data analytics and tracking capabilities on the system level. The following key features of a SIS have been identified:

1. Can any actor add a new coordination artifact?[2]
2. Can any actor contribute to parts of the coordination artifact of an other actor, thus change its state?
3. Are actors able to create system-internal links to connect coordination artifacts?[3]
4. Are state changes of selected artifacts traceable for all actors and/or forwarded to them (via dissemination mechanisms)?
5. Does the system have a user-driven recommender system?
6. Does the system keep track about the usage behavior of a single actor?[4]

A system has to meet all 6 features in order to comply with the SIS metamodel. The pilot results (see Table 1) show that the inspected features have been consistently found in the groups of social networking services, wikis, media sharing, marketplace, review and recommendation sharing, crowdsourcing and knowledge markets. All of the compliant systems are instances of modern social web applications. A feature, which should be observed in more detail in future research and which is unique to SIS-conform social web applications, is the linkability of artifacts using system-internal links. Although the terms 'folksonomies', tagging, and social graph have become buzz words in the last decade of web applications, preliminary results indicate that this feature is indeed pivotal. Another important feature is the creation of new artifacts by external users, which is also common to other established groupware systems like internet forums, mailing lists, version control systems and BitTorrent trackers.

6 Conclusions and Future Work

This work introduced a hypothetical architecture metamodel of social web applications, which embeds a stigmergy-like coordination model. The SIS metamodel defines key elements and their relations and organizes a system in the four layers of agent, artifact data, analysis & control and workflow. In a pilot survey we explored the metamodel's validity for various types of groupware and social web applications with a set of 6 characteristic key features derived from the metamodel. Results of the pilot study indicate that the metamodel is capable

---

[2] Access restrictions (password wall, pay wall, etc.) are not an exclusion criteria as long as they affect all actors in the same way.

[3] Examples are the friend-relationship in Facebook or Wikilinks in Wikipedia (http://en.wikipedia.org/wiki/Help:Link#Wikilinks) (last visited at 06/18/2014).

[4] Client-side tracking of usage behavior via cookies is not sufficient.

Table 1. Features mapped to representative groupware instances

Category	Example (SW-Tech)	1. Art	2. Ctb	3. Lnk	4. Dsm	5. Rmd	6. Trk
Internet Forum	forums.debian.net (phpBB)	✓	✓		✓		✓
Mailing List	Apache Software Foundation Mailing Lists (ezmlm)	✓	✓		✓		✓
Blog	mashable.com (WordPress)		✓		✓	✓	
Version Control System	git.kernel.org (Git)	✓					✓
CMS	huffingtonpost.com (Moveable Type)		✓		✓	✓	
BitTorrent Tracker	OpenBitTorrent.com (Opentracker)	✓					
Online Booking System	expedia.com		✓		✓	✓	
Social Networking Service	Facebook	✓	✓	✓	✓	✓	✓
Wiki	Wikipedia	✓	✓	✓	✓	✓	✓
Media/Content Sharing	YouTube	✓	✓	✓	✓	✓	✓
Marketplace	eBay	✓	✓	✓	✓	✓	✓
Review & Recommendation Sharing	Yelp	✓	✓	✓	✓	✓	✓
Crowdsourcing	InnoCentive	✓	✓	✓	✓	✓	✓
Knowledge Market	Stack Exchange	✓	✓	✓	✓	✓	✓

of describing certain types of social web applications and substantiate the hypothesis that a coordination-centric perspective like the SIS metamodel has the potential to provide a wider and more detailed viewpoint of the system.

For future work the following steps are planned: (1) Interviews with software architects to get feedback on the metamodel for soundness and further refinement. (2) A quantitative, comprehensive survey of systems from the field to evaluate the metamodel's validity and the identified key features, as well as to investigate commonalities and variations in features. (3) An architecture analysis of a representative social web application to map metamodel elements to system elements. Though it takes extensive validation in multiple steps to conclusively evaluate a metamodel that covers such a broad field, we see it as a promising architectural research agenda in the time of socio-technical platforms and networked societies.

Acknowledgments. This work was supported by the Christian Doppler Forschungsgesellschaft, the Federal Ministry of Economy, Family and Youth and the National Foundation for Research, Technology and Development, Austria.

References

1. Babaoglu, O., et al.: Design patterns from biology for distributed computing. ACM Trans. Autonomous and Adaptive Systems 1(1), 26–66 (2006)
2. Bonabeau, E., Dorigo, M., Theraulaz, G.: Swarm Intelligence: From Natural to Artificial Systems. Oxford University Press, New York (1999)

3. Ciancarini, P.: Coordination Models and Languages as Software Integrators. ACM Computing Surveys 28(2), 300–302 (1996)
4. Dorn, C., Taylor, R.N.: Architecture-Driven Modeling of Adaptive Collaboration Structures in Large-Scale Social Web Applications. In: Wang, X.S., Cruz, I., Delis, A., Huang, G. (eds.) WISE 2012. LNCS, vol. 7651, pp. 143–156. Springer, Heidelberg (2012)
5. Ducasse, S., Pollet, D.: Software Architecture Reconstruction: A Process-Oriented Taxonomy. IEEE Trans. Software Engineering 35(4), 573–591 (2009)
6. Favre, J.-M.: CacOphoNy: Metamodel-Driven Architecture Recovery. In: Proc. 11th Working Conf. on Reverse Engineering (WCRE 2004), pp. 204–213. IEEE CS (2004)
7. Girgensohn, A., Lee, A.: Making Web Sites Be Places for Social Interaction. In: Proc. ACM Conf. on Computer Supported Cooperative Work (CSCW 2002), pp. 136–145. ACM (2002)
8. Minder, P., Bernstein, A.: *CrowdLang*: A Programming Language for the Systematic Exploration of Human Computation Systems. In: Aberer, K., Flache, A., Jager, W., Liu, L., Tang, J., Guéret, C. (eds.) SocInfo 2012. LNCS, vol. 7710, pp. 124–137. Springer, Heidelberg (2012)
9. Musil, J., Musil, A., Winkler, D., Biffl, S.: A First Account on Stigmergic Information Systems and Their Impact on Platform Development. In: Proc. WICSA/ECSA 2012 Companion Volume (WICSA/ECSA 2012), pp. 69–73. ACM (2012)
10. Musil, J., Musil, A., Biffl, S.: Elements of Software Ecosystem Early-Stage Design for Collective Intelligence Systems. In: Proc. Int'l Workshop on Ecosystem Architectures (WEA 2013), pp. 21–25. ACM (2013)
11. Musil, J., Musil, A., Biffl, S.: Stigmergic Information Systems - Part 1: An Architecture Metamodel for Collective Intelligence Systems. Technical report, IFS-CDL 14-40, Vienna University of Technology (August 2014), http://qse.ifs.tuwien.ac.at/publication/IFS-CDL-14-40.pdf
12. Omicini, A.: Nature-Inspired Coordination Models: Current Status and Future Trends. In: ISRN Software Engineering 2013 (2013)
13. Omicini, A., Contucci, P.: Complexity and Interaction: Blurring Borders between Physical, Computational, and Social Systems. In: Bădică, C., Nguyen, N.T., Drezovan, M. (eds.) ICCCI 2013. LNCS, vol. 8083, pp. 1–10. Springer, Heidelberg (2013)
14. Omicini, A., Ricci, A., Viroli, M.: Artifacts in the A&A Meta-model for Multi-agent Systems. Autonomous Agents and Multi-Agent Systems 17(3), 432–456 (2008)
15. Papadopoulos, G.A., Arbab, F.: Coordination Models and Languages. Advances in Computers 46, 329–400 (1998)
16. Ricci, A., Omicini, A., Viroli, M., Gardelli, L., Oliva, E.: Cognitive Stigmergy: Towards a Framework Based on Agents and Artifacts. In: Weyns, D., Van Dyke Parunak, H., Michel, F. (eds.) E4MAS 2006. LNCS (LNAI), vol. 4389, pp. 124–140. Springer, Heidelberg (2007)
17. Tiwana, A., Bush, A.: A social exchange architecture for distributed Web communities. Journal of Knowledge Management 5(3), 242–249 (2001)
18. Van Dyke Parunak, H.: A Survey of Environments and Mechanisms for Human-Human Stigmergy. In: Weyns, D., Van Dyke Parunak, H., Michel, F. (eds.) E4MAS 2005. LNCS (LNAI), vol. 3830, pp. 163–186. Springer, Heidelberg (2006)
19. Weyns, D., Omicini, A., Odell, J.: Environment as a first class abstraction in multiagent systems. Autonomous Agents and Multi-Agent Systems 14(1), 5–30 (2007)

Using Policies for Handling Complexity
of Event-Driven Architectures

Tobias Freudenreich, Stefan Appel, Sebastian Frischbier,
and Alejandro P. Buchmann

Databases and Distributed Systems, TU Darmstadt, Darmstadt, Germany
lastname@dvs.tu-darmstadt.de

Abstract. Cyber-physical systems and the Internet of Things illustrate
the proliferation of sensors. The full potential of ubiquitous sensors can
only be realized, if sensors and traditional data sources are integrated
into one system. This leads to large, complex systems which are harder
to use and manage, and where maintaining desired behavior is increasingly difficult. We suggest a novel approach to handle the complexity
of these systems: users focus on the desired behavior of the system and
use a declarative policy language (DPL) to state these behaviors. An
enhanced message-oriented middleware processes the policies and automatically generates components which execute the policies. We compared
our approach against other approaches in a case study and found that it
does indeed simplify the use of cyber-physical systems.

1 Introduction

The number of sensors in today's environments increases steadily. In our homes
the sheer number but also the different kinds of sensors have increased in recent
years. Similarly, companies rely more and more on sensor data to improve and
steer their processes, especially in production and logistics. Trends like cyber-
physical systems (CPS) or the Internet of Things illustrate this evolution further.

This calls for a new perspective on software architecture. In Event Driven Architectures (EDAs) components get triggered by events [27]. In service Oriented
Architectures (SOAs) they are invoked by explicit calls. In modern architectures
both interaction paradigms coexist. This perspective shift comes at the price of
increased architectural complexity: EDAs are inherently distributed, the application does not have direct control over the control flow, and language-support for
event processing is but well-supported. We believe that this complexity must -at
least in part- be handled by a middleware, which abstracts from this complexity.

Event handling today is done via complex event processing (CEP), which
proposes to construct more complex events out of simple ones, according to a
set of rules [24]. An event query language (EQL), as for example found in Esper
or Software AG's Apama, allows for declaratively stating such rules. However,
this abstraction is still on a very low level. It requires expert developers to be
handled correctly. Even when handled by experts, the number of rules quickly

P. Avgeriou and U. Zdun (Eds.): ECSA 2014, LNCS 8627, pp. 114–129, 2014.

exceeds a manageable amount, creating a maintenance nightmare with (hidden) dependencies among the rules and no indication why a rule was created.

Our goal is to allow domain experts without a profound computer science background to use systems based on an EDA, as well as to provide developers with a mechanism which abstracts from the architectural complexity of EDAs. Thus, we introduce the abstraction of a *policy*. A policy is the conceptual representation of a set of fine grained rules, which cooperate towards a common goal. Policies abstract from rule management and architectural distribution. By allowing users to state policies declaratively, we enable them to focus on *what* they want to achieve, rather than *how* this is done exactly. Other approaches, sharing the goal of simplifying the use of EBS by providing higher level abstractions, focus on procedural workflows [2,19]. Declarative statements bear the advantage of abstracting from implementation details, while procedural statements provide more control of how a task is achieved. No concept is inherently superior.

We illustrate the idea of our approach with a typical example from the domain of situation monitoring originally proposed by Georgakopoulos et al. [18]: A company wants to ensure the following: guests are allowed to walk around the company area. However, in some restricted rooms, guests need to be accompanied by an employee, otherwise an alarm should sound. There are already many sensors in place to derive positions of people, e.g., RFID readers or cameras. [1]

Ensuring this policy involves several steps (querying the database for a person's status, calculating absolute positions, checking in which room a person is, correlating multiple position events). Each of these steps requires a number of low-level CEP rules to encode. A common approach to reduce the number of rules is to define event compositions, resulting in a more complex event hierarchy. When adding more "real-world" requirements, like different security clearances, the set of rules quickly becomes hard to manage. We therefore advocate a segmentation of the rule space into policies and a mechanism to express them declaratively[2]:

```
IF
      person A with attribute status='guest' IS INSIDE
      room R with attribute security='restricted ' AND
      person B with attribute status='employee'
          IS NOT WITHIN 5m of A
THEN
      sound alarm
```

We provide a generic middleware architecture and approach to automatically process such policies. It can be instantiated by providing a domain model and annotating data sources with metadata. Similar to a database expert creating a database schema, providing this information is done only once. With this information, we can generate *Event Enrichment Components (EECs)* which enrich

---

[1] We were able to verify the validity of such a scenario in discussions with Software AG (http://www.softwareag.com), a leading provider of business application software.

[2] Note that this policy does not enforce B to be in the same room as A. We omit this detail for presentation simplicity.

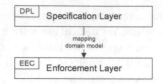

Fig. 1. Policies are specified in DPL and mapped to executable code in EECs

events with additional knowledge. EECs enforce policies by evaluating derived rules against incoming events.

Enabling domain experts to fully exploit CPS requires the following components (Figure 1 provides an illustration): a) A user-friendly way of stating the policies. We refer to this as the declarative policy language (DPL). b) A grammar underlying DPL. c) A mapping from DPL to executable code (EEC). d) A framework to capture domain concepts to support the mapping.

The contributions of this paper are:

- A novel approach to handle the complexity of cyber-physical systems and event-driven architectures in general.
- A generic, declarative language to state policies and a middleware architecture for processing them. The language can be mapped to multiple concrete languages and implementations.
- An implementation with modern message-oriented middleware to map DPL statements to executable code. Our implementation is in Java and based on Apache ActiveMQ, an industry-strength middleware.
- An approach that preserves the benefits of event-driven architectures: new sensors/producers can be added at runtime and the system remains flexible

The rest of this paper is structured as follows. Section 2 provides a detailed description of the parts comprising our DPL-enabled middleware, including how they interact. Section 3 compares our approach against Java and CEP-techniques in a case study. We discuss related work in Section 4 and conclude in Section 5.

2   Technical Overview

In this section, we detail how to get from a policy to executable code. Therefore, we first provide our domain model framework and the grammar for DPL. We follow up with the description of the architecture and close with an illustration of the interaction among the components with the example from Section 1

2.1   Domain Model Framework

We need domain models as background knowledge to generate executable code from a policy. The purpose of this section is not to discuss suitable representation languages, but rather state the requirements of our approach. We therefore introduce the individual elements and defer discussion about a suitable representation to Section 2.3.

Concepts and Attributes. Every policy will refer to certain *things*. In the example from Section 1 these are `person` and `room`. In that regard they are similar to entities in a database schema. However, we chose to call them *concepts* (similar to description logic) to avoid confusion. Concepts are described by attributes and may not have a direct representation (i.e. in a database). They might exist implicitly only (e.g., because various events refer to it)

Relationships. Relationships connect concepts. A relationship is backed by a relationship function, which evaluates for given instances if the relationship holds. A relationship function uses attributes of the related concepts. More than one relationship may exist between two concepts. For example, the employee and room can be connected by the relationship works in and meets customers in.

Figure 2 shows an example illustrating the concepts, attributes and relationships of our running example. The relationship *inside* refers to the attributes *position* and *coordinates* of two opposing corners of a rectangular room. Thus, when evaluating if a specific person is inside a specific room, the relationship function will be passed the values of position and coordinates as its arguments.

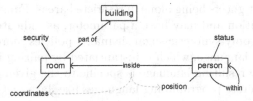

Fig. 2. Example domain model related to the policy from Section 1

To support relationships like *within*, which need an additional parameter (e.g., 5 meters), the framework must support parameterized functions.

Since relationship functions can be complex, we chose to keep them separate from the structural definition to support *separation of concerns*. In our example, one concern is to say that generally, persons can be inside rooms. Another concern is to say what exactly the semantics of being inside a room is.

Another advantage of keeping the definition of the relationship functions separate is reusability. Developers can reuse their function in different domain models and a set of functions can be directly shipped with the middleware.

2.2 Policy Grammar

With usability in mind, we believe that the determinism of a formal language outweighs the familiarity of natural language. Thus, policies must follow a formal syntax. Figure 3 shows the grammar that generates DPL in EBNF notation. The nonterminals concept, attribute, value, f-name, parameter and action are not explicitly given, as they can be arbitrary strings.

```
policy          ::= 'IF' conditions 'THEN' actions
conditions     ::= condition | conditions op conditions | '(' conditions ')'
condition      ::= concept-def function concept-ref
concept-def    ::= concept [alias],
     ['with attribute' (attribute attr-op value)*]
attr-op        ::= '=' | '!=' | '<' | '>' | '<=' | '>='
concept-ref    ::= concept-def | alias
function       ::= ['is'] ['NOT'] f-name [parameter] ['of']
op             ::= 'AND' | 'OR'
actions        ::= action+
```

Fig. 3. Grammar for policies in Extended Backus-Naur Form (EBNF)

Policies are divided into a situation description part and an actions part. The first part contains a set of conditions, describing the desired situation. Conditions are checked upon arrival of relevant events and, if met, the actions of the actions part are triggered. Thus, policies are similar to event-condition-action rules [10]. However, policies abstract from the notion of events and let users think in the descriptions of situations.

Concepts may have an alias for easier referencing within the policy. The with attribute statement allows for filtering out instances of a concept not relevant for the current statement. For example, guests and employees are persons, but we are concerned about guests being alone in restricted areas. Functions connect two concepts to a condition and may have a parameter, as indicated in Section 2.1. The element 'of' is only syntactic sugar: it makes policies more readable.

DPL is a generic language, which is instantiated by pairing it with a concrete domain model. The resulting language is specific to the given domain, but may map to several concrete programming languages like Java or C#.

2.3   Middleware Architecture

In event-driven architectures (EDAs), events (e.g., sensor readings) are reified as event notifications. Due to a typically high volume of data and the benefits of decoupling, EDAs adopt the publish/subscribe messaging paradigm [14]: software components with an interest in events issue subscriptions for them with a message-oriented middleware (MOM). Sensors act as event producers and send event notifications in the form of messages to the MOM. There, a message broker matches incoming messages against issued subscriptions and routes messages to interested consumers.

Figure 4 shows the generic architecture of the middleware enabling declarative behavior specification. We will detail the components in this section and illustrate how they interact. Components are loosely coupled and communicate asynchronously through a message bus. Interaction with the request/reply parts of the EDA also happen through messages (e.g., an event-driven SOA, where the action part of a policy fires a service-triggering event).

Message and Command Bus. A message bus connects event producers, auxiliary data sources (e.g., databases), the user interface, the policy engine as well

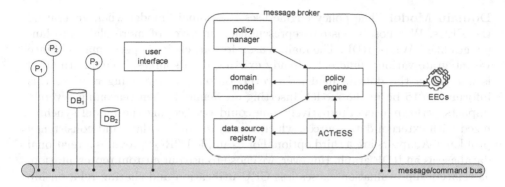

Fig. 4. Architecture of the DPL-enabled middleware

as the processing components. We use the existing messaging functionality of the MOM. The command bus consists of special message channels. Thus, each component is able to listen to commands asynchronously, which provides for good decoupling and easy distribution.

Producers send events via the publish/subscribe messaging facility. Since all messages pass through the broker, it can access message content.

User Interface. The user interface allows for creating, altering and deleting policies. Creating a policy just requires writing it, choosing a unique name and sending the policy to the middleware. We provide users with an Eclipse plugin with content assist, syntax highlighting and syntax checking. Thus, users cannot accidentally send erroneous policies to the middleware. Altering a policy follows similar steps, except that the user first retrieves the policy by its name. Deletion of a policy may happen implicitly or explicitly. An explicit deletion means the termination by a user action, while implicit deletion happens as part of a policy's action part.

Policy Engine. The policy engine is the heart of our DPL-enabled middleware. It serves as a coordinating component in a controller-like fashion: Upon receiving a policy, the policy engine uses the policy manager to analyze the policy. Based on the analysis, it generates *Event Enrichment Components* (EECs).

Conflicting Policies. Especially in multi-user environments policies might conflict. For example, one policy could state to close the windows if the temperature is less than 25°C (to preserve heat), while another policy requires opening the windows if the temperature is greater than 23°C (to preserve air quality).

Without proper semantic annotation of actions, it is impossible to automatically analyze, on a semantic level, what the *effect* of an action is. Such semantic analysis is out of scope of this paper and subject of future work. Currently, we support users by displaying *similar* policies to them as they edit theirs. Similarity is chosen based on the concepts and their attributes a policy is referring to.

Domain Model. The policy engine uses the domain model when generating the EECs. We chose a custom representation in favor of more elaborate languages like OWL or RDF. The main reason for our choice is performance. Since we integrate various, different, already existing data sources, their information is not yet in the domain model. However, ontological reasoning requires this information to be in the model. Inserting on demand, then reasoning severely impacts performance. Alternatively, one could try keeping the model synchronized with external data sources, which causes redundant data and consistency problems. Adapters are a third option. For example D2RQ[3] provides a relational database as an RDF graph. However, we chose to use our custom representation, as relationship evaluation causes less CPU utilization and sharing relationship functions across processing nodes is easier. Reusing existing ontologies/domain models is still possible, by simply registering them as an external data source.

Data Source Registry. The data source registry keeps track of all data sources. The example from Section 1 illustrates that the suggested middleware has to integrate various data sources. We distinguish between two categories of data sources: pull sources (e.g., databases) and push sources (e.g., sensors). Pull sources follow a request/reply paradigm, while push sources typically interact in a publish/subscribe fashion.

Data sources need to be annotated with metadata. The metadata specifies about which concept the data source provides information and which format the data have. For example, the employee table provides information about the concept person.

The position of sensors is useful information and thus also included in the metadata. Unlike location-based publish/subscribe [12,23], we use location information for enrichment, not routing.

Depending on the kind of data source, we distinguish between *static* and *dynamic* attributes: pull sources provide comparatively static, queryable information, while push sources provide volatile, high frequency data in an event-based fashion. Thus, we call attributes with associated pull sources *static* and those with associated push sources *dynamic* attributes.

Policy Manager. The policy manager keeps track of all registered policies. It is responsible for handling new and edited policies, as well as ensuring proper shutdown of all related components when a policy is deleted.

When a policy is created or edited, the policy manager creates a *policy logic tree*, based on the policy and the domain model. The policy logic tree represents the policy's concepts, their attribute constraints and relationships with other concepts. The tree then enables the policy engine to make educated judgments which data source to use for enrichment and which relationship functions to evaluate.

We want to illustrate this with the running example: Figure 5 shows the policy logic tree for our running example. The policy logic tree is then further analyzed.

---

[3] http://d2rq.org/

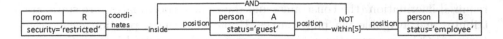

Fig. 5. Policy logic tree for the running example

For edges connecting a static attribute with a dynamic attribute (e.g., inside), the policy manager generates an EEC which is triggered for events providing information about the dynamic attribute (e.g., position) and enriches them. For edges connecting two dynamic attributes, the policy manager generates an EEC, which reacts to events from event streams and correlates them. The resulting events are further processed by nodes representing the logic operators. Changing the domain model might force re-analyzing policies and re-generating EECs, which our middleware can handle transparently.

ACTrESS. Cyber-physical systems are inherently heterogeneous systems, due to their many different sensors. One example for heterogeneity are different unit systems, e.g., Metric units vs. American Standard units. Thus, an event saying `temperature = 25` can only be interpreted correctly, if producer, broker, and consumer share the same understanding of what 25 means (and what `temperature` means). Heterogeneity becomes even more complicated when we take the structure and types of events into consideration.

In order to correctly interpret events, this heterogeneity has to be mediated. The correct interpretation is vital both for the subscription matching in the broker and handling of events at the consumers. To achieve this, we designed and built ACTrESS (Automatic Context Transformations in Event-based Software Systems), which transforms incoming events to the desired format and interpretation [15]. We proved ACTrESS to be type safe to avoid hard-to-trace runtime errors [16].

ACTrESS enhances message-oriented middleware, by allowing producers and consumers to tell the broker about their interpretation of data (independent of each other). Based on this information, the broker then automatically transforms messages.

For the DPL-enabled middleware we make use of ACTrESS. As pointed out in Section 2.3 producers provide their data format in the metadata. We feed this information into ACTrESS so it can transform incoming events to the needs of the EECs. For example, the generated EECs will always receive absolute Cartesian coordinates (x, y) , even if a sensor (e.g., a camera) sends events in relative, polar coordinates (r, θ).

EECs. We distinguish between query-EECs and correlation-EECs. We illustrate the need for this distinction with our running example:

Checking the `inside` edge of the policy logic tree (c.f. Figure 5) involves knowing a person's and the rooms' coordinates. Since `person.position` is a dynamic attribute (c.f. above), computation is triggered by position events. All other required information (the constraints and the rooms' coordinates) are static attributes and available via pull sources. Upon receiving a position event, the (query-)ECC can query the external sources for the required information and generate an enriched event based on the obtained information.

This is different from the `within` edge. In this case, both sides are dynamic attributes and thus, their information is not readily available when the EEC receives a position event. In this case, we must correlate multiple events. Such correlation is best left to event stream processing engines like Esper[4].

We designed EECs so they do not need to run on the same machine as the middleware. This helps in distributing processing and keeping the overall system scalable. EECs therefore subscribe to events from the message bus. At least one EEC per policy is also responsible for invoking the specified action when all conditions are met. Since EECs fulfill a certain event processing related task (enriching events/ taking action), they can be implemented with Eventlets[1]. Eventlets encapsulate tasks in event-based systems and have a managed lifecycle. This allows for instantiating one EEC per instance (e.g., one for every person), resulting in an automatically managed, highly modular (and thus parallelizable and scalable), distributed infrastructure.

The policy engine keeps track of all running EECs. We can stop an EEC if its corresponding policy was deleted. The policy engine also allows for getting various statistics about the EECs, e.g., how often they triggered the policy or even the triggering frequency. We use publish/subscribe monitoring tools like ASIA [17], to keep the monitoring overhead to a minimum.

2.4   Detailed Walkthrough

In this section, we want to illustrate the interaction between the components with our running example from Section 1. We assume that the system has been setup by an expert (e.g., loading the domain model and annotating data sources).

After receiving the policy, the policy engine analyzes it and generates three EECs, based on the policy logic tree: (1) A query-EEC, subscribing to position events and checking (by querying external sources) if the reported position belongs to an employee. If successful, the EEC generates an `EmployeePosition` event. (2) A query-EEC, subscribing to position events and checking if the reported position belongs to a guest and if that guest is inside a restricted room. Upon successful detection, the EEC generates a `GuestInsideRestricted` event. (3) A correlation-EEC, subscribing to `EmployeePosition` events and `GuestInsideRestricted` events and checking (using event stream processing) if the received events show a pattern which satisfies the policy's conditions.

Position sensors (e.g., RFID readers) produce `PositionEvent`s as shown in Figure 6. As discussed in Section 2.3, we use ACTrESS to transform the local position to a global one. After this transformation, the broker delivers the position event to the two query-EECs. Depending on the status of the person with

---

[4] http://esper.codehaus.org/

```
<PositionEvent>
   id = 5
   at = (5, 3)
</PositionEvent>
```

```
<EmployeePosition>
   id = 5
   at = (27.4, 40.3)
</EmployeePosition>
```

```
<GuestInsideRestricted>
   id = 5
   at = (27.4, 40.3)
   room = 205
</GuestInsideRestricted>
```

Fig. 6. Source event (left) and enriched events

id 5 (obtained by querying an external source), one of them generates an enriched event (c.f. Figure 6).

For guests, the EEC queries an external source to obtain the room which contains the position $(27.4, 40.3)$. Finally, the correlation-EEC uses a stream processing engine like Esper to correlate both event streams (e.g., with the EQL statement given in Figure 7)

```
select 1 from pattern
   [a=GuestInsideRestricted and not b=EmployeePosition]
where within(a.at, b.at, 5)
```

Fig. 7. EQL statement (simplified) used by the EEC

When the EEC detects such a pattern, it generates a `PolicyAction` event, which the middleware detects and invokes the alarm actuator.

3   Case Study

To strengthen and support our initial claim of simplifying the development of cyber-physical systems and event-based systems in general, we use a case study to compare three approaches along several criteria. The three competing approaches are Java, EQL (Event Query Language used by Esper) and DPL. They represent a solution to the evaluation example we give in the next section.

We do not provide a detailed performance analysis due to space reasons. In light of modern cloud infrastructures, single node performance is less important. Thus, we show that our approach is fully distributable (and thus parallelizable).

The generated EECs are autonomous components, which run independently of each other. As indicated in Section 2.3, EECs can be implemented as Eventlets. The execution of each EEC is thereby even further distributed. For example, the Eventlet middleware separates the guest-EEC along `id`. Each EEC instance then processes events for only a single person. The Eventlet middleware automatically manages distribution of instances efficiently. We thus achieve a very fine grained distribution/parallelism, which makes our approach easily scalable with virtually any load.

3.1   Complete Example

For the evaluation, we slightly expand the example from Section 1. There are publicly accessible areas in the company. For all other rooms, guests must be accompanied by employees. Furthermore, there exist restricted areas where guests are not allowed under any circumstances. We can express this in **DPL**:

```
IF
    person A with attribute status='guest' IS INSIDE
    room with attribute security != 'public' AND
    person B with attribute status='employee' IS NOT WITHIN 5m of A    OR
        A IS INSIDE room with attribute security = 'restricted'
THEN
    sound alarm
```

The exact **EQL** statements depend on the specifics of the stream processing engine, the host language and how much functionality is pushed to the streaming system. Thus, we outline how to achieve the above goal and try pushing as much functionality to the streaming system as possible.

We need to make data from the database available to the streaming system, by inserting them into a stream (for every table we need data from):

```
insert into UserStream select * from pattern[timer:interval(0)],
    sql:db1 ['select * from users']
```

We need to generate higher-order events based on the conditions, for example:

```
insert into NonPublicEvent select p.id, p.position, r.room
    from PersonPositions as p, RoomStream as r
    where inside(p.position, r.coordinates)
        and p.status = 'guest' and r.security != 'public'
```

The function `inside` is a host language function made accessible to the streaming system. This EQL statement assumes that there is a stream PersonPositions which combines position events with user data. This illustrates the dependency between different EQL statements. For our example, various such higher-order events are necessary, whose definition we omit for brevity.

Finally, an alarm triggering mechanism based on the given conditions must be specified:

```
insert into AlarmEvents select * from pattern
    [a=NonPublicEvent and not b=EmployeeEvent
    or c=ForbiddenEvent]
where within(a.position, b.position, 5)
```

The host language can subscribe to events matching this pattern, and upon reception of an event, trigger the alarm.

We omit the **Java**-only code for implementing the given scenario, as we believe the reader can imagine the effort to implement this in Java without any stream processing support (like Esper provides).

3.2   Criteria

We want to evaluate our three candidate solutions with the criteria **description similarity**, **number of instructions**, **control**, and **change**. We explain each criterion in more detail:

Description similarity indicates how similar the solution is to the original task (written in prose). We used the MCS method [26] which measures text similarity on a semantic level. Similarity is measured on a scale from 0 to 1, with a higher score meaning a higher similarity. We believe this metric to be a good indicator of how close a solution is to the mental model of the user.

Number of Instructions refers to the *length* of the solution. We use lines of code the solution requires as our metric. We do not count boilerplate code or setup-related code (e.g., registering JMS clients).

Control means how much direct control the user has over what happens inside the system. For example, choice of index structures and data structures.

Change indicates how well changes are supported. Changes might occur because the user wishes to change the behavior, but may also result from changes to the system (e.g., the addition of new sensors). We assume the presence of other policies in the system, which also need to work.

3.3   Results

Table 1 summarizes our results, which we detail in this section.

Table 1. Results of the Case Study

	Java	EQL	DPL
Description similarity	0.08	0.33	0.62
Number of Instructions	158	34	9
Control	++	+	−
Change	−−	−	++

Looking at the description similarity, the advantages for DPL are apparent. While it is nowhere close to a natural language definition, DPL still matches the description in some terms and the line of thought. EQL requires the definition of more complex events and access to database data, all of which is not part of scenario description. Java's syntax prevents coming close to a description in prose.

Implementing the given scenario with EQL requires considerably more instructions than using DPL. Many of the EQL statements are simply necessary to prepare the raw data so it can finally be used in a pattern-statement. By using DPL, the middleware takes care of all preparation through enrichment and lets the user focus on the important part. Thus, DPL requires much less effort to implement the scenario. Since the Java implementation cannot rely on stream processing libraries, it takes even more instructions.

On the other hand, more middleware-enabled functionality means less control for the end user. Thus, Java provides the most control, while stream processing libraries usually provide many optional settings. DPL clearly provides little control about how a policy is executed. Providing mechanisms for more control, would complicate the language and execution, which is not our goal.

Changing policies is also much better supported in DPL. For example, if we want to extend the restrictions to interns, in EQL, we will have to change the definition of a `NonPublicEvent`. However, other parts of the system might still depend on the current definition. Thus, the user has to either introduce a new definition besides `NonPublicEvent` with the risk of doing unnecessary work (if `NonPublicEvent` is in fact not used anywhere else), or the user has to analyze all other EQL-statements to see if and how they depend on `NonPublicEvent`. In Java, the user must analyze the code to check where the modifications need to be made and which other parts of the code might be affected, requiring similar effort. Assuming a correct setup of the additional knowledge (e.g., domain model), with DPL, the user simply modifies the query and leaves the rest to the middleware.

In summary, we see the arguments above as good and convincing evidence that DPL indeed, simplifies the development of event-driven architectures.

4   Related Work

Complex Event Processing (CEP) [24] is an active field of research. It is based on stream processing and active databases, aiming at providing higher-level abstractions with event patterns, filtering and aggregation. Low-level events are combined according to rules. There is a plethora of complex event processing and stream processing systems [9]. All systems however, try to improve performance [29] or the expressive power of their rule language. Other works are on improving the rule language design itself [22], but stick with the same concept. Eckert et al. surveyed CEP languages [11], but all of them operate on a lower abstraction than our approach and are thus comparable with EQL. Some approaches advocate integrating event processing directly into major languages like Java [13]. Reactive Programming [3] extends this idea by providing more built-in language support to avoid common problems such as value propagation inconsistencies. However, none of these approaches attempts changes as radical as our approach.

Situation monitoring suggests such a perspective shift [4,18]. They argue that users typically think of situations a computer system should be aware of and then define reactions based on them. They provide tools for defining these situations. Their approach faces some drawbacks in light of today's distributed, dynamic and heterogeneous systems: their approach does not use message-oriented middleware for forwarding events and they hard-wire information flows from specific sensors to specific processing components. Similarly, behavioral programming aims at "constructing reactive systems [...] from their expected behaviors" [20]. They advocate thinking about a system as the composition of its behaviors, where behaviors are reactions to events. However, they rely on explicitly defining the interactions and an a-priori knowledge of which events exist. Schiefer et al. developed a graphical tool for specifying event-condition action rules [28]. While their approach certainly helps tackling the complexity of event-based systems, it still requires the technical knowledge of how events can be combined.

The Alarm Correlation Engine (ACE) allows for declaratively specifying conditions and actions for alarms in a computer network, based on events [30]. Their motivation, too, is to give domain experts a tool for specifying policies. However, their approach is highly tailored to networks, with a predefined correlation database. Their solution is too rigid for modern event-driven architectures. Handling multiple, heterogeneous data sources with the help of an ontology has been explored in the field of query formulation [25,8]. Users are supported with suggestions to the queries they are trying to construct. Among other hints, query formulation systems suggest vocabulary based on the underlying ontology.

Higher-level approaches for simplifying the development of cyber-physical systems are Ukuflow, Event Stream Processing Units and MobileFog. Ukuflow allows users to define workflows, which are then deployed and executed in a wireless sensor network (WSN) [19]. Although targeted to WSNs, we believe the approach can be adopted to event-driven architectures in general. Similarly, Event Stream Processing Units (SPUs) support developers and domain experts by introducing an abstraction for event stream processing. Thus, event streams can easily be integrated into the business process modeling. MobileFog abstracts from the distributed nature of applications for event-driven architectures (called *Future Internet Applications*) [21], based on the paradigm of *fog computing* [5]. All three approaches rely on a procedural approach, while we use a declarative approach, each with its unique advantages.

Policies can be viewed as a grouping mechanism of CEP queries. For example, the policy given in Section 3.1 can be seen as a collection (group) of the EQL statements (not technically, but conceptually). In that regard, our approach is similar to constraint grouping techniques in DBMSs [7,6]. Constraint grouping aims at grouping database constraints into meaningful units, which can be plugged in and out, without worrying about other dependencies. However constraint grouping and query formulation have been designed for pull-based interactions, while we specifically target push-based interactions.

5   Conclusion

In modern software architectures SOAs and Event-driven architectures coexist. While the former has good architectural support the latter still suffers from a lack of good abstractions. Particular challenges are distribution and no direct control over the control flow. In this work we proposed a novel approach for handling this complexity. Our approach allows users to focus on the desired behavior of the event-driven parts, leaving architectural concerns like distribution to the middleware. We allow for stating the behavior in a declarative way, expressed in DPL. We implemented a prototype of our approach on top of a message-oriented middleware used as a communication infrastructure. We rely on computer experts to do the initial setup of the system, similar to a database developed by database experts for use by domain experts. Results from our case study show, that our approach makes event-driven architectures much easier to use.

Our approach yields some tradeoffs: using a declarative approach allows for easy specification but also means less control for the user. For example, window sizes or the degree/strategy of distribution is beyond the user's control. In terms of system qualities, our approach clearly favors scalability over some others: by automatically dividing the processing into small, independent processors, scaling out is handled automatically, which is especially useful for cloud environments. On the other hand, since we access messages and create new ones, encryption and signatures require trust in our middleware. Even with trust, the necessary key/certificate management becomes a challenge.

In future work, we want to exploit existing spatial database technology and incorporate enhanced event detection from image processing. Furthermore, we want to explore the benefits of dynamically moving EECs to other nodes in the system when CPU load becomes too high. Especially for settings where multiple users interact with a large system, we want to develop a policy conflict detection. This involves making the meaning of actions (and probably also conditions) explicit to the policy engine. We can then use standard conflict resolution strategies to avoid inconsistent system behavior.

Acknowledgment. Funded in part by the German Federal Ministry of Education and Research (BMBF) grant 01IS12054. The authors assume responsibility for the content.

References

1. Appel, S., Frischbier, S., Freudenreich, T., Buchmann, A.: Eventlets: Components for the Integration of Event Streams with SOA. In: SOCA (December 2012)
2. Appel, S., Frischbier, S., Freudenreich, T., Buchmann, A.: Event stream processing units in business processes. In: Daniel, F., Wang, J., Weber, B. (eds.) BPM 2013. LNCS, vol. 8094, pp. 187–202. Springer, Heidelberg (2013)
3. Bainomugisha, E., Carreton, A.L., van Cutsem, T., Mostinckx, S., de Meuter, W.: A survey on reactive programming. ACM Comput. Surv. 45, 52:1–52:34 (2013)
4. Baker, D., Georgakopoulos, D., Nodine, M., Cichocki, A.: From events to awareness. In: IEEE Services Computing Workshops, SCW 2006, pp. 21–30 (2006)
5. Bonomi, F., Milito, R., Zhu, J., Addepalli, S.: Fog computing and its role in the internet of things. In: MCC (2012)
6. Buchmann, A., Carrera, R.S., Vazquez-Galindo, M.A.: A generalized constraint and exception handler for an object-oriented CAD-DBMS. In: OODS (1986)
7. Buchmann, A., de Célis, C.P.: An architecture and data model for CAD databases. In: VLDB (1985)
8. Catarci, T., Di Mascio, T., Franconi, E., Santucci, G., Tessaris, S.: An ontology based visual tool for query formulation support. In: Meersman, R. (ed.) OTM-WS 2003. LNCS, vol. 2889, pp. 32–33. Springer, Heidelberg (2003)
9. Cugola, G., Margara, A.: Processing flows of information: From data stream to complex event processing. ACM Comput. Surv. 15, 15:1–15:62 (2012)
10. Dayal, U., Buchmann, A., McCarthy, D.: Rules are objects too: A knowledge model for an active, object-oriented database system. In: Dittrich, K.R. (ed.) OODBS 1988. LNCS, vol. 334, pp. 129–143. Springer, Heidelberg (1988)
11. Eckert, M., Bry, F., Brodt, S., Poppe, O., Hausmann, S.: A cep babelfish: Languages for complex event processing and querying surveyed. In: Helmer, S., Poulovassilis, A., Xhafa, F. (eds.) Reasoning in Event-Based Distributed Systems. SCI, vol. 347, pp. 47–70. Springer, Heidelberg (2011)
12. Eugster, P., Garbinato, B., Holzer, A.: Location-based Publish/Subscribe. In: 4th IEEE International Symposium on Network Computing and Applications (2005)

13. Eugster, P., Jayaram, K.R.: EventJava: An extension of java for event correlation. In: Drossopoulou, S. (ed.) ECOOP 2009. LNCS, vol. 5653, pp. 570–594. Springer, Heidelberg (2009)
14. Eugster, P.T., Felber, P.A., Guerraoui, R., Kermarrec, A.-M.: The many faces of publish/subscribe. ACM Comput. Surv. 35(2), 114–131 (2003)
15. Freudenreich, T., Appel, S., Frischbier, S., Buchmann, A.: ACTrESS - automatic context transformation in event-based software systems. In: DEBS (2012)
16. Freudenreich, T., Eugster, P., Frischbier, S., Appel, S., Buchmann, A.: Implementing federated object systems. In: Castagna, G. (ed.) ECOOP 2013. LNCS, vol. 7920, pp. 230–254. Springer, Heidelberg (2013)
17. Frischbier, S., Margara, A., Freudenreich, T., Eugster, P., Eyers, D., Pietzuch, P.: Aggregation for implicit invocations. In: AOSD (2013)
18. Georgakopoulos, D., Baker, D., Nodine, M., Cichoki, A.: Event-driven video awareness providing physical security. World Wide Web 10(1), 85–109 (2007)
19. Guerrero, P., Jacobi, D., Buchmann, A.: Workflow support for wireless sensor and actor networks. In: DMSN (2007)
20. Harel, D., Marron, A., Weiss, G.: Behavioral programming. Commun. ACM 55(7), 90–100 (2012)
21. Hong, K., Lillethun, D., Ramachandran, U., Ottenwälder, B., Koldehofe, B.: Mobile fog: a programming model for large-scale applications on the internet of things. In: MCC (2013)
22. Le, T.-G., Hermant, O., Manceny, M., Pawlak, R., Rioboo, R.: Unify event-based and rule-based styles for developing concurrent and context-aware reactive applications. Technical report, LISITE, France (2012)
23. Li, G., Wang, Y., Wang, T., Feng, J.: Location-aware publish/subscribe. In: SIGKDD (2013)
24. Luckham, D.C., Frasca, B.: Complex event processing in distributed systems. Technical report, Stanford University (1998)
25. Mahalingam, K., Huhns, M.: An ontology tool for query formulation in an agent-based context. In: COOPIS (1997)
26. Mihalcea, R., Corley, C., Strapparava, C.: Corpus-based and knowledge-based measures of text semantic similarity. In: AAAI, vol. 6, pp. 775–780 (2006)
27. Mühl, G., Fiege, L., Pietzuch, P.: Distributed Event-Based Systems, vol. 1. Springer, Heidelberg (2006)
28. Schiefer, J., Rozsnyai, S., Rauscher, C., Saurer, G.: Event-driven rules for sensing and responding to business situations. In: DEBS (2007)
29. Wu, E., Diao, Y., Rizvi, S.: High-performance complex event processing over streams. In: ACM SIGMOD (2006)
30. Wu, P., Bhatnagar, R., Epshtein, L., Bhandaru, M., Shi, Z.: Alarm correlation engine (ACE). In: NOMS (1998)

Architecture-Based Code Generation: From π-ADL Architecture Descriptions to Implementations in the Go Language

Everton Cavalcante[1,2], Flavio Oquendo[2], and Thais Batista[1]

[1]DIMAp, Federal University of Rio Grande do Norte, Natal, Brazil
[2]IRISA-UMR CNRS/Université de Bretagne-Sud, Vannes, France

evertonrsc@ppgsc.ufrn.br, flavio.oquendo@irisa.fr, thais@ufrnet.br

Abstract. Architecture description languages (ADLs) should consider both structural and runtime perspectives of software architectures, an important requirement for current software systems. However, most existing ADLs are disconnected from the runtime level, thus entailing architectural mismatches and inconsistencies between architecture and implementation. With the emergence of the new generation programming languages for large-scale, dynamic, and distributed systems, this problem becomes worse since most existing ADLs do not capture the features of this type of language. In this context, we investigate the generation of source code in the Go programming language from architecture descriptions in the π-ADL language as they are both based on the π-calculus process algebra. We define the correspondences between π-ADL and Go elements and present how architecture descriptions in π-ADL can be automatically translated to their respective implementations in Go through a real-world flood monitoring system.

Keywords: Software architectures, Architecture description languages, π-ADL, Programming languages, Mapping, Implementation, Go.

1 Introduction

The construction of new generation software systems requires languages that enable software architects to describe architectures of these systems by considering both structural and runtime perspectives, and such descriptions need to be supported by programming languages that provide facilities to tackle the features of these systems. However, as software architectures are typically defined independently from implementation, most existing software architecture description languages (ADLs) [1, 2] are disconnected from the runtime level, thus entailing architectural mismatches and inconsistencies between architecture and implementation mainly as the architecture evolves. Therefore, even if a system is initially built to conform to its intended architecture, its implementation may become inconsistent with the original architecture over time.

This decoupling between architecture descriptions and their implementation becomes worse with the emergence of new generation programming languages,

P. Avgeriou and U. Zdun (Eds.): ECSA 2014, LNCS 8627, pp. 130–145, 2014.
© Springer International Publishing Switzerland 2014

such as the Go language [3]. Most existing ADLs do not properly address the features of this type of languages, which are characterized by their purpose of easily taking advantage of the modern multicore and networked computer architectures, as well as providing concurrency capabilities. These features are not well supported by existing mainstream programming languages such as C++ or Java, thus increasing the required complexity for constructing large-scale and dynamic systems, which are becoming typical in several application domains.

In this context, this paper addresses the integration of π-ADL architecture description language [4] with the Go programming language for designing complex systems. On one hand, π-ADL provides a formal, theoretically well-founded language for describing dynamic software architectures by encompassing both structural and behavioral viewpoints, unlike most existing ADLs. In turn, Go is an easy general-purpose language designed to address the construction of scalable distributed systems and handle multicore and networked computer architectures. Such an integration is mainly fostered by their common basis on the π-calculus process algebra [5] and the straightforward relationship between elements of the languages, such as the use of connections in π-ADL and channels in Go as means of communication between concurrent processes. In this perspective, the purpose of this paper is twofold: (i) to define the correspondences between the elements of these languages, and; (ii) to present a process that defines how architecture descriptions in π-ADL can be automatically translated to their respective source code implementations in Go.

The remainder of this paper is organized as follows. Section 2 presents a brief overview about the π-ADL and Go languages. Section 3 introduces the mapping of π-ADL architectural descriptions to corresponding implementations in Go. In Section 4 we illustrate our proposal by specifying the architecture of a real-world flood monitoring system in π-ADL and showing how it can be automatically translated to its respective implementation in Go. Section 5 briefly discusses related work. Finally, Section 6 contains final remarks and directions to future works.

2 Background

2.1 The π-ADL Architecture Description Language

π-ADL [4] is a formal language for describing dynamic software architectures under both structural and behavioral viewpoints, i.e., in terms of the elements that compose such architectures and their operation at runtime. It is part of a family of languages designed to formally describe and refine dynamic software architectures and to support automated verification at both design time and runtime. In the last decade, π-ADL and its technologies have been applied in several real-world scenarios and pilot projects for critical and large-scale systems.

π-ADL has as theoretical foundation the higher-order typed π-calculus process algebra [5] (hence the name) and encompasses a formal transition and type system. Such a basis is conformed to the language design principles of correspondence, abstraction, and data type completeness [6]. Type completeness ensures first class citizenship to all data types, i.e., they can be declared, assigned, persisted, and have equality defined over them.

In π-ADL, an architecture is described in terms of components, connectors, and their composition. *Components* represent the functional elements of a software system, while *connectors* manage interactions among components since a component cannot be directly connected to another component. Components and connectors can be also composed to construct composite elements, which may themselves be components or connectors. Components and connectors also comprise a *behavior*, which expresses the interaction of an architectural element and its internal computation and uses connections to connect and transmit values. In π-ADL, architectures, components, and connectors are formally specified in terms of typed abstractions over behaviors.

As π-ADL is derived from π-calculus, it is grounded on the concept of *communicating processes* [7]. In π-calculus, communications/interactions between concurrent processes take place through *channels*, which are abstractions that enable the synchronization between such processes by sending and receiving messages (values or even channels). Analogously, in π-ADL a component can send/receive values via typed *connections*, which can send (output connections) and receive (input connections) any value of the existing types as well as connections themselves. In order to attach a component to a connector, at least a connection of the former must be attached to a connection of the latter. Such an attachment takes place by means of unification or value passing, so that attached connections can transport values, connections or even architectural elements.

Figure 1 depicts the main architectural concepts of π-ADL. From a black-box perspective, only connections of components and connectors and values passing through connections are observable. From a white-box perspective, internal behaviors of such elements are observable.

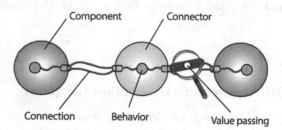

Fig. 1. Main architectural concepts of the π-ADL language

Figure 2 illustrates a π-ADL description[1] for a simple pipeline architecture composed of two components (filters) linked through one connector (pipe). Filter components transform data received from their input and send the transformed data to their output, while pipe connectors transmit the output of one filter

---

[1] More details about the syntax of architecture descriptions in π-ADL and its main elements can be found in [4, 8].

to the input of another filter. The `Filter` component (Fig. 2-a) is declared with two connections: (i) `inFilter`, an input connection for receiving data to be processed, and; (ii) `outFilter`, an output connection for sending processed data. The behavior of the `Filter` component encompasses the `transform` function, which receives data from the `inFilter` connection and returns data to be sent through the `outFilter` connection. In such an architecture description, the `transform` function is *unobservable*, i.e., internal. Similarly, the `Pipe` connector (Fig. 2-b) is declared with two connections: (i) an input connection (`inPipe`) that receives data as output of a filter, and; (ii) an output connection (`outPipe`) that sends data to the input of another filter. Finally, the `PipeFilter` architecture (Fig. 2-c) is specified as a composition in which two filter components (`F1` and `F2`) and one pipe connector (`P1`) are instantiated. The attachments of these architectural elements take place through the unification of the output connection of the filter `F1` with the input connection of the pipe `P1`, and the unification of the output connection of the pipe `P1` with the input connection of the filter `F2`. Therefore, data can be sent from filter `F1` to filter `F2` through the pipe `P1` via the declared connections.

2.2   The Go Programming Language

Go [3] is a new general-purpose language that was launched as an internal project at Google, Inc. in 2007 and became a public open-source project on November 2009. In 2012, Go was stably released as Go 1 by including a language specification [9], standard libraries, and custom tools. In the last years, Go has been used by Google and a variety of commercial and noncommercial organizations. It is also integrated to the Google App Engine [10], the Google's cloud-based development platform.

Go was designed to address the construction of new generation large-scale software systems, which are to be efficient, dynamic, and deployed on multicore and networked computer architectures. In order to achieve these purposes, the language aims to combine the lightweight, ease of use, and expressiveness of interpreted and dynamically typed languages, such as JavaScript and Python, with the efficiency and safety of traditional statically typed, compiled languages such as Java. Moreover, it is possible to directly compile even a large Go program to native code in few seconds.

One of the main features of Go is its lightweight support for concurrent communication and execution through high-level operations, in contrast to the considerable effort required to develop, maintain, and debug concurrent programs in mainstream languages such as C++ and Java. In this perspective, the solution provided by Go is threefold. First, the high-level support for concurrent programming enables programmers to easily develop concurrent programs. Second, concurrent processing is performed through *goroutines*, which are lightweight processes (similar to threads, but lighter), which can be created and automatically load-balanced across the available processors and cores. Finally, the automatic and efficient garbage collection relieves programmers of the memory management typically required by concurrent programs.

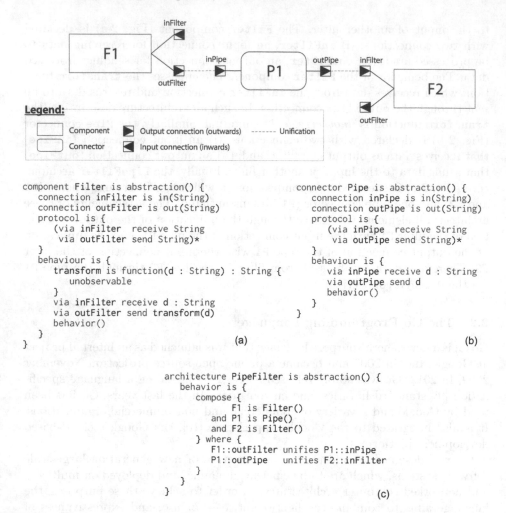

```
component Filter is abstraction() {          connector Pipe is abstraction() {
    connection inFilter is in(String)            connection inPipe is in(String)
    connection outFilter is out(String)          connection outPipe is out(String)
    protocol is {                                protocol is {
        (via inFilter  receive String               (via inPipe  receive String
         via outFilter send String)*                 via outPipe send String)*
    }                                            }
    behaviour is {                               behaviour is {
        transform is function(d : String) : String {     via inPipe receive d : String
            unobservable                             via outPipe send d
        }                                            behavior()
        via inFilter receive d : String          }
        via outFilter send transform(d)      }
        behavior()
    }
}                                     (a)                                                (b)
```

```
architecture PipeFilter is abstraction() {
    behavior is {
        compose {
            F1 is Filter()
            and P1 is Pipe()
            and F2 is Filter()
        } where {
            F1::outFilter unifies P1::inPipe
            P1::outPipe   unifies F2::inFilter
        }
    }
}
                                                    (c)
```

Fig. 2. Description of a simple pipeline architecture in π-ADL

In Go, goroutines communicate by using typed *channels*, which are used as means for sending and receiving values of any type. When a channel communication takes place, the sending and/or receiving channels (and their respective goroutines) are synchronized at the moment of the communication [7]. Therefore, explicit locking and other low-level details are abstracted away, thus simplifying the development of concurrent programs. Furthermore, due to its theoretical foundations on π-calculus, Go also supports the mobility of channels, i.e., channels are seen as first-class objects that can be transported via other channels.

Due to space restrictions, in Sections 3 and 4 we introduce just some elements of Go used in the implementation code generated from architecture descriptions in π-ADL. The interested reader is invited to refer to the complete specification of the language, its main elements, and details about its syntax in [9,11].

3 Mapping π-ADL Architectural Descriptions to Implementations in Go

This section presents how we can generate source code in the Go programming language from π-ADL architecture descriptions. Section 3.1 defines the correspondences between the elements of π-ADL to Go whereas Section 3.2 presents a process used to perform such a translation between the languages.

3.1 Correspondences between π-ADL and Go

Table 1 summarizes the relationships between the main elements of π-ADL and Go, each one detailed as follows.

Table 1. Summary of the correspondences between elements of π-ADL and Go

π-ADL	Go
Component	Function (goroutine)
Connector	Function (goroutine)
Behavior	Body of function (goroutine)
Connection	Channel
Architecture	Main function
Declaration of connections	Maps of channels
Unification of connections	Channels as parameters to goroutines
Basic types (except **Any**)	Primitive types
Any type	Empty interface
Unobservable elements	Empty body

Components, Connectors, and Their Behavior. In a π-ADL architecture description, components and connectors are created as abstractions that can be instantiated within the specification of the architecture. In Go, components and connectors are represented as functions that will be called as goroutines, thus being equivalent to the notion of communicating processes in π-calculus. Such functions are signed with the respective names of the components and connectors that they represent and the body of these functions comprises the behavior of such architectural elements.

Connections. As we have presented in Section 2, one of the main elements of the π-calculus process algebra are channels, which are used as means of communication and synchronization between concurrent processes. In π-ADL, connections are used to send and/or receive values between architectural abstractions (components and connectors) and their behaviors. Similarly (and then straightforwardly to π-calculus), the typed channels in Go are used to send and/or receive values between processes (goroutines to be synchronized), so that connections in π-ADL are mapped to channels in Go. The data type of the values that are transmitted through a channel is the one specified in the declaration of the connection.

Declaration of Connections. In the main function, maps[2] of channels are created in order to represent the set of connections associated to a component or connector. These $<string, channel>$ maps use as keys the names of the connections declared in the architecture description and map to the respective channel object that represent the connection. Such maps are used in order to enable the rastreability of the connection names when performing the translation from the architectural description π-ADL to the respective code in Go.

Unification of Connections. In π-ADL, a connection of a component can be attached to a connection of a connector in order to enable these elements to communicate. In Go, such a unification process takes place by passing the channels regarding the connections to be unified as parameters of the functions (goroutines) that represent behaviors of components and connectors. For example, in order to unify a connection of a component to a connection of a connector, the respective channel object regarding the former connection is passed as parameter to the goroutine that represents the connector.

Architecture. The main element of an architectural description is the architecture itself. In π-ADL, an architecture is specified as a composition of component and connector instances. In Go, it is represented by the main function (`func main`), which stands for the entry-point of a Go program (thus being the first function called when the program executes) and has no parameters and type. In order to create the instances of components and connectors, the goroutines that represent such architectural elements are called within the main function. In such calls, two parameters are provided: (i) the respective map of channels that represent the connections of the component/connector, and; (ii) the channel that represents the connection that will be unified to this component/connector.

Basic Types. π-ADL provides the following basic types: `Natural`, for non-negative (natural) numbers; `Integer`, for integer numbers; `Real`, for real numbers; `Boolean`, for Boolean logical values, and; `String`, for character strings. Such basic types are respectively mapped to the following Go primitive types: `uint64`, for unsigned integer numbers; `int64`, for signed integer numbers; `float64`, for floating point numbers; `bool`, for Boolean values, and; `string`, for character strings. π-ADL also provides a special basic type called `Any`, which represents an infinite union of types, so that values of the `Any` type consist of a value of any type with a representation of such a type. For similar purposes, the `Any` generic type is mapped to empty interfaces (`interface{}`), which are means of generic typing in Go. As empty interfaces do not have defined methods, any type is able to satisfy these interfaces.

Unobservable Elements. In π-ADL, an element (e.g., behavior, function, etc.) can be set as unobservable, i.e., internal. In Go, this is represented as an element with empty body.

---

[2] A *map* (a.k.a. associative array or hash table) in Go is an unordered, non-sequential collection of $<key, value>$ pairs. They are used to search for a value through a key, which works as an index that enables to access the value related to it.

3.2   Mapping Process

Figure 3 depicts the technical process performed to generate source code in the Go programming language from architecture descriptions in π-ADL. In the first step, the grammar of π-ADL was specified by using Xtext [12], a framework for developing programming languages and domain specific languages. Besides the specification of the syntactic rules and automatic generation of the language infrastructure, Xtext provides: (i) an abstract syntax tree, which is a tree representation of the abstract structure of a source code; (ii) a code formatter, integrated to a code editor; (iii) support tools for static syntactic analysis of the source code; (iv) a parser, and; (v) a code generator, which is able to generate code from a model in the defined language. From the grammar specification in the Extended Backus-Naur Form (EBNF) notation, Xtext also generates a conformed meta-model of the language with all abstract elements that are part of it and the relationships among them.

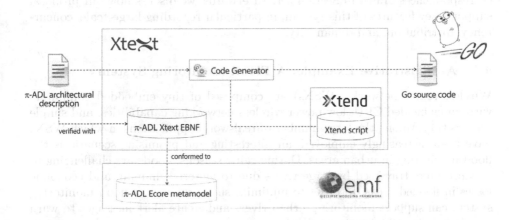

Fig. 3. Process for generating source code in Go from π-ADL architecture descriptions

From the grammar specification, Xtext uses a modeling workflow engine (MWE2) to generate the π-ADL language infrastructure, which encompasses components such as lexical analyzer, parser, and serializer, as well as source code in the Java programming language for implementing each abstract element of the language. Moreover, such an engine generates the entry point for implementing a code generator, which is used for generating source code from the textual model conformed to the grammar specification. This code generator was implemented by using facilities provided by Xtend [13], a dialect of Java that translates a textual model to source code. For this purpose, Xtend uses extension methods and template expressions to specify how a given abstract element in the input model can be translated to its representation in the source code to be generated. Therefore, these mechanisms provided by Xtend were used to translate the abstract elements defined in the π-ADL grammar to their respective implementation in Go based on the correspondences defined in Section 3.1. When specifying an architectural specification in π-ADL, if it is correct according to the syntactic rules of the language, the infrastructure automatically generates Go source code from this specification when it is saved in the language editor.

More details about the mapping process, the Xtext grammar specification of the π-ADL language, as well as the Eclipse-based projects used for generating Go source code are available at the following URL address:

http://consiste.dimap.ufrn.br/projects/PiADL2Go/

4   Application

In this section, we illustrate our proposal by specifying the architecture of a real-world flood monitoring system in π-ADL and showing how it can be automatically translated to its respective implementation in Go by following the correspondences drawn in Section 3.1. Afterwards, we discuss how our proposal supports key features of this system, in particular regarding large-scale, concurrency, distribution, and dynamicity.

4.1   An Illustrative Example: A Flood Monitoring System

Wireless sensor networks (WSNs) are composed of tiny embedded computers with an embedded CPU, low power wireless networking capabilities, and simple sensors [14]. Among the large number of real-world applications in which WSNs have been increasingly employed, an interesting and promising scenario is the flood monitoring in urban areas. During rainy seasons, floods are challenging to urban centers traversed by large rivers due to material, human, and economic losses in flooded areas. In order to minimize such problems, a flood monitoring system can support monitoring urban rivers and create alert messages to warn people in case of an imminent flood.

A successful example of WSN-based flood monitoring system is the one used to monitor the Monjolinho River in São Carlos, Brazil [15]. This system is composed of multiple sensor nodes, which measure the water depth of the river as an indicator of the risk of flood, and a gateway station, which collects, analyzes, and make such data available. Raw data measured by the sensors undergo some processing and are forwarded to neighbor sensors until reaching the gateway station. In case of an imminent flood, the system creates alert messages to warn people about the risks. The communications between sensors among themselves and with the gateway node take place through ZigBee wireless links. Figure 4 depicts the architecture of this WSN-based flood monitoring system, which is composed of two sensor components (S1 and S2), one gateway component (G), and a connector linking them (L1).

Figure 5(a) shows the specification of the Sensor component in π-ADL, which is composed of three connections: (i) the sense input connection is used for receiving raw data measured by the sensor; (ii) the pass input connection is used

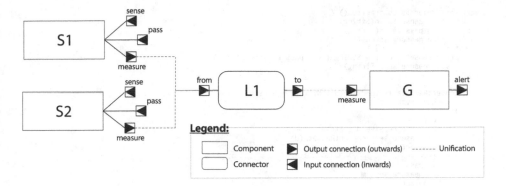

Fig. 4. Architecture of the WSN-based flood monitoring system

for receiving data from a neighbor sensor, and; (iii) the `measure` output connection is used for sending data. The behavior of this component encompasses the definition of the `convertRawData` function, which is responsible for preprocessing the sensed raw data. Moreover, such a behavior can proceed through two alternative options, as specified in the `choose` construct: (i) data received via the `sense` input connection are processed by the `convertRawData` function and then sent via the `measure` output connection, or; (ii) data received via the `pass` input connection are directly sent (i.e., without any processing) via the `measure` output connection. As partially shown in Fig. 5(b), this component is implemented in Go by the `Sensor` function, which receives as parameters the map of channels representing the set of named connections (as exemplified by the map `S1`) and a channel representing the connection to be unified when this goroutine is called within the main function. The `Sensor` function also comprises the declaration of a local function corresponding to the `convertRawData` function specified in the behavior. In order to represent the `choose` construct for alternative behavior options, the `select` instruction is used for selecting the pairs of channels according to the reception of messages. The value to be written to the `measure` output channel can be the one received in the `sense` input channel (sensed data) or the one received in the `pass` input channel (data from another sensor). The specification of the `Gateway` component in π-ADL and its corresponding implementation Go follow the same approach.

Figure 6(a) shows the specification of the `ZigBee` connector in π-ADL, which encompasses the `input` connection for receiving data and the `output` connection for sending data. In turn, as shown in Fig. 6(b), this connector is implemented in Go by the `ZigBee` function, which receives as parameters the map of channels representing the set of named connections (as exemplified by the map `L1`) and a channel representing the connection to be unified when this goroutine is called within the main function. In the `ZigBee` function, the unification effectively takes place through the assignment of the channel (connection) to be unified to the `input` channel of the connector. Afterwards, the value in the `input` channel is assigned to a variable (`d`) to be written to the `output` output channel.

```
component Sensor is abstraction() {
   connection sense is in(String)
   connection pass is in(String)
   connection measure is out(String)
   protocol is {
      ((via sense    receive String | via pass receive String)
        via measure send String)*
   }
   behavior is {
      convertRawData is function(d : String) : String {
         unobservable
      }
      choose {
         via sense receive d : String
         via measure send convertRawData(d)
         behavior()
      } or {
         via pass receive m : String
         via measure send m
         behavior()
      }
   }
}
```

(a)

```
func main() {
   S1 := map[string]interface{}{
      "sense"   : make(chan string),
      "pass"    : make(chan string),
      "measure" : make(chan string),
   }
   // ...
}

func Sensor(conn map[string]interface{},
   toUnify interface{}) {
   convertRawData := func(d string) string {
      // Empty body
   }
   select {
   case d := <- conn["sense"].(chan string):
      conn["measure"].(chan string) <- convertRawData(d)
   case m := <- conn["pass"].(chan string):
      conn["measure"].(chan string) <- m
   }
   Sensor(conn, toUnify)
}
```

(b)

Fig. 5. Description of the `Sensor` component in π-ADL and its corresponding implementation in Go

Finally, Fig. 7 shows the specification of the `WSNFloodMonitoring` architecture in π-ADL, which corresponds to the main executable function (`func main`). In this function, instances of the `Sensor` and `Gateway` components are created by calling the respective goroutines that represent such elements and their behavior with the respective maps of channels. The unifications of connections specified within the composition behavior (`compose`) take place by passing the channels as parameters to the goroutines. For instance, the calls to the `ZigBee` goroutine unify the output connection `measure` of the components `S1` and `S2` to the connector `L1`, so that the contents of the output channel of the formers are sent to the input channel of the later. Similarly, the call to the `Gateway` goroutine unifies the output connection `output` of the connector `L1` to the component `G`.

4.2   Discussion

After illustrating our proposal in small-scale with a simplified architecture composed of two sensor components, one gateway component, and one connector

```
connector ZigBee is abstraction() {
   connection input is in(String)
   connection output is out(String)
   protocol is {
      (via  incoming::input  receive String
       via outcoming::output send    String)*
   }
   behavior is {
      via incoming::input receive d : String
      via outcoming::output send d
      behavior()
   }
}
                        (a)
```

```
func main() {
   // ...
   L1 := map[string]interface{}{
      "input"  : make(chan string),
      "output" : make(chan string),
   }
   // ...
}

func ZigBee(conn map[string]interface{},
            toUnify interface{}) {
   conn["input"] = toUnify
   d := <- conn["input"].(chan string)
   conn["output"].(chan string) <- d
   ZigBee(conn, toUnify)
}
                                    (b)
```

Fig. 6. Description of the `ZigBee` connector in π-ADL and its corresponding implementation in Go

(Fig. 4), we will discuss how it is possible to scale-up the system and support distribution, concurrency, and dynamicity features.

In our mapping process from π-ADL to Go, components and connectors are implemented as goroutines, which are lightweight processes. In this perspective, increasing the number of architectural elements to be considered in the architecture in order to have a large-scale system does not promote a considerable impact mainly due to the efficient support to the execution of lightweight goroutines provided by Go. Moreover, Go also supports elastic platforms. This is the case of the flood monitoring system in which an increase of the number of sensors implies increasing the hardware execution platform, as each sensor node has its own processing unit.

Furthermore, Go natively provides an easy, lightweight support for the concurrent communication and execution of distributed programs mainly by using goroutines. In this perspective, as the architectural elements of the flood monitoring system are logically and physically distributed, such features provided by Go enable their concurrent execution and then foster an easy development of this type of system.

Finally, there may be cases in which it is necessary to add, remove or replace sensors or connections to the current flood monitoring system. Components and connectors can be dynamically added to the system as the creation of these elements is simply performed through new calls to the respective goroutines that implement them. In case of replacing components and connectors, it is necessary to make new calls to the goroutines that are to replace the elements and rearrange the communication channels in order to enable their synchronization. Finally,

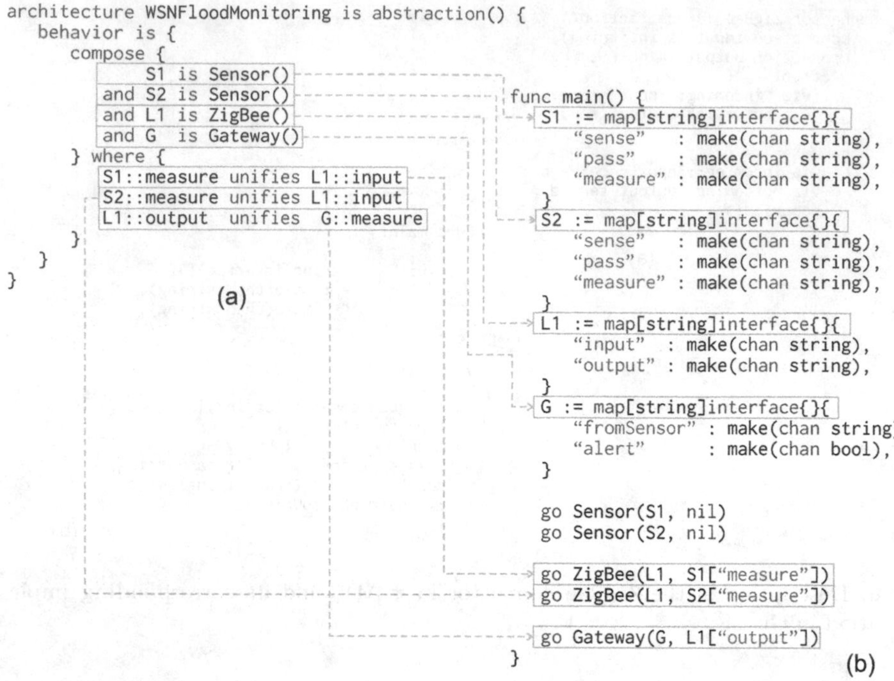

```
architecture WSNFloodMonitoring is abstraction() {
    behavior is {
        compose {
                S1 is Sensor()
            and S2 is Sensor()
            and L1 is ZigBee()
            and G  is Gateway()
        } where {
            S1::measure unifies L1::input
            S2::measure unifies L1::input
            L1::output  unifies  G::measure
        }
    }
}
```
(a)

```
func main() {
    S1 := map[string]interface{}{
        "sense"    : make(chan string),
        "pass"     : make(chan string),
        "measure" : make(chan string),
    }
    S2 := map[string]interface{}{
        "sense"    : make(chan string),
        "pass"     : make(chan string),
        "measure" : make(chan string),
    }
    L1 := map[string]interface{}{
        "input"   : make(chan string),
        "output" : make(chan string),
    }
    G := map[string]interface{}{
        "fromSensor" : make(chan string),
        "alert"       : make(chan bool),
    }

    go Sensor(S1, nil)
    go Sensor(S2, nil)

    go ZigBee(L1, S1["measure"])
    go ZigBee(L1, S2["measure"])

    go Gateway(G, L1["output"])
}
```
(b)

Fig. 7. Description of the WSNFloodMonitoring architecture in π-ADL and its corresponding implementation in Go

when removing these elements, the goroutines associated with them are to be blocked by closing the communication channels (connections) and the garbage collector of the Go language will be in charge of dealing with their destruction.

5   Related Work

Supporting code generation through the translation of architecture descriptions specified in an ADL to a programming language is not a new research subject [16,17], but it is still a relevant issue mainly due to the concern of maintaining conceptual integrity between architecture representations and its corresponding implementation code. However, as far as we are concerned, there is no work on the integration of ADLs with new generation programming languages in order to tackle the gap between architecture descriptions and their implementations. In this section, we briefly discuss some existing work on the integration of architectures with implementation and its limitations.

The Medvidovic et al.'s work [17] is one of the first works on the relationship between architecture descriptions and implementation languages. The proposed approach encompasses Dradel, an environment for modeling, analyzing, evolving, and implementing architectures described in C2SADEL (C2 Software Architecture Description and Evolution Language), which is an extension of the C2 language designed to support architecture-based evolution. A Java class is generated for each component specified in C2SADEL and a method in such a class is generated for each component service, with preceding preconditions and followed postconditions both marked as simple comments. In addition, developers need to provide an implementation for these application-specific methods.

ArchJava [18] is an extension to Java that tangles software architecture specifications to Java implementation code in order to ensure the traceability between architecture and code (that is, the conformation of the implementation with the specified architecture) and to support the co-evolution of both architecture and implementation. ArchJava adds new language constructs for specifying components, the connections among them and their ports, and behavior of components is implemented together the services that they provide. In terms of dynamicity support, components can be dynamically instantiated in a similar way to ordinary objects and connected at runtime. Although ArchJava presents a fresh approach as an architectural solution, it is limited in that it is more concrete than "pure" ADLs because the language has a stronger implementation basis. As it is essentially based on an informal Java foundation, an entire ArchJava architecture cannot be subjected to formal reasoning, despite the formally well-founded type system of the ArchJava component extensions [19]. Furthermore, the generated architectures are to be executed over a single Java Virtual Machine, which is not suitable to take advantage of multicore and networked computer architectures for the construction of large-scale and dynamic systems, as the Java programming language itself.

Finally, π-ADL.NET [20] is the result of the integration of π-ADL with the .NET platform. In π-ADL.NET, formal architecture descriptions in π-ADL are compiled to CIL (Common Intermediate Language), thus resulting in a code that is able to access the existing resources provided by the .NET platform. By enabling the execution of the architecture description, π-ADL.NET supports runtime analysis of the concrete architecture and it seeks to preserve architectural integrity of the system at the implementation level. Therefore, π-ADL based architectures remain formally verifiable at the implementation level. Despite its intention of bringing a formally founded ADL to an implementation platform, the main limitation of π-ADL.NET that makes it not well suited for new generation software systems regards the lack of counterparts when performing the mappings from π-ADL to CIL or the .NET platform. For instance, in π-ADL, behaviors and abstractions communicate through connections, which have no corresponding elements in CIL, so that a .NET class was developed by hand to emulate π-ADL connections, with requisite threading and synchronization functionality. In turn, due to their common π-calculus basis, π-ADL connections are straightforwardly mapped to channels in Go, which are first-class elements of the language and can be easily managed mainly when synchronizing processes. Furthermore, π-ADL.NET also lacks of support for distribution (that is easily and natively supported by Go), thus becoming a constraint when implementing distributed systems, a typical feature of new generation software.

6   Final Remarks

This paper addressed the integration of the π-ADL architecture description language with the Go programming language in order to tackle the existing gap between architecture descriptions and their respective implementations in the context of large-scale, dynamic, distributed and concurrent software systems. While π-ADL provides a formal and theoretically well-founded language for describing dynamic software architectures under structural and behavioral perspectives, Go is a general-purpose language suitable for building large-scale distributed systems deployed in multicore and networked computer architectures, which are features that are not well supported by the current mainstream programming languages. Due to their common basis on the π-calculus process algebra, one of the key features of π-ADL that fosters its integration with Go is the use of connections, which are represented in Go by channels and enable the communication and synchronization between behaviors, implemented as lightweight concurrent goroutines. In this perspective, we have defined a comprehensive mapping process between the elements of the π-ADL and Go languages, so that source code in Go can be automatically generated from architecture descriptions π-ADL by using facilities provided by Xtend extension methods within the Xtext framework for grammar specification and code generation. In order to validate our proposal, we have applied such a translation process to a real-world flood monitoring system.

In future works, we intend to expand our mapping process in order to address some elements of π-ADL that were not considered in this paper, such as constructed types and other behavior types. Moreover, we also intend to quantitatively evaluate our process by using model transformation metrics, as the one discussed in [21]. Finally, we also intend to address dynamic reconfiguration issued in terms of how reconfiguration actions specified at the architectural level take place at the implementation level and vice-versa. In this context, it is also important to verify and enforce structural, behavioral, and quality properties before, during, and after the reconfiguration process itself.

Acknowledgments. This work was partially supported by the following institutions: CAPES, grant 11097/2013-2; CNPq, PVE grant 400449/2013-7; INES, grant 573964/2008-4, and; the Brazilian National Agency of Petroleum, Natural Gas and Biofuels, PRH-22/ANP/MCTI Program.

References

1. Clements, P.: A survey of architecture description languages. In: 8th International Workshop on Software Specification and Design (IWSSD 1996), pp. 16–25. IEEE Computer Society, USA (1996)
2. Medvidovic, N., Taylor, R.N.: A classification and comparison framework for software architecture description languages. IEEE Transactions on Software Engineering 26(1), 70–93 (2000)
3. The Go Programming Language, http://golang.org

4. Oquendo, F.: π-ADL: An architecture description language based on the higher-order typed-calculus for specifying dynamic and mobile software architectures. ACM SIGSOFT Software Engineering Notes 29(3), 1–14 (2004)
5. Milner, R.: Communicating and mobile systems: The π-calculus. Cambridge University Press, USA (1999)
6. Oquendo, F., Warboys, B.C., Morrison, R., Dindeleux, R., Gallo, F., Garavel, H., Occhipinti, C.: ARCHWARE: Architecting evolvable software. In: Oquendo, F., Warboys, B.C., Morrison, R. (eds.) EWSA 2004. LNCS, vol. 3047, pp. 257–271. Springer, Heidelberg (2004)
7. Hoare, C.A.R.: Communicating sequential processes. Communications of the ACM 21(8), 666–677 (1978)
8. Oquendo, F.: Tutorial on ArchWare ADL – Version 2 (π-ADL Tutorial). Technical report, ArchWare Consortium (2005)
9. The Go Programming Language Specification, http://golang.org/ref/spec
10. Go Runtime Environment – Google App Engine, http://developers.google.com/appengine/docs/go/
11. Balbaert, I.: The way to Go: A thorough introduction to the Go programming language. iUniverse, USA (2012)
12. Xtext, http://www.eclipse.org/Xtext/
13. Xtend, https://www.eclipse.org/xtend/
14. Ueyama, J., Hughes, D.R., Matthys, N., Horré, W., Joosen, W., Huygens, C., Michiels, S.: An event-based component model for wireless sensor networks: A case study for river monitoring. In: 28th Brazilian Symposium on Computer Networks and Distributed Systems (SBRC 2010), pp. 997–1004. SBC, Brazil (2010)
15. Hughes, D., Ueyama, J., Mendiondo, E., Matthys, N., Horré, W., Michiels, S., Huygens, C., Joosen, W., Man, K.L., Guan, S.U.: A middleware platform to support river monitoring using wireless sensor networks. Journal of the Brazilian Computer Society 17, 85–102 (2011)
16. Shaw, M., DeLine, R., Klein, D.V., Ross, T.L., Young, D.M., Zelesnik, G.: Abstractions for software architecture and tools to support them. IEEE Transactions on Software Engineering 21(4), 314–335 (1995)
17. Medvidovic, N., Rosenblum, D.S., Taylor, R.S.: A language and environment for architecture-based software development and evolution. In: 21st International Conference on Software Engineering (ICSE 1999), pp. 44–53. ACM, USA (1999)
18. Aldrich, J., Chambers, C., Notkin, D.: ArchJava: Connecting software architecture to implementation. In: 24th International Conference on Software Engineering (ICSE 2002), pp. 187–197. ACM/IEEE Computer Society, USA (2002)
19. Aldrich, J., Notkin, D.: Architectural reasoning in archJava. In: Magnusson, B. (ed.) ECOOP 2002. LNCS, vol. 2374, pp. 334–367. Springer, Heidelberg (2002)
20. Qayyum, Z.: Realization of software architectures using a formal language: Towards languages dedicated to formal development based on π-ADL. Ph.D. Thesis, Université de Bretagne-Sud, France (2009)
21. Nguyen, P.H.: Quantitative analysis of model transformations. Master Thesis, Technische Universiteit Eindhoven, The Netherlands (2010)

Generating EAST-ADL Event Chains
from Scenario-Based Requirements Specifications

Thorsten Koch[1], Jörg Holtmann[1], and Julien DeAntoni[2]

[1] Project Group Mechatronic Systems Design, Fraunhofer IPT
Zukunftsmeile 1, 33102 Paderborn, Germany
{thorsten.koch,joerg.holtmann}@ipt.fraunhofer.de
[2] Univ. Nice Sophia Antipolis, I3S, UMR 7271 CNRS, Sophia Antipolis, France
julien.deantoni@polytech.unice.fr

Abstract. Real-time software-intensive embedded systems complexity,
as in the automotive domain, requires rigorous Requirements Engineering
(RE) approaches. Scenario-based RE formalisms like Modal Sequence Diagrams (MSDs) enable an intuitive specification and the simulative validation of functional requirements. However, the dependencies between
events occurring in different MSD scenarios are implicit so that it is
difficult to find causes of requirements defects, if any. The automotive
architecture description language EAST-ADL addresses this problem by relying on event chains, which make dependencies between events explicit.
However, EAST-ADL event chains have a low abstraction level, and their
relationship to functional requirements has seldom been investigated.
Based on the EAST-ADL functional architecture, we propose to use its
central notion of *event* to conciliate both approaches. We conceived an
automatic transformation from the high abstraction level requirements
specified in MSDs to the low abstraction level event chains.

Keywords: Requirements engineering, embedded systems, automotive,
scenario-based specification, EAST-ADL event chains.

1 Introduction

The growing functionality and complexity of today's embedded software-intensive
systems that are subject to real-time constraints, like in the automotive domain,
require rigorous development processes. This is especially true for the requirements engineering (RE) phase, since the detection and fixing of defects in the
system under development (SUD) in subsequent development phases cause costly
iterations [15].

On the one hand, scenario-based notations are well suited for the specification of requirements due to their intuitive representation [10]. Scenarios describe
sequences of events of tasks that the SUD has to accomplish [10]. In previous
work, we conceived a scenario-based RE approach based on a recent Live Sequence Chart (LSC) [3] variant, so-called *Modal Sequence Diagrams (MSDs)* [8].
The scenario-based nature of MSDs enables a visual and intuitive specification

P. Avgeriou and U. Zdun (Eds.): ECSA 2014, LNCS 8627, pp. 146–153, 2014.
© Springer International Publishing Switzerland 2014

of requirements. Furthermore, the underlying formal semantics allows validating the requirements by means of the Play-out algorithm, originally conceived for LSCs [9]. Our MSD Play-out approach implemented in the SCENARIOTOOLS[1] tool suite considers assumptions on the environment [2] as well as real-time constraints [1] and is applicable to hierarchical component structures [11], which makes it well suited for automotive systems.

On the other hand, the automotive architecture description language EAST-ADL allows the specification of particular events occurring in an automotive architecture [5]. The specification of so-called *event chains* causally relates these events to each other, which make dependencies between them explicit. Additional real-time constraints restrict the timing of the particular event occurrences. Furthermore, the formalization of EAST-ADL event chains and timing constraints [6,7] has recently made possible their validation by means of simulation in the TIMESQUARE[2] tool suite [4].

However, EAST-ADL event chains only describe requirements on event occurrences of an automotive software architecture. Functional requirements are not in their scope, and the relationship to scenario-based requirements has not been investigated, yet. This missing link to functional requirements is problematic, because the explicit dependencies between the events have to be specified in a modeling notation with a very low abstraction level. Thus, the requirements engineer has to manually extract the information in scenario-based requirements and specify it again in an awkward manner by means of EAST-ADL event chains, which is time-consuming and error-prone.

In order to bridge the gap between both formalisms, we conceived an automatic model transformation from MSDs to EAST-ADL event chains using the EAST-ADL functional architecture as a common basis. In this paper, we present a mapping from MSDs to EAST-ADL event chains, which acts as a link between both formalisms throughout a functional architecture. This enables an intuitive specification of scenario-based requirements and reduces effort to obtain a low abstraction level specification by means of EAST-ADL event chains.

We illustrate the approach by means of an electronic control unit controlling vehicle body functions, named Body Control Module (BCM). In the considered use case, the BCM has to unlock all vehicle doors after a crash was detected such that all passengers can safely escape or can be rescued from outside.

This paper is structured as follows: The following section introduces the fundamentals of MSDs and EAST-ADL event chains. Sect. 3 presents the transformation approach. Sect. 4 covers related work. Finally, Sect. 5 summarizes this paper and provides an outlook on future work.

2   Foundations

In this section, we introduce relevant foundations for the understanding of this paper: some basic concepts of MSDs (Sect. 2.1) and the EAST-ADL event chains (Sect. 2.2). Both are illustrated on the running example.

---

[1] http://scenariotools.org/
[2] http://timesquare.inria.fr/

2.1   Modal Sequence Diagrams

The MSD specification of our running example consists of the two MSDs CrashDetected and CrashDetected-Hazard, depicted in Fig. 1. The first MSD describes the
requirements that the doors of the vehicle must be opened (message open) as soon
as a crash has been detected (message crashDetected). The MSD CrashDetected-
Hazard specifies the requirements that if the open operation fails (message doorSta-
tus(false)), a hazard operation is performed (message hazardOpen) to ensure that
the passengers of the vehicle can safely escape or can be rescued from outside.

Basically, an MSD consists of lifelines and messages. Lifelines describe structural entities, which can be distinguished into *environment objects* and *system
objects*. Environment objects are depicted as cloud symbols and represent the environment that is sensed and manipulated by the SUD (e.g., lifeline cs:CrashSensor
in Fig. 1a). System objects represent components of the SUD (e.g., lifelines
bcm:BCM and dl:DoorLock in Fig. 1). Messages, represented by arrows between
lifelines, define requirements on the communication between objects. Messages
sent from environment objects are called *environment messages*, whereas messages sent from system objects are called *system messages*. They have a *temperature* and an *execution time*. The temperature of a message can be *cold* or *hot*
visualized by blue and red arrows in Fig. 1. It is used to distinguish between
provisional (cold) and mandatory (hot) behavior. The semantics of a hot message is that other messages specified by the MSD are not allowed to occur at
this point in time, while for a cold message, other messages may occur [2]. The
execution kind of a message can either be *executed*, depicted by solid arrows,
or *monitored* depicted by dashed arrows. An executed message indicates that
the message must eventually occur, whereas a monitored message can but need
not to occur [2]. The MSD CrashDetected contains an *alternative fragment*, which
describes different alternative continuations of the scenario.

The scenario-based nature of MSDs enables a high-level specification of requirements with separation of concerns. However, in big specifications the implicit event dependencies between several scenarios (e.g., message doorStatus(false)

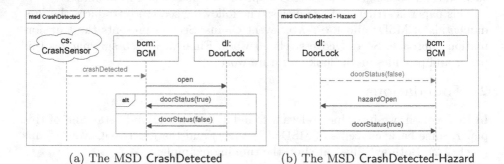

(a) The MSD CrashDetected   (b) The MSD CrashDetected-Hazard

Fig. 1. MSDs for the crash detection use case

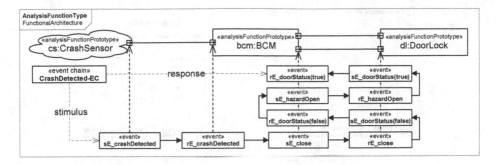

Fig. 2. The BCM example functional architecture in EAST-ADL including event chain for alternative (2) of MSDs in Fig. 1

in both MSDs) can complicate the investigation of requirements defects like an undesired activation of an MSD.

2.2 EAST-ADL Event Chains

The *Electronics Architecture and Software Technology - Architecture Description Language* (EAST-ADL) is an architecture description language for automotive embedded systems [5]. The EAST-ADL provides a unified notion for all important engineering information including the functional and non-functional properties of the system.

In the EAST-ADL [5, Part VI], an *event* is the abstract representation of a specific system behavior that can be observed at runtime. An *event chain* describes the causal order for a set of functionally dependent events. Each event chain has exactly one stimulus and response event, which describe the start and end point of the chain. Furthermore, an event chain can be hierarchically decomposed into an arbitrary number of sub-chains, so-called *event chain segments* that also have exactly one stimulus and response event.

Fig. 2 depicts the EAST-ADL functional architecture of the running example. Furthermore, we add events and the event chain CrashDetected-EC to illustrate the same interaction as specified in alternative (2) of the MSD CrashDetected activating the second MSD. Obviously, the specification of all particular events has a lower abstraction level than the specification of message exchange within MSDs, but the event chain makes the dependencies between both scenarios explicit.

3   Transformation Approach

In this section, we present our transformation approach for the generation of EAST-ADL event chains from MSD specifications using the EAST-ADL functional architecture as common basis. The transformation approach has been implemented in the SCENARIOTOOLS tool-suite and covers the MSD messages, alternative fragments and real-time constraints. However, due to space limitations,

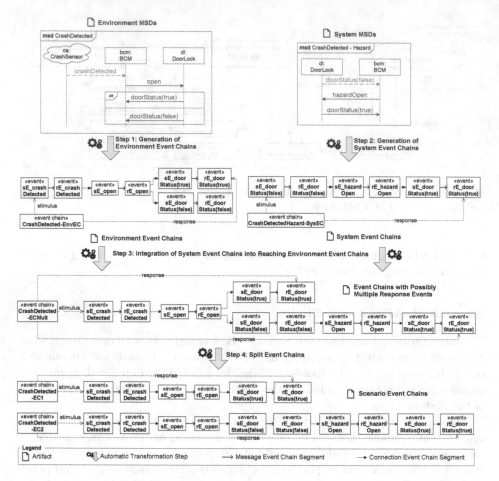

Fig. 3. Overview of the Transformation Approach

we do not detail the transformation of real-time constraints in this paper (please refer to [13] for more details about real-time constraint transformations).

Our transformation approach is implemented by means of QVT Operational [14] model transformations (partially supported by Java black-box libraries) and encompasses four steps, which are depicted in Fig. 3. In our approach, an EAST-ADL event chain is the description of the SUD's reaction to an environment message specified in an MSD. We call this type of event chain *scenario event chain*, which is the final result of our transformation (i.e., CrashDetected-EC1 and CrashDetected-EC2). The stimulus of a scenario event chain is always the sending event of an environment message. In the following, we describe each step by means of the running example.

Transformation Steps 1 and 2: For the first two steps, we divide the set of MSDs into *environment MSDs* and *system MSDs*. We qualify an MSD as an environment MSD, if its first message is an environment message; or as a system MSD, if its first message is a system message. These MSDs, representing a sequential order of messages, are respectively transformed into *environment event chains* and *system event chains*. For each MSD message, the transformation algorithm creates a *message event chain segment* by setting the sending event of the message as stimulus and the receiving event to the response.

Based on the running example, the transformation algorithm starts with the processing of the environment MSD CrashDetected. Therefore, it creates a new environment event chain CrashDetected-EnvEC and a message event chain segment for the first message crashDetected consisting of sE_crashDetected and rE_crashDetected.

The next element that occurs in the MSD is the open message. The transformation algorithm creates again a message event chain segment and in addition a *connection event chain segment*. A connection event chain segment preserves the order of two subsequent messages, e.g., crashDetected and open. Therefore, the stimulus of the connection event chain segment is set to the receiving event rE_crashDetected, and the response to the sending event of sE_open.

The next element that occurs in the MSD is the alternative fragment. MSD messages within the alternative fragment are transformed in the same way as other MSD messages. However, to preserve the order between the last message before the alternative fragment and the first message in each alternative, the transformation algorithm creates a set of connection event chain segments from rE_open to sE_doorStatus(true) and sE_doorStatus(false).

The two alternatives contain only one message, and thus, these messages are the last messages in the MSD. For a last message, the transformation algorithm has to consider two cases. First, if the message is not the first message in another MSD (e.g., doorStatus(true)), the currently considered alternative is terminated and the response event of the last message is added to the set of response events. Second, if the message is the first message in another MSD (e.g., doorStatus(false)), the transformation algorithm only marks the MSD as *reachable*. We call a system MSD *reachable*, if and only if its first message occurs in another processed MSD.

In the second step, the transformation algorithm processes the reachable system MSD CrashDetected-Hazard in the same manner, which results in the system event chain CrashDetectedHazard-SysEC.

Transformation Steps 3 and 4: In the third step, the transformation algorithm merges the system event chains with the event chains of the MSDs from which they are reachable. To accomplish this step, the event chain CrashDetected-EnvEC is first copied to a new event chain CrashDetected-ECMult. Afterwards, the event chain segments and the response events of CrashDetectedHazard-SysEC are attached to the event chain path that corresponds to the MSD message that has reached the MSD CrashDetected-Hazard (path containing sE_doorStatus(false) and rE_doorStatus(false)).

In Sect. 2.2, we stated that an event chain is only allowed to have one stimulus and one response event. However, in our running example, the event chain CrashDetected-ECMult contradicts this definition. Hence, in the fourth step, the transformation algorithm splits all event chains with multiple response events and creates a set of event chains; one for each response event (e.g., both occurrences of rE_doorStatus(true) in the event chain CrashDetected-ECMult). To accomplish this step, the transformation algorithm performs a backward search for each response event. After the completion of this transformation step, we obtain the two well-formed scenario event chains CrashDetected-EC1 and CrashDetected-EC2 that have exactly one stimulus and one response event.

After the application of the transformation approach, we can apply both simulation approaches in a complementary manner. On the one hand, requirements engineers can simulate the particular scenarios in SCENARIOTOOLS and investigate the behavior emerging from the interplay of multiple scenarios. On the other hand, they can simulate the resulting event chains within TIMESQUARE and visualize explicit event dependencies between different scenarios, enabling to detect requirements defects caused by undesired activations of MSDs.

4 Related Work

Chen et al. [17] propose a modeling approach for specifying timing requirements on the base of functional requirements. They have extended the Problem Frame formalism with the recent formalization [6,7] of EAST-ADL event chains and timing constraints. The event chains and timing constraints have to be specified awkwardly in the underlying formalization, which is in contrast with our more intuitive representation of scenario-based requirements. Klein and Giese [12] present Timed Story Scenario Diagrams (TSSDs), a visual notation for scenario specifications that takes structural system properties into account. In TSSDs, it is possible to specify time constraints that allow setting lower and upper bounds for delays. There is no mention of analysis support for TSSDs. Priesterjahn et al. [16] present an automatic approach that generates a timed failure propagation model from a system model for fault tolerance analysis based on timed automata. The transformation is similar to our approach, but they focus on reliability, while we focus on timed requirements.

5 Conclusion and Outlook

In this paper, we presented a transformation approach from high abstraction level scenario-based requirements to low abstraction level event chains while using an EAST-ADL functional architecture as common basis. We apply MSDs as concrete formalism for scenario-based requirements and EAST-ADL as modeling notation for event chains. Our approach combines intuitive but formal scenario-based requirements specifications on a high abstraction level with the possibility to visually inspect explicit event chains induced by the scenarios.

The future work encompasses several aspects. On the one hand, we want to evaluate our approach and the opportunities w.r.t. real-time requirements in combining the two simulative validation approaches in a complementary manner. On the other hand, we want to reuse the EAST-ADL event chains in the subsequent software development process within AUTOSAR.

Acknowledgments. This research is partially funded by the German Federal Ministry of Education and Research (BMBF) within the Leading-Edge Cluster "Intelligent Technical Systems OstWestfalenLippe" (it's OWL) and is managed by the Project Management Agency Karlsruhe (PTKA). This work is also partially supported by the ANR INS Project GEMOC (ANR-12-INSE-0011).

References

1. Brenner, C., Greenyer, J., Holtmann, J., Liebel, G., Stieglbauer, G., Tichy, M.: ScenarioTools real-time play-out for test sequence validation in an automotive case study. In: Graph Transformation and Visual Modeling Techniques (2014)
2. Brenner, C., Greenyer, J., Panzica La Manna, V.: The ScenarioTools play-out of modal sequence diagram specifications with environment assumptions. In: Graph Transformation and Visual Modeling Techniques (2013)
3. Damm, W., Harel, D.: LSCs: Breathing life into message sequence charts. Formal Methods in System Design 19, 45–80 (2001)
4. DeAntoni, J., Mallet, F.: TimeSquare: Treat your models with logical time. In: Furia, C.A., Nanz, S. (eds.) TOOLS 2012. LNCS, vol. 7304, pp. 34–41. Springer, Heidelberg (2012)
5. EAST-ADL Association. EAST-ADL Domain Model Specification: Version V2.1.12 (2013)
6. Goknil, A., DeAntoni, J., Peraldi-Frati, M.-A., Mallet, F.: Tool support for the analysis of TADL2 timing constraints using TimeSquare. In: ICECCS, pp. 145–154. IEEE (2013)
7. Goknil, A., Suryadevara, J., Peraldi-Frati, M.-A., Mallet, F.: Analysis support for TADL2 timing constraints on EAST-ADL models. In: Drira, K. (ed.) ECSA 2013. LNCS, vol. 7957, pp. 89–105. Springer, Heidelberg (2013)
8. Harel, D., Maoz, S.: Assert and negate revisited: Modal semantics for UML sequence diagrams. Software and Systems Modeling 7, 237–252 (2008)
9. Harel, D., Marelly, R.: Come, let's play: Scenario-based programming using LSCs and the play-engine. Springer (2003)
10. Hassine, J., Rilling, J., Dssouli, R.: An evaluation of timed scenario notations. Journal of Systems and Software 83(2), 326–350 (2010)
11. Holtmann, J., Meyer, M.: Play-out for hierarchical component architectures. In: 11th Workshop Automotive Software Engineering (ASE 2013). LNI, vol. P-220, pp. 2458–2472 (2013)
12. Klein, F., Giese, H.: Joint structural and temporal property specification using timed story scenario diagrams. In: Dwyer, M.B., Lopes, A. (eds.) FASE 2007. LNCS, vol. 4422, pp. 185–199. Springer, Heidelberg (2007)
13. Koch, T.: Combining scenario-based and architecture-based timing requirements. Master's thesis, University of Paderborn, Paderborn (2013)
14. Object Management Group. Meta object facility (MOF) 2.0 query/view/transformation specification: Version 1.1, OMG document number: formal/2011-01-01 (2011)
15. Pohl, K.: Requirements Engineering: Fundamentals, Principles, and Techniques. Springer (2010)
16. Priesterjahn, C., Heinzemann, C., Schäfer, W.: From timed automata to timed failure propagation graphs. In: 4th IEEE Workshop on Self-Organizing Real-time Systems (SORT 2013). IEEE (2013)
17. Chen, X., Liu, J., Mallet, F., Jin, Z.: Modeling timing requirements in problem frames using CCSL. In: APSEC, pp. 381–388 (2011)

Architecture Strategies for Cyber-Foraging: Preliminary Results from a Systematic Literature Review

Grace A. Lewis[1,2], Patricia Lago[2], and Giuseppe Procaccianti[2]

[1] Carnegie Mellon Software Engineering Institute, USA
[2] VU University Amsterdam, The Netherlands
glewis@sei.cmu.edu, {p.lago,g.procaccianti}@vu.nl

Abstract. Mobile devices have become for many the preferred way of interacting with the Internet, social media and the enterprise. However, mobile devices still do not have the computing power and battery life that will allow them to perform effectively over long periods of time or for executing applications that require extensive communication or computation, or low latency. Cyber-foraging is a technique to enable mobile devices to extend their computing power and storage by offloading computation or data to more powerful servers located in the cloud or in single-hop proximity. This paper presents the preliminary results of a systematic literature review (SLR) on architectures that support cyber-foraging. The preliminary results show that this is an area with many opportunities for research that will enable cyber-foraging solutions to become widely adopted as a way to support the mobile applications of the present and the future.

1   Introduction

Mobile Cloud Computing (MCC) refers to the combination of mobile devices and cloud computing in which cloud resources perform computing-intensive tasks and store massive amounts of data. Increased mobile device capabilities, combined with better network coverage and speeds, have enabled MCC such that mobile devices have become for many the preferred form for interacting with the Internet, social media, and the enterprise. However, mobile devices still offer less computational power than conventional desktop or server computers, and limited battery life remains a problem especially for computation- and communication-intensive applications.

Cyber-foraging is an area of work within MCC that leverages external resources (i.e., cloud servers or local servers called surrogates) to augment the computation and storage capabilities of resource-limited mobile devices while extending their battery life. There are two main forms of cyber-foraging. One is computation offload, which is the offload of expensive computation in order to extend battery life and increase computational capability. The second is data staging to improve data transfers between mobile devices and the cloud by temporarily staging data in transit.

P. Avgeriou and U. Zdun (Eds.): ECSA 2014, LNCS 8627, pp. 154–169, 2014.
© Springer International Publishing Switzerland 2014

The goal of this paper is to present the preliminary results of a Systematic Literature Review (SLR) to discover software architecture solutions that support cyber-foraging and set the stage for future and necessary research in this area. Section 2 presents a very brief summary of the SLR elements. Section 3 presents the analysis of the identified primary studies using a categorization of architecture decisions that are relevant for cyber-foraging systems. A summary of the observations and findings from the primary studies is presented in Section 4. Section 5 presents related work. Finally, Section 6 presents conclusions and the next steps in our research.

2   Research Method

To identify work related to architectures for cyber-foraging an SLR was conducted following the guidelines proposed in [1] and [2]. The research question was stated as "What software architecture and design strategies for cyber-foraging from mobile devices can be identified in the literature?" The main data source was Google Scholar and snowballing was used to complement the set of primary studies. Due to page limitations, the details related to inclusion and exclusion criteria, search string used, search string validation, results of the multiple search rounds, and threats to validity can be found at http://www.cs.vu.nl/~patricia/Patricia_Lago/Shared_files/SLR-ArchCyberForaging.pdf. A set of 57 primary studies was identified [1] Table 1 shows the computation offload systems found in the primary studies and Table 2 shows the data staging systems.

3   Analysis of Primary Studies

Defining an architecture for a system that uses cyber-foraging to enhance the computing power of mobile devices requires making decisions on where, when and what to offload, from the perspective of the mobile device. The systems from the primary studies were analyzed to obtain the answers to these questions.

3.1   Where to Offload

In cyber-foraging, computation or data is offloaded to resources with greater computing power. These resources are located in either single-hop or multi-hop proximity of mobile devices.

Most of the systems in the studies (16/60 or 27%) offload to only *Proximate Disconnected* resources, which are surrogates located in single-hop proximity of the mobile device that can operate without being connected to a cloud resource.

---

[1] The total of primary studies is 57 but the total of systems analyzed is 52 for computation offload and 8 for data staging for a total of 60 systems because two of the computation offload studies present two different systems and one study presents systems for both computation offload and data staging.

This is expected because of the advantages of lower latency and battery consumption that come from using WiFi or short-range radio instead of broadband wireless (e.g., 3G/4G) [3]. These systems therefore assume that the surrogate can function stand-alone and offload computation is pre-provisioned (i.e., at system deployment time) or provisioned at runtime from the mobile devices themselves. However, many of these systems could be adapted to work with remote cloud servers or any addressable offload target but would lose the advantage of lower latency due to proximity.

Table 1. Computation Offload Systems in Primary Studies

Column groups: **Where** = Prox. Disconnected, Prox. Connected, Remote; **When** = Runtime Decision, Always Offload; **What / Granularity** = Process, Function, Component, Service, Application, Computation; **What / Payload** = Partitioning Algo., Parameters, Application State, Device Context, Source Location, Setup Instructions, Continuous Data.

System	Prox. Disconnected	Prox. Connected	Remote	Runtime Decision	Always Offload	Process	Function	Component	Service	Application	Computation	Partitioning Algo.	Parameters	Application State	Device Context	Source Location	Setup Instructions	Continuous Data
mHealthMon [4]			X	X					X				X					
Mobile Agents [5]			X	X				X					X					
Clone-to-Clone (C2C) [6]	X		X			X							X					
Chroma [7]	X		X			X							X					
Collaborative Applications [8]	X		X			X							X	X				
Computation and Compilation Offload [9]	X		X			X							X					
Cloud Media Services [10]		X			X			X							X			
Roam [11]	X	X	X					X					X	X		X		
CloneCloud [12]	X				X	X							X					
MAUI [13]	X	X	X			X							X					
Kahawai [13]	X				X						X							X
HPC-as-a-Service [14]	X	X			X				X				X					
OpenCL-Enabled Kernels [15]	X	X	X					X				X	X					
Real Options Analysis [16]	X	X	X			X							X					
3DMA [17]			X	X				X					X					
Spectra [18]	X		X			X							X					
AlfredO [19]			X	X					X			X	X					
Collective Surrogates [20]		X	X	X						X							X	
Grid-Enhanced Mobile Devices [21]		X	X	X				X					X					
Cloudlets [22]	X			X							X	X	X					
Virtual Phone [23]		X		X				X							X			
Single-Server Offloading [24]	X			X		X							X					
Cloud Operating System [24]		X		X				X				X	X					
Android Extensions [25]			X	X				X					X					
ThinAV [26]		X	X	X						X			X					

Continued on next page

Table 1. *Continued from previous page*

System	Where			When		Granularity					Payload							
	Prox. Disconnected	Prox. Connected	Remote	Runtime Decision	Always Offload	Process	Function	Component	Service	Application	Computation	Partitioning Algo.	Parameters	Application State	Device Context	Source Location	Setup Instructions	Continuous Data
Cuckoo [27]	X		X	X				X			X		X					
ThinkAir [28]			X	X			X				X		X					
MACS [29]	X		X	X				X			X		X					
Scavenger [30]	X			X				X			X		X					
AMCO [31]	X		X	X				X					X	X				
MCo [32]		X			X			X			X		X					
PowerSense [33]	X			X						X			X					
AIDE [34]	X		X	X				X					X					
Application Virtualization [35]	X				X					X	X		X					
PARM [36]	X			X				X					X					
Resource Furnishing System [37]		X	X		X				X									X
Cloud Personal Assistant [38]		X	X		X					X			X					
SOME [39]			X		X	X							X					
SmartVirtCloud [40]		X			X			X			X		X					
Odessa [41]	X		X	X				X					X					
Smartphone-Based Social Sensing [42]	X		X	X				X					X					
MAPCloud [43]		X	X	X					X								X	
VM-Based Cloudlets [44]	X				X					X	X		X					
IC-Cloud [45]	X		X	X		X							X					
SPADE [46]			X		X			X					X					
Slingshot [47]		X			X					X			X					
Offloading Toolkit and Service [48]	X		X	X				X			X		X					
Mobile Data Stream Application Framework [49]			X	X				X						X	X			
Heterogeneous Auto-Offloading Framework [50]			X	X				X					X					
Weblets [51]			X	X				X					X					
DPartner [52]	X		X	X				X					X					
Elastic HTML5 [53]	X		X	X				X					X			X		

The second largest set of systems in the studies (15/60 or 25%) offloads to *Remote* resources, such as an enterprise cloud or data center. However, unless connectivity to an enterprise cloud is necessary for the system to function, these systems could also offload to proximate connected or disconnected nodes.

Tied for the second largest set of systems in the studies (also 15/60 or 25%) are those that offload to *Remote* or *Proximate Disconnected* resources. In

Table 2. Data Staging Systems in Primary Studies

System	Where			When		What — Data Type				What — Data Operations			
	Prox. Disconnected	Prox. Connected	Remote	Runtime Decision	Always Offload	Data Updates	Application Data	Data Files	Field-Collected Data	Pre-Fetching	In-Bound Processing	Out-Bound Processing	Storage
Edge Proxy [54]		X			X	X					X		
Mobile Information Access Architecture for Occasionally-Connected Computing [55]	X				X	X					X		
Trusted and Unmanaged Data Staging Surrogates [56]	X				X			X			X		
Android Extensions [25]			X		X	X							X
Telemedik [57]	X	X			X	X						X	
Feel the World [58]	X	X	X		X				X				X
Large-Scale Mobile Crowdsensing [59]		X			X				X			X	
Sonora [60]	X	X	X		X				X			X	

general, these systems have offload targets that can function stand-alone and are accessible over an IP network, whether local or remote.

The next set of systems (7/60 or 12%) offloads to *Remote* or *Proximate Connected* resources, which are surrogates located in single-hop proximity of the mobile device that need to be connected at runtime to a cloud resource. The offload targets in these systems need access to a cloud resource in order to operate properly, whether to obtain the code to be offloaded, access application data, or offload computation or data to other cloud resources (i.e., surrogate acts as an intermediary).

Finally, five out of 60 systems (5/60 or 8%) offload to only *Proximate Connected* resources, and there are two data staging studies that can offload to all three options (2/60 or 3%).

Most systems in the studies offload to a single known surrogate or cloud resource. The reason is that the focus of the studies is on demonstrating the validity or efficiency of portions of the architecture, such as optimization engines or partitioning algorithms, and not the operation of the full system. Some systems include a component in the architecture to discover and select offload targets based on (1) offload target broadcast, (2) a cloud directory service, (3) surrogate managers that manage available surrogates, (4) local offload target lists, or (5) an application or service directory.

3.2   When to Offload

In general, offloading is beneficial when large amounts of computation are needed with relatively small amounts of communication [61].

For most of the systems in the studies (33/60 or 55%) offloading is a *Runtime Decision*. The majority of these systems perform a runtime calculation (often called a utility function) to determine whether it is better to execute locally or to offload computation by comparing predicted local execution cost against predicted remote execution cost. Local execution cost typically takes into consideration the energy consumed by local execution as well as the local execution time. Remote execution cost typically considers the energy consumed by communication based on payload size and network conditions, the communication time based on payload size and network conditions, and remote execution time.

The systems that perform runtime calculations require developer input or static profiling to obtain the initial values or models that are used in the calculation, such as required compute cycles, payload size based on input and output parameters, and required energy for execution and communication. Other parameters such as current network conditions or load of the mobile device and offload target are obtained at runtime. In addition, some systems use runtime profiling to collect data at runtime to adjust the initial values. The goal is to obtain more realistic values based on actual execution data.

The rest of the systems in the studies (27/60 or 45%) *Always Offload* computation or data. For computation offload systems, the parts of the system that are considered computation-intensive, or that simply cannot run on a mobile device, are pre-determined and executed on offload targets. All the data staging systems fall in this category, which is expected, because by definition the idea is for the mobile device to send and receive data to and from an enterprise cloud, either directly or via a surrogate. The decision-making process is not whether it is efficient or not to stage data but when is the right time to do so.

3.3   What to Offload

What to offload involves two architecture decisions, but these are different for computation offload and data staging systems.

Computation Offload Systems. For computation offload, one decision has to do with the *Granularity* of the computation that is offloaded to the surrogate or cloud resource and another has to do with the *Payload* that is sent from the client to the surrogate or cloud resource in order to execute the offloaded computation. Although these seem like low-level decisions, they have architecture implications because they determine the components that are needed on the client and the offload target.

All the systems in the studies have an *offload client* that runs on the mobile device and an *offload server* that runs on the offload target to coordinate the offload operation. The majority of the systems are designed such that the applications at runtime are not aware that computation is being offloaded. What changes between systems based on granularity are the development, build and runtime dependencies between the offload client and target, as well as the amount of state synchronization to guarantee the correct execution of applications.

For *Granulairity*, most systems offload at the *Component, Class, Module, or Task* level (27/52 or 52%). The type of element that is offloaded varies greatly between systems, but in general they are software elements that execute inside specific containers or runtime environments such as Java Virtual Machines (JVMs), OGSi platforms, or custom-built environments that enable migration between local and remote execution. The advantage of offloading at this level of granularity is that for the most part these are self-contained elements, meaning that they store their own state. Once an element is offloaded there is no need to synchronize state with the local device unless the execution is returning to the local device. However, except for the systems that rely on more standard environments, such as JVMs and OGSi platforms, there are very tight dependencies between the mobile execution environment and the execution environment on the offload target, which creates limitations in terms of programming languages and increases the effort required for application reuse because of the need to use specific libraries and constructs to enable computation offload.

The second largest set of systems offloads *Functions, Methods, or Operations* (11/52 or 21%). In many of these systems, developers manually mark the functions that they consider offloadable. In addition to the same types of constraints and requirements for applications and offload targets outlined for the first set of systems, the challenge for these types of system is guaranteeing fidelity of results, which means that executing locally or remotely should produce the same results. Functions, methods and operations are part of a larger programming constructs such as classes or programs that maintain state at runtime, typically expressed as class attributes or global variables. This means that the system has to synchronize state such that it is the same locally and remotely, either periodically or sending it as an additional input/output of the offload operation.

Systems that offload full *Applications, Programs or Servers* of a client/server application represent the third largest set of systems in the studies (7/52 or 13%). The advantage of offloading at this level of granularity is that execution environments are much more generic, such as virtual machines or application servers. This also increases application reuse because servers do not have to be adapted to run on mobile devices. Clients are very thin and perform the functionality that cannot be offloaded, such as user interface and sensor operations. However, the rest of the computation is always offloaded, regardless of whether it would be more efficient or not to be executed on the mobile device.

The fourth largest set of systems in the studies offload *Services* (6/52 or 12%). Services in these studies are coarse-grained capabilities accessed via standardize interfaces that have been identified by system developers as computation-intensive. These systems do not have the requirements or constraints of the systems that offload functions or components because by definition services are self-contained. Once a decision is made to offload, the service is invoked and the system either waits for a reply or receives the reply when it is ready.

Finally, there is one system that offloads at the process level (1/52 or 2%). In this system the mobile device is fully cloned inside a VM running on the offload target. When the system encounters a computation block that is marked for offload, the process enters into a sleep state and process state is transferred from the mobile device to the clone VM. The clone VM integrates the process state, executes the computation block from beginning to end, and then transfers its process state back to the mobile device. The mobile device reintegrates the process state and wakes up the sleeping process to continue its execution. This system allows very fine-grained control of what portions of an application to offload, but requires a very stable network connection to support state synchronization.

Concerning *Payload*, for the majority of the systems the payload is the *Invocation Parameters* to execute the remote computation (27/52 or 52%). All these systems assume that the offloaded computation already exists on the offload target, which leads to a small payload that simply depends on the size of the parameter data types. However, these systems completely rely on the existence and currency of the offloaded computation on the offload target, which in turn would require more complex deployment processes.

For the next largest set of systems the payload is *Computation* and *Invocation Parameters* (12/52 or 23%). This means that both the actual computation (code) and its invocation parameters are sent from the mobile device to the offload target. The offload target deploys the computation inside a container or execution environment, executes it directly in a runtime environment, or distributes it to other offload targets for deployment. Once the computation is running, the mobile device sends the invocation parameters for the actual execution.

For the next set of systems the payload is *Application State* (2/52 or 4%). The state of the application on the mobile device is synchronized with the offload target so that the remote computation can be executed with the same state as that on the application running on the mobile device. In both of these systems the execution returns to mobile device and state is synchronized back in the same way.

For a small set of systems the payload is *Setup Instructions* and *Invocation Parameters* (2/52 or 4%). This means that the initial payload is the instructions of how to set up the computation on the offload target. Once the computation is running, the mobile device sends the invocation parameters for the actual execution.

In the next set of systems (2/52 or 4%) the payload is *Continuous Data from Offload Target to Mobile Device*. In Kahawai [13], a system targeted at GPU-intensive applications such as games, the offload target maintains a high-fidelity version of the graphics and a low fidelity version that matches the fidelity of the mobile device. It compares both and sends a compressed video stream of delta frames to the mobile device. The mobile device decompresses the stream and applies the deltas to the frames that it renders locally. In the Resource Furnishing System [37] the interaction with the offload target is done via a VNC client which means that GUI updates are continuously sent from the offload target to mobile devices and applied locally.

In addition to *Invocation Parameters*, two systems offload the *Partitioning Algorithm* that is part of the "When to Offload" decision to determine what computation executes locally and what computation is offloaded (2/52 or 4%).

For two systems the initial payload is local *Application State* so that the mobile device and the offload target can synchronize state before invoking the offloaded computation (2/52 or 4%). Once the computation is running, the mobile device sends the *Invocation Parameters* for the actual execution.

On a smaller scale, for one system the initial payload is the *Device Context* (1/52 or 2%), which in this case is device type, browser type, supported codecs, screen size, network bandwidth, and latency, such that the appropriate media processing components are selected. Once the computation is running, the mobile device sends the *Invocation Parameters* for the actual execution. For one system (1/52 or 2%), the initial payload is the *Source Location*, or where to obtain the computation for installation on the offload target. *Application State* is then transferred from the mobile device to the offload target. Once the computation is running and the state is synchronized, the mobile device sends the *Invocation Parameters* for the actual execution. Finally, for one system, the initial payload is the *Source Location* (URL) of the offloaded computation and then it sends the *Invocation Parameters* for the actual execution (1/52 or 1%).

Data Staging Systems. For data staging, one architecture decision has to do with the type of data that is being staged and the other has to do with the operations that are offloaded to the surrogate or cloud resource to be performed on the data. As with computation offload, the answer to this question has architecture implications because it requires different components on both sides depending on how data is stored and forwarded.

Concerning *Data Type*, *Field-Collected Data* is sent to an offload target for staging in three of the systems (3/8 or 38%). Staging sensor data addresses storage limitations on mobile devices. In addition, data collected by a surrogate can be shared by other mobile devices connected to the same surrogate or can be fused or pre-processed before sending it to the enterprise.

Application Data is staged in three of the systems (3/8 or 38%). Data that is like to be used by an application on the mobile device is retrieved from a cloud resource and staged on a surrogate. The advantage in this case is lower latency because the data resides in a nearby surrogate and not in a remote cloud.

One system uses the surrogate as an intermediary for *Data Updates* (1/8 or 13%). In Edge Proxy [54] the surrogate informs the mobile device when marked areas of a web page have changed, so that the mobile device is only notified when there are data updates. therefore limiting the amount of direct communication to remote resources.

Finally, one system stages *Data Files* (1/8 or 13%). In Trusted and Unmanaged Data Staging Surrogates [56] a surrogate stages data files that might be needed by the mobile device. The advantage, as in staging application data, is lower latency because the files reside on a nearby surrogate and not in a remote server. Access to the remote server is done by the surrogate and only when the file is not available on the surrogate (similar to a cache miss) or when data on the surrogate has changed and need to be consolidated with the data in the remote server.

Concerning *Data Operations on Surrogate*, two systems perform *Pre-Fetching* operations on the surrogate (2/8 or 25%). The goal is to pre-determine data that is likely to be used by connected mobile devices, retrieve that data from cloud resources, and then store it to reduce the latency of direct cloud access.

Two systems perform *In-Bound Filtering or Pre-Processing* of data that flows from the enterprise (or cloud) to the mobile device (2/8 or 25%). The goal is to pre-process data that is retrieved or pushed from cloud resources so that data is ready to be consumed, or filtered such that the mobile device only receives the data that it needs. The advantage is that the heavy computation and communication to remote servers happens on the surrogates and not on the mobile devices.

Two systems perform *Out-Bound Filtering or Pre-Processing* of data that flows from the mobile device to the enterprise (or cloud) (2/8 or 25%). The goal is for the surrogate to process data that is received from mobile devices such that the data that is sent on to the cloud resource is ready for consumption by the cloud resource (e.g., cleaned, filtered or merged data).

Finally, two systems use the offload target as an extension of the mobile device's storage system for *Data Storage* (2/8 or 25%). All data operations (i.e., CRUD operations) are performed on the surrogate.

4   Observations and Findings from Primary Studies

The primary studies show different and novel computation offload and data staging systems targeted at guaranteeing fidelity of results, and optimizing attributes such as energy consumption, network bandwidth usage, and performance. For computation offload systems, the offload mechanisms range from dynamic approaches in which the computation is provisioned from the mobile device to more static approaches where the computation already exists on the offload target. For data staging systems, the capabilities of the offload target range from an extension of the mobile device's storage to sophisticated algorithms that predict and stage the data that will likely be needed by the mobile device. As far as distribution, the number of computation offloading systems (52) is much larger than the number of data staging systems (8).

A preliminary analysis of the data shows the following gaps and opportunities for architecture strategies for cyber-foraging systems.

- Understanding of quality attributes beyond energy, performance, network usage, and fidelity of results: Many of the cyber-foraging systems, especially those that perform runtime partitioning and offloading decisions, have very complex algorithms for guaranteeing fidelity of results, and optimizing energy consumption, network bandwidth usage and performance. Disconnected operations and fault tolerance are supported by some systems in which the local computation is a fallback mechanism if the remote computation fails. However, there is very little consideration of other quality attributes that are relevant to cyber-foraging systems, such as ease of distribution and installation, resiliency, and security.

- System-level architecture analysis: Related to the previous point, the systems in the studies tend to focus on enabling cyber-foraging between one mobile device and one offload target. However, there is very little discussion of system-level attributes that have to be considered when moving from experimental prototypes to operational systems. For example:
  - How do the systems perform when there are multiple devices trying to offload to the same target?
  - If there are multiple offload targets available, how does the mobile device select the target that best fits its requirements?
  - What happens if the mobile device loses connectivity to the offload target?
  - In those mechanisms that require custom infrastructures or middleware, what are the mechanisms for ensuring currency and compatibility of mobile-side and server-side components if these may not have the same distribution mechanisms?
  - What are the tradeoffs between the quality attributes promoted by the system and other quality attributes such as ease of distribution and installation, resiliency and security?
- Large-scale evaluations: Most of the studies have very limited case studies or evaluations. For example, even though studies talk about mobile cloud computing the experiments are done in controlled environments over WiFi connections, which is not representative of a real mobile cloud environment with disconnections, high latency and multiple heterogeneous users and devices.
- Architectures for data staging systems: The low number of primary studies related to architectures for data staging, combined with an increasing number of data collection devices in the field and the Internet of Things (IoT), show that it is a potential area for developing architecture patterns or tactics that can be leveraged by software architects and developers of these types of systems.

5   Related Work

There are several studies that survey the field of MCC and identify cyber-foraging as a research area and challenge, but are not systematic literature reviews and do not have an architecture focus. Abolfazli et al [62] present a survey of cloud-based mobile augmentation (CMA) approaches, one of which is cyber-foraging. One of the challenges stated by this work is the lack of a reference architecture for CMA. Dinh at al [63] present a survey on MCC. Computation offload is discussed as a technique for extending battery lifetime of mobile devices and listed as one of the challenges for MCC. Fernando et al [64] present a more complete survey on mobile cloud computing. Some of the research that addresses efficient computation offload and distribution to the cloud and how it differs from traditional distributed systems is discussed in this paper. Kumar et al [65] present a survey on computation offloading but focus primarily on the algorithms used to partition and offload programs in order to improve performance or save energy. Finally, Yu et al [66] present a survey on seamless application mobility, which is the continuous or uninterrupted computing experience as a user moves across devices. Code offloading is mentioned as a future direction for seamless application mobility. The work that is most similar to ours is by Flinn et al [67] that presents a discussion of representative cyber-foraging systems and their characteristics. However, it is limited to a small number of systems and does not follow a systematic process. To the best of our knowledge, ours is the first systematic literature review related to architectures for cyber-foraging.

6   Conclusions and Next Steps

We presented preliminary results of an SLR in architectures for cyber-foraging systems and analyzed the primary studies using a categorization of architecture decisions related to what, when and where to offload computation and data from mobile devices. The analysis allowed us to identify gaps and opportunities for research in (1) quality attributes that are relevant to cyber-foraging systems, such as ease of distribution and installation, resiliency, and security, (2) system-level architecture analysis, (3) large-scale evaluations, and (4) architectures for data staging systems. Our next steps are to further refine the analysis and cluster the results to identify architectural tactics that can be employed by system architects to build systems that use cyber foraging, with an analysis of the quality attributes and tradeoffs related to each tactic.

Acknowledgments. This material is based upon work funded and supported by the Department of Defense under Contract No. FA8721-05-C-0003 with Carnegie Mellon University for the operation of the Software Engineering Institute, a federally funded research and development center. This material has been approved for public release and unlimited distribution (DM-0001173).

References

1. Dyba, T., Dingsoyr, T., Hanssen, G.: Applying systematic reviews to diverse study types: An experience report. In: First International Symposium on Empirical Software Engineering and Measurement, ESEM 2007, pp. 225–234 (September 2007)
2. Kitchenham, B., Charters, S.: Guidelines for performing systematic literature reviews in software engineering. Keele University and Durham University Joint Report, Tech. Rep. EBSE 2007-001 (2007)
3. Balasubramanian, N., Balasubramanian, A., Venkataramani, A.: Energy consumption in mobile phones: A measurement study and implications for network applications. In: Proceedings of the 9th ACM SIGCOMM Conference on Internet Measurement Conference, IMC 2009, pp. 280–293. ACM, New York (2009)

4. Ahnn, J., Potkonjak, M.: Toward energy-efficient and distributed mobile health monitoring using parallel offloading. Journal of Medical Systems 37(5), 1–11 (2013)
5. Angin, P., Bhargava, B.: An agent-based optimization framework for mobile-cloud computing. Journal of Wireless Mobile Networks, Ubiquitous Computing, and Dependable Applications (JoWUA) 4, 1–17 (2013)
6. Aucinas, A., Crowcroft, J., Hui, P.: Energy efficient mobile m2m communications. In: Proceedings of ExtremeCom 2012 (2012)
7. Balan, R.K., Gergle, D., Satyanarayanan, M., Herbsleb, J.: Simplifying cyber foraging for mobile devices. In: Proceedings of the 5th International Conference on Mobile Systems, Applications and Services, MobiSys 2007, pp. 272–285. ACM, New York (2007)
8. Chang, Y.-S., Hung, S.-H.: Developing collaborative applications with mobile cloud-a case study of speech recognition. Journal of Internet Services and Information Security (JISIS) 1(1), 18–36 (2011)
9. Chen, G., Kang, B.-T., Kandemir, M., Vijaykrishnan, N., Irwin, M.J., Chandramouli, R.: Studying energy trade offs in offloading computation/compilation in java-enabled mobile devices. IEEE Transactions on Parallel and Distributed Systems 15(9), 795–809 (2004)
10. Cheng, B., Probst, M.: Hbb-next i d4.4.1: Intermediate middleware software components for cloud service offloading. HBB-NEXT Consortium 2013, Tech. Rep. (2013)
11. Chu, H.-H., Song, H., Wong, C., Kurakake, S., Katagiri, M.: Roam, a seamless application framework. Journal of Systems and Software 69(3), 209–226 (2004)
12. Chun, B.G., Maniatis, P.: Augmented smartphone applications through clone cloud execution. In: Proceedings of the 12th Conference on Hot Topics in Operating Systems, p. 8. USENIX Association (2009)
13. Cuervo, E.: Enhancing mobile devices through code offload. Ph.D. dissertation, Duke University (2012)
14. Duga, N.: Optimality analysis and middleware design for heterogeneous cloud hpc in mobile devices. Master's thesis. Addis Ababa University (2011)
15. Endt, H., Weckemann, K.: Remote utilization of opencl for flexible computation offloading using embedded ecus, ce devices and cloud servers. In: Applications, Tools and Techniques on the Road to Exascale Computing. Advances in Parallel Computing, vol. 22, pp. 133–140. IOS Press EBooks (2011)
16. Esteves, R.G., McCool, M.D., Lemieux, C.: Real options for mobile communication management. In: 2011 IEEE GLOBECOM Workshops (GC Wkshps), pp. 1241–1246. IEEE (2011)
17. Fjellheim, T., Milliner, S., Dumas, M.: Middleware support for mobile applications. International Journal of Pervasive Computing and Communications 1(2), 75–88 (2005)
18. Flinn, J., Park, S., Satyanarayanan, M.: Balancing performance, energy, and quality in pervasive computing. In: Proceedings of the 22nd International Conference on Distributed Computing Systems, pp. 217–226 (2002)
19. Giurgiu, I., Riva, O., Juric, D., Krivulev, I., Alonso, G.: Calling the cloud: Enabling mobile phones as interfaces to cloud applications. In: Bacon, J.M., Cooper, B.F. (eds.) Middleware 2009. LNCS, vol. 5896, pp. 83–102. Springer, Heidelberg (2009)
20. Goyal, S.: A collective approach to harness idle resources of end nodes. Ph.D. dissertation, School of Computing, University of Utah (2011)
21. Guan, T.: A system architecture to provide enhanced grid access for mobile devices. Ph.D. dissertation, University of Southampton (2008)

22. Ha, K., Lewis, G., Simanta, S., Satyanarayanan, M.: Cloud offload in hostile environments. Carnegie Mellon University, Tech. Rep. (2011)
23. Hung, S.-H., Shieh, J.-P., Lee, C.-P.: Migrating android applications to the cloud. International Journal of Grid and High Performance Computing (IJGHPC) 3(2), 14–28 (2011)
24. Imai, S.: Task offloading between smartphones and distributed computational resources. Master's thesis, Rensselaer Polytechnic Institute (2012)
25. Iyer, A.N., et al.: Extending android application programming framework for seamless cloud integration. In: 2012 IEEE First International Conference on Mobile Services (MS), pp. 96–104. IEEE (2012)
26. Jarabek, C., Barrera, D., Aycock, J.: Thinav: truly lightweight mobile cloud-based anti-malware. In: Proceedings of the 28th Annual Computer Security Applications Conference, pp. 209–218. ACM (2012)
27. Kemp, R., Palmer, N., Kielmann, T., Bal, H.: Cuckoo: A computation offloading framework for smartphones. In: Gris, M., Yang, G. (eds.) MobiCASE 2010. LNICST, vol. 76, pp. 59–79. Springer, Heidelberg (2012)
28. Kosta, S., Aucinas, A., Hui, P., Mortier, R., Zhang, X.: Thinkair: Dynamic resource allocation and parallel execution in the cloud for mobile code offloading. In: 2012 Proceedings IEEE INFOCOM, pp. 945–953. IEEE (2012)
29. Kovachev, D., Klamma, R.: Framework for computation offloading in mobile cloud computing. International Journal of Interactive Multimedia and Artificial Intelligence 1(7), 6–15 (2012)
30. Kristensen, M.D.: Empowering mobile devices through cyber foraging. Ph.D. dissertation, Aarhus University (2010)
31. Kwon, Y.-W., Tilevich, E.: Reducing the energy consumption of mobile applications behind the scenes. In: Proceedings of the 29th IEEE International Conference on Software Maintenance, ICSM 2013 (2013)
32. Lee, B.-D.: A framework for seamless execution of mobile applications in the cloud. In: Qian, Z., Cao, L., Su, W., Wang, T., Yang, H. (eds.) Recent Advances in CSIE 2011. Lecture Notes in Electrical Engineering, vol. 126, pp. 145–154. Springer, Heidelberg (2012)
33. Matthews, J., Chang, M., Feng, Z., Srinivas, R., Gerla, M.: Powersense: power aware dengue diagnosis on mobile phones. In: Proceedings of the First ACM Workshop on Mobile Systems, Applications, and Services for Healthcare, p. 6. ACM (2011)
34. Messer, A., Greenberg, I., Bernadat, P., Milojicic, D., Chen, D., Giuli, T., Gu, X.: Towards a distributed platform for resource-constrained devices. In: Proceedings of the 22nd International Conference on Distributed Computing Systems, pp. 43–51. IEEE (2002)
35. Messinger, D., Lewis, G.A.: Application virtualizaton as a strategy for cyber foraging in resource-constrained environments. Carnegie Mellon Software Engineering Institute, Tech. Rep. (2013)
36. Mohapatra, S., Venkatasubramanian, N.: Optimizing power using a reconfigurable middleware. UC Irvine, Tech. Rep. (2003)
37. Ok, M., Seo, J.-W., Park, M.-S.: A distributed resource furnishing to offload resource-constrained devices in cyber foraging toward pervasive computing. In: Enokido, T., Barolli, L., Takizawa, M. (eds.) NBiS 2007. LNCS, vol. 4658, pp. 416–425. Springer, Heidelberg (2007)
38. O'Sullivan, M.J., Grigoras, D.: The cloud personal assistant for providing services to mobile clients. In: 2013 IEEE 7th International Symposium on Service Oriented System Engineering (SOSE), pp. 478–485 (2013)

39. Park, S., Choi, Y., Chen, Q., Yeom, H.: Some: Selective offloading for a mobile computing environment. In: 2012 IEEE International Conference on Cluster Computing (CLUSTER), pp. 588–591 (2012)
40. Pu, L., Xu, J., Jin, X., Zhang, J.: Smartvirtcloud: virtual cloud assisted application offloading execution at mobile devices' discretion. In: 2013 IEEE Wireless Communications and Networking Conference (WCNC): Services and Applications (2013)
41. Ra, M.-R., Sheth, A., Mummert, L., Pillai, P., Wetherall, D., Govindan, R.: Odessa: enabling interactive perception applications on mobile devices. In: Proceedings of the 9th International Conference on Mobile Systems, Applications, and Services, MobiSys 2011, pp. 43–56. ACM, New York (2011)
42. Rachuri, K.K.: Smartphones based social sensing: Adaptive sampling, sensing and computation offloading. Ph.D. dissertation, University of Cambridge (2012)
43. Rahimi, M.R., Venkatasubramanian, N., Mehrotra, S., Vasilakos, A.V.: Mapcloud: mobile applications on an elastic and scalable 2-tier cloud architecture. In: Proceedings of the 2012 IEEE/ACM Fifth International Conference on Utility and Cloud Computing, pp. 83–90. IEEE Computer Society (2012)
44. Satyanarayanan, M., Bahl, P., Caceres, R., Davies, N.: The case for vm-based cloudlets in mobile computing. IEEE Pervasive Computing 8(4), 14–23 (2009)
45. Shi, C., Pandurangan, P., Ni, K., Yang, J., Ammar, M., Naik, M., Zegura, E.: Ic-cloud: Computation offloading to an intermittently-connected cloud. Georgia Institute of Technology, Tech. Rep. (2013)
46. Silva, J.N., Veiga, L., Ferreira, P.: Spade: scheduler for parallel and distributed execution from mobile devices. In: Proceedings of the 6th International Workshop on Middleware for Pervasive and Ad-hoc Computing, pp. 25–30. ACM (2008)
47. Su, Y.-Y., Flinn, J.: Slingshot: deploying stateful services in wireless hotspots. In: Proceedings of the 3rd International Conference on Mobile Systems, Applications, and Services, MobiSys 2005, pp. 79–92. ACM, New York (2005)
48. Yang, K., Ou, S., Chen, H.-H.: On effective offloading services for resource-constrained mobile devices running heavier mobile internet applications. IEEE Communications Magazine 46(1), 56–63 (2008)
49. Yang, L., Cao, J., Yuan, Y., Li, T., Han, A., Chan, A.: A framework for partitioning and execution of data stream applications in mobile cloud computing. ACM SIGMETRICS Performance Evaluation Review 40(4), 23–32 (2013)
50. Zhang, Y., Guan, X.-T., Huang, T., Cheng, X.: A heterogeneous auto-offloading framework based on web browser for resource-constrained devices. In: Fourth International Conference on Internet and Web Applications and Services, ICIW 2009, pp. 193–199. IEEE (2009)
51. Zhang, X., Kunjithapatham, A., Jeong, S., Gibbs, S.: Towards an elastic application model for augmenting the computing capabilities of mobile devices with cloud computing. Mobile Networks and Applications 16(3), 270–284 (2011)
52. Zhang, Y., Huang, G., Zhang, W., Liu, X., Mei, H.: Towards module-based automatic partitioning of java applications. Frontiers of Computer Science 6(6), 725–740 (2012)
53. Zhang, X., Jeon, W., Gibbs, S., Kunjithapatham, A.: Elastic HTML5: Workload offloading using cloud-based web workers and storages for mobile devices. In: Gris, M., Yang, G. (eds.) MobiCASE 2010. LNICST, vol. 76, pp. 373–381. Springer, Heidelberg (2012)
54. Armstrong, T., Trescases, O., Amza, C., de Lara, E.: Efficient and transparent dynamic content updates for mobile clients. In: Proceedings of the 4th International Conference on Mobile Systems, Applications and Services, pp. 56–68. ACM (2006)

55. Bahrami, A., Wang, C., Yuan, J., Hunt, A.: The workflow based architecture for mobile information access in occasionally connected computing. In: IEEE International Conference on Services Computing, SCC 2006, pp. 406–413. IEEE (2006)
56. Flinn, J., Sinnamohideen, S., Tolia, N., Satyanarayanan, M.: Data staging on untrusted surrogates. In: Proceedings 2nd USENIX Conference on File and Storage Technologies (FAST 2003), San Francisco, CA, March 31-April 2 (2003)
57. Kundu, S., Mukherjee, J., Majumdar, A.K., Majumdar, B., Sekhar Ray, S.: Algorithms and heuristics for efficient medical information display in pda. Computers in Biology and Medicine 37(9), 1272–1282 (2007)
58. Phokas, T., Efstathiades, H., Pallis, G., Dikaiakos, M.D.: Feel the world: A mobile framework for participatory sensing. In: Daniel, F., Papadopoulos, G.A., Thiran, P. (eds.) MobiWIS 2013. LNCS, vol. 8093, pp. 143–156. Springer, Heidelberg (2013)
59. Xiao, Y., Simoens, P., Pillai, P., Ha, K., Satyanarayanan, M.: Lowering the barriers to large-scale mobile crowdsensing. In: Mobile Computing Systems and Applications (2013)
60. Yang, F., Qian, Z., Chen, X., Beschastnikh, I., Zhuang, L., Zhou, L., Shen, J.: Sonora: A platform for continuous mobile-cloud computing. Technical Report. Microsoft Research Asia, Tech. Rep. (2012)
61. Kumar, K., Lu, Y.-H.: Cloud computing for mobile users: Can offloading computation save energy? Computer 43(4), 51–56 (2010)
62. Abolfazli, S., Sanaei, Z., Ahmed, E., Gani, A., Buyya, R.: Cloud-based augmentation for mobile devices: Motivation, taxonomies, and open challenges. IEEE Communications Surveys Tutorials 16(1), 337–368 (2014)
63. Dinh, H.T., Lee, C., Niyato, D., Wang, P.: A survey of mobile cloud computing: architecture, applications, and approaches. Wireless Communications and Mobile Computing 13, 1587–1611 (2011)
64. Fernando, N., Loke, S.W., Rahayu, W.: Mobile cloud computing: A survey. Future Generation Computer Systems 29, 84–106 (2012)
65. Kumar, K., Liu, J., Lu, Y.-H., Bhargava, B.: A survey of computation offloading for mobile systems. Mobile Networks and Applications 18(1), 129–140 (2013)
66. Yu, P., Ma, X., Cao, J., Lu, J.: Application mobility in pervasive computing: A survey. Pervasive and Mobile Computing 9, 2–17 (2012)
67. Flinn, J.: Cyber foraging: Bridging mobile and cloud computing. In: Satyanarayanan, M. (ed.) Synthesis Lectures on Mobile and Pervasive Computing. Morgan & Claypool Publishers (2012)

Adapting Enterprise Architecture at a Software Development Company and the Resultant Benefits

Krzysztof Jamróz[2], Dariusz Pitulej[1,2], and Jan Werewka[1,2]

[1] Department of Applied Computer Science
AGH University of Science and Technology
al. Mickiewicza 30, 30-059 Kraków, Poland
{Jan.Werewka,D.Pitulej}@agh.edu.pl
[2] ATSI S.A. (Advanced Technology Systems International)
ul. Krakowska 386, 30-080 Zabierzów, Poland
info@atsisa.com

Abstract. This publication presents an approach to developing an enterprise architecture at a software development company. That type of company differs from other companies in relation to software usage and development, hence a corresponding approach should be used. An efficient solution based on own experience is proposed in this paper. The solution includes the following main set of activities: defining a motivation model, adapting architecture modeling tools, IT landscape creation products, building architecture capabilities in the organization, implementing standards and guidelines, applying architecture governance, defining the architect's roles, managing risks, using architecture governance. The proposed solution is introduced in an iterative way in the software development company.

Keywords: Software architecture, enterprise architecture, architecture governance, ArchiMate.

1   Introduction

Growing organizations, especially whose main business line is software development, have to face many complicated issues connected with:

- An increase in the developed systems complexity;
- The problematic integration of new systems with existing ones;
- A poor business alignment of the developed systems. Organizations have been facing growing obstacles in aligning these increasingly costly IT systems with the business needs of customers;
- Problems with managing competencies of engineers who have the biggest technical impact on software systems development;
- Too big mix of standards and technologies used by in-house developers.

Organizations wish to improve their effectiveness and competitiveness in all their business lines. Any organization can benefit from understanding its structure,

P. Avgeriou and U. Zdun (Eds.): ECSA 2014, LNCS 8627, pp. 170–185, 2014.
© Springer International Publishing Switzerland 2014

products, operations, technology and the relationships between them. To adopt IT solutions in the best possible way, it is necessary to implement an enterprise architecture.

An Enterprise Architecture (EA) can be regarded as a model describing the way in which an organization achieves its current and future business objectives, using IT. For an enterprise, it is important that, by applying enterprise architecture, it will align its business and IT and thus become as competitive as needed. The implementation of an enterprise architecture is important for all companies and gives them many benefits [1,2,3]. Implementing an enterprise architecture in a software development company is a very important task, which can have a two-fold effect. Firstly the company improves its own organization on the basis of IT systems used for software development, and secondly delivers software products to improve the customer's organization. The overall value of implementing the EA at IT enterprises varies depending on the size and the complexity of the enterprise, the types and complexity of the software products developed, the technological solutions used, and the software services provided. It is possible to roll out architecture governance based on a general-purpose architecture framework. However, tailoring such a universal tool that can be used in any industry may be labor-intensive. Most EA architecture models are two-dimensional and do not account for the influence and synergies between their elements. Synergies can be achieved by introducing lean, agile and participatory concepts. Consequently, an enterprise will be able to respond quickly to changes coming from its internal and external environments.

The methodology applied at a software house should differ from the standard solution and should use more responsive methods already adapted in the software development industry. This article describes an approach already adapted to particular needs of the software industry. The approach has to solve problems mentioned at the beginning of this section while maintaining:

- a holistic view of the software systems developed at the company;
- a concerted development of architects' competencies in all company divisions;
- an embeddedness of the company's business strategy in plans of the software development.

The authors of this paper present an enterprise architecture deployment and governance by using a holistic, lean approach at a software development company.

The paper starts with a review of the existing works. Since the authors did not find a solution that could be directly applied to a Software Development Company (SDC), a most suitable approach was adapted. Further sections describe the realization of key activities related to the introduction of EA at the company. The authors explain exactly which actions have been taken and present their thoughts and lessons learned from the implementation phase. In the concluding section of this paper, there are listed benefits resulting from the application of the described solution.

2   Related Works

In the process of adapting an enterprise architecture at a software development company, a typical approach is to focus on the most popular frameworks. The examples of how to apply enterprise prescriptive methodologies, such as TOGAF [5] and the Zachman Framework, are known and described in the literature, e.g. [2]. TOGAF is a general tool for organizing or adapting the method of developing an enterprise architecture and aims at providing a practical, easily-accessible, standardized and industrial method of designing the enterprise architecture.

From the viewpoint of a software development company, it is interesting how to align software development processes with the enterprise architecture. This very issue is widely explored and described in existing publications [6, 7]. The global IT industry also develops frameworks for wide sections of IT practice. The best-known are COBIT (Control Objectives for Information and Related Technologies) and ITIL (Information Technology Infrastructure Library). COBIT [12] enables clear policy development and good practices for IT control throughout organizations. COBIT 5 makes enterprise architecture a mandatory discipline and draws a direct link with the recommendations of TOGAF. The above mentioned reasons speak for using COBIT as a governance framework for SOA (Service Oriented Architecture) [3] or Information Technology [13]. ITIL outlines an extensive set of management procedures that are intended to support businesses in achieving both quality and value, in a financial sense, in IT operations. Paper [14] proposes a way of integration by approaching ITIL from an EA perspective and puts forward a mapping of ITIL concepts to EA, as well as a set of models representing the ITIL meta-model using the ArchiMate modeling language.

Communicating enterprise architecture solutions incorporating software development must be realized in a universal way. ISO/IEC/IEEE 42010 defines architecture description (AD) standards and specifies requirements regarding architecture descriptions [8]. Architecture description languages (ADL) are a form of expression to be used in architecture descriptions. To conform to the AD standard, an ADL must specify: the identification of concerns, the identification of stakeholders having those concerns, the types of models implemented by the ADL, any architecture viewpoints and correspondence rules. ArchiMate [9] is an architecture description language that is mostly used for modeling the enterprise architecture and is a very convenient tool for communicating solutions among business and technology staff. For supporting the EA modeling activity, paper [10] proposes a Model Driven Engineering (MDE) framework based on the ArchiMate language. In paper [11], an ontological analysis of the BSVC (Business Strategy and Valuation Concepts) of an ArchiMate extension and the associated notions of capability, resources and competences are proposed.

In the process of adapting the enterprise architecture at a software development company, the agile and lean approaches used in the IT branch must be taken into account. A vision for such approach is illustrated in [1].

Literature provides some case studies related to applying a structured approach in using enterprise architecture at software development companies. Paper [15] presents an integrated service-oriented enterprise system development framework (called the BITAM-SOA Framework), which focuses on business-IT alignment via communication, architecture and governance. In study [16], the joint effect of the developer team structure and an Open Source Software (OSS) architecture on the OSS development performance is examined. It was discovered that the developer team structure and the software architecture significantly moderate each other's effect on the OSS development performance. Case study [17] investigates a lean governance approach to software development. The Minimum Marketable Features (MMFs) approach was used to identify the most valuable feature a customer needed, and aimed to keep each software unit being built as small as possible. Decisions concerning the software, initial estimates, and how the work have been broken down into MMFs are recorded in the architecture. Developing, deploying and maintaining software solutions is a major challenge for both the organization developing and deploying the software and the one which is to use it. To ensure that these organizations cooperate effectively, it is necessary to build broader and deeper relationships that go beyond the simple rules of cooperation between the client and the contractor. In [4], SMESDaD (Synergetic Methodology for Enterprise Software Development and Deployment) is proposed. It concerns the operation and cooperation of two organizations. One of these organizations is an SDC supplying software for the main business line of the second company operating on the market.

3   Adapting Enterprise Architecture at a Software Development Company

As shown in *Related works,* there are many ways of implementing an enterprise architecture. TOGAF [5] is one of the most popular general solutions. One of its biggest advantages is the fact that it is a broadly accepted standard, and the first step to be taken by an organisation willing to implement it, is customising it for the purposes of given business needs. In practice, however, TOGAF might turn out to be too general for adjusting to the needs of a given type of enterprise. An example of a scenario in which TOGAF may seem too difficult to adjust is the implementation of enterprise architecture in a SDC type. TOGAF defines IT software as a set of services/tools that are to support the activities of various business lines within an organisation, but it does not by itself constitute an essence of the company operations. The situation is different in the case of software development companies. Here, the main systems that are developed simultaneously constitute the products whose market standing determines the success or failure of the whole enterprise. Another problem with implementing TOGAF or other general solution is the lack of a clear relationship between the enterprise architecture built around TOGAF and the IT systems architecture developed in the company. This problem can be particularly apparent in the software development type of companies, in which taking care of the right architecture of the developed systems represents one of the most important tasks of the organisation.

Another issue related to the introduction of general purpose frameworks, like TOGAF, is the difficulty of their adaptation to agile approach commonly used by SDCs. Architecture Development Method (ADM) proposed by TOGAF seems to be more suitable for waterfall management than for agile or lean methodologies (e.g. Scrum or Kanban).

In relation to the described issues with adjusting TOGAF to the needs of building the enterprise architecture in an SDC, the authors of this article were forced to look for alternative solutions that would better fit the specific nature of SDC-type companies. In book [1], the authors described eight main activities which should be undertaken by enterprise architects at an SDC.

Activities proposed in [1] may be treated as a reference model that is a base for developing the Enterprise Architecture methodology tailored to the specificity of SDCs. The proposed methodology should enable developing the architecture governance at an existing medium-sized company (50-500 developers). Bigger companies (over 500 developers) usually create their own methodology strictly designed to their own needs. For small companies (less than 50 developers) the cost of introducing architecture governance may be bigger than the expected profits. The created methodology is currently developed and deployed at a company employing about 250 developers.

The architecture governance developed in the described SDC company is composed from the following activities:

1) defining a motivation model;
2) adapting architecture modeling tools;
3) creating an IT landscape and mapping it to company products;
4) building architecture capabilities in the organization;
5) implementing standards and guidelines;
6) applying architecture governance;
7) defining the architect's role in software projects execution;
8) managing risk in IT solutions using architecture governance.

The presented activities make it possible to obtain the main gains coming from the enterprise architecture implementation in the organisation, i.e. the simplification of the company IT landscape and a better adjustment of IT systems to business needs. Additionally, a link can be found between the enterprise architecture-related activities and the creation of the software architecture of systems under development. The described approach integrates well with agile methodologies that are leveraged by IT companies.

In the following part of the article, the authors present the adjustments of the described eight activities to the purposes of implementing an enterprise architecture at a medium-sized IT company (50-500 developers).

4   Case Study

To verify the described approach, we have to ensure that all development activities of the SDC are properly aligned with its business goals. This can be done by adjusting the SDC's internal process and introducing mechanisms supporting software architecture governance within it. Ensuring that all architecture decisions are taken in accordance with the strategy of the enterprise is crucial.

4.1   Defining a Motivation Model as a Bridge between the Business and IT Solutions

The enterprise architecture should be modeled including, on the one hand, strategic concerns and goals, and on the other, the information and technology structure [18]. ArchiMate 2.0 is a comprehensive enterprise architecture modeling language in which a motivation layer was introduced, enabling modeling strategy with IT solutions. Extensions proposed to the ArchiMate motivation layer introduce additional concepts such as value, risks, resources, capabilities, competencies and constraints [19, 20].

Basing on the solutions, standards and in-house experience, an ORRCA (Open Robust Reference Collaborative Architecture) methodology for architecture governance was proposed and implemented. The best solution to create the correct architecture governance at the SDC is the transition from both customer-related and enterprise-architecture-related requirements to the final software architecture. The proposal constitutes an attempt to create a meta-model that fills the gap and moves from the enterprise architecture to software architecture. This gap is filled by creating the meta-model [21] of the motivation and business layer. The considered meta-model is based on the motivation and business layers described in the ArchiMate notation. The proposed meta-model concerns the development of software systems for which a bridge to business goals is essential.

The main task is to identify key requirements, goals and principles that are crucial for enterprise and software architectures. Something that motivates the change at an organization is modeled by a driver element in the ArchiMate motivation layer. Typical reasons for change originate from what a company wants to achieve: to reduce development costs, to be more competitive and to increase customer satisfaction. Fig. 1 shows relations originating from the driver called 'minimize costs of software development'. The assessment is performed using the SWOT analysis (S- strengths, W- weaknesses, O - opportunities, and T – threats). A principle is an element of the ArchiMate motivation layer defining [9] a standardizing property of all systems in a given context, or the way in which they are constructed. ORRCA defines the following set of principles: lean architecture, architecture governance, component reusability, integration readiness, portability, scalability, and data as an asset. The principles viewpoint [9] allows the analyst or designer to model the principles that are relevant to the design problem at hand, including the goals that motivate these principles. In addition, relationships between principles, as well as their goals and constraints, can be modeled. For example, principles may influence other meta-model elements positively or negatively.

The presented ORRCA meta-model can be used by the SDC to create its own architecture governance model facilitating the development of the system architecture for its products. An architecture governance model based on ORRCA includes all important factors that should be taken into account when creating a system architecture for a given organization.

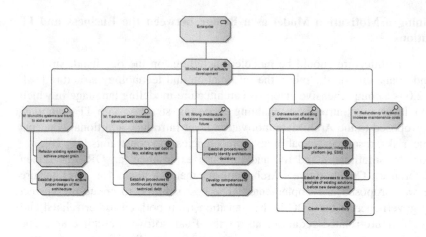

Fig. 1. Relations of drivers called 'minimize costs of software development'

Benefits: Defining a motivation model as a bridge between the business and IT solutions will promote better understanding and alignment with the development direction.

Lesson learned: The organization had problems with defining IT Strategy corresponding to its current market situation. An iterative approach turned out to be the right solution. The starting point was to identify external and internal motivation factors that influence IT development in the organization. Then, ArchiMate was used to model the definition of the motivation layer. Also goals, drivers, concerns and constrains were defined in ArchiMate. Defining the motivation layer allowed to reach common views and goals in various enterprise departments. The next step will be to create an IT Strategy whose subsequent steps will be mapped on the defined motivation layer.

4.2   Adapting Architecture Modeling Tools

In order to support the process of modeling an enterprise architecture, different tools were developed. An overall approach to modeling, communicating, and analyzing an enterprise architecture, presented in [2], is to design an integrated enterprise architecture workbench acting both as a modeling environment and the infrastructure for integration with the existing modeling languages and tools.

One important feature of the modeling tools is the possibility to be used by a broader audience. This means that models developed by the use of these tools should also be easy to understand for stakeholders with no IT experience. The basic tools which meet the demands of communicating the architecture are: BMC (Business Model Canvas), ArchiMate and BPMN. The problem of aligning the architecture with business is considered broadly. There are different tools proposed, but the BMC approach [22, 23] is gaining popularity due to its simplicity, understandability and expressiveness. The ArchiMate language was developed under the assumption that in order to build an expressive business model, it is necessary to use relations linking completely different fields: from business motivations to business processes, services and infrastructure. A good example in which ArchiMate is applied is the integration proposed in [14] by approaching ITIL from an EA perspective with a set of models representing ITIL in the ArchiMate modeling language. On the one hand, this proposal gives an architect the elements, relationships and models that represent best practices in the IT service management, and on the other, formally models ITIL for knowledge sharing, stakeholder communication and to contribute to the ITIL discussion and validation.

The Business Process Modeling Notation (BPMN) allows [25] enterprise architects, business analysts and application architects to work on the same readily understandable model in order to obtain a business-process-driven software system. To ensure a clear conceptual alignment between the business processes and the software architectures, a solution based on the BPMN notation is proposed [26].

Benefits: The considered SDC has different tools in use, like UML, ArchiMate, PBMN and BMC. In its communication with different stakeholders, ArchiMate, BPMN and BMC are the most valuable. The right choice of architecture notation tools allows useful viewpoints to be created for the architecture.

Lesson Learned: Proper modeling tools were chosen for particular areas of the company. The BPMN notation was used to model company processes. Despite having a complete process model, the creation of metrics to assess a quality of individual processes was unsuccessful. BMC was partially implemented in the Product Owner department. Unfortunately, BMC usage is still fragmentary and not optimal. The ArchiMate notation was used to describe systems. They were modeled at the level of components and relations between individual systems/components. Using BPMN, BMC and ArchiMate has another big advantage, i.e., it improves communication with stakeholders owing to the common language and the glossary of terms.

4.3   IT Landscape Creation and Mapping to Company Products

Before planning any changes and improvements within the enterprise, it is crucial to know and understand its current state. The larger SDC, the more challenging this task can be. A wide range of products, systems, and technologies in combination with many different dependencies between these elements make the overall analysis very complex. A useful tool for describing the 'as-is' state is the IT landscape. A properly created landscape will also form a valuable source of information during the process of planning future state and migration activities.

The SDC described in this article used the following approach:

1.   All products being developed within the SDC were identified and assigned to appropriate market segments.
2.   Products were divided into systems they consist of. Common and reusable parts were identified.

3. Additional properties were assigned to all systems, namely: a department responsible for development, technologies used, and business services provided.
4. Dependencies between systems were identified and documented.

During the development of the SDC's IT landscape, 307 elements (segments, products, systems, services, and technologies) and 1095 relations between them were defined. The collected data became a valuable source of information for further analyses and strategic planning.

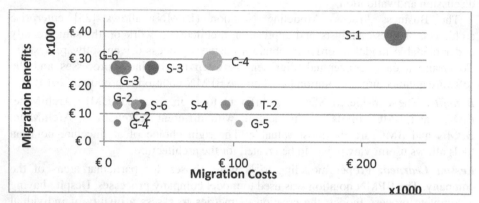

Fig. 2. Migration costs-benefit analysis based on data from IT landscape

It turned out that, in some cases, the chosen technology was not cost-effective, for example, software license fees were raising the deployment costs, although better alternatives were available. Data from the landscape was used to find a system that should be migrated to open-source technology alternatives. Fig. 2 presents the costs-benefit analysis of the possible migration.

Another significant issue was the redundancy across different systems. It was found that systems from different departments sometimes provide similar business services. To optimize the development efforts, they could be integrated in a long term period.

A large number of connections between systems grounds a high level of complexity. IT landscape helps to manage this complexity. The analysis of the gathered data revealed key systems that others depend on. Changes to these systems must be done cautiously, not to impair other related systems. Fig. 3 presents relations between systems. It is clear that some systems are strongly connected (e.g. T-45, G-62), while other have fewer or no connections (e.g. E-25, E-35). There are also notable relations between some groups of systems (e.g. T has many connections to G, while there are no connections between H and G).

The exemplary SDC discussed here proves that IT landscape can serve as a good starting point for introducing the Enterprise Architecture. It provides a good overview of SDC products and helps to identify areas that could be improved in the future.

Benefits: IT landscape allows us to understand the complex environment of the SDC. It can serve as a valuable source of information during the formulation of development plans concerning company products.

Lesson Learned: A need to make an inventory of IT artifacts was a cause for creating the IT landscape, which then proved to be more valuable that initially expected. What is more, the IT landscape turned out to be a good source of information about a selection of the technology stack, allocation of programming resources and interdependencies between systems.

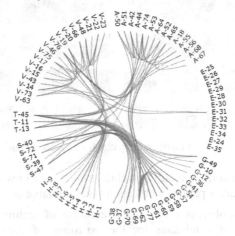

Fig. 3. Relations between systems (full names replaced by IDs to improve readiness)

4.4   Building Architecture Capabilities in the Organization

The basic requirement for architecture governance is that the architect (taking architectural decisions) should have the appropriate competences. Goals concerning architecture competence development can be achieved by fulfilling the following requirements: developing competences of software architects; continuously improving technical skills of the development teams; involving individuals with high domain knowledge and experience in projects; establishing processes that ensure the use of agile techniques in the development of a software architecture; including analysis and development of the software architecture in agile development processes.

Architects' capabilities should be assessed and improved at the SDC. At the examined company, architect positions were identified, roles and required competences were described, and finally, the candidates were selected.

Vertical and horizontal models of career paths for all positions in the company, including architects (fig. 4), were formulated. To be a solution architect, one has to be a programmer with four years of experience in the field and with four competence levels achieved one after the other: junior, specialist, senior and expert. The next career level for a solution architect is that of the enterprise architect. An infrastructure architect, on the other hand, can be previously an IT administrator, a tester or a support engineer at the expert competence level. The target career path for an infrastructure architect is the position of a solution architect.

This model of architect competence development and appraisal forms a part of the proposed consistent methodology of maintaining architectural governance in the company.

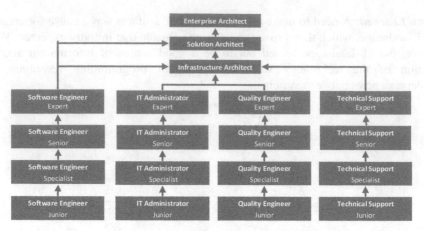

Fig. 4. A diagram of career paths for architects' positions

Benefits: The main benefit of building architecture capabilities is the clear definition of competences and career paths which help to gain valuable competences.

Lessons Learned: Employees received the creation of architectural positions very positively. Selection of candidates for the positions of architects was made by recruiting volunteers. This enabled to identify people involved and willing to undertake self-development. A talent management program was launched in the HR department which would deal with, among others, a choice of training paths for the candidates. Finally, the career paths and the role of architects were adapted to the organizational structure of the company.

4.5   Implementation of Standards and Guidelines

The SDC described in this paper started introducing architecture standards with defining Architecture Principles. Simply speaking, principles are sets of rules supporting the strategy of the enterprise. They play an important role by charting the direction of architecture activities and supporting the achievement of strategic goals. The SDC has chosen Architecture Principles included within the ORRCA methodology.

Further standards and guidelines were defined after the IT landscape had been created and the current state of the enterprise had been analyzed. One of the introduced guidelines specified a set of preferred technologies that should be used across projects carried out at the company. The common technology stack ensures compliance with the 'Integration Readiness' principle and additionally allows resources to be shifted between different departments.

Benefits: Properly defined standards and guidelines support the execution of the SDC strategy plans.

Lesson Learned: It was observed that one of the most important factors that determine a high complexity of the IT landscape is the lack of corporate standards and guidelines concerning, among others, the technology stack, a way of decomposing the systems, and methods of their deployment. At the same time, too complex standardization reduces the level of innovation and "flexibility" in the development groups. Currently, there are certain areas of the technology stack, including databases, in which the standardization process is ongoing.

4.6   Applying Architecture Governance in Project, Program and Portfolio Management

The IT landscape analysis should lead to choosing an appropriate approach to developing particular systems. Systems that are the most important to a current operation of the company and the ones without which it can still function should be identified.

In the presented example of an implementation, the company decided to divide all systems into four categories. A division was based on metrics which accounted for both technological and business aspects. The first category includes systems that are the most crucial for the current operation of the company. The sale of systems from this category brings the highest profit to the company and ensures its stable operation. The next group of systems encompasses those which will form the key source of income within approximately five years. The third category consists of systems whose sale is still bringing profits, but their development is costly and the return on sales is likely to fall. The last group contains systems whose costs currently exceed the profits and this is almost certain to continue in the future.

Basing on the division of systems according to the presented key, the results of this classification can be taken into consideration while planning the project work in the company. It is particularly important to take care of systems from the first two categories. It is obvious that the primary goal is to ensure that the requirements for the systems that currently secure the company's operation are fulfilled. However, it is also important to allocate resources to work on systems that will be important in the future. For systems from this category, paying attention to the regularity of the software architecture and supervising its implementation is as important as maintaining their continuous development. This stems from the fact that the planned lifecycle of such systems is long, and if architectural errors are committed at the beginning, they may be very difficult to rectify later on in the lifecycle. Additionally, the importance of the system architecture comes from the fact that the system should be easy both to develop and implement new requirements that are often not known beforehand.

For the systems classified to the third and fourth category, it is necessary to reduce development work wherever possible. One of the ways to cut the expenses is an attempt to substitute these systems by extending the versions of systems that are promising (category 2) or that have a stable position on the market (category 1). In such a case, at the same time we limit amount of work on the systems in which we do not plan to invest in the future, and we can work on the systems that we want to promote.

Benefits: Categorization of systems based on the current and expected future market position supports assigning priorities to projects carried out at the SDC.

Lesson learned: The result of the IT landscape analysis was a division of systems into four presented categories. The classification was based on metrics that took into account viewpoints of both technical and business persons. Unfortunately, introducing changes into the program portfolio and project management resulting from the conducted classification is much more difficult that classifying. Even more problematic is the implementation of changes (for instance, suspending the development of systems from the 4th category) in a way that do not disturb the value stream of systems delivered to customers.

4.7   Defining the Architect's Role in Software Project Implementation

An architectural team plays an important role at the SDC. It is responsible for ensuring the technological integrity of the delivered systems. Moreover, the architects have to accomplish the company's strategies pertaining to the overall direction of the developed systems.

In the presented implementation, the architectural team consists of enterprise architects, solution architects (who are at the same time software architects), and infrastructure architects. Systems developed in the company are divided into three main functional units and one enterprise architect is responsible for each unit. Furthermore, there are two additional enterprise architects responsible for the coordination of work among units and the overall implementation of the board's strategy. Work of these enterprise architects is not assigned to a particular project but rather consists in ensuring the compliance of all project work with the strategy resulting from the enterprise governance of the firm.

Solution and infrastructure architects directly engage in project work. One solution architect responsible for the preparation and supervision of the implementation of the whole solution architecture should be assigned to each project. Additionally, if the infrastructure is a key element of the project, the infrastructure architect takes part in the project work as well. His or her role is to ensure that the design of what will be used is correct. The work of solution architects is monitored by enterprise architects who are responsible for ensuring that the solution architecture is compatible with the strategy of the firm.

Solution architects should cooperate closely with project managers and other people responsible for collecting client's business requirements so that the developed solution suits the client's needs best.

Benefits: The right selection of the architecture team structure allows the enterprise architecture to be efficiently implemented within the SDC. Enterprise architects are responsible for the efficient implementation of strategy plans regarding the IT evolution within the company. Solution and infrastructure architects are responsible for a good alignment of systems to customer requirements by ensuring the technical integrity of the created solutions.

Lesson Learned: At the beginning, it was assumed that a solution architect would not be an active member of a project group. This solution proved to be incorrect because it would lead to a situation in which the solution architecture is developed independently of the implementation, and this might result in inconsistencies between them. Additionally, separating solution architects from development teams would require recruiting additional resources to the solution architects group. Unfortunately, external recruitment of architects was unsuccessful, since they lacked sufficient technical knowledge and experience. It turned out that the best solution for the above mentioned problems was to assign a role of the solution architect to a member of the development team who would be responsible for the development of the solution architecture. In addition, working as an active developer, he or she would be able to make sure that the implementation is compatible with the architecture.

4.8   Managing Risk in IT Solutions Using Architecture Governance

In an enterprise architecture, the risk management plays an important role and applies to all processes of an enterprise. General methods of dealing with risk at the enterprise have been developed [27]. The enterprise architecture should include a risk prevention and control mechanism. Paper [28] proposes an alignment between the risk management governance and enterprise activities. Another example [29] describes a business architecture model that describes the integration of the main processes for IT Governance, IT Risk Management and IT Compliance (IT GRC).

The approach proposed in the paper is very similar to governance, risk and compliance (GRC) solutions. The Integrated Governance, Risk and Compliance (GRC) is becoming one of the most important business requirements for organizations. The architecture governance proposed in this paper is structured in a way that should decrease risks. The defined principles, goals, and requirements should limit the possible risk. This does not mean that risk management should be omitted. On the contrary, it should be closely integrated with the proposed governance and motivation model. Integrating risk management into the organization means considering the strategy, processes, people and the technology used.

Benefits: At the SDC, the main benefits stemmed from the knowledge of risk, and this led to changes in some processes. Risk monitoring is included in the project, portfolio, operation and HR management.

Lesson learned: The SWOT analysis of products and processes was conducted at the SDC. It helps to make conscious decisions about changes in the products and processes portfolio.

5   Conclusions

It seems that introducing architecture governance represents a good approach to optimizing development activities of the SDC. The authors analyzed different architecture frameworks and used the experience gained to create their own solution that meets the specific needs and problems of the described enterprise. The proposed solution is inspired by the approach presented in [1], which can be treated here as a reference approach.

The Architecture Governance methodology ORRCA was introduced in the process of adapting EA in the SDC. The in-depth analysis of the IT landscape allowed to identify many areas with room for improvement. During the analysis, non-trivial problems including an inefficient structure of redundancy in the developed systems were found. To solve the discovered issues, a corrective action was planned and partially introduced. It was necessary to create an architecture team composed of enterprise, solution, and infrastructure architects with clearly defined responsibilities in order to ensure the correct implementation of these plans

The proposed methodology was introduced iteratively at the software company. Currently, the SDC described in this paper is at an early stage of introducing architecture governance. Activities which were performed concerned different areas and the experience gained is shortly described in lessons learned. The execution of all plans is now at the initial stage, but the current results look promising. Some of the solutions have already been successfully deployed, other need some organizational changes   before they can be thoroughly implemented, so that they do not disturb software product delivery to customers.

References

1. Bente, S., Bombosch, U., Langade, S.: Collaborative Enterprise Architecture: Enriching EA with Lean, Agile, and Enterprise 2.0 Practices. Morgan Kaufmann (2012)
2. Lankhorst, M.: Enterprise Architecture at Work: Modelling, Communication and Analysis. Enterprise engineering series. Springer (2009)
3. Hojaji, F., Shirazi, M.R.A.: A Comprehensive SOA Governance Framework Based on COBIT. In: 6th IEEE World Congress on Services, pp. 407–414 (2010)
4. Rogus, G., Skrzyński, P., Szwed, P., Turek, M., Werewka, J.: SMESDaD – a Synergetic Methodology for Enterprise Software Development and Deployment. In: Łebkowski, P. (ed.) Aspects of production engineering and management. AGH University of Science and Technology Press (2011)
5. The Open Group: TOGAF Version 9.1 (2009-2011), p. 692
6. Eeles, P., Cripps, P.: The Process of Software Architecting. Addison Wesley Professional (2010)
7. Rozanski, N., Woods, E.: Software Systems Architecture: Working with Stakeholders Using Viewpoints and Perspectives. Addison-Wesley (2011)
8. ISO/IEC/IEEE: Systems and software engineering – architecture description. ISO/IEC/IEEE 42010:2011(E) (Revision of ISO/IEC 42010:2007 and IEEE Std 1471-2000), pp. 1–46 (2011)
9. The Open Group: ArchiMate 2.0 Specification (2009-2012), p. 183
10. Pena, C., Villalobos, J.: An MDE approach to design enterprise architecture viewpoints. In: Seventh IEEE International Conference on E-Commerce Technology (CEC 2005), pp. 80–87 (2010)
11. Azevedo, C.L.B., Iacob, M.-E., Almeida, J.P.A., van Sinderen, M., Pires, L.F., Guizzardi, G.: An Ontology-Based Well-Founded Proposal for Modeling Resources and Capabilities in ArchiMate. In: 17th IEEE International Enterprise Distributed Object Computing Conference, pp. 39–48 (2013)
12. COBIT® 5: A Business Framework for the Governance and Management of Enterprise IT, ISACA, ISBN 978-1-60420-237-3. United States of America (2012)
13. Radovanović D., Lučić D., Radojević T., Šarac M.: Information technology governance - COBIT model, MIPRO 2011, Opatija, Croatia: pp. 1426-1429 (2011)
14. Vicente, M., Gama, N., da Silva, M.M.: Using ArchiMate to Represent ITIL Metamodel. In: IEEE International Conference on Business Informatics, pp. 270–275 (2013)
15. Chen, H.-M., Kazman, R., Perry, O.: From Software Architecture Analysis to Service Engineering: An Empirical Study of Methodology Development for Enterprise SOA Implementation. IEEE Transactions on Services Computing 3(2), 145–160 (2010)

16. Nan, N., Kumar, S.: Joint Effect of Team Structure and Software Architecture in Open Source Software Development. IEEE Transactions on Engineering Management 60(3), 592–603 (2013)
17. Middleton, P., Joyce, D.: Lean Software Management: BBC Worldwide Case Study. IEEE Transactions on Engineering Management 59(1), 20–32 (2012)
18. Cardoso, E.C.S., Almeida, J.P.A., Guizzardi, R.S.S.: On the Support for the Goal Domain in Enterprise Modelling Approaches. In: 14th IEEE International Enterprise Distributed Object Computing Conference Workshops, pp. 335–344 (2010)
19. Iacob, M.-E., Quartel, D., Jonkers, H.: Capturing Business Strategy and Value in Enterprise Architecture to Support Portfolio Valuation. In: IEEE 16th International Enterprise Distributed Object Computing Conference, pp. 11–20 (2012)
20. Azevedo, C.L.B., Almeida, J.P.A., van Sinderen, M., Quartel, D., Guizzardi, G.: An Ontology-Based Semantics for the Motivation Extension to ArchiMate. In: 15th IEEE International Enterprise Distributed Object Computing Conference, pp. 25–34 (2011)
21. Werewka, J., Jamróz, K., Pitulej, D.: Developing lean architecture governance at a software developing company applying archiMate motivation and business layers. In: Kozielski, S., Mrozek, D., Kasprowski, P., Małysiak-Mrozek, B. z. (eds.) BDAS 2014. CCIS, vol. 424, pp. 492–503. Springer, Heidelberg (2014)
22. Osterwalder, A.: The Business Model Ontology: a proposition in a design science approach. Dissertation, Universite de Lausanne, Ecole des Hautes Etudes Commerciales (2004)
23. Meertens, L., Iacob, M., Jonkers, H., Quartel, D., Nieuwenhuis, L., van Sinderen, M.: Mapping the business model canvas to ArchiMate. In: Proceedings of the 27th Annual ACM Symposium on Applied Computing, pp. 1694–1701. ACM (March 2012), http://doc.utwente.nl/82858/
24. Vicente, P., da Silva, M.M.: A Business Viewpoint for Integrated IT Governance, Risk and Compliance. In: IEEE World Congress on Services, pp. 422–428 (2011)
25. Business Process Model and Notation (BPMN), Version 2.0, OMG (2011), http://www.omg.org/spec/BPMN/2.0
26. Dahman, K., Charoy, F., Godart, C.: From Business Process to Component Architecture: Engineering Business to IT Alignment. In: 15th IEEE International Enterprise Distributed Object Computing Conference Workshops, pp. 269–274 (2011)
27. Practice Standard for Project Risk Management, Project Management Institute (2009)
28. Barateiro, J., Antunes, G., Borbinha, J.: Manage Risks through the Enterprise Architecture. In: 45th Hawaii International Conference on System Science (HICSS), pp. 3297–3306 (2012)

Service Development and Architecture Management for an Enterprise SOA

Thomas Kriechbaum[1], Georg Buchgeher[2], and Rainer Weinreich[3]

[1] RACON Software GmbH, Austria
thomas.kriechbaum@racon.at
[2] Software Competence Center Hagenberg, Austria
georg.buchgeher@scch.at
[3] Johannes Kepler University Linz, Austria
rainer.weinreich@jku.at

Abstract. We report on service development and architecture management practices for an enterprise SOA in the financial domain. First we describe how services are currently developed by one of the largest service providers for the financial domain in Austria. Then we show how we have introduced various practices and tools for architecture management over the last years. We have specifically implemented support for architecture extraction, architecture visualization, automatic architecture analysis, and architecture reviews as part of quality gates in the service development process. Finally, we report on lessons learned both in the area of service development and architecture management as well as on existing challenges and future work in this area.

Keywords: SOA, service-based development, enterprise architecture, architecture management.

1 Introduction

The GRZ IT Group is one of the major service providers for financial institutions in Austria and has been developing software for the financial domain for over 40 years. Within this period the various software solutions developed by the GRZ IT Group have evolved into a large scale Service-Oriented Architecture (SOA). Currently, the SOA consists of about 170 subsystems (also called service modules) providing about 1700 services. Each subsystem defines a number of related services for a specific task. Subsystems are the units of planning, evolution, and deployment, and constitute a large system of systems (SoS) architecture. In this paper we report on experiences with the development and architecture management of services in this enterprise SOA.

The contributions of this paper are as follows: A set of practices for the development of an enterprise SOA including a service development process model and central architecture management activities, lessons learned regarding the development and architecture management of an enterprise SOA, and a list of open research challenges in this field.

P. Avgeriou and U. Zdun (Eds.): ECSA 2014, LNCS 8627, pp. 186–201, 2014.
© Springer International Publishing Switzerland 2014

The remainder of this paper is organized as follows: In Section 2 we describe the context of the paper - this includes an overview of the domain, an architecture overview of the enterprise SOA, and an overview of the organization structure including essential stakeholders and their concerns. Section 3 describes the established service development and service life cycle process. In Section 4 we describe selected quality management activities performed by the architecture management team. Lessons learned, open challenges, as well as current and future work are discussed in Section 5. The paper is concluded in Section 6.

2   Context

GRZ IT Group develops and operates software for the financial domain in Austria, including software for end users (i.e., internet banking applications and portals) and software for employees in banks (front and back office applications). In 2013 the GRZ IT Group had 780 employees and a turnover of 153 million Euros. Applications are operated in multiple computing centers at different locations in Austria. Developed applications need to be highly scalable and performant in order to handle a large customer base. For example, in the second half of 2013 the internet banking application had to handle about 122 million page views per month on average.

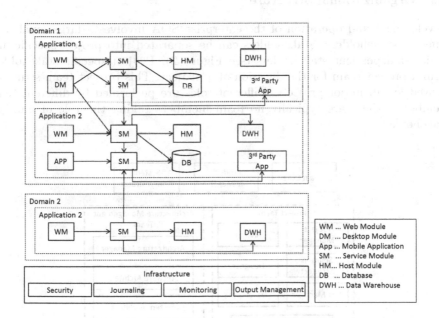

Fig. 1. SOA Overview

2.1   System Overview

Figure 1 provides a conceptual overview of the enterprise SOA. The system landscape is organized in multiple applications, which are clustered into business domains. An application is further decomposed into multiple modules, which are the units of versioning and deployment. Modules belong to different tiers of an application. The client tier encompasses different kinds of client modules, like web client modules (WM), desktop application client modules (DM), and mobile application client modules for smartphones (APP). Clients use functionality via web services provided by so-called service modules (SM) located in the service tier. Service modules interact with a number of different subsystems: They can use services provided by other service modules, they can call operations provided by host modules (HM) of the mainframe tier, they can access data from database management systems (DB) and from data warehouses (DWH) (e.g., reports), and they can interact with 3rd party applications. The business logic of enterprise applications is either implemented through services in service modules, or it is implemented in host modules at the mainframe. In the latter case services act as a facade for accessing the functionality implemented at the host. An infrastructure tier further provides fundamental crosscutting functionality like security, journaling, monitoring, and output management.

2.2   Organizational Structure

Development and operation of the enterprise SOA involves a large number of different stakeholders. Stakeholders can be separated into project-specific and project-independent stakeholders (see Figure 2). Project-specific stakeholders form a project team for the duration of a project. This project team structure is used for all major projects. Different roles are performed by different team members - there are typically no team members taking the role of multiple stakeholders.

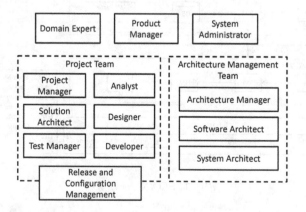

Fig. 2. Enterprise SOA Stakeholders

In the following we describe central stakeholders with their concerns.

Domain Expert. Domain experts are representatives of regional banks. They are the customers of the developed products and are responsible for negotiating requirements among different regional banks, and for initiating and funding new projects.

Product Manager. Product managers set the strategic direction of products. They identify potential features of a product and suggest these features to the domain experts. They also coordinate and prioritize system requirements on a coarse level. Product managers exist independently of a particular project and are not part of a project team.

Project Manager. Project managers are concerned with the management and controlling of all project-related development activities.

Solution Architect. Solutions architects (together with product managers) are responsible for defining the high-level architecture of a product, which includes identification and specification of dependencies to other applications (SOA subsystems) and the identification of service candidates based on the system requirements and the coarse-grained architecture. Further, they participate in quality gate reviews of applications developed by other teams.

Analyst. Analysts refine and manage the requirements provided by domain experts and product managers. These refined requirements are then used for refining the architecture and act as input for the designer. Analysts are not directly involved in the service development life cycle.

Designer. The designer uses the service candidate descriptions and the refined requirements and develops the detailed design of services. This includes the design of data structures, internal components, and the detailed design of service interfaces. Further, designers are responsible for negotiating modifications of existing service interfaces with other designers.

Developer. Developers are responsible for implementing applications, services, and unit tests.

Test and Quality Manager. Test and quality mangers are responsible for the specification, coordination, and execution of tests and for other quality control activities. This includes tests of functional correctness and of nonfunctional requirements like performance and scalability.

Release and Configuration Manager. Release and configuration managers are concerned with the coordination of all company-wide release activities, e.g., the management of dependencies between product releases.

System Administrator. System Administrators are responsible for operating released products in computing centers. This includes the runtime monitoring of the enterprise SOA in order to detect problems in terms of performance and scalability.

Architecture Manager. The architecture manager is the head of the architecture management group. His responsibilities include the coordination of team activities, the optimization of processes, and the development of architecture-related guidelines based on the global business strategies.

Software Architect. Software architects are responsible for the definition of the reference architecture (see Section 4) including the technology stack (see Section 3.1).

System Architect. System architects are responsible for the definition of the strategic system architecture (see Section 4).

3   Service Development and Service Lifecycle

Services and service modules (see Section 2.1) are at the heart of the enterprise SOA. In this section we present central principles guiding the development of services and service modules. This includes an overview of the technologies used (Section 3.1), the service development process (Section 3.2) and selected practices for service development (Section 3.3).

3.1   Technology Stack

The technology stack defines the implementation technologies (i.e., used programming languages, frameworks, and runtime environments) used for the service development. A main driver behind the definition of the technology stack was the aim to reduce the complexity and effort for implementing service-oriented applications. Therefore, the enforced policies (i.e., security, auditing, logging, monitoring, and standardized contracts) are covered by the provided frameworks and service-containers whenever possible. The utilization of standard technologies and de-facto standard frameworks is a strategic aim to ensure vendor-independence and to reduce any proprietary in-house development. The technology stack has evolved over the years as new technologies and standards were introduced by the Java EE platform itself. As some of our software applications have a long lifetime (10 years and longer) we currently have to support three different versions of the technology stack that all are required to run on a defined system infrastructure.

The first version of the technology stack, internally named *Java Platform 1*, is based on the Java EE 1.4 technologies and an extensive in-house framework that covers security, auditing, and configuration and composition of components. Services are exposed as JAX-RPC-based web-services. Service-requests are propagated to EJBs that encapsulate the business logic.

The second version, named *Java Platform 2*, is based on Java EE 5. The proprietary configuration and composition framework was replaced by the Spring framework. JAX-RPC was replaced by JAX-WS. EJB technology is still used for exposing external services and for integration into the application server.

With the upgrade to a Java EE 6 compliant application server, we introduced the third version of our technology stack, named *jRAP SOA*. In this version we reduced in-house developed frameworks to the areas security, auditing, and integration of business-logic on the mainframe, as these areas are not covered by any standard technology. In *jRAP SOA* these components have been refactored to ensure the required integration into CDI capable containers. Configuration and component composition is now based on CDI. CDI technologies and extension mechanisms allow us to expose and integrate services with different communication technologies as well as to annotate certain classes with important architecture information.

3.2 Service Development Process

Services are identified and developed as part of the product development process. Therefore, the service lifecycle has been embedded in the product development lifecycle, which itself is structured into the phases analysis and management of requirements, decomposition of the overall system into service- and client-components, integration of the components, and release of a new product or product version [9].

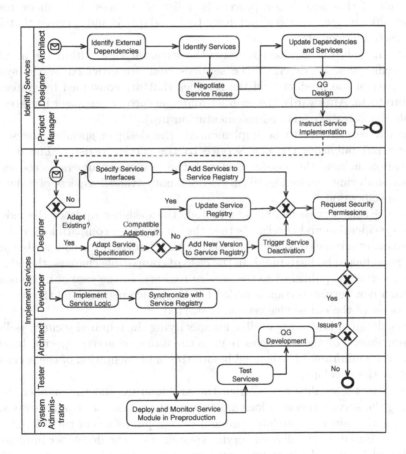

Fig. 3. Service Development Process

The service development process consists of a set of design/implementation activities, which are intercepted by so-called Quality Gate (QG) reviews [10].

Only if a QG is passed, the development may continue, otherwise developed products need to be reworked.

The service lifecycle is depicted in Figure 3. It starts with the solution architect identifying the required systems and subsystems and their external dependencies based on user requirements defined by the product manager. User requirements are provided as a requirements definition, which has been reviewed as part of the quality gate *Requirements Definition*. Depending on the required integration level (UI, process, service, data) and the required degree of decoupling of applications and subsystems, the solution architect identifies the potentially required services. Existing services are reused whenever possible.

The designer takes the list of proposed services (consumed and provided), analyzes the existing services interfaces in detail, and tries to negotiate any adaptation of existing service interfaces and service implementations if necessary. The result of this negotiation process is a list of services that can be reused without any changes, services that have to be adapted, and services that have to be newly implemented.

Next, the solution architect updates the external view within the architecture specification. He describes the services that are provided by the system that is part of the product, and the services that are consumed by systems of other products. Afterwards, the product manager/project manager initiates and controls the necessary service implementation projects.

If a new service has to be implemented, the designer specifies the service interface and publishes the new service to the service registry. The detailed specification includes the coordination with the service consumers, as the service negotiation during service identification does not cover all aspects of a detailed service specification.

If an existing service has to be adapted, the designer updates the existing service specification and checks whether the changes are compatible and do not break existing service consumers or whether the changes are incompatible and a new version has to be introduced. In the case of compatible changes, the adapted service interface is published to the service registry. In the case of incompatible changes, a new service version is added to the service registry and the deactivation process of the old service version is started.

As the designer is also responsible for specifying the required security policies, the enforcement of these policies (e.g. permissions to access specific business logic on the mainframe) is triggered before the implementation of the services is started by the developer.

As part of the quality gate *Design* the architecture and the detailed design including the service specifications are evaluated against the requirements specification and against the architecture and design guidelines of the reference architecture. Based on the defined service specification the developer implements the internal business logic or integrates existing (internal or external) services and service compositions. The model-driven approach as described in Section 4.3 ensures that external service interfaces are compliant to the enforced SOA guidelines. The developer is also responsible for implementing unit and integration tests that are executed during continuous integration and release builds.

As a precondition of the quality gate *Development* the developer extracts the implemented architecture directly from the source code (see Section 4) and synchronizes the extracted dependencies with the service registry. As part of the quality gate *Development* it is verified that the system implementation conforms to the specified architecture.

After deployment in pre-production zones, the test and quality team performs different kinds of tests that have been defined in a test specification. Possible tests are load and performance tests, tests of expected business functionality, and static code analysis. The result of the (nonfunctional) tests and the architecture extracted from the source code are checked by the solution architect. Any discovered issues are reported and discussed with the development team and the product-manager/project-manager to determine, if any fixes should be implemented before the service implementation can be released and transferred to the release- and configuration management team.

3.3   Development Practices

When developing services we try to minimize the amount of complexity by keeping a comprehensible set of concepts. As a result, the core business logic should be very clear and straightforward to implement, to test, and to understand. Dependencies to frameworks and technologies should be reduced to a minimum.

Development practices like Model-Driven Development (MDD), unit-testing and continuous integration, a transparent integration into the container on top of standard technologies, and a customized services registry based on a logical information model are key factors in our SOA efforts. Some of these practices have been optimized over years but are still part of a continuous adaptation process, as more and more mission critical products and even persons in external locations are using these concepts.

Model-Driven Development. Model-driven development has been introduced to support a top-down-strategy for specifying and implementing services. The designer not only provides a service-specification in the form of an informal document but also in the form of a formally defined UML-model. This UML-model contains all services as UML-interfaces and all entities modeled as UML-classes. These UML-elements are annotated with specific UML-stereotypes that allow providing information that is not covered by the UML-standard.

After the services and entities have been modeled, a code generator creates all necessary modules, configuration files and initial artifacts including service implementation stubs, and service client libraries that can be used by a service-consumer to integrate the provided services. The developer simply has to implement the service logic as CDI-managed beans and does not have to deal with container integration, protocol- and technology-specific endpoint-implementation, mapping-logic, security integration, etc. Model-driven development has proven to be an important success factor. For instance, the time required for integrating existing services could be reduced from up to one day to just a few minutes by simply adding a generated service client library as dependency.

Custom Annotations for Architectural Information. On top of standardized annotations we have developed a set of additional annotations for enriching the system implementation with architectural information. This information is used for automatically extracting the implemented architecture from the system implementation in order to keep architecture documentation (i.e., architecture models and information in the service registry) up-to-date over time and to automate architecture-related quality control activities (see also Section 4). For instance, custom annotations are used for distinguishing different component types (data access object components, service components, and components for accessing functionality provided by the mainframe), and for associating modules with applications and domains in order to automatically update information in the service registry.

Service Registry. Service development includes detailed planning activities for which information about existing services is required (see also Section 3.2). For instance, solution architects and designers need to be able to search for existing services for reuse, and they need information where a particular service is currently used, if an existing service has to be changed. Information about services is stored in a central service registry, which is updated whenever new services are being published, existing services are modified, or when services are being deactivated. Information in the service registry is based on a logical information model (see Figure 4) reflecting the enterprise SOA consisting of domains, applications, and modules. A module represents an installable software artifact and is the unit of deployment and versioning. A module is part of an application, whereas the overall capabilities of an application can be partitioned into multiple modules. Modules contain one or more components that can be services, UI components, processes, data marts, or host programs. These component types are technically defined as part of the reference architecture and managed within the service-registry.

To support the process of service identification and the requirement to add information to the service-registry as soon as possible in the service development process we introduced the concept of ports, which can also be found in the UML component model, as well as in the definition of WSDL. With ports is it possible, to add public integration points without the need of knowing the concrete interface or concrete component in advance. This permits managing dependencies between service consumers and providers at an early stage in the service lifecycle.

Stakeholders, e.g., designer, developer and architect, and additional documents (service specification, policies...) are assigned to modules to provide information about contact persons and documentation that should help to find the appropriate service for reuse.

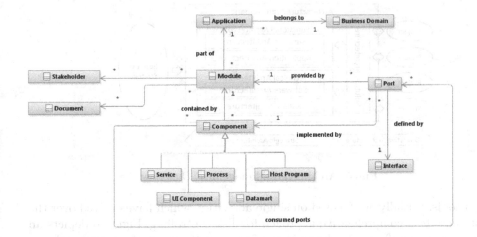

Fig. 4. Service Registry Information Model

4 Architecture Management

Architecture management within the GRZ IT Group is concerned with the *planning*, *development* and *controlling* of the enterprise architecture and concrete *solution architectures* (see Figure 5). The enterprise architecture acts as the foundation and framework for solution architectures of single applications constituting the enterprise SOA. It consists of the *business architecture* (i.e., the business processes, and the domain model), the *application architecture* (i.e., the functional description of the single applications of the enterprise SOA and their relationships), the *software architecture* (i.e., the company-wide reference architecture including technologies and frameworks for application development), and the *system architecture* (i.e., the runtime environment for the enterprise SOA including operating systems, application servers and databases).

In terms of the main architecture activities, *Architecture Planning* refers to the definition of the enterprise architecture. *Architecture Development* encompasses periodic evaluations and adaptations of the enterprise architecture in response to changes in business and technology. Finally, *Architecture Controlling* focuses on supporting solution architects during design activities and also supports compatibility checking with the technical enterprise architecture.

Architecture Controlling activities are resource-intensive in terms of required human resources. This high resource demand results from the huge number of SOA subsystems, which have to be analyzed on a regular basis, as well as from the fact that analysis activities (including their preparation activities) have to be performed manually. In 2010 a joint research project between the GRZ IT Group, the SCCH and the JKU started with the goal to reduce the resource demand for EA controlling activities. As part of this research project we investigated how different architecture-related activities can be automated and supported

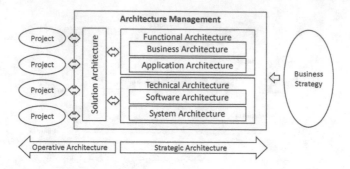

Fig. 5. Architecture Management Overview

with tools. Initially, we focused on single activities, which have evolved over the last years to a comprehensive approach for EA controlling. Figure 6 depicts an overview of our efforts. As shown in the figure, at the heart of our approach is a centralized architecture information repository, in which all architectural information is stored. Architectural information is *automatically extracted* from the system implementation of SOA subsystems. Information from the architecture information repository can be *visualized* with a view-based approach, *automatically analyzed*, and used to support *manual review processes* (i.e., quality gate reviews). Architecture information is *synchronized* with the service registry. In the following we describe these aspects in more detail.

Architecture Information Repository. In order to provide all stakeholders with the architectural information they need for their tasks, we have developed a centralized architecture information repository. By following a centralized repository approach all stakeholders are collaboratively working on a single information source (a single model). Changes made by one stakeholder (e.g., a review comment) are immediately visible to all other stakeholders. The architecture information repository is based on the LISA AIR model, a revision of the LISA model [6]. The LISA AIR model is semi-formally defined. This allows us to create large parts of the model automatically (along with manually defined parts). In addition, an architecture model can be maintained through incremental extraction and it can be analyzed automatically.

Architecture Extraction. Keeping architectural information up-to-date can be challenging since this is a time-consuming and tedious activity [3]. We automatically extract the actually implemented architecture from the system implementation [8]. Because the software architecture is typically not completely contained in the system implementation [4], we have defined a set of custom annotations (see also Section 3.3) as part of the latest technology stack to enrich the system implementation with architectural information and to facilitate architecture extraction. Architecture extraction is performed incrementally in order not to overwrite architectural information that has been defined manually.

Architecture Visualization. Information contained in the architecture information repository is visualized using a view-based approach. Currently views for

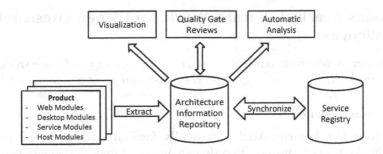

Fig. 6. Architecture Information Repository Overview

visualizing the internal configuration of service modules [8] and additional code and module views are available. Additional views like views for visualizing web and host modules, and a system of systems view focusing on the interaction between different service subsystems are under development. Architectural views are connected with the system implementation. This makes it possible to navigate from architectural views to the system implementation and vice versa.

Automatic Architecture Analysis. Architectural information contained in the architecture information repository can be automatically analyzed. A configurable set of predefined analyses continuously analyses information in the architecture information repository for model completeness, model consistency, and architecture/implementation conformance [2]. In addition, we have developed a rule-based approach for checking the conformance of service modules to reference architecture rules defined as part of the global architecture [7].

Quality Gate Reviews. Not all kinds of architecture analysis can be performed automatically. For example, quality gate reviews performed during the service development process have to be performed manually. For each quality gate the architecture management group has defined a questionnaire that has to be answered during the review. We are currently working on support for this kind of reviews in our architecture management infrastructure. Specifically, we provide dedicated editors for defining quality gate questionnaires and for answering these questionnaires during a quality gate review. Quality gate reviews are further supported by providing visualizations of the system architecture (see above). Review comments can be linked to architecture diagrams, which facilitates tracing and further discussion of detected issues. It is also possible to generate a detailed report for quality gate reviews.

Service Registry Synchronization. The service registry is a central means for searching for existing services, for tracking the life cycle of provided services, and for analyzing the service usage. Information in the service registry is kept up-to-date by synchronizing this information with information contained in the architecture information repository.

5   Lessons Learned, Future Work, and Open (Research) Challenges

In this section we report on our lessons learned, on current and future work, and on open (research) challenges regarding the development of an enterprise SOA.

5.1   Lessons Learned

Model-Driven Development. MDD drastically facilitates service development. Since technology/platform-specific code can be generated, developers can concentrate on the implementation of the business logic and do not require an indepth knowledge of the used frameworks and technologies any more. However, this can make technical problem analysis difficult and often requires the help of the framework/platform team for problem resolution. This means that developers still need to be educated in platform technologies. MDD also facilitates the migration to new implementation technologies because technology-specific code can be generated by reusing existing models. MDD also requires a shift in the service design process in which formally defined models need to be created. Not all designers are familiar with the creation of formal architecture models. Thus in many project teams the designers only create informal textual service descriptions, which then need to be converted into formal models by the developers.

Model-Based Architecture Management. Formally defined architecture models allow more efficient architecture controlling activities. Currently we automatically extract the actually implemented architecture from the system implementation, which can then be automatically analyzed for compatibility with the company-wide reference architecture. The extracted architecture can also be synchronized with the service registry and can be used as input for manual architecture review activities (quality gates). If additional architecture models, like a model of the intended architecture, are used in the development process, also the conformance of the actually implemented architecture to the intended/designed architecture can be checked automatically.

Architectural Information. Architectural information plays a vital role for many development activities like SOA governance, service design, implementation, test, and acquisition activities. For example, designers require architectural information for searching for reusable services; test managers require information for the development of test concepts; the architecture management group requires information for quality gate reviews and periodic assessments. Therefore it is important that this information is available, complete, and up-to-date. Concepts like a centralized service registry and a centralized architecture information repository help providing stakeholders with the required information.

SOA Governance. SOA governance processes are a prerequisite for the successful development of an enterprise SOA. Without governance, existing services are not reused but developed redundantly. Also a high number of parallel service versions would be in operation because clients would not be updated to new services versions.

5.2 Current & Future Work

Adaptations of the Technology Stack. Making adaptations to the technology stack is an ongoing activity performed as part of the architecture development process (see Section 4). Adaptations are necessary in response to new and emerging technologies (e.g., internet/web technologies like WebSocket and Java EE 7), and in response to negative experiences with currently used technologies. For instance, using web services with SOAP requires frequent releases, because even adding optional information to the response message of the service breaks the compatibility with defined contracts. Therefore, more tolerant technologies like RESTful services with JSON are currently investigated for future versions of the technology stack.

Architecture Information Repository. Our efforts of establishing an architecture information repository are still at the beginning. In the future we plan to extend our architecture information repository with additional views, i.e., a dedicated system of systems view for visualizing and analyzing the dependencies between client, services and host modules, and a dedicated context view for automatically analyzing dependencies between applications and the system context.

Runtime Monitoring. Currently the service registry only contains design time information about services. We plan to extend this design time view with runtime information about the actual service use. Such an integrated view allows the identification of frequently used services, of services with performance problems, and the exploration of runtime service interactions and dependencies. Further, this information can be used for strategic planning of the evolution of the enterprise SOA.

Architecture Reviews. Architecture reviews (quality gates) are often difficult to perform and results are often difficult to understand. The currently implemented tool support facilitates performing reviews and understanding review results but still requires validation and further adaptations with regard to the integration in the development process and the presentation of results to various stakeholders.

5.3 Open (Research) Challenges

Architecture and Testing. Currently testing is focused on individual applications and subsystems of a *System of Systems* (SoS). In an SoS context retesting the whole system in case of changes of individual components is infeasible. Testing needs to cross system boundaries. Better approaches for testing system of systems architectures are required. One could imagine using architecture information (e.g., dependencies to other systems) to analyze the impact of changes and to identify systems and components that should be retested.

Architecture and Agility. The development and evolution of our enterprise SOA currently follows a rather plan-driven process including strict analysis, design, implementation, documentation and governance activities. Literature and current trends in software development lead to the wish to introduce agile methodologies and techniques by development teams. However, in the context of enterprise applications and SOA as implemented for financial institutions with many restrictions and company-wide regulations, it still is unclear how an agile methodology can be established within existing organizational structures and business processes. Approaches like *Enterprise Scrum* aim to combine high-level business and governance processes and low-level agile development methodologies. In general, there is a tension between architecture-centric and agile methodologies [1], and this is even more evident in an enterprise SOA context. We need more research on how to combine architecture and agile methodologies for such large-scale systems with a long lifespan.

Architecture Management. Architecture information is not only a means for learning and evaluation in enterprise systems but also a central means for organizing government processes and for supporting development and quality control processes. In addition, many stakeholders are interested in different aspects of the available architectural information to address their concerns. The different stakeholders have already been addressed in architecture research and practice through different views [5] on architecture information, but there is additionally a need to provide the information in a central and timely manner. One way to address this concern could be to provide architecture information as a service which integrates architecture information from different sources. This also requires means for keeping the required information consistent over time.

Architecture Knowledge Sharing. A SoS as defined by the SOA in our context is characterized by different systems which are partly managed by largely independent organizational units. However, changes to a subsystem often are not only contained within the subsystem but may also affect other subsystems. However, such changes cannot be communicated globally because of the resulting information overload and subsequent ignorance by other organizational units. Thus we need effective means to efficiently provide architectural information to exactly the other organizational units and architect that might by affected by a change.

Service Development. A service-oriented software system as the one described in this paper has a long lifespan. This is quite natural because it is a main characteristic of such a system of systems that subsystems or individual components and services are upgraded, extended, modified, and removed during the lifespan of the system. A major problem in this regard is a change of the underlying technology platform because of side effects, which are hard to detect. For this reason, migrations to a new technology platform are currently typically avoided, because of the potential risks involved. This leads to additional costs for maintenance and operation of multiple different technology stacks. Therefore, we need approaches for minimizing the risks and for supporting platform evolution in such a system. One approach might be to specifically include architecture information to support such migrations as part of the system implementation.

6   Conclusion

The development of an enterprise SOA requires support for multiple stakeholders with different concerns and strict development and government processes. Architecture can be a central factor for supporting these stakeholders and processes. We have shown how architecture can be used to facilitate quality control activities within a SOA. But architecture might even be useful to address further challenges we have identified like focused and targeted testing in a SoS context, coordinating independently operating units through sharing of architectural knowledge, and facilitating platform migration in such a context. There are also open questions in terms of how to deal with agility in such a strictly controlled environment and how to provide architecture information in a central and consistent way to support the various stakeholders involved.

References

1. Abrahamsson, P., Babar, M.A., Kruchten, P.: Agility and architecture: Can they coexist? IEEE Software 27(2), 16–22 (2010)
2. Buchgeher, G., Weinreich, R.: Continuous software architecture analysis. In: Babar, M.A., Brown, A.W., Mistrik, I. (eds.) Agile Software Architecture. Aligning Agile Processes and Software Architectures, pp. 161–188. Newnes (2013)
3. Clements, P.: Documenting software architectures: views and beyond. Addison-Wesley, Upper Saddle (2010)
4. Hofmeister, C.: Architecting session report. In: WICSA 2005: Proceedings of the 5th Working IEEE/IFIP Conference on Software Architecture (WICSA 2005), pp. 209–210. IEEE Computer Society, Washington, DC (2005)
5. Rozanski, N., Woods, E.: Software systems architecture: working with stakeholders using viewpoints and perspectives., 2nd edn. Addison-Wesley, Upper Saddle River (2011)
6. Weinreich, R., Buchgeher, G.: Towards supporting the software architecture life cycle. Journal of Systems and Software 85(3), 546–561 (2012)
7. Weinreich, R., Buchgeher, G.: Automatic reference architecture conformance checking for soa-based software systems. In: 11th Working IEEE/IFIP Conference on Software Architecture (WICSA). IEEE Computer Society Press (2014)
8. Weinreich, R., Miesbauer, C., Buchgeher, G., Kriechbaum, T.: Extracting and facilitating architecture in service-oriented software systems. In: 2012 Joint 10th IEEE/IFIP Working Conference on Software Architecture & 6th European Conference on Software Architecture (WICSA-ECSA 2012). IEEE Computer Society Press, Los Alamitos (2012)
9. Weinreich, R., Wiesauer, A., Kriechbaum, T.: A service lifecycle and information model for service-oriented architectures. In: International Conference on Advanced Service Computing (Service Computation 2009), pp. 346–352 (2009)
10. Westfall, L.: The certified software quality engineer handbook. ASQ Quality Press, Milwaukee (2009)

Multi-tenant Architecture Comparison

Jaap Kabbedijk, Michiel Pors, Slinger Jansen, and Sjaak Brinkkemper

Department of Information and Computing Sciences
Utrecht University, The Netherlands
{J.Kabbedijk,M.Pors,Slinger.Jansen,S.Brinkkemper}@uu.nl

Abstract. Software architects struggle to choose an adequate architectural style for multi-tenant software systems. Bad choices result in poor performance, low scalability, limited flexibility, and obstruct software evolution. We present a comparison of 12 Multi-Tenant Architecture (MTA) patterns that supports architects in choosing the most suitable architectural pattern, using 17 assessment criteria. Both patterns and criteria were evaluated by domain experts. Five architecture assessment rules of thumb are presented in the paper, aimed at making fast and efficient design decisions. The comparison provides architects with an effective method for selecting the applicable multi-tenant architecture pattern, saving them effort, time, and mitigating the effects of making wrong decisions.

Keywords: Multi-tenancy, architecture patterns, quality attributes.

1 Introduction

As a consequence of the current shift of on-premises software to the cloud [4], software architects find themselves facing numerous new challenges related to the adequacy of architectures for cloud software. A commonly used technique in architecting for Software-as-a-Service (SaaS) is the use of the concept of multi-tenancy, which is defined for this research as *"a property of a system where multiple varying customers and their end-users share the system's services, applications, databases, or hardware resources, with the aim of lowering costs"* [11].

Multi-tenancy can bring about many benefits. By serving the software service from a centrally hosted location, clients are relieved from the responsibility of purchasing and maintaining expensive in-house servers. The total cost of ownership decreases, giving the SaaS provider access to new potential customers that previously could not afford the expenses [2]. In addition, the utilization rate of hardware in a multi-tenant environment is higher than in a single-tenant environment [12]. Furthermore, when multiple customers share application and data instances, the total number of running instances will be lower than in a single-tenant environment, catering the same number of customers. A low number of instances is beneficial for maintenance [9] and is beneficial for application development [1].

However, multiple barriers withhold service providers from massively switching to multi-tenant environments. The challenges for multi-tenancy adoption include

P. Avgeriou and U. Zdun (Eds.): ECSA 2014, LNCS 8627, pp. 202–209, 2014.

performance [10], scalability, security [7], and the re-engineering of current software applications [13]. Selecting the appropriate multi-tenant architecture is a complex problem due to the existence of numerous alternative architectural patterns. Benefits and barriers of multi-tenancy are identified and described in literature, but the aspect of choosing an appropriate multi-tenant architecture based on software vendors' preferences has received little attention in literature. Finding the most suitable multi-tenant architecture is crucial; it expresses a fundamental structural organization schema for a provider's software system. However, choosing the appropriate architecture is a wicked problem [5]. Accounting for all the challenges and benefits complicates the decision process considerably [8].

This paper presents a comparison of different Multi-Tenant Architecture (MTA) patterns, based on the the mixed method research approach used within this study (Section 2). The twelve different MTA patterns are shown in section 3, together the MTA comparison matrix in section 4. We conclude with a discussion on the comparison, together with threats to validity present and future work in section 5, focussing on the importance of evaluating more effective methods in architectural decision making.

2   Research Approach

The main research question of this research is formulated as follows:

RQ. *How can a SaaS provider be supported in the decision process of choosing an applicable multi-tenant architecture?*

Three sub questions are answered in order to develop a decision model that solves the main research question. The decision model consists of three fundamental elements, which need to be identified. The first element is a set of multi-tenant architectures to choose from. Hence, the first sub question is defined as follows:

SQ1. *What distinctive layers in multi-tenant architectures can be defined?* — Using a Structured Literature Research (SLR), the distinctive layers in multi-tenant architectures are identified in SQ1. For more details on the search query, criteria, strategy and construction of trail searches, please see [11]. Instead of searching directly for multi-tenant architectures and documenting them, a different approach is taken. First, different layers on which multi-tenancy can be applied are identified. Then, generic multi-tenant architectures are identified, based on these layers. The list of identified architectures is evaluated by domain experts to ensure the list is complete and concise. The expert evaluation is not only essential for checking the correctness of the list, but also to make sure the identified architectures reflect *relevant* and *implementable* architectures.

SQ2. *What are the relevant decision criteria for choosing an appropriate multi-tenant architecture?* — SQ2 aims at identifying the different decision criteria, or architecturally significant requirements, related to multi-tenant architectures.

The decision criteria are quantifiable attributes distinguishing between the different multi-tenant architectures. Similar to the identification of the MTAs, a structured literature research is carried out to identify the list of criteria. The identification process results in a large set of criteria, which is analyzed in order to merge similar and delete unimportant attributes. Consequently, the completeness and conciseness of the list is evaluated in an expert evaluation. Finally, the multi-tenant architectures must be evaluated using the decision criteria, resulting in performance scores. The final sub question is stated as:

SQ3. *How do the different multi-tenant architectures perform on the decision criteria?* — In SQ3, an evaluation is performed in which all MTAs are assessed by domain experts on the identified decision characteristics. The evaluation serves as a basis for MTA decision making.

3   Multi-tenant Architectures

The levels at which multi-tenancy can be applied, resulting from the literature study, are shown in Table 1. All levels are listed together with the frequency of occurrence (N) in literature. The different levels are depicted as layers in a stack with decreasing granularity from top to bottom in Figure 1. The granularity aspect translates to a sharing versus isolation continuum, where the lowest layer has the lowest level of sharing with the highest level of isolation. For the highest layer it is vice versa. When multi-tenancy is applied at a specific level, the levels below that level are shared among tenants as well, but isolation occurs at the levels above, i.e. for each tenant a dedicated instance is running. This applies to the application and data layer independently.

Table 1. Multi-Tenancy levels identified in literature

Multi-tenancy level	N
Application Instance	16
Database Server	16
Database	15
Operating System	15
Hardware	14
Schema	14
Middleware	12
Virtual Machine	9
Application Server	4

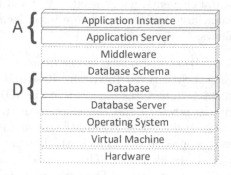

Fig. 1. Multi-tenancy computing stack. *'A' and 'D' relatively indicate the Application and Data related layer sets.*

The final two levels of the stack in the data layer are the *database* and *schema level*. These two levels were first described by Chong et al. [3]. When tenants are consolidated in a single database, each tenant operates its own set of tables. In schema-level multi-tenancy, isolation occurs at table row level.

The *application* related layer set (A) and the *data* related layer set (D) are stacks commonly used in enterprise architecture in order to separate concerns [6]. Within this research the application layers and data layers are identified as separate *layer sets*, each containing different sub layers, as can be seen in Figure 1.

Consequently, three tenancy levels, indicated by a two letter abbreviation, are identified in the *Application* related layer set (**A**). The different levels result from identifying ascending levels of sharing among all layers on the set:

1. **AD** - A Dedicated Application server is running for each tenant, and therefore each tenant receives a dedicated application instance.
2. **AS** - A single Application Server is running for multiple tenants and each tenant receives a dedicated application instance.
3. **AI** - A single application server is running for multiple tenants and a single Application Instance is running for multiple tenants.

The first level corresponds to multi-tenancy enabled at the hardware or virtual machine level. The second level is equal to application server multi-tenancy. The third level is the same as multi-tenancy enabled at the application instance level. In the *Data* related layer set (**D**) a service provider can select one the following four tenancy levels:

1. **DD** - A Dedicated Database server is running for each tenant, and therefore each tenant receives a dedicated database.
2. **DS** - A single Database Server is running for multiple tenants and each tenant receives a dedicated database.
3. **DB** - A single DataBase server is running for multiple tenants, data from multiple tenants is stored in a single database, but each tenant receives a dedicated set of tables.
4. **DC** - A single database server is running for multiple tenants, data from multiple tenants is stored in a single database and a single set of tables, sharing the same Database sChema.

The first level is equal to multi-tenancy applied at the hardware or virtual machine level. The second one corresponds to database server multi-tenancy. The third alternative is the same as multi-tenancy applied to the database and the final one is equal to database schema multi-tenancy.

From these options in both the application and data layer, the set of multi-tenant architectures (MTAs) are constructed. Based on the tenancy levels within the layers, the number of possible architectures is twelve. Because all MTAs prescribe a specific tenancy level in set A and D, each architecture is defined as a tuple:

$$MTA = \langle \{AD, AS, AI\}, \{DD, DS, DB, DC\} \rangle \qquad (1)$$

Each of the twelve MTAs can be seen as an architectural pattern in which tenants (Tenant A, B and C in the example MTAs) communicate with a software application consisting of an application layer and a data layer as shown in Figure 2. For a complete overview of all MTAs please see [11].

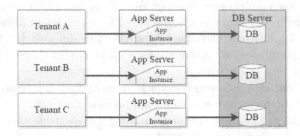

Fig. 2. MTA$\langle AD, DS \rangle$ - Dedicated Application Server & Shared Database Server

In Figure 2 the application layer is represented as a set of application servers running one or multiple application instances. The data layer is displayed as a set of database servers, running one or more databases, in which one or multiple database schema's exist. If one of these entities is shared among the tenants, its color is gray. If its dedicated to only one tenant, its colored white. For the sake of simplicity only three tenants are displayed in the architectures. A service provider can offer his software application to more than three tenants, the patterns merely presents possible arrangements of shared resources.

4   MTA Comparison Matrix

The MTA pattern comparison offers decision makers a method to make an informed and balanced decision on the MTAs to consider implementing for their software product. The MTA Comparison Matrix in Table 2 offers a high level of detail, while also giving a quick overview of the strengths and weaknesses of all patterns. Using the matrix, architects can get an overview of the consequences of all different MTA patterns and assess the weight of the consequences for their specific situation. Based on the consequences and the weights, architects can select a subset of patterns to evaluate more thoroughly. To help in selecting a subset for future analysis, this section presents some Rules of Thumb (RT) derived from the comparison matrix and are helpful in giving decision makers a quick overview of the most important consequences of an MTA assessment.

RT1. Focus on the database dimension — The effect of different MTAs on decision criteria is largest on the database dimension. The MTA Comparison Matrix shows the effect of database related decisions is higher than application related decisions. Choosing between a set of MTAs, focus on database related decisions first, and application related decisions after.

RT2. Sharing database tables enables serving of many tenants but harms robustness — Selecting an MTA in which the database schema is shared

Table 2. Multi-Tenant Architecture Comparison Matrix (In color) - **1.0** indicates a highly negative effect, by applying the pattern, on the decision criterion. **5.0** indicates a highly positive effect.

Decision Criterion	$\langle AD,DD \rangle$	$\langle AS,DD \rangle$	$\langle AI,DD \rangle$	$\langle AD,DS \rangle$	$\langle AS,DS \rangle$	$\langle AI,DS \rangle$	$\langle AD,DB \rangle$	$\langle AS,DB \rangle$	$\langle AI,DB \rangle$	$\langle AD,DC \rangle$	$\langle AS,DC \rangle$	$\langle AI,DC \rangle$	Dist. Factor (σ^2)
Time Behavior	5.0	4.0	4.0	4.0	4.0	3.0	4.0	3.5	3.0	3.5	3.0	2.0	0.6
Resource Utilization	2.5	2.5	3.0	2.5	3.0	3.0	3.0	3.0	4.0	3.0	3.0	4.5	0.4
Throughput	4.5	3.0	3.0	4.0	3.0	3.0	3.0	3.0	3.0	3.0	3.0	3.0	0.2
Number of Tenants	1.0	3.0	3.0	3.0	3.5	4.0	3.0	4.0	4.0	3.0	4.0	5.0	1.0
Number of End-Users	2.5	3.5	3.0	3.0	3.5	3.5	3.0	3.5	4.0	3.5	4.0	4.0	0.2
Availability	4.0	3.0	3.0	3.0	3.0	3.0	3.0	3.0	3.0	3.0	3.0	3.0	0.1
Recoverability	5.0	4.5	4.5	4.0	4.0	4.0	3.0	3.0	3.0	2.0	2.0	2.0	1.1
Confidentiality	5.0	4.5	4.0	4.0	4.0	4.0	3.5	3.0	3.0	2.0	2.0	2.0	1.0
Integrity	4.5	4.0	3.0	4.0	3.5	3.0	3.5	3.0	3.0	3.0	2.5	2.5	0.4
Authenticity	4.5	3.5	3.0	3.5	3.0	3.0	4.0	3.0	3.0	3.0	3.0	3.0	0.2
Maintainability	1.5	2.5	3.0	2.0	3.0	3.5	2.5	4.0	4.0	3.0	4.0	5.0	1.0
Portability	5.0	5.0	5.0	4.5	4.5	4.5	4.0	4.0	4.0	3.0	3.0	3.0	0.6
Deployment Time	1.5	3.0	3.0	2.5	3.5	4.0	3.0	4.0	4.0	3.0	4.0	5.0	0.8
Variability	5.0	4.0	2.0	5.0	4.0	2.0	4.5	3.5	2.0	2.5	2.0	1.0	1.9
Diverse SLA	5.0	4.0	3.0	4.0	3.5	2.5	4.0	3.0	3.0	3.0	2.5	2.0	0.7
Software Complexity	5.0	4.5	4.0	4.5	4.5	3.5	4.0	4.0	3.0	2.5	2.5	2.0	0.9
Monitoring	1.0	2.5	3.0	2.5	3.0	3.0	3.0	4.0	4.0	3.0	4.0	5.0	1.0

(i.e. $\langle A?, DC \rangle$[1]) is beneficial if the software product serves many tenants and end-users. The product is easy to maintain and monitor, and deployment time is minimal. The recoverability of the system, on the other hand, is greatly compromised. It is difficult to implement variability and tenant data may be at risk of unintentional sharing. Based on this trade-off, SaaS providers should select $\langle A?, DC \rangle$ when designing a large scale software product with limited variability requirements.

RT3. Sharing application instances helps maintainability and performance but harms variability — Choosing an MTA, decision makers can decide to share the application instance among tenants (i.e. $\langle AI, D? \rangle$). Doing so causes the maintainability and ease of monitoring to increase. Also the resource utilization is better and the deployment time low. The variability of the software product, however, is lower and more difficult to implement. Because of this, SaaS should choose $\langle AI, D? \rangle$ when maintainability and performance efficiency are important.

---

[1] '?' is used as a single character wild card.

RT4. Ease of implementing variability differs greatly per MTA — Out of all decision criteria, variability has the highest distinction factor. This means the variability of a software product is for a significant part determined by the implemented MTA. Choosing an MTA with a low tenancy level (i.e. $\langle AD, DD \rangle$, variability is relatively easy to achieve. Selecting an MTA with a high tenancy level however (i.e. $\langle AI, DC \rangle$), causes large problems implementing variability over all tenant instances.

RT5. Dedicated servers improve performance and variability, but hamper scalability — When choosing an MTA with dedicated servers (i.e. $\langle AD, DD \rangle$) the time behavior, recoverability, variability and confidentiality are expected to be good, and software complexity low. The downside to this approach is the low scalability of the system; when the number of tenants increases, dedicated servers become hard to maintain and hardware costs will rise. Choose $\langle AD, DD \rangle$ for software products with a small user base that need to have high performance and a high level of flexibility. Typically large enterprise applications fall in this category.

The rules of thumb listed in this section do not aim for completeness, but rather give software architects and decision makers a collection of rules to guide their architecture selection.

5   Discussion and Conclusion

The identification of the 12 different multi-tenant architecture patterns and the comparison of the patterns, along with a list of assessment criteria and rules of thumb, support SaaS providers in providing a concise and versatile method for multi-tenant architecture assessment. In case specific assessment criteria or MTAs are irrelevant to a decision maker for some reason, those elements can be easily removed from the analysis, simplifying the selection of a suitable architecture. If a SaaS provider feels important decision criteria are missing from the assessment model, extra decision criteria can be added in the analysis. However, performance values of the MTAs on these criteria can not be provided in this research.

We identify the following threats to validity to this study: 1. The small sample of 10 domain experts used may lead to biased results. A larger set would potentially increase the generalizability of the results. 2. All experts are from the same company. This threat is mitigated by the fact they are all employed at different independent projects. 3. The comparison matrix is not evaluated in practice in an extensive case study to test the applicability. By performing a case study, the appropriateness of the matrix can be validated.

All are threats to *external* validity, as defined by Yin [14]. We suggest further research to focus on demonstrating the analytic hierarchy process in conjunction with the comparison matrix at several companies. Then, the ratings can be evaluated more thoroughly resulting in possible adjustments for these performance values. Furthermore, the ratings provided in this research are based on subjective judgements of ten experts. The accuracy of the ratings can be increased by surveying a larger number of experts, causing a decrease of the standard deviation.

Acknowledgments. This research is funded by the NWO/ICT-Regie 'Product as a Service' grant. Special thanks to Leen Blom and the experts willing to cooperate in our research. We would also like to thank Hans van Vliet for providing valuable feedback.

References

1. Bezemer, C.P., Zaidman, A., Platzbeecker, B., Hurkmans, T., t Hart, A.: Enabling multi-tenancy: An industrial experience report. In: Proc. of the Int. Conference on Software Maintenance (ICSM), pp. 1–8. IEEE (2010)
2. Chong, F., Carraro, G.: Architecture strategies for catching the long tail. Tech. rep., MSDN Library, Microsoft Corporation (2006)
3. Chong, F., Carraro, G., Wolter, R.: Multi-tenant data architecture. Tech. rep., MSDN Library, Microsoft Corporation (2006)
4. D'souza, A., Kabbedijk, J., Seo, D., Jansen, S., Brinkkemper, S.: Software-as-a-service: Implications for business and technology in product software companies. In: Proceedings of the Pacific Asia Conference on Information Systems (PACIS), pp. 140–146 (2012)
5. Esfahani, N., Razavi, K., Malek, S.: Dealing with uncertainty in early software architecture. In: Proc. of the Int. Symposium on the Foundations of Software Engineering, p. 21. ACM (2012)
6. Fowler, M.: Patterns of enterprise application architecture. Addison-Wesley Professional (2003)
7. Guo, C.J., Sun, W., Huang, Y., Wang, Z.H., Gao, B.: A framework for native multi-tenancy application development and management. In: Proc. of the Int. Conference on E-Commerce Technology (CEC), pp. 551–558. IEEE (2007)
8. Kazman, R., Asundi, J., Klein, M.: Quantifying the costs and benefits of architectural decisions. In: Proc. of the Int. Conference on Software Engineering (ICSE), pp. 297–306. IEEE Computer Society (2001)
9. Kwok, T., Nguyen, T., Lam, L.: A software as a service with multi-tenancy support for an electronic contract management application. In: Proc. of the Int. Conference on Services Computing (SCC), pp. 179–186 (2008)
10. Lin, H., Sun, K., Zhao, S., Han, Y.: Feedback-control-based performance regulation for multi-tenant applications. In: Proc. of the Int. Conference on Parallel and Distributed Systems (ICPADS), pp. 134–141. IEEE (2009)
11. Pors, M., Blom, L., Kabbedijk, J., Jansen, S.: Sharing is caring - a decision support model for multi-tenant architectures. Tech. Rep. UU-CS-2013-015, Department of Information and Computing Sciences, Utrecht University (2013)
12. Sääksjärvi, M., Lassila, A., Nordström, H.: Evaluating the software as a service business model: From cpu time-sharing to online innovation sharing. In: Proc. of the Int. Conference e-Society, Qawra, Malta, pp. 27–30 (2005)
13. Tsai, C.-H., Ruan, Y., Sahu, S., Shaikh, A., Shin, K.G.: Virtualization-based techniques for enabling multi-tenant management tools. In: Clemm, A., Granville, L.Z., Stadler, R. (eds.) DSOM 2007. LNCS, vol. 4785, pp. 171–182. Springer, Heidelberg (2007)
14. Yin, R.K.: Case study research: Design and methods, vol. 5. Sage (2009)

Integrating Service Matchers into a Service Market Architecture*

Marie Christin Platenius, Steffen Becker, and Wilhelm Schäfer

Software Engineering Group, Heinz Nixdorf Institute,
University of Paderborn, Germany
{m.platenius,steffen.becker,wilhelm}@upb.de

Abstract. Service markets provide software components in the form of services. In order to enable a service discovery that satisfies service requesters and providers best, markets need automatic service matching: approaches for comparing whether a provided service satisfies a service request. Current markets, e.g., app markets, are limited to basic keyword-based search although many better suitable matching approaches are described in literature. However, necessary architectural decisions for the integration of matchers have a huge impact on quality properties like performance or security.

Architectural decisions wrt. service matchers have rarely been discussed, yet, and systematic approaches for their integration into service markets are missing. In this paper, we present a systematic integration approach including the definition of requirements and a discussion on architectural tactics. As a benefit, the decision-making process of integrating service matchers is supported and the overall market success can be improved.

Keywords: Service Matching, Service Markets, Software Architecture, On-The-Fly Computing.

1 Introduction

In the last decades, development turned from monolithic software products towards more flexible, component-based and service-oriented solutions. On *service markets*, service requesters can obtain software components that are provided in form of readily deployed services (Software-as-a-Service). Till date, there are only a few markets for this kind of services. However, following the example of markets for software products comparable to services, e.g., apps, we can expect service markets to rapidly increase in the future, too [12].

The more crowded service markets get, the more important becomes the quality and efficiency of the markets' service discovery mechanisms. While most established markets today are still limited to a relatively simple, keyword-based search, in academia, there is a mass of research for comprehensive *service matching* approaches, i.e., the analysis of whether the specifications of provided services satisfy a requested service [4,10] considering also structural, behavioral,

---

* This work was supported by the German Research Foundation (DFG) within the Collaborative Research Center "On-The-Fly Computing" (CRC 901).

P. Avgeriou and U. Zdun (Eds.): ECSA 2014, LNCS 8627, pp. 210–217, 2014.

and quality properties. However, integrating a service matcher component implementing such a matching approach into an existing service market is complicated as there are different architectural possibilities with different consequences on market success. For example, integrating a service matcher into the requester's client provides the benefit of customizability but it may lead to a bottleneck that can slow down the whole discovery because many matching processes have to be performed sequentially. On the other hand, integrating a service matcher into the provider's system can lead to serious security problems allowing service providers to manipulate matching results but, depending on further parameters, a better performance may be attainable. Problems like these lead to the conclusion that a more systematic approach for the integration of service matchers on the architectural level is needed. However, until now, in literature, architectural decisions wrt. service matchers have rarely been discussed and there is no systematic approach for their integration into a market. Also applying classic software architecture decision-making methods has not been analysed wrt. service matchers and their influence on markets yet.

In this paper, we present a systematic approach for the integration of service matchers into a service market. This includes the definition of requirements and a discussion on architectural tactics based on these requirements. The contribution of this paper is an approach that can be used to integrate matchers into existing markets. Thereby, the general success of service markets, impacted by the use of service matching approaches, can be improved. An extended version of this paper including an application example has been published as technical report [9].

In the next section, we briefly summarize the foundations for this work. In Section 3, we derive requirements which we use to discuss integration tactics in Section 4. Section 5 deals with related work. The paper is concluded in Section 6.

2   Service Markets and Matching

In this paper, we use the following definition of a *service*: A service is a software component that is deployed and running on a service provider's platform. One example is Google Maps. Google Maps is a service offered by Google and it provides the functionality of querying and showing a map of some location. A *service market* allows trading, i.e., buying and selling, such services.

Although paradigms like Service-Oriented Architectures and Service-Oriented Computing have been investigated for several years now, there are not many established markets for services in the sense of readily deployed software components till date. In the area of web services, there has been the service registry standard UDDI but it has been officially discontinued years ago. However, along with emerging cloud providers, some more platforms to obtain web services for usage in the cloud appeared, e.g., Amazon Web Services [1]. Furthermore, there are markets for software products similar to services, like software components in the form of plug-ins (e.g., Eclipse Marketplace [14]) or apps. Schlauderer and Overhage analysed StrikeIron [13], Salesforce's AppExchange [11], and Google's Apps Marketplace (now Google Play [5]) as leading markets in 2010 [12].

In service markets, there are different roles, e.g., *service requesters* and *service providers*. Service requesters are interested in buying a service that fits to their requirements. Providers offer and sell services. Furthermore, there can be trusted third parties, e.g., a *market operator*, who provides and manages the market [12]. An actor can play several roles, e.g., intermediaries act as both requester and provider at the same time.

Service providers make their service offers available to requesters by publishing service specifications that help to *discover* their services. In most of today's markets, service specifications are either informal, describing a service's functional and non-functional properties using plain text mostly, or simple technical descriptions, like the Web Service Description Language (WSDL) [3], limited to the services' signatures. In academia, there are already a lot of approaches for more comprehensive but also machine-readable service specifications including expressive formalisms like protocols, ontological semantics, pre- and postconditions, and many more [8]. Such comprehensive specifications enable a service discovery taking into account technical, behavioral, as well as quality information, based on *service matching*. Service matching is the process of comparing the specification of a requested service, i.e., a *request*, to the specification of a provided service, in order to determine whether the provided service satisfies the request. It can be part of many different use cases, e.g., automated service composition, or used by service end-users. As an output, a matcher delivers a matching result which denotes how well a provided service specification matches a request. For example, a very simple specification of Google Maps could be `getMap(Location):Map`. Following the principles of simple signature matching approaches, this provided specification would achieve a good matching result with a request like `searchMap(City):Map` with `City` being a subtype of `Location`. There are many automated and much more complex matching approaches in literature. For a classification and an overview of recent surveys, refer to our earlier work [10].

3   Requirements for Matcher Integration

Figure 1 depicts an overview of the requirements collected for the integration of matchers into service markets. A dependency from A to B means that the fulfilment of B supports the fulfilment of A. Neither the requirements, nor the dependencies are meant to be a complete collection as we focussed on the ones that are most important in our context.

Due to page limitations, in this paper, we focus only on some of the requirements depicted in Fig. 1. For the complete list, refer to our technical report [9]. There, we also give an overview of the process and methodology we used to elicit the requirements. The requirements we selected are described in the following.

(**R5**) *Performance:* Performance refers to the time to perform one matching process, i.e., the time to determine how much a particular service satisfies the request. It needs to be high in order to gain a good efficiency of the overall discovery process (*R4*).

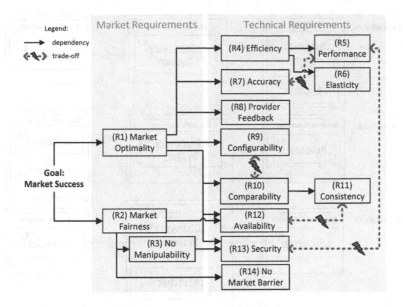

Fig. 1. Overview of the requirements for integrating a matcher into a market

(**R6**) *Elasticity:* Even if the performance of one matching process is good, the discovery's efficiency is still problematic when a huge amount of matching processes is required. Thus, similar to cloud computing systems, in service markets, the matching system needs to be elastic [6] in a way that it adapts to the amount of required matching processes.

(**R10**) *Comparability:* If different services are matched to the same request, services with the same matching result should satisfy the request equally well. Similarly, services with better matching results should satisfy the requester more than services with lower matching results. This has to hold, even and especially, if those services are offered by different providers.

(**R11**) *Consistency:* Matching results are only comparable if they are consistent. Dynamic markets, where providers can appear and disappear or change their offers at any time, can lead to situations in which several versions of a service or a service decription are available. It has to be avoided that this dynamics leads to inconsistent matching results between different providers so that comparability can be ensured.

(**R13**) *Security:* Matching results have to be secure so that they cannot be manipulated by any service provider. For example, if aspects like reputation of a service are matched, providers have to be prevented from cheating in a way that they claim to have a better reputation than they actually have.

Figure 1 shows trade-offs between requirements by dotted arrows annotated with a flash symbol. Because of such conflicting requirements, there may not be one general best solution for all service markets. For a description of these trade-offs, please refer to our technical report [9]

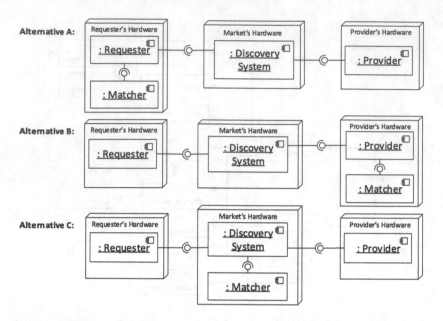

Fig. 2. Architectural alternatives for matcher integration

4   Integrating a Matcher Based on Architectural Tactics

When integrating the matcher into a market, there are different alternatives, as depicted in Fig. 2. In Alternative A, the matcher is integrated into the requester's system and, therefore, deployed on the requester's hardware. Here, the requester's system accesses the discovery system to get the specifications of the provided services and forwards them to the matcher. Alternative B lets the providers deploy the matcher on their own resources. In this case, the discovery system forwards the request to the providers, where each provider matches its service specifications against the request. In Alternative C, the matcher is part of the discovery system and deployed on the market operator's resources. Instead of the market operator, this role can also be played by another trusted third-party which is part of the market. The specifications of provided services could still be located at the providers, or, alternatively, stored on the market operator's resources, too. As we can see, the question of where to integrate the matcher is related to the question of who deploys the matcher.

Each of the three alternatives has different benefits and drawbacks and, in particular, a different impact on the fulfilment of our requirements. Table 1 lists these benefits and drawbacks with respect to the requirements collected in Section 3. A minus in the table means that it is difficult to satisfy the corresponding requirement, whereas a plus means that it is easier to satisfy it. Similarly to the architectural tactics described by Bachmann et al. [2], the table depends on bound and free parameters: Bound parameters are already fixed because their assignment is the same for all service markets. Free parameters (highlighted in italics) need

Table 1. Where to integrate the matcher?

	Alternative A: Requester	Alternative B: Provider	Alternative C: Market Operator	w
R5	- (no caching)	+	+	?
	depends on kind of requesters/providers			
R6	depends on number of providers and requests at a time			?
R10	+	- (conflict with R9 and R13)	- (conflict with R9)	?
R11	- (not insurable)	+	- (not insurable)	?
R13	+	- (high risk for manipulation)	+	?

further assumptions to be assigned, i.e., the evaluation can have a different result depending on the properties of a concrete service market. Furthermore, there is a column about weights in order to allow influencing the overall evaluation by assigning special priorities to some requirements. Weights can be positive (e.g., +1), if a requirement is particularly important, or negative (e.g., -1), if it is less important compared to the other ones. Similar to free parameters, weights depend on properties of concrete service markets, too. Thus, they are not yet assigned in this general version of the table.

The table only covers the requirements selected in Sec. 3. For the complete table, refer to our technical report [9]. In the following, we describe the evaluation shown in Table 1.

(**R5**) **Performance** Regarding the performance, Alternative A seems not to be a good solution. Matchers located at the service provider or a market operator provide the possibility to cache matching results and benefit from it when similar requests are received. This possibility is not available for matchers deployed at the requester's because it would only pay off, if one requester repeatedly states similar requests, which is not the case if the discovery scenario works well and the requester already gets a satisfying result after her first request. Furthermore, if the matcher runs on hardware with high computation power, e.g., compute centers, this could speed up the matching process, too. In contrast, if the matcher runs on a mobile device, a matching process takes longer. Which role can provide the more appropriate resources depends (amongst others) on the domain. For example, requesters in some technical domain could be assumed to have better hardware available than the typical hotel booking service user, whereas providers can be expected to have access to more computation power than the requesters in both cases.

(**R6**) **Elasticity** For Alternative A, the amount of matchers increases with each new requester and, thereby, also with the amount of stated requests. This is good if there are many requests but only few service offers. For Alternative B, the amount increases with each new provider, and, thereby, also with the amount of service offers. If we have a market with many providers but only few requesters, Alternative B is preferable. Alternative C suffers from the fact that the market operator has to provide or pay a cloud infrastructure in order to provide an elastic matching architecture.

(**R10**) **Comparability** Comparability is in conflict with configurability. This especially holds for Alternative B and C: if providers use different matching configurations, the matching results for services of different providers are not comparable for the requester. However, if the requester has the matcher and the possibility to configure it, this is no problem as all services from different providers are matched with the same configuration. Comparability among different requests is not needed as matching on service markets is one-sided, i.e., we search an optimal allocation of services to requests but not the other way around because software services are immaterial and (almost) not capacity-constrained. In addition, comparability is also influenced by security as, in the case of manipulation of matching results, comparability cannot be ensured. This is a disadvantage of Alternative B because it is most susceptible for manipulation (see *R13*). All in all, for *R10*, Alternative A is the best solution.

(**R11**) **Consistency** Regarding consistency, Alternative A as well as Alternative C both have the disadvantage that it is not necessarily ensured that they match the specification describing the provider's current offer. Compared to this, the provider has a better chance to ensure consistency because the provider manages the specifications herself.

(**R13**) **Security** Security becomes a problem, in particular, if the provider deploys the matcher. In this case, it is hard to keep the provider from manipulating matching results. In contrast, the requester or the (trusted) market provider can be assumed not to be interested in faking the results.

As we can see, there is no obvious answer to the question of where to integrate the matcher. Each alternative has its advantages and disadvantages and some aspects depend on the concrete environment, e.g., the market's size. For this reason, the table needs to be adapted to concrete application scenarios. For an example of such an adaption refer to our technical report [9].

5 Related Work

Even though there is a lot of research for the single areas of software architectures, service matchers, and service market mechanisms, the integration of service matchers into a market has not been addressed on the architectural level, yet. For example, Klusch [7] as well as Dong et al. [4] give overviews of semantic service discovery architectures and classifies them into centralized and decentralized architectures. However, the alternatives are not discussed with respect to requirements for a matcher's integration nor taking into account market mechanisms. Similarly, the architecture description of web services by the W3C [15] distinguishes between a centralized server-sided scenario (similar to our Alternative C) and an index or peer-to-peer client-sided matching scenario (Alternative A) However, only the requirements wrt. the dynamics and the scalability of the environment are taken into account.

6 Conclusions

In this paper, we presented a systematic approach for integrating a service matcher into a service market. This approach includes the definition of requirements and a discussion on architectural tactics in order to enable a more informed decision-making regarding architectural alternatives. Both practitioners and researchers benefit from this paper. In practice, our results can be used to integrate service matchers into existing or emerging service markets and thereby supporting both requesters and providers by achieving their goals. In research, this paper also represents a first attempt to bridge the gap between markets and the mass of existing matching approaches in literature.

References

1. Amazon Web Services. Website, aws.amazon.com (last access: June 2014)
2. Bachmann, F., Bass, L., Klein, M.: Deriving architectural tactics: A step toward methodical architectural design. Technical report, Software Engineering Institute, Carnegie Mellon University, CMU/SEI-2003-TR-004 (2003)
3. Chinnici, R., Moreau, J.-J., Ryman, A., Weerawarana, S.: Web Services Description Language Version 2.0 Part 1: Core Language. Technical report (2007)
4. Dong, H., Hussain, F.K., Chang, E.: Semantic Web Service matchmakers: state of the art and challenges. In: Concurrency and Computation: Practice and Experience, vol. 25, pp. 961–988. Wiley Online Library (2012)
5. Google. Google Play - Website, play.google.com/ (last access: June 2014)
6. Herbst, N.R., Kounev, S., Reussner, R.: Elasticity: What it is, and What it is Not. In: 10th Int. Conf. on Autonomic Computing. USENIX (2013)
7. Klusch, M.: Semantic web service coordination. In: CASCOM: Intelligent Service Coordination in the Semantic Web, pp. 59–104. Springer (2008)
8. O'Sullivan, J., Edmond, D., ter Hofstede, A.II.M.: Service description: A survey of the general nature of services. Distributed and Parallel Databases Journal (2002)
9. Platenius, M.C., Becker, S., Schäfer, W.: Integrating Service Matchers into a Service Market Architecture. Technical Report tr-ri-14-340, Heinz Nixdorf Institute (2014)
10. Platenius, M.C., von Detten, M., Becker, S., Schäfer, W., Engels, G.: A Survey of Fuzzy Service Matching Approaches in the Context of On-The-Fly Computing. In: 16th Int. Symposium on Component-based Software Engineering. ACM (2013)
11. Salesforce.com, Inc., Salesforce AppExchange, appexchange.salesforce.com (last access: June 2014)
12. Schlauderer, S., Overhage, S.: How Perfect are Markets for Software Services? An Economic Perspective on Market Deficiencies and Desirable Market Features. In: Proc. of the 19th European Conf. on Information Systems (2011)
13. StrikeIron. StrikeIron - Website, http://www.strikeiron.com (last access: June 2014)
14. The Eclipse Foundation. Eclipse Marketplace, marketplace.eclipse.org (last access: June 2014)
15. W3C. Web services architecture, w3.org/TR/ws-arch (last access: June 2014)

Towards a Process to Design Architectures of Service-Oriented Robotic Systems

Lucas Bueno Ruas Oliveira[1,2], Elena Leroux[2], Katia Romero Felizardo[1],
Flavio Oquendo[2], and Elisa Yumi Nakagawa[1]

[1] Dept. of Computer Systems, University of São Paulo - USP, São Carlos, SP, Brazil
[2] IRISA Research Institute, University of South Brittany, Vannes, France
{buenolro,katiarf,elisa}@icmc.usp.br,
{elena.leroux,flavio.oquendo}@irisa.fr

Abstract. Robots have supported several areas of society, making daily
tasks easier and executing dangerous, complex activities. The increasing
demand and complexity of these robots have challenged the design of
robotic systems, i.e., the software systems that manage robots. In this
context, Service-Oriented Architecture (SOA) has been pointed out as
a promising architectural style to structure such systems, arising the
Service-Oriented Robotic Systems (SORS). However, most of software
architectures of SORS are still developed in an ad hoc manner. This lack
of maturity reduces the potential of SOA in providing important quality
attributes, such as reusability and maintainability, therefore affecting
the overall quality of these systems. This paper presents ArchSORS, a
systematic process that supports the design of software architectures for
SORS. Experiment results have pointed out that ArchSORS can produce
architectures with more quality, thus contributing to robotics and the
areas of society that have gained with the use of robots.

1 Introduction

Over the last years, robots have increasingly supported different areas of society.
Robots are no longer used only inside factories, but inside houses [1] and on the
streets [2]. Due to this high demand, robotic systems used to control robots are
becoming larger and more complex, creating a great challenge to the development of this special type of software system. Researchers have been investigating
different architectural styles focused on providing more quality for robotic systems. Robotic systems development has evolved from procedural paradigm to
object-orientation, and thence to component-based architecture [3]. More recently, Service-Oriented Architecture (SOA) [4] become focus of attention as a
promising architectural style to develop more reusable, flexible robotic systems.

Using SOA, complex robotic systems can be developed by assembling functionalities provided by independent, distributed software modules called services.
Designing robotic systems using SOA allows integration of heterogeneous hardware devices and reuse of complex algorithms, since services are provided through
auto-descriptive standard interfaces. Due to its relevance, several works reporting the use of SOA in robotics are available in literature, such as those that we

P. Avgeriou and U. Zdun (Eds.): ECSA 2014, LNCS 8627, pp. 218–225, 2014.

identified in our previous work [5]. Besides that, development environments specially focused on the design of Service-Oriented Robotic Systems (SORS) can be also found [6,7]. Nevertheless, few attention has been paid to the development of SORS software architectures. Currently, most of software architectures are designed in an *ad hoc* manner, without a systematic approach of development, hampering the construction, maintenance, and reuse of robotic systems. The consideration of quality attributes since the software architecture design is a critical concern, as these systems are often used in safety-critical contexts.

The main objective of this paper is to present ArchSORS (Architectural Design of Service-Oriented Robotic System), a process that aims at filling the gap between the systematic development of service-oriented systems and the current *ad hoc* approaches used to develop SORS. The ArchSORS process provides prescriptive guidance from the system specification to architecture evaluation. Results from our experiment indicate that ArchSORS has positive impact in modularity, cohesion, and coupling of SORS software architectures, thereby improving important quality attributes such as reusability and maintainability.

The remainder of this paper is organized as follows. Section 2 presents Arch-SORS and describes its phases. Section 3 discusses on ArchSORS evaluation. In Section 4, we present our conclusions and perspectives of future work.

2   Defining ArchSORS Process

ArchSORS is a process that promotes the systematic development of SORS software architectures. It explicitly considers the identification and assessment of constraints and quality attributes that are essential to robotic systems. The process also encompasses the main phases proposed by the consolidated SOMA (Service-Oriented Modeling and Architecture) method [8]. ArchSORS was established based on SORS software architectures available in the literature [5], a set of reference architectures that encompass knowledge of how to structure robotic systems [9], and our expertise on critical embedded systems. Fig. 1 outlines the overall structure of the ArchSORS process.

ArchSORS process is divided into five phases that can be applied in an iterative, incremental manner. The phases are divided into a set of activities, which are detailed into a comprehensive set of tasks. However, for sake of space detailed information and diagrams are only available in the SPEM (Software & Systems Process Engineering Metamodel Specification) version of the process[1]. Since ArchSORS is an incremental process, SORS software architectures can be successively refined from reference architectures into concrete architectures. In short, to establish a software architecture using ArchSORS, it is first necessary to characterize the robotic application and to produce the document of requirements (Step RSA-1). Following, in Step RSA-2, requirements are used to model the application flow and to identify capabilities that the robotic system should provide. In Step RSA-3, the functional architecture is described and represented in terms of the services used to provide the identified capabilities. In Step RSA-4,

---

[1] http://goo.gl/ykQ2d9

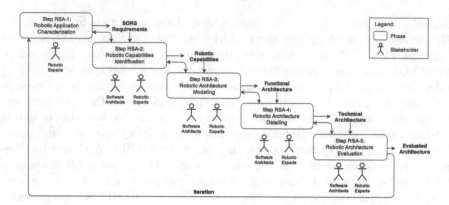

Fig. 1. ArchSORS: a process for developing SORS software architectures

services of the functional architecture are further described and decisions about hardware infrastructures are made, resulting in the technical architecture of the SORS. Finally, in Step RSA-5, the SORS software architecture is evaluated using architectural analysis methods. After that, if necessary, the evaluated architecture is refined through new iterations on the design process. Software architects (functional and technical) and robotics experts are involved and conduct the phases of the process. These phases are detailed as follows.

2.1 Phase RSA-1: Robotic Application Characterization

In Phase RSA-1, the application is described in terms of goals, activities, and characteristics about the robotic system and its operating environment. Additionally, applicable policies, rules, and constraints related to the robotic system are identified. As a result, the document of requirements of the robotic system is produced. The activities performed during this phase are detailed as follows.

RSA-A 1.1 – Initiate Project Activities: The main goals and characteristics of the robotic application are defined, described, and documented. Robotics specialists should perform brainstorm meetings to identify: (i) goals related to the robotic application; (ii) activities that the robotic system should perform to achieve these goals; (iii) the type of robotic system that will be developed, i.e., if the application involves a single robot, a team of robots, or a swarm; (iv) the type of robot (or types of robots) that will be used, the characteristics related to its mobility (if it will be mobile or non-mobile), the way it will move through the environment, its size, and so forth; and (v) the environment where the robot will be used (indoor, outdoor or both). At this point, no assumption is made on which hardware devices will be used in the robotic system.

RSA-A 1.2 – Identify Policies and Rules: Robotic applications must be conform with applicable policies and rules to be commercialized and used. A policy, for instance, can be defined by a law that regulates the operation of a given type of robotic system. Rules are restrictions on the robotic system design and operation that must be respected to comply with a given policy.

For instance, to comply with a given law, the robotic system should enforce safety by using redundant, independent sensors to measure distance from objects.

RSA-A 1.3 – Identify Constraints: Based on the decisions made in Activity RSA-A 1.1, constraints related to the robotic application are identified. These constraints are associate to both hardware requirements and real-time operation. Infrastructure requirements, such as battery consumption, processing power, network availability, and robot autonomy, are considered in the identification of hardware constraints. Use scenarios are carefully identified and described in the definition of real-time constraints. Afterwards, constraints associated to these scenarios are detected and prioritized. As robotic systems are often used in safe-critical domains, real-time constraints are very important and they must guide the rationale behind service identification and composition.

RSA-A 1.4 – Identify Standards: Robotic systems may need to be certificated to ensure the compliance with policies imposed to its operation. To obtain certification, development standards are applied both to robotic system and its development process. Thus, at this point, all standards related to the SORS are identified. Different standards can be applied to robotic systems and it depends on its own characteristics and on the environment where it will be used.

RSA-A 1.5 – Define Functional Requirements: Based on the outcomes of the previous activities, information related to the robotic system are obtained, resulting in a set of functional requirements. These requirements represent the functionalities that the SORS should provide to perform the robotic application.

RSA-A 1.6 – Define Quality Requirements: In this activity, quality requirements of the SORS are identified considering: (i) application goals; (ii) policies and rules; (iii) constraints; and (iv) standards associated to policies and rules. Afterwards, brainstorm meetings are carried out to prioritize the most important quality requirements. In a previous study [10], we have already identified a set of quality requirements considered as the most important to embedded systems. These requirements can be used as a starting point for this activity.

RSA-A 1.7 – Document SORS Requirements: Based on the results of the two previous activities, the document of the SORS requirements is created. This document will guide the description of the robotic application flow and support the identification of robotic capabilities. The document should be reviewed by all stakeholders to ensure that it is correct, complete, and in accordance with the robotic application goals and characteristics.

2.2 Phase RSA-2: Robotic Capabilities Identification

In Phase RSA-2, the robotic application is described in terms of functionalities necessary to achieve robotic system goals, the flow between these functionalities, and capabilities that are responsible for providing them. Thus, the application flow is modeled and then decomposed into different robotic capabilities. A capability is a service candidate that may either be already available or need to be developed. Descriptions of the activities of this phase are presented as follows.

RSA-A 2.1 – Model the Robotic Application Flow: During RSA-A 2.1, the flow of activities of the robotic application is described using description languages such as Unified Modeling Language (UML)[2] activity diagrams and Business Process Model and Notation (BPMN)[3]. The robotic application is described in terms of: (i) functionalities performed in parallel; (ii) functionalities performed in sequence, i.e., that depend on the result of the execution of previous functionalities; and (iii) functionalities that provide results based on the combination of results from other functionalities. Thereafter, the model is reviewed to check whether it fulfills all functional and quality requirements.

RSA-A 2.2 – Decompose the Robotic Application: Based on the defined model, the robotic application is decomposed into capabilities, which provide a set of functionalities of the SORS. To support this activity, we established a taxonomy that lists a comprehensive set of service candidates for SORS [11].

RSA-A 2.3 – Identify Available Capabilities: Robotics experts identify capabilities that are already available and can be reused. These capabilities are identified from different sources, such as: (i) robotic systems developed in previous projects; (ii) repositories of services for SORS; (iii) development environments, such as ROS and MRSD, which provide a set of native services for SORS; (iv) companies that provide device drivers and other capabilities related to their products; and (v) general purpose repositories, such as service brokers. To support this activity, we proposed a service repository[4] that automates the aforementioned taxonomy to enable the discovery of services for SORS.

RSA-A 2.4 – Identify Assets that Can Be Wrapped: Previous projects of non-service-oriented robotic systems are investigated to identify assets that can be provided as capabilities. These assets are packages, software modules, legacy applications, and algorithms (such as for localization and mapping) that can be wrapped as capabilities and then provided as services for the robotic system.

RSA-A 2.5 – Identify Assets that Can Be Refactored: Assets that are useful for the robotic system but can not be provided directly as robotic capabilities should also be identified. These assets have to be refactored in order to be reused as capabilities of the robotic system.

RSA-A 2.6 – Rationalize Capabilities: Services of the SORS are obtained based on the analysis of capabilities. Discussions are made to decide which capabilities will be exposed as services and which capabilities will be provided as components that support these services. As a result, a document is created to report: (i) capabilities related to the robotic application; (ii) functionalities provided by each capability; (iii) architectural elements used to provide each capability; and (iv) the design rationale related to these decisions.

2.3   Phase RSA-3: Robotic Architecture Modeling

During Phase RSA-3, services previously identified are described, modeled, and composed, resulting in the functional software architecture of the SORS.

---

[2] http://www.uml.org/
[3] http://www.bpmn.org/
[4] http://www.labes.icmc.usp.br:8595/RegistroServicoWeb/index.jsp

Therefore, interfaces, contracts, quality characteristics, and relationships of all robotics services should be created. The following activities are carried out in this phase.

RSA-A 3.1 – Specify Robotics Services: The document containing information about the robotic capabilities is updated and a detailed description of the roles played by each service is created. This document links the requirements of the robotic system to the requirements provided by each service.

RSA-A 3.2 – Model Robotics Services: Based on the updated capabilities document, services of the robotic system are modeled. As mentioned before, different types of ADL can be used to describe interfaces, contracts, and operations of the services in the architecture. In SORS, contracts, associated to the interfaces, usually enforce three types of interaction: (i) synchronous Remote Procedure Call (RPC); (ii) asynchronous RPC; and (iii) service subscription, which is a long-term interaction in which the service client implements a handler method to receive notifications from a service provider.

RSA-A 3.3 – Define Service Constraints: To ensure the compliance with the overall robotic system constraints, each service must guarantee its individual set of constraints. The clear description of constraints at architectural level is crucial to the determination of which participant (i.e., concrete service) will be able to provide a given service. Thus, the capabilities document is updated with information about the constraints of each robotics service of the architecture.

RSA-A 3.4 – Describe Quality Attributes: Based on the quality requirements of the robotic system and the services constraints, quality requirements related to each robotics service (i.e., QoS requirements) are identified and the capabilities document is again update. QoS requirements represent information about how functionalities of robotics services should be provided.

RSA-A 3.5 – Define Services Composition: The composition of robotics services is defined and the relationship among service partners are detailed. These partnerships are designed considering obligations of consumers and providers defined in the service contracts. In addition, complementary information about the interactions are described, such as service partners that should be hosted in the same infrastructure. These constraints are used to support decisions made during the design of the functional architecture described in the next phase.

RSA-A 3.6 – Specify Robotics Components: Robotics services are often abstractions of functionalities provided by the coordination of one or more components, i.e., capabilities that were not directly exposed as services. Thus, relationships among services and components of the SORS should be described and modeled using different representations, such as UML component diagrams.

RSA-A 3.7 – Document SORS Functional Architecture: The outcome of Phase RSA-3 is a document describing the SORS functional architecture. This document is produced by updating the capabilities document with all developed models, the design rationale applied in the modeling, and all useful information regarding the functional aspects of the robotic system.

2.4   Phase RSA-4: Robotic Architecture Detailing

In this Phase RSA-4, the functional architecture is detailed in terms of modules of software and hardware devices used to develop services of the robotic system, resulting in the technical architecture of the SORS. Descriptions of the activities conducted in this phase are presented as follows.

RSA-A 4.1 – Design of New Components: Services that are not available for reuse and need to be developed are further detailed and represented. Different diagrams can be designed, illustrating both design and runtime aspects of the services. The representation of the internal structure of services may be done by using ordinary object-oriented (OO) modeling and different design patterns.

RSA-A 4.2 – Design of Refactored Components: Services that provide capabilities from existing robotics assets are designed. To perform the refactoring, design documentation of the robotics assets is analyzed and new diagrams representing the robotics components are created.

RSA-A 4.3 – Rationalize Technical Decisions: Technical architects and robotics experts decide about hardware infrastructure and implementation strategies that will be used during the robotics services concretization. In addition, decisions are made on how the services of the robotic system will be deployed. As a result, a document reporting the rationale on service concretization is created.

RSA-A 4.4 – Detail SORS Concrete Architecture: Finally, the overall structure of the functional architecture is described in a document containing all information related to its design. Textual descriptions of the diagrams and design decisions are documented. Additional views of the architecture, such as deployment view, can also be created.

2.5   Phase RSA-5: Robotic Architecture Evaluation

In this phase, the SORS technical software architecture is evaluated and the compliance with requirements and systems constraints is assessed. Different evaluation methods can be used to perform this evaluation, such as inspection check lists and scenario-based methods. Moreover, the architectural description itself should evaluated to identify and eliminate defects related to omission, ambiguity, inconsistency, as well as strange and incorrect information. As a result, a more reliable software architecture version of the robotic architecture is achieved.

3   Experimental Evaluation

In order to evaluate the ArchSORS process, we have performed an experiment with 30 students of a preparatory course for the French national robotics competition[5]. These students were divided into two groups: (i) one to design the software architecture of a SORS using ArchSORS and (ii) other to design it in an *ad hoc* manner. The software architectures were evaluated using metrics of

---

[5] www.robafis.fr

coupling, cohesion, and modularity, since these metrics directly impact on quality attributes such as modifiability, reusability, and buildability. Results pointed out that students using ArchSORS designed software architectures that score better in these three metrics and, therefore, tend to present higher quality.

4   Conclusion and Future Work

SOA has been increasingly adopted for the development of SORS, getting advantages of SOA and resulting in more flexible robotic systems. The main contribution of this paper is to put forward ArchSORS, a process that intends to systematize the development of SORS software architectures and, as a consequence, to improve the quality of such systems. Experiment results point out that ArchSORS can positively impact on the quality of SORS. As future work we plan to perform a case study on the development of SORS using ArchSORS.

Acknowledgments. This work is supported by Brazilian funding agencies FAPESP (Grant N.: 2011/06022-0) and CNPq (Grant N.: 142099/2011-2 and 474720/2011-0), as well as the National Institute of Science and Technology on Critical Embedded Systems (INCT-SEC) (Grant N.: 573963/2008-8 and 2008/57870-9).

References

1. iRobots: iRobot Roomba Vacuum Cleaning Robot. Online (2014) http://www.irobot.com/us/learn/home/roomba.aspx (accessed in February 15, 2014)
2. Google: Google Driverless Car. Online (2014), http://goo.gl/NZ7Y2B
3. Brugali, D., Scandurra, P.: Component-based robotic engineering (Part I). IEEE Robotics Automation Magazine 16(4), 84–96 (2009)
4. Papazoglou, M.P., Traverso, P., Dustdar, S., Leymann, F.: Service-oriented computing: a research roadmap. International Journal of Cooperative Information Systems 17(2), 223–255 (2008)
5. Oliveira, L.B.R., Osorio, F.S., Nakagawa, E.Y.: An investigation into the development of service-oriented robotic systems. In: SAC 2013, Coimbra, Portugal, pp. 223–226 (2013)
6. Straszheim, T., Gerkey, B., Cousins, S.: The ROS build system. IEEE Robotics & Automation Magazine 18(2), 18–19 (2011)
7. Jackson, J.: Microsoft Robotics Studio: A technical introduction. IEEE Robotics & Automation Magazine 14(4), 82–87 (2007)
8. Arsanjani, A., Ghosh, S., Allam, A., Abdollah, T., Ganapathy, S., Holley, K.: SOMA: A method for developing service-oriented solutions. IBM Systems Journal 47(3), 377–396 (2008)
9. Feitosa, D., Nakagawa, E.Y.: An investigation into reference architectures for mobile robotic systems. In: ICSEA 2012, Lisbon, Portugal, pp. 465–471 (2012)
10. Oliveira, L.B.R., Guessi, M., Feitosa, D., Manteuffel, C., Galster, M., Oquendo, F., Nakagawa, E.Y.: An investigation on quality models and quality attributes for embedded systems. In: ICSEA 2013, Venice, Italy, pp. 523–528 (2013)
11. Oliveira, L.B.R., Osorio, F.S., Oquendo, F., Nakagawa, E.Y.: Towards a taxonomy of services for developing service-oriented robotic systems. In: SEKE 2014, Vancouver, Canada, pp. 344–349 (2014)

Scalable Architectures for Platform-as-a-Service Clouds: Performance and Cost Analysis

Huanhuan Xiong[1], Frank Fowley[1], Claus Pahl[1], and Niall Moran[2]

[1] IC4 – The Irish Centre for Cloud Computing and Commerce, Dublin City University,
Dublin 9, Ireland
{huanhuan.xiong,frank.fowley,claus.pahl}@dcu.ie
[2] Microsoft Ireland, Dublin 18, Ireland
nimoran@microsoft.com

Abstract. Scalability is a significant feature of cloud computing, which addresses to increase or decrease the capacities of allocated virtual resources at application, platform, database and infrastructure level on demand. We investigate scalable architecture solutions for cloud PaaS that allow services to utilize the resources dynamically and effectively without directly affecting users. We have implemented scalable architectures with different session state management solutions, deploying an online shopping cart application in a PaaS solution, and measuring the performance and cost for three server-side session state providers: Caching, SQL database and NoSQL database. A commercial solution with its supporting state management components has been used. Particularly when re-architecting software for the cloud, the trade-off between performance, scalability and cost implications needs to be discussed.

Keywords: Scalability, Platform-as-a-Service (PaaS), Session State Management, Windows Azure Platform.

1 Introduction

Cloud computing has emerged as a technology facilitating a movement to treat IT services as a commodity with the ability to dynamically increase or decrease capacity to match usage needs on a pay-as-you-go basis. Customers can benefit from moving their business to the cloud, in cost saving, improved scalability and performance and automatic updates and easy maintenance, etc.

In the cloud computing technology stack [1], infrastructure has matured faster than platform or software service technologies with respect to languages and techniques used for architecting and managing respective applications [2]. Platform-as-a-Service (PaaS) emerges as a focus for the near future with the increased complexity, compared to more structured data for Software-as-a-Service (SaaS) or more standardized structures of VMs and manipulation for Infrastructure-as-a-Service (IaaS).

PaaS is designed to support the entire application development lifecycle, allowing organizations to quickly develop, design and deploy live, scalable architectures. Thus, load-scalable architectures are largely handled by the PaaS providers, which increase

P. Avgeriou and U. Zdun (Eds.): ECSA 2014, LNCS 8627, pp. 226–233, 2014.

or decrease the capacities of allocated virtual resources on demand. However, PaaS users often consider re-architecting their software to make it cloud aware. Stateful architectures, however, often hinder scalability solutions as state is harder to transfer between virtual resources.

We present scalable architecture variants for PaaS that allow a service to allocate resources (e.g. virtual machines) dynamically and temporarily without directly affecting users. These architectures are based on different configurations of server-side session state management, providing a mechanism for multiple servers to process requests for the same session without losing the session state data, implementing loose coupling between state and application services.

We have implemented scalable solutions based on server-side session state management, deploying an online shopping application in Windows Azure, and measuring performance, scalability and cost under three server-side session state providers. We demonstrate that considering different architectural solutions while re-architecting for the PaaS cloud, we can have performance and scalability improvements as well as cost benefits, but often trade-offs between technical and cost factors are inevitable.

The remainder of this paper is organized as follows. Section 2 introduces scalability in cloud computing environments, including the scaling categories and metrics. Section 3 describes the stateful architecture and the proposed stateless architecture based on server-side session state management. Then, we set up an experiment and evaluate the performance and cost of three session state modes in a real cloud environment in Section 4, demonstrating and analysing the experimental results. Section 5 presents the related work to this project, and finally we give a conclusion in Section 6.

2   Scalability in Cloud Computing

Scalability is a significant feature in cloud computing [4], focussing on allocating and managing resources efficiently. There are two primary approaches to scaling [5]:

- Vertical scaling, or scaling up, means increasing the capacity of individual nodes through hardware improvements, e.g., change to other nodes with higher memory, or increase the number of CPU cores.
- Horizontal scaling, or scaling out, means increasing the overall application capacity by adding more nodes. Each additional node typically has the equivalent memory and CPU capacity.

Most cloud providers offer scaling up and scaling out solutions, such as Amazon EC2 and Windows Azure [8]. We focus on horizontal scaling, which takes full advantage of cloud technologies, i.e., we can use standard computers to implement high-performance computing, use capacity on demand and can upgrade without downtime.

Scalability is a measure of the number of users a system can effectively support at one time. Alternatively, if an application sustains consistent performance as the number of concurrent users grows, it is also scaling. Many scalability metrics have been proposed in distributed computing and parallel computing environments [9-13]. We propose three metrics to evaluate the scalability in our case: workload (concurrent users), resource utilization and response time. In addition, we add cost as a performance measure of a scalable cloud application.

3   Re-architecting Scalable Architectures for State Management

Internet applications often rely on HTTP - a stateless protocol that responds to each client request without relating it to other requests. Adding state is possible, with reduced scalability, but is necessary for applications in e-commerce or banking, for instance. In these applications, clients and servers need to exchange state information to place HTTP request and response into a larger context [14], called a session.

Many web applications use sticky sessions, which assign each user to a specific server node when they first visit. Once assigned, the load balancer directs all requests from one client within the same user session to the same sever instance. Sticky sessions are easy to code and fast to store session state, but reduce scalability.

Software [2] can be re-architected to benefit from stateless or properly managed stateful cloud architectures. We propose loosely coupled architectural options, out-of-process modes [15], for state management and services, allowing multiple server machines to share session state with each other, see Fig. 1.

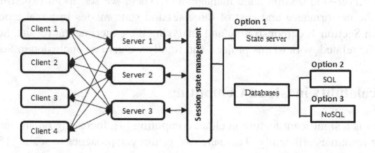

Fig. 1. The stateless architecture

Stateless architectures allow any server to receive a session request. This server fetches the session state from a state server or database before processing the request. Session state information can be stored and shared across all services with high scalability. There are 3 session state management modes: state server, SQL and NoSQL.

- State server: the principle is extracting the session ID from the request, performing a cache lookup for the state dictionary stored in a separate server, and marking the session as accessed to prevent its expiration.
- SQL database: the principle is extracting the session ID from the request and storing the state in an external SQL server database.
- NoSQL database: the principle is extracting the session ID from the request and storing the state in an external NoSQL database.

In the two database modes, clients can continually query the databases by using the unique session ID, and the application servers can save it in the databases for use across multiple requests or multiple clients. Additionally, in a cloud environment, we need scalability among session state providers as well as across multiple applications, using distributed cache, SQL state partitioning [16] or NoSQL database sharding. A single state server or database could be a bottleneck of a scalable architecture, but here, we focus on application scalability when deploying applications at PaaS level.

4 Experimental Evaluation

4.1 Experimental Platform

Windows Azure is Microsoft's cloud computing platform for IaaS (virtual machines), PaaS (cloud services) and applications. We deploy the testing environment and applications on Azure Virtual Machines, and scale out/down the instances on demand. At PaaS level, Azure offers different cloud services, such as Azure Cache, SQL Azure, Azure Storage (tables or blobs), which are the suitable solutions for the three session state modes. Then, we use CloudShop (online shopping cart software) as the testing application, implementing the re-architected stateful-session to stateless-session management solution. Furthermore, we utilize CSF telemetry [17] to monitor and collect the diagnostic information for the different state management providers. Thus, the experimental setting is described as follows:

- Cloud services (3 services): one for running the CloudShop App (2 small VMs scaled to 3VMs during scalability load test), one for running CSF telemetry (2 small VMs) and one for CSF scheduler (1 small VM).
- SQL Azure (3 instances): one for the CloudShop App product database, one for session states for SQL session management and one as a telemetry repository.
- Azure Storage (one storage account with 11 containers): five Table containers (four for telemetry data, one for session data for storage session management), six Blob containers (four for telemetry data, one for session data for storage session management and one for scheduling and sharding configuration data storage).

We ran 4100 tests; each test case started with 25 active clients sending requests, which gradually increased to 200 clients. All test cases had a duration of at least 10 min, simulating different loads varying the request per second (rps) from 80 to 90 rps.

4.2 Performance Analysis

Client-Side Performance. We measured the average page response time under the different session state providers with the following four operations: browsing products, adding items to cart, removing items from cart, and checking out, see Fig. 2. The horizontal axis represents the test time in *minutes:seconds* and the vertical axis represents the page response time in *seconds*. Fig. 2 shows that Caching and SQL Azure generally perform well, NoSQL database is almost the slowest solution. Caching is always fast, and the SQL database runs more smoothly, while NoSQL database takes approximate 2.5-3 times longer than caching.

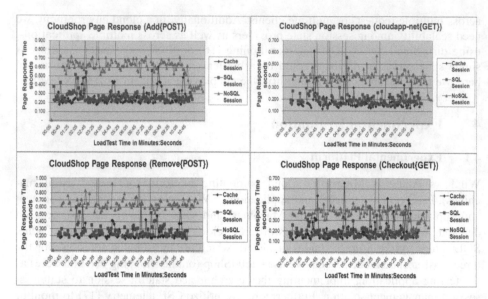

Fig. 2. The average page response time under three session state providers

Server-Side Performance. We measured CPU and memory usage under different session state providers, see Fig. 3. The horizontal axis represents the test time in *minutes:seconds*, and the vertical axis represents the % processor load time and committed memory in Mbytes separately. Fig. 3 shows that SQL Azure consumes the least CPU. Cache has the worst CPU performance. Memory in caches is similar to SQL Azure, while NoSQL has the worst memory performance.

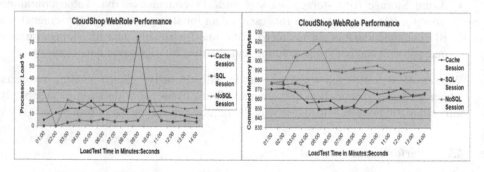

Fig. 3. The CPU and memory usage under three session state providers

4.3   Cost Analysis

Azure Pricing Model. Windows Azure (based on actual pricing for December 2013), serves as an example of a current Pay-as-you-go pricing model as follows:

- Computing: a virtual machine (small VM): 6.70 cent per hour or 49 euro per month
- Storage: 5 cent per GB per month, or 50 euro per TB per month

- Storage transactions: 7 cent every one million transactions
- SQL database: 7.40 euro per GB per month (no charge for SQL transactions)
- Data transfer out: 9 cent per GB (no charge for data transfer in)

Azure Consumption Results. We used 6 VMs running 92 hours in accumulative total. Three SQL database instances consumed 0.3 GB space, 11 storage containers utilized 0.06 GB storage space and consumed less than 2.5 million transactions, the data transfer out consumed 2.14 GB in total. Thus, the Cache is the most expensive solution; the NoSQL solution is the cheapest. One Worker Role means running a VM (we use a small size) as the worker role. Increased Web Role CPU means consuming part of the Web Role CPU originally used for running the application. Thus, the probability to scale out other homogeneous VM increases, as does acceleration of costs.

4.4   Discussion

The details of a comparison of the scalability, performance and cost for the three session state providers are shown in Table 1.

Table 1. Comparison of scalability, performance and cost for the three session state providers

	Azure Cache	Azure SQL	Azure NoSQL
Performance	Best performance in page response time in average	About 70ms slower than Azure Cache	About 400ms slower than Azure Cache
Cost	Highest (One Worker Role + 10% increased Web Role CPU)	About 1/3 cost comparing with Azure Cache	Negligible (storage cost +13% increased Web Role CPU)
Scalability	Scaling , consistent performance for end users as the number of concurrent users grows (according to Fig.2 and Fig.3, the page response time, CPU and memory usage is quite consistent by increasing the load amount)		

Caching is the most expensive with the best performance, while Azure NoSQL storage dose not perform well in state management probably due to the inefficient combination of Azure Blobs (for storage) and Azure Table (for index and query). As some of the results are unexpected, more investigations are required. However, Microsoft currently officially only supports caching as session state provider, which would explain the best performance as expected.

5   Related Work

So far the focus has been the migration process [2, 3], not re-architecting for performance and scalability. In the EU FP7 project REMICS [18], significant advances in languages and model-driven technologies for cloud migration have been explored, without specifically evaluating QoS and cost concerns. Agrawal et al. [4] investigate scalability, which relates to our work, but the problem is not approached from an architecture perspective. Tsai et al. [11] explore scalability for SaaS applications, which is less relevant to re-architecting. Ardagna et al. [6] propose scalability patterns. In this regard, our architecture configurations can be considered as patterns. Unlike these solutions, which link scalability to security concerns, ours takes costs into account and evaluates the trade-off. In a similar vein, [7] focusses on performance. These works consider earlier pre-cloud investigations as in [9] or [10].

The need for patterns, as in [6] or [19] emerges from the discussion here and elsewhere [20]. Our contribution would be three patterns specific to state management.

6   Conclusion

We looked at scalable architectures for PaaS-based server-side session state modes, including state sever, SQL databases and NoSQL databases. We implemented a loosely coupled architecture between state and services and enabled multiple server machines to share the session state with each other.

To evaluate scalability, performance and cost of the three session state modes in real cloud environments, we deployed an online shopping application in Windows Azure. The results have shown that 1) all three modes implement application scalability in session state management; 2) state service through caching has the best page response for end users, but does need a lot of computing resources, while NoSQL databases have the worst performance and SQL databases had the smoothest; and 3) caching was the most expensive solution, while NoSQL was the cheapest. This suggests that re-engineering software architectures for the cloud is beneficial.

The analysis presented in this paper leaves out some architectural configurations. We plan to focus on more cloud database solutions, comparing the performance and scalability between SQL partitioning technology and NoSQL databases. The indicated link between the trade-off results and their formal representation as rules in a dynamic configuration and load balancing solution shall be investigated.

Acknowledgments. The research work described in this paper was supported by the Irish Centre for Cloud Computing and Commerce, an Irish national Technology Centre funded by Enterprise Ireland and the Irish Industrial Development Authority.

References

1. Mell, P., Grance, T.: The NIST Definition of Cloud Computing. Communications of the ACM 53(6), 50–50 (2010)
2. Pahl, C., Xiong, H.: Migration to PaaS Clouds – Migration Process and Architectural Concerns. In: 7th IEEE International Symposium on the Maintenance and Evolution of Service-Oriented and Cloud-Based Systems (MESOCA 2013), pp. 86–91 (2013)
3. Pahl, C., Xiong, H., Walshe, R.: A Comparison of On-Premise to Cloud Migration Approaches. In: Lau, K.-K., Lamersdorf, W., Pimentel, E. (eds.) ESOCC 2013. LNCS, vol. 8135, pp. 212–226. Springer, Heidelberg (2013)
4. Agrawal, D., El Abbadi, A., Das, S., Elmore, A.J.: Database scalability, elasticity, and autonomy in the cloud. In: Yu, J.X., Kim, M.H., Unland, R. (eds.) DASFAA 2011, Part I. LNCS, vol. 6587, pp. 2–15. Springer, Heidelberg (2011)

5. Michael, M., Moreira, J.E., Shiloach, D., Wisniewski, R.W.: Scale-up x Scale-out: A Case Study using Nutch/Lucene. In: 2007 IEEE International Parallel and Distributed Processing Symposium, pp. 1–8. IEEE (2007)
6. Ardagna, C.A., Damiani, E., Frati, F., Rebeccani, D., Ughetti, M.: Scalability Patterns for Platform-as-a-Service. In: IEEE 5th International Conference on Cloud Computing, pp. 718–725. IEEE (2012)
7. Iosup, A., Yigitbasi, N., Epema, D.: On the performance variability of production cloud services. In: Proc. of IEEE/ACM CCGrid 2011, pp. 104–113. IEEE (2011)
8. Auto-scaling and Windows Azure, Microsoft pattern and practices, http://msdn.microsoft.com/ en-us/library/hh680945v=pandp.50.aspx
9. Jogalekar, P., Woodside, M.: Evaluating the scalability of distributed systems. IEEE Transactions on Parallel and Distributed Systems 11(6), 589–603 (2000)
10. Sun, X.: Scalability versus Execution Time in Scalable Systems. Journal of Parallel and Distributed Computing 62(2), 173–192 (2002)
11. Tsai, W., Huang, Y., Shao, Q.: Testing the Scalability of SaaS Applications. In: IEEE International Conference on Service-Oriented Computing and Applications (SOCA 2011), pp. 1–4. IEEE (2011)
12. Intel White Paper, Two Tools Measure the Performance Scalability of Your Application, http://software.intel.com/sites/products/Whitepaper/ MeasureApplicationPerformanceScalability_013012.pdf
13. Caceres, J., Vaquero, L., Rodero-Merino, A.P.L., Hierro, J.: Service scalability over the cloud. In: Furht, B., Escalante, A. (eds.) Handbook of Cloud Computing (2010)
14. Kristol, D., Montulli, L.: HTTP State Management Mechanism, Network Working Group, RFC 2965 (2000), http://www.ietf.org/rfc/rfc2965.txt
15. Patelis, A.: ASP.Net State Management Techniques, CODE Project (2007), http://www.codeproject.com/Articles/17191/ ASP-Net-State-Management-Techniques
16. Volodarsky, M.: Fast, Scalable, and Secure Session State Management for Your Web Applications. MSDN Magazine (2005), http://msdn.microsoft.com/en-us/magazine/cc163730.aspx#S7
17. Fairweather, E.: Telemetry-Application Instrumentation, Azure CAT, Microsoft Wiki Article (2013), http://social.technet.microsoft.com/wiki/contents/articles/ 18468.telemetry-application-instrumentation.aspx
18. Mohagheghi, P., Sæther, T.: Software engineering challenges for migration to the service cloud paradigm: Ongoing work in the REMICS project. In: IEEE World Congress on Services (SERVICES 2011), pp. 507–514 (2011)
19. Wilder, B.: Cloud Architecture Patterns. O'Reilly, Sebastopol (2012)
20. Jamshidi, P., Ahmad, A., Pahl, C.: Cloud Migration Research: A Systematic Review. IEEE Transactions on Cloud Computing (2013)

Enactment of Components Extracted from an Object-Oriented Application

Abderrahmane Seriai[1], Salah Sadou[1], and Houari A. Sahraoui[2]

[1] Université de Bretagne Sud, IRISA, Vannes, France
{abderrahmane.seriai,Salah.Sadou}@irisa.fr
[2] Université de Montréal, DIRO, Montréal, Canada
sahraouh@iro.umontreal.ca

Software architecture plays an important role for the application understanding before its maintenance. Unfortunately, for legacy systems code often there is no corresponding (or up to date) architecture. So, several work tackle this problem by extracting components from the legacy system and define their links. Although these components allow to get an architectural view of the legacy system, they still can't be easily implemented in a concrete framework. In fact, restructuring completely the legacy system facilitates the mapping between the architectural elements and their corresponding ones in the code. This paves the way to the future maintenance of the system.

Our approach aims to reach this complete restructuring. Thus it goes beyond what exists in the state of the art by proposing a technique that makes components extracted from object-oriented applications implementable within a concrete component model. This is done by using class instances that compose the extracted components to infer possible instances the components. Thus, we propose for each extracted component its provided and required interfaces, and a way to construct its instances. We validated the feasibility of the proposed approach through the Spring framework and we illustrated it through a legacy Java application.

1 Introduction

Most existing works on extraction of components from a legacy system have as a main aim the construction of an understandable architecture [10,17,2]. When the legacy system is implemented in the object-oriented paradigm, a component is represented by a cluster of classes with a set of provided methods and a set of required methods. Thus, the identification of the components consists in finding the groups of classes that are the most cohesive and loosely coupled. So, the obtained results have the advantage to offer a more abstract representation via a component-oriented architecture view of the object-oriented application.

The extracted software architecture facilitates the understanding of the legacy system. However it needs to be complemented by a mapping between architectural elements and their corresponding ones in the code in order to facilitate the achievement of maintenance. In fact, sets of classes, representing components, can not be easily projected onto a specific component model [2]. This problem is due to the shift from the concept of object instances to the concept of component instances. Indeed, it is not easy to infer a component instances from a set of class instances. Hence, the executable

P. Avgeriou and U. Zdun (Eds.): ECSA 2014, LNCS 8627, pp. 234–249, 2014.

version of the application remains in its old form and therefore has no direct corre-spondence with the architecture. Consequently, there is no direct mapping between the architecture and the running application.

To solve this problem, we need to be able to project the extracted components on a concrete component model. This will give the advantage of creating a direct mapping between architectural elements and their equivalents in the code of the application. To achieve this purpose, we need to (i) identify the interfaces of the extracted components to make them consistent with the component paradigm concepts, and (ii) determine how the concerned classes will be instantiated with respect to component instances. This second concern, which is neglected in literature on component extraction, is im-portant as it allows to formalize the notion of component instance, which is necessary to make the application executable and at the same time its components reusable by others applications.

In a recent work [16], we proposed a solution for the point (i) based on a static anal-ysis of the extracted components. In this paper, we propose a solution for the point (ii). Our approach considers that the extraction of components (cohesive groups of classes) is already performed. It is based on the hypothesis that an instance of a component consists of a connected set of instances of its classes. Thus, the objective is to iden-tify all instances of classes representing an instance of a component in order to build the component's factory. This will provide the necessary means for the framework to run the restructured application. Furthermore, the identification of the component in-stances allows us to propose a dynamic approach to the identification of the component interfaces.

To demonstrate the feasibility of our approach, we present its implementation within the Spring component framework. After that, we apply it on a Java application that we restructured into a component-based application with the approach presented in [2]. To validate the correction of the restructuring, we have replayed the application's case studies on its component-based version and the results were identical to those of its object-oriented version.

The rest of the paper is organized as follows: in the next section we describe the process of our approach. Sections 3 shows how to define instances of a component starting from the objects of its classes. Then, the definition of the component's inter-faces and the creation of its instances is described in Section 4. In Scetion 5 we show how our approach can be implemented using the Spring component framework. Before concluding, we present the related work in Section 6.

2 Approach

The group of classes, which represents a component, are part of the definition of the component descriptor. The descriptor of a component is equivalent to the class in the object-oriented paradigm. Thus, what is lacking with the group of classes is the way to build instances of the component. Indeed, to create a component-based application, as in the case of an object-oriented application, it requires creating component instances and binding them.

For this work, we propose the following definition for a component instance:

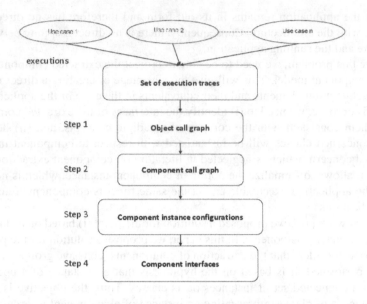

Fig. 1. Process of the proposed approach

Definition 1 : An instance of a component consists of all instances of its classes, which have had connections during the execution of the application and thereby forming a connected group.

Objects surrounded by a dashed line in figure 3 is an example of component instance. To build component instances, we must first identify the instances of classes that compose them and their links. This is why our approach, as shown in Figure 1, begins with the execution of the application's use cases in order to extract traces of method calls between objects. This information will be summarized in an object call graph (step 1 of the process).

The use of the application's use cases is a way to get only objects that actually play a role in the functionalities provided by the system. Thus, all the other objects from classes held by the application are naturally avoided and have no chance to infer in the proposed process.

By analysing all objects, instances of classes belonging to the same component, we can find several connected groups. It is these groups of objects that represent instances of the component. Thus, we can reduce the obtained object call graph to a component call graph in order to focus on the relationships between component instances (step 2 of the process).

The identification of component instances is interesting only to deduce a way to build them. For a given component, some of its instances may have similarities when considering the type of their involved objects. Thus, these component instances suggest a common constructor. Indeed, these component instances have a similar configuration of their constituent objects that we define as follows:

Definition 2 : Two instances of the same component belong to the same configuration if and only if their subsets of objects, which are directly concerned by the component's incoming calls, are similar.

Definition 3 : Two sets of objects are similar if and only if they contain the same number of class instances for **each involved class**.

Finding all possible instance configurations for each component is the goal of the step 3 of our process. Once the possible instance configurations of a component are identified, we need to define a constructor for each of them. Subsequently, to each configuration of instances, we associate a component provided interface (goal of the step 4). Thus, with our approach, each component interface highlights one of its aspect, which is emerged by the configuration. For a component, its required interfaces will be defined according to the identified provided interfaces of all components on which it depends.

In the following sections, we describe each step of our approach.

3   From Object to Component Call Graph

An important step in our approach is to identify component instances, and their bindings, by considering the classes they hold. The component instances will consist of objects from its classes. For this aim, we first construct an object call graph in order to transform it into a component instance call graph.

3.1   Object Call Graph

The first step of our approach consists of identifying all possible class instances for the entire application and build their links. This leads to the construction of a call graph specific to class instances (objects).

To get this call graph, we run the application with all its use cases to capture the execution traces. An execution trace corresponds to a directed tree $T(V, E)$ where V is a set of nodes and E a set of edges between nodes. Each node V_i represents an instance of the class (Cl_i). An edge $\langle V_i, V_j \rangle$ indicates that an instance i calls a method of an instance j. The root of $T(V, E)$ corresponds to the entry point of the system.

As shown in Figure 2(left), the nodes of the tree are labeled by the identifier, the actual types of the objects that are called and the concerned methods. As the execution traces are based on method calls, it is possible to have nodes containing the same object (same identifier) with calls on different methods. This is the case for object d0 which appears twice for two different methods (see left part of Figure 2). So, these nodes are grouped in the same one in order to get a graph where each object is represented by exactly one node. Thus, the resulting node contains all called methods. An example of such a transformation is given in the right part of Figure 2. The resulting graph corresponds to what we call Object Call Graph (OCG).

3.2   Component Call Graph

The identification of component instances is based on our definition of component instance (see Section 2). Thus, starting from the OCG of an application, we need to

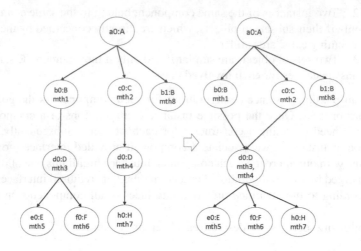

Fig. 2. Example of execution trace tree (left) and its corresponding object call graph (right)

identify the sub-OCG that may be associated with each component. Recall that our working hypothesis is that for each component, we know the classes composing it. Thus, finding the sub-OCG associated with a component leads to find the sub-OCG composed of all objects that are associated with the component.

Figure 3 (left side) shows examples of such a sub-OCG. Objects associated with the same component are marked with the same symbol (circle, triangle or square). For instance, the dimmed objects are associated with the same extracted component (triangle symbol), which holds the classes A, B, C, D, E and J. When an object is marked with several symbols, it means that it is used inside several components and thus, its class is used to define these components. This situation arises when components exchange object references through service calls. We will discuss the responsibility of creating this kind of objects in the next section.

By analyzing the sub-OCG of a component, we can identify sub-graphs. These sub-graphs correspond to possible instances of the component. Figure 3 (right side) provides a representation of the OCG that is reduced to component instances. That is what we call Component Call Graph (CCG). Thus, in a CCG, nodes are instances of components, and edges correspond to calls between components. In other words, edges correspond to calls between objects belonging to different components. For example, instances of the component represented by the dimmed sub-OCG in the right part of Figure 3 are shown as dimmed nodes in the right part of the same figure. One of these instances is Comp1.1, which contains objects a1, b1, d0 and e0. The listed methods (mth14, mth15) are those called on these objects by instances of other components. To each method name mthi, are associated the full method signature and the class to which it belongs.

In the case of an object that is shared by several component instances, all calls to (or from) this object, and coming from (or to) other objects held by these components,

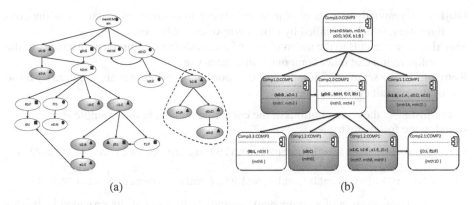

(a)   (b)

Fig. 3. (a) Example of sub-OCG, (b) Example of component call graph

are considered internal and therefore, not visible at the CCG level. For example, in the OCG of Figure 3, the object j0 belongs to two component instances of different types (square and triangle). Thus, the call from c1 to j0 is considered internal to the component instance of triangle type and the call from f1 to j0 is considered internal to the component instance of square type. This is why in the corresponding CCG (right part of the figure) there is no edge between the component instances Comp2.1 and Comp1.1.

4   Interface Identification

By analyzing the instances of a component, we can identify similar configurations of objects they contain. According to the definition given in Section 2, component's configurations help in defining its provided interfaces. At the same time, a configuration of a component reflects one of its aspects. Thus, we can also use the configuration to define a constructor for the component.

In the following, we describe our approach to identify configurations of a component as well as the constructors associated with them.

4.1   Configuration Identification

In Figure 3, the two instances Comp1.0 and Comp1.1 of component COMP1 have in common the fact that their accessible objects from outside (other components) are of the same type (b0 and b1 of type B and shown in bold). Thus, these component instances are associated with the same configuration. This configuration is characterized by the fact of exposing an object of type B as an interface to other components.

The two component instances, which have given rise to this configuration, show that only the methods mth1, mth2, mth14, and mth15 of the class B are used by the other components. Moreover, one of the two instances of the component (Comp1.0) requires an instance of another component (Comp2.0). As the latter belongs to a given configuration, so we can link the dependency to this configuration.

Thus, we define a configuration as a triple (ObjInt, MethInt, ReqConf) where:

ObjInt corresponds to a set of objects belonging to component instances of the configuration, which are called by other component instances.

MethInt corresponds to the union of sets of methods from component instances of the configuration that other component instances use.

ReqConf is the set of configurations of component instances that are required by those of the current configuration.

For instance, the configurations of the component given in the example above correspond to the following triplets:

```
({b0:B,b1:B},{mth1,mth2,mth14,mth15},{configuration1 of COMP2})
and
({c0:C,c1:C},{mth6,mth7,mth8,mth9},{configuration1 of COMP2})
```

From a configuration of a component, we can deduce one of its provided interfaces and some of its required interfaces. Indeed, the list of methods associated with the configuration correspond to a provided interface of the component. Thus, each provided interface is associated with one and only one configuration of the component. Furthermore, as the configuration requires configurations from other components, the provided interfaces associated with those configurations define the required interfaces of the targeted component.

Thus, the provided interfaces of a component correspond to the set of provided interfaces suggested by its configurations. And its required interfaces correspond to the union of the provided interfaces associated with the configurations required by its configurations. From the example given above, we deduce the following required and provided interfaces:

```
Provided interfaces = {{mth1,mth2,mth14,mth15},
                       {mth6,mth7,mth8,mth9}}
Required interfaces = {{mth3,mth4}}.
```

From the list of objects held by a configuration, we can also define the necessary constructors for the component instances associated with this configuration. We will show that in the next sub-section.

4.2   Component Constructors

With the notion of configuration, we have grouped a set of component instances around the same provided interface. Although these instances are used through the same types of objects, the way to create them is not necessarily the same.

Indeed, each object can have different constructors that can be used independently to create component instances associated with the same configuration. Thus, we must consider each component instance to analyse calls to constructors of its objects that are directly concerned with the provided interface. The objectives of this analysis are: (i) Identify objects whose construction is made by other components. (ii) Determine the precedence of creating these objects. iii) Determine the different combinations of constructors that are used to construct these objects.

Indeed, we are only interested in objects that are created outside of the component as the other objects are necessarily created by objects from the same instance component (connected graph).

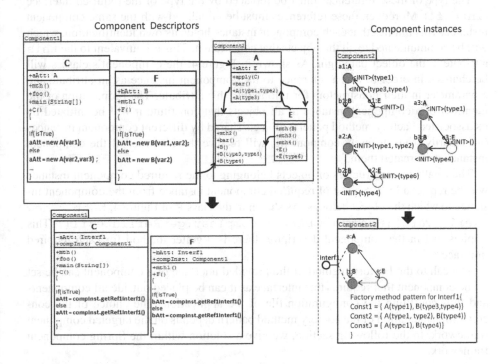

Fig. 4. Example of transformation of object constructors into a Factory method pattern

Figure 4 shows a component (Component1) that requires an interface of another component (Component2). This interface concerns only objects of types A and B. When tracing the different use cases, we distinguish three instances of component Component2 that are associated with this interface (see the right part of the figure). We note that the objects concerned by the interface were created by using different combinations of their constructors.

The different combinations of object constructors are grouped as a Factory method pattern. This pattern allows the construction of the various component instances that are associated with the same configuration (required interface). Thus, each provided interface of a component is associated with a Factory method pattern for the construction of component instances to be used through this interface.

Calls to object constructors of a component instance are actually dispersed in the component that uses this instance. Recall that each component instance is associated with a given provided interface. Thus, a component that uses a component instance will require an interface of the same type to which the component instance is associated with. Therefore, any references to objects of the component instance that is in the user component, must be transformed into a single reference to the component instance.

In the left part of Figure 4, component instances of Component1 use component instances of Component2 through object references (aAtt and bAtt) of type A and

B. The type of these references must be replaced by the type of the required interface (`Interf1`). Moreover, these references must be initialized with the same component instance. This implies that each component instance holds its own identification, which will be communicated to all the objects that constitute it. This is equivalent to the `this` attribute in the object paradigm. As shown in Figure 4, the component's classes will be changed in order to add a reference to the component instance as an attribute and a parameter in their constructors for initializing this attribute. The propagation of the identifier of a component instance to all objects that constitute it will be initiated by its associated Factory method pattern. Objects shared by different component instances (necessarily from different components) will receive the identifier of the component instance that created them.

Thus, calls to constructors of objects belonging to the required component instance will be replaced by a request of required component instance from the component instance to which the object belongs. As shown in the class F of Figure 4, `bAtt = new (var1, var2)` is replaced by `bAtt = compInst.getRef1Interf1()`. This implies that in the component descriptor, there is a getter method for each required interface.

The call to the Factory method of the provided interface of a component can be set in the component that requires this interface as it can be placed outside all components and thus constitute the configuration file of the application. The choice of the concrete implementation of the Factory method pattern depends on the targeted component framework. In the following section, we give a solution within the Spring component framework.

5   Case Study

The objective of our approach is to make components extracted from an object-oriented application projectable on a concrete component model. Thus, we chose the case of Spring as a concrete model and framework. Our approach relies on the existence of extracted components represented by sets of classes. In the past we had done this work on a concrete application called Logo.

Below we give a brief description of the Logo application, followed by the tools developed for the implementation of our approach and we conclude by showing how the components are projected onto Spring by using the Logo application as example.

5.1   Logo Application

The Logo application consists in a language for learning programming and its interpreter. The latter has a graphical interface which allows writing the code and a window, which shows the result of this code graphically. This system was selected for two reasons: (i) its reasonable size allows us to perform a deep analysis of the results. (ii) we already extracted its components. (iii) one of its developers was available to comment the results.

The component-based architecture of the Logo interpreter, which was extracted thanks to the approach proposed in [2], contains four components:

- The Language Parser component is used to read the logo code, to interpret it according to the Logo grammar, and to launch appropriate java treatments.
- The Evaluator that receives a list of instructions and evaluates them one after another in the current lexical environment.
- The Graphical Display component displays the results of a Logo program that makes the connection between the Logo code, its evaluation, and its visual results.
- The Graphical User Interface (GUI) component represents the graphical interface through which beginner programmers interact with the application.

The components above consist of sets of classes.

5.2   Process and Tools

We defined a tool for each step of our process (see Figure 1). All the tools were implemented in Java using JVMTI[1]. These tools are as follow:

Tracer: This tool allows the generation of execution traces (instances creation, method calls, attribute access, etc). This was made using a custom extraction agent written in C that utilizes the JVMTI API. This agent crops at each entrance or exit into/from a method, the relevant information, such as the class and the instance where the method is executed, the current thread, etc.

ObjectCallGraphBuilder: Using the traces provided by the Tracer, this tool constructs an object call graph.

ComponentConfigurationBuilder: Using information about contained classes for each component and the object, this tool uses algorithms from graph theory to generate connected sub-graph for each component (its different instances). It also provides the component's configurations.

ComponentInterfacesExtractor: This tool analyses dependencies between the objects involved in a configuration and those from the other components in order to define: (i) the provided interface associated with the configuration. (ii) the components that require this interface. (iii) the constructors for the component instances associated with the interface.

ComponentToSpring: This tool generates the classes representing component instances according to the Spring framework. It also modify classes of a component in order to make their objects aware about the component instance they constitute. Finally, it produces the configuration file for the application.

The first step of our experiment consists in executing scenarios corresponding to the 15 identified Logo use cases. Examples of such use cases are "file creation/saving", "code writing in the editor", "code interpretation", etc. Thanks to the Tracer, events that occur in the Logo application during the execution of these use cases are collected. Each event indicates which object calls which other object and on which method. Since we are interested only in events involving classes of the Logo application, we filtered

---

[1] Java Virtual Machine Tool Interface (JVMTI) API is a tool that provides both a way to inspect the state and to control the execution of applications running in the Java virtual machine (VM) (http://docs.oracle.com/javase/6/docs/technotes/guides/jvmti)

all the noises produced by the agent tracer. Indeed, the used extraction agent is listening to all events at each entrance or exit of methods, even those that come from libraries and mouse/ keyboard events, etc.

After that, the ObjectCallGraphBuilder, and the ComponentConfigurationBuilder are executed to build the component instance configurations for each component. After the identifying component interfaces thanks to the ComponentInterfaceExtracor, the ComponentToSpring tool produces the necessary classes to make the component-based version of the application according to the Spring framework.

Bellow, we detail how these classes are generated.

5.3   Generated Code for Spring

As shown in Figure 5, each component is represented by an abstract class. All its configurations correspond to concrete classes of the abstract class that represents it.

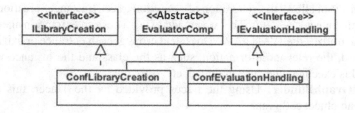

Fig. 5. Class diagram representing a component within the Spring framework

The interface associated with a configuration of a component is represented by a Java interface as shown in the example below. Thus, each configuration implements its corresponding interface.

```
public interface IEvaluationHandling {
  public void initEnv(HashMap<String, Object> penv);
  public Object evalList(ArrayList<Object> listInstruction);
}
```

Both interface method above come from two different classes. These are the classes of the objects involved in the configuration associated with the interface. This interface is implemented by the class that represents its configuration. The code below gives a brief description of such a class.

```
public class ConfEvaluationHandling extends EvaluatorComp
                      implements IEvaluationHandling {
  //required interface
  IErrorHandling  required1;

  //Objects of the configuration
  Library lib;
  InputOutout inOut;
```

```
// Constructor of component instances
public ConfEvaluationHandling(IErrorHandling  req1){
  //injection
  required1=req1;
  //creation of objects of component instances
  ObjectFactory();
  }

  //customized Factory for this configuration
  private void ObjectFactory(){
  lib = new Library (this);
  inOut = new InputOutout (this);
  }

  @Override
  public void initEnv(HashMap<String, Object> penv) {
    lib.initEnv(penv);
  }

@Override
public Object evalList(ArrayList<Object> listeInstruction){
  return lib.evalList(listInstruction);
  }
  ...
}
```

This class inherits from the abstract class representing the component. This is the way to associate a configuration to a component. The first attribute corresponds to the required interface. It will be injected via the constructor of the class using the configuration file (see below for an example). The two other attributes correspond to the objects that are directly involved in the configuration. The Factory method ObjectFactory creates the objects associated with the component instances. Note the "this" given to constructors of the objects that allows them to know the component instance to which they are associated. Methods of the interface are implemented as redirections to the corresponding objects.

Below you have an excerpt of the configuration file for the Logo application in its component-based version.

```
<!-- Definition for EvaluatorComp-instance2 bean -->
  <bean id="EvaluatorConf2"
      class= "com.irisa.evaluatorcomp.ConfEvaluationHandling">
      <constructor-arg ref="ParserConf1"/> </bean>
<!-- Definition for ParserComp-instance1 bean -->
  <bean id="ParserConf1"
      class="com.irisa.parsercomp.ConfErrorHandling">
      <constructor-arg ref="GuiConf2"/> </bean>
<!-- Definition for GuiComp-instance2 bean -->
  <bean id="GuiConf2"
      class="com.irisa.guicomp.ConfEventsHandling">
```

```
    . . .
</bean>
```

For the first created component instance (EvaluatorConf2) we can notice that the reference on the component instance (ParserConf1) is injected via the constructor of the component. This will be used for the required interface of the component instance (EvaluatorConf2).

The main statements in the launcher of the Logo application in its Sprint version are the follow:

```
IEventsHandling mainApp = (ConfEventHandling)
                         context.getBean("GuiConf2");
mainApp.main(args);
```

The first statement allows to retrieve an instance of the EventHandling component and to use it through its IEventsHandling interface. This component contains the class that holds the launcher (main method) of the Logo application, which is provided through the IEventsHandling interface. Thus, the second instruction starts the application.

To validate the component-based version of the Logo application, we replayed the 15 use cases, which were used to extract execution traces, and we got the same results. After that, we checked that the generated components can be used independently from each other. We reused the EvaluatorComp component in an application that allows to test the validity of Logo expressions through a command line. So we built a fairly simple component that allows to enter a Logo expression through the standard input. It requires the IEvaluationHandling interface of the EvaluatorComp component. It uses mainly the evalList method to submit the proposed expression. The returned result is translated into an understandable message and then printed on the standard output.

Obviously, we used an instance of ParserComp component that is required by the EvaluatorComp component. Apart from this component instance, which is perfectly appropriate, the reuse of the component do not generate any problem.

6 Related Work

The reverse engineering research community has been actively investigating techniques to decompose (partition) the structure of software systems into subsystems (clusters or component). In this section we target only work concerning the recovery of components in a legacy system.

6.1 Architecture Extraction

Software architecture plays an important role in at least six aspects of software development: understanding, reuse, construction, evolution, analysis and management [6]. Many approaches and techniques were proposed in the literature to support software architecture recovery [9,11,14,8,18,12,13], and often the problem is seen as a software clustering problem. The software clustering problem consists of finding a good partition of software modules based on various criteria, in particular, the dependencies among these modules [9]. Dependencies are extracted by static analysis, dynamic analysis, or using a combination of both (so-called hybrid approaches).

Among the approaches that use static analysis, Pourhaji Kazem et al. [11] proposed a genetic algorithm for clustering based on the weighted module dependency graph. Saeed et al. [14] used the Rigi tool to extract the function dependency graph and presented a new clustering algorithm called the "combined" algorithm to implement software architecture recovery. Mancoridis et al. [8] extracted the file dependency graph from the source code and used a clustering algorithm based on a genetic algorithm.

With regard to approaches that use dynamic analysis, Yan et al. [18] described a technique that uses run time observations about an executing system to construct an architectural view of the system. In a previous work, we proposed an approach to restructure an object-oriented application into a component-oriented one [2]. This approach is based on dynamic calls, *i.e.* actual calls at runtime with use cases, to determine the dependencies between classes. These dependencies are then used by a genetic algorithm to derive groups of classes representing components.

For hybrid approaches, Richner et al. [12] presented an environment supporting the generation of tailorable views of object-oriented systems from both static and dynamic information. Claudio Riva et al. [13] proposed a technique for combining the analysis of static and dynamic architectural information to support the task of architecture reconstruction.

All these work achieve the starting point of the approach proposed in this paper (ie, sets of classes representing components). Thus, these work are complementary to our approach.

6.2   Component Instance Identification

In the field of Component-oriented programming (COP) , where the components are created from scratch (bottom-up approach) [4], a component instance is uniquely identified with regard to the other instances, and is obtained from a component class (component descriptor), to enable use of the features associated with the component during the execution time. A variety of component-oriented languages have been proposed in the literature [4,3,5,19] to define components (component classes andor component instances). These component languages are either dedicated to only software specification and are not executable (eg. UML 2.0 [7]) or dedicated as well as to transform models [4,15] into executable codes or to write programs by hand. SCL [4] is an example of the latter case, which defines the component by a descriptor that can be instantiated.

Regarding the field of restructuring object-oriented systems into component-based systems, to the best of our knowledge, there is no work that identifies instances of extracted components.

7   Conclusion

The work presented in this paper aims to complete work on the extraction of components from legacy systems. Indeed, our approach allows to completely restructure an object-oriented application into a component-based application. Thus, it makes permanent mappings between elements from the extracted architecture and their corresponding ones in the code of the application. Identifying the different instances of a component highlights its various aspects. Defining the interfaces of a component based on the various configurations of its instances is a way to make it reusable according to its different aspects.

Thus, we performed this work as a continuation of the work we have already done on the extraction of components from an object-oriented application [2]. Given the assumption we made (ie, the components are represented as a set of classes), the proposed approach also applies to all work on the extraction of components from object-oriented applications. However, our approach requires the existence of use cases in order to identify instances of components.

We have shown that instances of a component can be used to define its interfaces. We have already proposed an approach for the identification of interfaces of a component through a static analysis (on source code) of its dependencies on other components [16]. We used the same application as a case study (Logo) and we found some differences in the identified interfaces. In fact, static analysis takes into account objects that may be created but do not really exist in the context of the application (polymorphism). On the other side, dynamic analysis allows to get objects related to classes dynamically loaded. But the obtained interfaces are related to the context of the concerned application.

In one of our old work we presented an approach for component extraction that relies on a combination of static analysis (on source code) and dynamic analysis (calls between objects) [1]. This combination of the two approaches of analysis allowed to better cover aspects of extracted components. We think this may be the case with the definition of component interfaces. Thus, we expect in a future work the definition of component interfaces based on a combination of the two types of analysis in order to deduce dependencies between instances of components and getting more reusable components.

References

1. Allier, S., Sadou, S., Sahraoui, H., Fleurquin, R.: From object-oriented applications to component-oriented applications via component-oriented architecture. In: 9th IEEE/IFIP Working International Conference on Software Architecture (WICSA), Boulder, Colorado, USA, pp. 214–223. IEEE Computer Society (June 2011)
2. Allier, S., Sahraoui, H.A., Sadou, S., Vaucher, S.: Restructuring object-oriented applications into component-oriented applications by using consistency with execution traces. In: Grunske, L., Reussner, R., Plasil, F. (eds.) CBSE 2010. LNCS, vol. 6092, pp. 216–231. Springer, Heidelberg (2010)
3. Bruneton, E., Coupaye, T., Leclercq, M., Quema, V., Stefani, J.-B.: An open component model and its support in java. In: Crnković, I., Stafford, J.A., Schmidt, H.W., Wallnau, K. (eds.) CBSE 2004. LNCS, vol. 3054, pp. 7–22. Springer, Heidelberg (2004)
4. Fabresse, L., Dony, C., Huchard, M.: Foundations of a simple and unified component-oriented language. Computer Languages, Systems & Structures 34(2-3), 130–149 (2008)
5. Fröhlich, P.H., Gal, A., Franz, M.: Supporting software composition at the programming language level. Sci. Comput. Program. 56, 41–57 (2005)

6. Garlan, D.: Software architecture: a roadmap. In: Proceedings of the Conference on the Future of Software Engineering, ICSE 2000, pp. 91–101. ACM, New York (2000)
7. Object Management Group. Unified modeling language 2.1.2 super-structure specification. Specification Version 2.1.2, Object Management Group (November 2007)
8. Mancoridis, S., Mitchell, B.S., Rorres, C.: Using automatic clustering to produce high-level system organizations of source code. In: Proc. 6th Intl. Workshop on Program Comprehension, pp. 45–53 (1998)
9. Martin, F., Kessentini, M., Sahraoui, H.: Deriving high-level abstractions from legacy software using example-driven clustering. In: International Conference on Computer Science and Software Engineering, CASCON 2011, pp. 188–199 (2011)
10. Medvidovic, N., Jakobac, V.: Using software evolution to focus architectural recovery. Automated Software Eng. 13(2), 225–256 (2006)
11. Pourhaji Kazem, A.A., Lotfi, S.: An evolutionary approach for partitioning weighted module dependency graphs. In: 4th International Conference on Innovations in Information Technology, IIT 2007, pp. 252–256 (November 2007)
12. Richner, T., Ducasse, S.: Recovering high-level views of object-oriented applications from static and dynamic information. In: Proceedings of the International Conference on Software Maintenance, ICSM 1999, pp. 13–22. IEEE (1999)
13. Riva, C., Rodriguez, J.V.: Combining static and dynamic views for architecture reconstruction. In: Sixth European Conference onSoftware Maintenance and Reengineering (CSMR), pp. 47–55. Nokia Research Center (2002)
14. Saeed, M., Maqbool, O., Babri, H.A., Hassan, S.Z., Sarwar, S.M.: Software clustering techniques and the use of combined algorithm. In: Proceedings of the Seventh European Conference on Software Maintenance and Reengineering, CSMR 2003, p. 301. IEEE Computer Society, Washington, DC (2003)
15. Costa Seco, J., Caires, L.: A basic model of typed components. In: Bertino, E. (ed.) ECOOP 2000. LNCS, vol. 1850, p. 108. Springer, Heidelberg (2000)
16. Seriai, A., Sadou, S., Sahraoui, H., Hamza, S.: Deriving component interfaces after a restructuring of a legacy system. In: 11th IEEE/IFIP Working International Conference on Software Architecture (WICSA), Sydney, Australia. IEEE Computer Society (April 2014)
17. Washizaki, H., Fukazawa, Y.: A technique for automatic component extraction from object-oriented programs by refactoring. Sci. Comput. Program. 56(1-2), 99–116 (2005)
18. Yan, H., Garlan, D., Schmerl, B., Aldrich, J., Kazman, R.: Discotect: A system for discovering architectures from running systems. In: International Conference on Software Engineering, pp. 470–479 (2004)
19. Zenger, M.: Keris: evolving software with extensible modules. Journal of Software Maintenance 17(5), 333–362 (2005)

Gossiping Components for Cyber-Physical Systems

Tomas Bures[1,2], Ilias Gerostathopoulos[1], Petr Hnetynka[1], Jaroslav Keznikl[1,2],
Michal Kit[1], and Frantisek Plasil[1]

[1] Faculty of Mathematics and Physics, Charles University in Prague,
Prague, Czech Republic
[2] Institute of Computer Science, Academy of Sciences of the Czech Republic,
Prague, Czech Republic
{bures,iliasg,hnetynka,keznikl,kit,plasil}@d3s.mff.cuni.cz

Abstract. Developing software for dynamic cyber-physical systems (CPS) is a complex task. One has to deal with the dynamicity and unreliability of the physical environment where the software resides in, while, at the same time, provide sufficient levels of dependability and scalability. Although emerging software engineering abstractions, such as dynamic ad-hoc component ensembles, provide a convenient way to structure software for dynamic CPS, they need to be mapped to robust decentralized execution schemes in real-life settings. A particular challenge in this context is the robust distributed data dissemination in dynamic networks. Gossip-based communication stands as a promising solution to this challenge. We argue, that exploitation of application-specific information, software architecture in particular, has a large potential for improving the robustness and performance of gossip-based communication. This paper proposes a synergy between high-level architectural models and low-level communication models to effectively enable application-specific gossiping in component-based systems. The synergy is exemplified on the DEECo component model which is tailored to the needs and specifics of CPS, and evaluated on an emergency coordination case study with realistic network configurations.

Keywords: Component, Ensemble, Gossip, Cyber-Physical Systems, MANET.

1 Introduction

Cyber-physical systems (CPS) are complex networked systems where the interplay of software control with the physical environment has a prominent role. Examples range from intelligent navigation systems (cars that communicate with each other and with street infrastructure to minimize traffic congestion, fuel consumption, etc.) to emergency coordination systems. Modern CPS are inherently distributed on a large scale and consist largely of mobile devices. They are also increasingly depending on software which has actually become their most intricate and extensive constituent [1].

Building software for large-scale software-intensive CPS via systematic software engineering approaches is a notoriously difficult task. This stems from the fact that CPS invalidate most of the assumptions that typically hold in software engineering of general-purpose systems [2]. Whereas the challenges and opportunities of CPS cover

P. Avgeriou and U. Zdun (Eds.): ECSA 2014, LNCS 8627, pp. 250–266, 2014.

a range of areas, in this paper we focus on the communication requirements of CPS. In CPS, the physical substratum continuously evolves following the movement of mobile devices. Locality of devices directly affects reachability and connectivity. Communication between devices is opportunistic; there are no guarantees regarding the stability and reliability of the established links. The network topology itself is dynamic and often relies on ad-hoc means without any managing infrastructure. Finally, the environments where CPS operate (e.g., road networks, emergency sites) are highly dynamic and inherently unpredictable.

At the same time, CPS have also a number of specifics that can be advantageously exploited, such as the fact that by moving around in the environment, the wireless devices effectively enlarge the physical area where information can be disseminated [3]. Physical locality and location-dependency of data offer also a natural way to partition the system and provide built-in scalability and robustness.

Looking at the state-of-the-art in distributed communication, gossip and epidemic protocols provide an efficient way to address the aforementioned specifics. Gossip protocols cope with node and network failures, are scalable due to their symmetric nature, and can exploit the physical mobility of gossiping nodes [3]. The gossiping paradigm has already been applied with success in both Internet-based systems and wireless mobile ad-hoc networks (MANETs) [4].

The central idea in gossip protocols is the periodic and probabilistic data transmission from a source node to a set of selected peers [4–6]. They typically combine probabilistic forwarding with counter-based, distance-based, and location-based mechanisms. These mechanisms and configuration parameters are, however, only available at the lower level of the software stack, often transparent to the application/architecture layer. While this is reasonable for uniform data dissemination, it becomes problematic when the spread of data depends on the architectural configuration in question.

The problem lies in a significant abstraction gap between gossip protocols and application-level architecture design using component models tailored to CPS.

In this paper, we aim at bridging this gap by incorporating concerns of gossiping into sound software engineering abstractions, which allow for (i) systematic engineering of CPS via gossiping components and (ii) application-specific, scalable, and efficient gossip-based communication. We do so in the context of DEECo [7] – a component model that specifically targets dynamic, ever-changing architectures of CPS by relying on the concepts of autonomous (soft) real-time components, and dynamic ad-hoc component ensembles. Our approach is not limited to DEECo though, since it is based on the generic synergy between a set of high-level architectural abstractions supporting dynamicity and low-level primitives of gossip-based protocols.

The rest of the text is structured as follows. In Section 2, we elaborate on a scenario from an emergency coordination case study that provides the motivation for architecture-based decentralized solution. Section 3 presents our approach and its integration into DEECo, while Section 4 outlines the implementation. Following, Section 5 presents the simulation-based evaluation results. Section 6 discusses key contributions and emerging related challenges. Finally, in Section 7 we survey the related work and in Section 8 we present our conclusions.

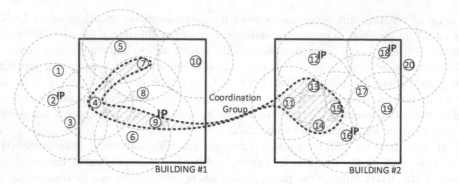

Fig. 1. Motivating scenario: Mobile and stationary nodes cooperate via ad-hoc coordination groups that span within designated boundaries

2   Motivating Scenario

To illustrate the need for effective mapping of architecture-level concepts to decentralized communication schemes in CPS, we use a scenario taken from a firefighter coordination case study[1], which is a real-world real-scale case study for evaluating distributed adaptive systems.

In the scenario, firefighters belong to tactical groups corresponding to the mission in hand. In case of an emergency, a scouting team composed of a team leader and several team members is initially dispatched to the operation site with the goal to assess the criticality level of the situation in hand, so that appropriate strategic decisions can be taken (e.g., mission escalation, request for additional teams). A strong requirement for the effective cooperation of team members is efficient data dissemination – every member has to be notified in a timely manner about important events and threats (e.g., low oxygen level in a particular room, firefighter in danger because of high temperature level) so that the team can act collaboratively and proactively.

Firefighters are equipped with low-power devices with sensing and actuating capabilities that are integrated into their personal protection equipment (being thus mobile). The devices communicate primarily via wireless mobile ad-hoc network (MANET) protocols (e.g., IEEE 802.15.4); additionally, some devices have IP connectivity. Advantageously, the firefighters may exploit other devices on the fire scene (e.g., on-site access points or devices of other emergency personnel) as network relays to boost their wireless coverage and performance. For illustration, consider an operation site that consists of two buildings (Fig. 1).

Obviously, the key challenges stem from the dynamicity of the whole scenario; in particular, the issues to be addressed include (i) MANET management and efficient use of the communication medium and (ii) seamless inclusion of the related concepts

---

[1] http://daum.gforge.inria.fr/

```
1.   role TemperatureSensor:
2.      missionID, temperature
3.
4.   role TemperatureAggregator:
5.      missionID, firefightersInDanger, temperatures
6.
7.   component Firefighter13 features TemperatureSensor:
8.      knowledge:
9.         ID = 13, missionID = 1024, position = {50.075306, 14.426948}, oxygenLevel = 90%, temperature = 35.2
10.     process measureTemperature (out temperature):
11.        temperature ← Sensor.read()
12.        scheduling: periodic( 1000ms )
13.     ... /* other process definitions */
14.  ... /* other firefighter definitions */
15.
16.  component Leader features TemperatureAggregator:
17.     knowledge:
18.        ID = 2, missionID = 1024, position = {50.075310, 14.426952}, firefightersInDanger = {1,3, ...},
19.        temperatures = {{1,30.7}, {2,25.0}, {3,35.2},...}
20.     process findFirefightersInDanger(in temperatures, out firefightersInDanger):
21.        firefightersInDanger ← analyze(temperatures)
22.        scheduling: periodic( 500ms )
23.     ... /* other process definitions */
24.
25.  ensemble TemperatureUpdate:
26.     coordinator: TemperatureAggregator
27.     member: TemperatureSensor
28.     membership:
29.        member.missionID == coordinator.missionID
30.     knowledge exchange:
31.        coordinator.temperatures ← {  (m.ID, m.temperature) | m ∈ members }
32.        scheduling: periodic( 500ms )
```

Fig. 2. Examples of DEECo components and ensembles of the firefighter coordination case study

in the high abstraction level employed in the design of the corresponding software architecture.

2.1   A DEECo-Based Solution

A promising approach for developing software of dynamic CPS is to employ the DEECo component model and its related methods and tools [7].

The design process in DEECo starts with identifying the main system components and dynamic ad-hoc coordination groups – *ensembles* – that the components should establish in order to cooperate for a common goal. In the scenario, ensembles reflect the groups of firefighters exchanging measured data (e.g., temperature, oxygen level) and the groups of officers exchanging strategic information (e.g., mission updates, orders from the chief officer). For illustration, consider the ensemble definition in Fig. 2, lines 25-32. Here, the goal is to enable the members of a firefighting team to propagate information on the measured temperature to the leader of the team so that the leader can determine which firefighters are in danger. In general, an ensemble definition in DEECo contains a condition specifying which components should be considered for membership (lines 28-29), and a function that specifies knowledge exchange among the members (lines 30-31). A particular ensemble (i.e., an instance of an ensemble definition) is identified by its coordinator which features a specific role (line 26). It is instantiated and dissolved by the DEECo runtime environment (Runtime further on), which periodically (line 32) checks the membership of potential groups of coordinator-members. Within an established ensemble, Runtime periodically performs the knowledge exchange, which transfers data between the coordinator and members.

A component in DEECo is an independent unit of computation and deployment. In the scenario, components correspond to the actors of the system (active firefighter, officer, relay node, etc.). For illustration, consider the two components in Fig. 2. Their state is captured by knowledge (lines 8-9, 17-19) and functionality by processes (lines 10-12, 20-22). Every component features a number of roles, i.e., sets of knowledge fields (lines 1-2, 4-5), which are used as the contract between the component and ensembles. Processes are executed by Runtime in a time- or event-triggered fashion (lines 12, 22). Each process execution consists of atomically reading (a part of) the knowledge of the component, executing the process body, and atomically updating the knowledge with the result.

Note that components in DEECo do not explicitly communicate with each other; their only means of communication is knowledge exchange mediated by the ensembles to which the components belong. A component may belong to a number of ensembles at a time (i.e., ensemble instances may overlap).

2.2   Challenges in DEECo-Based Solution

As shown above, DEECo provides a comprehensive set of concepts at a high level of abstraction, coping with the dynamicity by means of component roles and ensembles. However, mapping the concepts into a scalable and robust DEECo implementation is challenging. The particular challenge lies in how and where to evaluate the membership condition for every possible ensemble. This typically requires reasoning at the system level, exploiting some form of global view over the system state. If this reasoning is encapsulated into a special-purpose entity in Runtime, this entity becomes a bottleneck – single point of failure. In particular, such a centralized solution does not scale when ensembles are to be formed among large numbers of components.

3   Gossiping in Ensembles

In order to mitigate the above issue, we have adopted a fully decentralized and robust approach relying on gossiping for establishing ensembles and performing knowledge exchange. In principle, we replace the network communication layer of DEECo by gossip-based communication and extend the DEECo architectural model (the definition of ensembles in particular) by the concept of a *communication boundary* so as to allow efficient functioning of the underlying gossiping mechanism.

To connect components at the architectural level with their physical deployment, we define *node* as a hardware/software platform where a number of DEECo components are deployed (hosted in an instance of Runtime). Nodes communicate with each other via their network interfaces depending on the available networking infrastructure. Thus, component communication is constrained by the available networking infrastructure between the nodes the components are deployed on. Inspired by the motivating scenario, we focus on combinations of IP-based networks (wireless and wired) and MANET networks (which allow only for short range broadcast communication). As a product of distributed communication among nodes, each node obtains copies – *replicas* – of the knowledge of components hosted on (some of) the other nodes.

The main principles of our approach to gossip-based ensemble creation and knowledge exchange can be characterized by the following points:

1. A node has its own awareness of ensemble instances existing in the system, specifically of those that include the components deployed on the node. This awareness is based on evaluating the membership with respect to the current knowledge of local components and replicas of other components.
2. Based on the awareness obtained in (1), a node performs only knowledge exchange that results in updating the knowledge of the local components using, again, the current knowledge of the local components and replicas of others.
3. A node proactively disseminates component knowledge, so that every other node has the replicas necessary for realization of (1) and (2).

The following describes the individual elements of our approach in more detail – points 1 and 2 are explained in Section 3.1, while point 3 is elaborated in Sections 3.2 and 3.3.

3.1   Decentralized Evaluation of Ensemble Membership/Knowledge Exchange

Instead of forming ensembles by looking at a snapshot of the whole system (which would imply that a global view on the system has to be available), we take a node-centric approach. Every node periodically iterates over all known ensemble definitions and checks whether a local component can act as a member or coordinator in an instance of the ensemble definition, given its replicas. For each such ensemble instance, it performs the corresponding knowledge exchange, which results in updating the local components' knowledge (but not the replicas).

As an example, consider an instance of the TemperatureUpdate ensemble (Fig. 2) evaluated on the site of the coordinator. In this case, the knowledge exchange results into updating the coordinator's field temperatures.

Note that a consequence of this technique is that degradation of system performance when no connectivity is available (e.g., due to appearance/disappearance/ mobility of nodes) is gradual: each Runtime effectively operates on the locally available replicas until they become too outdated to rely upon. Here, we count on one of the specifics of CPS, namely on the fact that the values of most magnitudes in CPS (e.g., temperature in Fig. 2) evolve gradually according to physical laws [8]. Practically this means that a belief which is not too old may still be at least partly relevant. Another consequence is that, due to belief outdatedness causing belief inaccuracy, it is possible for a component to behave as if it were in ensemble with a coordinator, which is not aware of it (and vice-versa). These consequences are further analyzed in Section 6.2.

3.2   Asynchronous Knowledge Dissemination via Gossip

The decentralized solution presented in Section 3.1, requires that each node possesses all the necessary replicas from the components that can potentially participate in ensembles with its local components. We enable this by asynchronous gossip-based knowledge dissemination between all the components of a DEECo application.

The main idea is that every node periodically publishes the knowledge of its local components on the network. For MANETs, this translates to periodic broadcast within the wireless range of the node. For IP networks, it translates to periodic sending to randomly selected nodes. Upon reception of a component's knowledge, a node probabilistically decides whether to retransmit the received knowledge. The nodes that perform such re-transmission then act as relays. Here, we rely on the probabilistic convergence of gossip protocols [9], which ensures that every node will eventually receive the knowledge of every component in a bounded number of steps. The nodes that dynamically appear in the system join the publication and re-transmission of knowledge automatically.

Note that this dissemination scheme dictates that all nodes potentially perform the retransmission, not only the ones that are interested in the disseminated knowledge (i.e., nodes hosting components that could be members of the ensemble which the disseminated knowledge relates to).

3.3   Bounding the Gossip

Although the aforementioned gossip-based knowledge dissemination successfully propagates the knowledge of all nodes to all nodes, it raises performance issues. Specifically, if a DEECo application is considered as a ubiquitous ecosystem in a real environment, the application is potentially boundless w.r.t. network reachability. In such a system, unlimited gossiping is not a viable option. Advantageously, in contrary to the assumption of traditional gossip protocols discussed above, not every node is interested in all the data being disseminated by all the components. Thus, certain application-specific bounds should be established for knowledge dissemination.

For this purpose, we define for each ensemble its *communication group* as the set of nodes to which the ensemble's knowledge dissemination is limited. This set consists of all the nodes where components forming the ensemble are hosted and all the relays necessary for knowledge propagation. Relying on the fact that data is disseminated via gradual flooding, we define a *communication boundary* as the predicate determining the limits of a particular communication group w.r.t. network topology. The relays not satisfying the communication boundary will not participate in the dissemination. In a way, a communication group forms a dynamic, architecture-specific network overlay for knowledge dissemination.

Naturally, a communication boundary includes all the nodes "potentially interested" in the disseminated replicas, while excluding as many of the other nodes as possible. Thus, a communication boundary forms a conservative approximation of the ensemble membership. For example, given the pervasive application from Fig. 1, the communication boundary for the ensemble definition in Fig. 2 can be formulated as follows:

"For every mission, include all components within all the areas   in which the participants of the mission operate."

In this example, the communication boundary reflects the fact that all components satisfying the membership condition of the ensemble, i.e., those participating on the same mission, operate in one of the predefined areas. Note however, that the communication boundary predicate is generic w.r.t. a particular mission – it determines a number of different communication groups (thus approximating a number of different ensemble instances), namely a distinct group per distinct mission.

To achieve its desired functionality, a relay has to evaluate a communication boundary much more efficiently than membership condition, preferably using exclusively locally-available information. Thus, we specify communication boundary as a predicate over the local knowledge of the relay and the particular knowledge being disseminated.

Since "communication group" is an application-specific concept relating to application architecture (namely to ensemble membership), we capture it by extending the ensemble definition with a definition of the communication boundary. In addition, we extend the existing concept of "role" to be applicable also at the level of nodes – we say that a node supports a role if one of the components (representative) deployed on the node has structurally-matching knowledge (structural matching enables designing open-ended architectures).

Technically, a communication boundary is defined by a set of predicates (lines 13-16 in Fig. 3). Each of these predicates, given a relay role and a replica role, determines whether a node that has a representative matching the relay role meets the communication boundary for a replica that matches the replica role. Formally, the communication boundary is a conjunction of these predicates (having the form of implications). A relay role has to be either the coordinator or member role.

As an example, in Fig. 3 we show a revised version of the ensemble definition from Fig. 2. Specifically, given a replica corresponding to the member role (TemperatureSensor), the communication boundary includes all relay nodes featuring the TemperatureRelay role, which are in one of the mission areas specified by the replica. This is captured on lines 13-14, which semantically form an implication: the line 13 forms the antecedent (i.e., "if the relay has the role TemperatureRelay and the replica corresponds to the member's role"), while line 14 forms the conclusion. Note, that we have extended the TemperatureSensor role and the knowledge of all the related components to provide the information about mission areas. Similarly, on lines 15-16 the predicate prevents any relaying of replicas matching the coordinator role (as there is no knowledge exchange towards the member). This can be illustrated on Fig. 1 as follows. Provided that all nodes feature the TemperatureRelay role and given that the node 6 participates in a mission that is different to the mission of 9 and localized only to the building #1, then this communication boundary prevents 9 disseminating knowledge of 6 to building #2, as well as 3 from disseminating knowledge of 4. On the other

```
1.  role TemperatureRelay:
2.    position
3.
4.  role TemperatureSensor:
5.    missionID, missionAreas, temperature
6.
7.  ensemble TemperatureUpdate:
8.    coordinator: TemperatureAggregator
9.    member: TemperatureSensor
10.   membership:
11.     member.missionID == coordinator.missionID
12.   boundary:
13.     case relay: TemperatureRelay, replica: roleOf(member):
14.        ∃area ∈ replica.missionAreas: isInArea(relay.position, area)
15.     case relay: any, replica: roleOf(coordinator):
16.        false
17.   ip-registry: 10.10.16.35, 10.10.16.112
```

Fig. 3. Example of a communication boundary definition in DEECo

hand, 9, as well as any node in building #1, will disseminate the knowledge of 6 within the building #1. Moreover, 9 will disseminate knowledge of #4 and #7 also to the building #2 via IP.

This part of specification of communication boundary aligns well with the knowledge dissemination in MANETs, where the set of potential recipients is limited by their geographical locality. On the other hand, in large networks that enable routing based on global addressing, such as IP networks, a necessary performance optimization is to disseminate replicas only to recipients which themselves meet the communication boundary (rather than blindly pollute the entire IP network). To do this, given a replica, a sender has to be able to (at least partially) assess the validity of the communication boundary with respect to the recipient.

To address this issue, we assume that well-known registries exist providing a relay node the information which other IP-based nodes are part of a communication group (given a particular replica). To avoid unnecessary centralization, such a registry is ensemble specific. The registry either provides statically-defined recipients (well-known relay nodes) or evaluates the communication boundary with respect to a recipient. In the latter case, the potential recipient relay nodes provide the registry with the required relay knowledge. Syntactically, the communication boundary definition contains a set of IP addresses identifying the registries that are specific to the corresponding ensemble (line 17 in Fig. 3). Note that due to the nature of gossip, we do not require all the registries in a given ensemble specification to contain the same information.

3.4   Gossip-Based Semantics

To allow for formal analysis of functional and timing properties and precise simulations, as for instance given in Section 4, we have formalized the computational model described in the previous section in terms of operational semantics, which also acts as a thorough, detailed description of the computational model. Technically, based on our previous work [10] we represent the semantics via a state transition system generated by a set of inference rules. Additionally, considering (soft) real-time properties of CPS, the formalization allows only transition traces that are admissible with respect to real-time periodic scheduling of the system processes, ensemble knowledge exchange, and (gossip-based) knowledge dissemination. In a way, these restrictions impose a fairness constraint on the transition traces. Due to space constraints, we refer the interested reader to the technical report [11] for a description of the semantics.

4   Implementation

We have implemented[2] the proposed approach by extending the current implementation of jDEECo (a Java implementation of DEECo Runtime). Specifically, we have added support for the concept of communication boundary and the gossip-based knowledge dissemination and ensemble evaluation presented in Section 3. Since these concepts are closely connected to the network layer, we have also integrated jDEECo with the OMNet++ simulation framework[3] that provides an appropriate abstraction for the network infrastructure, enabling precise discrete-time simulations (Fig. 4).

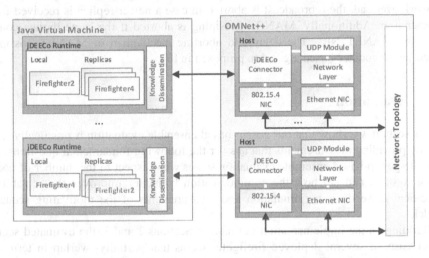

Fig. 4. jDEECo Runtime Framework – OMNet++ integration overview

From the perspective of the OSI (Open Systems Interconnection) model [12], our implementation glues together the application layer given by jDEECo Runtime (along with the deployed components and ensembles) with the underlying layers implemented in OMNet++ (Fig. 4). An instance of jDEECo Runtime reflects a single unit of network deployment (e.g., a mobile device). Apart from managing components, scheduling of component processes' execution and ensemble evaluations, jDEECo Runtime automates knowledge management, including network communication

---

[2] https://github.com/d3scomp/JDEECo
[3] http://omnetpp.org/

needed for knowledge replica dissemination. Each jDEECo Runtime continuously advertises the knowledge of the locally deployed components and, additionally, acts as a relay.

At the network layer, each jDEECo Runtime is bound to its OMNet++ counterpart (namely OMNet host), with which it communicates via JNI (Java Native Interface) calls. Every OMNet host is equipped with two kinds of Network Interface Cards (NICs): one for MANET-based wireless (IEEE 802.15.4) and one for IP-based (Ethernet) communication. Direct communication is implemented via UDP on top of the Ethernet NIC, while MANET-oriented broadcast communication is performed via the wireless NIC. For implementation, we relied on two extensions of OMNet++: the MiXiM plugin delivering a detailed model of the 802.15.4 protocol and the INET framework implementing the whole Ethernet stack.

Each jDEECo Runtime gossips knowledge replicas obtained from the network. We specifically distinguish two cases: gossiping via MANET and direct gossiping. In the case of MANET gossiping, a jDEECo Runtime calculates a probabilistic rebroadcast delay relying on RSSI (Radio Signal Strength Indicator); in case of direct gossiping the data is retransmitted to a random set of peers using a fixed delay. To prevent network overload, the rebroadcast is aborted in case a newer replica is received from another peer. Additionally, MANET gossiping is aborted if the same replica comes from the MANET NIC. The delay and aborting mechanism of MANET gossip is based on the counter-based algorithm proposed in [6].

5   Evaluation

In this section, we show that our gossip-based ensemble evaluation is practically feasible by providing measurements that answer the following fundamental questions: (1) how the gossip-based ensemble evaluation scales with respect to the number of nodes in the system, and (2) how the communication boundary improves the scalability. Specifically, we do it by simulation and measurements of the motivating scenario model.

Building on the implementation outlined in Sections 2 and 3, the evaluated scenario consists of several deployed firefighter teams that partially overlap in terms of radio signal coverage. Each team uses the other teams' members as relays for knowledge dissemination in the overlapping areas to ensure the necessary wireless coverage. The objective of this scenario is to illustrate the performance gain of employing communication boundary, which limits data sharing strictly to the overlapping regions. Note that the communication boundary being used (Fig. 3) allows any node that monitors its position, such as a device of other emergency personnel, to be equally included into the scenario and act as a relay; for brevity we include only firefighters. The scenario combines MANET-based gossiping (with evenly distributed nodes in the area) and direct gossiping realized by Ethernet-enabled nodes (a small fraction of the nodes).

The scenario is affected a large number of factors, such as network density, size of the overlapping regions, wireless communication range, gossip protocol configuration, etc. Therefore, we have simulated our system under a variety of configurations; however, due the space limits, this paper presents results for configurations varying in the number of overlapping teams (thus also in the total number of nodes), while maintaining a fixed node density (close to the highest density safely manageable by the implemented MANET gossip protocol, as evaluated by Williams and Camp in [4]). The detailed information on the configuration parameters, which were set to match the realistic case described in Section 2 as close as possible, as well as the simulation results for various set-ups, can be found on the DEECo project website[4].

The results presented in Fig. 5 show the leader-member end-to-end communication time in a firefighting team (in particular, the time it takes a leader node to learn that a member of its team is in danger, normalized by the hop distance between the two nodes). Specifically, we compare the cases with and without communication boundary. Not using communication boundary results into propagation of a team's data across all nodes; this causes global degradation of end-to-end communication performance (corresponding to the performance limitations of the implemented gossip protocol). On the other hand, communication boundary localizes the team's data dissemination and prevents the communication channels from overloading, which results in stable performance (as long as the dynamic communication boundary does not grow). Specifically, the communication boundary reduces the utilization of the shared communication medium by preventing "outside" data from penetrating deeper (than necessary) into the team's area. This reduces the overhead of the communication medium; the freed capacity can be now utilized to handle dissemination of the team's data.

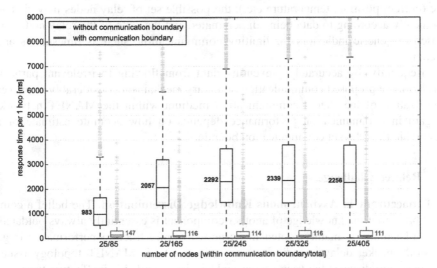

Fig. 5. Time for discovering a team Member in danger by a corresponding Leader

---

[4] http://d3s.mff.cuni.cz/projects/components_and_services/
deeco/simulations

6   Discussion

In this section we review the key contributions of our approach and discuss the main related challenges that stem from the decentralized decisions on ensemble membership and gossip-based communication.

6.1   Key Contributions

Integrating the DEECo concept of ensemble with gossip-based communication enables for efficiently dealing with scenarios where system architecture is open-ended and changes continuously; e.g., systems with high mobility of components or largely unreliable communication links. To this end, the autonomicity of DEECo components and best-effort style of communication provided by the gossip-based implementation of ensemble knowledge exchange deliver means for assuring high infrastructural resilience.

Although, due to the dynamic nature of ensembles, the gossip-based implementation of knowledge exchange requires disseminating knowledge to all the potential members, possibly requiring all nodes to act as relays, communication boundary provides means to accurately reduce the dissemination to only those nodes, which are actually needed considering the application-logic point of view. Moreover, as the knowledge dissemination governed by the communication boundary exploits the contextual information available at the application level in the form of component knowledge (current position, temperature etc.), the possible set of relay nodes may change dynamically according to data being disseminated and the state of the relay nodes, as opposed to generic indicators for limiting communication, such as timestamps and hop count.

Consequently, by accurately preventing data from flowing to irrelevant parts of the system, the proposed communication boundary mechanism considerably improves the utilization of the shared communication medium within the MANET network. The gain in communication performance depends on how accurate estimate of a membership the relevant communication boundary is.

6.2   Related Challenges

Belief Inaccuracy in Asynchronous Knowledge Dissemination. The belief a component has about the knowledge of another component is essentially always outdated. This outdatedness is mainly rooted in (i) network infrastructure performance (e.g., bandwidth, packet delays, medium access rate, etc.) (ii) MANET topology issues (e.g., large hop distance between sender and receiver), and (iii) ineffective tuning of the employed gossip algorithm (e.g., too long (re)transmission period).

The outdateness of belief determines its inaccuracy, i.e. the difference between the value of the belief and the actual value of the knowledge. Depending on the nature of data (i.e., continuous or discrete domain, rate of change), slight incoherence between knowledge and belief might be tolerated or accounted for during design [8].

Advantageously, this is the case with most of CPS where real-world phenomena (e.g., position, oxygen level, velocity) are to be captured.

Split-Brain Situations in Ensembles. Due to the belief outdatedness and isolated membership evaluation by each potential member, situations where different nodes arrive at conflicting conclusions regarding ensembles may arise. This results in a member acting as if it were in an ensemble having a coordinator who is not aware of it (or vice-versa). As an example, consider an ensemble that is formed of the firefighter components (each hosted on a separate node) whose positions lie within a 10-meter perimeter from a leader (coordinator). When a firefighter node steps out of the designated area, the corresponding firefighter component should not be part of the ensemble. The coordinator, however, will only learn about that at the next time its host node receives an up-to-date replica of that component. Until then, it will falsely consider the firefighter component as a legitimate member of its ensemble.

In cases where belief outdatedness and topology dynamicity are not too high these "split-brain" situations are of temporal nature. For deeper analyses, system simulations (see Section 4) and timing analysis can be used to provide measurements of the distribution of such inconsistencies and their duration.

Gossip Implementation. For our experiments we employed a basic version of counter-based gossiping [6] without emphasis on its optimization, as we did not intend to evaluate the gossip protocol per se but rather the practical feasibility of gossiping ensembles and the impact of the communication boundary. One of such optimizations of the communication that we identified as an absolute necessity was stripping down the size of the disseminated replicas. This is especially critical in MANET settings, where the bandwidth is limited and larger replicas (more than approx. 128 bytes) lead to fragmentation. In combination with the CSMA/CA medium access technique and the hidden node problem [13] this leads quickly to network contention.

7   Related Work

The solution presented in this paper brings about the convergence of software component models for CPS and gossip-based communication. Although there are some attempts to achieve synergy between the two areas ([14–16]), they are set on a significantly different track than our approach. In [14], the authors propose a conceptual architecture and design framework for gossip. The framework is based on reusable building blocks, where individual protocols are treated as monolithic black boxes. In [15], the authors propose an API for programming gossip-based systems by analyzing the identified recurrent design dimensions of gossip protocols – namely randomness, neighborhood, and communication. Finally, in [16], the authors introduce a component framework GossipKit, which aims at facilitating the development and testing of gossip protocols by relying on reusable and modular gossip abstractions and standard component-based composition techniques. In all of these approaches the focus is on providing an architectural solution for building gossip-based middleware by means of ready-made components/interfaces. We, in contrast, focus on modeling application logic by means of autonomous components which use gossip internally and partially transparently as the primary means of their communication.

Regarding the state of the art in gossip-based communication, different variations of the basic gossiping scheme have been proposed for different application domains and with slightly different semantics ([17–19]). In MANETs gossiping translates to probabilistic broadcasting within the wireless range of each node [3]. Probabilistic forwarding is often combined with some other locally computable mechanism, such as counter-based [6], location-based [20], distance-based [21], energy-based [22], or a combination of these, to further reduce the number of retransmitted messages (with respect to blind flooding). In our work we do not intend to extend or evaluate the state of the art in gossip-based communication, but provide a method for architecting CPS using abstractions that facilitate the efficiency of the gossip by relying on the architecture-level context information.

Regarding component models and architectures supporting distributed dynamic systems such as CPS, different approaches related to self-adapting/self-organizing systems [23, 24], self-managing architectures [25], component-based architectures [26, 27], and architectural models at runtime [28] have been proposed. The common denominator of these approaches is the fact that they do not support high dynamicity (which does not scale with the ever-changing landscape of CPS) or they do not readily map to decentralized architectures. DEECo, on the other hand, fits better the specifics of CPS by relying on dynamic component grouping and implicit component communication.

8 Conclusions

In this paper, we presented a synergy of software component model abstractions and gossip-based communication primitives as a promising solution for engineering scalable dynamic decentralized cyber-physical systems. Our approach relies on providing architecture-level descriptions that feature communication groups (captured by communication boundaries) and allow us "driving" the gossip efficiently. The presented experiments show that our approach is in principle feasible. Our current and future work involves improving the scalability of our approach by various optimizations of the gossip protocol (e.g., employing location-based algorithms where GPS-enabled devices are required). Another direction is investigating timing constraints on the gossip-based knowledge dissemination and exchange which will supplement the strict real-time constraints already imposed on local component behaviors.

Acknowledgments. This work was partially supported by the EU project ASCENS 257414 and by Charles University institutional funding SVV-2014-260100. The research leading to these results has received funding from the European Union Seventh Framework Programme FP7-PEOPLE-2010-ITN under grant agreement n°264840.

References

1. Beetz, K., Böhm, W.: Challenges in Engineering for Software-Intensive Embedded Systems. In: Model-Based Engineering of Embedded Systems, pp. 3–14. Springer (2012)
2. Lee, E.A.: Cyber Physical Systems: Design Challenges. In: Proc. of ISORC 2008, Orlando, FL, USA, pp. 363–369 (2008)
3. Friedman, R., Gavidia, D., Rodrigues, L., Viana, A.C., Voulgaris, S.: Gossiping on MANETs: The Beauty and the Beast. ACM SIGOPS Oper. Syst. Rev. 41, 67–74 (2007)
4. Williams, B., Camp, T.: Comparison of Broadcasting Techniques for Mobile Ad Hoc Networks. In: Proc. of MobiHoc 2002, pp. 194–205. ACM, Lausanne (2002)
5. Eugster, P.T., Guerraoui, R., Handurukande, S.B., Kouznetsov, P., Kermarrec, A.-M.: Lightweight probabilistic broadcast. ACM TOCS 21, 341–374 (2003)
6. Tseng, Y.-C., Ni, S.-Y., Chen, Y.-S., Sheu, J.-P.: The Broadcast Storm Problem in a Mobile Ad Hoc Network. Wirel. Networks 8, 153–167 (2002)
7. Bures, T., Gerostathopoulos, I., Hnetynka, P., Keznikl, J., Kit, M., Plasil, F.: DEECo – an Ensemble-Based Component System. In: Proc. of CBSE 2013, pp. 81–90. ACM, Vancouver (2013)
8. Ali, R., Al, B.T., Gerostathopoulos, I., Keznikl, J., Plasil, F.: Architecture Adaptation Based on Belief Inaccuracy Estimation. To appear in Proc. of WICSA 2014 (2014)
9. Drabkin, V., Friedman, R., Kliot, G., Segal, M.: RAPID: Reliable Probabilistic Dissemination in Wireless Ad-Hoc Networks. In: Proc. of SRDS 2007, pp. 13–22. IEEE, Beijing (2007)
10. Barnat, J., Benes, N., Bures, T., Cerna, I., Keznikl, J., Plasil, F.: Towards Verification of Ensemble-Based Component Systems. In: Fiadeiro, J.L., Liu, Z., Xue, J. (eds.) FACS 2013. LNCS, vol. 8348, pp. 41–60. Springer, Heidelberg (2014)
11. Bures, T., Gerostathopoulos, I., Hnetynka, P., Keznikl, J., Kit, M., Plasil, F.: Computational Model for Gossiping Components in Cyber-Physical Systems. Charles University in Prague, TR no. D3S-TR-2014-03
12. OSI: OSI Basic Reference Model: The Basic Model - ISO/IEC 7498-1, http://standards.iso.org
13. Yoo, J., Kim, C.-k.: On the Hidden Terminal Problem in Multi-rate Ad Hoc Wireless Networks. In: Kim, C. (ed.) ICOIN 2005. LNCS, vol. 3391, pp. 479–488. Springer, Heidelberg (2005)
14. Rivière, E., Baldoni, R., Li, H., Pereira, J.: Compositional gossip: A conceptual architecture for designing gossip-based applications. ACM SIGOPS Oper. Syst. Rev. 41, 43–50 (2007)
15. Eugster, P., Felber, P., Le Fessant, F.: The "Art" of Programming Gossip-based Systems. ACM SIGOPS Oper. Syst. Rev. 41, 37–42 (2007)
16. Taiani, F., Lin, S., Blair, S.G.: GossipKit: A Unified Component Framework for Gossip. IEEE Trans. Softw. Eng. PP, 1–17 (2013)
17. Branco, M., Leitão, J., Rodrigues, L.: Bounded Gossip: A Gossip Protocol for Large-Scale Datacenters. In: Proc. of SAC 2013, pp. 591–596. ACM, Coimbra (2013)
18. Khelil, A., Suri, N.: Gossiping: Adaptive and Reliable Broadcasting in MANETs. In: Bondavalli, A., Brasileiro, F., Rajsbaum, S. (eds.) LADC 2007. LNCS, vol. 4746, pp. 123–141. Springer, Heidelberg (2007)
19. Kermarrec, A.-M., Van Steen, M.: Gossiping in distributed systems. ACM SIGOPS Oper. Syst. Rev. 41, 2–7 (2007)
20. Karp, B., Kung, H.T.: GPSR: Greedy Perimeter Stateless Routing for Wireless Networks. In: Proc. of MobiCom 2000, pp. 243–254. ACM, Boston (2000)

21. Cartigny, J., Simplot, D.: Border Node Retransmission Based Probabilistic Broadcast Protocols in Ad-Hoc Networks. In: Proc. of HICSS 2003, pp. 303–312. IEEE, Hawaii (2003)
22. Miranda, H., Leggio, S., Rodrigues, L., Raatikainen, K.: A Power-Aware Broadcasting Algorithm. In: Proc. of PIMRC 2006, pp. 1–5. IEEE, Helsinki (2006)
23. Serugendo, G.D.M., Fitzgerald, J., Romanovsky, A.: MetaSelf – An Architecture and a Development Method for Dependable Self- * Systems. In: Proc. of SAC 2010, pp. 457–461. ACM, Sierre (2010)
24. Liu, H., Parashar, M., Hariri, S.: A Component Based Programming Framework for Autonomic Applications. In: Proc. of ICAC 2004, pp. 10–17 (2004)
25. Kramer, J., Magee, J.: Self-managed systems: an architectural challenge. In: Proc. of FOSE 2007, pp. 259–268. IEEE, Minneapolis (2007)
26. Baresi, L., Guinea, S., Tamburrelli, G.: Towards Decentralized Self-adaptive Component-based Systems. In: Proc. of SEAMS 2008, pp. 57–64. ACM, Leipzig (2008)
27. Peper, C., Schneider, D.: Component engineering for adaptive ad-hoc systems. In: Proceedings of SEAMS 2008, pp. 49–56. ACM, Leipzig (2008)
28. Morin, B., Barais, O., Jezequel, J.-M., Fleurey, F., Solberg, A.: Models at Runtime to Support Dynamic Adaptation. Computer (Long. Beach. Calif.) 42, 44–51 (2009)

A Property Description Framework
for Composable Software

Alexander Frömmgen, Max Lehn, and Alejandro Buchmann

Databases and Distributed Systems Group (DVS), TU Darmstadt, Germany
{froemmge,mlehn,buchmann}@dvs.tu-darmstadt.de

Abstract The composition of software components can be used to fit specific application needs. Finding feasible and, moreover, optimal compositions demands extensive domain knowledge from the developer—with respect to both application requirements and used components. Frameworks can provide support for the composition selection based on requirements, component properties, and their dependencies. Their description, however, becomes complex in practice.

In this paper, we propose the *ProDesc* framework. It contains a property description language with a bespoke type system for describing properties of software components and their operations. *ProDesc* can express compositional variability, including dependencies of properties on the environment and on other components. A UML-like graphical notation and transformations to feature diagrams support the software developer.

The most suitable component composition is selected based on a utility function, which is evaluated during runtime. Our approach raises the abstraction level, leads to a clear separation of concerns, reduces the development time, and facilitates optimized software.

1 Introduction

Modern software development uses components as a central abstraction. The composition of multiple components provides a certain functionality with particular properties. Developers need domain knowledge and time to choose the most suitable composition; or they simply choose any feasible composition. Depending on the use case, different properties of the components are of importance and influence the composition. This is particularly important if components, e.g. those of the Java collection framework, are used for a variety of purposes in different scenarios. Desktop applications, for example, should be optimized for high responsiveness, application servers should have a high throughput, and mobile apps should focus on energy savings.

Consider a software developer who needs a map in their application for storing key-value pairs. The key-value store interface is implemented by multiple components that use different data structures, e.g. trees and hash-tables. Different data structures have different properties, e.g. with respect to computational and memory complexity. Based on the knowledge about the usage scenario and therefore its requirements, the developer has to choose between the different

P. Avgeriou and U. Zdun (Eds.): ECSA 2014, LNCS 8627, pp. 267–282, 2014.
© Springer International Publishing Switzerland 2014

options. Furthermore, the key-value store component that is based on a hash-table uses one of several available hash algorithms. As these algorithms can in turn be provided by different components, the properties of the key-value store component depend on the properties of the selected hash-component.

Obviously, the developer needs profound knowledge about all available components and their properties to select the most suitable component composition. Particularly challenging is the consideration of properties that depend on the properties of other components. Finally, such design decisions are in most cases not explicitly documented.

In this paper, we target the problems described above and introduce the property description framework *ProDesc* for composable software. This framework contains a description language with a bespoke type system to support the developer. *ProDesc* allows to resolve the dependencies of properties between different components and balances between detailed modeling and ease of use. We propose to use utility functions to express the requirements and preferences on component compositions. During the development of the software, the component properties and utility functions are specified. At compile time, a verification of the properties and components ensures the correctness of the model. Assuming a valid property description, *ProDesc* determines optimal compositions at runtime. Additional tools such as transformations to feature diagrams support the developer.

In Section 2, we discuss existing approaches for property description and component selection. Based on this, we present an extended overview of the description model (Section 3), the type system (Section 4), and the property description language (Section 5) of *ProDesc*. Afterwards, we describe a UML-like graphical notation (Section 6). In Section 7, we present two model transformations to feature diagrams. Section 8 describes how the preferences of the software developer are covered by the utility function. Additionally, we present an algorithm to determine the optimal component composition. In the case study and evaluation (Section 9), we discuss multiple examples and show performance measurements. We close with a discussion and outlook.

2   Related Work

Several domains in software engineering deal with property description and optimization based on these descriptions. Before going into detail, we want to emphasize that *ProDesc* intentionally does not distinguish between functional, non-functional and extra-functional properties [1], characteristics [2], attributes [3], qualities [2], or service parameters [4], as those terms are used differently in the literature. We handle all of them as *properties* because a differentiation is neither needed nor constructive for our approach. In contrast to most related work, the presented approach is domain agnostic and does not introduce a vocabulary or ontology. In the following, we discuss related work in the domains of UML, component based systems, web service composition, and self-adaptive systems.

UML Based Approaches: Based on the observation that "most modeling languages provide support for the description of functional behavior, [but] describe non-functional requirements merely using simple comments or informal structures" [2], the *UML Profile for Modeling Quality of Service and Fault Tolerance Characteristics and Mechanisms* [2] introduces a catalog with QoS characteristics and categories. The *UML Profile for Schedulability, Performance and Time* [5], which models real-time characteristics, specifies properties like *response time, delay,* and *is blocking.* Both profiles, however, do not provide a general framework for specifying properties. In particular, there is no systematic approach to represent dependencies between components, properties and the composition. Additionally, there is only minor support for a specification of requirements and preferences based on the modeled properties.

Several approaches provide a more flexible definition of properties. Cysneiros et al. [6] propose a *Language Extended Lexicon* to define vocabulary and to reflect non-functional requirements in UML. Espinoza et al. [7] annotate non-functional properties for quantitative analysis. Therefore, they distinguish between quantitative (measurable, countable, and comparable) and qualitative properties and introduce concrete non-functional property types (duration-type, rate-type, probability-type, size-type). Nevertheless, dependencies between properties and an explicit notion of compositional variability are still missing.

Component Based Systems: Automated software component retrieval systems focus on an increased software reuse. Morel et al. [8] use specifications to abstractly represent implementations and theorem-provers to formally verify reusability. In contrast, we assume that the developer already knows the required interface and therefore concentrate on optimizing the component composition.

Multiple property description approaches are proposed for component models. Zinky et al. [9] propose a QoS Description Language (QDL) complementary to the interface description language (IDL) of CORBA. However, their concepts concentrate on distributed systems and the middleware layer and do not consider dependencies between multiple components in a composition.

Eichberg et al. [10] enrich the interface description of components using feature models. Based on a list of desired variants, the so-called feature requirement specification, a suitable component is determined. Lacking an explicit assessment of different properties, only the number of instantiated components is optimized.

Web Service Composition: Dustdar et al. [11] present a comprehensive survey on web service composition and the different composition approaches. For example, the automated web service composition in [12] uses ontologies of QoS metrics. The Web Service Level Agreement Language [4] (WSLA) can specify properties of web services. A systematic description of the variability and their properties is missing in all the presented approaches.

Leitner et al. [13] discuss cost-based web service composition optimization. Rosenberg et al. [14] additionally use a QoS-aware composition model to apply metaheuristic optimizations. Their findings might be transferred to our optimization problem. However, these concepts concentrate on the optimization and provide only limited property description support.

Adaptive Systems: Compositional adaptation uses dynamic recomposition at runtime to achieve adaptable behavior. Therefore, a representation of the possible compositions is required. Bencomo et al. [15] use two domain-specific languages. The *OpenCOM DSL* is used to specify components and interfaces. As *OpenCOM* does not provide property description concepts, the *Transition Diagrams DSL* specifies the possible adaptability as on-event-do-action policies. The visualization of the variability as feature diagram is comparable with our *Component-as-Feature* Transformation (Section 7.2).

Hallsteinsen et al. [16,17] use a utility function to determine and adapt to the most suitable composition. Therefore, they annotate components with properties. The authors conclude that it is hard for developers to express properties and utility functions. However, their approach lacks a clear type system and a language to express these properties. Together with the support for complex compositions and dependencies we believe that our approach enables the developer to express a wide range of properties and utility functions.

3   Overview of the Description Model

In this section, we give an extended overview of our description model and present the meta-model of *ProDesc*.

A software developer who uses components has to choose between different components which implement the same interface. We assume that the software developer knows the interface she requires. In the example in Figure 1, the two components C_1 and C_2 provide different properties. The properties of component C_1 might even depend on the component used for interface I_2. The developer needs time to choose the most appropriate component composition or simply chooses any feasible composition. However, the developer's choice is most probably not explicitly documented in the source code. Additionally, the choice might depend on environment variables, e.g. the network availability, the energy supply, CPU features or the display resolution.

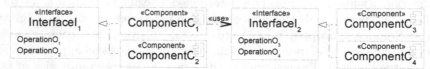

Fig. 1. Simple variability example with multiple components and interfaces

Figure 2 illustrates the meta-model of *ProDesc*. The entities *Component, Operation*, and *Interface* (top right box) have a direct counterpart implemented in the host programming language. We assume a component is a modular unit with well-defined interfaces (e.g. a single class or a class which encapsulates more complex structures). The semantic of the three entities matches those of object oriented languages. Like in UML, a component can *use* and *realize* interfaces [18]. Interfaces specify operations that the realizing component has to implement.

Interfaces, Components, Operations, and the *Environment* have *Property Instances*. A property instance has a name and refers to a property. The set of

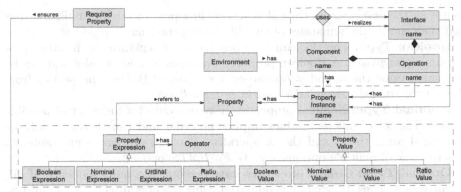

Fig. 2. The meta-model of *ProDesc*

property instances builds the vocabulary for the property description. The developer therefore has to specify the required property instances. A property can be a concrete value or an expression which refers to other properties. Thus, an expression can compose multiple properties. The type system and the different types (bottom box) are explained in Section 4. A *uses* relationship between a component and an interface can have multiple *Required Properties*, which are *Boolean Expressions* and specify additional constraints.[1]

ProDesc concentrates on the domain of property description of composed components. Following a clear separation of concerns, *ProDesc* only specifies components, interfaces and operations as far as needed for the presented approach to minimize the modeling overhead.

The current implementation of *ProDesc* assumes that the concrete component instance graph at runtime is an arborescence. However, it might be interesting to weaken this assumption and add support for acyclic directed graphs in the future. *ProDesc* does not assume a certain host language. A system might even contain multiple components implemented in different programming languages or wrappers for Web Services. In conjunction with the strategy pattern [19], a component can represent an algorithm.

4   The Property Type System

ProDesc is designed to easily express and evaluate properties for complex compositions of components. Therefore, it has a *strong type system* which assigns each expression an unambiguous type. Additionally, the language is *statically typed*, which enables compile time checking and thus supports the software developer.

ProDesc has four built-in types which are inspired by Steven's scales of measurement [20]. The language does not use the common base types such as integer, double, or char, as these are improper for property description. Instead, the built-in types are specifically chosen to support property description and to be easy

---

[1] The *Required Properties* should not be confused with the Object Constraint Language (OCL). OCL expresses constraints on the known UML elements, e.g. classes, attributes, and associations. *Required Properties* use the *ProDesc* properties.

to use for the developer. In the following, we first present the four built-in types and then specify the semantics of the different operations:

Boolean Type: The Boolean type has the same semantics as in other programming languages. A Boolean property evaluates to *true* or *false* and can be compared using the = and ≠ operators. Examples of Boolean properties from the network domain are *reliable* and *in order delivery*.

Nominal Type: Nominal properties have one out of a finite set of possible values. The set of different values implies no order and can therefore only be compared using the = and the ≠ operator. Nominal properties are useful to describe one of multiple options, e.g. *WiFi, UMTS,* or *LTE*.

Ordinal Type: Ordinal properties have one out of a finite sequence of different values. Thus, they can be compared using the operators =, ≠, <, and >. However, the distance between the different values is not specified. Therefore, operations like addition and multiplication are not valid. Ordinal properties are suitable for modeling properties, as they allow a good balance between modeling detail and overhead. The developer can express a qualitative relation without the need for expressing the exact quantitative difference, e.g. the execution time could be *low, medium,* or *high*.

Ratio Type: Ratio properties have numeric values and are internally represented by double precision floating point values. They support most common operators (Table 1) but require more detailed domain knowledge than the other types. The Ratio type allows an accurate modeling of quantitative properties such as the *execution time in seconds* and *availability*.

Table 1 specifies the operations based on the four built-in types, where $[t]$ denotes a property or expression of the type t. The operations are used to compose or aggregate other properties. Most of the operations have intuitive semantics, e.g. the $[t_1] = [t_2]$ operator evaluates to *true* iff $[t_1]$ and $[t_2]$ have the same type and the same value. The $[o_1] := inc([o_2])$ operator returns the next higher value of $[o_2]$. If $[o_2]$ is the highest possible value, $[o_2]$ is returned. The $[o] := min([o], ...)$ operator returns the minimal value of the provided properties. The additional ternary operator **if** $[b]$ **then** $[t_1]$ **else** $[t_2]$ allows a case distinction. Depending on the evaluation of the Boolean expression $[b]$, $[t_1]$ or $[t_2]$ is returned.

We intentionally do not support user-defined types, as this would increase the complexity of both description and utility expression. However, the native

Table 1. The operations on the four built-in types of *ProDesc*

Type	Operations			
Boolean	$[b] := [b] = [b]$	$[b] := [b] \neq [b]$	$[b] := [b]\ \&\&\ [b]$	$[b] := [b]\ \|\|\ [b]$
Nominal	$[b] := [n] = [n]$	$[b] := [n] \neq [n]$		
Ordinal	$[b] := [o] = [o]$	$[b] := [o] \neq [o]$	$[b] := [o] < [o]$	$[b] := [o] > [o]$
	$[o] := inc([o])$	$[o] := dec([o])$	$[o] := min([o], ...)$	$[o] := max([o], ...)$
Ratio	$[b] := [r] = [r]$	$[b] := [r] \neq [r]$	$[b] := [r] < [r]$	$[b] := [r] > [r]$
	$[r] := [r] + [r]$	$[r] := [r] - [r]$	$[r] := [r] * [r]$	$[r] := [r] : [r]$
	$[o] := min([o], ...)$	$[o] := max([o], ...)$		

support of additional types and their operations such as probabilities and their distribution, and support for θ-notation might be added in future releases.

5 Modeling Language

Based on the meta-model and the type system, we present the *ProDesc* description language syntax. In the following we describe the four parts of *ProDesc* using simple examples. [ ] brackets emphasize optional keywords.

Property Definition: The property definition is used to specify property instances with unique names. This is the vocabulary of the domain. Listing 1 shows an example for each built-in type. For nominal and ordinal properties, the possible values are enumerated as sets and sequences respectively.

```
1   property Reliable as boolean;
2   property Encryption as nominal {RSA, ECC, None};
3   property ExecutionTime as ordinal (Low, Medium, High);
4   property BatteryStatus as ratio;
```

Listing 1. Example of the property definition in ProDesc.

Environment Definition: Properties of the environment are specified in the optional *environment* definition. Listing 2 shows the definition of an external environment variable. External variables are used for properties whose values are not available at design time and therefore retrieved at runtime.

```
1   environment {
2       BatteryStatus = [volatile] retrieveFromStaticMethod(
3           "InternalClass", "getBatteryStatus");
4   }
```

Listing 2. Environment definition in ProDesc.

The *ProDesc Framework* supports two kinds of external variables. The developer can either specify a host language method which is invoked at runtime, or explicitly set the value at runtime using a setter-method provided by the framework. The retrieve methods are black boxes for the *ProDesc Framework* and should have no side effects. The *volatile* attribute specifies that the external variable might change during runtime. Therefore, *ProDesc* reads the variable each time an optimal composition is determined. The externally retrieved values are dynamically type checked and converted to the built-in types. Additional sources for external variables (e.g. Web Services) can be used with a wrapper in the host language. The Web Service Level Agreement Language [4] supports a similar approach which allows to specify Web Services as a source for variables.

Interface Definition: The interface definition (Listing 3) specifies the properties of the implementing components and their operations. The implementing component can override the property values and expressions of the interface.

```
1    interface IFoo {
2        Reliable;
3        Encryption = None;
4        operation IOp {
5            ExecutionTime = Medium;
6        }
7    }
```

Listing 3. The definition of an interface with properties in ProDesc.

Component Definition: The component definition (Listing 4) contains multiple parts. The Boolean *requires* expression (line 2) determines under which conditions the component can be instantiated. Based on the implemented interfaces (line 1), the definition of concrete property values or expressions for all properties specified in the interfaces is enforced. This is comparable with object-oriented languages, where a class has to provide all methods of the implemented interfaces. The used interfaces (line 3) specify an alias which refers to the concrete instance. A used interface can express requirements on the used components as Boolean expression. Additionally, used interfaces can be *optional*.

```
1    component CFoo implements IFoo {
2        requires Environment.BatteryStatus > 20;
3        uses [optional] IBar as alias [requires alias.reliable =↩
         true];
4        Reliable = alias.reliable [optional false];
5        Encryption = RSA;
6        operation IOp {
7            ExecutionTime = inc(alias.IOp.ExecutionTime);
8        }
9    }
```

Listing 4. The definition of a component in ProDesc.

Expressions use the type system and operations presented in Section 4 to compose properties based on the used components. The *dot* syntax allows to reference components (line 4), operations (line 6), and the environment (line 2). In case optional components are specified, the *ProDesc Framework* enforces that each property value can be evaluated (line 4).

ProDesc can generate a description language template based on the interfaces and classes in Java and generate Java templates based on the *ProDesc* description. Additional imports and exports (e.g. XMI-based) to support other tools such as a model driven development infrastructure can be implemented easily.

Even though it violates the separation of concerns, properties can also be specified in the host language. This reduces the modeling overhead. For Java, *ProDesc* supports annotations as shown in Listing 5.

```
1    @Property(name="EexecutionTime", value="High")
2    public void insert(String key, String value) {
```

Listing 5. Example of the Java annotation for property specification.

6   Graphical Notation

The graphical notation of *ProDesc* (Figure 3) is based on the well known class and component diagrams in UML [18]. Interfaces are visualized using an explicit notation (*InterfaceI*$_2$) or the ball-and-socket notation (*InterfaceI*$_1$). Components are visualized as rectangles containing their properties, operations, and the properties of their operations. Required properties are annotated on the connecting edge between the component and the interface or the socket.

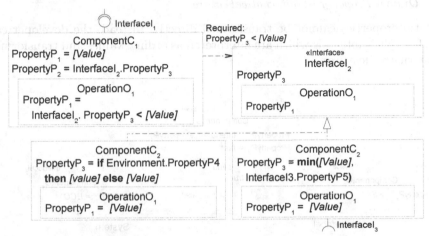

Fig. 3. Example of the UML-like graphical representation of *ProDesc*

ProDesc therefore provides its own viewpoint on the overall architecture. While the host language and UML class diagrams specify the attributes of components, *ProDesc* describes the properties of components and their operations.

7   Feature Models

ProDesc can be transformed into *feature models* which are used in the *Feature Oriented Design Analysis* to describe the feature-variability of systems. Features "are user-visible aspects or characteristics of the domain" [21]. *ProDesc* benefits from the established feature model analysis, such as the number of possible configurations, core features which exist in all configurations, dead features which are not available, and atomic sets of features which always appear together [22].

Feature diagrams, the graphical representation of feature models, introduce a new viewpoint on the specification and allow domain experts to validate the *ProDesc* description at design time. Thus, a feature configuration is an instance of the model with concrete values for each feature.

In the following, we introduce the *Property-as-Feature* and the *Component-as-Feature* transformation as simple rules. More sophisticated approaches, e.g. QVT[2], could be used as well.

---

[2] http://www.omg.org/spec/QVT/1.1/

7.1 Property-as-Feature Transformation

The *Property-as-Feature* transformation interprets the properties as features (Figure 4 left). This leads to a feature diagram which helps to reason about possible property combinations. A feature configuration contains concrete values for the properties and thus a concrete instantiation of a composed component. Depending on the property type, different transformation rules are executed:

$$Boolean\ Property \mapsto optionalFeature$$
$$Nominal\ Property \mapsto alternativeFeature$$
$$Ordinal\ Property \mapsto alternativeFeature$$

Ratio properties cannot be transformed directly. Instead, the developer can specify explicit intervals which are interpreted as ordinal values and transformed to alternative features.

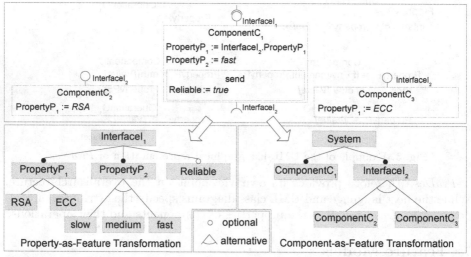

Fig. 4. The Property-as-Feature and the Component-as-Feature transformation

7.2 Component-as-Feature Transformation

Interpreting a component as a feature leads to a feature diagram which shows possible component instantiations. A feature configuration of this model contains the component instances that are created for one component composition. Figure 4 (right) shows an example of such a transformation. The transformation algorithm determines the dependencies between the components and creates an alternative feature for mutually exclusive components.

8 Choosing the Optimal Composition

So far, we have described the property modeling. In this section, we show how to express the utility function and how the optimal composition is determined.

8.1 Expressing Utility

ProDesc strictly separates the property description and the assessment of properties. A general-purpose goal for a single component would be misleading, as it depends on the requirements of the application. Even obvious assessments like *decrease memory consumption* might be undesirable in cases where the application focuses on energy consumption. Therefore, we propose to use a utility function as the central connection between the modeled properties and the actual application. *ProDesc* propagates the requirements through the entire component composition graph. Based on this, the optimal composition is determined.

Listing 6 shows a utility function which minimizes the *size* and enforces *ECC* (line 1). If there are multiple instances with the same *size*, the *speed* is maximized. In line 2, an instance of the component composition which implements the *IKeyValueStore* interface is retrieved. The *this*-reference is needed to resolve the calling instance and the dependencies in the composition.

```
1   UtilityFunction uf = new UtilityFunction().min("size").
2       required("encryption=ECC").maxLowPrio("speed");
3   IKeyValueStore store = model.retrieveInstance(this, "alias",
4       IKeyValueStore.class, uf);
```

Listing 6. Example of a utility function in Java.

Thus, the utility function makes the assumptions, design decision, and the trade-offs of the software developer explicit. Different utility aggregation methods (e.g. weighted sums or products) can be specified easily. *ProDesc* supports the generation of the overall utility function and provides additional analysis such as a *what-if analysis*.

The utility function supports the following eight expressions:

- *requires*   A boolean expression which has to evaluate to *true*.
- *prefers*   A boolean expression which is prefered to evaluate to *true*.
- *min, max*   An ordinal or ratio expression which should be minimized or maximized.
- *minLowPrio,*   An ordinal or ratio expression which should be minimized
  maxLowPrio   or maximized if the decision is not unique.
- *minUntil,*   An ordinal or ratio expression which should be minimized
  maxUntil   or maximized until the specified value is reached.

8.2 Determining the Optimal Composition

Basic Algorithm: The design of *ProDesc* is driven by the goal of evaluating the utility and determining the optimal composition. Figure 5 shows a basic algorithm. The calculation of the utility (Step 2.2) is a recursive evaluation of the utility expression (Section 8.1) and all their referenced properties.

Please note that the algorithm does not keep the whole composition space in memory in Step 2. Instead, an iterator generates compositions sequentially and therefore limits the memory consumption. Additionally, a composition only has to specify variant points which influence the properties of the utility function. Compositional decisions which have no effect on the utility can be ignored.

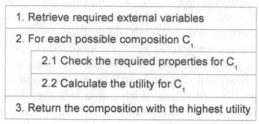

Fig. 5. The basic algorithm to determine the optimal composition

The restricted support of external variables (method invocations without parameters and side effects) is important for a fast execution of the algorithm. In order to decrease the selection overhead, our implementation of the *ProDesc* framework compiles the optimization algorithm for a given property description to Java byte code. The algorithm's time complexity, however, is dominated by the exponential explosion of the composition space.

Parallel Algorithm: A parallelized version of the presented basic algorithm reduces execution time. Assuming that the composition space iterator requires a small fraction α of the total time, we use one thread per core to parallelize step 2.1 and 2.2 with minimal synchronization overhead. Following Amdahl's Law, we expect a speedup s for n cores of $s = \frac{1}{\alpha + \frac{1-\alpha}{n}}$. The efficient parallization of the iterator is more difficult and might be implemented in the future.

Further Optimizations Options: Due to the exploding size of the composition space, further optimizations could become necessary. Preprocessing at compile time might reduce the computation at runtime, e.g. through the use of generated rules. In the area of artificial intelligence, algorithms inspired by statistical physics (simulated annealing) and evolutionary biology (genetic algorithms) execute a nondeterministic search. Therefore, they might not find the optimal composition but significantly reduce search complexity. Similar approaches are applied for web service composition [13].

9　Case Study and Evaluation

In order to evaluate the presented approach, we have implemented the *ProDesc* framework for Java. This includes a development environment as well as a runtime environment. In the following, we discuss properties from a selection of domains, such as the Java class library and networking, and show a concrete modeling example. Additionally, we present performance measurements of the selection algorithm.

9.1   Use Cases

In the following, we exemplarily discuss properties of the Java class library, and of the performance, the security, and the network domain.

Java: The Java class library contains several examples that could benefit from *ProDesc*. The Java collections API provides interfaces for different collections, e.g. *Set*, *List*, and *Map*. The developer has to choose between implementations with different properties. As she might anticipate the concrete requirements (e.g. that the insert performance is important but elements will not be deleted), a utility-based selection is suitable and makes the design decision explicit. Based on this abstraction, it would be even possible to provide more specialized implementations in the library without overwhelming the developer.

The various *Stream*, *Reader*, and *Writer* classes of the *java.io* package are further examples. Currently, the developer chains implementations, e.g. a compressing *GZIPOutputStream* and an encrypting *CipherOutputStream* to achieve the desired functionality. A utility function that specifies that *compression* and *encryption* are required improves the selection and code maintainability.

Performance: *ProDesc* can express the estimated *execution time* of operations as *ratio* or *ordinal* property. Since it is challenging to express the *execution time* quantitatively, the *ordinal* type simplifies property description in most scenarios. Operations which use other operations can express their *execution time* as the sum (sequential execution) or maximum (parallel execution) of the involved operations. These concepts can be used for *space requirements* as well.

Security: Different *encryption schemes* from the security domain can be expressed as *nominal* properties. The properties and parameters of the schemes (e.g. key size) can be expressed as well. *ProDesc* supports fundamental *Boolean* properties like *authentication* or *authorization*. As components can abstract web services, the properties from the different WS-* specifications, e.g. WS-Security and WS-Trust, can be expressed as well.

Network: *ProDesc* can express properties from all layers of the networking domain. For example, *latency* and *bandwidth* are *ratio* or *ordinal* properties; *reliability* and *ordered delivery* are *Boolean* properties. Semantics in the area of distributed systems as *at most once* or database isolation levels can be likewise expressed easily.

9.2   Example

Based on the *ProDesc* description, shown in its graphical notation in Figure 6, a software developer who requires a *KeyValueStore* can express the requirements as a utility function. The selected composition for the utility function

   require(Encryption!=None).require(Persistent).min(put.ExecutionTime)

depends on the environment (the hardware support for RSA) and leads to another composition than

   require(Encryption!=None).min(put.ExecutionTime).

The developer can use the optimal *KeyValueStore* without detailed knowledge about the actual component composition. Newly developed components can be easily described and added to the composition space.

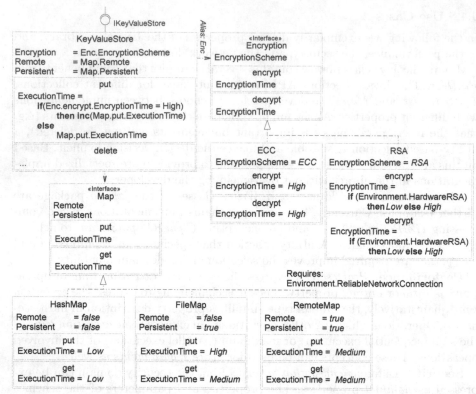

Fig. 6. Graphical notation of an extended example with multiple components

9.3 Performance

We evaluated the performance of the selection algorithm for different numbers of interfaces and components (Table 2). For typical use cases, we expect less than 30 different components, which leads to a composition space size less than 1000. This can be solved in a few milliseconds, which is acceptable for most usage scenarios. The Java collections framework, for example, contains about 22 different collection implementations. As the results show, parallelization improves the execution time as expected by up to 62%.

10   Discussion and Outlook

The presented property description framework *ProDesc* enables the convenient and general-purpose description of properties of components and operations. Its static type system and explicit representation of the compositional variability simplifies the expression of property dependencies. The transformation to feature diagrams allows additional analysis. Utility functions make design decisions more explicit and enforce a clear separation of requirements and properties. The *ProDesc* framework increases the loose coupling of components, because the application benefits from newly added components without any adjustment. All

Table 2. Performance measurements for different numbers of components

	Composition Space Size	20 [12 Comp.]	50 [15 Comp.]	100 [20 Comp.]	1,000 [30 Comp.]	10,000 [40 Comp.]
1 Thread	Iterator	1.1 ms	1.1 ms	1.1 ms	1.2 ms	1.3 ms
	Calculation	4.1 ms	4.2 ms	6.1 ms	11.2 ms	85.1 ms
	Total Time	5.2 ms	5.3 ms	7.2 ms	12.4 ms	86.4 ms
2 Threads	Iterator	1.1 ms	1.1 ms	1.2 ms	1.2 ms	1.3 ms
	Calculation	3.8 ms	4.0 ms	5.6 ms	7.3 ms	51.8 ms
	Total Time	4.9 ms	5.1 ms	6.8 ms	8.5 ms	53.1 ms

these features facilitate a valid property description and an optimal component composition, which leads to improved software. Even though *ProDesc* is developed to support composed components, it is well-suited for single component selections.

Besides further performance optimizations of the selection algorithm, there are multiple areas for future work. Based on the explicit variability model and requirements of the components, automated testing could be extended to the whole composition space. A runtime comparison between monitored properties and the modeled properties might support the property modeling.

The presented approach allows to choose an optimal composition at runtime based on the environment. However, the environment might change as well as the utility function. We believe that the *ProDesc* framework can serve as a foundation of compositional runtime adaptation [23].

Acknowledgments. This work has been funded by the German Research Foundation (DFG) in the Collaborative Research Center (SFB) 1053 "MAKI - Multi-Mechanism Adaptation for the Future Internet".

References

1. Glinz, M.: On Non-Functional Requirements. In: 15th IEEE International Requirements Engineering Conference, RE 2007, pp. 21–26 (October 2007)
2. UML Profile for Modeling Quality of Service and Fault Tolerance Characteristics and Mechanisms Specification (2008)
3. Chung, L., Nixon, B.A., Yu, E.: Non-Functional Requirements in Software Engineering. The Kluwer International Series in Software Engineering. Kluwer Academic (2000)
4. Ludwig, H., Keller, A., Dan, A.: Web Service Level Agreement (WSLA) Language Specification. Technical report, IBM (2007)
5. UML Profile for Schedulability, Performance, and Time Specification (2005)
6. Cysneiros, L.M., Sampaio do Prado Leite, J.C.: Using UML to Reflect Non-functional Requirements. In: CASCON. IBM Press (2001)

7. Espinoza, H., Dubois, H., Gérard, S., Medina, J.L., Petriu, D.C., Woodside, C.M.: Annotating UML models with non-functional properties for quantitative analysis. In: Bruel, J.-M. (ed.) MoDELS 2005. LNCS, vol. 3844, pp. 79–90. Springer, Heidelberg (2006)
8. Morel, B., Alexander, P.: SPARTACAS: Automating Component Reuse and Adaptation. IEEE Transactions on Software Engineering 30(9) (2004)
9. Zinky, J., Bakken, D., Schantz, R.: Architectural Support for Quality of Service for CORBA Objects. Theory and Practice of Object Systems (1997)
10. Eichberg, M., Klose, K., Mitschke, R., Mezini, M.: Component Composition Using Feature Models. In: Grunske, L., Reussner, R., Plasil, F. (eds.) CBSE 2010. LNCS, vol. 6092, pp. 200–215. Springer, Heidelberg (2010)
11. Dustdar, S., Schreiner, W.: A survey on web services composition. Journal of Web and Grid Services 1(1), 1–30 (2005)
12. Tosic, V., Patel, K., Pagurek, B.: WSOL - web service offerings language. In: Bussler, C.J., McIlraith, S.A., Orlowska, M.E., Pernici, B., Yang, J. (eds.) CAiSE 2002 and WES 2002. LNCS, vol. 2512, pp. 57–67. Springer, Heidelberg (2002)
13. Leitner, P., Hummer, W., Dustdar, S.: Cost-Based Optimization of Service Compositions. IEEE Transactions on Services Computing 6(2), 239–251 (2013)
14. Rosenberg, F., Müller, M.B., Leitner, P., Michlmayr, A., Bouguettaya, A., Dustdar, S.: Metaheuristic Optimization of Large-Scale QoS-aware Service Compositions. In: 2010 IEEE International Conference on Services Computing, pp. 97–104 (July 2010)
15. Bencomo, N., Grace, P., Flores, C., Hughes, D., Blair, G.: Genie: Supporting the Model Driven Development of Reflective, Component-based Adaptive Systems. In: Proceedings of the 30th International Conference on Software Engineering, ICSE 2008, pp. 811–814. ACM, New York (2008)
16. Hallsteinsen, S., Geihs, K., Paspallis, N., Eliassen, F., Horn, G., Lorenzo, J., Mamelli, A., Papadopoulos, G.A.: A development framework and methodology for self-adapting applications in ubiquitous computing environments. Journal of Systems and Software 85(12) (2012)
17. Geihs, K., Barone, P., Eliassen, F., Floch, J., Fricke, R., Gjorven, E., Hallsteinsen, S., Horn, G., Khan, M.U., Mamelli, A., Papadopoulos, G.A., Paspallis, N., Reichle, R., Stav, E.: A comprehensive solution for application-level adaptation. Software: Practice and Experience 39(4), 385–422 (2009)
18. OMG Unified Modeling Language, Superstructure (2011)
19. Gamma, E., Helm, R., Johnson, R., Vlissides, J.: Design Patterns. Addison Wesley, Reading (1995)
20. Stevens, S.S.: On the Theory of Scales of Measurement. Science 103(2684) (1946)
21. Kang, K.C., Cohen, S.G., Hess, J.A., Novak, W.E., Peterson, A.S.: Feature-oriented domain analysis (foda) feasibility study. Technical report, Carnegie-Mellon University Software Engineering Institute (November 1990)
22. Benavides, D., Segura, S., Ruiz-Cortés, A.: Automated analysis of feature models 20 years later: A literature review. Information Systems (2010)
23. McKinley, P.K., Sadjadi, S.M., Kasten, E.P., Cheng, B.H.C.: Composing adaptive software. Computer 37(7), 56–64 (2004)

Layered Connectors

Revisiting the Formal Basis of Architectural Connection for Complex Distributed Systems

Amel Bennaceur[1,*] and Valérie Issarny[2]

[1] The Open University, Milton Keynes, UK
[2] Inria Paris-Rocquencourt, France

Abstract. The complex distributed systems of nowadays require the dynamic composition of multiple components, which are autonomous and complex that they can be considered as systems in themselves. These components often use different application protocols and are implemented on top of heterogeneous middleware, which hamper their successful interaction. The explicit and rigorous description and analysis of components interaction is essential in order to enable the dynamic composition of these components. In this paper, we propose a formal approach to represent and reason about interactions between components using *layered connectors*. Layered connectors describe components interaction at both the application and middleware layers and make explicit the role of middleware in the realisation of this interaction. We provide formal semantics of layered connectors and present an approach for the synthesis of layered connectors in order to enable the dynamic composition of highly heterogeneous components. We validate our approach through a case study in the area of collaborative emergency management.

Keywords: Component interaction, Layered connectors, Middleware, Dynamic composition, Architectural mismatches.

1 Introduction

In 1994, Allen and Garlan published their seminal paper on formalising architectural connection [1], for which they received the ICSE most influential paper award 10 years later. The authors put forward a vision, and a supporting theory, that improved our understanding of software architecture by relying on the elegance of formal methods to highlight the relation between the different entities of a software system. These entities are *components*, which are meant to encapsulate computation, and *connectors*, which are meant to encapsulate interaction [22].

At the same time, another vision that focuses on the implementation of distributed systems has received an increasing attention among developers, that of *middleware*. Middleware is a software entity logically placed between the application and the operating system that provides an abstraction that facilitates the

---

* This work was performed when the author was at Inria.

P. Avgeriou and U. Zdun (Eds.): ECSA 2014, LNCS 8627, pp. 283–299, 2014.
© Springer International Publishing Switzerland 2014

communication and coordination of distributed components [25]. Fortunately, the two visions are by no means antagonistic. Indeed, the influence of middleware on the architecture of software systems has long been recognised [21] and it has been admitted that middleware plays an important role in implementing connectors [15,19]. However, this influence has not been explicitly formalised and the relation between connectors and middleware remains ill defined. In this paper, we show how the formalisms used in the literature to describe and analyse architectural connection can be extended to reason about components interaction at the middleware layer. Considering both the software architecture and the middleware perspectives allows us to better understand the digital world surrounding us and also empowers us with methodologies to solve many of the problems inherent to this complex digital world.

One critical problem is that of *architectural mismatches* [9]. Architectural mismatches occur when composing two, or more, software components to form a system and those components make conflicting assumptions about their environment. Components may exhibit disparate data types and operations, and may have distinct business logics, which results in *application heterogeneity*. Components may also rely on different communication standards (e.g., CORBA or SOAP) which define disparate data representation formats and induce different architectural constraints, which results in *middleware heterogeneity*. Architectural mismatches must be solved in order to enable components to be composed successfully. Since connectors model the exchange of information between components and the coordination of their behaviours, solving architectural mismatches often amounts to finding or creating the appropriate connector that enables their successful interaction. This connector acts as a translator that performs the data conversions necessary to solve differences between components' interfaces and as a controller that coordinates components' behaviours. The implementation of this connector should also consider the different middleware solutions used by the components involved.

As the modern digital world become increasingly populated with mobile and ubiquitous computing technology, the scope and boundary of software systems can be uncertain and can change. As a result, the connectors that regulate components interaction cannot be designed and implemented beforehand, but rather synthesised dynamically. Although much work has been carried out on connector synthesis [13], existing solutions have not fully succeeded in keeping pace with the increasing complexity and heterogeneity of modern software, and meeting the demands of runtime support. Solutions either (i) focus on application heterogeneity and generate the connector that enable the composition of the components, based on some domain knowledge, but fail to deploy them on top of heterogeneous middleware [18,24,12,26,17], or (ii) deal with middleware heterogeneity while assuming developers to provide all the data translations and behavioural coordinations that need to be made, as is the case with Enterprise Service Buses (ESB) [10]. At the best of our knowledge, only Starlink [6] attempts to tackle both application and middleware heterogeneity by providing a runtime execution engine that allows developers to deploy translators and controllers dynamically. However, it is the role of the developers to specify these translators and controllers, which might be somehow restrictive considering the domain expertise necessary to provide these specifications.

We argue that architectural mismatches are a cross-cutting concern and solutions thereof must consider both application and middleware heterogeneity. On the one hand, the application layer provides the appropriate level of abstraction to reason about architectural mismatches and synthesise the appropriate connectors based on knowledge specific to the application domain. On the other hand, the middleware layer offers the necessary services for realising the synthesised connector and instantiating the specific data structures and protocols expected by the components at hand. Therefore, we propose a rigorous approach to model and reason about components interaction from the application down to the middleware layer. The objective is to provide a systematic solution for solving architectural mismatches. To this end, we make the following contributions:

- *Formalisation of components interactions at both the application and middleware layers.* We build upon pioneering work on the formalisation of architectural connection by Allen and Garlan [1] to describe the role of middleware in the formal description of connectors. The goal is to identify the mechanisms used by middleware solutions to coordinate the behaviours of components and their influence on components interaction regardless of the specific middleware implementation. We also make explicit the semantics of actions used by the components, using ontologies. The result is the formal definition of *layered connectors* that explicitly describe the coordination and the data exchange between components at both the application and middleware layers. Consequently, we can verify the ability to specify and implement connectors regulating the interaction between highly heterogeneous components.
- *Synthesis of layered connectors in order to solve architectural mismatches.* We define an approach that exploits recent advances in both the fields of software engineering and distributed systems to enable the synthesis of layered connectors in order to allow the composition of heterogeneous components. Note that rather than focusing on a specific technique for translator or controller synthesis, which we tackle elsewhere [4], we show how these techniques can be made to work together in order to solve application and middleware heterogeneity.
- *Experimentation with a real-world scenario.* To validate our approach, we consider one representative application domain, that of emergency management, as illustrated by the GMES[1] initiative. GMES gives a special interest to the support of emergency situations (e.g., forest fire) across different European countries. Indeed, each country defines an emergency management system that encompasses multiple components that are autonomous, designed and implemented independently, and do not obey any central control or administration. Nonetheless, there are incentives for these components to be composed and collaborate in emergency situations. In [2], we used this scenario to illustrates the role of models@runtime is supporting interoperability; in this paper, we specifically focus on the formal specification and

---

[1] Global Monitoring for Environment and Security –http://www.gmes.info/

synthesis of layered connectors to allow the dynamic composition of hetero-geneous components.

The paper is structured as follows. Section 2 describes background work. Section 3 presents the formal semantics of layered connectors and presents our approach for their synthesis. Section 4 illustrate the approach using the emergency management scenario. Finally, Section 5 concludes the paper and discusses future work.

2 Background on Connectors

In this section we introduce the foundational concepts of our approach and explain the relation with existing solutions for the formal description, synthesis, and implementation of connectors.

Formal Basis of Architectural Connection. We consider as our starting point the formalisation of architectural connection introduced by Allen and Garlan [1], which uses process algebra to model the behaviours of components together with their interaction. More specifically, we use FSP (Finite State Processes) [16] based on the follow-up work by Spitznagel and Garlan [24]. The behaviour of a component is modelled using *ports* while a connector is modelled as a set of *roles* and a *glue*. The roles specify the expected behaviours of the interacting components while the glue describes how the behaviours of these components are coordinated. The ports, roles, and glue are specified as FSP processes. The syntax of FSP is summarised in Table 1 while we will assume that the reader has some familiarity with FSP in what follows.

Table 1. FSP syntax overview

Definitions	
set S	Defines a set of action labels
$[i : S]$	Binds the variable i to a value from S
Primitive Processes (P)	
$a \rightarrow P$	Action prefix
$a \rightarrow P \| b \rightarrow P$	Choice
$P(X =' a)$	Parameterised process: P is described using parameter X and modelled for a particular parameter value, $P(a1)$
$P/\{new\_1/old\_1, ...\}$	Relabelling
Composite Processes ($\|P$)	
$P\|Q$	Parallel composition
forall $[i : 1..n]$ $P(i)$	Replicator construct: equivalent to the parallel composition $P(1)\|...\|P(n)$
$a : P$	Process labelling

A component can be attached to a connector only if its port is *behaviourally compatible* with the connector role it is bound to. Behavioural compatibility between a component port and a connector role is based upon the notion of refinement, which implies the inclusion of the traces of the expected behaviour of the component in those of the observed behaviour of the component [1]. In other words, it should be possible to substitute the role process by the port process. Verifying behavioural compatibility allows us to check the presence or absence of architectural mismatches. To solve architectural mismatches, we must find or create a connector whose roles are behavioural compatible with components' ports.

Synthesis of Connectors. It is not always possible to find an existing connector for managing interactions between heterogeneous components and it is difficult and time consuming to design and implement a new connector from scratch [19]. There are several compositional approaches for connector construction by reusing existing connector instances [24]. Nevertheless, with the increasing emphasis on mobility and ubiquity of software systems, there is a growing interest on synthesis of connectors. Rather than expecting a developer to specify how the connector instances should be composed, solutions for connector synthesis seek to analyse the ports of components in order to generate the connector that enables their successful interaction. More specifically, the roles of this connector are assumed to be same as the ports of the components involved, and a glue is synthesised which guarantees that the components interact without errors (e.g., deadlocks) and exchange meaningful data.

Formal methods focus on the behaviour of components, which they rigorously analyse in order to reveal potential inconsistencies, ambiguities, and incompleteness. Once potential execution errors are detected, they can be solved either by eliminating the interactions leading to the errors or by introducing a controller that forces the components to coordinate their behaviours correctly. Only the introduction of a controller can keep the functionality of the system intact by enabling its components to achieve their individual functionalities. Existing solutions for the generation of controllers (e.g., [26,17,12]) often operate on a high-level abstraction, which makes turning the generated controller into an implementation challenging. Moreover, they often assume that the behaviours of the components are described using the same set of actions or the correspondence between the actions of components' interfaces is provided.

Semantic Web technologies allow us to infer the translations necessary to reconcile the differences between components' interfaces. Ontologies play a key role in the Semantic Web by formally representing shared knowledge about a domain of discourse as a set of concepts, and the relationships between these concepts [11]. Ontologies have been extensively used to automate the reasoning about the information exchanged between software components, especially in ubiquitous computing environments, so as to infer the translations necessary to reconcile the differences in the syntax of this information [18]. However, ontology reasoning techniques focus on differences at the application layer alone, assuming the use of the same middleware underneath.

Middleware to Implement Connectors. The implementation of a connector is often based on middleware since middleware provides reusable solutions that facilitate communication and coordination between components [15,19]. However, while components and connectors are conceptually separate, middleware solutions are often invasive since they influence the implementation of the components as well. As a result, components implemented using different middleware solutions are not able to work together. For example, a SOAP client cannot invoke a REST service even if they use the same application data and obey the same business logic. Therefore, other middleware solutions have been proposed in order to reconcile the differences between middleware [10]. However, when these middleware solutions follow different interaction patterns, e.g., shared memory and publish/subscribe, the differences are such that they cannot always be solved [7].

The connector classification introduced by Mehta *et al.* [20] provides a convenient framework that helps selecting the appropriate connectors according to application requirements. It is also used to create a set of guidelines that specify the conditions under which connectors can be composed. However, this set of guidelines are based on some intuitive understanding and rules of thumb and lack the formal basis necessary to make the solution sound and future proof.

The Need for Layered Connectors. In order to enable the dynamic composition of components, it is important to find the right level of abstraction so as to reason about the interaction of these components automatically while keeping enough details to turn the conclusions drawn during the reasoning phase into a concrete artefact. It is difficult to deal with implementation-level differences, as it involves managing many details that, although crucial, make the reasoning very difficult, if not impossible. But an excessive abstraction is also useless as the decision space toward refining the result of the reasoning and turning it toward a concrete solution would be immense. Furthermore, knowledge about the domain in which the components evolve is necessary in order to capture the meaning of the information they exchange.

We introduce the concept of layered connector in order to capture the application-level semantics of components interaction as well as the semantics of the associated middleware solution. Through the concept of layered connectors, we consolidate the techniques and solutions proposed in the fields of software engineering and middleware in order to describe the semantics of components interaction precisely. The goal is to reason about components interaction at a level of abstraction that would allow us to solve architectural mismatches by synthesising the appropriate layered connectors that act as (i) translators by ensuring the meaningful exchange of data between components, (ii) controllers by coordinating the behaviours of the components to ensure the absence of errors in their interaction, and (iii) middleware by enabling the interaction of components across the network so that each component receives the data it expects at the right moment and in the right format.

3   Formal Specification and Synthesis of Layered Connectors

We first show how the semantics of middleware solutions can be formalised using a combination of formal methods and ontologies. Then, we describe how to represent the relation between these middleware solutions and the application implemented on top. Finally, we describe how to synthesis layered connectors in order to enable heterogeneous components to interact successfully.

3.1   Middleware-Layer Connectors

Communication in distributed systems is always based on low-level message passing as offered by the underlying network. Expressing communication through message passing is harder than using primitives proposed by middleware solutions [25]. While middleware solutions and implementations define diverse IDLs and message formats, their interaction protocols follow comparably few interaction patterns, a.k.a., communication paradigms/types [25] or coordination models/paradigms [10]. An interaction pattern defines the rules to coordinate the behaviours of the components. In Mehta *et al.* connector classification [20], these interaction patterns match with the connector types that provide communication and coordination services. Our approach seeks to identify, capture and separate the core of a middleware solution, represented by the interaction pattern it uses, from specific details related to the format of messages. To this end, we introduce, for each interaction pattern, an ontology that models the essential primitives of this interaction pattern, which we use to specify the behaviours expected by the components implemented using a middleware solution based on this interaction pattern as well as how these behaviours are coordinated. A specific middleware solution is modelled using specialisation over the ontology that represents the interaction pattern on which the middleware solution is based. While in [14] we gave initial thoughts about an ontology for middleware solutions, the lack of behaviour description for the interaction patterns made it impossible to make a formal analysis of these solutions as well as to verify transformations between different interaction patterns.

Remote Procedure Call. Remote procedure call (RPC) [5] represents the most common interaction pattern in distributed systems. RPC directly and elegantly supports client/server interactions with servers offering a set of operations through a service interface and clients calling these operations directly as if they were available locally. The interaction is supported by a pairwise exchange of messages from the client to the server and then from the server back to the client, with the first message containing the operation to be executed at the server and associated arguments and the second message containing any result of the operation. To interact according to RPC, the client and the server must agree on the format of the messages they exchange as well as the encoding of the data, which represent the arguments and results, enclosed in these messages.

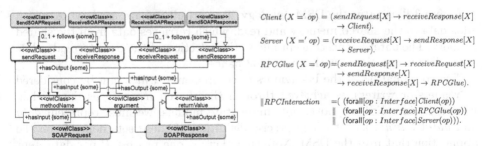

$Client\ (X =' op) = (sendRequest[X] \rightarrow receiveResponse[X]$
$\rightarrow Client).$

$Server\ (X =' op) = (receiveRequest[X] \rightarrow sendResponse[X]$
$\rightarrow Server).$

$RPCGlue\ (X =' op) = (sendRequest[X] \rightarrow receiveRequest[X]$
$\rightarrow sendResponse[X]$
$\rightarrow receiveResponse[X] \rightarrow RPCGlue).$

$\|RPCInteraction\quad =(\ (forall[op : Interface]Client(op))$
$\|\quad (forall[op : Interface]RPCGlue(op))$
$\|\quad (forall[op : Interface]Server(op))).$

Fig. 1. The RPC ontology specialised with SOAP [14]

Fig. 2. RPC behavioural description

Figure 1 depicts the RPC ontology. The invocation of an operation is achieved using sendRequest, which specifies the operation invoked using methodName and the associated argument, possibly followed by a receiveResponse, which includes the operation invoked together with the results returnValue. The server gets the operation call using the receiveRequest primitive. If the result of this operation is not empty, the server returns it using the sendResponse primitive. Figure 1 further shows how the RPC ontology is specialised to describe SOAP. Note that even though SOAP supports the sending and reception of messages independently, it is often used to realise RPC-based interactions, especially in the context of Web Services. In this context, SOAPRequest includes methodName and argument while SOAPResponse encompasses methodName and returnValue.

Figure 2 describes how the behaviours of the client and server are coordinated. The variable *op* defines the operation signature that is made up of the methodName, argument, and returnValue. The set of all operations signatures is denoted by *Interface*. The precise definition of the *Interface* set is specific to the application.

Distributed Shared Memory. Distributed Shared Memory (DSM) provides developers with a familiar abstraction of reading or writing (shared) data structures as if they were in their own local address spaces. A DSM-based middleware enables components to read and write data in the shared memory, regardless of the exact location of the data. Nevertheless, the structure of the shared data is defined at the application layer and the middleware does not provide any guarantee about when data is made available and how long it will reside in the shared memory. In other words, the synchronisation between the readers and writers also needs to be managed at the application layer.

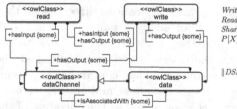

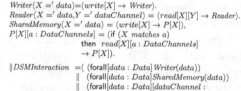

Fig. 3. DSM ontology [14]   **Fig. 4.** DSM behavioural description

Figure 3 illustrates the DSM ontology. Two primitives are used: write, which adds data to the shared memory and read, which retrieves data from the shared memory. The dataChannel concept allows the selection of the data to read, while every data is associated with some dataChannel.

The coordination of the behaviours of components, which can be considered as readers or writers, is achieved through the shared memory as depicted in Figure 4. Since FSP supports only finite state models, we must represent *data* and *dataChannel* as sets. The precise definition of these sets depends on the application that uses the DSM. Note that there is one process P per data item, which deals with the several reads assuming that the data are persistent, i.e. the data can be read infinitely often. The *matches* function indicates whether the data channel specified in the read corresponds to the data managed by P. It is the role of the middleware to implement the *matches* function.

Publish/Subscribe. Many applications require the dissemination of information or items of interest from a large number of producers to a similarly large number of consumers. Publish/subscribe middleware solutions provide an intermediary service, a *broker*, that ensures that information generated by producers is delivered to the consumers that want to receive it. In other words, publish/subscribe middleware solutions (sometimes also called distributed event-based middleware) allow subscribers to register their interest in an event, or a pattern of events, and ensure that they are asynchronously notified of events generated by publishers. The task of the publish/subscribe middleware is to match subscriptions against published events and ensure the correct delivery of event notifications. The expressiveness of publish/subscribe middleware solutions is determined by the type of event subscriptions they support: either subscriptions are made using specific topics (also referred to as subjects) which the events belong to, or based on the content of the event.

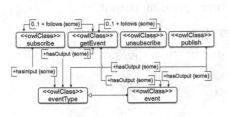

$$Publisher(X =' event) = (publish[X] \rightarrow Publisher).$$
$$Subscriber(X =' event, Y =' eventType)$$
$$= (subscribe[Y] \rightarrow getEvent[Y] \rightarrow Subscriber).$$
$$Broker = P,$$
$$P = (subscribe[eventType : EventTypes]$$
$$\rightarrow MATCH[eventType]$$
$$| publish[Events] \rightarrow P),$$
$$MATCH[eventType : EventTypes]$$
$$= (publish[event : Events] \rightarrow$$
$$\text{if } (event \text{ matches } eventType) \text{ then}$$
$$getEvent[event] \rightarrow MATCH[eventType]$$
$$\text{else } MATCH[eventType]).$$
$$\| PubSubInteraction = ((forall[event : Events]Publisher(event))$$
$$\| (Events : Broker)\{publish/Events.publish\}$$
$$\| (forall[event : Events][eventType :$$
$$EventTypes]Subscriber(event, eventType))).$$

Fig. 5. Publish/Subscribe ontology [14]   **Fig. 6.**   Publish/Subscribe behavioural description

Figure 5 depicts the Publish/Subscribe ontology. The subscribe primitive, which is parameterised by eventType that defines a filter over the set of all possible events, is used to express an interest in a set of events. The events are delivered to subscribers using getEvent. The unsubscribe primitive is used to revoke a subscription. The publish primitive is used to disseminate an event event to interested subscribers.

The behaviours of publishers and subscribers are coordinated using a broker as described in Figure 6. Similarly to DSM, we represent *event* and *eventType* as sets while the precise definition of these sets depends on the application that uses the publish/subscribe middleware. Note that we define several $MATCH$ processes, each of which manages the subscriptions related to one specific event type. The *matches* function indicates whether the published event is of the type managed by the specific $MATCH$ process. The middleware is in charge of implementing this function.

To sum up, there are different interaction patterns that define specific rules to coordinate the behaviours of components. While we present and formalise the interactions patterns most commonly used in the development of middleware solutions, we are aware that some middleware are not represented, e.g., stream-based middleware solutions. The case of streaming solutions is to be explored in future work.

3.2 Bridging the Application and Middleware Layers

Whether expressed as operation calls, data read and write, or event publication, component interactions mainly consists in the production and consumption of information. The production of information in the environment is modelled using provided actions while the consumption from the environment is modelled using required actions, with the understanding that required actions are received from and controlled by the environment, whereas provided actions are emitted and controlled by the component. More specifically, a required action $\langle op, i, o \rangle$, where the symbols $op, i,$ and o are references to concepts in a domain ontology $\mathcal{O}$, represents a consumption of a functionality op by sending the appropriate input data i and receiving the corresponding output data o. The dual provided action[2] $\langle \overline{op}, i, o \rangle$ uses the inputs and produces the corresponding output.

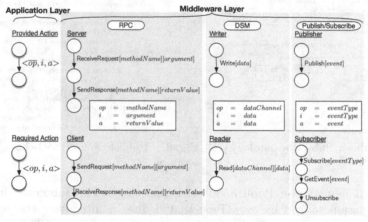

Fig. 7. Mapping interaction patterns primitives to required/provided actions

All middleware solutions, regardless of the interaction pattern they are based on, provide an abstraction that represents required and provided actions. Figure 7, which revisits that in [14], shows how the primitives associated with each interaction pattern, and defined in the associated ontology, are mapped to required/provided actions. In RPC, the server provides an action whose functionality is expressed by the *methodName*, it uses as input *argument* and generates *returnValue*. The associated client requires this same action. In DSM, it is the writer that provides an action while the functionality is enclosed in the data itself as *data* is associated with a specific *dataChannel*. The reader selects *data* available on some *dataChannel*. In publish/subscribe, the publisher provides an

---

[2] We use the overline as a convenient shorthand to denote provided actions.

action whose functionality is represented by the event type. The subscriber selectively consumes these events by subscribing to a specific *eventType*, recalling that each *event* is associated with some *eventType*.

The formalisation of middleware interaction patterns allows us to define, and verify, transformations between required actions implemented using one interaction pattern and provided actions implemented using another interaction pattern. Furthermore, since every middleware solution specialises some interaction pattern, these transformations can also be specialised with the primitives of specific middleware solutions. For example, consider the case of a required action implemented using RPC and a provided action implemented using DSM, i.e. interaction between Writer and Client[3]. We can specify a transformation between Writer and Client that consists in intercepting the request and converting the *methodName* and *arguments* into *dataChannel*. Then, using *dataChannel* to read *data*, which is transformed into the appropriate *returnValue* and sent back as a response to the client. This is formally specified as follows:

$$Client \ (X =' op) \quad = (sendRequest[X] \rightarrow receiveResponse[X] \rightarrow Client).$$
$$Writer(Y =' data) = (write[Y] \rightarrow Writer).$$
$$RPC2DSMGlue(X =' op, Y =' dataChannel, Z =' data) = (receiveRequest[X] \rightarrow translate[X][Y]$$
$$\rightarrow read[Y][Z] \rightarrow translate[Z][X] \rightarrow sendResponse[X] \rightarrow RPC2DSMGlue).$$
$$\| RPC\text{-}DSM \quad = (\ (forall[op : Interface] \ Client(op)) \ \| \ (forall[op : Interface] RPCGlue(op))$$
$$\| \quad (forall[data : Data] \ Writer(data)) \ \| \ (forall[data : Data] SharedMemory(data))$$
$$\| \quad (forall[op : Interface][data : Data][dataChannel : DataChannels]$$
$$RPC2DSMGlue(op, data, dataChannel))).$$

where the sets *Interface*, *Data*, and *DataChannels*, as well as the translations $translate[X][Y]$ and $translate[Z][X]$ performed by *RPC2DSMGlue*, are specific to the application. We can easily verify that $\| RPC\text{-}DSM$ is free from deadlocks. Note that the specification of this connector depends on the translations performed at the application layer. In the subsequent section, we show how these transformations between interaction patterns can help implementing the layered connector that regulates components interaction from the application down to the middleware layer.

3.3 Synthesis of Layered Connectors

To enable the dynamic composition of highly-heterogeneous components, i.e. components featuring differences at both the application and middleware layers, we must synthesise the layered connector that ensures that each component receives the data it expects at the right moment and in the right format. Because of space considerations and because the focus of the paper is on describing an approach to solve architectural mismatches between highly-heterogeneous components rather than on devising a specific approach for translator or controller synthesis, we will present the gist of each synthesis step while details can be found elsewhere [3].

The first step consists in using domain knowledge, which is represented using the adequate domain ontology, to calculate the correspondences between the

---

[3] The description of all other possible cases can be found in [3].

actions required by one component and those provided by the other, that is *translator synthesis* (see Figure 8, ❶). For each correspondence identified, we associate a *matching process* that synchronises with each component and performs the translations necessary to reconcile the differences in the syntax of the input/output data used by each component.

The second step consists in composing the matching processes in a way that guarantees that the components will reach their termination states without errors such as deadlocks, that is *controller synthesis* (see Figure 8, ❷). In [3] we propose an approach that combines constraint programming and ontology reasoning to compute the correspondences between the actions used by the components, which we then use to synthesise the controller.

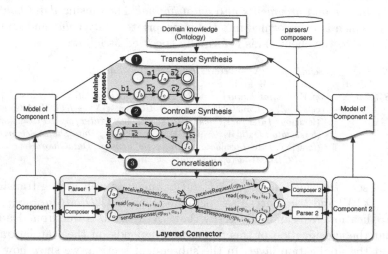

Fig. 8. Overview of our approach to the synthesis of layered connectors

Finally, *concretisation* entails the instantiation of the data structures expected by each component and their delivery according to the interaction pattern defined by the middleware based on which the component is implemented (see Figure 8, ❸). To this end, we rely on the mappings defined in Section 3.2 to refine the matching processes. In addition, the middleware ontologies, which are specialised with the middleware solutions used by each component (see Figure 1), serve specialising the transformations between the different interaction patterns. We also assume that *parsers and composers* dedicated to specific middleware solutions, can be used. A middleware-specific parser intercepts network messages conforming to the associated middleware solution and processes them in order to extract the relevant data. For example, a SOAP parser allows us to access the methodName and argument fields without a need to parse the network messages. In a dual manner, a middleware specific composer creates adequate network messages given the necessary data. For example, a SOAP composer allow us to create an appropriate SOAP response by simply giving the methodName and returnValue. More specifically, we rely on the Starlink framework [6] to generate parsers and composers for different middleware solutions.

4   Layered Connectors in Action: The GMES Case

To provide insight into the benefits of using the synthesis of layered connectors to support the dynamic composition of heterogeneous components, we now present the experiment we conducted in the context of the GMES initiative [8]. GMES is the European Programme for the establishment of a European capacity for Earth Observation. In particular, a special interest is given to the support of emergency situations (e.g., forest fire) across different European countries. GMES makes a strong case of the need for solutions to enable multiple, and most likely heterogeneous, components to collaborate in order to perform the different tasks necessary for decision making. These tasks include collecting weather information, locating the agents involved, and monitoring the environment.

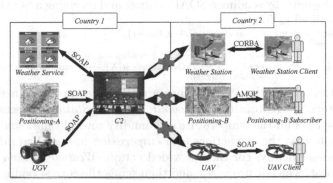

Fig. 9. The GMES example

Figure 9 depicts the case where the emergency system of *Country 1* is composed of a Command and Control centre (*C2*) which takes the necessary decisions for managing the crisis based on the information about the weather provided by the *Weather Service* component, the positions of the various agents in field given by *Positioning-A*, and the video of the operating environment captured by *UGV* (Unmanned Ground Vehicle). The components of *Country 1* use SOAP to communicate. *Country 2* assists *Country 1* by supplying components that provide *C2* with extra information. These components are *Weather Station*, *Positioning-B*, and *UAV* (Unmanned Aerial Vehicle). However, *C2* cannot use these components directly. Indeed, *Weather Station* is implemented using CORBA and provides specific information such as temperature or humidity whereas *Weather Service*, which is used by *C2*, returns all of this information using a single operation. Furthermore, *Positioning-A* is implemented using SOAP whereas *Positioning-B* is implemented using AMQP and hence communicates according to publish/subscribe. Furthermore, *UGV* requires the client to login, then it can move in the four cardinal directions while *UAV* is required to takeoff prior to any operation and to land before logging out. Table 2 summarises the differences between *Country 1* and *Country 2* components. We refer the interested reader to [8] for further details about each component. To enable *C2* to use the components provided by *Country 2*, the appropriate layered connectors

Table 2. Application and middleware differences in GMES cases

Case	Application Differences	Middleware Differences
Weather	one-to-many	SOAP vs. CORBA
Positioning	one-to-one	SOAP vs. AMQP (RPC vs. Pub/Sub)
Vehicle Control	extra actions	—

have to be synthesised. For space considerations we only describe the Weather case in the following; the detailed description of all the cases can be found in [3].

The interface of *C2* includes three required actions *login*, *getWeather*, and *logout*. *C2* first logs in, invokes *getWeather* several times, and finally logs out. Since *C2* interacts using SOAP, then each of the required actions is realised by invoking the appropriate operation *op*, which belongs to the set {*login*, *getWeather*, *logout*}, by sending a SOAP request and receiving a SOAP response, which is formalised as follows:

set $C2\_weather\_actions = \{login, getWeather, logout\}$
$C2\_weather\_role \quad = (req.login \rightarrow P1),$
$P1 \quad = (req.getWeather \rightarrow P1 \mid req.logout \rightarrow C2\_weather\_role).$
$SOAPClient \ (X =' op) = (req.[X] \rightarrow sendSOAPRequest[X] \rightarrow receiveSOAPResponse[X]$
$\rightarrow SOAPClient).$

The interface of *Weather Station* encompasses three provided actions *login* *getTemperature*, *getHumidity*, and *logout*. *Weather Station* expects clients to login first, then ask for the temperature or humidity several times, and log out to terminate. Note that the two actions *getTemperature* and *getHumidity* can be performed independently. For each provided action, *Weather Station* receives a CORBA request, which it processes, and then sends the corresponding response:

set $WeatherStation\_actions = \{login, getTemperature, getHumidity, logout\}$
$WeatherStation\_role \quad = (prov.login \rightarrow P2),$
$P2 \quad = (\ prov.getTemperature \rightarrow P2 \mid prov.getHumidity \rightarrow P2$
$\mid \quad prov.logout \rightarrow WeatherStation\_role).$
$CORBAServer \ (X =' op) = (prov.[X] \rightarrow receiveCORBARequest[X]$
$\rightarrow sendCORBAResponse[X] \rightarrow CORBAServer).$

The first step is to compute the necessary translations between the actions of *C2* and *Weather Station* given some knowledge about the application domain represented by the GMES ontology [8]. Beside the semantic correspondences between the *login* and *logout* required and provided actions, there is also one between the *getWeather* action required by *C2* and the sequence of actions *getTemperature* and *getHumidity* provided by *Weather Station*. Once the correspondence identified, we must compute the associated translation functions. Therefore, in addition to the domain ontology, we also use XML schema matching techniques to identify related elements between the schema of the input/output data of the actions [23].

Each correspondence is associated with a matching process. Note though that *getWeather* may be translated into *getTemperature* followed by *getHumidity* or *getHumidity* followed by *getTemperature*, which results in some ambiguity with which the controller must deal by selecting one of the matching processes. This selection may be motivated by some non-functional property or the length of the sequences of actions. In our example, let us assume that the selected matching process translates the *getWeather* action required by *C2* into the sequence of *getTemperature* followed by *getHumidity* provided by *Weather Station*. In addition, the controller must compose the matching processes in the right order, i.e. first matching the *login* actions, then *getWeather* with *getTemperature* followed by *getHumidity*, and finally the *logout* actions. The resulting controller is as follows:

$$
\begin{aligned}
Controller &= (req.login \rightarrow prov.login \rightarrow P), \\
P &= (req.getWeather \rightarrow prov.getTemperature \rightarrow prov.getHumidity \rightarrow P \\
&\quad | \ req.logout \rightarrow prov.logout \rightarrow Mediator).
\end{aligned}
$$

Finally, the concretisation step involves dealing with differences between the middleware solutions used to implement the two components. Let *SOAPImpl* and *CORBAImpl* denote the middleware-layer connectors associated with the SOAP and CORBA middleware solutions respectively, each of which is associated with dedicated parsers and composers. Even though the format of the requests/responses is different, the interaction pattern is the same and can be transformed into primitives from the RPC ontology. The resulting layered connector (|| *WeatherSystem*) is described as follows:

$$
\begin{aligned}
\| WeatherSystem = &(C2\_weather\_role \ \| \ WeatherService\_role \ \| \ Controller \\
\| \ &(forall[op : C2\_weather\_actions] \ SOAPImpl(op)) \\
&/\{sendSOAPRequest/sendRequest, \ receiveSOAPResponse/receiveResponse\} \\
\| \ &(forall[op : WeatherStation\_actions] \ CORBAImpl(op)) \\
&/\{receiveCORBARequest/receiveRequest, \ sendCORBAResponse/sendResponse\}).
\end{aligned}
$$

We can verify (using LTSA) that the synthesised layered connector is free from deadlocks.

To evaluate the performance of our approach, we measured the time necessary to execute each step of the synthesis. The results are reported in Table 3. While the controller synthesis, which is performed using the approach described in [3] and involves FSP behavioural analysis, takes few milliseconds to execute, the translator synthesis and the concretisation necessitates around $1s$ as they also requires dealing with XML and ontology processing. Still, the overall time for the synthesis of layered connectors remains less than $2s$. Furthermore, the synthesis is performed only once and is definitely faster than hand-coding the layered connector or even specifying it. In summary, the synthesis of layered connectors allows us to deal with architectural mismatches by reconciling the differences in the implementations of components at both the application and middleware layers.

Table 3. Processing time (in ms) for each synthesis step in the GMES scenario

Case	Weather	Positioning	Vehicle Control
Translator Synthesis	10031	9709	10256
Controller Synthesis	2	<1	7
Concretisation	809	903	465

5   Conclusion and Future Work

Enabling the dynamic composition of software components and solving their potential architectural mismatches is a complex challenge that can only be solved by appropriately combining different techniques and perspectives. In this paper, we consider both the software architecture and the middleware perspectives and propose an approach that brings together and enhances the solutions that seek to solve architectural mismatches from these perspectives. Our core contribution stems for the principled and rigorous approach to reason about components interaction using layered connectors, which formally describe components interaction at both the application and middleware layers. In addition, the systematic approach for synthesising layered connectors lays firm foundations for supporting dynamic composition in an increasingly heterogeneous world. The main idea is to first extract the data translations using knowledge about the application domain and to synthesise the appropriate controller that enables the components to interact successfully, then to refine this controller by taking into account the characteristics of the middleware solutions underneath.

As part of our future work, we would like to study the impact of errors or incompleteness in the specifications of the components or the domain ontology in the synthesis of layered connectors. This is even more relevant when the specifications are inferred using learning techniques. Therefore, we have to keep monitoring the components and their environment to detect changes and update the connectors accordingly. In this context, the incremental re-synthesis of layered connectors would allow us to respond efficiently to changes in the individual components or in the ontology. Another direction is to consider the security aspect, both on how enabling composition may induce unanticipated threats, but also how the increased ability to compose components dynamically may help securing software systems by rapidly reacting to newly discovered threats.

Acknowledgments. We acknowledge ERC Advanced Grant no. 291652 (ASAP).

References

1. Allen, R., Garlan, D.: Formalizing architectural connection. In: Proc. of ICSE (1994)
2. Bencomo, N., Bennaceur, A., Grace, P., Blair, G., Issarny, V.: The role of models@run.time in supporting on-the-fly interoperability. Computing (2013)
3. Bennaceur, A.: Dynamic Synthesis of Mediators in Ubiquitous Environments. Ph.D. thesis, Université Paris VI (2013), http://hal.inria.fr/tel-00849402/en
4. Bennaceur, A., Chilton, C., Isberner, M., Jonsson, B.: Automated mediator synthesis: Combining Behavioural and Ontological Reasoning. In: Hierons, R.M., Merayo, M.G., Bravetti, M. (eds.) SEFM 2013. LNCS, vol. SEFM, pp. 274–288. Springer, Heidelberg (2013)
5. Birrell, A., Nelson, B.J.: Implementing remote procedure calls. ACM Trans. Computing System (1984)
6. Bromberg, Y.-D., Grace, P., Réveillère, L., Blair, G.S.: Bridging the interoperability gap: Overcoming combined application and middleware heterogeneity. In: Kon, F., Kermarrec, A.-M. (eds.) Middleware 2011. LNCS, vol. 7049, pp. 390–409. Springer, Heidelberg (2011)
7. Ceriotti, M., Murphy, A.L., Picco, G.P.: Data sharing vs. message passing: synergy or incompatibility?: an implementation-driven case study. In: Proc. of SAC (2008)

8. Connect Consortium: Connect Deliverable D6.4: Assessment report: Experimenting with CONNECT in Systems of Systems, and Mobile Environments. FET IP Connect EU project (2012), http://hal.inria.fr/hal-00793920
9. Garlan, D., Allen, R., Ockerbloom, J.: Architectural mismatch or why it's hard to build systems out of existing parts. In: Proc. of ICSE (1995)
10. Georgantas, N., Bouloukakis, G., Beauche, S., Issarny, V.: Service-oriented distributed applications in the future internet: The case for interaction paradigm interoperability. In: Lau, K.-K., Lamersdorf, W., Pimentel, E. (eds.) ESOCC 2013. LNCS, vol. 8135, pp. 134–148. Springer, Heidelberg (2013)
11. Gruber, T.R.: A translation approach to portable ontology specifications. Knowledge Acquisition (1993)
12. Inverardi, P., Tivoli, M.: Automatic synthesis of modular connectors via composition of protocol mediation patterns. In: Proc. of ICSE (2013)
13. Issarny, V., Bennaceur, A.: Composing distributed systems: Overcoming the interoperability challenge. In: Giachino, E., Hähnle, R., de Boer, F.S., Bonsangue, M.M. (eds.) FMCO 2012. LNCS, vol. 7866, pp. 168–196. Springer, Heidelberg (2013)
14. Issarny, V., Bennaceur, A., Bromberg, Y.-D.: Middleware-layer connector synthesis: Beyond state of the art in middleware interoperability. In: Bernardo, M., Issarny, V. (eds.) SFM 2011. LNCS, vol. 6659, pp. 217–255. Springer, Heidelberg (2011)
15. Issarny, V., Kloukinas, C., Zarras, A.: Systematic aid for developing middleware architectures. Commun. ACM (2002)
16. Magee, J., Kramer, J.: Concurrency: State models and Java programs. Wiley (2006)
17. Mateescu, R., Poizat, P., Salaün, G.: Adaptation of service protocols using process algebra and on-the-fly reduction techniques. IEEE Trans. Software Eng. (2012)
18. McIlraith, S.A., Son, T.C., Zeng, H.: Semantic web services. IEEE Intelligent Systems (2001)
19. Medvidovic, N., Dashofy, E., Taylor, R.: The role of middleware in architecture-based software development. Int. Journal of Soft. Eng. and Knowledge Eng. (2003)
20. Mehta, N.R., Medvidovic, N., Phadke, S.: Towards a taxonomy of software connectors. In: Proc. of ICSE (2000)
21. Nitto, E.D., Rosenblum, D.S.: Exploiting adls to specify architectural styles induced by middleware infrastructures. In: Proc. of ICSE (1999)
22. Shaw, M.: Procedure calls are the assembly language of software interconnection. In: Proc. of ICSE Workshop on Studies of Software Design (1993)
23. Shvaiko, P., Euzenat, J.: A survey of schema-based matching approaches. In: Spaccapietra, S. (ed.) Journal on Data Semantics IV. LNCS, vol. 3730, pp. 146–171. Springer, Heidelberg (2005)
24. Spitznagel, B., Garlan, D.: A compositional formalization of connector wrappers. In: Proc. of ICSE (2003)
25. Tanenbaum, A., Van Steen, M.: Distributed systems: principles and paradigms. Prentice Hall (2006)
26. Yellin, D.M., Strom, R.E.: Protocol specifications and component adaptors. ACM TOPLAS (1997)

Effort Estimation for Architectural Refactoring to Introduce Module Isolation

Fatih Öztürk[1], Erdem Sarılı[1], Hasan Sözer[2], and Barış Aktemur[2]

[1] Vestel Electronics, Manisa, Turkey
{fatih.ozturk,erdem.sarili}@vestel.com.tr
[2] Department of Computer Science, Ozyegin University, Istanbul, Turkey
{hasan.sozer,baris.aktemur}@ozyegin.edu.tr

Abstract. The decomposition of software architecture into modular units is driven by both functional and quality concerns. Dependability and security are among quality concerns that require a software to be decomposed into separate units isolated from each other. However, it appears that this decomposition is usually not aligned with the decomposition based on functional concerns. As a result, introducing module isolation forced by quality attributes, while preserving the existing decomposition, is not trivial and requires a substantial refactoring effort. In this work, we introduce an approach and a toolset to predict this effort prior to refactoring activities. As such, a selection can be made among potential decomposition alternatives based on quantitative estimations. These estimations are obtained from scalable analysis of module dependencies based on a graph database and reusable query templates. We discuss our experiences and evaluate our approach on a code base used in a commercial Digital TV and Set-top Box software.

Keywords: Software architecture, reverse engineering, refactoring, module isolation, effort estimation, dependability, security.

1 Introduction

Modularity is a key principle in software architecture design [12]. Decomposing the system into separate, modular units is driven by functional concerns and a set of relevant quality concerns such as dependability and security [2]. These quality concerns usually require that certain modules are decomposed and isolated from each other. For instance, distrusted modules must be isolated from the rest of the system to increase security. This is usually achieved by sandboxing [15] and placing each module into its own address space. Without such a fault isolation, errors can propagate among the modules of the system.

Isolation is usually supported by the operating system (e.g., process isolation [9]) or a middleware (e.g., encapsulation of Enterprise Java Bean objects [4]). Regardless of the underlying infrastructure, the application software architecture must be decomposed so that certain parts of the system can be quarantined. However, it appears that the required decomposition for module isolation

P. Avgeriou and U. Zdun (Eds.): ECSA 2014, LNCS 8627, pp. 300–307, 2014.

is usually not aligned with the decomposition based on functional concerns. The redesign and implementation of the whole system is likely to be an impractical approach for large-scale legacy systems. On the other hand, refactoring the existing systems is not trivial either; it requires that the interactions of a module with all the other parts of the system are captured and appropriately isolated [13].

In this work, we propose an approach and a toolset for predicting the refactoring effort for decomposition and implementation of software architecture for module isolation. As such, a selection can be made among potential decomposition alternatives based on quantitative estimations. In our approach, dependencies among the software modules are captured with a compiler frontend and stored in a graph database. These dependencies are queried based on a set of reusable query templates. Queries are instantiated according to the evaluated decomposition alternative. The novelty of our work is to facilitate the use of scalable and interactive architectural queries. We discuss our experiences in the application and evaluation of our approach by introducing module isolation to a set of modules taking part in a commercial Digital TV (DTV) and Set-top Box (STB) software architecture. We were able to estimate the required refactoring effort for a large code base with 85% accuracy on the average.

The remainder of this paper is organized as follows. Section 2 presents the industrial case study and a motivating example. We introduce our approach in Section 3. The evaluation of the approach is presented in Section 4. Related studies are summarized in Section 5. Finally, in Section 6, we provide our conclusions and discuss future work directions.

2   Industrial Case Study: DTV/STB Software

In this section, we introduce an industrial case study and a running example to be used in the rest of the paper. We investigated a software system being developed and maintained by Vestel[1], which manufactures DTV and STB systems. Conditional access (CA) system providers are among the customers of the company. These customers have various requirements that are subject to certification tests. One of these requirements is module isolation. Due to many different external interfaces such as USB and Ethernet, DTV and STB systems are exposed to an increasing number of dependability and security threats. Therefore, CA system providers require that certain modules of the system are isolated from each other by running them on different processes.

Vestel has a legacy code base that includes approximately 8M lines of code (LOC) in C/C++ excluding the chipset drivers (33M LOC including the drivers). The overall code base is composed of 4 layers: *i) Driver*: includes the platform-related software that is mostly in the kernel space; *ii) Platform Integration Layer*: provides abstraction for the functions provided by the Driver layer; *iii) Middleware*: implements the main business logic; *iv) Application*: implements the user interface. Module isolation requirements usually affect the 3rd and the 4th layers.

---

[1] http://www.vestel.com.tr

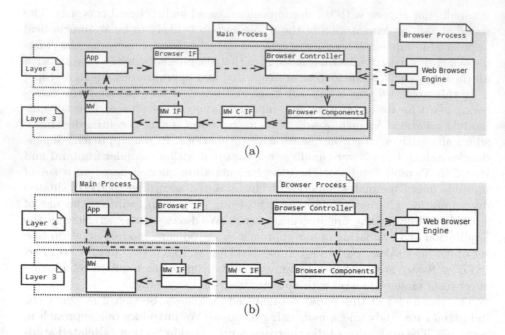

Fig. 1. Decomposition alternatives for the isolation of the web browser engine

For instance, it was required by a CA system provider[2] that the web browser functionality should be isolated from the rest of the system. To satisfy this requirement, the corresponding module was planned to be isolated in a separate process as depicted in a module view of the software architecture in Figure 1(a). Refactoring a system for process isolation is not trivial for large code bases. It requires that the interactions of the isolated module(s) with all the other parts of the system are captured. All the function calls and direct accesses to shared data must be redirected through inter-process communication (IPC). As a result, additional glue layers and wrappers have to be developed [13].

There are usually many decomposition alternatives that satisfy a module isolation requirement. The implementation of these alternatives require different amounts of effort based on the module inter-dependencies. In fact, it was figured out later in the architectural refactoring phase that the decomposition depicted in Figure 1(b) was a better alternative in terms of effort. The development team abondoned the attempts to do decomposition given in Figure 1(a), resulting in wasted time and man-hours, and instead focused on Figure 1(b). In the following section, we introduce our approach for estimating the refactoring effort to evaluate various decomposition alternatives with automated and scalable analysis.

---

[2] Customer identity is undisclosed due to confidentiality agreements.

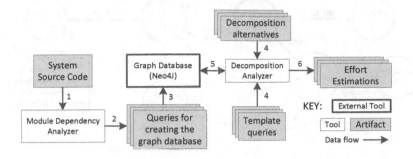

Fig. 2. The overall approach

3   The Approach

The overall approach is depicted in Figure 2. First, a static code analysis, called the *Module Dependency Analyzer*, is applied to the system source code to identify module inter-dependencies. The analyzer is implemented as an LLVM [10] compiler pass that runs on intermediate level code. (Therefore, the pass is runnable on software written in any programming language provided that there is an LLVM front-end that translates the code to LLVM Intermediate Representation. In our case study, the code base is written in C/C++.) The output of the module dependency analyzer is a set of Cypher queries that build a graph database with Neo4J [8] (step 2). Then, these queries are executed to create a graph representation of all the identified module inter-dependencies (step 3). In our case, two modules shown in Figure 1 were analyzed. These modules are 20K LOC in total. The size of the generated queries was 76K LOC. It took around 3.5 hours to complete the execution of all the queries on a desktop computer. The graph had 25K nodes and 60K edges. A small, representative example is depicted in Figure 3. The graph database is built only once per code base. Then, it can be utilized many times to evaluate various decomposition alternatives (step 5). *Decomposition Analyzer* takes decomposition alternatives and template Cypher queries [8] as input (step 4). Each decomposition alternative specifies the set of modules that are separated from each other. Figure 1 depicts only the top level modules, each of which comprises many more modules. In our case study, we specified 10 module interfaces that are separated as a result of implementing the decomposition alternative depicted in Figure 1(b). Template queries are instantiated based on the evaluated decomposition alternatives. They also have coefficients to be adjusted based on the implementation. The execution of the queries outputs effort estimations (step 6). In our case study, executing the queries to evaluate 10 module interfaces took around 10 minutes.

We calculate the effort in terms of LOC to be written for glue layers and wrappers [13] required for realizing a decomposition alternative. These LOC mainly comprises IPC calls, callback handlers, and data (de)serialization implemented

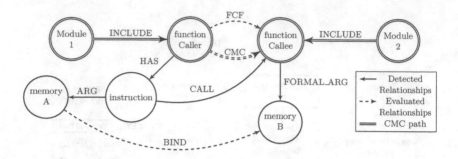

Fig. 3. Representation of module inter-dependencies as nodes and edges

for coupled modules that are isolated in different processes. Hence, the effort is related to the amount of and the type of coupling among the isolated module interfaces. The queries that are instantiated for evaluation first detect function calls among such interfaces. Then, parameter bindings between formal and actual parametres are analyzed. For every call to be redirected, complexity of parameters and return value is calculated based on the use of pointers and nesting level of classes and structures. Finally, effort required for each cross-modular function call is summed up to represent total cost required for isolation of the given two modules. Figure 3 represents a simple parameter binding between the function *Caller* defined in *Module 1* and the function *Callee* defined in *Module 2*. Here *FCF* represents function call, *CMC* represents cross-modular function call, and *BIND* represents parameter binding between two memory locations.

A sample truncated query for evaluating module dependency is given in Listing 1. Hereby, *env.module2* and *env.module1* are parameters that define the separated modules (Line 5). The coefficient *SIMPLE_PARAM* (Line 9) defines the unit effort to handle a simple function argument. Nested argument structures are captured and the corresponding unit effort is calculated separately (Line 12).

The utilization of a graph database and reusable template queries provides scalability and genericity. Our analysis addresses the amount of coupling at the module view level. However, the approach can also be applied to different types of architectural views [5] by using appropriate set of template queries. In our case, the toolset can provide an effort estimation based on the decomposition structure and coefficients for unit costs. The coefficients can be adjusted based on the underlying isolation framework.

4   Evaluation and Discussion

We examined the implementation depicted in Figure 1(b) for the 10 module interfaces that are separated. We manually measured the real effort required for the realization of this decomposition in terms of *effective LOC* [6]. We also applied our approach on the previous version of the source code, before the

```
1  . . .
2  match (x:folder)-[:INCLUDE*1..]
3     ->(caller:function)-[:FCF]->(callee:function)
4     <-[:INCLUDE*1..]-(y:file) where
5     x.name = env.module2 and y.name = env.module1
6     create unique
7     caller-[:CMC{param_point:0, return_point:0}]->callee;
8  . . .
9  match a-[r: BIND]->b set r.point = SIMPLE_PARAM;
10 match b<-[bind:BIND]-a-[LOAD*0..1]->()-[CAST*0..1]
11    ->()-[:IS_A]->(strct) with a,b,bind,strct
12    set bind.point = strct.point;
13 . . .
```

Listing 1. A truncated query template for dependency evaluation

decomposition is implemented. We obtained estimations regarding the separation of the 10 module interfaces. We compared the estimated effort and measured effort in terms of the *relative error* [1] measure. Results are listed in Table 1. Estimations are 85% accurate per interface on the average. (We think that the per-interface average of relative error is a better indicator of accuracy than the relative error on the *overall effort*, which is much smaller: 1359 vs. 1306 ⇒ 4% error.) In fact, if we do not consider the two exceptional interfaces, H and I, the accuracy is 91%. In the following, we discuss the reasons for estimation errors regarding these interfaces.

The measured effort is much less than the estimated effort for *Interface H*. This interface is generally composed of getter functions that return primitive C

Table 1. Comparison of measured and estimated effort

Interface	Measured Effort	Estimated Effort	Relative Error
A	128	133	0.04
B	94	78	0.17
C	175	189	0.08
D	102	88	0.14
E	80	66	0.17
F	321	302	0.06
G	65	68	0.05
H	165	211	0.28
I	125	70	0.44
J	104	101	0.03
Total	1359	1306	-
Average	-	-	0.15

types. Serialization and extraction of the return values are identical for several functions. Therefore, such identical operations are implemented in a helper function, which reduce the effort to a large extent. On the other hand, the estimated effort is much less than the measured effort for *Interface I*, because this interface employs complex C structs with callback function pointers. The use of these callback functions are scattered among many modules. Hence, the isolation of *Interface I* required extra effort for transferring these functions through IPC.

5   Related Work

Vespucci tool [11] captures structural dependencies in multiple complementary views called *slices*. Each slice captures different types of dependencies to be analyzed separately. In this work, we capture all the dependencies in a graph database and query all types of dependencies regarding a certain part of the system, which is subject to refactoring for module isolation.

The FLORA framework [13] comprises a set of tools to estimate the performance overhead introduced by module isolation and optimize the software architecture decomposition [14]. The estimation is based on a dynamic analysis that collects statistics about the frequency of performed function calls and the data access profile of the system. In this work, we aim at estimating the maintenance effort for introducing module isolation. As such, we utilize static analysis. We also utilize a graph database and a declarative graph query language to achieve scalability [8].

Micro-kernel architectures [7] and operating systems with *sealed processes* [9] have been introduced for flexible multiprocessing support and better isolation to improve dependability and safety. To be able to exploit the multiprocessing support for isolation, the application software must be partitioned to be run on multiple processes. Our approach supports such a refactoring and predicts the re-engineering effort for making use of the multiprocessing support.

There have been also other approaches [3, 4] to isolate software components from each other. However, they do not consider the restructuring and partitioning of legacy software to introduce this isolation.

6   Conclusion and Future Work

Module isolation can be necessary to satisfy several quality concerns. However, it appears that the required decomposition for module isolation is usually not aligned with the decomposition based on functional concerns. Therefore, the realization of this decomposition requires substantial maintenance effort. We have introduced an integrated toolset that predicts the refactoring effort to introduce module isolation by preserving the existing structure. We have illustrated our approach in the context of an industrial case study to introduce module isolation to a set of modules in a large code base. We obtained accurate estimations of the refactoring effort. As such, our approach proved to be practical for large-scale systems to support module isolation in software architectures.

As future work, we are planning to utilize our observations summarized in Section 4 to improve the accuracy of our estimations. We also plan to perform additional case studies.

Acknowledgements. We thank the software developers and managers at Vestel Electronics for sharing their code base with us and supporting our analysis.

References

1. Alsmadi, I., Nuser, M.: Evaluation of cost estimation metrics: Towards a unified terminology. Journal of Computing and Information Technology 21(1), 23–34 (2013)
2. Avizienis, A., Laprie, J.C., Randell, B., Landwehr, C.: Basic concepts and taxonomy of dependable and secure computing. IEEE Transactions on Dependable and Secure Computing 1(1), 11–33 (2004)
3. Buskens, R., Gonzalez, O.: Model-centric development of highly available software systems. In: de Lemos, R., Gacek, C., Romanovsky, A. (eds.) Architecting Dependable Systems IV. LNCS, vol. 4615, pp. 163–187. Springer, Heidelberg (2007)
4. Candea, G., Fox, A.: Crash-only software. In: 9th Workshop on Hot Topics in Operating Systems (HotOS), pp. 67–72. USENIX Assoc., Berkeley (2003)
5. Clements, P.C., Bachmann, F., Bass, L., Garlan, D., Ivers, J., Little, R., Merson, P., Nord, R., Stafford, J.A.: Documenting Software Architectures: Views and Beyond, 2nd edn. Addison-Wesley (2010)
6. Fenton, N., Pfleeger, S.: Software Metrics: A Rigorous and Practical Approach, 2nd edn. Thomson Learning Inc. (2002)
7. Herder, J.N., Bos, H., Gras, B., Homburg, P., Tanenbaum, A.S.: Failure resilience for device drivers. In: 37th IEEE/IFIP International Conference on Dependable Systems and Networks, Edinburgh, UK, pp. 41–50 (2007)
8. Holzschuher, F., Peinl, R.: Performance of Graph Query Languages: Comparison of Cypher, Gremlin and Native Access in Neo4J. In: EDBT/ICDT 2013 Workshops, pp. 195–204. ACM, New York (2013)
9. Hunt, G., Aiken, M., Fähndrich, M., Hawblitzel, C., Hodson, O., Larus, J., Levi, S., Steensgaard, B., Tarditi, D., Wobber, T.: Sealing OS processes to improve dependability and safety. SIGOPS Oper. Syst. Rev. 41(3), 341–354 (2007)
10. Lattner, C., Adve, V.: LLVM: A compilation framework for lifelong program analysis & transformation. In: Int. Symposium on Code Generation and Optimization (CGO), pp. 75–87. IEEE Computer Society, San Jose (2004)
11. Mitschke, R., Eichberg, M., Mezini, M., Garcia, A., Macia, I.: Modular specification and checking of structural dependencies. In: 12th Int. Conference on Aspect-oriented Software Development (AOSD), pp. 85–96. ACM, New York (2013)
12. Parnas, D.L.: On the criteria to be used in decomposing systems into modules. Communications of the ACM 15(12), 1053–1058 (1972)
13. Sozer, H., Tekinerdogan, B., Aksit, M.: Flora: A framework for decomposing software architecture to introduce local recovery. Software: Practice and Experience 39(10), 869–889 (2009)
14. Sozer, H., Tekinerdogan, B., Aksit, M.: Optimizing decomposition of software architecture for local recovery. Software Quality Journal 21(2), 203–240 (2013)
15. Wahbe, R., Lucco, S., Anderson, T., Graham, S.L.: Efficient software-based fault isolation. SIGOPS Operating Systems Review 27(5), 203–216 (1993)

Interoperability-Related Architectural Problems and Solutions in Information Systems: A Scoping Study

Hadil Abukwaik, Davide Taibi, and Dieter Rombach

University of Kaiserslautern
Gottlieb-Daimler-Straße 47
67663 Kaiserslautern, Germany
{abukwaik,taibi,rombach}@cs.uni-kl.de

Abstract. [*Context*] With the increasing industrial demands for seamless exchange of data and services among information systems, architectural solutions are a promising research direction which supports high levels of interoperability at early development stages. [*Objectives*] This research aims at identifying the architectural problems and before-release solutions of interoperability on its different levels in information systems, and exploring the interoperability metrics and research methods used to evaluate identified solutions. [*Methods*] We performed a scoping study in five digital libraries and descriptively analyzed the results of the selected studies. [*Results*] From the 22 studies included, we extracted a number of architectural interoperability problems on the technical, syntactical, semantic, and pragmatic levels. Many problems are caused by systems' heterogeneity on data representation, meaning or context. The identified solutions include standards, ontologies, wrappers, or mediators. Evaluation methods to validate solutions mostly included toy examples rather than empirical studies. [*Conclusions*] Progress has been made in the software architecture research area to solve interoperability problems. Nevertheless, more researches need to be spent on solutions for the higher levels of interoperability accompanied with proper empirical evaluation for their effectiveness and usefulness.

Keywords: Software interoperability, software architecture, information systems, scoping study.

1 Introduction

Interoperability among software systems endows them with the capability to meaningfully communicate and exchange information and services [1, 2]. However, interoperability faces many challenges, e.g., different communication protocols, incompatible architectures, heterogeneous data models, ambiguous meaning of information exchanged, and more. In response, several solution approaches have been proposed. On one hand, integration solutions that focus on solving interoperability problems after they happen are the most suggested ones. However, adopting any of these integration solutions to overcome systems' heterogeneity is expensive and requires significant effort [3]. On the other hand, before-release architectural solutions are proposed to build interoperability potentials in software systems with reduced cost. These architectural design

P. Avgeriou and U. Zdun (Eds.): ECSA 2014, LNCS 8627, pp. 308–323, 2014.

decisions have an immediate impact on systems' components and connectors that can be the main obstacle impeding interoperability [4]. Such a promise from the architectural solutions makes them a powerful base for interoperability and hence they are the main interest of this paper.

With the increasing complexity of information systems (ISs) and their interoperability requirements, software architects need to choose from existing solutions that support before-release interoperability. However, this task becomes a challenge with the proliferated architectural solutions that are scattered across research fields [5] (such as component-based software, open systems, enterprise application, etc.) with focus on multiple interoperability issues (such as syntax, structure, semantics, etc.). Also, having no evaluation results for proposed solutions is a significant issue which questions their effectiveness and real value gained when adopting these solutions [6].

In the light of the big magnitude and high business value of interoperability among ISs [7], it is important to alleviate the aforementioned task complexity and to support software architects in choosing appropriate interoperability solutions. Hence, in this research we performed a systematic scoping study in order to (1) identify the state-of-the-art of interoperability architectural problems and before-release solutions in ISs, and to (2) explore the state of evidence on the quality of the identified solutions. This study helps practitioners to understand the state of research on interoperability-related architectural approaches and to consider adopting them. Also, the findings provide researchers with insights regarding future research topics to cover the identified gaps.

The rest of this paper is structured as follows. Section 2 introduces a background, Section 3 overviews related work to our study and Section 4 outlines the design of the scoping study. Section 5 reports the results and Section 6 discusses their implications. While Section 7 presents the study limitations, Section 8 summarizes the conclusions.

2   Interoperability Levels - Background

Multiple classification models have been built for defining and organizing interoperability levels in software systems. These models help in defining the compatibility level between systems and the amount of effort required to enable them to work jointly. Examples of interoperability models include: (1) the Levels of ISs Interoperability (LISI) [8], (2) NC3TA Reference Model for Interoperability (NMI) [9] and (3) the Levels of Conceptual Interoperability Model (LCIM) [10]. Whereas the LISI and NMI focus on the technical level of interoperability, LCIM provides a more comprehensive classification from data sharing capabilities point of view which we see it as an essential goal of interoperation in ISs. Therefore, we select LCIM to be our reference model for interoperability levels in this study.

LCIM encompasses seven levels which increase from no interoperability level to conceptual interoperability level. Here we present a brief description for each of the seven levels of the LCIM model: (1) **No Interoperability**: no connection or data sharing with other systems. (2) **Technical Interoperability**: physical connection and data exchange with other systems. (3) **Syntactic Interoperability**; similar structure for information exchange and unambiguous data formats. (4) **Semantic Interoperability**:

shared reference model for information exchange and clear data meanings. (5) **Pragmatic interoperability**: methods and procedures used by participating systems are known by the others. Besides, understanding the context of the exchanged information and how they are used is unambiguous. (6) **Dynamic Interoperability**: changing data and operations over time in a participating component are comprehended by other components. The effect of exchanging information is explicitly announced. (7)**Conceptual Interoperability**: concepts and assumptions that components of the domain operate on are aligned. This requires documenting conceptual models by engineering methods allowing engineers to interpret and evaluate them.

3   Related Work

Sedek et al. [11] have systematically reviewed the current architecture-based approaches used for building interoperability in e-government portal until 2011. Sedek et al. reviewed previous works to identify a suitable approach for creating architectures with higher interoperability. They identified 17 studies and analyzed them with respect to: important characteristics of architectural aspect of e-government portal, the interoperability and reliability achievements of the current e-government portal architecture and the common limitations and strengths of the existing e-government architectures. Sedek's study concluded that current approaches lack improving the architecture towards a high level of interoperability and reliability. They stated that SOA and layered architectures are common in e-government portals. Also, they found that mediators are incorporated in architectures to resolve technical and semantic mismatches using approaches like Semantic Mediator Model and User Ontology.

To the best of our knowledge, the previously mentioned study is the only related work to this scoping study. Our research extends the work of Sedek et al. by: (1) reviewing both architectural problems and solutions of interoperability on different interoperability levels and (2) considering all types of ISs from different application domains rather than focusing only on enterprise systems from the e-government domain. These extensions broaden the scope of the research along with its collected data and strengthen the validity of the conclusions we build regarding the ISs interoperability. Moreover, we aim at exploring the evidence on the identified solutions' quality by looking for used evaluation method which supports or rejects their claims.

4   Research Methodology

In this research we systematically study the nature and extent of software architecture researches about interoperability problems and before-release solutions in ISs, to collate, summarize and disseminate research findings, and to identify research gaps. Therefore, we performed a scoping study following the process proposed by Petersen et al. [12] along with a data extraction form. Different than systematic literature review [13], we aimed at a broad analysis for literature rather than an in-depth analysis and quality assessment for selected papers. All materials of this study are available at the scoping study webpage[1].

4.1 Research Questions

The goal of this scoping study is to identify architectural problems and before-release solutions of interoperability in the context of ISs from the view point of researchers and software engineers. This goal is translated into the following research questions:

- *RQ1: Which levels of interoperability are handled in literature with architectural solutions?* This question intends to determine the extent to which architecture research addresses interoperability in terms of the levels of LCIM model.
- *RQ2: What are the architectural problems faced when building interoperability among ISs?* This question intends to identify the issues and key drivers that need to be considered while designing ISs to support the desired interoperability property.
- *RQ3: What are the architectural solutions for handling the identified problems?* This question intends to identify the architectural design decisions and activities proposed in literature to handle the identified interoperability issues.
- *RQ4: How are architectural solutions for interoperability evaluated?* This question intends to explore the evidence provided on the quality of identified solutions in terms of the used evaluation method.
- *RQ4.1: What interoperability measures are used to evaluate the architectural solutions?* This question intends to investigate interoperability metrics used as a part of the evaluation.

4.2 Data Sources and Search Strategy

According to the recommendations of Dybå et al. [6], we looked for published papers in journals and conference proceedings of the following databases: IEEE Xplore, ACM Digital Library, Springer Digital Library, Google Scholar, and Science Direct. Having the data sources selected, we performed trial searches using various combination of search terms derived from our research questions. Based on the results we defined our search terms as: (T1) Interoperability AND Architecture, (T2) Interoperation AND Architecture, (T3) Interoperability AND Architectural Design, and (T4) Interoperation AND Architectural Design. The search process was carried as follows:

- **Stage 1**: Pilot search the databases using the defined terms T1 to T4 separately and then combined with the "OR" operation to remove duplicates. The search was applied on the titles and abstracts (4128 studies).
- **Stage 2**: As abstracts from stage 1 showed irrelevance to the research questions, the database search was refined to be applied on titles only (246 studies).

---

[1] http://wwwagse.informatik.uni-kl.de/staff/abukwaik/pub/
ECSA14/scoping-study.htm

- **Stage 3**: Inclusion/exclusion criteria, described in subsection 4.3, were applied on the 246 studies based on keywords, abstracts, and conclusions (22 studies).

We note that the primary studies included in Sedek's review were not a subset of our study. This was beacause the titles of these studies focused on eGoverment rather than interoperability and architecture. Consequently they were not retrieved in stage 2.

4.3   Inclusion and Exclusion Criteria

A study got included if it met all the inclusion criteria and none of the exclusion criteria, otherwise it got excluded. Inclusion criteria are:

- I1. Studies with a main focus on interoperability problems and architectural solutions in ISs.
- I2. Studies with architectural solutions supporting interoperability before release.

While exclusion criteria are:

- E1. Studies with writing language other than English.
- E2. Gray studies with unclear peer-review process (e.g., technical reports, short papers, keynotes, abstracts, etc.).
- E3. Secondary studies about interoperability problems and solutions (i.e., related works to this research).
- E4. Studies with minor interest in interoperability architectural aspects.
- E5. Studies proposing solutions for specific projects under restricted settings and conditions that cannot be generalized to ISs

Separately, two researchers applied the criteria on the studies and in discussion sessions, decisions about discrepant results were taken based on reached consensus. The search was conducted in November 2013, and had no timeframe limitations to get a broader coverage of studies related to our research questions. Note that we did not contact authors of included studies seeking unpublished evaluation or other related researches.

4.4   Data Extraction Strategy

Table 1 shows the fields that correspond to our predefined research questions. One researcher extracted the data from the 22 included studies and another checked it against the studies to ensure completeness and correctness of the extraction process.

4.5   Data Analysis

Qualitative data analysis was performed using an initial coding schema in a tabular form including interoperability problems, interoperability levels, architectural solutions, architectural components, and evaluation types. The coding schema provided definition of concepts, categories, and criteria that guided the translation of raw data into descriptions that answer the research questions.

Table 1. Data extraction form

	Field	Description	RQ
F1	Title	Title of the paper	Documentation
F2	Author	Writer(s) of the paper	
F3	Year	Year of publishing the paper	
F4	Publication	Name of Journal / Proceeding	
F5	Keywords	Keywords of the paper	RQ1
F6	Objectives	Stated goals of the study by the authors- free text	RQ1
F7	IS type	Kind of IS application which the study focuses on	RQ2
F8	Interoperability problem(s)	Object of the study which the study tries to solve (i.e., problem of interest) - free text	RQ2
F9	Interoperability level	Level of LCIM that the study handles (see section 2)	RQ1
F10	Architectural solution(s)	Subject of the study that is proposed to solve the object (i.e., solution of problem) - free text	RQ3
F11	Solution elements	Concrete elements of the proposed subject (i.e., components of architectural solutions) - free text	RQ3
F12	Technology used	Technologies supporting implementation of proposed subjects (e.g., XML, Web Services ... etc.)	RQ3
F13	Solution evidence	Evidence provided on the quality of proposed subjects (e.g., discussion, controlled experiment, case study, etc.)	RQ4
F14	Interoperability Metric	Quantitative measures used in the study evaluation to describe the interoperability property achieved	RQ4.1
F15	Comments	Additional notes provided in the study (i.e., claimed benefits, tradeoffs, limitations, or challenges) - free text	RQ2.1

5   Results

5.1   Overview

The identified primary studies were 22 that were performed in diverse application domains (e.g., eGovernment, eCommerce, eLearning, geographical, military, and biomedical systems). As seen in Fig. 1, there is a little increase in the number of studies on interoperability after 2004.

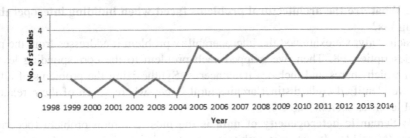

Fig. 1. Year-wise distribution of selected studies

Studies were conducted in academic and industrial environments with 10 of 22, 45%, collaboration between the two. Almost all studies (21 of 22, 95%) were published in conferences, while one study appeared in a journal. Remarkably, there is no a dominating venue publishing many studies on interoperability architectural problems and solutions, i.e., each venue published one study except for one which published two studies. Also, one conference found dedicated to software interoperability named "Distributed Applications and Interoperable Systems".

5.2   Interoperability Architectural Problems and Solutions

RQ1: Which levels of interoperability are handled in literature with architectural solutions?

To determine the interoperability concerns of each study, we analyzed its keywords F5, objectives F6, problem description F8, and solution advantages F15. Afterwards, we compared these concerns to the description of LCIM levels.

Figure 2 illustrates the distribution of the handled levels of interoperability over the included studies. Some studies addressed more than one level, e.g., S3 addressing both the semantic and pragmatic levels. Note that, semantic has the biggest share of the studies' focus with a growing interest along the years while the pragmatic has a low share and disappeared after 2007. Syntactic and technical levels have convergent shares. In recent years, especially 2012 and 2013, the technical level grasps the attention of the inter-Cloud systems researchers (S18 and S22). Both the dynamic and conceptual levels got no share in the studies at all.

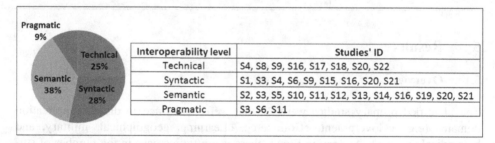

Interoperability level	Studies' ID
Technical	S4, S8, S9, S16, S17, S18, S20, S22
Syntactic	S1, S3, S4, S6, S9, S15, S16, S20, S21
Semantic	S2, S3, S5, S10, S11, S12, S13, S14, S16, S19, S20, S21
Pragmatic	S3, S6, S11

Fig. 2. Interoperability-level distribution over selected studies

RQ2: What are the architectural problems faced when building interoperability among ISs?

For each study, we examined the interoperability problem it addresses from the problem description F8. Then, we mapped each problem to the corresponding level of LCIM which shares and includes its concerns. Synthesizing the problems of all studies, we identified eight distinct architectural issues where seven of them related to LCIM levels as seen in Table 2.

P1: Semantic heterogeneity of data is the most common problem (occurrence number (N) = 11). It concerns architects about designing interoperable systems that correctly interpret the meaning of data elements being exchanged among them. For example, the authors of (S11) investigated designing interoperability among different

GIS systems, and stated that it was a challenge due to the growing number of heterogeneous spatial data sources with semantic differences.

P2: Syntactical heterogeneity of data has been reported frequently (N = 7). It requires architects to take into account the differences in data types, formats, and modeling languages of interoperating systems. For instance, in (S6), Carvalho et al. stated that exchanging geographic data among different layers on GIS required resolving its different representations first.

P3: Heterogeneity of communication protocols, platforms, and technical standards are considered as serious architectural problems (N = 7). It is essential for interoperability to make design decisions that enable the system to establish communication with systems of different technical properties. In (S9), Rabhi observed that developing cooperation among financial market systems required enormous effort due to their variant technologies, communication interfaces, and network protocols.

P4: Heterogeneity of data context has been reported as a problem in the context of financial and GIS systems (N=3). It is important for architects to reflect the context in which the designed system functionalities and data can be used to assure meaningful interoperability. For example, (S11) described possible context heterogeneity to happen in interpreting a domain value of a CropType attribute in the designed system. While in one land it could be "Wheat", in the other it could be "Corn".

Other stated problems include: **P5: Heterogeneity of method signatures; P6: Misunderstanding of the sematic interoperability meaning; P7: Redundancy of data; and P8: Inadequacy of architecture framework supporting interoperability**.

Table 2. Overview LCIM levels with their identified problems and solutions in the studies

Interoperability Level	Problem ID	Solution ID	Study ID
Technical	P3	Sol5	S4
		Sol7	S9, S16, S17, S18, S20, S22
		Sol10	S8
Syntactical	P2	Sol5	S6
		Sol7	S15, S16, S20
		Sol8	S3
		Sol9	S9
	P5	Sol6	S4
	P7	Sol13	S1
Semantic	P1	Sol1	S14, S21
		Sol2	S3, S5, S10, S12, S13
		Sol4	S11
		Sol3	S16, S19, S20
	P6	Sol11	S2
Pragmatic	P4	Sol2	S3, S11
		Sol5	S6
n/a	P8	Sol12	S7

RQ3: What are the architectural solutions for handling the identified problems?

For each study we studied the interoperability solution it proposed from the architectural solution F10, its components F11, and the used technology F12. Then we mapped the solutions to the identified problems in RQ2 (see Table 2).

Sol1: Standards address semantic interoperability problems, e.g., (S21) unambiguous semantic metadata is achieved through a standard-based metadata repository which provided formal description for the meaning of data types used in classes and attributes of data systems. Also, (S14) proposed standard-based modeling for processes and data between collaborating organizations.

Sol2: Ontologies solve semantic and context interoperability problems. For example, (S13) proposed ontology-based blackboard architecture to facilitate user retrieval for the correct service offered by eGovernment system based on his needs with less effort. This was by modeling the basic concepts of services from a user perspective.

Sol3: Semantic mediator aligns semantically related concepts. We identified three identified forms of mediators: *formal-methods-based mediator* aligns the behavior of systems using their LTS models (S16), *thesaurus-based mediator* mediates concepts using knowledge structures simpler than ontologies (S19), and *standard-based mediator* facilitates standardized information exchange and orchestration (S20).

Sol4: Wrapper encapsulates local data sources in export schema comprising the main concepts of the real world entities. As described in (S11), a wrapper receives queries from interoperating systems and translates them into a local form to enable processing them and to retrieve the required information from the local system.

Sol5: Adaptor The adaptor embeds the connection state and logic to one or more external systems, e.g., it can encapsulate a telnet-based connection to a remote Unix host (S4). Also, (S6) proposed using adaptor component to transform data among interfaces of different GIS devices.

Sol6: Facets provides different implementations for a standard interface of an action. Hence, the action can be invoked by different system types through its corresponding facet. In (S4), these facets are automatically generated by specialized tools.

Sol7: Middleware handles heterogeneities in communication protocols and data formats. In (S16), Bennaceur et al. presented how on-the-fly middleware component dynamically resolved heterogeneity of data formats in messages being exchanged between distributed systems.

Sol8: External data models are concerned with representing all sources of data that the system may exchange with other interoperating systems. In (S3), the authors gave examples on external data to include relational database sources, XML sources, HTML web wrapper sources, and computational procedures modeled as relations.

Sol9: Internet data formats are proposed to be used on the data level of distributed systems to ensure wide applicability of the associated components (S9), i.e., using XML and its variants like FIXML with CORBA for handling the communication.

Sol10: Technical reference model guides in expeditiously selecting technical standards using common vocabulary. According to (S8), this fosters interoperability by providing appropriate system standard profiles.

Sol11: Semantic reference model guides developing semantic interoperability capabilities in systems by fulfilling a set of semantic requirements. In (S2), these requirements are categorized as policy and governance, organization, and technology.

Sol12: Enterprise architecture framework provides a systematic blueprint to build interoperability among enterprise IS. In (S7), the identified framework resolves weakness   es comparatively determined in legacy enterprise architecture frameworks.

Sol13: Central repository allows cooperative sharing of information among systems. For example, (S1) proposed using a central repository for installed applications on a phone device to enable sharing resources and context data among them.

A recurring theme we observe in the findings is basing the identified solutions on the service oriented architecture style (SOA), and implementing it with the web service technology. This theme was reported in nine studies (S5, S6, S10, S12, S13, S14, S17, S18, and S22). Also, we found that the different solutions are not associated with particular application domain or research field, i.e., they are applicable in general ISs.

5.3   Evidence on the Quality of the Identified Solutions

RQ4: How are architectural solutions for interoperability evaluated?
As seen in Fig. 3, 8 out of the 22 identified studies did not provide any evaluation of their proposed solutions. Because of the lack of empirical evidence regarding the quality of the identified solutions, it was not possible to determine their effectiveness.

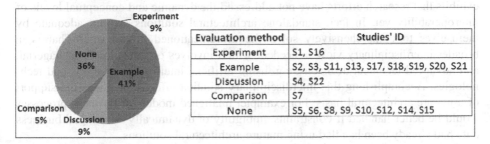

Evaluation method	Studies' ID
Experiment	S1, S16
Example	S2, S3, S11, S13, S17, S18, S19, S20, S21
Discussion	S4, S22
Comparison	S7
None	S5, S6, S8, S9, S10, S12, S14, S15

Fig. 3. Evaluation-method distribution over selected studies

RQ4.1: What interoperability measures are used to evaluate the architectural solutions?
None of the studies included in this scoping study used interoperability metrics to appraise achieving it in the systems.

Studies with empirical evaluation focused only on assessing: *performance* in terms of query execution time (S1), *feasibility* in terms of concepts' understandability and development easiness (S7), and *validity* in terms of overcoming the interaction and application heterogeneity (S16). Noteworthy, neither (S7) nor (S16) was accompanied with quantitative data.

Studies with toy examples described their solutions' benefit against different interests: (S2) argued providing a good base for evaluating the maturity level of semantic interoperability capability of agencies; (S3) showed allowing context mediation without rigidity imposed by changing original context models; (S13) explained how end-users were provided with appropriate interfaces for published services; (S17) illustrated how groupware requirements diversity could be more easily fulfilled by controlling concurrency access to shared documents; (S19) clarified the feasibility of achieving semantic interoperability with simpler structures rather than ontologies; (S20) explained gained adaptivity, flexibility, and security; (S21) presented the feasibility to make semantically interoperable data using ontologies and standards.

Studies with no evidence claimed to achieve autonomy, flexibility, and extensibility (S11) and to allow optimized provisioning of computing, storage, and networking resources (S18). No reflection of such claims was found in the given examples.

6   Discussion

The study results reveal that software interoperability architectural problems and solutions have been studied especially on the syntactic and semantic levels over the last fifteen years. However, only a few studies proposing solutions to the higher LCIM levels have been published. Also, results demonstrate the low evidence level of the studies as the quality of their solutions was not properly evaluated in the included papers of our scoping study. Consequently, we want to draw the attention to the following issues that should be overcome to advance the research area:

Architectural basis for Higher Levels of Interoperability. This scoping study exhibits that research efforts have not addressed the dynamic and conceptual levels of interoperability yet. In fact, standalone architectural solutions are not adequate by themselves to comprehensively solve the aforementioned high levels. That is, a broader interdisciplinary view is needed, which involves organizational, managerial, and advanced technical decisions, e.g. using artificial intelligence methods and technologies. Accomplishing this interdisciplinary solution effectively needs the support of a mature architectural basis. For example, unaligned models of business processes would be better handled if constraints ambiguity of dynamically exchanged business data had already been handled using mature architectural solutions.

Accordingly, we emphasize on the importance to reach a reasonable degree of architectural maturity in backing interoperability on its higher levels. As indicated by [14] , achieving a clear interoperability maturity level determines systems' strengths and weaknesses in terms of their likelihood to interoperate; and hence defines the improvement priorities towards successful interoperability.

Prior Architectural Solutions to Support Interoperability Before Release. The results show that researchers tend to deal with interoperability problems after facing them, i.e., expensive posterior solutions [3]. Contrary, adopting prior architectural solutions can save time and effort, e.g., designing and implementing an interface adaptor for under construction system is less expensive than modifying a released system and integrating it with new components [3]. Therefore, we call for pushing the wheels of research in the direction of prior architectural solutions for interoperability.

Architectural Practices to Support Software Interoperability. In this study, only architectural design decisions have been found as architectural. However, software architecture includes other activities that affect systems characteristics like architectural analysis, synthesis, evaluation, and documentation [15]. It is thus of significant importance to direct such activities towards improving interoperability potentials of ISs and facilitating its tasks. For instance, it would be useful to have studies about best practices to evaluate design patterns with regards to interoperability. Also, studies about architecture documentation activities that introduce specialized interoperability views can help in analysis phases. Hence, researches on architectural activities supporting interoperability are required and should reserve a place in future studies.

Empirical Evidence on the Quality of Proposed Solutions. Based on our collected data, the majority of the identified architectural solutions have not been associated with reliable validation. This can lead to difficulties for practitioners to properly adopt interoperability solutions and to systematically enhance them in future works. Thus, it is important to provide trustworthy evidence like empirical evaluations to raise the reliability of a solution and encourage adopting it. Such evaluation should analyze a solution with respect to its achieved interoperability level, costs, and any other claimed benefits. The experience reported in the field of evidence-based software engineering explains the necessity of empirical evaluation to enable fast adoption of good practices, improve products' quality and minimize projects' failures [6].

Comparisons among Interoperability Architectural Solutions. The results show that the identified interoperability architectural solutions have not been compared to the already existing ones in literature. This is absolutely acceptable if solutions aim at solving interoperability problems that have not been addressed before. However, a proper justification on the preference of adopting a new solution over others addressing the same problem would be needed. Specifically, we call for comparing the experimental results of new solutions with results obtained from previous ones. Similar recommendation has been proposed by Aleti et al. [16] in the context of building new software architecture optimization methods. Moreover, it would be of additional help if trade-offs of solutions are declared too. In this sense, the community would benefit also from publicly sharing evaluation results to enable conducting comparisons.

Interoperability Metrics for Assessing Solutions. The included studies are inconsistent in estimating the benefits of their solutions, i.e., they differ in both the qualities they assessed and the metrics they used. This lack of consistency impedes comparing the solutions and thus we could not infer the architectural characteristics that influence the interoperability property of systems. Another issue is that, some studies measured interoperability using indirect metrics that have unclear relation to interoperability, e.g., autonomy, resource provisioning, security, and concurrency.

Hence, reporting bias represented in both inconsistency and indirectness should be overcome through using valid and reliable measures of interoperability, These measures include interoperability models like: the Levels of Information Systems Interoperability (LISI) model [8], the Operational Interoperability Model (OIM) [17], the LCIM [10], the System of Systems Interoperability (SOSI) model [18], and others. Using these interoperability models can be a good base for reporting the results of the previously discussed empirical evidence and comparisons on the quality of interoperability solutions. Though, it would be of greater benefit to come up with metrics that can precisely quantify systems' interoperability and clearly draw the lines between semantic, pragmatic, and conceptual levels.

Combining interoperability solutions' empirical evaluation, consistency in reporting results, and directness in assessing interoperability, we can definitely improve the strength of evidence of these solutions. Thus, estimating effectiveness and interoperability achieved when adopting these solutions can be more certain and trustworthy.

Reference Rules for Selecting Appropriate Interoperability Architectural Solutions. Currently, various interoperability architectural solutions have been identified and some are addressing similar problems. Therefore, it is important to provide guiding rules that define interoperability problems and assign them to their most suitable architectural solutions. For example, it would be a valuable assistance for junior interoperability architects facing a semantic data heterogeneity problem to have precise directions on how to choose from alternative solutions like ontology-based, standards-based and thesaurus-based mediations. Certainly, designers of such rules need to carefully take into account the different factors that may influence the effectiveness of adopting a specific solution. These factors include available resources, system components' modularity and dependency, targeted interoperability level, system domain, project size, developers' experience, etc.

Tool Support for Interoperability. Another useful support for practitioners designing and building interoperability would be to aid them with software tools that can automatically identify potential interoperability problems between two systems from their architectural models. More helpful these tools can be, if they can also suggest plausible architectural solutions for the detected problems using the aforesaid guidelines. For example, this can be implemented as a plug-in, to an existing software architecture modeling language (e.g., UML), which provides an interoperability view, reports architectural mismatches, and supports resolving these mismatches.

7   Limitation of This Study

Researcher Bias. (1) To produce unbiased conducting for the study, the selection criteria and data extraction protocol were derived from the research questions and reviewed by an independent researcher. For the same purpose, the study selection was performed by two researchers. (2) To ensure correct inference in extracting data from studies with poor or insufficient description, data extraction was performed by one researcher and reviewed by another with discussions as needed. (3) To increase the confidence about the outcome of interpreting the qualitative data, analysis results were reviewed and discussed until agreement among the researchers. This was important in cases where interoperability was described using different or no models. (4) For a transparent and replicable study, data and results of each step were documented.

Publication Bias. Although we did the search in large electronic databases, we did not contact authors to identify unpublished evaluation or other related researches. Also, even with deriving the search terms from the research questions, software engineering keywords are not standardized. Consequently, relevant studies might be missed due to our search terms choice. For these reasons, we do not claim generalizing the results for the whole research field. However, this research covered a significant part of the literature and provided valid results.

8   Conclusion

We have performed a scoping study to identify the architectural problems and solutions for interoperability in ISs. Also, we pursued evidence on the identified solutions' benefits in the selected 22 studies. The studies were published between 1999 and 2013.

Our study contributes by listing faced interoperability problems in IS and mapped them to the identified solutions. The study results reveal that while the technical, syntactical, semantic, and pragmatic interoperability problems are addressed, dynamic and conceptual ones still in need for research attention. The identified architectural solutions vary to include ontologies for semantic issues, adaptors for syntactical differences, middlewares for technical variations, and mediators for pragmatic problems.

Although most of the included studies justify their solutions using examples, many did not present any evaluation method. Besides, no direct interoperability metric is used to appraise the sought out interoperability.

In order to advance the software architecture research towards being a cornerstone in achieving interoperability, we conclude the necessity for further research to: (1) address interoperability on its higher levels, (2) provide empirical evidence for solutions using reliable interoperability metrics, and (3) support interoperability architects and developers with reference rules and tools. Findings also indicate a need to raise the recognition of the interoperability topic within software architecture venues.

Acknowledgments. This research was performed as part of the PhD research of Hadil Abukwaik under the supervision of Prof. Dieter Rombach. We thank Mohammed Abufouda for replicating the selection of studies and the data extraction. Our thanks also go for Liliana Guzmán, Dr. Matthias Galster, Dr. Matthias Naab, and the anonymous reviewers for their valuable comments and guidance.

A   Appendix: Selected Studies

ID	Reference
S1	A. Brodt et al.: A mobile data management architecture for interoperability of resource and context data. In MDM (2011)
S2	A. Ojo et al.: Semantic interoperability architecture for electronic government. In dg.o (2009)
S3	A. Moulton et al.: Semantic Interoperability in the fixed income securities industry: A knowledge representation architecture for dynamic integration of web-based information. In HICSS (2003)
S4	G. Hatzisymeon et al.: An architecture for implementing application interoperation with heterogeneous systems. In DAIS (2005)

S5	L. Xianming et al.: Research on the Portlet Semantic Interoperability Architecture. In WCSE (2009)
S6	D. de Carvalho et al.: Functional and device interoperability in an architectural model of geographic information system. In SIGDOC (2007)
S7	J. Kim et al.: An enterprise architecture framework based on a common information technology domain (EAFIT) for improving interoperability among heterogeneous information systems. In SERA (2005)
S8	S. Zhu et al.: Army enterprise architecture technical reference model for system interoperability. In MILCOM (2009)
S9	F. Rabhi: Towards an open architecture for the integration and interoperability of distributed systems. In Ent-Net at SUPERCOMM (2001)
S10	B. Powers: A multi-agent architecture for NATO network enabled capabilities: enabling semantic interoperability in dynamic environments (NC3A RD-2376). In SOCASE (2008)
S11	E. Leclercq et al.: ISIS: a semantic mediation model and an agent based architecture for GIS interoperability. In IDEAS (1999)
S12	M. Paul: Enterprise geographic information system (E-GIS): A service-based architecture for geo-spatial data interoperability. In IGARSS (2006)
S13	G. Lepouras et al.: An active ontology-based blackboard architecture for web service interoperability. In ICSSSM (2005)
S14	C. Schroth et al.: UN/CEFACT Service-Oriented Architecture-Enabling Both Semantic And Application Interoperability. In KiVS (2007)
S15	P. Arapi et al.: ASIDE: An Architecture for Supporting Interoperability between Digital Libraries and ELearning Applications. In ICALT (2006)
S16	A. Bennaceur et al.: Towards an architecture for runtime interoperability. In ISoLA (2010)
S17	R. Maciel et al.: WGWSOA: A service-oriented middleware architecture to support groupware interoperability. In CSCWD (2007)
S18	Y. Demchenko et al.: Intercloud Architecture for interoperability and integration. In CloudCom (2012)
S19	D. Arize et al.: ThesIS: A semantic interoperability service for a middleware service oriented architecture. In CSCWD (2013)
S20	R. Crichton et al.: An Architecture and Reference Implementation of an Open Health Information Mediator: Enabling Interoperability in the Rwandan Health Information Exchange. In FHIES (2013)
S21	G. Komatsoulis et al.: caCORE version 3: Implementation of a model driven, service-oriented architecture for semantic interoperability. In J-BHI (2008)
S22	A. Mohtasebi et al.: Analysis of Applying Enterprise Service Bus Architecture as a Cloud Interoperability and Resource Sharing Platform. In KMO (2013)

References

1. IEEE Standard Computer Dictionary, IEEE Std 610. A compilation of IEEE standard computer glossaries (1991)
2. ISO/IEC 2382-1: Information technology, vocabulary, Part 1: Fundamental terms (1993)
3. Gonçalves, R., Müller, J., Mertins, K.: Enterprise Interoperability III: New Challenges and Approaches. Springer (2007)
4. Davis, L., Payton, J., Gamble, R.: How system architectures impede interoperability. In: Proceedings of the 2nd International Workshop on Software and Performance, pp. 145–146 (2000)
5. Land, C.I.: Existing approaches to software integration–and a challenge for the future. Integration 40, 58–104 (2004)

6. Dybå, T., Kitchenham, B., Jørgensen, M.: Evidence-based software engineering for practitioners. IEEE Software 22(1), 58–65 (2005)
7. Loukis, , Charalabidis, : An empirical investigation of information systems interoperability business value in European firms. Computers in Industry 64(4), 412-420 (2013)
8. C4ISR Interoperability Workig Group: Levels of information systems interoperability (IISI). Technical Report, Department of Defense (1998)
9. Powers, B.J.: A multi-agent architecture for NATO network enabled capabilities: enabling semantic interoperability in dynamic environments (NC3A RD-2376). In: Kowalczyk, R., Huhns, M.N., Klusch, M., Maamar, Z., Vo, Q.B. (eds.) SOCASE 2008. LNCS, vol. 5006, pp. 93–103. Springer, Heidelberg (2008)
10. Turnitsa, C.: Extending the levels of conceptual interoperability model. In: Proceedings IEEE Summer Computer Simulation Conference. IEEE CS Press (2005)
11. Sedek, K., Sulaiman, S., Omar, M.: A systematic literature review of interoperable architecture for e-government portals. In: 2011 5th Malaysian Conference on Software Engineering (MySEC), pp. 82–87 (2011)
12. Petersen, K., Feldt, R., Mujtaba, S., Mattsson, M.: Systematic mapping studies in software engineering. In: 12th International Conference on Evaluation and Assessment in Software Engineering, vol. 17 (2008)
13. Kitchenham, B.: Procedures for undertaking systematic reviews,Joint technical report. Computer Science Department, Keele University and National ICT Australia (2004)
14. Guédria, W., Chen, D., Naudet, Y.: A Maturity Model for Enterprise Interoperability. In: Meersman, R., Herrero, P., Dillon, T. (eds.) OTM 2009 Workshops. LNCS, vol. 5872, pp. 216–225. Springer, Heidelberg (2009)
15. Hofmeister, C., Kruchten, Nord, Obbink, Ran, America, P.: Generalizing a model of software architecture design from five industrial approaches. In : 5th Working IEEE/IFIP Conference on Software Architecture, pp.77–88 (2005)
16. Aleti, A., Buhnova, B., Grunske, L., Koziolek, A., Meedeniya, I.: Software architecture optimization methods: A systematic literature review. IEEE Transactions on Software Engineering 39(5), 658–683 (2013)
17. Clark, T., Jones, R.: Organisational interoperability maturity model for C2. In: Proceedings of the 1999 Command and Control Research and Technology Symposium (1999)
18. Edwin, M., Linda, L., Patrick, P., Daniel, P., Meyers, B.: System of systems interoperability (SOSI): Final report. Tech. rep. (2004)

fUML-Driven Design and Performance Analysis of Software Agents for Wireless Sensor Network*

Luca Berardinelli, Antinisca Di Marco, and Stefano Pace

Dept. of Information Engineering, Computer Science and Mathematics,
University of L'Aquila, 67100 L'Aquila, Italy
{luca.berardinelli,antinisca.dimarco,stefano.pace}@univaq.it

Abstract. The growing request for high-quality applications for wireless sensor network (wsn) demands model-driven approaches that facilitate the design and the early validation of extra-functional properties by combining design and analysis models. for this purpose, uml and several analysis-specific languages can be chosen and weaved through translational approaches. however, the complexity brought by the underlying technological spaces may hinder the adoption of uml-based approaches in the wsn domain. the recently introduced foundational uml (fuml) standard provides a formal semantics to a strict uml subset, enabling the execution of uml models.

Leveraging fUML, we realize the Agilla Modeling Framework, an executable fUML model library, to conveniently design agent-based software applications for WSN and analyze their performance through the execution of the corresponding fUML model. A running case study is provided to show our framework at work.

Keywords: fUML, Model-Driven Analysis, Tool Support, WSN.

1 Introduction

A Wireless Sensor Network (WSN) consists of spatially distributed autonomous sensors that cooperate to accomplish a task. Sensors are small, low-cost, wireless and battery-powered devices. They can be easily deployed to monitor several environmental parameters and they create large-scale flexible architectures. Sensors can be distributed everywhere and they enable different applications such as domotics, disaster relief and alternate reality game.

The specific nature of sensors complicates the development of applications, mainly because the quality of the services they provide is influenced by factors like network availability, battery levels, and so on. Despite this, a WSN must continue providing its services as long as possible, and with the best effort trying to guarantee network longevity.

Traditionally, WSN applications have been developed following a code-and-fix approach, that is, by directly programming nodes with the use of low-level primitives. This approach, neglecting design and quality validation phases, results in

---

* This work is partially supported by the EU-funded VISION ERC project (ERC-240555), and by PRESTO ARTEMIS project (GA n. 269362).

P. Avgeriou and U. Zdun (Eds.): ECSA 2014, LNCS 8627, pp. 324–339, 2014.

not structured, hard to maintain code with the risk of missing extra-functional requirements and compromising the system usability. Indeed, the system's extra-functional properties must be considered as earlier as possible in the system life-cycle to guarantee their fulfillment.

In this respect, the Model-Driven Engineering (MDE) paradigm may play a capital role in the WSN domain. In MDE, models are used as the main system specification throughout the whole development process for both design and analysis purposes. Such models are then weaved through model transformations. For example, architectural models can be defined on a high level of abstraction and continuously refined until an executable system is (semi-) automatically derived [1]. Similarly, different analysis models (e.g., queuing networks) can be generated from design artifacts [2].

Translational approaches for model-driven analysis have the advantage that existing techniques and tools for the target language can be directly exploited. The major drawback, however, is that an additional level of indirection and complexity is inevitable. Implementing the translation of models from the source language (e.g., UML) into models of the target language used for the analysis is a complex task, requiring a deep knowledge not only of the semantics of source and target languages, but also of model transformation techniques.

Another challenge in developing translational approaches is translating back the analysis results from the target language back to the source one. If this backwards translation is missing, the analysis results may not be comprehensible for the modelers, as they are usually only familiar with the source language. The complexity of translating the analysis results back to the source language lead to the unsatisfactory fact that only very few translational model-driven analysis approaches provide the results on the level of the source models (cf. [2] pointing this out for the software performance engineering domain). As a result, these approaches do not gain the adoption they deserve outside the academia, including also researchers and practitioners in the WSN domain.

These challenges are even more evident with UML, the most adopted general-purpose modeling language in the MDE domain (as reported in a recent survey on architectural languages [3]) as well as one of the most criticized languages due to its lack of formal semantics. Adopting UML as the main notation for *live* design models (i.e., not just for postmortem documentation purposes) requires model transformations to generate analyzable and executable artifacts. As a consequence, UML-based approaches usually span different technological spaces [4] and require a non-negligible effort to set up a model-driven working environment in terms of stakeholders' know-how and tool support. To face these challenges, France et al. [1] suggested the integration of the analysis algorithms directly with the modeling language used in systems development.

Following this suggestion and with the aim of bringing the benefits of the MDE paradigm into the WSN domain, we propose in this paper the Agilla Modeling Framework (AMF). AMF is a model-driven, tool-supported approach to design and analyze Agilla applications [5] through the Foundational UML (fUML) [6], a new standard of the Object Management Group (OMG) that defines the operational semantics of a (strict) UML subset. AMF provides a fUML model library that supplies, at the same time, i) reusable design modeling elements and ii) analysis algorithms for fUML models of Agilla applications.

The rest of the paper is organized as follows. Section 2 provides a quick background on Agilla and fUML. Section 3 illustrates the AMF framework and its functionalities with the help of a case study. In Section 4, we focus on the performance analysis functionality. Section 5 discusses about the opportunities and current limitations of our approach. Finally, Section 6 reviews related works and Section 7 concludes the paper outlining future research directions.

2   Background on Agilla and fUML

Agilla [5] is a bytecode-like programming language and a middleware (Agilla MW) for mobile agents running on WSNs, based on TinyOS operating system [7]. The Agilla MW runs on all the nodes of a WSN and allows creating, migrating and destroying software agents at run-time, without service interruption. An agent behavioral specification consists of a list of statements from an Agilla Instruction Set Architecture (ISA)[1] and interpreted by an ad-hoc virtual machine. The Agilla ISA includes general-purpose instructions to perform basic tasks (e.g., obtaining a neighbor list, sensing) and migration instructions that allow an agent to move or clone to another node. A code fragment is shown in Figure 2. To support agent communication and migration, the Agilla MW provides a shared memory based on tuple spaces [8]. A unique and distinct tuple space is available on each node. For this reason, Agilla ISA also includes *tuple space* operations to allow agents to both locally and remotely manage the content of tuple spaces. The Agilla MW also provides further data structures like a *stack* and three *registers*, namely an agent id, a program counter, and a condition code. At run time, the *stack* stores input parameters and output results of instructions and, combined with values of registries, determines the next instruction and task to execute.

Foundational UML (fUML) [6] is a new standard of the standardization body OMG. It defines the operational semantics of a strict UML subset. The standard goes along with a Java-based reference implementation[2] of an *fUML virtual machine* for executing *Classes, Common Behaviors, Activities*, and *Actions* UML language units. Since fUML does not introduce any heavyweight extension, any fUML model is compliant to UML. At run time, the fUML VM is in charge of generating the so called *instance model* from given fUML model where InstanceSpecifications, Links, and Slots model elements represent the run time counterpart of Classes, Associations and Properties, respectively. In this respect, the execution of fUML activities add, delete or modify elements of the instance model. In essence, fUML enables the execution of UML models where i) structural elements are classes with their own properties, operations, and associations while ii) the behavioral specification is modeled through UML activities.

---

[1] http://mobilab.wustl.edu/projects/agilla/isa.html
[2] http://fuml.modeldriven.org

3 The Agilla Modeling Framework

AMF is an ongoing work[3] that aims at providing a fUML-based modeling and simulation environment to design and analyze Agilla applications.

Figure 1 sketches the fUML-driven approach supported by AMF. Artifacts and functionalities are depicted as rectangles and rounded boxes, respectively, while dashed arrows connect functionalities and related artifacts with labels detailing their relationships. In its first version ([9]), AMF supported a *canonical* translational approach for generating Agilla code from annotated UML Activities. From [10] on, we started its porting process from UML to fUML. As a result, AMF is now a fUML executable model library to be reused across UML-based design artifacts. The AMF model library provides a predefined set of structural and behavioral elements (namely, *patterns*) to design the software architecture of Agilla applications as executable fUML models. In addition, following the suggestion given in [1], it integrates analysis algorithms directly in fUML (i.e., as fUML Activities) for the sake of performance analysis of Agilla applications.

The choice of fUML as the main modeling notation stems from a recent survey on industrial needs on architectural languages [3] where the authors document the still growing and predominant adoption of UML but also the need for more powerful analysis functionalities and tool support for UML-based approaches. In addition, the need for a precise UML semantics is cleanly stated in [1]. In this respect, AMF is an attempt to exploit and assess the potential benefits brought by fUML in model-driven approaches. The main benefit is avoiding translational approaches to different external notations and related technological spaces [4] by integrating algorithms and results directly within the modeling

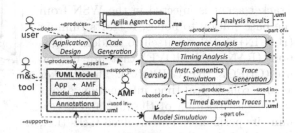

Fig. 1. Actors, functionalities and artifacts in AMF

language used in systems development, as suggested by France et al. [1].

The AMF's algorithms and related data structures are modeled through activities and classes, respectively, and are part of an executable *model library* [11]. A UML model library is analogous to a class library in object-oriented programming languages. It includes reusable classes, properties as well as operations with their associated behaviors (a.k.a, *methods* [11]) as UML activities. The modeling elements from a library can be suitably enriched with structural and behavioral ones from the user-defined models by establishing relationships (e.g., generalizations, associations) and invoking operations (e.g., through call operation actions).

The AMF model library provides five functionalities, *parsing*, *instruction semantics simulation*, *trace generation*, *timing analysis*, and *performance analysis*),

---

[3] http://sealabtools.di.univaq.it/tools.php

all implemented in fUML, i.e., through classes and activities. These functionalities are illustrated below with the help of a case study.

Case Study. The Wildfire Tracking Application (WTA) is an existing case study taken from [5]. The WTA software is deployed on a WSN distributed into a region that is prone to fires. It must detect a fire and determine its perimeter. When a fire starts, its movements are unpredictable and WTA is implemented to continuously re-adapt the perimeter of the fire. The original WTA is composed by five Agilla agents. We choose two of them, namely the *Tracker* and *Reader* agents, to show our approach and tool at work. The agents' code with its TASKS and fragments of their inner **instructions** are shown in Figure 2. The Reader runs on all the WSN nodes and is programmed to **sense** the temperature at regular time intervals and to send the value to a base station connected to a PC, where the temperature level is evaluated and where eventual alarms are triggered. Once a fire has been detected, a Tracker agent is injected in the WSN from the base station to nodes. It starts running (BEGIN) and clones itself to random neighbors (RANDOM MOVE) that are not on fire (CHECK_NEIGHBORS). The Tracker agents collect real-time information about the precise position of the fire, and determine its perimeter. The involved tasks (i.e., those labeled with BARRIER) are repeated until the Tracker runs on all the neighbors of the burning nodes (BARRIER_DONE).

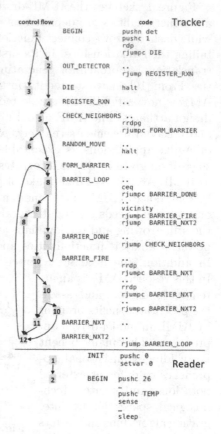

Fig. 2. Agents' code and control flow

Application Design. The AMF user models the structure and behavior of an Agilla application using class and activity diagrams. Figure 3 shows an excerpt of the structure and behavior of both the WTA and the AMF model library. The AMF model library provides the generic structural elements, i.e., *AppComp*, *AgentComp*, *TaskComp*, and *InstrComp*, from which the user-defined software components have to be specialized. A hierarchy of user-defined classes is then obtained, where the WTA agents, *Reader* and *Tracker*, have distinct associations for each inner task. Given the class diagram of the WTA application architecture, the fUML VM is able to generate, at run time, its corresponding instance model. The link between the agent and task components and the corresponding behavioral specifications is obtained through *main()* operations, added to both agents and tasks components. As prescribed by fUML, the behavioral specifications of all these operations are given by executable UML activities: Figure 3 depicts the main() operations for the Tracker agent and its task BEGIN.

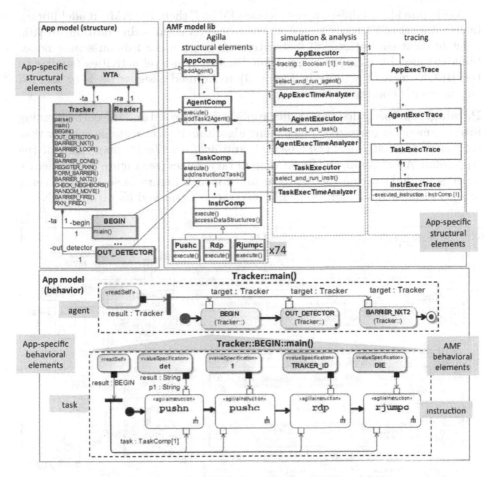

Fig. 3. Design of the WTA through the AMF model library

Additionally, further operations are required on agents for each owned TASK, using its label as name: the Tracker agent requires, for example, twelve operations as many as the tasks on its code (see Figure 2). These task-specific operations are then invoked, through call operation actions [11], within an *main()* operations than model the agent's behavior. Figure 3 shows this main() operation for the Tracker. While the agent-level behaviors are completely modeled by the AMF user, task-level behaviors can be created with the help of the AMF library through predefined `instructions` taken from the AMF library. For example, the white actions in the BEGIN::main() activity in Figure 3 can be dragged and dropped from the library to be further refined by the user with instruction parameters. In this respect, strings and integers can be modeled through Val-ueSpecification actions [11]. At run time, their actual values flow through input and output pins, depicted in Figure 3 as small black and white boxes on actions, respectively.

Agilla provides 74 different instructions [5] and, then, the AMF model library included a set of 74 ready to use instruction-level actions. In addition, In [10], a set of recurrent patterns of instructions (e.g., to make leds on sensor nodes blinking) are also included as predefined instruction-level activities (similar to the BEGIN::main() activity in Figure 3) to be used assigned as is or merged within main() operations of tasks.

Parsing. A properly designed Agilla application is parsed and the corresponding instance model is generated. The parsing algorithm is an executable activity that calls the *addAgent()*, *addTask2Agent()*, and *addInstr2Task()* operations of the AppComp, AgentComp, and TaskComp library classes (see Figure 3) to generate objects and links within the fUML instance model. Figure 4a shows an excerpt of such instance model for the WTA, its Tracker agent and its task BEGIN.

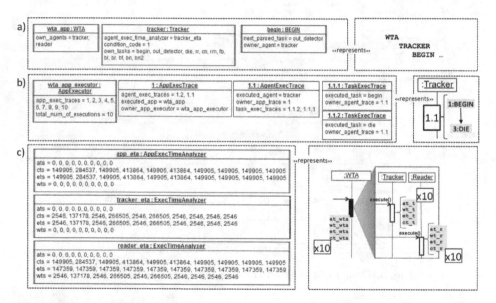

Fig. 4. Excerpts from the WTA instance model: a) instances of Agilla structural units, b) execution trace, c) performance analysis results

Instruction Semantics Simulation. In Agilla, the instruction semantics is implemented as modifications of data structures provided by the Agilla MW like the stack, the condition code registry and the tuple space [5].

In particular, we first model the semantics of two sets of Agilla instructions[4]: i) those that access and modify the value of the condition code registry (like rdp, rrdp, rrdpg, ceq and vicinity) and ii) those that determine the application

---

[4] We refer the reader to [5] for further details on these and similar Agilla instructions.

control flow both by (un)conditionally jumping to a certain task ($\mathtt{rjump}$, $\mathtt{rjumpc}$) with(out) reading the current value of the condition code registry or by stopping the agent execution ($\mathtt{halt}$). The Tracker's code in Figure 2 shows how such instructions can be combined within tasks to determine the its control flow.

In AMF, the instruction semantics is defined in fUML, i.e. through executable activities associated to the execute() operations of InstrComp library classes (see the *Pushc, Rdp, Rjumpc* library classes in Figure 3). The AMF library represents the Agilla data structures in fUML through classes and properties so that, at run time, the corresponding instance specifications and slot values are available within the fUML instance model of any Agilla application.

Any InstrComp library class provides its own *execute()* operation with the corresponding executable activity implementing its own instruction semantics (i.e., whose actions directly access and modify the Agilla data structures). Instruction-level executions always occur within the owning task and, in turn, within the owning agent, like in a Russian wooden doll. For this reason, the AMF compound structural elements, AgentComp and TaskComp, provide their own execute() operation. Finally the correct scheduling of all these execute() operations is up to *Executor* library classes (*AppExecutor, AgentExecutor* and *TaskExecutor*)[5]. Their scheduling algorithms are modeled again by fUML activities associated with their *select_and_run* operations. Currently, AMF supports a First-In-First-Out (FIFO) scheduling policy. Explicitly modeling the semantics of instructions as part of the AMF library frees the AMF users from explicitly modeling the control flow of agents as required and shown in [10].

Timed Trace Generation. The AMF library includes a *trace model* represented as a hierarchical set of classes. *AppExecTrace, AgentExecTrace, TaskExecTrace,* and *InstrExecTrace* library classes are instantiated during the model simulation when the corresponding behavioral units are scheduled. As a result, an execution trace is built at run time and is part of the fUML instance model as linked lists of instance specifications. Each trace corresponds to a path over the control flow graphs shown in Figure 2. As an example, a BEGIN-DIE trace for the Tracker is illustrated in Figure 4b. During the execution of the performance analysis algorithm, these traces are further enriched with slots containing timed values (e.g., the execution time of each unit) and exploited for the sake of timing and performance analyses.

Timing Analysis. This AMF functionality has been originally presented in [10] where we also explain how we measured the execution times of Agilla instructions over a predefined hardware platform [12]. In this new version of AMF, we redesign the timing analysis algorithm (i.e., the corresponding executable activities) to make the timing analysis operating over execution traces, not available in [10]. Now, given a timed execution trace of InstrExecTrace objects, the application, task and agent execution times (*ets*) are calculated by summing the *ets* of AgentExecTrace, TaskExecTrace and InstrExecTrace instances, respectively. For

---

[5] Being a basic behavioral unit, an InstructionExecutor library class is not necessary and its role is played directly by the execute() operations.

redesign this functionality, we followed the same design strategy applied for the schedulers by distributing the implementation of the timing analysis algorithm over operations provided by three TimeAnalyzer library classes (*AppExecTime-Analyzer*, *AgentExecTimeAnalyzer*, and *TaskExecTimeAnalyzer*).

Performance Analysis. This is the new analysis functionality by AMF introduced in this paper. The performance analysis algorithm leverages the Timing Analysis and (then) the Timed Trace Generation functionalities to calculate the average, minimum, and maximum response time of the modeled Agilla application over a set of application-level execution traces. Section 4 illustrates this functionality in detail.

Tool Support. Both the AMF library and the user-defined fUML model of an Agilla application are UML models. Therefore any UML-compliant tool can manage all the UML-based artifacts (boxes with the .uml tag) in Figure 1. However, only UML modeling tools also capable of simulating fUML models (the m&s actor in Figure 1) can exploit all the AMF functionalities. The fUML standard is accompanied by a reference Java-based VM implementation and it is available as plug in for open source and commercial UML modeling tools like Papyrus[6] and MagicDraw UML[7], respectively. For AMF, we choose MagicDraw UML and its plug in Cameo Simulation Toolkit to model and to simulate fUML models, respectively. These two tools play a double role: i) they assist both the AMF users in modeling and simulating an Agilla application and ii) they provide us, as tool developers, an industrial-strength environment to design and simulate our framework.

Figure 5a sketches the workflow of the AMF functionalities in Figure 1 through a state machine-like notation. Given a properly designed fUML model of an Agilla application extended by the AMF library, AMF runs all its functionalities atop the fUML model simulation capability. After the parsing step that build up the software structures within the fUML instance model, the Agilla instructions (and then the containing tasks and agents) are scheduled and their timed execution traces saved at the same time. Then, timing and performance analysis steps follow. In [10], we described how the execution times of the Agilla instructions were measured on a real hardware platform [12] and how such timings were used as parameters to run the timing analysis step. The next section illustrates the new AMF performance analysis functionality applied on the WTA case study.

4   Performance Analysis with AMF

The performance analysis scenario for the WTA case study is graphically depicted on a sequence-like diagram in Figure 4c and replicated for clarity in Figure 5b. It is not part of the WTA fUML model and used for the sake of illustration.

---

[6] www.papyrusuml.org
[7] http://www.nomagic.com/

Currently, AMF is able to simulate a single, multi-agent Agilla application running on a sensor node. In this respect, the proposed scenario for WTA includes two agents, Tracker and Reader. The corresponding application-level execution traces are generated accordingly, tracking the executed tasks and instructions for both agents. Graphically, these execution traces correspond to the execution occurrences over lifelines as shown in Figure 4b.

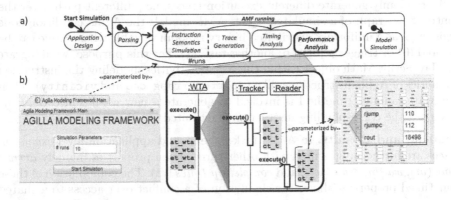

Fig. 5. a) AMF functionalities workflow and b) the performance analysis step

The performance analysis algorithm requires two main input parameters: i) the *execution times* (*et*) of each Agilla instruction and ii) a collection of application-level execution traces. By leveraging such execution traces, AMF can calculate the mean, maximum, and minimum response times (RTs) for the simulated Agilla application and all its agents and tasks. We detail the performance analysis tasks in the following.

Analysis Inputs. The execution times (*ets*) quantify the time required by a seized resource to process a (software) request. In AMF, such requests are the Agilla basic behavioral unit (instructions) and compound ones, (tasks, agents and the whole application).

The AMF user has to input the instruction-level *ets* through a graphical user interface (GUI)[8] as shown in Figure 5b. We reuse, for our performance scenario, the *ets* measured on the same target hardware platform used in [10]. As a consequence, the analysis results shown later can be considered platform-specific, even though the reference hardware platform [12] has not been explicitly modeled in the WTA model.

The second input to the performance analysis algorithm is a collection of timed execution traces as generated by several simulation runs. In our performance scenario, a couple of execution traces, one for Tracker and one for the Reader agents, are generated for each simulation run and a new set of timed execution traces are generated as part of the fUML instance model.

---

[8] The GUI has been designed using the prototyping capabilities of MagicDraw(r).

The AMF user has to input the maximum number of runs as shown in Figure 5b. It acts as a stopping condition. In our performance scenario, we set this value to 10. In accordance with the workflow sketched in Figure 5a, AMF repeats the Instruction Semantics Simulation, Trace Generation, Timing Analysis and Performance Analysis steps 10 times. As a consequence, we collect in our scenario 10 distinct sets of application-level traces, each containing a Tracker and Reader timed execution trace.

To randomly generate different execution traces, i.e., different paths over the control flow graph of a simulated agent, AMF models the Agilla condition code register [5] as a uniformly distributed binary random variable whose value can be ignored (0) or trigger a jump to another task (1). For this purpose, we integrate the JavaScript Math object within the fUML activities modeling the instruction semantics of Agilla instructions (like `rdp`, `rrdp`, `rrdpg`, `ceq` and `vicinity`). Then the Math.random() method is invoked to generate a new condition code value whenever the corresponding instruction is executed.

Analysis and Results. In AMF, task-, agent- and application-level execution traces are further augmented with other three timed properties, namely *arrival time* (*at*), *waiting time* (*wt*), and *completion times* (*ct*). The combination of these four timed properties allows the simulation of a conflict over access to a shared computing resource among agents running on the same node. All these timed properties are modeled as integer values representing times in microseconds (μs). In particular:

- *at* is the time when the Agilla behavioral unit is ready to be run by the proper Executor instance.
- *wt* quantifies the time elapsed before the behavioral unit access the shared computing resource.
- *ct* is the time when the behavioral unit has completed its execution and releases the shared resource.

All the remaining timed properties are calculated by the performance analysis algorithm and assigned to the proper execution traces. In particular, in our performance scenario, we consider both Tracker and Reader agents ready for execution when the WTA application starts (i.e., *at*=0). Once all the timed properties of the collected execution traces have been calculated, the RT of the WTA application can be obtained. In our scenario, the RT can be intuitively quantified as the time required to execute the sequence diagram in Figure 5b, i.e. the interval between the instant when the WTA application starts and the instant when the Reader agent stops. For example, the application-level RT is obtained as the difference between the *ct* of the latest executed agent (in this case, the Reader) and the *at* of the first one (i.e., the Tracker). In a similar way, the RTs can be calculated for each agent and task by considering only *ct*s and *at*s saved on the corresponding AgentExecTrace and TaskExecTrace instances. Figure 4c shows how the performance results are saved within the WTA instance model: they are modeled as ordered lists of slot values associated to the right properties (*at*s, *wt*s, *et*s, and *ct*s) within instances of AppExecTimeAnalyzer, AgentExecTimeAnalyzer, and TaskExecTimeAnalyser library classes.

We finally collect and display the results in the bar charts in Figure 6. The WTA RT varies from a minimum of 149905 μs to a maximum of 413864 μs. In particular, the Reader RT is a constant value across all the simulation runs (147359 μs) due to its simple control flow graph (two sequential tasks always executed at each run, see Figure 2) while the RT of the Tracker may vary according to the complexity of its randomly generated execution trace. For sake of illustration, we

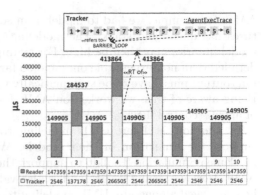

Fig. 6. RT (in μs) of the whole WTA and its Tracker and Reader agents

report the execution trace analyzed during the fourth and sixth runs by the ids of the corresponding tasks (see the control flow graph in Figure 2). In particular, for these two runs, AMF tracked 13 task executions including the three loops starting from the BARRIER_LOOP task (id=5).

5   Discussion

It is worth noting that, in this paper, we are extending the analysis capabilities of AMF with the intent of showing the suitability of fUML for i) the design and analysis of WSN applications, and ii) the design of more and more complex analysis tools as fUML model libraries, at the same time. In accordance with our background and research goals, we primarily focus on assessing the exploitation of fUML and related technologies in the WSN and extra-functional analysis domains.

We consider AMF and, more in general, the underlying fUML-driven approach proposed in this paper, an initial as well as a first practical evaluation of the impact that fUML and its related technologies may have i) on expectations from UML practitioners and ii) on future research directions in MDE [1,3]. With this work, we show that both the design and analysis of WSN as well as tool development are feasible activities with fUML. While pursuing our goals, we experienced both opportunities and limitations related to the usage of fUML.

fUML is a young OMG standard, published on February 2011. It makes a strict (and then easier to learn) subset of UML executable. By leveraging their current background in UML, both researchers and practitioners can already adopt it for their specific purposes. At the time of writing, the (positive or negative) impact of fUML on daily modeling activities still has to be assessed (e.g., [3] was concluded in July 2011).

fUML promotes model reuse through executable model libraries, like AMF, and it may be compared to a new programming language that, however, still suffers from the lack of an adequate support in term of built-in libraries. In

AMF, for example, we had to model from scratch common auxiliary data structures like queue and stack. The modeling effort required to create executable model libraries may then be high. For example, fUML activities are much more detailed than non-executable ones and so far usually disregarded details, like input/output pins, have to be systematically modeled to allow a correct execution. Being aware of this, we worked on AMF for its users to simplify the modeling of agents' control flows.

In addition, still few UML modeling tools exist that provide plug ins to support the simulation of their models. We choose MagicDraw and its plug in Cameo Simulation Toolkit to support the modeling and simulation tasks in AMF. However, being fUML models also valid UML models, such artifacts may be exchanged among any UML modeling tools supporting common serialization formats (e.g., XMI and Eclipse UML).

In this work, we are adopting fUML to design, from scratch, an analysis tool.From [10] on, the AMF executable model is growing fast to support its new functionalities, including also possibly heavy computational tasks, like performance analysis is.

To the best of authors' knowledge, AMF represents the first attempt to design performance analysis algorithms through fUML-compliant activities as part of a reusable UML model library. During this task, we experienced some scalability issues that limited the complexity of our performance scenario (e.g., larger workloads). For example, Tatibouet et al. [13] pinpointed the lack of central control unit in charge of managing discrete events and their timings. They also provided solution in the form of a fUML model library that both extends and preserves the original fUML semantics. Moreover, AMF can be seen as a layered tool infrastructure and all the AMF functionalities run within a hosting UML Modeling environment that, in turn, run on top of a Java Virtual Machine. This layered infrastructure may worsen the perceived scalability issues for analysis tools, like AMF, running on the topmost layer. Even though assessing the maturity level of fUML and its underlying technology for performance analysis is out of scope of this paper and left for future work, we imagine that the possible integration of [13] with our library will help both in re-designing the current AMF's performance analysis algorithms and in modeling new ones. The experience gained in designing AMF will help in widening our research goals to integrate other (existing) model-based analysis approaches (e.g., reliability), possibly applied on industrial case studies [14].

6   Related Work

In this work, that directly stems from [10], as well as in [15] and [16], we pursue a similar goal but aiming at a tighter integration between fUML and analysis methodologies. In particular, we showed in [15] and [16] how performance analysis can be conducted on annotated fUML models by generating and analyzing traces compliant with a fUML run time metamodel [17]. Tool support is provided through a Java-based Eclipse plug-in that suitably interacts with the fUML VM during its execution. In [10] and in this subsequent work, we further emphasize the role and importance of fUML by directly designing (that is, implementing) the analysis tool as a fUML model library.

In [10,15,16] and in this work as well, the expected benefits of directly utilizing the execution of UML models for carrying out model-based analysis are twofold: *(i)* the costly translation of UML models into formal languages dedicated to specific analysis purposes is avoided and, hence, *(ii)* the implementation and maintenance of supporting analysis tool sets is eased significantly. With AMF approach presented in this paper, we offer both of these benefits and showcase them by developing a performance analyzer that implements an analysis method directly on UML models for WSN applications. A translation of UML models into a performance model can now be omitted and it is not necessary to use additional external tools for performance analysis purposes.

[18] presents a model-driven framework based on MathWorks tools, in which an application developer can model a WSN application by using Stateflow constructs and then generate code. In [19], the authors introduce a UML-based framework where a system model *(i)* is extended with a new profile for representing NesC application along with the supporting hardware platform, and *(ii)* is annotated with performance parameters defined in MARTE. Thereafter they apply a set of transformations to this enhanced UML model that targets a Queueing Network performance model to carry out a performance analysis of the WSN application. AMF differs from [18,19] since it targets Agilla agents and the analysis technique is based on simulation of UML without demanding a transformation to different notations for analysis purposes. The current supported analyses are functional, timing and performance ones.

In [20], the OMNeT++ simulation environment is presented. It is a complete environment capable of simulating various kinds of networks, including WSNs. Even if OMNeT++ is a complete environment, it is difficult to use and, instead of directly providing simulation components for computer networks, queuing networks or other domains, it provides the basic machinery and tools to write such simulations. In addition, while Omnet++ models are created with a specific description language with its own graphical editor, our models as well as our simulation environment are both based on UML, shortening the learning curve for developers that are not expert in functional simulation, timing and performance analysis.

In [21], a model-driven approach is used to separately model the software architecture of a WSN, the low-level hardware specification of the WSN nodes and the physical environment where nodes are deployed in. The framework uses these models to generate executable code to analyze the energy consumption of the modeled application.

Finally, there are several ongoing research efforts towards the exploitation of fUML in MDE approaches for verification and validation activities. Benyahia et al. [22] evaluate how well the current fUML semantics supports the formalization of concurrent and temporal semantic aspects, which is required for the design and analysis of real-time embedded systems. They illustrate how the standard fUML execution model, as well as the fUML VM, have to be extended for this purpose to explicitly incorporate a *scheduler* into fUML that, at each step of the model execution, determines the activity node to be executed next according to certain scheduling policies (e.g., first-in-first-out (FIFO)). The same limitation has been addressed by Abdelhalim et al. [23]. In contrast to Benyahia et al. [22], they do not propose an extension of the standard fUML execution model but rather present a model-based framework that translates fUML activities into communicating sequential processes (CSP) for performing a deadlock analysis detecting possible scenarios leading to deadlocks shown on UML sequence diagrams.

7   Conclusion

We developed a model-driven approach that allows both modeling and the trace-driven performance analysis of software for WSN nodes running the Agilla mobile agents-based middleware. We adopted fUML, a strict executable UML subset, as design notation for AMF users and as well as development language for AMF itself. We provided modeling guidelines to AMF users in order to obtain an executable specification directly in UML, without the need of learning ad-hoc notations and tools. In this respect, thanks to its fUML native compatibility with UML, our approach is tool-supported by construction and can leverage many existing, industrial-strength UML-based tools. AMF is an ongoing work and, in this paper, we highlighted its new performance analysis capabilities. We show the modeling framework and the performance analysis at work on the WTA case study.

As future research goals, we plan to improve the design and scalability of existing analysis algorithms in fUML. We also plan to integrate new analysis algorithms for the sake of energy consumption, reliability, and trade-off analyses.

References

1. France, R.B., Rumpe, B.: Model-driven development of complex software: A research roadmap. In: Future of Software Engineering, pp. 37–54 (2007)
2. Cortellessa, V., Di Marco, A., Inverardi, P.: Model-Based Software Performance Analysis. Springer (2011)
3. Malavolta, I., Lago, P., Muccini, H., Pelliccione, P., Tang, A.: What industry needs from architectural languages: A survey. IEEE Trans. Softw. Eng. 39(6) (2013)
4. Bézivin, J.: Model driven engineering: An emerging technical space. In: Lämmel, R., Saraiva, J., Visser, J. (eds.) GTTSE 2005. LNCS, vol. 4143, pp. 36–64. Springer, Heidelberg (2006)
5. Fok, C.L., Roman, G.C., Lu, C.: Agilla: A mobile agent middleware for self-adaptive wireless sensor networks. ACM Trans. Auton. Adap. 4(3), 16 (2009)
6. OMG. Semantics of a foundational subset for executable UML models (2011)
7. TinyOS Operating System for WSNs, http://www.tinyos.net/
8. Gelernter, D.: Generative communication in Linda. ACM Trans. Program. Lang. Syst. 7(1), 80–112 (1985)
9. Di Marco, A., Pace, S.: Model-driven approach to Agilla agent generation. In: IWCMC 2013 Conference - Wireless Sensor Networks Symposium (July 2013)

10. Berardinelli, L., Di Marco, A., Pace, S., Marchesani, S., Pomante, L.: Modeling and timing simulation of agilla agents for WSN applications in executable UML. In: Balsamo, M.S., Knottenbelt, W.J., Marin, A. (eds.) EPEW 2013. LNCS, vol. 8168, pp. 300–311. Springer, Heidelberg (2013)
11. OMG. UML, Superstructure, Version 2.4.1 (2011)
12. Memsic MicaZ mote, http://www.memsic.com/wireless-sensor-networks/
13. Tatibouet, J., Cuccuru, A., Gérard, S., Terrier, F.: Principles for the realization of an open simulation framework based on fuml (wip). In: Proc. of the Symposium on Theory of Modeling & Simulation-DEVS Integrative M&S Symposium, p. 4. Society for Computer Simulation International (2013)
14. Gouvêa, D.D., et al.: Experience with model-based performance, reliability, and adaptability assessment of a complex industrial architecture. Software and System Modeling 12(4), 765–787 (2013)
15. Berardinelli, L., Langer, P., Mayerhofer, T.: Combining fUML and profiles for nonfunctional analysis based on model execution traces. In: QoSA (2013)
16. Fleck, M., Berardinelli, L., Langer, P., Mayerhofer, T., Cortellessa, V.: Resource contention analysis of service-based systems through fUML-driven model execution. In: Proc. of NiM-ALP, p. 6 (2013)
17. Mayerhofer, T., Langer, P., Kappel, G.: A runtime model for fUML. In: Proc. of the Int'l Workshop on Models@run.time (MRT 2012) at MODELS (2012)
18. Mozumdar, M.M.R., Lavagno, L., Vanzago, L., Sangiovanni-Vincentelli, A.L.: Hilac: A framework for hardware in the loop simulation and multi-platform automatic code generation of WSN applications. In: Symposium on Industrial Embedded Systems (SIES), pp. 88–97. IEEE (2010)
19. Berardinelli, L., Cortellessa, V., Pace, S.: Modeling and analyzing performance of software for wireless sensor networks. In: Int'l Workshop on Soft. Eng. Sensor Network App. (SESENA), pp. 13–18. ACM (2011)
20. OMNeT++ project web site, http://www.omnetpp.org/
21. Doddapaneni, K., Ever, E., Gemikonakli, O., Malavolta, I., Mostarda, L., Muccini, H.: A model-driven engineering framework for architecting and analysing wireless sensor networks. In: Int'l Workshop on Soft. Eng. Sensor Network App. (SESENA), pp. 1–7 (2012)
22. Benyahia, A., Cuccuru, A., Taha, S., Terrier, F., Boulanger, F., Gérard, S.: Extending the standard execution model of UML for real-time systems. In: Hinchey, M., Kleinjohann, B., Kleinjohann, L., Lindsay, P.A., Rammig, F.J., Timmis, J., Wolf, M. (eds.) DIPES 2010. IFIP AICT, vol. 329, pp. 43–54. Springer, Heidelberg (2010)
23. Abdelhalim, I., Schneider, S., Treharne, H.: An integrated framework for checking the behaviour of fUML models using CSP. Int'l Journal on Software Tools for Technology Transfer, 1–22 (2012)

Runtime Enforcement of Dynamic Security Policies

Jose-Miguel Horcas, Mónica Pinto, and Lidia Fuentes

Universidad de Málaga, Andalucía Tech, Spain
{horcas,pinto,lff}@lcc.uma.es
http://caosd.lcc.uma.es/

Abstract. The security policies of an application can change at runtime due to several reasons, as for example the changes on the user preferences, the lack of enough resources in mobile environments or the negotiation of security levels between the interacting parties. As these security policies change, the application code that copes with the security functionalities should be adapted in order to enforce at runtime the changing security policies. In this paper we present the design, implementation and evaluation of a runtime security adaptation service. This service is based on the combination of autonomic computing and aspect-oriented programming, where the security functionalities are implemented as aspects that are dynamically configured, deployed or un-deployed by generating and executing a security adaptation plan. This service is part of the INTER-TRUST framework, a complete solution for the definition, negotiation and run-time enforcement of security policies.

Keywords: Security enforcement, Security policy, Aspect-Oriented Programming, Dynamicity.

1 Introduction

A security policy is a set of rules that regulate the nature and the context of actions that can be performed within a system according to specific roles (i.e. permissions, interdictions, obligations, availability, etc) to assure and enforce security [1]. The security policies have to be specified before being enforced. This specification can be based on different models, such as OrBAC [2], RBAC [3], MAC [4], etc. and describes the security properties that an application should meet. Once specified, a security policy is enforced through the deployment of certain security functionalities within the application. For instance, the security policy "the system has the *obligation* of using a digital certificate to authenticate the users that connect using a laptop" should be enforced by deploying, within the application, "an authentication module that supports authentication based on digital certificates".

However, the security policies of an application can change at runtime due to many reasons, as for example the changes on the user preferences, the lack of enough resources in mobile environments or the negotiation of security levels between the interacting parties. As these security policies change, the application code that copes with the security functionalities should be adapted in order to enforce at runtime the changing security policies. In this sense, the use

P. Avgeriou and U. Zdun (Eds.): ECSA 2014, LNCS 8627, pp. 340–356, 2014.

of the Autonomic Computing (AC) paradigm [5] is nowadays widely accepted by the distributed systems community to endow distributed systems with this dynamicity or self-management capacities.

Following the typical MAPE-K loop of the AC paradigm, where "MAPE" stands for Monitoring-Analysis-Plan-Execution and 'K' stands for Knowledge, the development of a software system with self-adaptation of the security functionalities consists on providing support to: (1) model the security information, including the identification of those features that are foreseen that may change at runtime and the mapping with the security functionalities (Knowledge); (2) model the security functionalities that need to be deployed in order to enforce a required security level (Knowledge); 3) monitor the runtime environment to listen for changes (e.g. contextual changes, user preferences changes, changes on the resources availability) that may affect security (Monitor); 4) analyze how the occurred changes affect the security configuration of the application (Analysis); 5) define a plan with the set of changes that need to be performed in the current security configuration (Plan Generation), and 6) dynamically adapt the security configuration according to the plan generated (Plan Execution).

In this paper we focus on presenting how the security knowledge can be modeled making use of a Dynamic Software Product Line (DSPL) [6] approach, and how the generation and execution of the reconfiguration plan can be developed using Aspect-Oriented Programming (AOP) [7]. On the one hand, DSPL are an accepted approach to manage the runtime (security) variability of applications. DSPLs produce software capable of adapting to changes, by means of binding the variation points at runtime [6]. This means that the variants of the DSPL are generated at runtime. On the other hand, the AOP technology is very appropriate to implement the dynamicity that is required in our approach. AOP produces more modular software with a better separation of concerns and this facilitates the runtime weaving and/or unweaving of the security functionality. The rest of the MAPE-K loop (i.e. the monitoring and analysis phases) are out of the scope of this paper.

Part of this work has been developed in the context of the FP7 European Project INTER-TRUST [1]. INTER-TRUST is a framework for the specification, negotiation, deployment and dynamic adaptation of inter-operable security policies. Concretely, the modules that perform the dynamic generation and execution of the security adaptation plan are also part of INTER-TRUST[1]. However, the use that we make of DSPLs to represent the security information and to generate the security configurations at runtime is specific of our approach.

After this introduction, the paper is organized as follow. Section 2 presents our proposal following the MAPE-K loop. Section 3 describes the knowledge, while Section 4 explains how to generate a new security configuration from the security policies. Section 5 and Section 6 describes the generation of the adaptation plan and the execution of the plan respectively. Section 7 evaluates our proposal.

---

[1] They are open source and can be downloaded from https://github.com/Inter-Trust/Aspect_Generation/tree/demonstrator-version

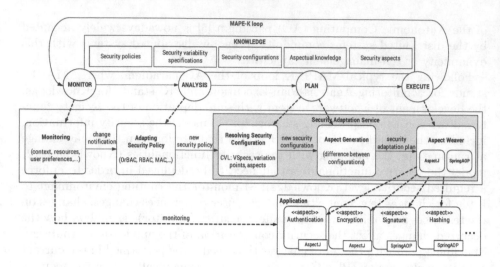

Fig. 1. Our MAPE-K loop approach and the Security Adaptation Service

Finally, Section 8 discusses the related work, and Section 9 presents conclusions and future work.

2   Our proposal

Figure 1 provides an overview of our proposal. As previously said, we follow the MAPE-K loop of the AC paradigm. An important part of the MAPE-K loop is the Knowledge, which in our approach represents all the information that is needed to adapt the applications to the changes on the security policies. The details about the Knowledge are provided in Section 3.

In the MAPE-K loop, the dynamic adaptations are driven by changes on the runtime environment. As shown in Figure 1, in our approach these changes are monitored and analyzed by the Monitoring and the Adapting Security Policy modules. These modules will depend on: which changes the application is interested on, such as changes in the context, changes in the user preferences, lack of enough resources in mobile environments, or negotiations of the security levels between interacting parties; the languages used to define the security policies (e.g. OrBAC [2], RBAC [3], MAC [4]), and the reasoning engine used to analyze and adapt those policies. The proposal presented in this paper is independent of a concrete design and/or implementation of these modules and thus the details about them are out of the scope of this paper. Basically, we will rely on existing approaches. For instance, in the context of the INTER-TRUST framework the monitoring is performed by the Montimage Monitoring Tool (MMT) [8] and the security policies are specified and analyzed using OrBAC [2].

Thus, this paper mainly focuses on the Resolving Security Configuration, the Aspect Generation and the Aspect Weaver modules that form the Security Adaptation Service (gray shaded in Figure 1). Firstly, the Resolving Security

`Configuration` module is in charge of selecting the proper configuration of the security functionality that needs to be deployed into the application in order to fulfill the requirements specified in the new security policy. All the possible security configurations are specified using a DSPL. Concretely, we use the Common Variability Language (CVL) [9] to specify and resolve the variability of the security functionalities. The details of this approach can be found in [10]. The main difference of both papers is that in [10] we used a SPL based on the use of CVL to generate a particular configuration of security during the design of applications. Now, we have extended that approach to use those security models at runtime and to integrate it in our `Security Adaptation Service`. These security functionalities are encapsulated into aspects by using AOP.

Secondly, the new security configuration is sent to the `Aspect Generation` module that dynamically generates a generic *security adaptation plan* with the actions that need to be performed with the security aspects (e.g. add a new aspect, remove an aspect, re-configure an aspect,...), taken into account the difference between the current security configuration deployed within the application and the new security configuration required, and using the available aspectual knowledge of the application (e.g. pointcuts and advices definitions).

Finally, the `Aspect Weaver` module executes the security adaptation plan at runtime by performing the particular actions of the AOP framework being used (e.g. weave/unweave). This module supports different AOP frameworks (AspectJ and Spring AOP) since the use of a unique AOP solution does not cover all the dynamicity, expressiveness, versatility, and performance requirements that the applications may need. For instance, Spring AOP allows weaving aspects at runtime (in contrast to AspectJ), and thus, we can add new security functionalities at runtime that were not taken into account when the application was initially deployed.

The Security Adaptation Service represents a generic solution that can be applied to many types of applications (e.g. pervasive applications, service-oriented applications, etc.) and can be used for the adaptation of any functionality, not only security. For instance, to illustrate our approach, we use an e-voting case study which is one of the demonstrators of the INTER-TRUST project where security requirements are complex and can change at runtime. This case study is provided by a enterprise partner of INTER-TRUST and a complete description of the e-voting application can be found in [1].

3   Knowledge

The knowledge represents all the information required in order to adapt the applications to changes on the security policies. The knowledge is available at runtime and includes: (1) the security policies that can be specified in any security model (e.g. OrBAC); (2) the security variability specifications; (3) the current security configuration deployed within the application; (4) the security aspectual knowledge; and (5) a repository with the security aspects files (i.e. class files, jar files, xml files,...).

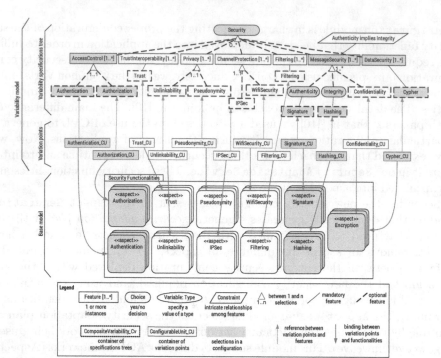

Fig. 2. Modeling security concepts in CVL

On the one hand, as previously said, the security knowledge is specified making use of DSPLs to manage the security variability at runtime. Figure 2 represents the security variability modeled in CVL. Top of Figure 2 shows the abstract part in which all the security concerns, functionalities, attributes and parameters that can be re-configured at runtime are specified — i.e. the variability specifications tree for security. Bottom of Figure 2 shows a representation of the particular implementation of the security functionalities encapsulated into aspects. Details of the parameters of each security concern in the variability specifications tree and in the aspects are hidden in Figure 2 to simplify it. Figure 3 shows a complete example for the authentication functionality and will be detailed in the next section. Finally, the security features of the tree and the specific functionality of the aspects are linked by using the CVL variation points[2] (middle of Figure 2). A particular selection of the features in the tree defines a particular configuration of the aspects. This configuration will be generated by the `Resolving Security Configuration` module, taking as input the requirements specified in the security policies.

On the other hand, the aspectual knowledge used by the `Aspect Generation` module depends on the application and on the implementation of the aspects since this information includes the points of the application where the security

---

[2] A complete description of CVL can be found in http://www.omgwiki.org/variability/

Listing 1.1. Security aspectual knowledge.

```
1  <ak:pointcuts>
2    <ak:pointcut id="Voter" expression="execution(* * Connection.*(
         Voter, ..)) && this(VoterClient)" />
3    <ak:pointcut id="sendingVoteJP" expression="execution(public *
         ElectionVote.sendVote(Vote, ..)) && args(Vote)" />
4  </ak:pointcuts>
5  <ak:advices>
6    <ak:advice id="certificateAuth" classname="uma.caosd.sas.
         Authentication"><ak:functionalities>
7      <ak:functionality id="authentication#digCertificate" />
8      <ak:functionality id="authentication#x509certificate" />
9    </ak:functionalities></ak:advice>
10   <ak:advice id="userPassAuth" classname="uma.caosd.sas.
         Authentication"><ak:functionalities>
11     <ak:functionality id="authentication#userPassword" />
12   </ak:functionalities></ak:advice>
13   <ak:advice id="encrypt" classname="uma.caosd.sas.Encryption"><
         ak:functionalities>
14     <ak:functionality id="confidentiality#encrypt" />
15     <ak:functionality id="confidentiality#rsa-encryption" />
16   </ak:functionalities></ak:advice>
17 </ak:advices>
18 <ak:advisors>
19   <ak:advisor id="certAuth" advice-ref="certificateAuth" pointcut-
         ref="Voter" />
20   <ak:advisor id="userPassAuth" advice-ref="userPassAuth" pointcut
         -ref="Voter" />
21   <ak:advisor id="encryptRSA" advice-ref="encrypt" pointcut-ref="
         sendingVoteJP" />
22 </ak:advisors>
```

functionality can be incorporated (i.e. the pointcuts definitions) and the list of functionalities provided by each aspect (i.e. the advices). The aspectual information is represented in a mapping table with the information needed to relate the different security functionalities required by the security configuration with the available advices implemented in the aspects. This information also includes the associations between the defined pointcuts and the advices — i.e. the advisors, following the Spring AOP terminology. The excerpt XML file in Listing 1.1 is an example of the aspectual knowledge for the e-voting application. We observe the lists of pointcuts (lines 2–7), the list of advices with the functionalities provided by each aspect (lines 9–38), and the list of advisors (lines 40–50).

4   Resolving Security Configurations

This section describes the generation a new security configuration that enforces the new security policy received from the Adapting Security Policy module.

When a request of a new security policy is received, the Resolving Security Configuration module extracts the security information from the rules of the security policy, selects the proper security features, and assigns the appropriate parameters in the security variability specifications tree of the DSPL. For instance, Figure 3 shows a particular configuration for the authentication functionality in the e-voting application, and thus the required configuration for the attributes and parameters of the authentication aspect. The configuration includes the use of an X.509 digital certificate as authentication mechanism; this

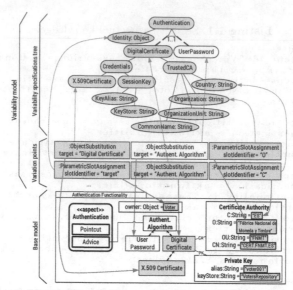

Fig. 3. Variability Modeling of Authentication functionality

Listing 1.2. New security configuration aspects.

```
1  <sca:aspects>
2    <sca:aspect  id="Authentication">
3    <sca:joinpoint  id="Voter"  />
4    <sca:functionalities>
5      <sca:functionality  id="authentication#digCertificate"  />
6      <sca:functionality  id="authentication#x509certificate"  />
7    </sca:functionalities><sca:configuration>
8      <sca:parameter  name="SessionKey">
9        KeyAlias="voter001",  KeyStore="VotersRepository"
10     </sca:parameter><sca:parameter  name="TrustedCA">
11       C="ES",  O="Fabrica  nacional  de  moneda  y  timbre",  OU="FNMT",  CN
           ="CERT.FNMT.ES"
12     </sca:parameter></sca:configuration></sca:aspect>
13 </sca:aspects>
```

means that the authentication aspect must use an advice that implements an authentication algorithm based on digital certificates. Moreover, the configuration also includes the parameters for the certificate authority (`TrustedCA`) such as the information about the organization that issued the certificate, and the values of the session key to be used with the certificate (`KeyAlias` and `KeyStore`). Note that only one kind of authentication mechanism can be selected at the same time for the same instance of the aspect. But, the variability model allows creating and configuring different instances of each aspect.

Then, when the CVL engine is executed at runtime, it resolves the variability and automatically generates a configuration of the security aspects that enforces the new security policy. Listing 1.2 shows the new configuration generated for the authentication aspect. This new configuration must be deployed within the application, so this configuration is notified to the `Aspect Generation` module.

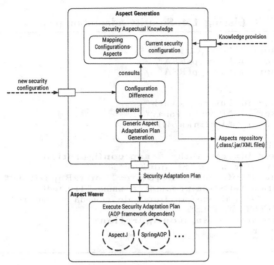

Fig. 4. Aspect Generation and Aspect Weaver architecture overview

Listing 1.3. Current security configuration deployed in the application.

```
1  <sca:aspects>
2    <sca:aspect  id=" Authentication ">
3      <sca:joinpoint  id=" Voter "  />
4      <sca:functionalities>
5      <sca:functionality  id=" authentication#userPassword "  />
6      </sca:functionalities></sca:aspect>
7    <sca:aspect  id=" Privacy "  ...  />
8    <sca:aspect  id=" Signature "  ...  />
9    <sca:aspect  id=" Hashing "  ...  />
10   <sca:aspect  id=" Pseudonymity "  ...  />
11   <sca:aspect  id=" Unlinkability "  ...  />
12 </sca:aspects>
```

5   Aspect Generation

The Aspect Generation module receives notifications about a new security configuration to be deployed, and dynamically generates a generic security adaptation plan with the actions that need to be performed with the security aspects currently deployed in the application. This module is independent from the AOP framework used to weave the aspects. Its architecture and internal components are specified in top of Figure 4.

The Security Aspectual Knowledge component represents the part of the knowledge related to the security aspects (e.g. classnames, functionalities) and to the applications (e.g. pointcuts) that the Aspect Generation module requires (Listing 1.1), as well as the current security configuration of the aspects deployed in the application (Listing 1.3). The information is incorporated at the initialization of the module and can be updated at runtime, including the incorporation of new aspects (pointcuts and/or advices) to the aspect repository.

The Configuration Difference component analyses the notified new configuration and the aspectual knowledge and determines whether the security aspects, currently instantiated in the application, fulfil the new configuration or

Listing 1.4. Security adaptation plan

```
1 <sap:ADD>
2    <sap:advisor id="certAuth" />
3    <sap:advisor id="encryptRSA" />
4    <sap:advisor id="decryptRSA" />
5 </sap:ADD>
6 <sap:REMOVE>
7    <sap:advisor id="userPassAuth" />
8    <sap:advisor id="Pseudonymity" />
9    <sap:advisor id="Unlinkability" />
10 </sap:REMOVE>
11 <sap:CONFIGURE>
12    <sap:advisor id="certAuth" ><sap:configuration>
13      <sca:parameter name="SessionKey">
14        KeyAlias="voter001", KeyStore="VotersRepository"
15      </sca:parameter><sca:parameter name="TrustedCA">
16        C="ES", O="Fabrica nacional de moneda y timbre", OU="FNMT", CN
              ="CERT.FNMT.ES"
17      </sca:parameter></sap:configuration>
18    </sap:advisor>
19 </sap:CONFIGURE>
```

some changes must be done in the deployed aspects. To do that, we calculate the difference between the current security configuration deployed in the application and the new requested configuration. Then, using the aspectual knowledge and the security configuration calculated, the **Generic Aspect Adaptation Plan Generation** component generates a list of actions that need to be performed within the aspects in order to satisfy the security configuration calculated — i.e. generates the security adaptation plan. The list of actions are independent from the AOP framework and are based on the concept of advisor — i.e. the advice with the functionality and the associated pointcut defining the points of the application where the functionality takes place (see the aspectual knowledge in Listing 1.1). The possible actions are:

1. **ADD**. Deploys a new advisor within the application.
2. **REMOVE**. Undeploys an advisor currently deployed in the application.
3. **CONFIGURE**. Re-configures the parameters of an advisor currently deployed in the application or to be deployed.

For instance, as a result of the difference between the current security configuration deployed in our e-voting application (Listing 1.3) and the new configuration to be deployed (Listing 1.2), the list of actions to fulfill the calculated new configuration are presented in Listing 1.4. Since the authentication mechanism has changed, we need to remove the **userPassAuth** advisor and add a **certAuth** advisor, but we also need to configure the new **certAuth** advisor with the appropriate parameters (lines 16–28). Moreover, there are some other advisors to be added (**encryptRSA** and **decryptRSA**) and to be removed (**Pseudonymity** and **Unlinkability**) — see the selections of Figure 2. Advisors related to the **Privacy**, **Signature**, and **Hashing** aspects do not change, so no actions need to be performed for these three aspects.

The security adaptation plan is the input to the `Aspect Weaver` module described in the next section.

6   Aspect Weaver

The `Aspect Weaver` module receives a security adaptation plan and dynamically weaves, unweaves, and configures the security aspects at runtime interacting directly with them. Bottom of Figure 4 overviews the architecture of this module.

Since the security aspects can be implemented in more than one AOP framework in order to fulfill all the application needs, the `Aspect Weaver` module works as a wrapper that translates the generic security adaptation plan to the particular syntax of the AOP weaver being used (AspectJ, Spring AOP, etc). This means that different instantiations of the `Execute Security Adaptation Plan` component of this module for using different AOP weavers are available. The output of this component is a direct interaction with the selected AOP weaver in order to add, remove, and configure the corresponding aspects into the applications.

The specific actions to be performed depend on the dynamicity provided by each AOP weaver. On the one hand, the AspectJ weaver only supports compile-time and load-time weaving, while the Spring AOP weaver supports run-time weaving. This means that, in case of the AspectJ weaver, the security aspects need to be woven with the application at compile- or load-time weaving. However, we improve the dynamicity of our solution by using the `if()` pointcut constructor that AspectJ provides to define a conditional pointcut expression which will be evaluated at runtime for each candidate join point[3]. This mechanism increases the degree of dynamicity by coding patterns that can support dynamically enabling and disabling advice in aspects [11,12]. An example of the use of this mechanism to increase the dynamicity of the AspectJ aspects is shown in Listing 1.5. The `Authentication` aspect includes two advisors (`certificateAuth` and `userPassAuth`) that can be enabled or disabled at runtime by changing the advisor status. These advisors associate the pointcut with the proper advices defined in the aspect. The execution of each advice is based on the conditional pointcut to be evaluated at runtime. So, in this case, the action of adding (deploying) an advisor corresponds to enabling an advisor, and removing (undeploying) an advisor corresponds to disabling an advisor. This is done by the custom instance of the `Execute Security Adaptation Plan` component for AspectJ.

On the other hand, in the case of the Spring AOP aspects, the actions corresponding with the addition/deletion of an advisor are real operations allowed by the Spring AOP API[4] and are implemented following the proxy-based mechanism used by the Spring AOP framework to perform the run-time weaving. In this case, the instance of the `Execute Security Adaptation Plan` component for Spring AOP is in charge of managing all the Spring artifacts (e.g. advisors, proxies, XML configuration files,...) and performing the appropriate actions specified in the adaptation plan.

---

[3] http://eclipse.org/aspectj/doc/released/progguide/index.html
[4] http://projects.spring.io/spring-framework/

Listing 1.5. Authentication aspect in AspectJ.

```
1  public aspect Authentication {
2    ...
3    pointcut Voter(VoterClient v): execution(* * Connection.*(Voter,
         ..)) && this(v);
4    pointcut certificateAuth(VoterClient v): if(AdvisorsStatus.
         isEnabled("certificateAuth")) && Voter(v);
5    pointcut userPassAuth(VoterClient v): if(AdvisorsStatus.isEnabled(
         "userPassAuth")) && Voter(v);
6
7    Object around(VoterClient v): certificateAuth(v) {
8      CertificateAuthentication auth = new CertificateAuthentication(
         AdvisorsParameters.getParams("certificateAuth"));
9      if (auth.authenticate(v.getVoter()))
10       proceed();
11   }
12
13   Object around(VoterClient v): userPassAuth(v) {
14     UserPassAuthentication auth = new UserPassAuthentication(
         AdvisorsParameters.getParams("userPassAuth"));
15     if (auth.authenticate(v.getVoter()))
16       proceed();
17   }
18   ...
19 }
```

7 Evaluation

Our approach uses consolidated software engineering technologies (DSPLs and AOP), and a proposed standard language (CVL). So, in this section we first qualitatively discuss our work to argue about its correctness, maintainability, extensibility, separation of concerns, and reusability, from the point of view of the use of DSPLs and AOP. Regarding AOP, in spite of its benefits, the main concern about the use of this technology in real projects is the performance overhead introduced by AOP. This means that a critical part of the evaluation of our approach should be the evaluation of the performance overhead introduced by the use of a specific AOP weaver. As part of our participation in the INTER-TRUST project, the `Aspect Generation` and the `Aspect Weaver` modules presented in this paper has been used to implement a demonstrator of the project that provides dynamic adaptation of security for an e-voting application[5]. This demonstrator has been evaluated both quantitatively, by controlled tests performed for the implementation of the `Aspect Generation` and `Aspect Weaver` modules, and qualitatively, by collecting the opinion of software developers with different expertise on both security and AOP. The main results of this evaluation are discussed in this section.[6]

---

[5] The code and the documentation of this demonstrator can be downloaded from `https://github.com/Inter-Trust/Aspect_Generation/tree/demonstrator-version`

[6] For more detailed information the reader can consult the project deliverables [13,14].

7.1   Qualitatively Results

Correctness. DSPLs and AOP do not improve the correctness of applications or security functionalities as such. However, modularizing security functionalities in separate modules with AOP considerably facilitates the verification of the security properties of an application since a security expert does not have to check all the modules in the base application to ensure that all security requirements are correctly enforced. Instead, only the code of the aspects and the definition of the pointcuts where the aspects will be introduced need to be checked. Additionally, it is well-known that the use of AOP can introduce vulnerabilities and security risks [15]. In our proposal, the `Monitoring` module is responsible for testing the behavior of the aspects [8] preventing these kinds of issues.

Separation of Concerns. The use of AOP improves modularization by allowing the separation of crosscutting concerns (i.e. the security functionalities in our approach). Moreover, following the MAPE-K loop we separate the different phases of our approach maintaining the independence of each module and facilitating the replacement of them.

Maintainability and extendibility. The use of DSPL allows us to easily reconfigure the security functionality according to the changes in the security policies. The variability model used (Figure 2) can also be extended to cover more security concerns.

Reusability. Our proposal is a generic solution that can be applied to many types of applications. The main drawback is that we cannot reuse completely the generated aspects for all the applications because they contain application dependent knowledge (e.g. pointcuts in the case of AspectJ). However, the security functionality (advices) can be reused in different contexts.

7.2   Performance overhead of AOP

AOP has important benefits in comparison to OO, such as achieving a better modularization of crosscutting concerns, improving the maintainability and the dynamic evolution of applications both at design and at runtime. These benefits are at the cost of a certain performance overhead, produced by the weaving process. In this evaluation, the main goal is to measure this performance overhead for the different AOP weavers and weaving mechanisms that we have used in the `Aspect Weaver` module, so we can reason about the suitability of using AOP for the `Security Adaptation Service`.

We have measured the time overhead introduced by the weaving process based on the lifetime of the application (compile-time, load-time, and run-time weaving) when the aspects are instantiated (Table 1) and when the advices of the aspects are executed (Table 2). We also consider the scalability of our solution when more than one aspect are applied at the same join point of the application. Results are summarized in Figure 5 and Figure 6. We observe that the overhead introduced by the AOP weavers is lower than the one initially expected. According to the data in Table 1, there is a penalty when the aspects are instantiated,

Table 1. Aspect weavers performance: aspects instantiation time (in milliseconds)

#aspect at the same join point:	1	5	10	20	50	100	1000
Compile-time weaving (AspectJ)	58.79	61.40	64.54	71.51	92.69	119.34	535.31
Load-time weaving (AspectJ)	19.81	20.91	30.11	53.72	109.46	196.22	1410.35
Run-time weaving (Spring AOP)	28.81	29.25	28.48	29.36	23.73	23.84	32.77

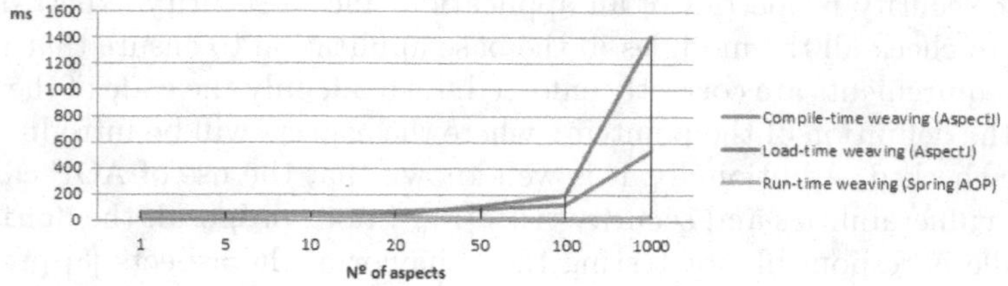

Fig. 5. Aspect weavers performance: aspects instantiation time

but, once the aspects have been created, the execution of them are faster (see Table 2). In any case, the results are similar for both the compile-time and load-time weaving. However, as expected, the runtime weaving introduces more overhead when the aspects are executed. Moreover, both AspectJ and Spring AOP weavers provide a great degree of scalability since a high number of aspects can be simultaneously applied at the same join point without reaching a non-acceptable performance overhead.

7.3 Results of the Software Developers Questionnaire

In [14] you can find a questionnaire about the usefulness of the INTER-TRUST framework in general, and in particular about the 'Aspect Generation and Aspect Weaver' demonstrator. That questionnaire was filled by evaluators that were selected mainly among software developers with different backgrounds and different levels of knowledge and experience in security issues and AOP.

Five participants who were experts in security modeling and negotiation answered the questions related to the Aspect Generation and Aspect Weaver demonstrator. In general, the results obtained are mainly in line with the expected target values (see [14] for more details about the metrics used to evaluate the demonstrator and the expected target values). However, some answers indicate that improvements can still be done for the next version of the demonstrator (and consequently, for the next version of the Aspect Generation and the Aspect Weaver modules). For instance, some evaluators were not convinced about the capacity of the Aspect Generation and Aspect Weaver modules to automatically deploy the security policies using aspects, its capacity for weaving the proper aspects or the runtime management of security policies and contextual information.

Additionally, five participants who were experts in security testing and monitoring also answered the questions related to the demonstrator. As for the experts on security modeling and negotiation, the results obtained were mainly in line with the expected target values.

Table 2. Aspect weavers performance: aspects execution time (in nanoseconds)

#aspect at the same join point:	1	5	10	20	50	100	1000
Compile-time weaving (AspectJ)	683	1280	1706	2560	5120	9813	106665
Load-time weaving (AspectJ)	426	854	1280	2560	4693	8960	111785
Run-time weaving (Spring AOP)	443301	439035	457808	474447	447568	479140	451408

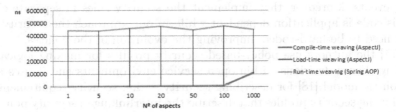

Fig. 6. Aspect weavers performance: aspects execution time

Finally, four participants who were experts in AOP answered the questionnaire. In general, we can say that the results obtained from AOP experts are better than the expected target values. Only one expert in AOP has considered that the security rules are not automatically deployed in the application original code. Since the rest of answers to this question are 'quite likely/extremely likely', we understand than the reviewer probably did not understand well either the question or how the modules functions regarding the automatic deployment of the aspects.

7.4 Discussion

The evaluation results obtained support our decision to use DSPLs and AOP in the design and implementation of our runtime Security Adaptation Service. However, we need to complete the evaluation with more interesting and conclusive empirical experiments. For instance, we need to evaluate the overhead of using AOP when different degrees of dynamicity are considered (e.g. when adding/removing advices and pointcuts) or when different instantiation models are used (e.g. aspect per object, aspect per control cflow,...). Moreover, we have not evaluated the global overhead introduced by the complete Security Adaptation Service, but only for the aspect solutions. Also, we need to increase the number of participants in the evaluation questionnaire in order to evidence the benefits and usefulness of our approach.

8 Related Work

There are a lot of works that try to deal with runtime adaptation of security. For instance, in [16] the authors present a policy-based approach for automating the integration of security mechanisms into Java-based business applications. They use security@runtime, an Domain Specific Language (DSL) for the specification of security configurations based on authorization, obligation and reaction policies. Our approach, in contrast, is suitable for using security policies specified in any model (e.g. OrBAC), since the mapping between the policies and the security functionalities is made in an abstract level of the variability model. Another difference with our approach is that we separate the monitoring of changes in the application and the integration of the security functionality following the MAPE-K loop while they integrate the security functionalities at the same monitoring events. Moreover, they implement the security rules in separate classes but this code is application dependent while in our approach the security rules do not need to be hard-coded, improving the evolution of the policies.

In [17] the authors use policy-based security profiles for making logical and knowledge-based decisions within open service environments and it uses a layered holistic model [18] for describing security — i.e. security requirements are defined using security profiles that describe the interlinking of security policies to instances of services. However, in our approach, the security policies are decoupled from the specific knowledge of the application and from the implementation of the security functionality in aspects, and this improves the reusability of both the security policies and the security functionalities.

Model-Driven Security (MDS) are often used to adapt dynamically security following different approaches: UMLSec [19], SecureUML [20], OpenPMF [21,22], SECTET [23], etc. For instance, in [24], models@runtime is used to keep synchronized an architectural model with a policy, but this approach only supports access control policies and not any kind of security functionality as in our security adaptation service. This is a general limitation in many security policy based approaches because they are mainly focused only on access control or authorization concerns ([21,22,25,26]) or focused only on a specific domain such as mobile cloud ([27]) or Service Oriented Architecture (SOA) ([21,22,23,25]).

There are also some generic approaches for reconfiguration at runtime that are not focused only on security concerns. In [28], Gamez et al. propose a reconfiguration mechanism that switches among different architectural configurations at run-time. The configurations are based on the specialization of feature models, and the reconfiguration plans are automatically generated from the differences among them. They propagate changes in configurations at architectural level instead of directly aspects implementation, as we do.

9   Conclusions and Future Work

We have presented a complete solution for the run-time enforcement of security policies following the MAPE-K loop of the AC paradigm that endow multiple kinds of applications with this dynamicity and self-management capacities. We have described in detail a security adaptation service based on the combination of DSPL and AOP technologies, where the security functionalities are implemented as aspects that are dynamically configured, deployed or un-deployed by generating and executing a security adaptation plan. These technologies bring significant benefits to our proposal, including a better modularization, maintainability, extendibility, and reusability.

As part of our future work, we plan to complete the evaluation of our `Security Adaptation Service` with empirical studies in order to evidence its benefits and usefulness.

Acknowledgment. Work supported by the European INTER-TRUST FP7-317731 and the Spanish TIN2012-34840, FamiWare P09-TIC-5231, and MAGIC P12-TIC1814 projects.

References

1. FP7 European Project INTER-TRUST: Interoperable Trust Assurance Infrastructure, http://www.inter-trust.eu/
2. Kalam, A., Baida, R., Balbiani, P., Benferhat, S., Cuppens, F., Deswarte, Y., Miege, A., Saurel, C., Trouessin, G.: Organization based access control. In: POLICY, pp. 120–131 (2003)
3. Ferraiolo, D.F., Sandhu, R., Gavrila, S., Kuhn, D.R., Chandramouli, R.: Proposed NIST standard for role-based access control. ACM Trans. Inf. Syst. Secur. 4(3), 224–274 (2001)
4. Sandhu, R.: Lattice-based access control models. Computer 26(11), 9–19 (1993)
5. IBM: Autonomic Computing White Paper - An architectural blueprint for autonomic computing. IBM Corp. (2005)
6. Hallsteinsen, S., Hinchey, M., Park, S., Schmid, K.: Dynamic Software Product Lines. Computer 41(4), 93–95 (2008)
7. Kiczales, G., Lamping, J., Mendhekar, A., Maeda, C., Lopes, C., Loingtier, J.M., Irwin, J.: Aspect-Oriented Programming. In: Akşit, M., Matsuoka, S. (eds.) ECOOP 1997. LNCS, vol. 1241, pp. 220–242. Springer, Heidelberg (1997)
8. Mallouli, W., de Oca, E.M., Wehbi, B., Fuentes, L., Pinto, M., Horcas, J.M., Benab, J.B., Prez, J.M.M., Ayed, S., Cuppens, N., Cuppens, F., Toumi, K., Cavalli, A., Kerezsi, E.: Specification and design of the secure interoperability framework and tools - first version. Deliverable D4.2.1, FP7 European Project INTER-TRUST (2013), http://inter-trust.lcc.uma.es/documents/10180/15714/INTER-TRUST-T4.2-MI-DELV-D4.2.1-SpecDesSecInterFram
9. Haugen, O., Wąsowski, A., Czarnecki, K.: CVL: Common Variability Language. In: SPLC 2012, vol. 2, pp. 266–267 (2012)
10. Horcas, J.M., Pinto, M., Fuentes, L.: Closing the gap between the specification and enforcement of security policies. In: TrustBus (2014)
11. Andrade, R., Ribeiro, M., Gasiunas, V., Satabin, L., Rebelo, H., Borba, P.: Assessing idioms for implementing features with flexible binding times. In: CSMR, pp. 231–240 (2011)
12. Andrade, R., Rebelo, H., Ribeiro, M., Borba, P.: Aspectj-based idioms for flexible feature binding. In: SBCARS, pp. 59–68 (2013)
13. Arrazola, J., Merle, L.: Specification of the evaluation criteria. Deliverable D5.2, FP7 European Project INTER-TRUST (2013), http://inter-trust.lcc.uma.es/documents/10180/15714/INTER-TRUST+-++D5.2+Specification+of+the+evaluation+criteria/72c26aff-51fa-4117-b9ba-7afcac8468e0

14. Bernab, J.B., Perez, J.M.M., Skarmeta, A.F., Pasini, R., Viszlai, E., Mallouli, W., Toumi, K., Ayed, S., Pinto, M., Fuentes, L., Horcas, J.M., Arrazola, J., Merle, L., Frontanta, J.L.V.: Results of first evaluation. Deliverable D5.3, FP7 European Project INTER-TRUST (2013), http://inter-trust.lcc.uma.es/documents/10180/15714/INTER-TRUST-T5.3-UMU-DELV-D5.3-ResultsFirstEval-V1.00.pdf/f8547c6e-bdbe-4be2-ade9-0698876d4423

15. Win, B.D., Piessens, F., Joosen, W.: How secure is AOP and what can we do about it? In: SESS, pp. 27–34. ACM (2006)

16. Elrakaiby, Y., Amrani, M., Le Traon, Y.: Security@runtime: A flexible mde approach to enforce fine-grained security policies. In: Jürjens, J., Piessens, F., Bielova, N. (eds.) ESSoS. LNCS, vol. 8364, pp. 19–34. Springer, Heidelberg (2014)

17. Tan, J.J., Poslad, S.: Dynamic security reconfiguration for the semantic web. Engineering Applications of Artificial Intelligence 17(7), 783–797 (2004)

18. Tan, J.J., Poslad, S., Titkov, L.: A semantic approach to harmonizing security models for open services. Applied Artificial Intelligence 20(2-4), 353–379 (2006)

19. Jrjens, J.: Secure Systems Development with UML. Springer (2010)

20. Basin, D., Doser, J., Lodderstedt, T.: Model driven security: From UML models to access control infrastructures. ACM Trans. Softw. Eng. Methodol. 15(1), 39–91 (2006)

21. Lang, U.: OpenPMF SCaaS: Authorization as a service for cloud amp; SOA applications. In: CloudCom, pp. 634–643 (2010)

22. Lang, U.: Cloud & SOA application security as a service. In: ISSE 2010 Securing Electronic Business Processes, pp. 61–71 (2011)

23. Katt, B., Gander, M., Breu, R., Felderer, M.: Enhancing model driven security through pattern refinement techniques. In: Beckert, B., Bonsangue, M.M. (eds.) FMCO 2011. LNCS, vol. 7542, pp. 169–183. Springer, Heidelberg (2012)

24. Morin, B., Mouelhi, T., Fleurey, F., Traon, Y.L., Barais, O., Jézéquel, J.M.: Security-driven model-based dynamic adaptation. In: ASE, pp. 205–214 (2010)

25. Dong, W.: Dynamic reconfiguration method for web service based on policy. In: Electronic Commerce and Security, 61–65 (2008)

26. Gheorghe, G., Crispo, B., Carbone, R., Desmet, L., Joosen, W.: Deploy, adjust and readjust: Supporting dynamic reconfiguration of policy enforcement. In: Kon, F., Kermarrec, A.-M. (eds.) Middleware 2011. LNCS, vol. 7049, pp. 350–369. Springer, Heidelberg (2011)

27. Cho, H.S., Hwang, S.M.: Mobile cloud policy decision management for mds. In: Lee, G., Howard, D., Kang, J.J., Ślęzak, D. (eds.) ICHIT 2012. LNCS, vol. 7425, pp. 645–649. Springer, Heidelberg (2012)

28. Gamez, N., Fuentes, L.: Software product line evolution with cardinality-based feature models. In: Schmid, K. (ed.) ICSR 2011. LNCS, vol. 6727, pp. 102–118. Springer, Heidelberg (2011)

Architectural Support for Model-Driven Performance Prediction of Distributed Real-Time Embedded Systems of Systems

Vanea Chiprianov, Katrina Falkner, Claudia Szabo, and Gavin Puddy

School of Computer Science
University of Adelaide
name.surname@adelaide.edu.au

Abstract. Systems of systems (SoS) are large-scale systems composed of complex systems with difficult to predict emergent properties. One of the most significant challenges in the engineering of such systems is how to predict their non-functional properties such as performance, and more specifically, how to model non-functional properties when the overall system functionality is not available. In this paper, we define an approach to SoS performance prediction based on the modelling of system interactions and their impacts. We adopt an Event Driven Architecture to support this modelling, as it allows for more realistic and flexible performance simulation, which enables more accurate performance prediction. We introduce a generic architecture and present its instantiation in a software architecture for the performance prediction of defence SoS. Our architecture allows for loose coupling, interoperability, and adaptability and facilitates sustainable evolution of the performance model of the SoS.

1 Introduction

Systems of systems (SoS) are large-scale concurrent and distributed systems that are comprised of complex systems [1]. SoS are complex systems themselves, and thus are distributed and characterized by interdependence, independence, co-operation, competition, and adaptation [2]. In the context of defence, SoS are concerned with interoperability and synergism of Command, Control, Computers, Communications, and Information (C4I) and Intelligence, Surveillance, and Reconnaissance (ISR) systems [3]. Defence SoS are characterized by long life-cycles, hard constraints on non-functional properties to meet the requirements of space, weight and power, and conformance to regulations and standards. These characteristics are reflected at the SoS level as well.

These challenges imply it is necessary to explore the expected performance by investigating several alternatives to system architecture, incorporating performance and space, weight and power requirements within the analysis. As they are conducted at the architecture level, such investigations provide a coarse grain prediction about the performance of a defence SoS, and not precise predictions. Investigating non-functional properties of SoS comprise all the issues

P. Avgeriou and U. Zdun (Eds.): ECSA 2014, LNCS 8627, pp. 357–364, 2014.
© Springer International Publishing Switzerland 2014

associated with the investigation of non-functional properties of composing systems. Moreover, there are challenges related to the specific nature of SoS [1], [2]. The decentralized, distributed nature of SoS require an emphasis on interface architecting to foster collaborative functions among its composing independent systems. The heterogeneity of the composing systems require interoperability and integration approaches. All these factors increase the difficulty of analysing non-functional properties of SoS.

One approach to allow the early checking of meeting non-functional performance requirements is *performance prediction modelling*. In this paper, we adopt the definition of *software performance prediction* introduced by [4]: 'the process of predicting (at early phases of the life cycle) and evaluating (at the end) based on performance models, whether the software system satisfies the user performance goals'. Similarly, we require that our understanding of performance prediction be based upon the provision and evaluation of an existing *performance model*. Prediction of software performance has developed from early approaches based on abstract models to *model-driven engineering* [5] based approaches. Model-driven engineering techniques use *Domain Specific Modelling Languages (DSMLs)*. A DSML is defined in this paper to be a language that offers expressive power focused on a particular problem domain through appropriate notation and abstractions.

System execution modelling (SEM) [6], a recent development from research into measurement-based performance prediction, provides detailed early insight into the non-functional characteristics of a DRE system design. System execution modelling supports the evaluation of overall (software) system performance, incorporating component interactions and the performance impact of 3rd party software such as middleware. These approaches [6], [7], [8] support detailed performance modelling of software systems, thus enabling predictions of performance through execution of representative source code of behaviour and workload models deployed upon realistic hardware testbeds.

While these approaches address the challenges of performance prediction of *individual* systems, cf. a review in Section 5, new mechanisms are needed to address the performance prediction of SoS. We review the requirements for such mechanisms, in Section 2. To fulfil them, we introduce in this paper a software architecture pattern for the SEM-based performance prediction of SoS, in Section 3. This generic software architecture provides a rich connection mechanism between performance models of individual, standalone, composing systems. Being based on event driven architecture, it allows for more realistic and flexible performance simulation, which enables more accurate performance prediction. We instantiate this generic architecture into a specific architecture for the performance prediction of defence SoS, in Section 4.

2   Requirements

To determine the requirements for the modelling environment designed to support the performance prediction of SoS within defence DRE systems, we undertook extensive discussions with stakeholders from the defence industry. The requirements detailed below influence our proposed software architecture.

1. *Loose coupling.* The systems that form an SoS are independent, but also need to interoperate and interact. Towards this, a mechanism that allows the description of loosely coupled interactions is needed.

2. *Interoperability of composing systems.* Different formalisms or modelling languages may be used to model performance prediction across the SoS. Moreover, to simulate realistic interconnectivity conditions between systems, different simulators (e.g. network simulators) may be used. A means to interconnect all these heterogeneous performance prediction models is necessary.

3. *Interaction specification.* The mechanism allowing the specification of loose interactions between composing systems of the SoS needs to be precise enough so as to limit the emergence of unexpected interactions to the point that they can be analysed as part of the performance prediction process. This also implies that the mechanism should allow for repeatability.

4. *Time and data distribution.* Because of its distributed nature, the performance prediction model of an SoS needs time and data distribution mechanisms between its composing performance models.

5. *Adaptability.* Both at the composing system and the SoS level, architectural reconfigurations (e.g. different types of middleware) within the performance models are necessary in order to analyse different architectural alternatives. Thus, a mechanism to generate code for a specific architectural configuration is necessary.

6. *Sustainable evolution.* The performance model of an SoS needs to accommodate models of composing systems being added, removed, and changed. The addition of new models, conforming to new formalisms, is related to the interoperability challenge. Removing models may impact the interaction specifications.

3   Software Architecture for Performance Prediction of Systems of Systems

The software architecture of our system addressing the requirements defined above is presented in Fig. 1, described in a formalism inspired from UML component diagrams. To predict the performance of a SoS, the performance of each of the composing systems needs to be predicted. This is due to the independent nature of the standalone composing systems of the SoS. Therefore, for each composing system, a Performance Model of the System (PeMS) is necessary. For each of these composing PeMS we use a SEM approach. In addition to the composing PeMS, a mechanism to specify the interaction of the loosely coupled interoperable composing systems is necessary.

The performance models of a system are integrated in our architecture using an event-driven approach. We base our architecture on the Event Driven Architecture (EDA) [9]. In an EDA, a notable event is immediately disseminated to all interested parties (human or automated). The interested parties evaluate the event, and optionally take action. The creator of the event (event generator) has no knowledge of the event's subsequent processing, or of the interested

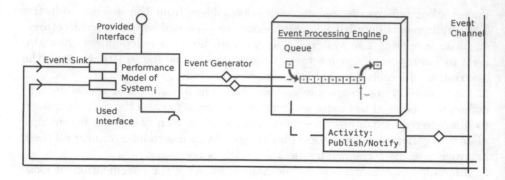

Fig. 1. Generic Software Architecture for Performance Prediction of SoS

parties (event sink). This makes EDA an extremely loosely coupled and highly distributed architecture. In terms of implementation, after an event has been triggered, a notification is produced and propagated to an event processing engine. The engine may order events according to a priority criteria, or may do other type of processing specified in the activity associated with the event. Next, it publishes the event notification on the event channel, which propagates it to all interested parties. The event sinks detect and decide whether to consume it.

In addition to addressing the loose coupling requirement, EDA also addresses the sustainable evolution requirement. Since the EDA event generator knows nothing about the event sinks, this enables an open-ended extension approach, in which event generators do not need to be modified to include new event sinks. Therefore, adding, removing and changing PeMS is simplified. The EDA event channel can be enhanced with a time and data distribution management bus. Such a bus, as long as it is independent of technologies used to describe PeMS, and is distributed, enables the interoperability of the PeMS.

The PeMS may be thought of as a component that provides an interface, and may use other interfaces, as shown in Fig. 1. It is described using a specific formalism. Independent of this formalism, we model the interactions with other PeMS using *event generators* and *event sinks*. The event generators of a PeMS produce event notifications that are sent to an *Event Processing Engine*, which orders them in a queue using a priority criteria. The engine processes the first event in the queue, and executes its associated activity. It next publishes the event notification on the *Event Channel*. The event channel may use different patterns, such as Reactor or Proactor [10], and propagates the event notification to all interested parties. The event sinks of all other PeMS detect it and may decide on an action. Event generators and sinks are introduced in the PeMS in ways specific to their formalism.

There may be multiple *Event Processing Engines* within the architecture. Each orders, in a queue, the events generated by several PeMS. The choice of which PeMS events should be ordered by a certain *Engine* may be decided through loading algorithms. Alternatively events may be grouped as Complex Events, that can be handled by the Complex Event Processing component of that Engine. All *Event Processing Engines* publish the event notifications directly on the *Event Channel*. This ensures a highly distributed, loosely coupled architecture that facilitates scalability and fault tolerance as the possibility of single point of failures or choke-points is reduced.

We introduce a Scenario domain specific modelling language (DSML) to specify interactions. It is built on top of the SoS performance prediction software architecture, containing concepts specific to EDA, and thus generic with respect to the composing PeMS. It is used to describe interactions between composing PeMS. The Scenario DSML also contains entities that are specific to the type of SoS whose composing systems' interactions are being described. For example, a defence SoS will contain Organisations with Units in an Environment, while an enterprise SoS may contain Actors interacting with Components, Devices, following certain Processes, etc. The Scenario DSML is presented in more detail in [11]. Complementary to it, we allow the user to interact with the model, to visualise its performance results. This visualisaton component can be extended to replace the Scenario DSML only with user commands.

The Scenario DSML uses model-driven engineering and code generation techniques to facilitate adaptability. For example, from the scenario model, code can be generated to different middleware implementations of the event channel or bus. The adaptability requirement is met also inside the PeMS, as it is possible to reconfigure each model with a different middleware.

In summary, the software architecture of our system answers the identified requirements, and is generic with respect to the composing PeMS, being agnostic of them, with the exception of event generators and sinks.

4 Specific Software Architecture for Performance Prediction of DRE Defence Systems of Systems

We have instantiated the Software Architecture for Performance Prediction of Systems of Systems to the domain of Defence. As part of this instantiation, the performance model of a system is modelled as a system execution model, using the Component Workload Emulator Utilization Test Suite (CUTS) formalisms, as described in Section 4.1. To instantiate the Event channel, we chose the Data Distribution Service (DDS), due to its extensive support of non-functional properties through QoS policies that support various time and data management mechanisms. We adopt a global wall clock time management pattern. DDS uses a Publisher-Subscriber (Observer) pattern.

The Event Generator is modelled specifically for the SEM, as an Effector worker, which describes the behaviour of the model when it sends an output. As discussed above, the Effector worker is a mechanism to implement the Event Generator in a way specific to the formalism used to describe the performance model. Similar to the Event generator, the Event sink is modelled in a way specific to the performance model formalism we chose, i.e., the system execution model, as a Sensor worker. A Sensor Worker models the system execution model behaviour when it receives an input. To communicate with the Event channel, i.e. the DDS bus in our case, a DDS subscriber - a mechanism specific to DDS - is necessary as well. Complementary, to send information on the DDS bus, the Activity attached to an Event must have a DDS publisher mechanism.

The Event Processing Engine is implemented in C++, containing a generic queue for all types of events. The priority criterion for ordering the events in the queue is based the conditions that guard the triggering of an event, e.g., conditions based on specific values of input parameters. These conditions are part of the Scenario DSML, described below.

4.1   Software Architecture for Performance Prediction of DRE Defence Standalone Systems

For completeness, we include here a discussion on our performance analysis and prediction process for a standalone SEM, described using CUTS formalisms. It has five steps: Model; Execute; Predict; Evaluate; and Evolve [12]. A DRE system is first modelled from different points of view. The modelling step includes the modelling of the DRE system's performance constraints together with scenarios of exercising the system in different conditions. From these models, distributed code is generated for different platforms of interest. The generated code is executed in the second step and information about its execution on various platforms is captured and aggregated into performance metrics. In the evaluation step, the metrics are shown to the expert through context-specific visualisations, such that (s)he can decide if the model fulfils the performance requirements. Depending on the expert's decision, modifications may be proposed to the initial models. These modifications may explore several alternatives, and each may result in a new generation of alternatives in the evolution step. The process continues from the modelling step and stops only when the expert decides to do so. We defined an architecture and associated tools to implement this process [13]. Executing the SEM code within its indicated deployment produces Execution traces and Basic metrics about the system performance.

5   Related Work

Predicting the performance of SoS has a number of approaches, e.g. a systematic review [14] identifies nine. For example, [15] presents a data-centric, capability-focused process for analysing architectures of SoS. An executable model of the architecture and the performance of the SoS is defined and its results are used to analyse and evaluate the performance of the SoS architecture. However, the SoS is treated like a standalone system; one model is defined for the entire SoS, not a model for each of its composing systems, as we do. Other approaches deal with developing metrics for performance measurement. For example, [16] adapts the notion of technical performance measure to SoS, proposing a hierarchical metric called SoS performance measure. However, it focuses strictly on defining a measurement metric, while our approach is much more complete.

There are numerous works on model-based performance engineering, including comprehensive surveys [4], [17], [18] that explore the many approaches, methodologies, and case studies. Several researchers explore the potential for modelling performance based on a complete understanding of the system architecture. UML MARTE defines a UML profile, which provides for the inclusion of non-functional requirements (i.e. performance, reliability, scalability) as UML models, which can be analysed as part of the development process. Our approach is complementary to that provided by MARTE, in that we provide support for emulation of performance models above existing middleware and hardware to support early performance evaluation within multiple realistic deployment scenarios, in addition to integrated analysis and visualisation.

6 Conclusion and Perspectives

In this paper, we proposed a software architecture for predicting the performance of SoS. We focused on SoS for which event-based modeling and simulation is pertinent. Based on the Event Driven Architecture, our architecture allows connecting heterogeneous performance models of composing systems (PeMS) using Event Channels. It is generic with respect to the composing PeMS, being agnostic of them, with the exception of event generators and sinks. We instantiated this generic architecture into an architecture for predicting the performance of Distributed Real-time Embedded defence SoS.

The PeMS are assumed to be solved by simulation. The Performance Modelling process for each composing system of the SoS has five steps: Model; Execute; Predict; Evaluate; and Evolve. To implement this process we used System Execution Modelling tools and Modelling Languages and tools that we defined using a Model Driven Engineering approach, but other ways of defining the Performance Models can be envisaged and easily included, for example with UML MARTE. This shows the genericity of our architecture in including heterogeneous performance modeling formalisms.

However, several avenues for future work still exist. In the generic software architecture, we are investigating alternatives for the Event Processing Engine(s) to allow the specification of various loading and other complex event processing criteria. In the specific architecture, we are looking into ways to integrate network and other simulators to provide for even mode detailed performance analysis.

References

1. Jamshidi, M.: System of systems engineering - new challenges for the 21st century. IEEE Aerospace and Electronic Systems Magazine 23(5), 4–19 (2008)
2. Dagli, C.H., Kilicay-Ergin, N.: System of Systems Architecting, pp. 77–100. John Wiley & Sons, Inc. (2008)
3. Manthorpe, W.H.: The Emerging Joint System of Systems: A Systems Eng. Challenge and Opportunity for APL. J. Hopkins APL Tech. Digest 17, 305–310 (1996)
4. Balsamo, S., Marco, A.D., Inverardi, P., Simeoni, M.: Model-based performance prediction in soft. dev.: a survey. IEEE Trans. on Soft. Eng. 30, 295–310 (2004)

5. Beydeda, S., Book, M., Gruhn, V. (eds.): Model Driven Software Development. Spinger (2010)
6. Hill, J., Schmidt, D., Slaby, J.: System Execution Modeling Tools for Evaluating the Quality of Service of Enterprise Distributed Real-time and Embedded Systems. In: Designing Software-Intensive Systems: Methods and Principles, pp. 335–371 (2008)
7. Paunov, S., Hill, J., Schmidt, D., Baker, S., Slaby, J.: Domain-Specific Modeling Languages for Configuring and Evaluating Enterprise DRE System Quality of Service. In: 13th IEEE Intl Symp and Wksh on Eng. of Comp. Based Sys. (2006)
8. Hill, J., Schmidt, D., Edmondson, J., Gokhale, A.: Tools for continuously evaluating distributed system qualities. IEEE Software 27(4), 65–71 (2010)
9. Michelson, B.M.: Event-driven architecture overview. Technical report, Patricia Seybold Group (2006)
10. Schmidt, D.C., Stal, M., Rohnert, H., Bushmann, F.: Pattern-oriented Software Architecture: Patterns for Concurrent and Networked Objects. Wiley (2000)
11. Falkner, K., Chiprianov, V., Falkner, N., Szabo, C., Puddy, G.: Modeling scenarios for the performance prediction of distributed real-time embedded systems. In: Military Communications and Inf. Systems Conf., Canberra, Australia, pp. 1–6 (2013)
12. Falkner, K., Chiprianov, V., Falkner, N., Szabo, C., Puddy, G.: A model driven engineering method for DRE defence systems performance analysis and prediction. In: Bagnato, A., Indrusiak, L.S., Quadri, I.R., Rossi, M.G. (eds.) Industry and Research Perspectives on Embedded System Design. IGI-Global (accepted, 2014)
13. Falkner, K., Chiprianov, V., Falkner, N., Szabo, C., Hill, J., Puddy, G., Fraser, D., Johnston, A., Rieckmann, M., Wallis, A.: Model-driven performance prediction of distributed real-time embedded defence systems. In: The 18th Intl Conf. on Engineering of Complex Computer Systems, Singapore, pp. 155–158 (2013)
14. Klein, J., van Vliet, H.: A Systematic Review of System-of-systems Architecture Research. In: The 9th Intl ACM Sigsoft Conf. on Quality of Software Architectures, QoSA 2013, pp. 13–22. ACM, New York (2013)
15. Ge, B., Hipel, K.W., Yang, K., Chen, Y.: A data-centric capability-focused approach for system-of-systems architecture modeling and analysis. Systems Engineering 16(3), 363–377 (2013)
16. Volkert, R., Stracener, J.T., Yu, J.: A framework for performance prediction during development of systems of systems. Intl J. of System of Syst. Eng. 3, 76–95 (2012)
17. Smith, C.: Introduction to soft. performance engineering: origins and outstanding problems. In: 7th Intl. Conf. on Formal Meth. for Perf. Evaluation, pp. 395–428 (2007)
18. Koziolek, H.: Performance evaluation of component-based software systems: A survey. Performance Evaluation 67(8), 634–658 (2010)

Safety Perspective for Supporting Architectural Design of Safety-Critical Systems

Havva Gülay Gürbüz, Bedir Tekinerdogan, and Nagehan Pala Er

Department of Computer Engineering, Bilkent University, Ankara 06800, Turkey
havva.gurbuz@bilkent.edu.tr,
{bedir,nagehan}@cs.bilkent.edu.tr

Abstract. Various software architecture viewpoint approaches have been introduced to model the architecture views for stakeholder concerns. To address quality concerns in software architecture views, an important approach is to define *architectural perspectives* that include a collection of activities, tactics and guidelines that require consideration across a number of the architectural views. Several architectural perspectives have been defined for selected quality concerns. In this paper we propose the *Safety Perspective* that is dedicated to ensure that the safety concern is properly addressed in the architecture views. The proposed safety perspective can assist the system and software architects in designing, analyzing and communicating the decisions regarding safety concerns. We illustrate the safety perspective for a real industrial case study and discuss the lessons learned.

Keywords: Software architecture design, software architecture modeling, software architecture analysis, safety-critical systems.

1   Introduction

To address quality concerns in software architecture views, an important approach is to define *architectural perspectives* that include a collection of activities, tactics and guidelines that require consideration across a number of the architectural views [6]. In this context, Rozanski and Wood define several architectural perspectives for selected quality concerns such as security, performance, scalability, availability and evolution. In order to capture the system-wide quality concerns, each relevant perspective is applied to some or all views. In this way, the architectural views provide the description of the architecture, while the architectural perspectives can help to analyze and modify the architecture to ensure that system exhibits the desired quality properties.

An important concern for designing safety-critical systems is safety since a failure or malfunction may result in death or serious injury to people, or loss or severe damage to equipment or environmental harm. It is generally agreed that quality concerns need to be evaluated early on in the life cycle before the implementation to mitigate risks. For safety-critical systems this seems to be an even more serious requirement due to the dramatic consequences of potential failures. For coping with safety several standard and implementation approaches have been defined but this has not been directly considered at the architecture modeling level. Hence, we propose the *Safety*

P. Avgeriou and U. Zdun (Eds.): ECSA 2014, LNCS 8627, pp. 365–373, 2014.

Perspective that is dedicated to ensure that the safety concern is properly addressed in the architecture views. The proposed safety perspective is defined according to the guidelines as described by Rozanski and Woods [6]. The safety perspective can assist the system and software architects in designing, analyzing and communicating the design decisions regarding safety concerns. We illustrate the safety perspective for a real industrial case study and discuss the lessons learned.

The remainder of the paper is organized as follows. Section 2 presents the proposed safety perspective. Section 3 illustrates the safety perspective for an industrial case study. Finally, section 4 presents the conclusion.

2   Safety Perspective

Rozanski&Woods provide the following guidelines [6] to define a new perspective:
- The perspective description in brief in *desired quality*
- The perspective's *applicability to views*
- The *concerns* which are addressed by the perspective
- An explanation of *activities for applying the perspective* to the architectural design.
- The *architectural tactics* as possible solutions when the architecture doesn't exhibit the desired quality properties the perspective addresses
- Some *problems and pitfalls* to be aware of and risk-reduction techniques
- *Checklist* of things to consider when applying and reviewing the perspective to help make sure correctness, completeness, and accuracy

Table 1 shows the proposed safety perspective description including the above points. In the following we shortly discuss the each point.

Table 1. Brief Description of Safety Perspective

Desired Quality	The ability of the system to provide an information about safety-related decisions and ability to control and monitor the hazardous operations in the system
Applicability	Any systems which include hazardous or safety-critical operations
Concerns	Failures, Hazard, Risks, Fault Tolerance, Availability, Reliability, Accuracy, Performance
Activities	Identify hazards, Define risks, Identify safety requirements, Design safety model, Assess against safety requirements
Architectural Tactics	Avoid from failures and hazards, Define failure detection mechanisms, Mitigate the failure consequences
Problems and Pitfalls	Describing the fault tolerance, No clear requirements or safety model, Underestimated safety problems

Table 2 shows how the safety perspective affects each of the architectural views as defined by Rozanski and Woods [6]. For all the seven views the safety perspective seems to be useful and can reshape the corresponding view. The activity diagram in Fig. 1 shows the activities for applying the safety perspective. The first step includes the identification of the hazards followed by the definition of risks. This is followed by identifying and detailing the safety requirements. After the safety requirements safety models are designed and the safety requirements are assessed. In the following section we explain each activity using an industrial case study.

Table 2. Applicability of Safety Perspective to Architectural Views

View	Applicability
Functional View	The functional view allows determining which of the system's functional elements considered as safety critical.
Information View	The information view helps to see the safety-critical data in the system
Concurrency View	While designing the safety-critical systems, some elements need to be isolated or integrated in runtime. Therefore this will affect the system's concurrency structure.
Development View	Applying this view can help to provide a guideline or constraints to developers in order to raise awareness for the system's safety critical elements.
Deployment View	Applying this view can help to determine the required hardware, third-party software requirements and some constraints for safety.
Operational View	Safety implementation includes critical and complex operations. Therefore, operational view needs to consider safety critical elements to describe system's operation properly.
Context View	Applying this view can help to understand which types of users will use the system and which external systems are necessary to make sure the system operates correctly.

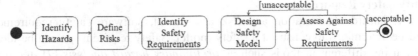

Fig. 1. Applying the Safety Perspective

3 Case Study

In this section we show the application of proposed safety perspective approach by using an avionics control system project of a company. To illustrate the application of the proposed safety perspective we have selected *"displaying aircraft altitude data"* as an example requirement for our case study. Altitude is defined as the height of the aircraft above sea level. Pilots depend on the displayed altitude information especially when landing.

3.1 Activities for Safety Perspective

This section explains how the activities given in Fig. 1 are applied to our case.

Identify Hazards

In order to identify and classify hazards, preliminary hazard analysis can be conducted which should include the list of all hazards, their probable causes and consequences, and the severity. Hazard severity levels are defined as *catastrophic, critical, marginal* or *negligible* in [2]. Hazard identification activity is performed with domain experts (avionics engineers and pilots), system engineers and safety engineers.

We have selected *"displaying wrong altitude data"* hazard related to selected requirement as an example hazard to illustrate the remaining activities. The possible causes of this hazard are loss of/error in altimeter device, loss of/error in communication with altimeter device and error in display device. Aircraft crash is identified as the possible consequence of this hazard. Severity of this hazard is identified as catastrophic since possible consequence of the hazard is aircraft crash.

Define Risks
To define risks, estimation of probability of hazard occurrence for each hazard should be carried out. In [2], occurrence definitions are defined as *frequent, probable, occasional, remote* or *improbable*. Based on the hazard severity and hazard occurrence class identification, risks should be assessed and categorized as *high, serious, medium* or *low* [2]. After the risk definition, risk assessment should be conducted by methods such as fault tree analysis, event tree analysis, simulation etc. For our case study, our design criterion is to design the system such that the probability of occurrence of all catastrophic failures should be improbable. Since the selected hazard is catastrophic hazard, the probability of occurrence is improbable. According to severity category and probability of occurrence, the risk category of the selected hazard is medium.

Identify Safety Requirements
After the hazard identification and risk assessment, software safety requirements should be determined to construct a safety model. Safety requirements can be identified by using different methods such as *preliminary hazard analysis* [7], top-down analysis of system requirements and specifications [7] and *fault tree analysis* [5]. Additionally, there are some other methods which combine the several existing techniques to derive safety requirements. To illustrate this step, we produce *"Probability of displaying wrong altitude should be improbable"* as a high-level safety requirement related to selected hazard. Many low-level safety requirements can be generated from this high-level safety requirement. Examples of the generated low-level safety requirements are (1)*"Altimeter data should be received at least two independent altimeter devices."*, (2) *"If the difference between two altimeter values received from two altimeter devices is more than a given threshold, the altimeter data should not be displayed and a warning should be generated."*, (3)*"Altimeter data should be shown on at least two independent display devices ".*

Design Safety Model
To present the safety-critical elements or components in the system a safety model is needed that can be derived from safety requirements. One way to create a safety model of the system is defining an extension mechanism to UML models [3]. UML extension can be achieved by adding stereotype to UML diagrams. Another approach to design a safety model is defining a domain-specific language [12]. Another way to express safety model is using automata [14].

This activity is an iterative process. The models are created first and then they are checked against the safety requirements. The models can be changed according to these checks. We prefer to show two versions of the architecture for our case study.

The first version is designed without considering the safety requirements. It is modified after safety requirements are identified, that is, after safety perspective is applied, which results in the second version. The reasons of the modifications will be explained in the next section (assessment section). The left part of the Fig. 2 shows the deployment diagram of the first version, which includes one avionics control computer (AvionicsComputer), one altimeter device (Altimeter), and one display device (GR_Display). The deployment diagram of the second version, after applying the safety perspective, is shown in the right part of the Fig. 2. The second version includes two avionics control computers (AvionicsComputer1 and AvionicsCompu-ter2), two altimeter devices (Altimeter_1 and Altimeter_2), and two display devices (GR_1_Display and GR_2_Display). Avionics control computer contains following modules: M1153 Manager (M1553), A429 Manager (A429), Navigation Manager (NAV), Graphics 1 Manager (GR_1), Graphics 2 Manager (GR_2), Health Monitor (Health_Monitor).

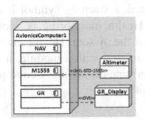
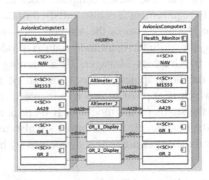

Fig. 2. Deployment View for the First Version (left) and for the Second Version(right)

M1553 Manager receives data from the devices connected to MIL-STD-1553 communication channels. Similarly, A429 Manager receives data from the devices on the ARINC-429 communication channels. MIL-STD-1553 and ARINC-429 are two widely known communication standards used in avionics systems. These two managers just receive the data and send it to the required modules. They do not make any calculations on the data. Navigation Manager receives the altimeter data from M1553 Manager and A429 Manager and makes the range check and difference check calculations on the altimeter data. If the difference between two altimeter values received from two altimeter devices is more than a given threshold, a warning data is produced. The altimeter data and warning data are sent to Graphics Managers. Graphics Managers drive two graphical displays according to the received data. A well-known standard called DVI is used to drive graphical displays. *SC* (Safety Critical) stereotype is defined to tag the safety-critical modules in the second version of the deployment diagram. *SC* stereotype differentiates the safety-critical modules from the rest of the modules.

Assess Against Safety Requirements

After designing the system's safety model, it should be assessed to check whether it is consistent with identified safety requirements. There is only one altimeter device and one display device in the first version of the architecture so low-level safety requirements 1 and 3 are not satisfied. We adapted the first version and included one additional altimeter device and one additional display device in the second version of the architecture. There are two different altimeter devices and two different display devices in the second version so low-level safety requirements 1 and 3 are satisfied.

Redundancy is also accomplished for the avionics control computer in the second version of the architecture. There are two avionics computers which can communicate to each other for heartbeat messages (through UDP protocol). They run according to master/slave paradigm. Only one of the avionics computers can be master at a given time. If slave avionics computer cannot receive heartbeat messages, it can become master. Both of them can receive altimeter data and can display it on graphical display devices but only the master computer does it.

Safety requirement 2 is also satisfied in the second version of the architecture. Navigation Manager checks the altitude data and produces either the altitude data or a warning for altitude. If altitude data is produced, it is displayed on both graphical devices by Graphics Managers. If a warning is generated, a warning symbol is displayed on the graphical devices instead of altitude. Health monitoring is another tactic which is applied in order to increase the safety of the system. Health monitor checks the status of the modules. If there is a problem related with a module, it can restart the module. Health monitors are also used to determine master/slave condition. Heartbeat messages are sent and received by health monitors.

3.2   Architectural Tactics

Architectural tactics can be considered as possible solutions when the architecture does not exhibit the required quality properties addressed by the perspective. In order to avoid from failures and hazards, one way is making the system as simple as possible. Another way is applying *redundancy* [13] by replicating the components in the system. The other way is N-version programming proposed by Chen and Avizienis [1]. By using N-version programming technique, different designs can be created for each version of the system in order to determine design faults from safety perspective. If hazards and failures occur, system should be able to detect them. In order to detect the failures, failure detection mechanisms can be derived from safety requirements [8]. Another tactic for failure detection is *heartbeat* [ref] which offers a mechanism for periodically monitoring the aliveness and arrival rate of independent runnables. At the architecture design level, based on the hazard identification and risk definition, consequences of failures can be predicted and reduced/prevented. *Redundancy* and *replication* also can be used in order to mitigate from the failure consequences.

Several architectural tactics are utilized for our case study. The first architectural technique is redundancy. Several parts of the system are designed as redundant in order to satisfy both safety requirements and high availability needs. This technique is applied to avoid from failures and mitigate the failure consequences. Health monitoring technique is applied for failure detection of the safety-critical modules. Table 3 summarizes the applied tactics. Similar tactics can be applied for other identified catastrophic hazards.

3.3   Checklist

In this section, we provide checklists in Table 4 for requirements capture and architecture definition to consider when applying and reviewing the perspective to help make sure correctness, completeness, and accuracy. We have applied the checklist to our case study. Results are presented in third column of Table 4. All items in the checklist are answered as yes except for the item 9. Since our case study doesn't include any safe state, this question is answered as not applicable.

Table 3. Architectural Tactics for the Case Study

Tactic	Avoid.	Detect.	Mitigate
If one of the altimeter devices produces wrong altimeter output, this fault is detected by Navigation Manager and a warning is generated	✓	✓	✓
If one of the display devices crashes and cannot display altitude data, the other one continue to display it.	✓		✓
If master avionics computer is not available, the slave avionics computer becomes master and starts to operate.	✓		✓
If a safety-critical module fails, this failure is detected by health monitor. The module is re-started.		✓	✓

Table 4. Checklist Table

No	Explanation	Y/N/NA
1	Have you identified safety-critical operations in the system?	Yes
2	Have you identified possible failures and hazards including causes and consequences of them?	Yes
3	Have you worked through the hazard severity and occurrence information to define the risks?	Yes
4	Have you identified availability needs for safety of the system?	Yes
5	Have you worked through example scenarios with your stakeholders so that they understand the planned safety risks the system runs?	Yes
6	Have you reviewed your safety requirements with external domain experts?	Yes
7	Have you addressed each hazard and risk in the designed safety model?	Yes
8	Is the design of safety model as simple as possible and highly modular?	Yes
9	Have you identified safe states and fully checked and verified them for completeness and correctness?	NA
10	Have you produced an integrated overall safety design of the system?	Yes
11	Have you defined the fault tolerance of the system?	Yes
12	Have you applied the results of the safety perspective to all effected views?	Yes
13	Have domain experts reviewed the safety design?	Yes

3.4   Applicability to Views

Table 5 lists the application of safety perspective to the views for our case study.

Table 5. Safety Perspective Application for the Case Study

View	Applicability to the case study
Functional	Safety-critical modules are determined (see right part of the Fig. 2)
Information	Safety-critical data is determined (altitude data)
Concurrency	Not applicable
Development	Requirement Standard, Coding Standard, Design Decisions, Reviews / Checklists and common processing required are defined.
Deployment	There are two avionics control computers, two altimeter devices and two display devices. (see right part of the Fig. 2)
Operational	Check the correctness of the loaded binaries, Software Configuration Management and Software Problem Reporting for safety-critical defects are defined, maintenance and user training are provided.
Context	External devices related with safety-critical features are determined.

4   Conclusion

Safety-critical systems need to be carefully designed and analyzed because a failure may result in death or serious injury to people, or severe damage to equipment. Hereby, the architecture design plays a crucial role to support the overall design and realization of the system and ensure the required level of safety. Addressing quality concerns at the architecture view level has been actually based on either defining a new viewpoint [2] or using architecture perspectives [7], each with their own merits. In our earlier work we have considered the explicit modeling of viewpoints for quality concerns [9][10][11]. Unfortunately, so far no architectural perspective has been defined for the safety concern. Based on the guidelines by Rozanski and Woods [7] we have proposed a safety perspective that can be used in the design of safety-critical systems. We have applied the safety perspective in a real industrial context. The safety perspective helps the designers to explicitly reason about and document the design decisions regarding the safety concern. In this respect, the safety perspective appeared not only to be useful as a guidance tool for assisting the safety engineer and the architect, but it also helped in the early analysis of the architecture. In our future work we aim to apply the safety perspective for several other domains and consider the trade-off analysis with the perspectives for other quality concerns. Further we also aim to define a viewpoint for safety.

References

[1] Chen, L., Avizienis, A.: N-Version Programming: A Fault-Tolerance Approach to Reliability of Software Operation. In: Fault Tolerant Computing, FTCS-8, pp. 3–9 (1978)

[2] Clements, P., Bachmann, F., Bass, L., Garlan, D., Ivers, J., Little, R., Nord, R., Stafford, J.: Documenting Software Architectures: Views and Beyond, 1st edn. Addison-Wesley (October 2002)

[3] MIL-STD-882D, Standard Practice for System Safety, Department of Defense (2000) (retrieved January 22, 2014)

[4] Pataricza, A., Majzik, I., Huszerl, G., Várnai, G.: UML-based design and formal analysis of a safety-critical railway control software module. In: Proc. of Symposium Formal Methods for Railway Operation and ControlSystems (FORMS 2003), Budapest, pp. 125–132 (2003)

[5] Ramezani, R., Sedaghat, Y.: An Overview of Fault Tolerance Techniques for Real-Time Operating Systems. In: 3th International Conference on Computer and Knowledge Engineering, pp. 1–6 (2013)

[6] Rausand, M., Hoylan, A.: System Reliability Theory, Models, Statistical Methods, and Applications. Wiley, USA (2004)

[7] Rozanski, N., Woods, E.: Software Architecture Systems Working with Stakeholders Using Viewpoints and Perspectives, 1st edn. Addison-Wesley (2005)

[8] Software Safety Guide Book, NASA Technical Standard (2004)

[9] Sojer, D., Christian, B., Knoll, A.: Deriving Fault-Detection Mechanisms from Safety Requirements. In: Computer Science- Research and Development, pp. 1–14. Springer (2011)

[10] Sözer, H., Tekinerdogan, B.: Introducing Recovery Style for Modeling and Analyzing System Recovery. In: 7th IEEE/IFIP Working Conference on Software Architecture, Vancouver, Canada, February 18-22, pp. 167–176 (2008)

[11] Sözer, H., Tekinerdogan, B., Aksit, M.: Optimizing Decomposition of Software Architecture for Local Recovery. Software Quality Journal 21(2), 203–240 (2013)

[12] Tekinerdogan, B., Sözer, H.: Defining Architectural Viewpoints for Quality Concerns. In: Crnkovic, I., Gruhn, V., Book, M. (eds.) ECSA 2011. LNCS, vol. 6903, pp. 26–34. Springer, Heidelberg (2011)

[13] Wasilewski, M., Hasselbring, W., Nowotka, D.: Defining requirements on domain-specific languages in model-driven software engineering of safety-critical systems. In: Lecture Notes in Informatics Software Engineering Workshopband, pp. 467–482 (2013)

[14] Wu, W., Kelly, T.: Safety Tactics for Software Architecture Design. In: 28th Annual International Computer Software and Applications Conference, Hong Kong, pp. 368–375 (2004)

[15] Yu, G., Wei Xu, Z.: Model-Based Safety Test Automation of Safety-Critical Software. In: International Conference on Computational Intelligence and Software Engineering, pp. 1–3 (2010)

How Do Software Architects Specify and Validate Quality Requirements?

Andrea Caracciolo, Mircea Filip Lungu, and Oscar Nierstrasz

Software Composition Group, University of Bern, 3012 Bern, Switzerland
{caracciolo,lungu,oscar}@iam.unibe.ch
http://scg.unibe.ch

Abstract. Software architecture is the result of a design effort aimed at ensuring a certain set of quality attributes. As we show, quality requirements are commonly specified in practice but are rarely validated using automated techniques. In this paper we analyze and classify commonly specified quality requirements after interviewing professionals and running a survey. We report on tools used to validate those requirements and comment on the obstacles encountered by practitioners when performing such activity (*e.g.*, insufficient tool-support; poor understanding of user's needs). Finally we discuss opportunities for increasing the adoption of automated tools based on the information we collected during our study (*e.g.*, using a business-readable notation for expressing quality requirements; increasing awareness by monitoring non-functional aspects of a system).

Keywords: Software architecture, empirical study, quality requirements, validation.

1 Introduction

The primary task of a software architect is to define and specify a suitable high-level design solution that fulfills all major technical and operational requirements. The document describing the architecture provides requirements and guidelines that will help in maintaining the conceptual and technical integrity of a software product. Quality requirements describe expected characteristics of specific aspects of the system, from its implementation to its observable behavior. They may refer to externally visible product qualities (*e.g.*, performance requirements) or to implementation details that support them (*e.g.*, legitimate module dependencies). Ensuring the enforcement of quality requirements and their deriving constraints should prevent architectural decay and make the system more adaptable to new, emerging requirements [3].

In this study we set out to survey whether the definition of quality requirements is a common practice in IT companies. We want to understand whether this activity is systematic and supported by tools and processes or rather based on personal assumptions and using makeshift tools. Finally, we are interested whether quality requirements, given their importance, are also automatically validated as the software system evolves.

P. Avgeriou and U. Zdun (Eds.): ECSA 2014, LNCS 8627, pp. 374–389, 2014.
© Springer International Publishing Switzerland 2014

Previous studies [7,8,13] propose solutions for specifying architectural invariants. Other studies [1,18,19,10] rank non-functional qualities (*e.g.*, performance, usability, availability, *etc.*) by carrying out surveys. In neither case is effort made to explore quality attributes from the point of view of practitioners.

In our study we focus on the following research questions:

1. What kind of quality requirements do architects define in practice?
2. How are quality requirements specified?
3. How are quality requirements validated?

To answer these questions, we use empirical methods to identify quality attributes that practitioners consider when designing their architecture. Furthermore we analyze how practitioners specify quality requirements in their documentation and explore the various techniques that are used for validation.

We observe that architects do not always adopt automated techniques to validate quality requirements and when they do, they automatically verify only a small subset of all the specified requirements. We discuss possible obstacles that might cause this situation as well as research opportunities that could lead to a general improvement in the practice of quality requirements validation (Section 5). Among the identified opportunities we consider the advantages of adopting a business-readable declarative language for specifying quality requirements. We also explore the benefits of promoting architectural visibility by introducing continuous validation support for user-defined quality requirements in current monitoring platforms (*e.g.*, Sonarqube).

2 Research Method

This paper uses a mixed research methods strategy: *sequential exploratory design* [4]. This approach consists of two different research methodologies: a qualitative investigation followed by a quantitative validation survey which triangulates the results of the first.

In the first study, we focused on collecting qualitative data. The goal of this study was to gain a possibly comprehensive overview of the state of practice in the definition and validation of quality requirements. The questions have been iteratively refined by conducting three internal pilot interviews with PhD and master students with professional experience in the field. The final list of questions, used as loose guideline for the actual interviews, is available on our web site[1]. Fourteen people working for six different organizations agreed to participate in our study (Table 1). More than 70% of the participants have been contacted indirectly through an intermediary and had no relevant links to the academic community. The remaining subjects were contacted directly and belonged to our industrial collaboration network. All interviews were carried out independently, leading to a set of complementary and partially overlapping observations. A total of approximately 18 hours of conversation have been recorded.

---

[1] http://scg.unibe.ch/research/arch-constr/study

Table 1. Interview study participants. Candidates with an asterisk worked in projects aimed at supporting architectural design. The remaining candidates worked as software architects or project managers in medium to large projects and have more direct experience in architectural design.

#	Role	Org.	Project (domain; type)	team size
A	CEO, architect	C1	government / enterprise	<5
B	business manager	C2	government / enterprise	10-50
C	project manager	C3	insurance / enterprise	>50
D	architect	C4	logistic / enterprise(integration)	<5
E	developer	C4	logistic / enterprise(integration)	<5
F	CTO	C5	banking / enterprise	>50
G	architect	C2	government / enterprise	5-10
H	architect	C2	government / enterprise	10-50
I	architect	C6	logistic / enterprise(migration)	>50
J*	developer	C2	government / development support tool	<5
K	architect	C5	banking / enterprise	5-10
L	architect	C6	transportation / control systems	5-10
M*	developer	C5	banking / source code analysis	>5
N*	architect	C5	banking / development support tool	5-10

The main outcome of this qualitative study was the list of quality attributes presented in Table 2. These quality attributes were inferred by analyzing the interviews and synthesizing the main concerns using coding techniques [17]. To support this activity, we identified and labeled quality requirements in interview transcriptions as well as the documentation files (*i.e.*, Software Architecture Documents, Developer guidelines) that we collected at the end of several interview sessions. To gather more evidence that the observations coming from the first study actually reflected the state-of-practice of a broader community, we created an e-survey. Over a time span of two months we collected 34 valid and complete responses. Invitations were sent to professionals selected among industrial partners and collaborators (*i.e.*, convenience sampling method), including people involved in the first phase of the study. The survey was also advertised in several groups of interest related to software architecture hosted by LinkedIn and on Twitter[2] (*i.e.*, voluntary sampling method). Survey participants were asked to specify whether the quality attributes identified in the first study were ever encountered in a past project, their perceived level of importance (on a scale from 1 to 5, with 5 being the highest), the formalism adopted to describe them and the testing tool used for their validation. A complete copy of the survey can be found on our web site[1].

3   Learning from Practitioners: A Qualitative Study

During interviews, we tried to elicit a possibly wide range of distinct architecturally significant quality attributes. We asked our respondents to enumerate

---

[2] http://www.linkedin.com; http://www.twitter.com

those concerns that could be considered fundamental for their architecture. For each of those, we asked them to describe their main properties and the form in which they were typically specified. Table 2 shows all identified quality attributes. For each quality attribute, we also present additional details collected during our quantitative study (columns 3-6 in Table 2).

Quality attributes are categorized based on the closest matching ISO-25010[11] quality characteristic. For simplicity's sake, we decided to pair each attribute with one single category. For clarity, we also published some explanatory requirements for all presented quality attributes on our web site[1].

Table 2. Taxonomy of quality requirements (grouped by supported quality characteristic). Columns (from left to right): Matching quality characteristic; Quality requirement; Evaluated importance (first, second and third quartile); Participants who encountered the requirement in a previous project (familiarity); Participants who specified the requirement using a formal notation. Columns 3-6 contain data collected during our quantitive study.

Quality Characteristic	Quality Attribute (Internal / External / Process)	Importance Q_1	Q_2	Q_3	Fam.	Form. Not.
Performance	Response time (E)	3	4	5	15%	14%
	Throughput (E)	3	4	4	26%	13%
	Hardware infrastructure (I)	2	3	4	29%	0%
Compatibility	Signature (I)	3	4	4	18%	52%
	File location (I)	1	3	4	29%	18%
	Data structure (I)	2	3	4	29%	47%
	Communication (I)	2	4	4	15%	22%
Usability	Visual design (E)	2	3	3.5	9%	21%
	Accessibility (E)	1	2	3.5	50%	0%
Reliability	Availability (E)	4	4	5	15%	14%
	Recoverability (E)	2	3	5	32%	5%
	Data integrity (I)	3	3	4	18%	23%
	Event handling (I)	2	3	4	35%	25%
	Software update (P)	1	2	3	59%	0%
Security	Authorization (E)	4	4	5	3%	23%
	Authentication (E)	3	4	5	21%	12%
	Data retention policy (I)	2	3	4	12%	13%
Maintainability	Meta-annotations (I)	1	3	4	32%	39%
	Code quality (I)	2	3	3.5	15%	19%
	Dependencies (I)	2.5	3	4	18%	53%
	Naming conventions (I)	2	3	3	12%	38%
Portability	Software infrastructure (I)	3	3	4	24%	8%

3.1 Identified Quality Attributes

We now comment on the identified quality attributes.

Performance: performance was often mentioned as being a key concern. Requirements on *response time* and *throughput* are commonly part of the acceptance criteria defined with the customer at the beginning of a project. Several respondents (*e.g.*, **A**, **B**) define latency requirements on the execution of specific tasks (*e.g.*, The system has to answer each request within 10 ms). Others (*e.g.*, **A**, **D**) set limits for the accepted throughput (*e.g.*, The system must be able to execute a certain task 10'000 times per hour). These requirements are often validated by collecting timestamps during execution or simulating high traffic load with a script. *Hardware infrastructure* requirements, specifying the hardware resources required to support a specific software implementation, also play a role in determining performance.

Compatibility: multiple interviewees (**B**, **F**, **J**) mentioned *communication* as one of the most important aspects in their architecture. **F** built a client simulator to test conformance with the prescribed communication protocol and check syntactical/semantical data consistency. **N** defined a guideline stating that data has to be passed from one layer to the other using Data Transfer Objects. **G** wrote a detailed specification of all service interfaces composing his application (*signature* attribute). This included details regarding accepted parameter values and activity diagrams describing the message exchange protocol. Interoperability between different components and tools often requires files to be placed into pre-determined folders or structure files according to a given shared schema (*file location* attribute).

Usability: *visual design* and compliance to *accessibility* guidelines were mentioned as typical requirements for application front-ends. **H** developed a web interface that had to conform to a set of rules defined in the corporate visual style guide. This requirement was satisfied by defining global stylesheets and forcing their inclusion into all related applications.

Reliability: robustness and fault-tolerance are important features for almost any kind of application. **H**'s application was required to guarantee 96% *availability* and a clear recovery procedure was defined for each type of fault that was likely to occur. *Data integrity* is also a major concern. **K** managed to maintain internal data consistency by defining data type classes for all supported business value types. **H** and **G** constrained field values specifying Hibernate or Spring formatting annotations. Specific rules were also defined to regulate strategies for *handling events* (*e.g.*, exceptions, notifications) and *update software* packages (*e.g.*, libraries).

Security: security is also considered critical and is often tested thoroughly. Verification becomes a necessity when the system is directly exposed to a large untrusted audience. Testing seems to have lower priority if the application is just deployed within an intranet (**E**). Most of the time, widely known frameworks (*e.g.*, JAAS) are used to implement *authentication* and *authorization* rules.

Maintainability: class *dependencies* and syntactic code invariants are commonly considered tightly related to software architecture. **H** even claims that "dependencies between modules are the main characteristic of a software architecture". Requirements on these two aspects are defined to support architectural principles (loose coupling, high cohesion) and minimize the cost of future maintenance.

Portability: requirements related to *software infrastructure* configuration are common. Prescriptions on technologies to be adopted can be found in almost every specification document. **J**, for example, specifies that the "persistence layer" of his application must use Hibernate as a persistence framework. Software infrastructure requirements are often related to rules addressing compatibility issues (*i.e.*, file location, data structure).

3.2   Specifying Quality Requirements

All the participants of our study describe their quality requirements in one or more text documents. The vast majority adopt a well-known standard template (*e.g.*, 4+1[12], togaf[3], arc42[4]). Textual documentation is always complemented with diagrams based on a common shared visual language (*e.g.*, UML, BPML, BPEL, flowchart, informal notation).

Documentation Audience. Documentation is written to satisfy the needs of three main stakeholders: customers, architects and developers.

For Customers: documentation is written to meet contractual requirements. In this case documentation is often seen as a burden for the architect and provides limited support to practitioners working on the project. It provides a non-technical specification that can be used to prove compliance to agreed requirements during a post-development validation phase (**G**).

For Architects: documentation is written to maintain a general overview of the system and support high-level design reasoning. Some respondents believe that developers are not interested in reading about architecture. "Developers only care about functionality and tend to ignore non-functional properties" (**E**). This assumption supports the idea that architecture and implementation are on different levels of abstraction and are hard to link together. Low effort is usually dedicated to keep documentation aligned and up-to-date with changes originated in the implementation. **I** stated that he rarely got any sort of feedback from the assumed recipients of his documentation work.

For Developers: documentation is a map, providing a high-level description of the system to technical users involved in the development process. It is particularly useful as an initial entry-point for new developers learning about the system. **D** said that "new developers start by reading the documentation, look into the code and finally sort out remaining doubts by talking with colleagues". Documentation is used to transfer knowledge, is open for change and needs to be kept up-to-date.

Documentation Intent. In our study we identified two type of documentation styles: descriptive and prescriptive.

---

[3] http://www.opengroup.org/togaf
[4] http://www.arc42.de

Descriptive Documentation: is meant to provide sufficient evidence to support developers in decision making activities. It is not written to set precise guidelines and rules but to help developers in evaluating alternatives and make good design choices. Architects writing "descriptive documentation" are usually skeptical about enforcing design rules through documentation. **D** said that "documented rules are often perceived as pedantic and restrictive". He added that "forcing developers to learn them beforehand is a failing strategy and often leads to poor results" because "they could be ignored and neglected". Apparently a much better approach is to provide useful feedback to developers when they break such rules.

Prescriptive Documentation: is more oriented towards the definition of strict guidelines and rules. The goal is to limit developers in their design choices in order to guarantee high-level properties (*e.g.*, maintainability). In this case, it's often convenient to express quality requirements in a clear and objective way. Most of the documents collected during our studies contained coding guidelines (general practices and syntax format rules) and quality requirements regarding data values and event handling.

Formalization of Quality Requirements. Quality requirements are rarely described formally. Formal specification is only used in practice to support specific verification tools. In this case, users are forced to extract architectural rules from the specification document and encode them in a separate file using a tool-specific notation.

In rare cases, companies develop their proprietary description language. **N** worked in a company where all developed applications are documented as visual diagrams based on a proprietary meta-model. Their models include a hierarchically organized set of interlinked logical components. All types of entities are characterized by various properties (*e.g.*, interface structure for components; message format, protocol, integration type for communication links). Each system, consisting of a set of components, is mapped to the specific infrastructural entity on which it is supposed to be deployed. This last information is used to feed a semi-automatic process for verifying the actual deployment configuration. **N** said that the documentation model adopted in his company is very helpful for keeping information consistent, accurate and closed to interpretation.

In other cases, users face the lack of usability of current specification mechanisms. **D**, for example, decided to verify package dependencies using a specific testing framework (JDepend). Unfortunately the test specification required by the adopted tool was not readable enough to be included in the official documentation. To solve this problem, he decided to specify the requirements in a spreadsheet and build a parser to generate a corresponding set of tests. In this case, having a simplified and testable representation of architectural rules justified the cost for building a conversion tool.

3.3 Validating Quality Requirements

We observed that quality requirements are validated using various approaches.

Manual Validation. According to the answers collected during our study, one way of validating quality requirements is simply by running the system and manually checking some operational properties (*e.g.*, *Response time*, *Authentication*). This validation strategy is usually preferred when automated testing tools are not available or exist but are too expensive to buy or customize. Scalability is sometimes verified by generating a large number of requests using a script and evaluating responsiveness by interacting with the application through an additional session. Properties that manifest themselves in source code (*e.g.*, *Code conventions*), are often checked through code reviews. As mentioned by **L**, "the number of existing [testing] tools is far from being exhaustive". He said that "companies rarely see the value of investing time in researching new testing techniques". In many cases manual validation seems to be the most viable and frequently chosen alternative.

No Validation. Some respondents avoid the need for direct verification by relying on a framework or code generator. If the framework is not developed internally, the fact that certain quality requirements are actually fulfilled is based on trust. **J**, responsible for the development of an internal framework used across multiple company projects, said that "frameworks should not be invasive but support the developer by simplifying his tasks and reducing possible design decisions in a non-invasive way". Frameworks that are built to limit implementation choices, as confirmed by **M**, are not well perceived by developers. A framework should convince developers to use its functions by offering useful services that contribute to reducing the cost of development (**J**). Code generators are typically used to simplify the maintenance and creation of modules that depend on business needs that vary through time. Our interviewees agreed on the fact that building testing tools is usually not an economically viable option. Building testing tools is also seen as a challenging task requiring advanced programming skills.

Automated Validation. When possible, architects prefer to use automated techniques. This can be done by writing programmatic tests or relying on tools developed by a third party. Existing tools do not always fit the needs of our respondents. Multiple respondents said that some of the currently available tools were lacking in flexibility and usability. **F** worked on a project where components could be identified by looking at the suffix of class names. All the tools he tried supported package name matching as the only mapping strategy. **K** was working on a system based on the OSGi framework[5]. He was not aware of any tool that allowed him to automatically check whether the specified dependencies existing between the OSGi bundles composing his system were actually consistent with the architectural specification. The only way to verify the alignment between implementation and specification was to manually inspect large XML configuration files.

---

[5] http://www.osgi.org/

Most of the tools force users to operate on an overly technical level. This fact prevents non-technical stakeholders from accessing valuable information and introduces new costs for setting-up and maintaining architectural tests. Current testing solutions require the user to specify testing rules in separate files. Quality requirements must be specified twice: in the official documentation using natural language (for supporting communication and reasoning) and in a purpose-built formal specification file (for supporting a specific testing solution). The resulting fragmentation leads to increased costs for maintaining multiple specifications aligned and consistent.

4   Corroborating the Evidence: A Quantitative Study

To confirm the validity of our impressions on a larger scale, we developed a second study. This study was aimed at obtaining a more uniform overview on how quality attributes (identified in the first study and presented in Table 2) are considered by practitioners.

We now report some of the main observations resulting from the analysis of the obtained results.

O1. Most requirements are not formally specified: Our survey confirms that very few requirements are formally or semi-formally specified (Table 2). In fact, only 2 quality requirements (*Signature, Dependencies*) out of 22 are formally specified more than 50% of the time. *Signature* quality requirements are specified using UML with custom profiles, XSD and IDLs (OMG IDL, MIDL, WSDL). *Dependencies* are described using tool-specific notations (*e.g.*, JDepend, ndepend, macker, DCL, SOUL), Java annotations and UML with custom profiles. Others (*Data structure, Naming conventions*) are also quite frequently formalized. *Naming conventions* can be specified using regular expressions, EBNF grammars, tool-specific notations (*e.g.*, SOUL for IntensiVE) or Java (*e.g.*, plugins for Checkstyle and PMD). *Data structure* quality requirements are either specified using standard schema definition languages (DTD, XSD) or semi-formal modeling notations (ER, UML).

O2. Automated testing is not commonplace: Results show that the use of automated techniques (*i.e.*, using white-/black-box testing or tools) for validating quality requirements is not commonplace (Figure 1). On average, 59% of the surveyed population adopts non-automated techniques (*e.g.*, code review or manual validation) or avoids validation completely. Based on the results of our survey (Figure 1), the following quality requirements are mostly validated manually: *Dependencies* (10 users), *Visual design* (8), *Naming conventions* (7), *Communication* (5). Quality requirements that remain most often unvalidated are: *hardware infrastructure* (50% of respondents), *recoverability* (48%) and *software update* (44%). Automated validation is not commonplace and is mostly adopted to validate quality requirements regarding end-user properties (*e.g.*, *Response time, Throughput*) and security (*e.g.*, *Authorization, Authentication, Data retention policy*). Table 3 shows which tools are used by the participants of our survey to validate the identified quality attributes.

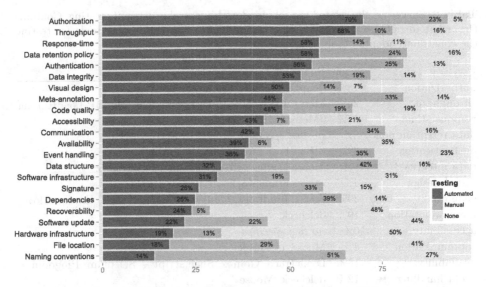

Fig. 1. Survey results: various approaches for validating quality requirements

O3. Tool support for automated validation is insufficient: One of the reasons why automated validation is not widespread seems to be related to the scarce availability of industrial-strength tools matching some practitioner's needs. A number of quality attributes (*e.g.*, *Code dependencies*, *Naming conventions*) can be checked with a large number of tools, while others (*e.g.*, *Data integrity*, *Meta-annotations*), considered as equally important, can only rely on a much smaller range of solutions.

O4. User's needs are still not completely recognized: Figure 1 shows that several requirements are also more frequently validated manually than automatically. The most striking examples are *Data structure, signature, dependencies*. This suggests the possibility that some requirements are still left unaddressed and need to be investigated further by conducting on-the-field studies. We believe that further analysis of emerging requirements could lead to new opportunities for future research in the field of tool development and tool building support.

O5. Emphasis is given to secondary requirements: Another interesting observation is that quality attributes that have been most frequently encountered in past work experiences (*e.g.*, *Software update, accessibility*) generally do not have a significant impact on the outcome of an industrial project (See "familiarity" and "importance" columns in Table 2). Further studies should analyze current design and specification methodologies and propose improvements on existing documentation practices.

Table 3. Survey results related to tool-aided architectural constraints testing. Columns (from left to right): Constraint name; respondents using third-party tools for testing the constraint; adopted tools.

Constraint	Tool	Reported Testing Tools
authorization	15%	SoapUI / *other:* Framework (JAAS)
throughput	26%	Meter, LISA, Selenium, Lucust, Gatling, HP LoadRunner
response-time	17%	JMeter, LISA, Selenium
data retention policy	8%	*no tool specified*
authentication	3%	*other:* Framework (JAAS, Spring)
data integrity	8%	Moose / *other:* db-constraints, Framework
visual design	4%	*other:* Framework
code quality	39%	Sonar, Findbugs, Code critics, Checkstyle, Emma, Clover
meta-annotation	19%	dclcheck
accessibility	0%	*no tool specified*
communication	8%	Moose, dclcheck
availability	10%	DynaTrace, Gomez, Shell script + Selenium, Pingdom
event handling	12%	dclcheck, Moose
data structure	16%	Moose / *other:* Custom tools
software infrastr.	8%	*other:* Automated declarative provisioning
signature	7%	Moose, JMeter, soapUI
dependencies	22%	SAVE, dclcheck, Patternity, Jdepend, Ndepend, Macker, IntensiVE, SmallLint, DSM tool
recoverability	0%	*no tool specified*
software update	0%	*no tool specified*
hardware infrastr.	6%	*no tool specified*
file location	0%	*other:* Guaranteed by framework
naming conventions	11%	Code critics, Checkstyle, PMD, FxCop, IntensiVE, Petit-Parser

O6. Tools do not take advantage of existing formalizations: Figure 1 shows that some constraints (*e.g., dependencies, naming conventions*) are more often formally specified than automatically validated. However, formally specifying constraints without automatically verifying them is less than optimal. Based on our analysis, we observe that some adopted notations do not provide sufficient details to support validation (e.g. UML for describing *signature*) and other notations are not fully taken advantage of by the existing tools (e.g. regular expressions for describing *naming conventions*). We think that more empirical studies are needed in order to expose actual formalization practices. The results of these studies might expose common flaws of existing notations and provide concrete evidence of practitioner's needs.

5   Discussion

In this section we discuss some general strategies that could help address the issues raised in the previous section.

Reduce the Gap between Specification and Implementation. As observed, many of the current tools force the user into a needlessly technical exercise. Several dependency testing tools (*e.g.*, JDepend, Dependometer), for example, not only require the test specification to be written using a technical notation (*i.e.*, Java or XML), but also offer poor documentation on how to do so.

Architects should be able to express their concerns in a single uniform format. Respondent **G** said that having the option to embed a formal (yet readable) test specification of his architectural rules in a Word document would be extremely appealing to him. This would allow him to write well-formed testing rules in a familiar environment with the additional benefit of automatic validation.

Terra *et al.* [20] and Marinescu *et al.* [15] proposed two different DSLs (Domain Specific Languages) for expressing quality requirements (See section 7). Both languages serve the purpose of encoding valuable information in a testable yet readable format. Unfortunately the expressiveness of such DSLs is strongly defined by the capabilities of the underlying tool. Völter [21] reports on a case study where a DSL is defined progressively by interacting with the customer. The language, grammar and support tooling is developed iteratively and will eventually be used as the basis for code generation and analysis. Cucumber[6], a behavior-driven development framework, is based on a similar concept. Tests are written by non-technical stakeholders and are checked by building an interpreter that translates the text into actual unit tests.

These approaches show that having business-readable descriptions of relevant design properties helps keeping alive the conversation between all involved stakeholders. It also shows that a well engineered DSL is useful for encoding information in a uniform and unambiguous manner, which can turn useful for supporting more sophisticated testing activities. We believe that users should not be asked to describe their quality requirements within the boundaries defined by a testing tool. Instead, tools should be employed to verify user-defined rules on a best effort basis.

Increase Awareness through Continuous Feedback. Several respondents (**G, H, J**) use Sonarqube as a guide for driving code review activities. Sonarqube aggregates code analysis reports from multiple sources and presents them in a customizable web-based interface. Information is constantly kept up-to-date, well integrated and easy to navigate. All aspects exposed by the tool relate to general low-level characteristics of the system that are typically of little interest for architects. The strength of Sonarqube mostly seems to be bound to its integrability (analysis can be configured to run as a build step in a wide range of continuous integration servers), the concreteness of its result and the fact that all information are current and kept up-to-date.

Having seamless access to a comprehensive set of system-wide properties and infringed rules is a good way to exercise control over non-functional aspects of an implementation. If architects had the chance to define domain-specific

---

[6] http://cukes.info

rules for testing design constraints that are relevant for their architecture, they would be able to reach a higher and more targeted level of control. Our intuition is that monitoring platforms, such as Sonarqube would largely benefit from being integrated with highly customizable DSL-based tools (*e.g.*, DCL[20], InCode.Rules[15]). Being able to specify similar and more articulated rules on this and other aspects of the system would eventually reduce the generality of the results minimizing the number of false warnings and optimizing review-time.

6   Threats to Validity

Internal Validity. During our first study, we tried to gather impressions and opinions by conducting semi-structured interviews. Our goal was to gather a clear answer to all the research questions presented in the introduction. All discussions have therefore been partially moderated by the interviewer. We did our best to minimize the influence of the interviewer on the respondent, but we cannot exclude the existence of biased answers. Some observations or questions made by the interviewer might have induced the respondent to articulate his answer in an unnatural way. The effect of a similar threat should have been mitigated by the number of different answers to the same question.

Users taking part in the survey had the right to remain anonymous. 41% of them chose not to share any identifying personal information (*i.e.*, email address). Among those, 71% (29% of the total population) did not specify their professional title. Due to this lack of information, we are unable to make general statements over the population participating to the survey. It would anyway be reasonable to assume that most of the people were either architects or professionals playing a comparable role. The fact that we contacted people belonging to our industrial collaborators network and that we posted invitations only on architecture-oriented virtual communities should support our hypothesis.

External Validity. Another limitation could be seen in the relatively modest number of participants who participated in each phase of the study. The first study involved 14 respondents, while the survey counted 34 valid results. These numbers could appear small, but in fact are comparable to those reported by similar studies. Four out of five of all the interview-based studies centered around non-functional requirements [1] involve 14 or fewer participants. If we consider the surveys related to the same topic [1], we see that two out of four studies draw their conclusions based on fewer than 34 responses.

7   Related Work

In our work we discuss the nature of quality requirements and report on the techniques used for their verification. We examine both topics from a very pragmatic point of view, taking in consideration concrete examples and specific information. To the best of our knowledge, no other empirical study covers the same topics adopting a similar standpoint.

Several surveys related to NFRs (non-functional requirements) have been carried out (See related work by Ameller *et al.* [1]). The main outcome of all these studies often consists of a ranking showing how non-functional requirements compare based on the level of importance attributed by the users. All these studies focus on generic quality characteristics ignoring actual quality attributes that practitioners address in the requirements. Our study provides new insights from a complementary point of view, showing which quality attributes are considered relevant and providing details of their validation.

Poort *et al.* [18] found a statistical correlation between the verification of NFRs and project success. According to their results, the benefits of verification are also more significant if NFRs are verified in early stages of a project. In our study we explore how NFRs get actually validated in practice.

Various research contributions show that architecture-related requirements can be formalized using ADLs (architectural description languages). ADLs allow to model an architecture as a set of interlinked components enriched with a pre-defined meta-annotations. These models are typically weakly related with the implementation. Tools are sometimes provided for checking the semantic consistency of relationships and annotations but only at the model level. Moreover, there is scarce evidence that the general concepts defined in ADLs (*i.e.*, Components, Ports, *etc.*) actually reflect the the way architects think about their architecture. Case studies, showing evidence of the practical utility of the language, can only be found for a few of the most prominent ADLs (*i.e.*, AADL [6,5] and xADL [2]). We think that the lack of support for testing concrete architectures combined with the possible mismatch between offered features and real needs can be the cause of the — by now confirmed [14] — failure of adoption of ADLs by the general public. In this paper we draw observations that could help making ADLs more effective and useful.

Recent research efforts try to make up for these limitations by proposing more test-oriented ADLs. Terra *et al.* [20] proposed a specification language for expressing restrictions on the existence of certain types of relationships (*e.g.*, access, extension) between sets of classes. Marinescu *et al.* [15] supports the specification of undesired dependencies and class-level anti-patterns. Both ADLs are supported by custom-built testing tools that enable rule verification at the code level. Other languages (*i.e.*, SOUL [16] and LePUS3/Class-Z [9]) are more formal and support more complex specifications. They provide the means to validate quality requirements at code level, but also require considerable training before usage.

8   Conclusion

We presented the results of two empirical studies that explore how quality requirements are defined and validated in practice. The studies show that architects care about the validation of quality requirement but are often unable to make best use of the currently available tools.

We observe that the present offering of tools is limited in number and that several solutions are not able to satisfy common requirements (see section 5).

Practitioners are rarely willing to develop solutions for governing architectural decay and are not motivated to formalize their quality requirements. Current formalization notations are typically strongly tied to specific testing solutions and are often lacking in readability. To improve this situation, we propose some ideas for specifying quality requirements and for reducing the cost of validation. Future testing solutions should take advantage of existing formalizations and provide functionalities that fulfill empirically recognized requirements.

In the future we plan to apply some of the discussed ideas by experimenting with new solutions for supporting the specification and validation of quality requirements.

Acknowledgment. We thank Erwann Wernli for valuable discussions regarding the content of this paper, and we thank the anonymous reviewers and the shepherd assigned to this paper for their many helpful suggestions. We gratefully acknowledge the financial support of the Swiss National Science Foundation for the project "Agile Software Assessment" (SNSF project No. 200020-144126/1, Jan 1, 2013 - Dec. 30, 2015). We also thank CHOOSE, the special interest group for Object-Oriented Systems and Environments of the Swiss Informatics Society, for its financial contribution to the presentation of this paper.

References

1. Ameller, D., Ayala, C., Cabot, J., Franch, X.: How do software architects consider non-functional requirements: An exploratory study. In: 2012 20th IEEE International Requirements Engineering Conference (RE), pp. 41–50 (September 2012)
2. Boucké, N., Garcia, A., Holvoet, T.: Composing structural views in xADL. In: Moreira, A., Grundy, J. (eds.) Early Aspects Workshop 2007 and EACSL 2007. LNCS, vol. 4765, pp. 115–138. Springer, Heidelberg (2007)
3. Carrière, S.J., Kazman, R.: The perils of reconstructing architectures. In: Proceedings of the Third International Workshop on Software Architecture, ISAW 1998, pp. 13–16. ACM, New York (1998)
4. Creswell, J.W., Vicki: Designing and Conducting Mixed Methods Research, 1st edn. Sage Publications, Inc. (August 2006)
5. Feiler, P., Gluch, D., Hudak, J., Lewis, B.: Embedded systems architecture analysis using SAE AADL. Technical Report CMU/SEI-2004-TN-005, Software Engineering Institute, Carnegie Mellon University, Pittsburgh, Pennsylvania (2004)
6. Feiler, P., Gluch, D., Woodham, K.: Case study: Model-based analysis of the mission data system reference architecture. Technical Report CMU/SEI-2010-TR-003, Software Engineering Institute, Carnegie Mellon University, Pittsburgh, Pennsylvania (2010)
7. Feiler, P.H., Gluch, D.P., Hudak, J.J.: The architecture analysis & design language (AADL): An introduction. Technical report, DTIC Document (2006)
8. Garlan, D., Monroe, R.T., Wile, D.: Acme: Architectural description of component-based systems. In: Leavens, G.T., Sitaraman, M. (eds.) Foundations of Component-Based Systems, ch. 3, pp. 47–67. Cambridge University Press, New York (2000)
9. Gasparis, E., Nicholson, J., Eden, A.: Lepus3: An object-oriented design description language. In: Stapleton, G., Howse, J., Lee, J. (eds.) Diagrams 2008. LNCS (LNAI), vol. 5223, pp. 364–367. Springer, Heidelberg (2008)

10. Haigh, M.: Software quality, non-functional software requirements and it-business alignment. Software Quality Control 18(3), 361–385 (2010)
11. ISO/IEC. ISO/IEC 25010 — Systems and software engineering - Systems and software Quality Requirements and Evaluation (SQuaRE) — System and software quality models (2010)
12. Kruchten, P.B.: The 4+1 view model of architecture. IEEE Software 12(6), 42–50 (1995)
13. Magee, J., Dulay, N., Eisenbach, S., Kramer, J.: Specifying distributed software architectures. In: Botella, P., Schäfer, W. (eds.) ESEC 1995. LNCS, vol. 989, pp. 137–153. Springer, Heidelberg (1995)
14. Malavolta, I., Lago, P., Muccini, H., Pelliccione, P., Tang, A.: What industry needs from architectural languages: A survey. IEEE Transactions on Software Engineering 39(6), 869–891 (2013)
15. Marinescu, R., Ganea, G.: inCode.Rules: An agile approach for defining and checking architectural constraints. In: 2010 IEEE International Conference on Intelligent Computer Communication and Processing (ICCP), pp. 305–312 (August 2010)
16. Mens, K., Kellens, A.: IntensiVE, a Toolsuite for Documenting and Checking Structural Source-Code Regularities. In: Proceedings of the 10th European Conference on Software Maintenance and Reengineering, CSMR, pages 10, pp. 239–248 (2006)
17. Miles, M.B., Huberman, M.: Qualitative Data Analysis: An Expanded Sourcebook, 2nd edn. Sage Publications, Inc. (1994)
18. Poort, E.R., Martens, N., van de Weerd, I., van Vliet, H.: How architects see non-functional requirements: Beware of modifiability. In: Regnell, B., Damian, D. (eds.) REFSQ 2011. LNCS, vol. 7195, pp. 37–51. Springer, Heidelberg (2012)
19. Svensson, R., Gorschek, T., Regnell, B., Torkar, R., Shahrokni, A., Feldt, R.: Quality requirements in industrial practice — an extended interview study at eleven companies. IEEE Transactions on Software Engineering 38(4), 923–935 (2012)
20. Terra, R., Valente, M.T.: A dependency constraint language to manage object-oriented software architectures. Software: Practice and Experience 39(12), 1073–1094 (2009)
21. Voelter, M.: Architecture as language: A story. InfoQ (February 2008)

Recommending Refactorings
to Re-establish Architectural Consistency

Sebastian Herold[1] and Matthias Mair[2]

[1] Lero–The Irish Software Engineering Research Centre
University of Limerick, Limerick, Ireland
[2] Department of Informatics, Clausthal University of Technology
Julius-Albert-Str. 4, 38678 Clausthal-Zellerfeld, Germany

Abstract. Keeping the software architecture of a system and its implementation consistent can be tough. The larger and more complex a software system is, the more likely software architecture erosion occurs. This effect can lead to a decrease of quality with respect to adaptability, maintainability, or reusability.

Refactorings can help to reverse software architecture erosion through systematically applying them to resolve architecture violations. However, it can be difficult in complex systems to manually resolve all violations in an efficient way due to the complex interdependencies between them.

In this paper, we propose a new approach to the automatic recommendation of refactorings to resolve architecture violations based on a meta-heuristic search for an efficient set of refactorings. The approach is applied to resolve architectural dependency violations using the "move class" refactoring.

1 Motivation

The software architecture of a software system influences greatly quality properties regarding its development and maintenance such as adaptability, maintainability, or reusability [4]. An appropriate intended software architecture manifesting the most fundamental design decisions enables a system to evolve and to be adapted to changing requirements more easily.

However, the more complex a software system is and the longer it evolves, the more likely software architecture erosion occurs [10]. This term describes the divergence of the intended software architecture and its realization. The reasons for architecture erosion are manifold, e.g., bug-fixing or adapting to new requirements [7]. In the long term, progressing erosion leads to unmaintainable software that requires to be replaced by completely and expensively redeveloped systems [12].

One way to deal with software architecture erosion is to repair architecture violations, e.g., through reengineering and refactoring techniques [3]. In these approaches, architectural violations are identified and refactorings are applied in order to resolve them and to restore architecture consistency.

However, repairing architecture erosion requires a broad understanding of the—rather complex—system, the causes of violations, and interdependencies between them. Thus, it might be difficult for software engineers to find a good or even optimal way to refactor it. For example, violations of dependency constraints (e.g., caused by misplaced

P. Avgeriou and U. Zdun (Eds.): ECSA 2014, LNCS 8627, pp. 390–397, 2014.

classes) defined by the software architecture might influence each other; moving classes to resolve a violation can create new ones; violations might become obsolete of others are resolved in a certain way.

In this article we present preliminary results of our work on developing an approach which leverages flexible first-order logic architecture checking mechanism and combines it with meta-heuristic search techniques to recommend a suitable set of refactorings. The developed algorithm is tested in experiments in which consistency with architectural dependency constraints is re-established. The results show that the recommended refactoring sequences are effectively computed and represent efficient measures to repair the detected violations.

2 Problem

According to Eden et al. [2], a software architecture can be represented as set of logical constraints about possible realisations. A realization conforms to an architecture, if and only if it fulfils that set of logical statements. For example, the layered architecture pattern defines constraints about allowed dependencies among elements of the system's realization. Repairing software architecture erosion can hence be understood as transforming a realization not fulfilling the logical statements of an architecture into a realization that does. Refactorings can be understood as the available basic repair actions to construct this complex transformation.

As outlined in [8], the problem of finding an optimal set of repair actions for an eroded system is undecidable. This implies that we have to perform an exhaustive search for the optimal sequence. However, the search-space of this problem is very "broad" depending on the number of available repair actions and possible places for application, making an exhaustive search impossible for large systems. The *Move Class* refactoring alone has c^{p-1} possible applications for c classes and p possible places to move classes [3].

Hence, most related approaches limit themselves to special cases of the general problem by reducing the set of considered architectural aspects, e.g. dedicated bad smells, and by considering a fixed set of refactorings. This might simplify consistency checking to something less complex than first-order logic model checking but naturally reduces the cases of erosion that can be detected; in particular, user-defined or system-specific violations and repair actions cannot be considered.

3 Related Work

The following approaches all aim at providing automatic tool support for finding places for adequate refactorings in a software system. They differ in the kind of architectural erosion they can detect, the refactorings they support, and the technique they use to determine the refactorings to be applied.

Seng et al. describe in [13] an approach to determine refactorings to improve class structures. They apply a genetic algorithm to optimize a given object-oriented system with a vector of several metrics as fitness function. The refactorings they consider are those from Fowler's catalog that focus on the internal structure of classes.

The approach proposed by Dietrich et al. detects four different motifs in dependency graphs of programs [1]. Motifs are graph representations of general antipatterns; motif detection can basically seen as graph pattern matching. The only repair action that is considered to remove motifs in a software system is to remove dependencies. A meta-heuristic search is applied which executes the removal resolving the largest number of motifs first.

Shah et al. apply *Move Class* refactorings to resolve dependency cycles in software systems [14]. They apply a meta-heuristic search technique according to first-ascent hill-climbing [11] whereas the number of dependency cycles is the function to mini-mize. The result is a set of class movements that resolves as many dependency cycles as possible.

In [15], architectures are specified using the *Dependency Constraint Language*. Its main elements are coarse-grained components, that are mapped to source code units, and dependency constraints. A consistency checking tool for this kind of architectures is complemented by a recommendation system for refactorings. However, recommenda-tions are made only locally, i.e. for each single violation, not taking inter-dependencies between refactorings into account.

It can be concluded that most existing approaches that are applicable to determine a set of refactorings restrict the kind of architectural constraints that can be checked and support only a fixed set of repair actions. In contrast to these approaches, we propose an approach that tries to tackle the problem without reducing the expressiveness of supported architectural constraints and allowing user-defined repair actions.

4 Proposed Approach

The proposed approach consists of three main components: detection of architecture violations in a software system, specification of refactorings for violations, and recom-mendation of a set of refactorings for a given set of violations.

4.1 Detecting Architectural Violations with ArCh

In order to detect architecture violations, we use the Architecture Checker *(ArCh)* tool [6]. It implements the approach to architecture consistency checking proposed in [5] which focuses on applicability in heterogeneous development scenarios in which many different architectural aspects require to be checked on a large set of different artefacts. For this purpose, models/source code of a software system are transformed into a joint instance of an ontology that abstracts from specific meta models/languages[1]. Architec-tural constraints can be specified by a software architect as first-order logic expressions over this ontology.

ArCh is able to deal with user-defined architectural meta models and user-specific architectural constraints, given a transformation into the applied ontology, and speci-fications of the constraints as annotations complementing the meta model. The archi-tectural model used in this paper—to which ArCh is *not* restricted— is based on very

---

[1] Currently, transformations for Java, UML, and several domain-specific architectures are available.

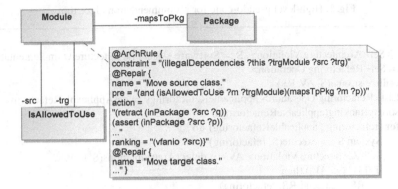

Fig. 1. Meta Model for Architectural Modules and Annotation for ArCh

simple module and dependency concepts captured in the meta model depicted in Fig. 1. Architectures define modules that can be understood as coarse-grained logical units. A mapping defines how modules are mapped to packages/namespaces of the source code (mapsToPkg). A relationship between modules indicates that modules may use other modules (isAllowedToUse). The actual dependencies in the source code must be local to packages mapped to the same module, or "run parallel to" the dependencies in the architecture. The annotation indicates that for each instance of Module the logical proposition *illegalDependencies*(...) will be checked, which captures this constraint on dependencies and returns every tuple of source code elements violating it. The specification of this expression is omitted for the sake of brevity and can be found in [5].

4.2   Defining Repair Actions

In order to define what should be done if violations of architectural constraints are found, the annotation of architectural meta model elements can contain Repair sections. In Fig. 1, the annotation for Module contains two Repair sections[2]. Each repair section consists of a precondition part and an action part. The precondition expresses (in terms of the available relationships of the ontology used in ArCh) which condition has to hold for the action to be applicable. For example, the upper precondition in Fig. 1 describes that for the following action, we are only interested in modules ?m and corresponding packages ?p that are allowed to access ?trgModule, which restricts the corresponding candidate set of packages for the "move class" refactoring.

The corresponding action part describes the refactoring as a sequence of operations on ArCh's knowledge representation and reasoning system. The command retract removes a fact from the knowledge base while assert adds a fact. Our repair action consists simply of moving a class to a different package by updating the package the class is contained in. We also allow post-processing steps after refactorings, e.g. to execute renaming of classes to avoid name conflicts if there exists a class in the target package with the same name as the moved one. We omit the details of this renaming for the sake of brevity.

---

[2] We depict only the first in detail, the second one is specified analogously.

Fig. 2. High-level pseudo-code for recommendation algorithm

Input:
    AV := Set<Architecture Violation>, S := Software system (architecture ∪ implementation)
    RS := Set<Refactoring Operation>
1: **procedure** SEARCH(S, AV, RS)
2:    List<Refactoring Operation> applicableRefactorings := getApplicableRefactorings(AV)
3:    sortByRanking(applicableRefactorings)
4:    **for** (refactoring : applicableRefactoring) **do**
5:        System S' := execute(S, refactoring)
6:        Set<Architecture Violation> AV' := detectArchViolations(S')
7:        **if** ($|AV'| < |AV|$) **then**
8:            RS := append(RS, refactoring)
9:            SEARCH(S', AV', RS)
10:          **break**
11:        **end if**
12:    **end for**
13: **end procedure**
Output:
    RS := Recommended set of refactoring operations

4.3 An Algorithm for Recommending Sets of Repairs

As outlined in Sec. 2, the search space for the problem of finding sets of repair actions is very broad. Meta-heuristic search algorithms hence seem to be an appropriate solution to this problem. In the given scenario, the goal of such an algorithm is to minimize the number of architectural violations with as few refactoring steps as possible for a given system and given set of available repair actions.

Due to the characteristic of a heuristic search, it is not possible to guarantee an over-all optimal output—fewest refactoring steps to minimize the number of violations—and hence the best set of refactoring operations. However, such algorithms often produce sufficiently good solutions for practical problems in reasonable time. The proposed algorithm is a variant of the first-ascent hill-climbing search algorithm [11]. Starting at position x_0, this algorithm tries to minimize/maximize a function $f(x)$ by computing the function for elements in the neighbourhood of x. If it finds an element y with $f(y) < f(x)$ or $f(y) > f(x)$, respectively, it repeats the search for y. It terminates, if no such y is found. In our case, the starting position is a software system (software architecture and implementation). The function to minimize is the number of violations. The neighbourhood of a position (a software system) consists of all software systems that could result from executing an applicable refactoring to one of the violations.

The high-level pseudo-code in Fig. 2 describes the search algorithm. The input parameters are the system description in form of the intended architecture and the given implementation, a set of architecture violations AV, and a set of refactoring operations RS which is initialized with the empty set and will contain the recommended sequence after the algorithm has terminated.

The method "getApplicableRefactorings" in line 2 computes all applicable refactoring operations for the architecture violations AV specified by the annotations described in Sec. 4.2. The applicable refactorings are ranked; in contrast to a "pure" first-ascent hill-climbing algorithm, we do not randomly select an element from the neighborhood. The ranking function is declared in the annotation (s. Fig. 1). The movement of a class into a different module should be ranked higher, the more likely that class is at a wrong place. We define[3]

$$vfanio(c) := \frac{1}{2}\left(\frac{IncomingViolations(c)}{IncomingDeps(c)} + \frac{OutgoingViolations(c)}{OutgoingDeps(c)}\right)$$

It holds that $0 \leq vfanio(c) \leq 1$. Informally spoken, the value of this metric for a classifier is great, if the ratio of architecture violating dependencies is high for the class. The applicable refactorings are primarily ranked by their specific ranking function and secondarily by the total number a refactoring has been computed as possible solution to any violation.

Given this ranking, the algorithm executes a repair action virtually (line 5). If it resolves more violations than it raises, the repair action is added to the recommended set of repair actions, and the algorithm is called recursively for the (virtually) modified system. The algorithm terminates if there are no more violations or no more improving repairs.

5   Experimental Results

The presented algorithm has been tested by applying it in experiments with synthetic software systems since it is difficult to get access to a representative group of eroded real-life systems for which both intended architecture and implementation are accessible. However, the investigated kind of architecture is motivated by industrial practice; we hence think that the experiments are generalizable.

For the experiments, random realizations of an architecture consisting of give modules were generated. The allowed usage relationships ordered modules hierarchically into a layering, allowing accesses only from upper modules to lower modules. A set of 1,000 classifier was generated and inserted into the packages following a uniform distribution. After that, 5,000 usage dependencies were generated between classifiers in a way that was architecturally consistent. After that, classes were moved to different modules with a certain probability to simulate erosion; different degrees of erosion were simulated by varying this probability. Among other values, we recorded for each run of the experiment (a) the relative size of the recommended set of refactorings compared with number of initial classifier movements introducing violations, and (b) the number of architecture consistency checks executed during search. We compared the values for the proposed algorithm with those measured for a simple first-ascent hill-climbing search.

The results over five test runs showed that both algorithms are able in nearly every test run to recommend a set of refactorings that would resolve all dependency violations.

---

[3] More precisely: if there are no incoming/outgoing dependencies for a class, the corresponding fraction is replaced by 0.

The proposed algorithm, however, misplaces classifiers in less cases to modules different from the original system structure. Moreover, the sequences generated by the proposed algorithm are significantly shorter than the sequences computed by first-ascent hill-climbing. Their relative lengths are on average 107.7% for the proposed algorithm vs. 153.7% for first-ascent hill climbing. These results let us assume that the violation fan-in fan-out metric used to rank possible refactorings leads to a significant improvement for the selection of constructive refactorings.

The most striking result is the significantly outperforming runtime behaviour of the proposed algorithm. The function that is minimized by the algorithms, the number of violations, is computationally complex since it is basically first-order logic model checking. Nearly the complete runtime of the search algorithm is spent checking architecture conformance after virtually executed refactorings. In our experiments, each single check took about 200ms. The proposed algorithm outperforms first-ascent hil-climbing by about factor 7–10.

One threat to validity of the experiments is the question whether they are valid representatives of real-life, eroded systems. In the experiments, erosion was created by moving classifiers to different modules, such that it is quite logical to resolve violations of dependency constraints by moving classifiers back to a valid position.

We tested the algorithm also for the open-source text editor jEdit for which a layered structure was identified in [9]. 325 dependency violations were identified and a set of refactorings eliminating ca. 70% was recommended. Reason for the lower results are the causes of violations that could not (or should not) be removed by moving classifiers, such as cyclic dependencies, callbacks, etc. This example, however, also shows that there is a need for a flexible approach that can be extended for new violations and refactorings; in our immediate future work, we plan to define more heterogeneous sets of repairs and to evaluate the proposed algorithm again. Furthermore, it has to be investigated how the approach performs when different kinds of violations have to be repaired; this case has not been considered by the experiments yet.

Finally, the consideration of the human effort leads to a discussion of the pragmatics of the proposed approach. The costs of maintaining the additional information, i.e., specification of architectural rules and of actions resolving violations, which constitute additional artefacts, must not eliminate the benefits of preserving architecture consistency.

6   Conclusion

This article describes a new approach that aims at repairing software architecture erosion by recommending refactorings to resolve architecture violations. Most of the approaches of the state of the art focus on a small subset of erosion cases. In contrast to these approaches, we combine a very general and expressive consistency checking technique with a simple meta-heuristic search algorithm to compute efficient refactoring sets. We show in experiments for a limited set of constraints and available refactorings that the proposed algorithm performs well.

The results, however, are preliminary since the very expressive consistency checking technique to avoid architecture erosion is applied to only a single aspect of architecture erosion, namely dependency violations. In the immediate future, we will apply it to more complex architectures with heterogeneous sets of constraints and more possibilities to refactor a system back to architectural consistency again. Nevertheless, the results are promising steps towards an extensible framework providing effective means for reversing architecture erosion and re-establishing consistency.

Acknowledgement. This work was supported, in part, by Science Foundation Ireland grant 12/IP/1351 to Lero - The Irish Software Engineering Research Centre (www.lero.ie).

References

1. Dietrich, J., McCartin, J., Tempero, E., Shah, S.M.A.: On the existence of high-impact refactoring opportunities in programs. In: Australasian Computer Science Conf., vol. 122, pp. 37–48. ACS (2012)
2. Eden, A., Hirshfeld, Y., Kazman, R.: Abstraction classes in software design. IEE Proc. - Softw. 153(4), 163–182 (2006)
3. Fowler, M.: Refactoring: Improving the Design of Existing Code. Addison-Wesley (1999)
4. van Gurp, J., Bosch, J.: Design erosion: Problems and causes. J. Syst. Softw. 61(2), 105–119 (2002)
5. Herold, S.: Architectural Compliance in Component-Based Systems. Ph.D. thesis, Clausthal University of Technology (2011)
6. Herold, S., Rausch, A.: Complementing model-driven development for the detection of software architecture erosion. In: 5th International Workshop on Modeling in Software Engineering (MiSE) at ICSE 2013, pp. 24–30 (2013)
7. Lindvall, M., Muthig, D.: Bridging the software architecture gap. IEEE Computer 41, 98–101 (2008)
8. Mair, M., Herold, S.: Towards extensive software architecture erosion repairs. In: Drira, K. (ed.) ECSA 2013. LNCS, vol. 7957, pp. 299–306. Springer, Heidelberg (2013)
9. Patel, S., Dandawate, Y., Kuriakose, J.: Architecture recovery as first step in system appreciation. In: 2nd Workshop on Empirical Studies in Reverse Engineering (WESRE) at the 13th Working Conference on Reverse Engineering, WCRE 2006 (2006)
10. Perry, D.E., Wolf, A.L.: Foundations for the study of software architecture. ACM SIGSOFT Softw. Eng. Notes 17, 40–52 (1992)
11. Russell, S.J., Norvig, P.: Artificial Intelligence: A Modern Approach. Pearson (2003)
12. Sarkar, S., Ramachandran, S., Kumar, G.S., Iyengar, M.K., Rangarajan, K., Sivagnanam, S.: Modularization of a large-scale business application: A case study. IEEE Softw. 26(2), 28–35 (2009)
13. Seng, O., Stammel, J., Burkhart, D.: Search-based determination of refactorings for improving the class structure of object-oriented systems. In: Proc. 8th Conf. on Genetic and Evolutionary Computation, pp. 1909–1916. ACM (2006)
14. Shah, S.M.A., Dietrich, J., McCartin, C.: Making smart moves to untangle programs. In: Proc. 16th Europ. Conf. on Software Maintenance and Reengineering, pp. 359–364. IEEE (2012)
15. Terra, R., Valente, M.T., Czarnecki, K., da Silva Bigonha, R.: Recommending refactorings to reverse software architecture erosion. In: Proc. 16th Europ. Conf. on Software Maintenance and Reengineering, pp. 335–340. IEEE (2012)

A Consistency Framework for Dynamic Reconfiguration in AO-Middleware Architectures

Bholanathsingh Surajbali[1], Paul Grace[2], and Geoff Coulson[3]

[1] Smart Research Development Centre, CAS Software AG, Karlsruhe, Germany
b.surajbali@cas.de
[2] IT Innovation, University of Southampton, Southampton, UK
pjp@it-innovation.soton.ac.uk
[3] School of Computing and Communication, Lancaster University, Lancaster, UK
geoff@comp.lancs.ac.uk

Abstract. Aspect-oriented (AO) middleware is a promising technology for the realisation of dynamic reconfiguration in distributed systems. Similar to other dynamic reconfiguration approaches, AO-middleware based reconfiguration requires that the consistency of the system is maintained across reconfigurations. AO middleware based reconfiguration is an ongoing research topic and several consistency approaches have been proposed. However, most of these approaches tend to be targeted at specific narrow contexts, whereas for heterogeneous distributed systems it is crucial to cover a wide range of operating conditions. In this paper we address this problem by exploring a flexible, framework-based consistency management approach that cover a wide range of operating conditions ensuring distributed dynamic reconfiguration in a consistent manner for AO-middleware architectures.

1 Introduction

A fundamental challenge for distributed systems is their need to support dynamic reconfiguration in order to maintain optimal levels of service in diverse and changing environments. In response to this challenge, aspect-oriented AO-middleware [1], [2], [3], [4] has recently emerged as a suitable architecture to build reconfigurable distributed systems. The core concept of AO-middleware is that of an aspect: a module that deals with one specific concern and can be changed independently of other modules. Aspects are made up of individual code elements that implement the concern (advices) which are deployed at multiple positions in a system (join points).

Dynamic reconfiguration of distributed systems requires assurances that the reconfiguration does not leave the system in an inconsistent state that can potentially lead to incorrect execution or even complete system failure. In AO-middleware environments reconfiguration inconsistencies arise from a range of characteristic sources - for example, if an encryption mechanism is added to the source of a communication channel, a corresponding decryption mechanism must be added to the sink of the channel; a given system must be reconfigured transactionally such that a given change is applied either to all of a specified set of targets, or to none; or a given system must be reconfigured such that it must not expose more security vulnerabilities than it was exposed to initially. In general, avoiding these sources of inconsistency is a difficult task due to the

P. Avgeriou and U. Zdun (Eds.): ECSA 2014, LNCS 8627, pp. 398–405, 2014.

diversity of distributed applications (e.g. centralised/decentralised, static/mobile, small scale/large scale etc) and also because of diverse application-specific factors (e.g. varying dependability requirements, or varying trade-offs between consistency and scalability). Relying on the application developer to ensure the consistency of the system is not feasible under such heterogeneous conditions. Moreover, a one-size-fits-all approach to consistency management is not feasible either. Instead, multiple consistency strategies should be supported within a framework-based approach so that appropriate strategies can be applied to each set of arising circumstances.

This paper therefore focuses on this latter perspective: that of identifying and mitigating the numerous incidental threats that can lead to inconsistent reconfigurations in AO-middleware systems. To address this perspective we present a novel distributed consistency framework, named COF for AO middleware environments that maximises the probability of consistent dynamic reconfiguration in the face of incidental factors. A key contribution is our approach itself is highly configurable and reconfigurable, as the frameworks mechanisms for detecting and repairing threats are themselves composed of dynamically woven aspects.

The rest of the paper is organised as follows. Section 2 presents, a threat taxonomy of the various threats to consistency to AO-middleware architectures prone. Then, in Section 3, we describe the COF framework, followed by Section 4 evaluating COF performance overhead. Finally, Section 5 discusses related work and we offer our conclusions in Section 6.

2   Threat Taxonomy

In this section, we present a list of threats which may jeopardise the consistency of a critical distributed system due to dynamic reconfigurations. To illustrate the "big picture" of our approach we present Fig.1 a generalised system model of an AO-middleware platform; this illustrates one AO-middleware instance for simplicity but the model is repeated across nodes in the distributed system. The model consists of five core entities: (i) the *reconfiguration agent* representing the entity initiating reconfiguration requests; (ii) a *configurator*, which acts on the reconfiguration request; (iii) an *AO-middleware platform* providing the necessary abstraction to support the composition and reconfiguration of distributed aspects to underpin the distributed application services; (iv) a set of *infrastructure servers* providing a set of infrastructure services to the system, such as hosting the system repositories (containing aspect software) and (v) the *communication service* providing exchange of messages and events among the different address spaces (referred as nodes) in the distributed environment. Also within the model, we identify a set of core join points (numbered 1 to 5 in Fig.1) at which aspects can be woven within a given instance of the AO-middleware deployed at each node. Hence, these are the points where the consistency framework solutions (in the form of threat aspects) are deployed to ensure consistency is achieved.

Compositional Threats. These relate to conflicting dependencies of reconfiguration resulting in negative interactions between system entities. For instance, some aspects are inherently dependent on each other such as a decryption aspect is dependent on the corresponding encryption aspect. Therefore, the order in which aspects are woven is

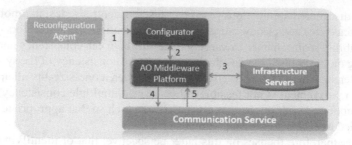

Fig. 1. Generalised model for AO-middleware platforms

crucial: e.g., encryption must be put in place before its associated decryption. Further, "remote aspects" [1] which are used by several distributed client nodes can be a source of inconsistency; for example, if a cache implemented as a remote aspect is removed without the consent or even the awareness of its client nodes, errors can arise when clients attempt to communicate with the cache. Finally, semantic conflicts can occur due to incompatibilities of the reconfigured aspect with the rest of the system as may arise in the deployment of logging and privacy aspects [10]. Moreover, the composition order in which aspects are woven can also affect their interactions, for example, if a cache advice is executed before an authentication advice, clients may be able to get access to resources without first authenticating themselves.

Operational Threats. The inherently unstable characteristics of the networks and nodes employed in the scenario increase the chances that a reconfiguration will be compromised. For example, application nodes may fail to apply a requested reconfiguration if: i) the node is overloaded or has crashed; ii) the node's local policy forbids it to make the requested change; iii) aspects may still be performing computations when an attempt is made to remove or recompose them. Such factors can clearly lead to parts of the intended reconfiguration not being carried out, and consequent inconsistency. Further, aspects to be reconfigured into the system are typically stored in infrastructure service repositories which may get congested with requests, or themselves crash, meaning that aspects may not be available to be deployed in some cases or at some times. Additionally, different repository instances may have different versions of the aspects: e.g. different versions of the encryption aspects may be produced over time, so that different nodes configure different versions and be inconsistent with each other. Finally, if reconfiguration-related messages are lost, re-ordered, duplicated or delayed, the consistency of the reconfiguration can be compromised. For example, a fragmentation aspect may be deployed but not the corresponding reassembly aspect.

User Threats. These refer to threats introduced to the AO-middleware system model by the reconfiguration agent; this can be the developer/administrator, or software runtime code initiated by some authority manager (e.g. in self-managed systems). For example, if a reconfiguration request is not properly checked, it may proceed while containing errors (for example wrongly formed declarative reconfiguration specifications) which may lead to incorrect actions and system inconsistency when the reconfiguration is applied. Similarly, a reconfiguration request may be unauthorised or reconfiguration

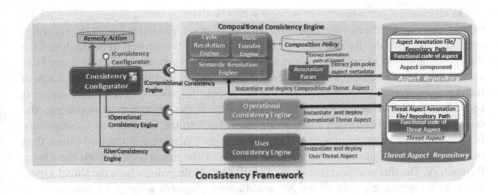

Fig. 2. Consistency Framework (COF)

messages may be spoofed by malicious nodes in an attempt to compromise consistency. In addition, reconfiguration requests may arise simultaneously in the system so that reconfiguration-related messages relating to distinct requests may be interleaved and potentially received in different orders at different nodes. For example, one request may ask to replace the fragmentation aspect with a different algorithm, while another asks for it to be removed. There will clearly be different outcomes depending on the execution order of these two requests and furthermore the outcomes might be different at different nodes.

3 Consistency Framework (COF)

The consistency framework (COF) as shown in Fig.2 addresses the reconfiguration threats defined in the threat taxonomy. Importantly, COF defines a canonical set of threat aspects that mitigate the threats found in the taxonomy, and an associated set of join point strategies to guide the application of the threat aspects within diverse AO-middleware implementations.

3.1 Consistency Configurator

The Consistency Configurator acts as a unit of autonomy making decisions about when and how to perform consistent reconfiguration. The Consistency Configurator is connected to the Remedy Action repository providing appropriate remedy actions to the Consistency Configurator for each reconfiguration. The Remedy Action uses a "condition action" approach that evaluates the reconfiguration request and instructs the Consistency Configurator to deploy appropriate threat aspects using the three main consistency engines. The consistency engines each evaluate the corresponding join points if they already have the required threat aspects. If the join points are present, an acknowledgement is returned to the Consistency Configurator, otherwise threat aspects are loaded from the Threat Aspect Repository and deployed at the defined join points.

On receiving a reconfiguration request with consistency threat aspects, the Consistency Configurator checks the aspect threat specification, associated with the reconfiguration script with the Remedy Action. The list of aspects required to be deployed for the reconfiguration is returned to the Consistency Configurator, which then sends to each consistency engine the list of threat aspects required at the join points. Each of the consistency engines then checks using the Aspect Repository if the threat aspect is present at the AO-middleware platform join point. If the threat aspect is present, the consistency engine returns an acknowledgement back to the Consistency Configurator for the reconfiguration to proceed. If no threat aspect is woven at the join point, then the consistency engines requests the instantiation of the threat aspect from the Threat Repository. The threat aspect instances, as well as the join point where the threat aspect needs to be woven are sent to the AO-middleware platform weaver. In case, a threat aspect is already woven and needs to be replaced, the Consistency Configurator first ensures that the reconfigured threat aspect is not performing any computation.

3.2 Compositional Consistency Engine

The Compositional Consistency Engine (CCE) addresses compositional threats in AO-middleware architectures by encapsulating and deploying:

- a *coordination protocol* such as Necoman protocol [5] and a *transaction protocol* encapsulated as an aspect and woven as a "before" advice at the top of the communications stack at join points 4 and 5 to address *dependency inconsistencies*.
- a *caretaker aspect* that proxies the aspect being reconfigured at join point 2 to address *unsynchronised unbinding of distributed aspects*; such that on receiving a message from a client the caretaker instructs the client that the aspect has been removed.
- *semantic reasoning and resolution engine (SRE)* [6] to query and resolve possible sources of inconsistency at join points 1 and 4 to detect semantic conflicts from incoming reconfiguration requests (from the reconfiguration agent) or from reconfiguration requests sent from the network.
- the Resolving *Cyclic* Dependencies *Engine* (ReCycle) [7] to detect cyclic inconsistencies from incoming reconfiguration requests from the reconfiguration agent or from incoming requests from the network by encapsulating and weaving ReCycle as aspect at join points 1 and 4.

3.3 Operating Environment Consistency Engine

The operating environment consistency engine component addresses the various distributed operating environment reconfiguration threats by encapsulating and deploying:

- a *transaction aspect* at the communication interface (join point 5) to detect *local node disruptions* and provide consensual decision making on what to do when these occur (e.g. accept the partial failure or roll back).
- *replication* [8] and *load balancing strategies* [9] aspects at the interface to the infrastructure services (join point 3) to detect*infrastructure service failures*.
- a *reliability* threat aspect at join points 4 and 5 to create a reliable communication service to handle *communication failures*.

3.4   User Consistency Engine

The user consistency engine component addresses the various user defined reconfiguration threats by encapsulating and deploying:

- a *reconfiguration validator aspect* to validate the reconfiguration script against policies to ascertain the correctness of the reconfiguration operation at join point 1 to resolve *badly formed requests*.
- an *authentication aspect* as "before" advice at the AO-middleware platform's communication interface at join points 4 and 5 to address *unauthorised reconfigurations*. This ensures only authentic users can adapt the system. Furthermore, in an un-trusted environment, additional *encryption and decryption aspects* can be woven at the communication interfaces (i.e. join point 4 and 5 respectively) of the sender and receiver (e.g. public or private cryptography algorithms can be used).
- a *distributed concurrency aspect* at join point 1 so that each reconfiguration request is isolated within a critical section addressing *simultaneous reconfigurations* inconsistencies.

4   Performance of COF

We now assess the performance characteristics of COF in two AO-middleware platforms we have considered (i.e. AO-OpenCom [4], and the JBoss AOP version of DyReS [10]). For this we use an experimental setup based consisting of a small network of four standalone workstations employed as shown in Fig.3a: a 1.8 GHz Core Duo 2 PC with 3GB RAM (node A); a 3.4 GHz Pentium IV PC with 1GB of RAM (node B); and a 2.8GHz Pentium IV PC with 1 GB of RAM (node C); a 1.33 GHz Core Duo 2 laptop with 2GB of RAM (node D). All of these are connected via a 100Mbps local area network. Each evaluation machine was installed with the AO-OpenCom and DyReS framework which was executed on a Java 1.7 virtual machine (VM). Based on this setup, the different threat aspect are represented in Fig.3b and the reconfiguration we perform is to *dynamically weave a symmetric AES [11] encryption/decryption aspect across each of the nodes*. The overhead results are shown in Table 1. It should be pointed that we do not claim that these results are in any sense definitive. Rather, they are indicative of the order of magnitude of overhead to be expected of COF deployments. In particular, the numbers are specific to our implementations.

Table 1. Reconfiguration of COF with AO-OpenCom and DyReS

	Overhead Using COF (ms)		Steady State Latency Time (ms)	
	AO-OpenCom	DyRes	AO-OpenCom	DyRes
Without COF	1994	5311	1724	5852
With COF	2995	7241	1724	5860

We can see that the base time to perform the reconfiguration without COF varies considerably across the two platforms: AO-OpenCom is fastest, with DyReS taking 2.66 times longer. The longer time taken by DyReS over AO-OpenCom is attributed mainly to the former's use of the NeCoMan coordination protocol [12], which seems to incur

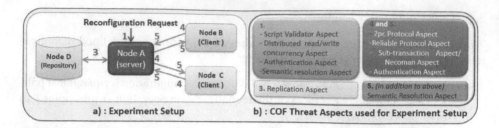

Fig. 3. Experimental setup to evaluate COF

a high degree of inter-node chattiness. In terms of the COF-induced overheads, AO-OpenCom and DyReS respectively take 1.25 and 1.36 times longer than their respective without-COF baselines, indicating that the overheads of COF are stable across all two implementations. Furthermore, the fact that the with-COF case for AO-OpenCom takes less time than DyReS indicates that COF overheads seem to be well within acceptable ranges.

5   Discussion and Related Work

Threat aspects are not completely orthogonal - in particular, the order in which they are composed is important, and executing aspects at some common join point in a "wrong" order could lead to problems (e.g. situations in which a message needing to be processed by a particular aspect has already been consumed by another). This ordering issue is particularly important for join points at the top of the communication stack (join point 4, 5) at which point numerous aspects are woven; for example, where both the consensus and reliability threat aspects are woven, the reliability aspect should come first to ensure that the consensus protocol uses a reliable communications service. In general, COF mandates a particular order for the weaving of the threat aspects and enforces this order using attributes attached to each aspect.

Few AO middleware platforms have addressed the challenges of performing consistent dynamic reconfiguration. DyMac [1], FAC [13] and CAM/DAOP [2] are component and aspect-based middleware frameworks that take a more principled approach to distribution by offering distributed aspects. They both support distributed aspect composition but no support for consistency and dynamic reconfiguration. Damon [3] is a distributed AO-middleware offering dynamic reconfiguration with remote pointcut and remote advice capabilities similar to AO-OpenCom and DyMac. However, the approach does not provide any consistency mechanisms for use during reconfiguration. Both DJasCo [14] and ReflexD [15] use a consistency protocol to ensure that whenever an aspect is woven at a specific host, mirrors are also woven at other involved hosts. However, they do not consider any other consistency threats as discussed in the threat taxonomy. Lasagne [2] offers semantic consistency support to prevent dangerous combinations of aspects, and offers atomic weaving of aspects. It also checks for unauthorised clients requesting aspect composition. However, it does not offer solutions for operating-environment threats and several other threats.

6   Conclusions and Future Work

In this paper we have presented a framework-based approach to consistency maintenance over dynamic reconfiguration operations for AO-middleware platforms. We believe that our threat taxonomy is representative of the type of threats that should be considered by all dynamic AOP platforms. Importantly, COF applies an aspect-oriented approach to consistency management, so the solutions it identifies are described in terms of "threat aspects" and can be applied using the native compositional model of the target AO-middleware platform. Furthermore, the evaluation result show COF: i) ability to handle reconfiguration threats; ii) flexibility of the framework as applied to two AO-middleware platforms; and iii) overheads are acceptable. In future we plan to investigate embedding our approach in a self-managing, autonomic environment in which reconfiguration requests are initiated by the platform itself as opposed to the user.

References

1. Lagaisse, B., Joosen, W.: True and transparent distributed composition of aspect-components. In: van Steen, M., Henning, M. (eds.) Middleware 2006. LNCS, vol. 4290, pp. 42–61. Springer, Heidelberg (2006)
2. Loughran, N., Parlavantzas, N., Colyer, A., Pinto, M., Sánchez, P., Webster, M.: Survey of aspect-oriented middleware (2005)
3. Mondejar, R., Garcia, P., Pairot, C., Urso, P., Molli, P.: Designing a distributed aop runtime composition model. In: Proc. of ACM Symposium on Applied Computing. ACM (2009)
4. Surajbali, B., Grace, P., Coulson, G.: Ao-opencom: An ao-middleware architecture supporting flexible dynamic reconfiguration. In: 17th ACM Sigsoft Conference on Component-Based Software Engineering. ACM (2014)
5. Janssens, N., Joosen, W., Verbaeten, P.: Necoman: middleware for safe distributed-service adaptation in programmable networks. Distributed Systems Online (2005)
6. Surajbali, B., Grace, P., Coulson, G.: A semantic composition model to preserve (re) configuration consistency in aspect oriented middleware. In: Proceedings of the 8th International Workshop on Adaptive and Reflective Middleware. ACM (2009)
7. Surajbali, B., Grace, P., Coulson, G.: Recycle: Resolving cyclic dependencies in dynamically reconfigurable aspect oriented middleware (2010)
8. Beloued, A., Gilliot, J.M., Segarra, M.T., André, F.: Dynamic data replication and consistency in mobile environments. In: Proc. Doctoral Symposium on Middleware. ACM (2005)
9. Minson, R., Theodoropoulos, G.: Adaptive support of range queries via push-pull algorithms. In: Principles of Advanced and Distributed Simulation. IEEE (2007)
10. Truyen, E., Janssens, N., Sanen, F., Joosen, W.: Support for distributed adaptations in aspect-oriented middleware. In: Proc. of the 7th International Conference on AOSD. ACM (2008)
11. Nechvatal, J., Barker, E., Bassham, L., Burr, W., Dworkin, M.: Report on the development of the advanced encryption standard (aes). Technical report, DTIC Document (2000)
12. Truyen, E., Joosen, W.: Run-time and atomic weaving of distributed aspects. In: Rashid, A., Akşit, M. (eds.) Transactions on Aspect-Oriented Software Development II. LNCS, vol. 4242, pp. 147–181. Springer, Heidelberg (2006)
13. Pessemier, N., Seinturier, L., Duchien, L., et al.: A component-based and aspect-oriented model for software evolution. Journal of Computer Applications in Technology (2008)
14. Navarro, L., Benavides, D., Südholt, M., et al.: Explicitly distributed aop using awed. In: Proc. 5th International Conference on AOSD. ACM (2006)
15. Tanter, É., Toledo, R.: A versatile kernel for distributed AOP. In: Eliassen, F., Montresor, A. (eds.) DAIS 2006. LNCS, vol. 4025, pp. 316–331. Springer, Heidelberg (2006)

Author Index